PANATI'S
PARADE OF
FADS, FOLLIES,
AND MANIAS

BOOKS BY CHARLES PANATI

Supersenses, 1974

The Geller Papers (editor), 1976

Links (a novel), 1978

Death Encounters, 1979

Breakthroughs, 1980

The Silent Intruder (with Michael Hudson), 1981

The Pleasuring of Rory Malone (a novel), 1982

Panati's Browser's Book of Beginnings, 1984

Panati's Extraordinary Origins of Everyday Things, 1987

Panati's Extraordinary Endings of
Practically Everything and Everybody, 1989

Panati's Parade of Fads, Follies, and Manias, 1991

PANATI'S PARADE OF FADS, FOLLIES, AND MANIAS

The Origins of Our Most Cherished Obsessions

Charles Panati

HarperPerennial

A Division of HarperCollins*Publishers*

Illustration credits are as follows:

Library of Congress: pages 50, 93, 314
UPI/Bettman Newsphotos: pages 13, 14, 30, 32, 33, 36, 39, 52, 61, 113, 123, 133, 149, 455
Picture People: pages 16, 18, 54, 63, 64, 127, 137, 160, 161, 178, 203, 207, 223, 238, 271, 446, 473, 475, 476
Lester Glassner Collection: pages 85, 185, 190, 194, 204, 225, 229, 259, 261, 352, 373, 386, 413, 473
Neal Peters Collection/Lester Glassner: pages 173, 240, 247, 277, 282, 284, 293, 300, 304, 308, 309, 341, 343, 353, 355, 358, 360, 361, 364, 417, 421, 436, 462, 474, 478, 481

FIRST EDITION

Designed by Alma Orenstein

Library of Congress Cataloging-in-Publication Data

Panati, Charles, 1943-
   Panati's parade of fads, follies, and manias:the origin of our
most cherished obsessions/Charles Panati.—1st ed.
      p.   cm.
   ISBN 0-06-055191-7. — ISBN 0-06-096477-4 (pbk.)
   1. Fads—United States—History—20th century. 2. United States—
Popular culture—History—20th century. 3. Curiosities and
wonders—United States—History—20th century. I. Title.
   E169.1.P19   1991
   306′.0973—dc20   90-56433

91 92 93 94 95 CC/RRD 10 9 8 7 6 5 4 3 2 1
91 92 93 94 95 CC/RRD 10 9 8 7 6 5 4 3 2 1 (pbk.)

This book is dedicated to my mother

Contents

(A Partial Listing)

Swallowing / Spin-off Crazes / Supermarket / Shopping
Cart / Great Dirigibles / Smoking on Board / Mass Death
and Media Coverage / Shirley Temple Dolls and Polka Dot
Dresses / M-I-C-K-E-Y M-O-U-S-E / Mousketeers /
Bingo / Yahtzee

Journey" / "I'm Always Chasing Rainbows" / *Carousel* / "Rum and Coca-Cola" / "Doin' What Comes Natur'lly" / "They Say It's Wonderful" / "Chestnuts Roasting on an Open Fire" / "Come Rain or Come Shine" / "How Are Things in Glocca Morra" / "Old Devil Moon" / "The Heather on the Hill" / "Near You" / "Time After Time" / "Buttons and Bows" / "A—You're Adorable" / "It's a Most Unusual Day" / "I've Got a Lovely Bunch of Coconuts" / *South Pacific* / "Diamonds Are a Girl's Best Friend" / "Baby It's Cold Outside" / "That Lucky Old Sun" / "Rudolph, the Red-Nosed Reindeer"

BESTSELLING BOOKS   231

Book Club Mania / Paperback Books / *How Green Was My Valley* / *For Whom the Bell Tolls* / *Ten Little Indians* / *While England Slept* / *Bet It's a Boy* / *Berlin Diary* / *The White Cliffs* / *Blood, Sweat, and Tears* / *The Last Time I Saw Paris* / *The Moon Is Down* / *The Song of Bernadette* / *The Robe* / *Forever Amber* / *A Tree Grows in Brooklyn* / *The Razor's Edge* / *Anna and the King of Siam* / *The Egg and I* / *The King's General* / *This Side of Innocence* / *Gentleman's Agreement* / *The Naked and the Dead* / *Raintree County* / *The Young Lions* / *Sexual Behavior in the Human Male* / *Common Sense Book of Baby and Child Care*

TELEVISION HITS   238

Listeners Become Viewers / "Milton Berle's Texaco Star Theater" / The Vaudeo Era Begins / "Toast of the Town" / "Your Show of Shows" / Sitcoms / "The Goldbergs" / "The Life of Riley" / "Mama" / Kiddie TV and Toy Fads / "The Howdy Doody Show" / Howdy is Born / Howdy Merchandising Madness / "Kukla, Fran and Ollie" / To Prime Time / "Hopalong Cassidy"

CHAPTER 7 The Fabulous Fifties: 1950 to 1959   253

The Do It for the Kids Decade / The Joneses Versus the Beatniks

FADS, FOLLIES, AND TRENDS   255

California Ranch House / Fallout Shelters / Split Level House / At Home Wear / Television Fashions / Credit Cards / Diners Club / American Express / 3-D Movies / Glamarama / Davy Crockett Hats and Haute Cowture / Wiffle Ball / Silly Putty and Slinky / Lego / Barbie Doll / Hula Hoop / Frisbee / Scrabble / Panty

Contents

INTRODUCTION

◻

A Century of Popular Culture

1890s to 1990s

THROUGHOUT THIS BOOK you'll encounter four themes that repeatedly surface and commingle: the pervasiveness of popular culture, the power of nostalgia, the mass appeal of faddishness, and something that makes possible the enjoyment of popular culture, nostalgia, and fads: leisure time—for people did not always have the time (to say nothing of the means) to engage in the kinds of behavior chronicled in these pages. A hundred and fifty years ago, the average work week in the United States was seventy hours.

This book begins with the Gay Nineties, a transitional decade that marked the waning of Victorian life and the dawning of modern America, the beginning of a century like none before it, a span of one hundred years now that can be charted—as is done in these pages—by the emergence of leisure and a devotion to popular culture. We've come a long way: from Handy Man *(Homo habilis)* to Craftsman *(Homo faber)* to Upright Man *(Homo erectus)* to Wise Man *(Homo sapiens)* to Leisure Time Man *(Homo ludens)*. And we began to enter this last stage around 1890.

The Gay Nineties was a historic turning point for several reasons. The Wild West frontier had officially been tamed and closed when the 1890 census revealed Americans settled from the Atlantic to the Pacific. The continent was a country. And its people began to experience a shifting away from sedate, Victorian pastimes to more uninhibited, carefree American behaviors. That is, the nation experienced a mood change from the earlier belief "idleness debases" to the then-contemporary pleas for "the right to be lazy" and one's "civil right" to follow the "gospel of relaxation." This transformation set the stage for the trends, crazes, manias, and luxuries presented in the following ten chapters—a chapter for each decade from 1890 into the 1990s.

First, a few words on the book's major themes:

1

Origin of Popular Culture

O, the times! O, the customs!
—Cicero

Perhaps Cicero pressed his temples and shook his head as he lamented the fickleness in his time. A century later the satirist Juvenal lambasted the masses for their interest in only two things, *panem et circenses,* "bread and circuses." Today he might have said Twinkies and sitcoms.

The point is, highbrows have always disparaged the pleasures and amusements of the majority. Until recently, they viewed popular culture as "the stale fodder of the conforming multitude," in contrast to "superior or refined culture" that boldly ventures down new avenues, daringly opens closed doors.

But as we'll see throughout this book, in countless instances, it is popular culture that today generates new styles and ideas, which are embraced by people regardless of social rank.

Popular culture is defined, if a bit harshly, as throwaway culture. Here today, trendy and profitable; gone the way of the trash tomorrow. Do you, for instance, still fondly cling to your pet rock, pillbox hat, dashboard troll doll? On the other hand, how many of us cherish "I Love Lucy" reruns, or collect art deco artifacts, classic baseball cards, or toy trains?

Popular culture seems at first glance to be a modern phenomenon. We might imagine that its offerings depend on a consumer-obsessed, technologically oriented world to explain their existence. Here, appearances are deceiving.

Folklorist Michael Bell, in *Concise Histories of American Popular Culture,* states that something is popular when it is created to respond to the values of the majority, and when it is "understood by that majority without the aid of special knowledge or experience." In a nutshell, when it has immediate mass appeal. Every society, in every era, had craftsmen who produced such popular materials. A difference between then and now is, of course, one of quantity. People in past centuries waded in shallow pools of popular culture, whereas we swim (some say drown) in a sea of it.

We are the first society to define popular culture's nature, estimate its worth, and offer Ph.D.s for its study. And we are the first society to clearly distinguish it from folk culture and elite culture—distinctions that are important for the material in these pages. In brief, from Bell:

Elite culture is exclusive. Elite creators seek to produce "classics"—something new that nevertheless can be evaluated in relation to the great works of the past. Elite audiences accept the creation as aesthetically pleasing, novel, maybe even daring, and they usually know (by name at least) the creator. Picasso; Cubism. Puccini; Italian opera.

Folk culture is personal, the culture of everyday life. Folk creators work with the facts of ordinary experience; creator and audience are bound together by generational traditions. Those who create folk culture never strive for the shock of the new. Convention and continuity are the guiding principles.

Popular culture, our concern here, is comprehensive, a kind of mass culture. Unlike the case with folk or elite culture, its creators are seldom known to their audiences—unless, that is, their audiences read this book, since I've taken great pains to present the originators of our major fads, trends, and manias. These creators strive to satisfy as many people as possible—and, equally as important, to offend as few as possible. They seek neither complexity nor profundity, only to reach and delight as many of us as possible. At a net profit.

We, the audience for popular culture, seek, most of all, to be entertained. Or to have a product that serves a functional purpose. We want novelty, but we don't want that novelty to be overwhelming. We insist that we be able to recognize ourselves and our values in the creation. Thus popular culture, which shoots for consensus, is responsive to the marketplace—if not entirely dependent on it these days.

As Juvenal, envisioning the degeneration of Rome, criticized the people for wanting only bread and circuses, modern popular culture has even harsher critics. They charge that the pioneering benefits of elite culture and the nurturing spin-offs of folk culture are being eroded by the short-term, instant gratification of popular culture. That, like Rome, we're headed for a fall.

In *Bread and Circuses: Theories of Mass Culture as Social Decay,* Patrick Brantlinger details how today's critics have taken up Juvenal's banner. The idea is that our modern society is consumed with trendiness; with the season's favorite sitcoms, pop songs, "in" dances, gadgets, and the like. You know: what's hot and what's not. All to the exclusion of serious matters.

As Juvenal lamented centuries ago: "The public has long since cast off its cares; the people that once bestowed commands, consulships, legions and all else, now meddles no more and longs eagerly for just two things—Bread and Circuses!"

Brantlinger counters this argument—which he calls negative classicism— by showing that it has existed among critics of popular culture for centuries. Each new invention of mass appeal—from mass-produced books and machine-produced goods, from radio to films to television—was viewed as the axe that would fell civilization. I have attempted throughout this book to quote the condemnations leveled against each new invention, and the dire forecasts made for every new fad or trend.

There are, to be sure, amusing (and perhaps thought-provoking) parallels to be found in Juvenal's satire. Rome did, after all, fall. He argued that the pleasure-loving Roman populace abandoned its political responsibilities for doles of food, the lure of the racetrack, and the thrill of the sports arena. In modern parlance, as the critic's parallel might go, the masses have abandoned political involvement in favor of welfare programs, get-rich gambling games, and the numbing distractions of the mass media.

Well, on one hand, that argument sounded convincing to me. I wondered if I should pursue writing a book that details through fads and follies the decay of modern civilization. Or, as a harsher critic views the dire consequences of widespread popular culture: "the betrayal of the Enlightenment ideal of democracy based on an educated, egalitarian public and the emergence of fascist and socialist tyranny, the final totalitarian shapes of mass society." That I did not wish to encourage.

Then I happened upon Herbert Gans's *Popular Culture and High Culture,* which persuasively argues that popular culture is not a pathological byproduct of American capitalism and democracy, nor does it threaten elite culture or society as a whole. Releasing a sigh, I proceeded with the writing of this book.

For I realized that America, more than any other society, comprises many cultural tastes, coexisting, occasionally commingling to generate a new hybrid with mass appeal. Our strength is rooted in our capacity to be serious one moment, silly the next. We can, as a society, dance the watusi, watch "Mr. Ed," twirl hula hoops, bet on the state lottery, play Nintendo, collect Smurfs and Hummels, bask in tanning salons, wear Nehru jackets and pillbox hats (even at the same time), and read comic books by the light of lava lamps—and not fear the collapse of civilization. Loving both bread and circuses, I certainly hope this is true.

Origin of Nostalgia

> Nostalgia is not what it used to be.
> —**Anon.**

The sage Anon told a half-truth; a wiser man, Will Rogers, got it right: "Things aren't like they used to be—and they probably never were."

Hand in hand with popular culture goes the phenomenon—and emotion—of nostalgia. "The Honeymooners." Barbie dolls. Pinball machines. LP records. "Inner Sanctum." The words alone spin a magic spell. They evoke, usually with longing, an earlier, easier, more carefree time—which is often only wishful thinking; nostalgia is not called magic for no reason.

Nostalgia, though, was once considered a disease and treated with medication, even surgery. Patients were "cured." How did nostalgia go from a treatable ailment to the basis of a modern multibillion-dollar memories industry? The basis, indeed, of this book.

It can be argued that if nostalgia was once a disease, today, when selling a sweet image of the past brings big bucks, nostalgia is an American epidemic, fast becoming a global pandemic. We are continually in the grip of another nostalgia fever.

The word nostalgia is from the Greek *nostos,* "to return home," and *algia,* "a painful condition"—thus, a painful yearning to return home.

Coined by the Swiss physician Johannes Hofer in the late seventeenth century, the term designated a condition of extreme homesickness among Swiss mercenaries fighting far from their native land. The symptoms, said Hofer in his 1688 "Medical Dissertation on Nostalgia," were despondency and melancholia, including profound bouts of weeping, anorexia, and, not infrequently, attempts at suicide.

Physicians pinpointed the disease in the brain, where, as Hofer waxed, nostalgia was caused by "the quite continuous vibration of animal spirits through those fibers of the middle brain in which impressed traces of ideas of the Fatherland still cling." Hofer believed that nostalgia was strictly a Swiss disease.

With the development of mass armies and the introduction of universal conscription by European states in the late eighteenth century, it was soon discovered that soldiers of other countries on military duty far from home were equally subject to the disease of nostalgia. But only with the word's unmooring from its pathological base did it begin to acquire the connotations it has today. Believe it or not, only in the 1880s did the word disappear as a disease from the *Oxford English Dictionary.*

Around this time, and notably in America, nostalgia first entered into popular parlance with connotations like "bittersweet," "it was all for the best," "a nice sort of sadness." It took on a positive aspect.

In America, especially after the 1950s, nostalgia came to evoke a desirous blend of yearning, of joy clouded with sadness, of pleasant past moments that cannot be repeated, only remembered.

The remembrance of things past is today even deemed therapeutic. Nostalgia can ease life's anxiety-provoking transitions. The groups most inclined to feel nostalgia are adolescents, longing for socially simpler days; the aging, longing for lost youth and innocence; and anyone muddling through a life crisis, who tends to remember as "the good old days" any period not containing the current crisis. We escape the present and its unpleasantness by slipping into another time, another place. There is so much stress in modern life that the marketing of nostalgia has become big business.

In a book such as the one you're holding, whose entire contents is the stuff of nostalgia, it is worth taking a moment to get technical about the subject. In *Yearning for Yesterday: A Sociology of Nostalgia,* sociologist Fred Davis defines three varieties of the emotion, not all pleasant.

Simple nostalgia is that subjective, unexamined state that tells you things were better, healthier, happier, more civilized, and more exciting then than they are now. Pure escapism.

Reflexive nostalgia goes a step deeper than sentimentalizing the past. Here you question, if only slightly, the validity of that warm emotion you feel. Was the time really that good? Was I actually happier then? More to the point: Am I forgetting the unpleasant things that occurred? Such truthful questioning, says Davis, enriches simple nostalgia, making it "a more complex human activity" from which we "can better comprehend ourselves and our past."

Interpreted nostalgia moves beyond escapism and historical accuracy. It gets problematic. You ask: Is something lacking in my life today to make me long for the past? Am I afraid of anything new, fearful of the future?

In today's world, advertisers play on the escapism of simple nostalgia, psychologists employ the therapeutic probing of reflexive nostalgia, psychiatrists treat the neuroses of interpreted nostalgia.

As you browse through this book, I hope the material will evoke the spontaneous flush of simple nostalgia and the honest questioning of reflexive nostalgia. It is not my intent to open the Pandora's box that is interpreted nostalgia.

"What do you suppose it means," asks one woman of another in a famous *New Yorker* cartoon, "when everything that's going on consists of stuff that's coming back?"

Be assured of this: As you read through this book's material, there exists the likelihood that any entry—a dance, a sitcom, a fad toy, or a behavioral folly—could, at this very moment, be on its way back into vogue. That is the nature of a popular culture fired by the big business of nostalgia. To be sure, a fad is happening now.

Origin of Fads

> Each age has its own follies, as its majority is made up of foolish young people.
>
> —**Ralph Waldo Emerson**

One might imagine that Emerson was no longer young when he penned that snipe. Since Emerson's day, the fad—that trivial fancy pursued for a brief time with irrational zeal—has changed . . . though only in order of magnitude. What a change that's been!

We'll see that during the hula hoop mania of the 1950s, 100 million of the $2 plastic rings were sold, suggesting that almost half the people in the country had one. That for three months in 1975, the pet rock craze convinced a million adults to plunk down $5 for a "quiet, well-behaved" rock. That for two years during the 1920s, mah-jongg held the country captive, with 15 million people playing the game. That the Trivial Pursuit mania of the 1980s generated retail sales of $850 million.

Mass communications, of course, accelerated fads, until we are at the stage today when we can truly say that it's a fad, fad, fad, fad world. One expert claims that if the hula hoop craze blossomed today, twice as many rings would be sold, but the mania would last only half as long as it did in the Fifties.

We'll see that many fads are ridiculous, that most fads are trivial, that all fads are short-lived. Also, that the true test of a fad is not its durability, but its desirability; its quantity, not its quality. For a fad to succeed, it must provide fun—pleasure is the primary excuse for a fad's existence. Aside, that is, from profit. The pleasurable aspect of a fad lays down in our brain a memory trace that on recall is nostalgia.

Whereas past centuries had occasional fads, our century can be charted by their continual creation and consumption—a realization that led me to arrange this book chronologically, as a sort of history text, though of a type not found in schools.

All fads, ancient and modern, depend on the amazing phenomenon of crowd behavior, a momentary madness of emotional contagion. "Anyone taken as an individual is tolerably sensible and reasonable," wrote the poet Schiller. "As a member of a crowd, he at once becomes a blockhead."

Or as Charles Mackay expressed collective behavior in his classic work, *Extraordinary Popular Delusions and the Madness of Crowds:* "Men . . . think in herds, while they recover their senses slowly, and one by one."

Finally, a word on leisure time.

Origin of Leisure Time

The right to be lazy.
—**Paul Lafargue**

The Right to Be Lazy was the title of a caustically witty tract by French physician Paul Lafargue, who championed shorter work weeks and more leisure time in a century characterized by debilitating overwork and underpay for most people.

A Marxist revolutionary who married Karl Marx's daughter, Lafargue inherited a fortune from his mother, enabling him to enjoy considerable leisure time himself. Practicing what he preached, he loved to "feast, socialize, and loaf." So committed was he to leisure that when his capital ran out in 1911 and he faced the prospect of spending his dotage in deprivation, the good-life physician injected himself with a lethally final solution. "I kill myself before pitiless old age, which carries away the pleasures and joys of existence one by one, paralyzes my energy, breaks my will," he explained in a farewell letter. To spare his wife, Laura, a life without leisure, he killed her, too.

However, his idea of leisure time for one and all lived on.

I don't mean to create a false impression. Mass leisure, long weekends, and month-long vacations were, in the 1890s, still decades away for most people. In England, France, and America, men, women, and even children could be forced to work a twelve-hour day. But, as we'll see in Chapter 1, the atmosphere of the Gay Nineties was abuzz with serious talk about a future "civilization of leisure," about a "civil right" to do what *you* wanted at least occasionally, not always constrained to do what someone else ordered of you.

In an earlier time, idleness had been the root of all gentle virtues. Leisure time then belonged to the aristocratic classes, the only people who engaged in trendy behavior and vogue attire. But that idleness fell into disgrace after the Industrial Revolution, with the rise of the hardworking middle class and the emergence of the modern edifice of commerce and industry. In time, the aristocrat who gloried in having nothing to do became a virtually extinct species.

With the death of idleness, the new and fairer notion of leisure time began to take shape in the minds of bosses and workers.

The right to work less and to enjoy more free time took its most distinctive shape in late Victorian times. This was one factor in my decision to begin this book in that historic period. In a relatively short time, many ordinary folk were enjoying such signs of leisure as music halls, café concerts, wax museums, bicycles, picture postcards, music boxes, and dressing up like the Gibson girl and the Gibson man—all social gathering spots and faddish pursuits unknown decades earlier. The attitude that all men and women, not just the aristocratic classes, were entitled to pursue trends and crazes had caught on—and could not be quashed.

In America, the pursuit of happiness was taking on a meaning broader than any imagined by the Founding Fathers. Today, we take it for granted that each of us is entitled to leisure, if not luxury—an attitude unimagined only a decade before the time frame of this book.

At your leisure,

Nostalgic browsing,
Charles Panati

CHAPTER 1

□

The Gay Nineties

1890 to 1899

The First Americans

The Gilded Age. The *Belle Epoque.* The Mauve Decade. Of all the labels affixed to the decade, none has stuck with more nostalgic might than the Gay Nineties. Its origin may come as a surprise.

That carefree-sounding phrase became popular in America in the not-so-gay Depression years of the 1930s. People looked backed with longing to the halcyon days of their parents' lives or of their own untroubled youth. Since then, the Gay Nineties has tagged an era in which Victorian elegance and formality waned, replaced by manners, lifestyles, and dress less formal and typically called American.

Actually, there was a lot of gaiety in the Nineties. The period was a happy, carefree time for many Americans, for whom the word gay meant "informal," and "to get gay" meant to take liberties unimaginable a decade earlier.

Money, the fuel of fads and leisure, was more abundant than ever. The American millionaire had become such a commonplace that the *New York Tribune* scanned the states and tallied heads for its readers: 4,047 American millionaires in the country; 145 of them living in San Francisco, 280 in Chicago, 155 in Brooklyn, 1,103 in Manhattan. At the time there was no income tax.

Mansions sprang up rapidly along New York's Fifth Avenue. "There are three at the corner of Fifty-seventh Street alone," gushed a Manhattan newspaper, "each worth more than a half-million—and the Vanderbilts, Astors, Belmonts, and many others are bringing over European paintings and statuary by the boatload." (That these shrewd families were often ruthless in business at home and worse in plundering antiquities abroad was seldom mentioned.) On the burgeoning of summer mansions in Newport, another newspaper commented that "not even a one-hundred-foot ballroom can hold all the rich." The

Nineties were quite gay for the rich (as all times have been), but the great difference was that for the first time increasing numbers of the not-so-rich were also gay.

In fashion, a stylish woman was still bundled up to the chin and robed to the floor, her feet discreetly hidden in shoes that had to be laboriously fastened with a buttonhook—an inconvenience that would lead in 1893 to the invention of the zipper. Her modish waist was created by an almost impregnable corset— which in a few years would give way to the invention of the modern bra.

We'll see in this chapter a gradual waning of the Victorian influence in the United States (several Gay Nineties fads had distinctly European roots), and the emergence of things uniquely American—dances, songs, personalities, and world's fairs, Yankee-style. Perhaps that creature who came to be known as the American was no better defined for all times than by the first vogues we'll examine, the Gibson girl and the Gibson man—a couple social historians call the first *real* Americans.

FADS, FOLLIES, AND TRENDS

Gibson Girl

Tall and stately, superbly dressed, artful but never wicked, she was an idealized woman, a raven-haired embodiment of every man's dream. Overnight the Gibson girl, who first appeared in the Nineties 10-cent humor magazine *Life*, became the idol and model for a generation of women. She was as much a label of her times as the bobbed-hair flapper who characterized a later decade.

But the Gibson girl was more. She was, in a very important sense, America's first lady.

Before illustrator Charles Dana Gibson synthesized his ideal woman, the image of the American girl—at home and abroad—was "vague, nondescript, inchoate," as the *New York World* archly reported: "As soon as the world saw Gibson's ideal it bowed down in adoration, saying: 'Lo, at last the typical American girl.' " Though that may be overstating the case slightly—given the reality that no girl may have actually resembled Gibson's fantasy—the image was all-American and highly influential on a generation and on the blossoming twentieth century.

Idealized women had accounted for a large share of faddish imitation in the late 1800s. But those women were European by nationality, Victorian by morality. Gibson's liberated creation defined for the world the American ideal of femininity at the turn of the century. With her high pompadour, tight waist, and aloof beauty, she became America's first pin-up, the undisputed goddess of an era. She influenced fashion (until the Twenties), popularizing the Gibson girl blouse, a starched, tailored shirtwaist with leg-of-mutton sleeves and a high collar with an ascot tie at the neck; the dark, floor-length Gibson girl skirt, worn over Gibson girl petticoats; and the divided skirt that Gibson girl imitators favored for bicycling. She even popularized the phrase hourglass figure.

From America in the twentieth century, there would come a long line of faddish female icons—the **Ziegfeld girl** (1900s), the **vamp** (1910s), the **flapper** and the **It girl** (1920s), the **Miss America Bathing Beauty** (1930s), the **sex kitten** and the **sweater girl** (1940s), the **sex symbol** (1950s), the **playmate** and the **bunny** (1960s)—but the Gibson girl was the first. Fiction that she was, the Gibson girl also exuded what was being called the American personality. And as Oscar Wilde sagely summed up history: "It is personalities, not principles, that move an age."

How the fad was launched:

Commercialization of an American Image. Charles Dana Gibson, born on September 14, 1867, in Roxbury, Massachusetts (he died December 23, 1944, in New York City), was an artist and illustrator. After studying for a year at the Art Students' League in Manhattan, Gibson began contributing stylish pen-and-ink drawings to the humor weekly *Life*. His Gibson girl drawings, characterized by a fastidious refinement of light ink lines, were modeled after his wife. So in demand did Charles Gibson become that at one point *Collier's Weekly* paid him $50,000—the largest amount then ever paid to an illustrator—for a single double-page illustration every week for a year. And so popular was one series of drawings, "The Education of Mr. Pipp," that it became the basis for a highly successful play.

From the Nineties until the First World War, most American women between the ages of fifteen and thirty yearned to look like the dazzling, self-assured visions that floated through the situational drawings of Charles Gibson. The success of his pen-and-ink ladies astonished their creator, who saw himself more as a social satirist than a fashion trendsetter. He initially created his idealized woman only to serve as a character in his political and social cartoons. Instead, she became the center of attraction. "If I hadn't seen it in the papers," he said, referring to the countless references to his creation, "I should never have known that there was such a thing as a Gibson girl."

The American image quickly traveled abroad, through pirated illustrations and romanticized hype. A European commentator exclaimed of America's Gibson girl wannabes: "Parents in the United States are no better than elsewhere, but their daughters! Divinely tall, brows like Juno, lovely heads poised on throats Aphrodite might envy." Artist Joseph Pennell, after a stroll in Manhattan, remarked, "Fifth Avenue is like a procession of Gibsons."

The commercialization of an image was nothing new in the Nineties, and in short time Gibson licensed his girls. Glazed on china plates, etched into silverware, embroidered on pillows and tablecloths, and decaled on whisk-broom holders, as well as any other surface that would take an imprint, the Gibson girl became in its day a financial bonanza like . . . well, Schulz's "Peanuts," or Henson's Muppets. Before Charles Dana Gibson was thirty-five, he'd published nine volumes of his drawings—which also appealed to Americans because they always lampooned social climbers, expatriates smitten with all things European, and the foibles of society.

So ubiquitous and influential was the Gibson girl image that its creator was charged with competing against the then-famous Butterick dress patterns—the first, and enormously popular, paper dress cut-arounds which in the Nineties were selling at the rate of more than 10 million a year. A woman who wished to make herself over was said to be "taking the Gibson cure."

As sharp a businessman as he was an illustrator, Gibson made the most of his worldwide publicity. When an automobile manufacturer asked him to create a Gibson girl drawing for an industry advertising contest, offering a cash prize to the winning illustrator but demanding the right to keep the drawings of all losing artists, Gibson wrote back: "I am running a competition for automobiles. Kindly submit one of yours. If acceptable, it wins an award. If rejected, it becomes my property."

Gibson Man

This imitative fad was not so large as its female equivalent, but it did change the way in which many men saw themselves. In illustrations, the Gibson girl was often accompanied by a handsome swain who, also to Gibson's surprise, became known as the Gibson man. Physically patterned on Gibson himself (as well as on the popular author Richard Harding Davis), this escort was strong-jawed, straight-backed, resolutely clean-shaven, and straightforward in manner and address.

Until the Gibson man appeared, American males had prided themselves on the lush beards and distinguished mustaches copied from European aristo-crats—continental gentlemen. Within a short time the hirsute appearance was out, and a clean-cut American handsomeness was in. Bachelors who were Gibson men were encouraged to decorate their apartments in Gibson girl wallpaper and to pad their suit jackets to achieve the broad-shouldered Gibson man ideal.

Today, Gibson's drawings evoke both nostalgia and full-blown images of life in the Gay Nineties. Historically, they are significant in that they drew a diffuse young nation, still satisfied with copying its European parent, into sharp focus, establishing a look and a feel and a style distinctly American.

Bicycling as a National Pastime

In the Nineties, the bicycle (bi, "two"; Greek kuklos, "wheel") was not itself new. But the safety bicycle (essentially the model we know today), the bicycle built for two, and the nickname bike were new, as was the national mania for bicycling, as well as the gynecological side effects of the pastime. The Georgia Journal of Medicine and Surgery reported that "the pedaling machine" produced a dangerous female disorder, especially at exhilarating speeds when "the body is thrown forward, causing the clothing to press against the clitoris, thereby eliciting and arousing feelings hitherto unknown and unrealized by the young maiden."

Whether Sunday bicycling aroused feminine feelings at all new is uncertain, but it was such a craze that in 1896 Scientific American reported that watch-

makers and jewelers were going out of business because people were spending their "luxury" money for bikes. "The tailor, the hatter, the bookseller, the shoemaker, the horse dealer, and the riding master," exclaimed the journal, "all tell similar tales of woe."

Tailors complained that cyclists so often dressed in their "cheap bicycle suits" that people no longer wore out their quality tailor-made clothes. Theater owners offered discounts to lure cyclists off their wheels and into music hall seats.

The issue got to Congress. Mad hatters claimed that bicycling kept people from purchasing hats because at the speeds attained by bikes, headwear was an impracticality. One congressman introduced a proposal that would have required every bike rider to buy two hats a year. Due to the popularity of biking, which caused the relative unpopularity of most other diversions, the *New York Journal of Commerce* reported that in one year alone merchandisers of competing goods lost $117 million. Booksellers, reported *Scientific American,* complained that "people who are rushing about on wheels, days, nights, and Sundays, no longer read anything." Claims were made that before the turn of the century America would be a nation of physically exhausted illiterates. The clergy, who would later lambaste "automobiling" as an invitation to sin, denounced cyclists for the utter idleness of the cycling vice, and the fact that it enabled young couples to escape from the watchful eyes of their elders. Cy-

"Wheels of Happiness."

IT'S A COLUMBIA.

When all the world's on wheels, there'll be no sorrow here below — for all the world'll be happy, and there'll be health and good digestion everywhere — and the best part of the world will ride Columbias, for Columbias are sound, one priced, beautiful to look upon, of lasting durability.

Book about Columbias, free at Columbia agencies. By mail for two 2-cent stamps. Pope Mfg. Co., Boston, New York, Chicago, Hartford.

BEAUTIFUL PICTURE. The above is a wood engraving of it — on plate paper, — as large as most oil paintings — printed in 16 water colors — the most exquisite picture ever given away — artistic enough for any drawing-room — mounted for hanging without frame, or for framing. Sent for five 2-cent stamps to pay for packing and postage. Address, Art Department, Pope Mfg. Co., Boston, Mass.

clists, preached one priest, were "condemned to a place where there is no mud on the streets because of its high temperature."

How big was the fad in numbers? In 1884, the year the safety bike began to challenge older models, Americans bought about 20,000 vehicles. By 1895 the number had climbed to an astonishing 10 million—a truly remarkable figure considering that bikes were never cheap: Versions of the safety bike cost between $50 and $150.

Yet people from all walks of life clamored for bikes. Doctors pedaled to house calls, students pedaled to school, salesmen cycled through their rounds. For the average woman, the bike was a liberating invention that enabled her to venture beyond the confining radius of her home—a fact that troubled preachers and husbands alike. As for the cost of a bike, keep in mind the comparative expense of owning a horse and buggy: The animal had to be fed, groomed, sheltered, and doctored, and the carriage required continual maintenance.

Safety Bike and Bicycle Built for Two.   The bicycle—one of the most efficient means of converting human energy into propulsion—was invented in 1839 by Scottish blacksmith Kirkpatrick MacMillian, and it sparked no fad. Called boneshakers, early bikes had large front wheels, small back wheels, and metal-rimmed tires that transmitted every jolt from the dirt or cobble road. In 1876 a London inventor introduced the **spoked tension wheel,** whose light weight and high strength allowed for the design of an extraordinary variety of bicycles. Then in 1888 John Dunlop guaranteed all future cyclists a smooth ride by introducing the air-filled **pneumatic tire.**

What launched the bicycling fad of the Nineties was the 1884 **safety bicycle,** with its pneumatic tires, medium-sized wheels of equal diameter, chain linkage, adjustable handlebars, cushioned seat, coaster brakes, and comfort and ease of riding. What also promoted bicycling was the **bicycle built for two**—both the gadget and the hit song of that title. The tandem bike was perfected in the early years of the Nineties. Greatly popularized by the publicized Sunday rides of Diamond Jim Brady and Lillian Russell in New York's Central Park, the tandem bike allowed couples to cycle together, another irritant for the clergy.

Hit Bike Songs. In 1892 the tandem bicycle was immortalized in Harry Dacre's song "Daisy Bell," popularly known as **A Bicycle Built for Two.** The tune swept the nation and was quickly followed by a host of songs celebrating all aspects of the bike culture: The boastful **The Cycle Man;** the women's militant **The March of the Bloomers** (referring to the cycling garb for women, invented by feminist Amelia Jenks Bloomer); the facetious **When Trilby Rides a Wheel** (referring to the era's Trilby fad; see page 48); the liberated lover's **I Love You, Bicycle and All;** and the mournful tribute to a woman who had forsworn the cycling vice, **Her Bloomers Are Camphored Away.**

Men used the bike to display to girlfriends and wives their mechanical ingenuity. "Purchase a vehicle, then soup it up" was the strategem—one later used on automobiles. The national bicycling mania was, however, relatively short-lived. True, some sages had forecast that cycling was a passing fad, "a toy of which people will grow weary." Others argued that "the time will soon come when the horse will resume his place in the interest and affections" of men and women. What no one had foreseen, though, was the advent of the horseless carriage—the car. The horse, of course, never returned to its former glory, and bicycling has returned periodically as a pastime and as a means of exercising, but not as the craze it once was.

Interestingly, bicycling existed not among the wealthy classes, who preferred their elaborate, showy horse-drawn carriages. The bike craze was largely created by the middle class, which was growing faster than at any time in history, and enjoying more leisure time. By 1910 the bicycle fad had considerably died down, with bikes relegated to Christmas gifts for children. Adults had begun their love affair with the automobile (see page 93).

Music Box

The late-1800s love affair was with large, cabinet-sized instruments that, through the change of a brass cylinder or disc, played a repertory of opera arias, folk songs, and popular tunes of the day. Immensely popular and found in many homes, this music box—technically an idiophone, an instrument with resonating parts that are plucked rather than vibrated by percussion—was the phonograph of its day. Its changeable cylinders or discs were the equivalent of later records.

"Instant music! Notewise perfection!" heralded one advertisement, and within the means of the burgeoning middle class. In an era when most people did not have ready access to classical concerts or bandstands, the music box brought "automatic music" into the home, and its mass acceptance in America was made possible through the mail-order catalogs of the era, known as wish books. Sears, Roebuck and Montgomery Ward devoted pages to the instruments, describing the beauty of the hardwood cabinets, the clarity of sound, and the availability of discs.

Music then was often bought not by title but by lot: "Trust us," ran an ad, "to send you a very pleasant selection." Here is one "trust us" medley from a Montgomery Ward catalog: "The musical casket will play hymns, popular airs, sets of Quadrilles, Polkas, Waltzes . . . Reels, Hornpipes, Operatic and the most difficult pieces," all heard with "cleanness, accuracy, and a degree of execution which but a few performers can equal." All ads stressed that "a false note is impossible." Not only were the boxes popular in homes, but they provided music in ice-cream parlors, stores, and churches. Their heyday of popularity and perfection, ironically, coincided with Thomas Edison's refinement of the phonograph—the fatal competition.

The music box with disc "records" originated in Switzerland near the end of the eighteenth century. The boxes developed from the miniaturization of a wide range of musical clocks, instruments, and novelty gadgets like the singing bird—all so popular that serious composers wrote for the devices. Beethoven composed "The Battle of Cittoria" in 1813 for the panharmonium; Haydn composed a medley for three musical clocks; Mozart wrote "Fantasies in F Minor" for a mechanical flute, as well an "Adagio for the Harmonica"; Berlioz wrote a part for the harmonica in his "Fantasia on the Tempest."

By the Gay Nineties, a family could have instant music in the home with simply the turn of a crank. American inventors also conceived of giant-sized, coin-operated public music boxes (forerunner of the jukebox), and throughout the United States people could choose selections from penny-in-slot or nickel-in-slot machines. At their peak of perfection in the Nineties, music boxes chimed in the turn of the century—a tune that was simultaneously their death knell.

Phonograph.　Edison's early phonographs of the 1880s had provided no real competition for the home music box. The clarity of notes from the music box was perfection, whereas the sound of music (and voice) from the phonograph was atrocious—to say nothing of the new invention's high price tag. Initially, the phonograph was itself thought of as merely a novelty, a curious fad. Few people at the start of the Nineties imagined that the music box, with its seemingly endless supply of new discs, could ever be shouldered aside.

The aspect of the phonograph that most seriously doomed the music box, though, was that it exactly reproduced not only music, but the human voice. By the close of the decade, Edison's talking machine had begun to relegate the music box from the living room to the attic. A sign of the times, and of recorded music's future, occurred when the popular Regina Music Box Company of New Jersey—located not far from Edison's laboratory—abandoned manufacturing their boxes for an entirely nonmusical product: vacuum cleaners. Prices for the elaborate boxes had plummeted, advertisements stopped appearing in newspapers, and the music box, once a home luxury, was banished to barns, cellars, or junk shops, or—as was often the case—was scrapped for war material during World War I. In time the passion of owning the latest music box became the obsession of collecting antique boxes.

*Thomas Edison
with phonograph.*

Fern Terrarium

The 1970s saw the fad of indoor plants: showy coleus, stately dracena, hanging baskets, jade plants, and ficus trees. It was not the first time that people brought nature indoors with a passion bordering on pretension.

Growing exotic ferns in sealed bottles was a mid-Victorian obsession, and how-to books poured from the presses exploiting the fad—which had a name: pteridomania (*pteris,* Greek for "fern," which is itself from *pteron,* meaning "feather," for the fern's featherlike resemblance). Sealed fern terrariums, called Wardian cases, were prominently displayed in homes and seductively described by fern-writers (like Shirley Hibberd) as "plumy emerald green pets," a personification not unlike the hype surrounding the later pet rocks.

How the faddish indoor keeping of what Shirley Hibberd called "vegetable jewelry" began is a fascinating tale of the popularization of a scientific discovery.

One day in 1829, British surgeon Nathaniel Ward, an amateur entomologist, found a developing moth cocoon and brought it home in an attempt to hatch it, sealing it in a bottle for winter. Come spring, no moth had emerged, but something completely unexpected had occurred: A tiny fern had sprouted from the damp mold on which the cocoon was lying—*without having been watered.* Ward had accidentally discovered that plants enclosed in airtight glass cases and exposed to sunlight are self-sustaining.

After the fern had continued to thrive for *two decades,* Ward displayed it at London's Great Exhibition of 1851. By this time, the discovery's commercial potential was being exploited. While scientists used Wardian cases to safely import exotic plants from the far-off tropics (long sea voyages and salt-air spray had doomed earlier efforts), florists sold "plumy green pets in glittering crystal palaces" (ferns in a bottle) for the home.

The fad appealed to women, particularly young, unmarried women with the luxury of leisure time. They bought ferns, collected other specimens from the wild, and mastered their tongue-twisting Latin names. "Your daughters, perhaps, have been seized with the prevailing Pteridomania," wrote Anglican clergyman Charles Kingsley, one of the first churchmen to support Darwin's theories. He advised parents not to fret, for their daughters were probably "more active, more cheerful, more self-forgetful" pursuing the fad, while "dreamy idleness has all but vanished from your drawing-room."

The fad and the scientific breakthrough progressed apace for a number of years. Botanists ferried exotic species around the world in Wardian cases, establishing China tea as a cash crop in India and South American rubber as an industry in Malaya. Meanwhile, young ladies, calling themselves pteridomaniacs, denuded the countryside of ferns, housing them in elaborate cases that mimicked Westminster Abbey, Oriental pagodas, and the Crystal Palace. A botanist warned that rarer ferns were virtually extinct in England.

In *The Victorian Fern Craze,* David Allen documents the mania as one of the major fads of the era. Young women not only grew ferns, but stenciled fern patterns on fabrics, wallpaper, and greeting cards, and collected fern-decorated china, textiles, woodwork, and frilly kerned wrought-iron garden furniture. At the height of the mania, florists hawked rare ferns on the street, while suppliers boasted of digging up "five tons of ferns in a single foray." The fad began in England and spread, on a lesser scale, to America, which was still coping with things British.

What kills a fad fastest is widespread popularity, and once every young lady had succumbed to the passion, the hobby lost its chic. Indeed, as one writer commented, "ferns became—horrible thought!—a little vulgar." Time was ripe for another craze, and it came, significantly, as an inspired offshoot of Ward's accidental discovery.

Goldfish Aquarium

Nathaniel Ward had experimented with adding chameleons and toads to his sealed fern terrariums, and ornamental fish to his tanks of aquatic plants. But it was fellow scientist Robert Warington, a chemist, who first fully enunciated the aquarium principle in 1850 and set the stage for the pet fish fad.

Previously, people who kept fish had to change or oxygenate the water regularly. Many wealthy women in the 1800s followed the lead of a Mrs. Anna Thynne, who had her maid aerate her fish tank by pouring the water backward and forward every day for an hour at a time. "This was doubtless a fatiguing operation," she conceded, "but I had a little handmaid, who, besides being rather anxious to oblige me, thought it rather an amusement."

Most people, though, did not have handmaids, and keeping an aquarium was a hobby bound to disappoint, since the most exotic fish invariably died. What catapulted keeping pet fish to a craze was the discovery that if plants were added to the water, they gave off enough oxygen to support animal life. Some enthusiasts had discovered this on their own, but Warington was the first person to fully explain and publicize the fact, having kept two goldfish and a *Valisneria spiralis* plant cohabiting in a 12-gallon tank for a year without changing the water. Furthermore, he announced that a few pond snails added to the tank kept the water and sandy floor clean. As Nathaniel Ward was the eponym of the Wardian case, Robert Warington was immortalized for a time in the Warrington case (even if his name was misspelled), which was advertised as an "Aquatic Plant Case or Parlor Aquarium."

The fad of fish-keeping on a large scale fell to naturalist Philip Gosse, who independently pursued the same experiments as Warington. Gosse promoted the idea of public aquariums, "zoos for fish," and assisted in the construction and stocking of an impressive tank for the London Zoo. He further piqued the public's attention by suggesting that self-sustaining "elegant vases" (home aquariums) could safely be stocked with small exotic fish and sea anemones.

Shortly after the publication of Gosse's how-to bestseller *The Aquarium,* the fish-keeping fad took off. "Elegant vases" popped up in drawing rooms in England and America. Often they were reconverted Wardian cases; passé ferns displaced by au courant fish. So rapidly did the craze spread that for a while it had no name. Gosse contemplated "vivarium," then "aqua-vivarium," and concluded, "Let the word AQUARIUM then be the one selected to indicate these interesting collections of aquatic animals and plants."

How-To Bestsellers.   Aquarium mania launched a cottage industry. Costly exotic fish were transported from the tropics, and quantities of fresh water and sea water were brought by railroad to suppliers. There were special fish foods to buy, as well as how-to books—a popular one, *Wonders of the Shore,* was by Charles Kingsley, who had documented the fern fad. Gosse topped his own first bestseller with *Handbook to the Marine Aquarium,* which sold two thousand copies in a few weeks. Virtually all the aquarium books were pirated in America. One New York publisher advertised twenty aquarium books, all by English authors.

The first American text was *Life Beneath the Waters; or the Aquarium in America* by Arthur M. Edwards. Edwards assured fish hobbyists that "objects for the purpose of stocking the Aquarium can be now purchased in New York City, and may soon be on sale in other of our large cities." New York enthusiasts hoping to save money, said Edwards, could, for a six-cent subway ride, find their own specimens by combing the shoreline of the East River at ebb tide.

Fish aquariums, like fern terrariums, were largely a female fad. Men did not yet keep brightly colored, delicate fish. Edwards emphasized both the fashionability of fish-keeping and the feminine delicacy of the hobby. "The lady part of the community," he wrote, will soon be "taking as much delight in the fitting up and management of these beautiful parlor ornaments as their sisters on the other side of the Atlantic."

The fad had a beneficial effect: the construction of major public aquariums. An early and famous one at Brighton, England, was advertised as "The Largest and most Beautiful Building devoted to Piscatorial Science in the World." It boasted fish "of great rarity," "Tanks nightly Illuminated," as well as "Promenade Concerts every Saturday—Band plays thrice daily."

It is hard for us to imagine the excitement of a person in the Nineties gazing for the first time at a creature as exotic and strange as an octopus: "The arrival of the octopus," wrote one public aquarium keeper, "attracted almost as much attention as the visit of a foreign emperor." At another aquarium the death of a porpoise was "mourned as a national calamity."

All fads end. Most vanish entirely. Others, though, evolve into hobbies. Aquariums, public and private, are still around, but not as the great novelties they once were. In fact, before the turn of the century the fad of the home aquarium had ended, while many public aquariums had been turned into freak shows. The Brighton Aquarium, for instance, to attract a steady influx of oglers, titillated with displays of human giants, midgets, Zulu chieftains, and Javanese temple dancers—none a piscatorial attraction. Philip Grosse's son, Edmund, was livid over the desecration of his father's invention. He did not comprehend that the public must always be given something new. A friend, more attuned to the nature of trends, observed, "Aquarium fever, which once swept through the country, has run its course, like hundreds of similar epidemics."

Dog Shows

The Victorian cult of the pet—to which we owe much—was at a feverish pitch in the Nineties. Whereas a dog show today is perhaps an annual event, in the Gay Nineties there were competitions almost weekly, and in England, birthplace of the phenomenon, almost every day of the year: 217 dog shows in 1892, 257 in 1895, 307 in 1897, and 380 in the last year of the decade. Showing a dog was the newest vogue, and owning a purebred was a status symbol for the upwardly mobile.

What, specifically, do we owe to the turn-of-the-century cult of the pet? That we now feed our pets from the table; dress them in elaborate outfits; build them houses; allow them to inconvenience human members of the household; chauffeur them to be professionally clipped, shampooed, and blow-dried—all of these relative commonplaces stem from an attitude toward pets that is rooted in a late-1800s passion. At that time, the middle class, copying the wealthy, began to pamper their dogs as pets. Previously, among the middle classes, a family dog was a combination of draft animal, spit turner, sheep herder, and home protector. Throughout the Renaissance, pet dogs remained the province of the upper classes, almost exclusively of women. Charles II is thought to be the first man to declare a public passion for pets. And when his animals were stolen, the king was inconsolable, advertising in a newspaper for their return. His brother, James II, shared this fondness, and from that time on dogs began to sit for formal portraits—either their own, or as a member of their human family.

Pampering pets did not become respectable among ordinary citizens until early in the nineteenth century—around the time of an increased public indulgence in what were called "the softer emotions." When Lord Byron buried his Newfoundland dog Boatswain within "the precincts of the sacred Abbey of Newstead," many people shared his sentiment that a dog offered greater loyalty and affection than a human friend—or as Byron expressed it on the monument: "all the Virtues of Man without his vices." By mid-century, the cult of the pet was well established.

First Official Show.   The first dog show was held in Newcastle, England, on June 28, 1859. It was sponsored by a Mr. Pape, a local sporting-gun maker; sixty pointers and setters competed. The prizes, provided by Mr. Pape, were guns from his store. Shows quickly sprang up all over England, then America. Within a decade, international dog shows were being staged in London and New York.

As the mania grew, so too did new commercial opportunities. Entrepreneurs began to market the first dog products: brass collars, monogrammed ceramic eating bowls, "Fibrine Dog Cakes," "Ashworth's Patented Metallic Comb-Brush," and "Mr. Paul's Dog's House and Yard Combined"—all faddish novelties. Of course, such purchases pointed to the status of the owner rather than that of the dog; a family that could pamper its pet had socially arrived. In the Gay Nineties, it was not uncommon for dog owners to have their monograms clipped into the pets' fur.

Signs of the cult were everywhere. In 1891 champion collies and St. Bernards sold for more than $2,000. Dog fancier magazines appeared, featuring articles such as "Portraits of Fox Terrier Men," and with regular departments including "Biographies of Celebrated Canines," "Gossip," "Debutantes" (animals appearing in their first dog show), and "Dog Visits" (a euphemism for who was being mated with whom; some owners introduced the "bride" to the "groom" in a "satin wedding coat"). At the height of this idolatry, professional dog stealers would abscond with a cherished "Debutante" or "Celebrated Canine," then offer to restore it for a price. Pet ransom was a flourishing business.

The rich had long kept idle animals; now, in a metonymic attempt at assimilation, the middle class borrowed the custom. Certain breeds became status symbols—as they still are. Queen Victoria fancied collies and Pomeranians, setting the mode. In the Gay Nineties, ownership of mongrels was thought to display commonness.

The countless dog shows of the decade were mostly regional affairs, offering fanciers the chance to show off their pets and to prepare for the big time. In 1890 almost fifteen hundred dogs competed at the Kennel Club show (the club originated at the height of the pet cult), and over seventeen hundred were entered in a show at the Crystal Palace.

Shows sorted people as well as dogs. The first dog show to become the world's most famous, later named the Crufts Show (after its originator, Charles

Cruft), was staged in Britain in 1891. By 1897 an encyclopedia on dogs described 274 distinct breeds. In this period the French created a bulldog, the British discovered the Basenji in Africa, and the Boston terrier—a cross between the English bulldog and bull terrier—appeared in the United States.

By the start of World War I, the cult mania had calmed. More than fifteen thousand dogs were called into service by the Allied forces, and almost a third of these were killed or lost in action—a war tale seldom told. Their tasks ranged from guard duty and patrol to carrying messages, munitions, and medical supplies to the front lines. Byron would have appreciated this noble use of the man's best friend, as Victorian cultists would certainly understand the celebrity of modern dogs like Lassie and Rin-Tin-Tin.

Calling Card Albums

Adolescent girls today might collect pictures of rock idols and hang them on their bedroom walls; in the Gay Nineties it was adult women—Queen Victoria among them—who collected pictures of celebrities, royalty, war heroes, and politicians, as well as scenes of exotic places, pasting them into *carte de visite*, or calling card albums. The fad was known as cartomania, and Victoria herself boasted of owning 110 albums—a veritable gallery of notables and a travelogue.

Carte de visite meant a photographic calling card, which began in mid-century; it was a 4-inch by 2½-inch visitor's card, bearing his or her photographic portrait. The idea was hatched by Parisian portrait photographer Andre-Adolphe-Eugene Disderi, who patented the four-lens *carte de visite* camera in 1854. Its mass-produced images (eight at a time) were cut into inexpensive portraits and separately mounted on calling cards, which the French called *nom de plume*.

The calling cards became a wildly popular fad for two reasons: the great novelty of inexpensive portraits, and the fact that French Emperor Napoleon III posed for Disderi, catapulting the photographer and his process to sudden fame. In time, *cartes de visite* not only were presented when calling on someone, but were exchanged on birthdays and holidays, and were obsessively cherished and displayed in albums in homes. During the American Civil War, *cartes de visite* of famous generals and heroes were a booming business in major cities— bequeathing to us an unexpected pictorial legacy of the era.

Today, a family album contains pictures relating in some way to family, its members and their adventures. But during the height of cartomania, women traded and fought over pictures of notable persons, exotic scenes, or works of art, and purchased others from magazines like *Godey's Lady's Book* for the sum of 15 cents each, or eight for a dollar. Ladies were advised that at this low price, they could furnish their albums at comparatively small cost and feature a stunning variety. By analogy, this would be like ordering from *Cosmopolitan* photographs of Elizabeth Taylor, Kurt Russell, and George Bush, as well as images of the Empire State Building and the Grand Canyon, and pasting them into your album alongside family pictures.

Today, when the visual image is a glut verging on an intrusion, we cherish only the most personally meaningful images. But in the early days of photography, almost any clear image was a gem to treasure. And, too, most people had never seen the visages of famous people, or the landscapes of Africa, the Orient, and other exotic places. The *carte de visite* album became something of a paste-up hybrid of *US* magazine and *National Geographic.*

The Pose.   A trip to a photography studio in the Gay Nineties was an elaborate undertaking. There was endless concern with proper attire, correct makeup (for men and women), and the most flattering pose and expression. Women were advised against "wearing excessive trappings" (jewelry caused photographic glare), and gentlemen were told not to wear "too closely fitting garments."

Many people believed that "if the features are unnaturally inanimate, heavy and dull while sitting, the picture must necessarily depict some degree of mental imbecility." Ladies tightly compressed their lips to make the mouth appear "small, dainty, and pretty"—vogue of the day. There were technical problems due to exposure times and lighting. A dark-complexioned man, for instance, whose face required more projected light, could not pose between two women of light complexion—the lower light requirement for the women could blacken the man's face, whereas brighter light for the man would wash out the women's features. And the time requirement to hold a pose meant that babies and small children often appeared as blurs, unless they were threatened into motionlessness.

At the height of cartomania, New York City had more than ninety portrait galleries, which churned out tens of thousands of small "study" shots for individuals and families eager to have their images preserved. CDVs, as the *cartes* are now called, were produced by the millions, and today photographs of ordinary folk are worth no more than a dollar or two apiece, whereas quality *cartes* of the era's true notables command considerably more.

Kodak Brownie

What helped put an end to the fad of cartomania—in addition to its own excess of overproduction—was the invention and popularization of George Eastman's inexpensive Kodak camera, the Brownie, which launched a do-it-yourself photographic fad. The first camera to use roll film (as opposed to individual plates), it came factory-loaded with a hundred-exposure film pack that users mailed back to the company for development. Kodak's slogan, "You press the button and we do the rest," convinced millions of technology-shy Americans that they could be their own best photographers. Introduced in the first year of the new decade, 1900, the Brownie sold for a dollar, and replacement film cost 15 cents a roll. The model was made of heavy cardboard, reinforced with wood and covered with black imitation leather. Each roll of film produced 2¼-inch by 2¼-inch pictures.

In choosing the name Brownie, Eastman tipped his hat in thanks to his manufacturing collaborator Frank Brownell, and also to the artist Palmer Cox, whose elfin "brownie" cartoon characters appeared in ads for the camera as well as on the Brownie box itself. The simplicity of the camera made it an immediate hit, and the dollar price tag put it in reach of millions of Americans who at the turn of the century were still marveling at the magic of "instant" pictures. The sheer quantity of do-it-yourself photographs quickly devalued the worth of *cartes* of even the deservedly famous. Once every family owned a camera and snapped its own pictures, the *cartes* became unwanted parlor room clutter.

Picture Postcards

Another fad to blossom from the novelty of the photographic image was collecting picture postcards. Today, at poolside during a Caribbean vacation, we might dash off a few gloating words to friends back home on the back of a picture postcard that, when received, is glanced at, read, and discarded. However, a century ago the Western world was in the throes of "postcarditis," and the travelogue pictures were saved in shoeboxes to be passed on to the next generation.

One cynic of the fad claimed that "postcarditis causes fatty degeneration of the brain." A noted stage actress boasted of owning 73,445 picture postcards. At one point, fanatical collectors picketed in front of U.S. post offices that placed their cancellation stamps on the *back* of a postcard and not on its image-bearing front, for cards that bore the mark of a distant place on the picture were enviously prized. Today, anyone wishing to comprehend the scope of this collecting mania and the lavishness of its cards can visit the extraordinary postcard collection at the New York Public Library.

To backtrack slightly. Before the picture postcard there was the **blank postcard.** These straw-colored cards (decades later they would be bleached white), for bearing a message through the mail at a cost less than the envelope letter rate, were first issued in Austria in October 1869 and called, fittingly, a *Korrespondenz Karte.* The idea was picked up by other European countries, and the U.S. Postal Service inaugurated postcard use on May 13, 1873. Almost at once American businesses realized the cards could be used for advertising, and companies began printing product names (and addresses of sales locations) on the blank side and mailing the cards in large numbers to potential customers— early junk mail.

A fad was launched around 1880 when pictures began appearing on one side of postcards. The first images were mostly primitive engravings of buildings and lithographed pictures of ships, animals, and human figures. Extremely popular, picture postcards sold in numbers upward of several million a year. The fad exploded in the Gay Nineties when the first cards printed by private enterprises, called private mailing cards, were permitted to be sold in the United States. By this time improvements in lithography made possible the reliable production of brilliantly colored cards in quantity.

Golden Era. The early years of the new century are considered the golden era of postcard production. During this time, lavish, well-constructed cards were imported from Germany and England.

American postcard mania is traced back to the Columbian Exposition in Chicago in 1893 (see page 33). There millions of fairgoers glimpsed their first picture postcards and had an opportunity to purchase them—not necessarily to mail to someone else, but to hoard for their own perusing pleasure. Themes were an important part of collecting. A lover of cats, for instance, collected cat cards. Not surprisingly, postcards of foreign capitals were in vogue at a time when people were genuinely surprised at how small the world was becoming. It was standard traveling practice that when arriving in a foreign city, one headed first to a picture postcard store, made purchases, addressed cards back home, and only then commenced with sightseeing.

The faddish aspect of collecting had ended before World War I, done in by a glut of the cards, a decrease in their quality, and, in no small measure, the popularity of George Eastman's do-it-yourself Brownie camera. And, too, around this time companies like Hallmark began promoting inexpensive folded greeting cards, which allowed for a longer and more private message. Picture postcards have, of course, lasted; they are found now on racks at corner drugstores, in the vestibules of European cathedrals, and in the souvenir shops of art museums. No longer the vicarious eye-openers they once were, today they are hoarded only by deltiologists (postcard collectors) and admiringly discussed as much for their intrinsic beauty as for their exchangeable worth.

3-D Viewers

A third fad to spring from the novelty of the photographic image was the hand-held stereoscopic viewer, a crossbow-shaped item for fusing three-dimensional scenes in space. Called a stereopticon in the Nineties, it was something of the hologram of its day, providing an illusion of reality that was at once believable and sensational. To see 3-D in fixed perspective was every bit as magical then as holography's wraparound image is today. The well-appointed drawing room or parlor had at least one stereopticon viewer. People who seldom traveled beyond the outskirts of their town were able to glimpse in 3-D such exotica as "Gypsies by the Walls of Jerusalem" from the Holy Land series, one of the most popular purchases of the day.

The stereoscope is made possible because our eyes operate with binocular vision: The left-eye view and the right-eye view of a scene are perceived from different angles. In the brain, the separate perceptions are combined and interpreted in terms of depth. The stereopticon—which in a plastic version would become a fad in the 1950s—sold in the Gay Nineties for less than 15 cents, while a hundred right-left 3-D cards, from a wide range of scenes, could be purchased for less than a dollar.

Not that the stereopticon was new in the 1890s—it was invented within a decade of the birth of photography; stereoscopic cameras photographed American Civil War scenes. But the early view holder and its 3-D cards were priced beyond the reach of the middle class. The fad erupted on a large scale when view holders and right-left paired cards (which measured about 7 inches by 3 inches) were priced for the masses.

What images did people most wish to see in 3-D? Travelogues and daring adventure series were bestsellers. In particular, views of donkey trips through the Grand Canyon and of the gushing geysers of Yellowstone Park, as well as the harrowing images of whalers harpooning and of Robert Peary's trekking expeditions in the Arctic. On the more voyeuristic side, ordinary folk bought up hundreds of series on how the wealthy lived in European castles and stately country homes—a curiosity not unlike that behind the success of television's "Lifestyles of the Rich and Famous." Men prized (and concealed) their "girlie" cards, like the hootchy-kootchy shenanigans of belly dancer Little Egypt from the 1893 Chicago Columbian Exposition.

Today, the cards and view holders are staple items in museums and antique shows. The devices were so wildly popular, with hundreds of thousands of cards produced by a single manufacturer, that they provide us with a rich visual record of the Gay Nineties. Early in the 1900s, when stereopticon cards began appearing as giveaways in cereal boxes, their faddish appeal vanished. These freebies were of poor quality and glutted a market that was already over-crowded. The stereopticon fad, taken with the era's manias for *cartes de visite* and picture postcards, presaged the obsessive romance the twentieth century would have with the visual image.

Pigs in Clover Puzzle

The phrase "like pigs in clover" originated in the early 1800s as an expression of blissful happiness, where "clover" was a polite stand-in for "shit." Near the end of the century the phrase was the name of a game that swept the country like, as a toy authority said, "a plague of locusts." Pigs in Clover was phenomenally popular—particularly in the nation's capital, where the symbolism of the spoils system was obvious—and underscored the carefree shift in attitude of the Gay Nineties.

Previously, moralistic games were bestsellers. Mid-century, the Mansion of Happiness game created a fad with its goal of teaching adolescents the "Virtues of Industry, Honesty, and Sobriety." Then came the militantly moralistic Game of Pope or Pagan, with its auspicious subtitle "The Siege of the Stronghold of Satan by the Christian Army." The firm of Milton Bradley introduced its tremendously popular Checkered Game of Life, in which, with providence's luck, you might land on squares labeled "Happiness," "Industry," "Virtue," or, through grave misfortune, land on "Gambling," "Poverty," or "Suicide." The game mimicked the full spectrum of life's vicissitudes, and the word checkered in the title was appreciated by one and all. Popular, too, were Civil War games, replete with heroics, slaughter, and bloodshed. In terms of faddishness, these games were the Rubik's Cube or Trivial Pursuit of their seasons, but with a difference: They taught moral lessons. In one sense, this enabled games to overcome the still-strong Puritan scruples against frivolous play.

Then came the Gilded Age and . . .

Games of Greed.   The new fad games reflected the freer times and new-found self-interests. Parker Brothers introduced the self-explanatory Game of Banking, while the 1889 Montgomery Ward catalog highlighted the hit Money

Makes Money, followed in 1895 by the popular Game of Business. In The Monopolist, players moved around a board "in the great struggle between Capital and Labor," where, "if the players are successful, they can break the Monopolist, and become Monopolists themselves." No moral lessons there.

But the most sensational game of the period, which sold in the hundreds of thousands, was Pigs in Clover. Conceived by Charles Crandall of Waverly, New York, a veteran inventor of toys, Pigs hit the public fancy immediately. Three weeks after its introduction in 1889, the *Waverly Free Press* reported that Crandall's "toy works are turning out 8000 a day and are twenty days behind in their orders." A New York headline read: EVERYBODY DRIVING PIGS—SOMETHING ABOUT THE LATEST TOY AND ITS GENERAL EFFECT.

At parties society folk cajoled, "Have you driven the pigs yet?" And people macabrely joked that only two things could have swept the country faster: "A conflagration and the cholera." The novelty was a hand-held puzzle that required the player to maneuver four marbles through a circular maze into a central enclosure. Sounds dull. But call the marbles pigs, the maze fences, the enclosure their pen, and the maneuvering driving, and you have one stampede of a fad.

It was a frivolous game, and serious people went wild for it. "Pig-driving," reported the *New York World,* "has become the fashionable occupation in Gotham. Everybody is crazy over it from the society belles on Fifth Avenue down to the little cash girls, and from the Wall Street bankers to the Italian bootblacks." It was billed by newspapers and magazines as "the sensation of the day," and the hyped comparison was leveled that "Barnum's greatest show on earth is nothing to it." Congressmen played it in the Capitol. The *New York Tribune* reported that senators from Alabama, Louisiana, Mississippi, and West Virginia "sent a page to buy a half dozen of the puzzles which they played for an hour in Senate Chambers."

Rip-offs. Even with modern mass-production techniques, a novelties manufacturer is often caught short by the unexpected success of a product. This was the case with Pigs, and with its selling agent, Selchow & Righter (who six decades later would experience the same bind with Scrabble). Public demand was such that the *New York Evening Sun* sent a reporter to the distribution warehouse. Mr. Righter explained, "We have sold out 200,000 so far," forecasting that while "It is impossible to say how many will be sold before the craze runs its course, a million puzzles will probably fall short of the number." Astute about the nature of fads, he predicted, "When it dies it will go very suddenly. All booms die suddenly."

Because of a delay in filing for a patent, Charles Crandall found that part of the country's mania for Pigs in Clover was being filled by such rip-off games as Pigs in Sty and Pigs Running Wild. The public could not get enough pigs—in any form. A store in Cleveland constructed a giant replica of the game in its window with live pigs in the maze. For hours each day a farmboy attempted to drive the pigs into their pen. "The crowds that congregate," reported a paper, "blockaded the streets and had to be dispersed by the police."

Pig fever spread across the Atlantic. The *New York Herald* ran a story from London headlined: A NEW AMERICAN DEVICE FOR THE PROPAGANDA OF INSANITY IN GREAT BRITAIN. "Apparently an infant's plaything," the article claimed, "it can take a strong man in its octopus-like tentacles and swirl him in the wildest abyss of insanity as easy as rolling off a log."

After several months, the fad did indeed die suddenly—replaced with a new Crandall game, Growth of a Century, a tie-in with the nationwide celebration of the hundredth anniversary of the Constitution and Washington's inauguration. (Interestingly, another Selchow & Righter game of the period, Parcheesi, never achieved faddish mass appeal, but sold modestly year after year, building a following.)

Charles Crandall, who better than anyone of his time understood the fickle appeal of a fad, died in Waverly, New York, on June 30, 1905. A magazine said, "He devoted his whole life to inventing clever devices to amuse the old and delight the young, and his success has surpassed that of any other inventor on either side of the Atlantic." The *New York Tribune* eulogized, "In his day, he probably furnished more pleasure through toys and puzzles than any other person in the country."

Leisure Time Games for Kids

Beginning in the Gay Nineties, with reduction in the length of the work week for children (who previously worked as long and hard as adults), there was a major attempt to redefine toys and games for children. Today, when playthings are pitched directly to children, it's hard to imagine a time when kids were not thought of as a vast and lucrative market. Most social observers agreed that nonworking children were largely idle in their free time. A survey in Milwaukee, Wisconsin, concluded that 50 percent of nonworking children "did nothing" on a typical day. A Cleveland study found 40 percent idle and bored. To help remedy the problem, in 1906 educators founded the Playground Association, which marked the beginning of organized children's games and sports in the United States.

Those children who did have time to play most often engaged in what are called street games, and the most popular of the period were Old World hand-me-downs.

Simon Says.   The mimicry game was popular in England as early as 1850, known as Wiggle-Waggle. One person, the leader, shouts rapid-fire commands prefaced with "Simon says," which the players must enact. Unless, that is, the leader omits the prefacing phrase, which is grounds for an inattentive player to be out.

Supposedly the American version was called Do This, Do That, until it was unveiled in the Borscht Belt of New York's Catskill Mountains by a social director named Simon. He renamed the game, and it quickly swept the East Coast, bringing him a modicum of fame.

Giant Steps.   Played in Israel under the name Aba, for Father May I? and in the Fatherland Germany as Mother May I? it came to America—from England, where it might have derived from a game of despotism called Judge and Jury—and became immensely popular as Giant Steps.

A game leader calls out commands, and the players must beg permission to follow them with the phrase "May I?" Forgetting the politeness, a player is out. Game authorities claim that only in America was it played by both sexes; elsewhere it was a girls' game.

Leapfrog.   References to the game of children leaping over the backs of other children are ancient, and in *Henry V* Shakespeare writes, "If I could win a lady at leapfrog." It hit Europe in a big way in the late Middle Ages, and is depicted in the paintings of Breughel and Hayman.

Blindman's Bluff.   This game in which a blindfolded person must catch and identify the people around him or her was a popular sport two thousand years ago among Greek boys, who called it Muinda, or Brazen Fly. While one boy was blindfolded, his playmates whipped him with papyrus husks until one of them was caught.

For husks, the Elizabethans substituted knotted rope, and the sightless boy donned a hood. Later, fondling replaced hitting, and the game reached its all-time popularity among adults as a rollicking form of court play (which was as often foreplay). The Victorians banished the fondling, instituted spinning the blindfolded person until dizziness was induced, and required only a tag-touch

Blindman's bluff.

to score a player "out." Identifying the caught child required too much body touching. As the game was played in the 1890s, it was less violent and sexual than its historical antecedents.

Hopscotch.   The word scotch in hopscotch refers to a stone, which is tossed into one section after another of a drawing made on the ground. A player hops along the partitions to pick up the stone. In the Nineties version, the drawing consisted of numbers from one to ten. But the game is ancient, and in the early years of Christianity various ground drawings had symbolism, representing the journey of the soul from earth to heaven. The uppermost square was heaven and everlasting glory.

It was as a religious game that hopscotch came to America with the early settlers. By the Gay Nineties it had lost its symbolism and was a street game played only by girls.

FAIRS AND EXPOS

Meet Me at the Fair

Between Reconstruction and the First World War (roughly from 1876 to 1916), millions of Americans flocked to international expositions or world's fairs in cities from Chicago to New Orleans, Philadelphia to San Diego. Fairs were *the* extravaganzas of the period, offering people a bold new image of America as an emerging world leader, a country rich in economic, intellectual, and artistic resources. The fairs were blueprints for the future that was the twentieth century—even the name seemed to burst with portent.

Today, world's fairs compete with myriad other events, but in the years heralding our century, they had no competition. People attended with grand passion and giddy expectation, and they were never disappointed. Between Reconstruction and the First World War, America staged *twelve* international expositions to, in effect, show off her newfound identity. Atlanta, Nashville, Omaha, Buffalo, Saint Louis, Portland, San Francisco, Seattle, Chicago, New Orleans, Philadelphia, and San Diego played host to tens of millions of people in an era when traveling a distance was a travail. The number of fairs alone attests to the country's mania for internationally flaunting its industry, future promise, and, not least, popular culture.

Before we look at one of the greatest fairs of the era in detail—Chicago's Columbian Exposition of 1893—here is a glimpse of the earlier expositions and why they drew such fanatical attendance, such public devotion.

County Fair to World's Fair

Americans have gone to fairs since the mid-1600s, when "fair" meant a market day. By 1800 a fair was an exhibition of produce, cattle, and arts and crafts, with

Court of Honor, Columbian Exposition, 1893.

musical entertainment; and the terms *country fair, state fair,* and *fairgrounds* had entered the American vocabulary.

The first world's fair was held in London in 1851, at the famous Crystal Palace; it was sponsored by Queen Victoria and Prince Albert. The British launched it as an experiment, to see if an international exposition—that is, a global chance to display one's wares—could stimulate new inventions, world commerce, and industrial manufacturing processes. The answer was a resounding yes.

America, a young country, all future potential, immediately appreciated the opportunity of an international extravaganza for proud self-promotion. Two years after the London show, America hosted its own world's fair, also in a "Crystal Palace" in New York's Reservoir Square (now Bryant Park behind the New York Public Library on Fifth Avenue). It covered 13 acres and cost nearly three-quarters of a million dollars; almost a million and a half people attended. It so effectively promoted international trade and technological advances—and popular culture, an export overlooked in the early years of fairs—that America worked aggressively to stage many of the future international fairs and expositions. In less than a decade the country hosted **Chicago's 1893 Columbian Exposition, San Francisco's 1894 California Midwinter, Atlanta's 1895 Cotton States, Omaha's 1898 Trans-Mississippi,** as well as **Buffalo's 1901 Pan-American.** Americans had a love affair with extravaganzas that advertised the nation's resources and ingenuity for invention.

Consider the marvels people glimpsed (many for the first time) at **Philadelphia's 1876 Centennial Exposition.** Costing $9 million, covering 236 acres, the fair encompassed 167 buildings and featured Bell's **telephone,** Sholes's **typewriter,** Singer's improved **sewing machine,** and Westinghouse's **air brakes** (a safety godsend made compulsory on all U.S. trains in 1893).

But the most talked about fair of the Gay Nineties—often considered *the* event of the decade—was held in Chicago to celebrate the four hundredth anniversary of Columbus's discovery of America. Perhaps no fair since has presented such a display of what the future held for America.

Chicago's World's Columbian Exposition: 1893

The theme of this fair was **electricity,** and its promise of unlimited power for the new century. From the White House, President Grover Cleveland opened the fair by pushing a "magic button" that, a thousand miles away, turned on the fairground's electric power.

Attended by 21 million people, the expo set the country abuzz with talk of Edison's **light bulb,** Tesla's **electric coil,** and Westinghouse's **alternating-current dynamo** and **electric transformer and motor**—all on display. Westinghouse had purchased the patent rights of several of Tesla's inventions, establishing the Westinghouse Electric Corporation, which lit the fair. The entire show was dubbed the White City because of its white, classical buildings (spread over 686 acres), which were magnificently illuminated at night. "The long lines of white building were ablaze with countless lights," wrote one

Aerial view of Columbian Exposition.

chronicler, forecasting: "The people who could dream this vision and make it real . . . would press on to greater victories than this triumph of beauty—victories greater than the world had yet witnessed."

Any visitor not impressed with electric lights and motors could glimpse the first **Ferris wheel**. Thousands of adults and children stood in long lines for a ride on the monster "bridge on an axle" invention of George Washington Gale Ferris. Ferris's wheel was a blatant challenge to the star attraction at the Paris Exposition four years earlier: Eiffel's Tower. In three months, 175,000 brave fairgoers shrieked in delight and terror on the wheel.

Little Egypt, Darling of the Nile.   Many accounts of the fair claim that Little Egypt—Fahreda Mahzar, a sleek Egyptian beauty who had come to America with a troupe of Syrian dancers—outshined all the expo's electric novelties with her scandalous *coochee-coochee* belly dance. It was the talk of the Nineties. Later called the hootchy-kootchy, the dance is thought to be named after the state of Cooch Behar in Bengal, and its promoters, seeking public acceptance through artistic pretensions, billed it as the "Oriental *danse du ventre*," which fooled no one.

From coast to coast, rumor was that she danced the coochee-coochee nude; actually the bewitching bellyrina wore a semitransparent skirt. Her writhing antics inspired the fair's public relations man, future New York Congressman Sol Bloom, to compose one of the era's hit songs, **The Hootchy Kootchy Dance,** which was soon parodied in lyrics like "Oh, they don't wear pants in the southern part of France." Bloom never denied his devotion to Little Egypt, and in his *Autobiography* takes credit for the song that helped spread her fame.

The fair made Fahreda Mahzar famous, and vice versa: Seeing Little Egypt became synonymous with going to the fair. She launched a belly dancing fad; in a short time there were twenty-two hootchy-kootchy dancers hip-thrusting at New York's Coney Island alone, each claiming to be the original sinner.

Three years later the real Fahreda Mahzar was arrested by New York police in a raid on the famous Sherry's restaurant, caught dancing her specialty, this time stark-ravingly naked, at a stag party given by a grandson of P. T. Barnum. Throughout the decade of the Nineties, made all the gayer by Little Egypt's escapades, she entertained at countless stag parties, where men paid $10 apiece to see what was then a rarity: a nude woman. The exposure paid well; Fahreda Mahzar died in 1908 leaving an estate of a quarter of a million dollars.

Frederick Olmsted, Stanford White, and Louis Sullivan.   America, engaged in a search for its own identity and shedding Victorian ties, created an indelible international image with the 1893 exposition. "Expositions are the timekeepers of progress," said President William McKinley, shortly before his assassination at the 1901 Pan-American Exposition at Buffalo. "They record the world's advancement. They stimulate the intellect of the people and quicken human genius." And never before had so much home-grown genius been on display than in Chicago in 1893.

Many cities—including New York, Boston, and Philadelphia—had vied to host the exposition honoring Columbus's discovery. But a group of Chicago's elite argued that nowhere had American ingenuity flourished finer and faster than in the expansion of their city; a village by a swamp transformed into a metropolis of a million and a half people—all in sixty years. That, they said, was America!

Winning the honor to host the fair, Chicago gave free creative rein to the country's best architects: Frederick Law Olmsted, who had laid out New York's Central Park; Stanford White, of international fame; and Louis Sullivan, father of the skyscraper and mentor to Frank Lloyd Wright. They—with the help of thousands of unsung workers—transformed a bleak South Side beach area into a magnificently landscaped fairgrounds. Olmsted would later redesign the area as Jackson Park, and the mile-long expanse called the fair's midway became the campus of the University of Chicago. Many architects today regard the 1893 fair-building effort to be the greatest in the history of international expositions.

Midway Sideshows and the First Theme Parks.   The 1893 Columbian Exposition's midway was the first of its kind in the country and was a sensation with the public. It would be copied in endless variations throughout this century. Tourists, for instance, strolled past a German village, an Austrian city, an Irish pub, a Moorish palace, a reproduction of Mount Vernon, and a Buddhist temple. Or they gazed curiously at a group of Dahomeyan huts with sixty native warriors, traded for knicknacks in a Chinese market or a Japanese bazaar, and listened to the caterwaul of thousands of parrots in a tropical jungle. In other words, they traipsed through theme parks.

In fact, the midway was an American invention and the springboard for later theme and adventure parks. This midway, as well as later ones, was, by today's standards, shockingly racist in portraying minorities, especially American blacks and native Africans. Midways also crudely highlighted the handicapped in freak shows, for which the Nineties public had an insatiable curiosity.

The landmark fair also had midway entertainment staged by a promoter named Flo Ziegfeld, who would go to New York and become, though his Follies, the world's leading king of revues. Another midway attraction, billed as the Houdini Brothers, featured Dash and Harry; the latter would go on to international acclaim. Then, too, the Chicago exposition gave thousands of visitors their first glimpse of a novelty that would sweep the next century as a pop culture mania: moving pictures. Eadweard Muybridge, the first person to apply the principle of still photography to motion, lectured on the future potential of moving pictures and flabbergasted onlookers with his images of birds flying and athletes wrestling.

Americans' love for the 1893 fair, and the fair's flair for promotion of everything American, was succinctly captured by a phrase in a review in the *New York Times:* "The late P. T. Barnum should have lived to see this day." The fair was a sensation. In so many ways it was the future.

DANCE CRAZES

Gotta Dance

Two major dances swept the Gay Nineties: one from the Old World, the waltz; one from the New World, the two-step. The latter was America's first contribution to social dance, and from that outstepping Americans cast aside hand-me-down dances from Europe to create a panoply of styles that, ever since, have launched crazes worldwide. Throughout this book we'll look at those frenzied fads decade by decade, and in this chapter we examine the pandemonium created by the waltz and the two-step. But first to backtrack a bit—to the origin of dance and the dawning of what we call popular dance.

Man has always danced. First with himself. Then with other men. Then, sensibly, with women. This last development, though, came late, arriving in Europe around the twelfth century in the form of the gliding estampie, regarded by dance historians as the first real couples dance. That is, one man, one woman—no groups of people holding hands in configurations of chains or circles.

The earliest dances—for enhanced fertility, victory in battle, or bountiful harvest—had earnest portent. Even later court dances were staged for special occasions—and engaged in only by the nobility. Only in recent times have great masses of ordinary folk danced without purpose, for pleasure. This fad-generating phenomenon is called popular dance, and it developed entirely within the Western world. Unlike ancient dance, popular dance requires no audience, no commemorative occasion, no training (though some may be helpful).

Even social dancing throughout most of the 1800s celebrated occasions such as weddings and holidays. People as yet did not go out on a Saturday night to kick up their heels just because it was the weekend. Further, these social dances, like folk dances, had prescribed steps that dancers performed in unison. On the other hand, fad dances of the twentieth century are based on certain steps but open to creative interpretation, if not personal abandon. Dance authorities say that modern popular dance is not performed to express a group's mood, but that of each dancer.

But we're getting ahead of the story.

Waltz

The waltz was, frankly, the dirty dancing of its day. The older generation downright denounced it; younger people danced it nonstop. From Frankfurt to Philadelphia, guardians of the old order poured out a steady stream of criticism of the waltz and the sinfulness it portended. A New York paper complained that the critics of the waltz viewed it "as if it were the only really *deadly* sin . . . worse than Perjury, and scarcely equalled in its enormity by malicious Homicide." Objections centered around two things: Couples held each other temptingly close, and they turned at speeds that intoxicated the brain—a sure-fire prescription for sin. On top of this, the music was the gayest ever orchestrated.

The waltz's history, from its folksy beginnings to its transatlantic popularity, is a generation tale of the young against the old, tradition against innovation and experimentation, a battle that would be repeated with countless faddish dances in our century, as is documented in subsequent chapters.

A ruckus was already in the air in 1812 when the dance waltzed from its homeland, Germany, into England. "Will-corrupting," "disgusting," "immodest," ran the reviews; a romp in which couples not only "embrace at the pelvis" but "whirl about in the posture of copulation." In an era when couples danced holding fingertips, full-body contact was, depending on one's point of view, decadence or delicious propinquity. Ironically, Lord Byron, himself no prude, displayed extraordinary hostility toward the dance and stirred the controversy with an anti-waltz poem:

> Hot from the hands promiscuously applied,
> Round the slight waist, or down the glowing side . . .
> The breast thus publicly resigned to man
> In private may resist him—if it can.

Byron claimed he objected to the "Lewd grasp and lawless contact" between dancers in public, arguing that the dance would not "leave much mystery for the nuptial night." However, what seemed to trouble him every bit as much—if not more—was the waltz's hearty adoption by the lower classes— they adored it; and this alone should have been approbation against society doing the dirty dance. (More on this later.)

Nonetheless, the waltz was rapidly becoming the vogue at European courts. In the summer of 1816 the waltz was first danced at a royal ball, and the London *Times* viewed its "voluptuous intertwining of limbs, and close compressure of the bodies," as a threat to "national morals." "So long as this obscene display was confined to prostitutes and adulteresses," the paper said, "we did not think it deserving of notice; but now that it is attempted to be forced upon the respectable classes . . . we feel it a duty to warn every parent against exposing his daughter to so fatal a contagion." The paper's public condemnation almost overnight increased the dance's popularity.

To this day debate exists as to the exact origin of the waltz, whose name is from the German *walzen,* "to revolve." Many authorities credit Germany with fathering the dance, Though it's as feasible that it began (in a modified form) as an Alpine folk dance. The earliest related "turning" dance dates from about 1670, but the waltz we know today became recognizable after being blended into three other dances: the Austrian *Ländler* (a hand-holding stamping dance in which couples turn), the German *Weller* (a rapid ancient turning dance), and the related *Spinner* (whose name is self-explanatory). But it was the German version of the dance, popular in the late 1700s, that would launch a craze on two sides of the Atlantic.

Strauss Fever

The first wave of waltz mania erupted in Vienna in the 1820s, due in large part to the pulsating beat of compositions by the Strauss family. Vienna was "waltz mad," and it quickly became the waltz capital of the world. Strauss waltzes would dominate popular dance music of the world for the remainder of the nineteenth century, with such international favorites as **The Blue Danube** (1867), **Tales from the Vienna Wood** (1868), **Wine, Women and Song** (1869), and **Vienna Life** (1873).

The waltz first reached America around 1816, and the turning dance made heads spin in more ways than one. For more than half a century, the dance suffered every imaginable indignity. Parents forbade their children to dance it. Waltz instrumental music was outlawed. Ministers, politicians, and educators lambasted both the gushing dance and its gay music, as well as titles like "Wine, Women and Song." Danced in private, behind closed doors, the waltz not only survived but flourished, such that by 1885 it was *the* fad dance. Not only had the times radically changed, but the generation that had so vociferously condemned the dance had either died off or was too moribund to make their views count.

Dance historians like to point out that the waltz was the first dance to gain wide popularity without the sanction of royal courts or dancing masters; rather, it was ordinary folk, driven by the rhythm of the music, who would not let the dance fade away. In this regard, the waltz was the first modern fad dance, beginning with the younger, non-monied masses and spreading upward through all levels of society. Byron had glimpsed the future.

Why was the waltz so immensely popular in Victorian times? For one thing, it was the only legitimate way during that socially repressive period for young couples to touch intimately in public.

Its popularity in the Gay Nineties was unprecedented for a dance. Allen Dodworth, one of America's most celebrated dance teachers of the period (admission to his school required three letters of recommendation), pronounced the waltz as "the culmination of modern society dancing . . . The dance which has for fifty years resisted every kind of attack is today the most popular known." His one concession to old guard decency was that the man should never put a *bare* hand on the woman's waist; if caught without a glove he should interpose a handkerchief.

Though many people had railed against the waltz, the dance truly expressed the spirit of its age. Only with the outbreak of World War I did the German dance lose preeminence. There was, however, another faddish import which Americans danced in the Gay Nineties.

Polka

The polka, a lively folk dance, originated in the 1830s in Bohemia (now Czechoslovakia). Its name is related to the Czech *pulka,* "half"; a half-step is continually repeated in the dance. The dance's catchy rhythm—as well as the vigorous movement of the feet, head, trunk, and arms—accounted for its immediate popularity in Europe and America after its performance on a Paris stage in the

Polka.

1840s. The polka was, quite simply, fun to dance. The London *Times* reported that "politics is for the moment suspended in public regard by the new and all absorbing pursuit, the Polka." Unlike the oom-pah-pah waltz, the da-da-dum polka experienced considerably little opposition, and it became the waltz's chief rival. People felt it mixed a decent modicum of the intimacy of the waltz with the heady vivacity of the Irish jig.

In New York and other large cities, the demand to learn the polka outstripped the supply of dance teachers. The common complaint among instructors was that the dance's sheer fun led couples to forfeit training and decorum for wild improvisation. What often raised old guard eyebrows was not the dance itself, but the often accompanying Polish-style costumes—short peasant skirts, high boots, and coquettish caps—which many women favored at balls. Arbiter of fashion, the *Illustrated London News* complained that no country had ever "imported anything more ridiculous or ungraceful" than the polka and its costume. The peasant dance, the paper claimed, is "a hybrid confusion of Scotch Lilt, Irish Jig, and Bohemian Waltz, and needs only to be seen once to be avoided forever." Well, not forever. For a month later, conceding to overwhelming popular—*and royal*—sentiment, the paper printed detailed instructions on how to dance the latest fad—which it now found to be "elegant, graceful and fascinating in the extreme," whereas it termed the polka's once "ridiculous" folk costume now "authentic wear."

Royalty had embraced the polka, and the year it hit the London scene, the Duke of Wellington danced it six times at a ball given to celebrate the queen's birthday. American papers commented on the dance's wonderfully militaristic, marchlike tempo—da-da-dum. For sheer delight, the polka was the darling dance of its day, infecting all levels of society with its quickening pace—which mirrored that of the times. Even more than the gliding, aristocratic waltz, the polka, in terms of its mass appeal, was closer to later fads like the Charleston and the shimmy—dances in which young people cut loose.

America Takes the Lead

As mentioned earlier, America made its first contribution to the field of social dance with the two-step in 1890. But before that time Americans danced; not the Puritans exactly, but certainly their Southern counterparts, the Cavaliers.

To backtrack briefly:

Contrary to popular belief, the Puritans allowed dancing done "for the Glory of God" on religious occasions (as does the Bible); and "unmixed" dancing (all one sex or the other). Dance instructions could be given by "Grave Persons" who taught "Decency of Behavior." Needless to say, these were not fad dances; more often than not they were sexless versions of British court vogues.

Some New Englanders dared to be more open-minded. A leading Massachusetts Bay minister, the Reverend John Cotton, advocated dancing that was not "lascivious . . . with amorous gestures and wanton dalliances." The country's first dietary health nut, Dr. Sylvester Graham (advocate of crackers that now bear his name), said, "Dancing . . . is one of the most salutary kinds of social enjoyment . . . Religious prejudice against dancing is altogether ill-founded." The historical record is so replete with condemnations against dance, one is forced to conclude that a great many Puritans took pleasure in dancing.

The early American South, on the other hand, swooned from dance fever. The first families of Virginia retained their English manners, fashions, and passion for dance. Many who made fortunes from tobacco plantations sent their sons and daughters back to England for an all-around education, which included dance, for among the rising gentry, dancing was a passport to polite society. Plantation architecture included spacious ballrooms, and dance parties were commonplace, with music provided by the females of the family, or by servants and slaves. Still, though, vogue dances in America were those of the British court.

By the eighteenth century, the Puritan challenge to dancing began to wane—at least among the socially privileged. Balls were held even in Boston, while New York and Philadelphia vied to be the center of cosmopolitan gaiety, boasting of the lavishness of their society bashes. Gotham's Horticultural Society Ball, the famous Firemen's Ball, and the Bachelor's Ball were the highlights of the mid-century social season.

George Washington, a Virginian, had an insatiable appetite for dancing. He once danced for three hours nonstop with the wife of General Nathanael Greene, whom he described as "a little frisk." Thomas Jefferson planned a schedule for his daughter in which she was to spend three hours every other morning dancing. And the young John Quincy Adams as a law student engaged in marathon dance sessions at Newburyport, confiding to his diary he'd spent a whole afternoon "in rigging for the ball." Dancing had become a social grace, but steps were still European: the minuet, the cotillion (an English square dance whose name means "petticoat"), the allemande, the schottische (a German waltzlike turning dance), and the quadrille (originally an Italian square dance).

By the time of the Civil War, Americans had reached an enthusiasm for dance that exceeded that of the English and rivaled that of the French. America was dancing, and it was about to take the lead with the . . .

Two-Step

It was the rousingly popular and patriotic "Washington Post March" of John Philip Sousa, introduced in 1889, that gave birth to America's first contribution to the field of social dance. It's no coincidence that a country which was forging its own image for the coming century proclaimed itself to the world of dance with full-blooded, if not belligerent, musical bombast. Called the March King, Sousa began his musical career at age eleven as a violinist in a dance band. He first achieved his formidable reputation as head of the U.S. Marine Corps Band. The "Washington Post March" had been preceded a year earlier by "Semper Fidelis," another favorite through the Nineties.

It's no exaggeration to say that Americans could not get enough of Sousa's patriotic marches. Resigning from the marines to form his own band, he composed tunes that, as he bluntly proclaimed, should make even "a man with a wooden leg step out." They may well have. For the entire nation, on the dance floor and around bandshells, galloped in two-step to every one of Sousa's sprightly tunes—and there were many (about 140 total). As he had opened the decade with his "Always Faithful" march, he closed it with the even more popular "Stars and Stripes Forever."

It's important to appreciate the national climate in which Sousa's robust marches flourished, and in which the militaristic two-step—a quick march with skips—achieved its popularity. In addition to America's break from Victorian influences, Teddy Roosevelt had led his Rough Riders through Cuba in the Spanish-American War, and Admiral George Dewey won the battle of Manila Bay by beating the Spanish Pacific fleet. America had acquired empires in the Caribbean and the Pacific, as well as a reputation as an international power, and the nation was heady with patriotic fervor. No music more aptly fit the tenor of the times than Sousa's marches. Musically speaking, America marched into the twentieth century.

The "Washington Post March" and the two-step dance—with its erect posture and galloping strides—exploded with a sense of self-confidence. The rhythms were uniquely American, the dance steps so lively that one could not imagine the generation of Victorians grown old with a cloistered queen keeping tempo. The march and the dance displayed power—as well as a shift in power on the international stage.

Anyone who took the time to listen could realize that the march and the dance spearheaded the American cultural invasion of Europe. The continent was by no means on the verge of collapse, but its influence was waning, and it could no longer regard the United States with a patronizing indulgence. This is not to deny that America's national assertiveness in the Gay Nineties was often crude, arrogant, and exploitative; it was, more often than not.

At the close of the decade, another thoroughly American dance craze was afoot.

Cakewalk

Originally a dance done by Southern blacks—featuring prancing struts, shuffling feet, and exaggerated sways—the cakewalk was similar to later spotlight dances that involve the elimination of couples in competition to outshine each other. It originated among slaves who, for the amusement of their white masters, used the dance as a comic satire on the pompous elegance of formal ballroom styles. Southern belles may not have enjoyed the jibe, but their men, who often had to be coaxed to formal dances, delighted in the spoof. So did the millions of Americans who made the cakewalk a favorite step from 1898 to 1904. From a satire on ballroom dancing, it became a popular ballroom dance itself.

In the white version, couples formed a square with the men on the inside and, high strutting to a sprightly tune, paraded imaginatively around the figure. Judges looked for regal bearing in the man, grace in the women, and all-around inventiveness; the winning couple took home an elaborately decorated cake.

Most significantly, the cakewalk contributed to the birth of later dances based on jazz rhythms, and its music influenced the growth of ragtime in the next decade. The frenetic rhythms and rollicking melodies of ragtime fit the cakewalk's high-energy creative abandon. After dancing to the syncopated rhythms of the cakewalk, people craved what was called "ragged" music, which led to a craze for the "rag" of composers like Scott Joplin. This dance fad marked the beginning of a close relationship between jazz and social dance.

From a spoof on elegance, the dance became a grand occasion to dress up in long-tailed black coats and sleek white gowns and exude elegance to strains of the "Maple Leaf Rag." From America, the fad spread to England and France, and it remained popular until ousted in the next decade by the even more trendy "animal" dances like the bunny hug and the kangaroo hop. In fact, it was the grotesquely exaggerated postures that cakewalkers had to invent continually that gave birth to the animal muggings (see page 70). Interestingly, at the turn of the century, when Joplin's "Maple Leaf *Rag*" was all the rage, waning in popularity was an earlier hit called the "Maple Leaf *Waltz.*" Joplin's song was at first turned down by publishers because of the similarity in titles. Joplin waited—and won, as the vogue in song and dance turned from waltz to rag.

POPULAR SONGS

Hits Before Your Hit Parade

Pop music is easier defined by what it is *not;* it is neither folk music nor classical music, but that broad, tuneful domain in between. People in earlier centuries had their favorites—**Greensleeves** (1580), **Three Blind Mice** (1609), **Sally in Our Alley** (1715), **The Campbells Are Coming** (1745), **Cockles and Mussels, Alive, Alive O!** and **Lavender's Blue, Diddy Dilly** (1750), and **Comin' Thro' the Rye** (1796).

Popular they were, but bestselling hits they were not, at least not in our century's money-making connotation of that phrase. Not even such patriotic favorites as **Yankee Doodle** (1753) and **The Star Spangled Banner** (1814) fall into that unique category—because, quite simply, there was as yet no such category. Much-loved tunes suffered several handicaps: a poor system of sheet-music merchandising, no radios or phonographs, and no publicity machine for plugging a mass-appeal melody. "If only a few hundred people bought a song," writes music historian Sigmund Spaeth, "or a few thousand heard it sung, it could be considered a success comparable to the seller of a million copies today."

Starting in the 1820s, though, events in the music industry began, so to speak, to go pop. With a burgeoning number of new publishers and improved sheet music distribution, Americans began to turn songs into nearly commercial hits; that is, tunes that made a profit for the composer and the publisher. If there was one landmark song above all others that successfully made the crossover from being merely popular to becoming a popular hit, it was the homey, sentimental ballad . . .

Home, Sweet Home!

> Be it ever so humble, there's no place like home.

Americans liked to emphasize the song's lyrics for their sentimentality, but more so because they were written by a fellow countryman—John Howard Payne, born in New York City (or possibly East Hampton, Long Island) in 1791. The melody was by British composer Sir Henry Bishop, and the tune first appeared in the 1823 London production of the opera *Clari, or The Maid of Milan,* adapted from a French play.

Payne—who, ironically, never settled down long enough to have a home of his own—as a young man went to London to become a playwright. Unable to support himself on his literary output, he eventually entered public service, becoming the American consul in Tunis, where he would die. In the "multinational" opera *Clari* (the story is French, the setting Italian, the composer British, the lyricist American), "Home, Sweet Home!" was sung by the heroine, Clari, then repeated by a chorus of villagers who welcome her back to her hometown. "It is the song of my native village," explains the Maid of Milan, "the hymn of the lowly heart, which dwells upon every lip there . . . It is the first music heard by infancy in its cradle." Actually, Sir Henry Bishop stole the tune from himself; he'd composed it for an earlier opera, then published it as a "Sicilian Air" in a collection of national melodies.

"Home" was an immediate hit, in Europe and America. Rossini inserted it into *The Barber of Seville,* and popular sopranos like Jenny Lind pulled it out for concert encores. Americans hummed it incessantly; though writer Robert Louis Stevenson (himself always traveling in search of an ideal climate for his tuberculosis) found the homey sentiment "wallowing naked in the pathetic." This was a minority opinion on the song Spaeth calls "the greatest home song of all time." In terms of its widespread distribution, it was a landmark in the history of American popular music—a hit, though not a million-seller. That magical distinction—to become a standard benchmark for a music's popularity—goes to one of the favorite songs of the Gay Nineties: "After the Ball."

First, though, a final sad note on the peripatetic and often-pecunious John Payne. From an entry in his diary, found after his death in 1852 in Tunis: "How often have I been in the heart of Paris, Berlin, London or some other city, and have heard persons singing or hand-organs playing *Home, Sweet Home,* without having a shilling to buy myself the next meal, or a place to lay my head. The world has literally sung my song until every heart is familiar with its melody, yet I have been a wanderer from my boyhood."

After the Ball: 1892

With the music industry rapidly expanding in the mid-1800s, there were many hits after "Home, Sweet Home!" Here is a chronological list of several of the biggest:

She Wore a Yellow Ribbon: 1838
Skip to My Lou: 1844
Oh! Susanna: 1848
I Gave My Love a Cherry: 1850
Old Folks at Home, or Way Down Upon the Swanee River: 1851
Jeanie With the Light Brown Hair: 1854
The Yellow Rose of Texas: 1858
Dixie: 1860
Frankie and Johnny Were Lovers: 1875
My Bonnie Lies Over the Ocean: 1881
When Strolling Through the Park One Day: 1884

In addition, the decade of the Gay Nineties opened with a freak smash hit, **Ta-ra-ra-boom-deay,** a jumble of nonsense syllables—which decades later would serve as the tune for "It's Howdy Doody Time."

But historians claim that the modern epoch of popular music probably began in 1892, when sheet music sales first soared into the millions. Sheet music sales for "After the Ball" totaled $5 million. The chorus of the song all America was singing, in lush waltz time, went:

> After the ball is over,
> After the break of morn,
> After the dancers' leaving,
> After the stars are gone.
> Many a heart is aching,
> If you could read them all;
> Many the hopes that have vanished,
> After the ball.

What do the words mean and why was the song such a hit?

"After the Ball" was written by pop music publisher Charles Harris (previously a bellhop and pawnbroker), who from his New York City headquarters advertised "Songs Written to Order," and revealed his secrets for success in *How to Write a Popular Song.* In those days the music business was called song manufacturing (whereas today it might be called song marketing). An instinctive tunesmith (he could neither read nor write music) and superb businessman, Harris, on a banjo, pluckily manufactured melodies for marriages, public events, births, and deaths.

One evening in 1892, he spotted a young couple quarreling after a dance, each lover going home alone "after the ball." He composed a mawkishly sentimental story ballad and had it interpolated in a variety revue called *A Trip to Chinatown*—not that "After the Ball" has the slightest thing to do with anything Oriental. It was inserted into the show (which, by the way, turned out to be Broadway's first significant long-running musical) simply for exposure—that is, a test of the public's reaction. If audiences applauded the tune, Harris would publish it in sheet music; the greater the clapping, the more copies he'd print—a sort of Gay Nineties version of product test marketing and a practice used by many songwriters.

Audiences went wild—as did John Philip Sousa, who played the tune daily at the bandshell of the 1893 Chicago World's Fair. Charles Harris had the country's first million-seller song. Ironically, this pioneering song in sales was thoroughly Victorian in sentiment: It tells of a little girl who climbs on an old man's knee, inquiring why he has no children, no family, no home. He once had a sweetheart, he says, but caught her kissing another man after a ball. Never could he forgive her, and he would not listen to her explanation. Years later, after her death, he learned that the man she kissed was her brother. Thus, the old man suffered for the years of heartache he caused his lover: "Many the hopes that have vanished, / After the ball."

Harris's specialty was teary, sentimental ballads written for middle-class ladies (especially spinsters) to perform at home on the piano. In the Gay Nineties, before the phonograph was a commonplace, there were more pianos in America than anywhere else in the world, and, it seemed, more lady pianists. It was women—largely young to middle-aged women from the middle classes—who created the first hit single. As composer, lyricist, and publisher, Harris made a windfall: $25,000 a week during the song's peak popularity. It eventually sold 10 million copies and was translated into scores of languages. And, of course, the blockbuster melody was interpolated by Jerome Kern into his 1927 Broadway hit *Show Boat.*

Never did Charles Harris have another such smash hit—nor did he have to; he died in New York City in 1930, having lived comfortably off royalties. And an entire industry—Tin Pan Alley—realized the profits to be reaped from pop music hits. Better than anyone, Harris knew the fickle nature of fads. In his book *How to Write a Popular Song,* he cautioned would-be composers, "Styles in songs change as quickly as ladies' millinery." It is music legend that Charles Harris cried every time he sang the sad words of "After the Ball," but surely these were tears of joy.

BESTSELLING BOOKS

A Top Ten List: 1895

There were bestselling books before 1895—that is, fiction and nonfiction that appealed to a wide readership—but they did not come under that big-business rubric bestseller, a word that is a wish as much as a windfall.

The term—as in bestseller list—was the brainchild of Harry Thurston Peck, and made its first official appearance in 1895 in the literary magazine he edited, *The Bookman.* The bestseller list then, compiled from scores of stores in America and a few in Canada, included Anthony Hope's swashbuckling romance **The Prisoner of Zenda;** Richard Davis's **Princess Aline,** illustrated by Charles Dana Gibson, then causing a stir himself with his Gibson girl drawings; and the exotic adventure *Trilby,* by George du Maurier. *Trilby,* we'll see, was more than a mere bestseller: It was the kind of book that launches nationwide spin-off crazes.

The bestseller list was an idea whose time had come. The number of public schools in America had increased since 1880 by almost fifty percent, creating a veritable outbreak of literacy. New public libraries opened at such a rate that by 1898 they numbered over seventeen hundred, each with a collection of more than five thousand volumes. And, too, passage of the International Copyright Law in 1891 brought an orderliness to publishing that, in fact, made possible the compiling of a bestseller list. The combined effect of the newfound literacy on the part of readers and honesty on the part of publishers produced a book boom in the Gay Nineties: Some seven hundred new works of fiction were published in 1894; by the close of the decade the annual number had snowballed to over two thousand.

What were Americans reading?

Predominantly fiction—specifically romances among women readers— which accounted for a full quarter of the books issued. Placing second was biography and history, with a poor third-place showing made by theology, which was once the undisputed champion among top-selling books. Times had changed. Interests had broadened. Education of the masses was altering America's tastes in reading material. Not everyone was pleased. Preachers denounced the wave of sentimental domestic novels written by and about women that had begun to appear mid-century. They also criticized books by women authors with such alluring titles as the temperance tract *Ten Nights in a Bar-Room,* and the independent-minded *Self-Raised,* which eventually sold over two million copies. Complained Nathaniel Hawthorne, "America is now wholly given over to a damned mob of scribbling women."

The term "bestseller" did not appear in a major dictionary for almost a decade after its introduction. And during that intervening period, it was used by many people disparagingly, as if it smacked of a short-term trendiness (which in many cases it did). One publication, commenting on the short shelf-life of books in the burgeoning new market (which was already squeezing out the likes of Dickens, Cooper, Thackeray, Stevenson, and Twain), observed, "Fortunately the 'best sellers' are the worst survivors"—meaning, of course, that they sell strongly, then fade from memory.

Yet the label "bestseller" thrived, suiting the commercialism of the era that created it—and of the century that would follow. In 1912, the industry magazine *Publishers Weekly* began to run bestseller lists (which I've used as a standard), and the concept proved profitable for the promotion of books through clubs like Book-of-the-Month Club (founded in 1926) and Literary Guild (1928).

In the Gay Nineties, though, one bestseller launched a national mania.

Trilby: 1894

In terms of product spin-offs, George du Maurier's romance *Trilby,* released in 1894, was the *Jaws* of its day. Women nibbled Trilby chocolates, danced to Trilby waltzes, dressed in Trilby hats and coats, donned jewelry shaped like Trilby's foot, scuffed about in Trilby slippers, and cultivated a Trilby-type beauty. An enterprising real estate man even named a Florida town Trilby—it had a Svengali Street.

Who was Trilby? A beautiful, young Irish girl with the surname O'Ferrall, who, as the novel's heroine, seeks fame in the city of Paris. Racy by the standards of the time, the book contains graphic descriptions of Trilby's bare feet, said to be "lovely and slender," and has the impetuous heroine immodestly kicking off her slippers to expose what she boasts is "the handsomest foot in all Paris"—sexually suggestive elements these, when gowns concealed women's feet. Besides, a woman who free-spiritedly kicked off her shoes in mixed company in the Gay Nineties signaled that she'd take off just about anything.

The story paints a colorful picture of bohemian life in the French Latin Quarter, where Trilby, an artist's model, falls under the hypnotic power of Svengali. Hypnotism was also a hot subject of the day, with people endlessly debating what unsavory behavior a hypnotist could elicit from a subject. Many readers wondered in earnest if anyone, under the magic of a Svengali-like trance, could be made to sing as beautifully as Trilby. Outrageous claims being made for hypnosis in the era only helped popularize the book. And that the sweetly innocent Trilby posed as a model in the nude scandalized many people and further boosted sales. Trilby's foot was so famous that butchers shaped sausages like feet—in an era when Freudian analysts saw in the foot a phallus. Summer evenings at bandshells across America, people sang a fifty-year-old song, "Ben Bolt," just because George du Maurier mentioned it in the novel.

The book was in tremendous demand. Chicago, then a city of a million people, had twenty-six copies in its public library and announced to a local newspaper that it "could use 260 and never find a copy on the shelves." The St. Louis library accumulated a whopping four hundred copies, all page-worn. Despite the novel's hefty cost of $1.75, within a few months a hundred thousand copies were sold, and it remained high on the new bestseller list throughout the year of 1895. The Trilby tale became a popular drama, touring the nation, playing to audiences mesmerized by the sight of the leading lady's bare feet. It was parodied in titles like *Biltry* and *Drilby,* and spiced up in a burlesque operetta appropriately called *Thrilby.* The bestselling book was a fad phenomenon and more; it was also a forward glimpse of the spin-off mania that would become standard business in the coming century.

CHAPTER 2

————————— ☐ —————————

The Innocent Oughts

1900 to 1909

Welcome to the Twentieth Century

At the stroke of midnight on the last day of the year 1899, the twentieth century dawned. Parents allowed children to stay up late to welcome in a new era, and from Rome Pope Leo XIII told Roman Catholics the world over that a midnight Mass was permissible on this exceptional night.

America had as much railroad track on the ground as telegraph wire overhead. The flag flew over forty-five states, the Constitution had fifteen amendments, and women could not vote to elect a president. On the brighter side, the world was free of gasoline fumes and income tax—though it also was missing radio and television.

The population of the United States stood at 76,094,000. New York was the most populous state (7,268,894), Nevada the least (42,335). Male life expectancy was 47.3 years; for a female 46.3 years; for blacks 33.0 years.

The three leading causes of death at the start of the century were heart disease, influenza with pneumonia, and tuberculosis. Cancer ranked number five—followed by diphtheria, typhoid, malaria, measles, and whooping cough.

The average American worker put in fifty-nine hours a week at his or her job—for a weekly wage of $12.98, or 22 cents an hour. Only seventeen out of every thousand people owned a telephone.

The country's top three companies were United States Steel (assets of $1.8 billion), Standard Oil ($800 million), and American Tobacco ($286 million). The largest portion of the work force, though, was engaged in agriculture.

The cost of men's clothing: pants, $1.25; shirt, 50 cents; suspenders, 25 cents; linen collar, 25 cents; shoes, $1.25.

The cost of ladies' clothing: skirt, $4; blouse, 35 cents; corset, 40 cents; shawl, 50 cents; silk petticoat, $5; beaded purse, 59 cents; shoes $1.50.

49

Grocery prices: coffee, 15 cents a pound; lemons, 15 cents a dozen; butter, 18 cents a pound; eggs, 12 cents a dozen; loaf of bread, 5 cents; salt, 20 cents for a hundred pounds. For meat and poultry: chicken, 7 cents a pound; beef, veal, pork, and turkey, 10 cents a pound; bacon, 12 cents a pound.

The total number of motor vehicle deaths in the first year of the new century would be 96; the total number of lynchings, 115. That year 4,490 new books would be published, and a teacher in the public school system could expect to take home an annual salary of $325.

Every American over the age of thirty-five had been living during the Civil War.

Gotta Shop: A Consumer Society Is Born

Though the first decade of the twentieth century has never been dubbed with a catchy nickname, it's popularly imagined as one long merry assault on the last

Nickelodeon.

vestiges of Victorianism. With its gaslights and horse-and-buggy lifestyle, the era evokes images of innocence, though on closer inspection it was a time of rapid and profound change. Even though three out of every five Americans lived in rural communities (with fewer than twenty-five hundred residents) and seldom traveled more than a day's journey from home, the advent of mail-order merchandising—raised to a high art by Sears, Roebuck and Montgomery Ward—allowed country folk a taste of city treasures. We'll see how mail-order catalogs—or "wish books" as they were dreamed of and paged through—gave the first hint of the "gotta shop" mania that would come to characterize our consumer society. At the turn of the century most Americans rated the Sears catalog as their favorite book after the Bible. Third was the Montgomery Ward catalog. Who could deny that Americans already loved to shop?

In the cities, entertainment was becoming big business. Huge crowds flocked to amusement parks built at the end of trolley lines, featuring Ferris wheels and roller coasters. More futuristic was Edison's Kinetoscope: drop in a coin, peer down a peephole, and for a few minutes marvel at a scene in motion—often decidedly naughty motions; men frequented these penny arcades not unlike today's teenagers elbowing each other to get at arcade games. The newest fad in 1905 was the **nickelodeon,** where for a nickel you enjoyed a moving picture projected onto a screen. Within three years ten thousand nickelodeons were in operation, and at the close of the decade some 10 million Americans went weekly to a local moving picture theater.

Buzzwords

For women who wanted to work, the invention of the typewriter was a godsend, creating countless openings for **typewriter secretaries.** Previously only teaching and nursing were proper female endeavors, and in 1870 fewer than a thousand women worked in offices. By 1910 America had more than 386,000 **typewriters,** as the pioneers were professionally known. The term **female secretary** sounds sexist by today's standards, but during the decade of the suffrage movement it was aggressively feminist.

Perhaps there is no better image of America in the early 1900s than that of a nation in a hurry. Buzz phrases of the time were **go-getter, time management,** and the **scientific study of efficiency.** The nation's first efficiency expert, Frederick Taylor, lectured on how to reorganize an office and revamp an industry, and he even instructed masons on how to stack and carry bricks efficiently. Seminars on **time efficiency** were popular. Clearly, a tempo was being set for the century: *Allegro con brio.*

More than a tempo, too. Freud visited America in the Oughts and proclaimed the sexual urge as the basis of human personality, the motivation behind so many of our seemingly altruistic actions. Ears burned, faces flushed, but the idea took root. The president's own daughter, Alice Roosevelt, in many ways typified the new woman with her devil-may-care doings. Her father, Teddy, admitted she danced till dawn, let "unsuitable" gentlemen monopolize her dance card, and hardly rose before noon. And he did not discipline her.

Future Forecasts

The start of a new century is important. And as the twentieth century dawned, novelist H. G. Wells, then thirty-four years old and already with a reputation as a seer, wrote six essays predicting what our time would be like. Wells had already published *The Time Machine, The Invisible Man,* and *War of the Worlds,* this last a story that, three decades later, radio personality Orson Welles would transform into an elaborate hoax that precipitated a national panic (see page 194). H. G. Wells foresaw trends on the horizon in the year 1900 that would affect the lives of all Americans.

On Cars.   The automobile was still only a rich man's plaything and roads were of dirt and dangerous. "Roads will be very different," predicted Wells. "They will be used only by soft-tired conveyances; the battering horseshoes . . . will never wear them . . . Their traffic in opposite directions will probably be strictly separated."

On Travel.   In an era when people still limited themselves to a radius of about four miles from their city's center, Wells claimed, "There will develop the hired or privately owned motor carriage . . . It will be capable of a day's journey of three hundred miles or more. One will change nothing—unless it is the driver. One will be free to dine where one chooses, hurry when one chooses, travel asleep or awake, stop and pick flowers."

On Electricity.   "The house of the future will probably be warmed in its walls from some power-generating station," Wells believed; many homes were then being wired for electric lights. "One always imagines a cook working with a crimsoned face and bare, blackened arms" over a fire stove, Wells said. "But with a neat little range, heated by electricity, and provided with a thermometer, with absolutely controllable temperatures and proper heat screens, cooking might very easily be made a pleasant amusement."

On Morality.   "For one Morality, there will be many moralities. Each human being will, in the face of circumstances, work out [events] as his or her character determines. Although there will be a general convention . . . it will only be with persons who have come to identical or similar conclusions in the matter of moral conduct." Wells concluded, "Life is already most wonderfully arbitrary and experimental, and for the coming century this must be its essential social history, a great drifting and unrest of people, a shifting and regrouping and breaking up again of groups, great multitudes seeking to find themselves."

FADS, FOLLIES, AND TRENDS

Ping-Pong

Ping-Pong—the name is an echoic from the nearby "ping" of the ball against your racket and the farther away "pong" against your opponent's—is also known as table tennis, a British invention of the 1890s, its name a registered trademark. Simply, it was a scaled-down, indoor game of lawn tennis, to allow play on that country's renowned rainy days. The upper class played lawn tennis, and its inexpensive mimic became a fad among the upwardly aspiring middle class. They, too, could play "tennis," even if it was on the kitchen table.

Eventually the game became popular around the world, and in many countries—notably China and Japan—it's a highly organized competitive sport. In the early 1900s it became a fad in America. Exactly why is unclear, though opinions have been proffered: The century was new, people craved novelty, and Ping-Pong was *the* latest vogue in England. Further, America as yet had neither public lawns nor clay tennis courts; the courts that existed were at exclusive country clubs. And since Ping-Pong allowed everyone to play an aristocrat's game, it seemed democratically tailored for the United States.

In its fad years in America it went by many inventive onomatopoeias: wick-wack, click-clack, whiff-whaff, and flim-flam. Department stores experienced shortages of nets, paddles, and balls, and newspapers throughout the country extolled the virtues of the sport, as well as fanning its popularity with pedestrian rhyme: "The pinging of the ball against the racquet's hide / Is answered by the ponging when it hits the other side" *(Denver Post);* "Where are you going, My Pretty Maid? / I'm going a ping-ponging, my sir, she said" *(Boston Post).*

Books proliferated on the subject. Doctors treated "Ping-Pong ankle" and warned of wrist tendonitis from marathon playing—itself a fad. The smash Broadway musical of the period, *Florodora,* featured references to the game, as well as a character who was a Ping-Pong set salesman. The short-lived craze—enjoyed at men's sporting clubs, at political gatherings, in boardrooms, on board luxury liners, and at family picnics—was dubbed by the press "Ping-Pongitis."

As a sport and pastime, Ping-Pong has lasted a century, but as a feverish fad it held on barely two years. It has on occasion returned with fervor—in the video game Pong, and when President Richard Nixon visited China, where tournaments are of a world-class order.

Teddy Bears

Toys are a rich source for fads, and "Teddy's bear" mania is the craze that kicked off our century's love affair with stuffed animals. It resurfaced most notably in the Eighties with the pricey likes of Lauren Bearcall, Humphrey Beargart, Zsa Zsa Gabear, Kareem Abdul-Jabbear, and Bear Mitzvah. Else-

Theodore Roosevelt.

where (in *Extraordinary Origins*), I've written of the origin of the Teddy bear toy; here I'm concerned with the magnitude of the nationwide Oughts fad.

In brief, its origin story goes like this: In November 1902 President Theodore (Teddy) Roosevelt visited Mississippi to negotiate a boundary dispute between that state and its neighbor Louisiana. Taking time off from his official duty—to "draw a line" between the states—he went bear hunting. Presented by his host with an easy set-up shot at a cub (that is, a photo opportunity), the president refused to take down the helpless target. Clifford Berryman, cartoonist for the *Washington Star* and one of the country's best-known newspaper illustrators, depicted Roosevelt forgoing the kill, captioning the picture with the double entendre "Drawing a line"—a phrase that swept the country as something of that day's equivalent of a sound bite.

Reprinted in New York papers, the cartoon initially drew no special attention, except, that is, from Morris Michtom, proprietor of a toy store in Brooklyn. Inspired by the cartoon, Michtom and his wife cut out and stuffed their own plush brown bear, giving it movable arms and legs and button eyes. They put the toy in the window with a copy of the Berryman cartoon and a sign saying "Teddy's Bear." That bear sold quickly, and another took its place in the sun. And so on and so forth, until the flake of a fad would roll into a snowballing mania.

Morris knew marketing, and he wrote to Roosevelt, candidly requesting permission to use the president's name to sell a stuffed animal. Astonishingly, Roosevelt returned a handwritten note saying that he doubted his name would carry weight in the toy business, but that Michtom was welcome to it. Times were simpler then.

All of this took time, as did securing financing and manufacturing services to mass-produce Teddy's bear. Thus, whereas the cartoon appeared in 1902—and Michtom continued to make animals on a small scale—the bear craze arrived in the fall of 1905. By this time there were a variety of Teddy rip-offs on the market; some from Europe, many from American manufacturers who in those days had not the slightest compunction about copying anything fast-selling.

Spin-off Fads.   Product spin-offs from a fad were already an established marketing ploy at the turn of the century. And from bearmania sprang the Teddy and the Bear bank, which featured the president and the cowering cub; a board game called Hunting With Roosevelt; a battery-operated toy called the Electric Bright Eye Teddy (with eyes lighting up either red or white); plus ceramic and porcelain novelties with names like Roosevelt's Bear and the White House Teddy Bear. A newspaper of the day observed that anybody with the money to own a car could mount special clip-on 36-inch teddys on the side lamps. And, too, you could buy "Teddy's" stationery, a squeeze ball, a hammock, and kiddie's pedal car—all bearing the name of the nation's president. None of this name stealing, it might be added, was objected to by the First Family; quite the contrary, as we'll see.

Manufacturers today have no monopoly on spin-off overkill. *Toys in Amer-*

ica makes this clear in terms of the national obsession with the teddy bear in the years from 1906 to 1908: "There were Teddy Bear targets, paper dolls, party games, banks, blocks, wagons, scarf pins, rubber stamps, water pistols, postcards, candy boxes, cotillion favors, balloons, bags, brief cases (of plush, of course), books, card games, shooflies, rocking 'horses', muzzles and leashes." To say nothing of such species crossovers as a Teddy with a doll's face, and a doll with a bear's face.

The circus at Madison Square Garden cashed in on the fad by dressing its clowns as bears and its performing dogs as cubs. In many vaudeville shows chorus girls paraded in bear costumes, while a comic told the joke *du jour:* "If Theodore Roosevelt is president with his clothes on, what is he with his clothes off?" Answer: "Teddy bare."

This craziness persisted for almost three years—and worried a number of serious-minded people. A priest claimed that bearmania among little girls, who had all but abandoned dolls, destroyed the very instincts of motherhood, threatening extinction of the species. Most troubled of all, though, were doll manufacturers, one of which asked rhetorically in an ad, "Is it as pretty a sight when a little girl mothers a bear as when she mothered a doll?"

Meanwhile, Back at the White House. Throughout all the Teddy hoopla, the real Teddy was delighted that his name was so loved as to launch a national craze. He was photographed with plushes, autographed other bears, and in speeches made reference to the fad. After his death, when his Long Island home, Sagamore Hill, was converted into a memorial to the president, Morris Michtom's son donated one of the original bears, which is on display there today. Mrs. Theodore Roosevelt Jr. requested that her children be photographed with several of Michtom's original bears, and another family member recounted the creation of the stuffed animal on a radio program. The real Teddy had busted trusts, initiated digging of the Panama Canal, and mediated the Russo-Japanese War, but perhaps he lives on most nostalgically as the namesake for a stuffed animal.

And what of Morris Michtom? While many of his competitors vanished along with the fad, his company, Ideal Toy, grew into a giant. Many of those early teddys are now collectors' items. At Christie's in London in May 1989, a German-made bear (by the renowned company Steiff) fetched $19,630, then four months later at Sotheby's another teddy sold for $88,000. It was bought by American Paul Volpp, a retired West Coast manufacturer of construction equipment and collector of teddy bears, as a gift to his wife on their forty-second wedding anniversary. Volpp estimated that the bear might sell for about $23,000 but instructed his bidder to "Buy that bear!" Bidding was fierce—which attests to a theme mentioned at the opening of this book: nostalgia. Paul Volpp bought nostalgia. Eighty-eight thousand dollars' worth.

Wish Books

Few events stirred more expectancy in the rural home of the Oughts than the arrival of the latest Sears, Roebuck or Montgomery Ward catalog. For women, a mail-order wish book meant furnishings "as seen in your finest Homes" and fashions that "Society's finest" were sporting in Chicago and New York. For men, pages devoted to farm implements, guns, pocket watches, and tools were a marvel of technology. Children ogled pictures of toys, puzzles, live pets, and dolls. The excitement lasted until the arrival of the next catalog. At a time when rural folk's only shopping was at a ma-and-pa grocer's, catalogs filled a need— and created countless others.

Wish books were read (and reread) with more savory interest than one might lavish on a novel. Jealously guarded, selectively shared, they put sixty percent of the American population (the rural sector) in pocketbook's touch with "The Most Complete Store on Earth"—a boast both Sears and Ward trumpeted. The turn-of-the-century Sears catalog opened with the title-page assurance "Cheapest Supply House on Earth," then greeted the perspective buyer with "Kind Friend." On the other hand, Ward's wish book—"Suppliers for Every Trade and Calling on Earth"—went straight for its major consumer with "Ladies, for the Spring and Summer try . . ." Ward's book of desiderata ran for 624 pages, Sears's for 1,162.

The concept was ground-breaking, buying gizmos and gewgaws through the mail, an innovation that transformed the look—and correspondingly the attitude—of rural America faster than anything prior to the automobile. This, brought about by a book, a book of dreams come true. In homes across America the decor of pioneer simplicity was spiced with metropolitan sophistication—a tuffeted chaise, flocked wallpaper, an art nouveau etched gas lamp—and a rural mentality was reshaped. In addition, labor-saving devices for the kitchen and farm gave rural Americans their first tantalizing breath of leisure time. Today we realize that an Eastern bloc or third world country cannot embrace the manufactured goods of free-market capitalism without eventually accommodating its philosophy. So too, to a lesser degree, did welcoming big-city goods into the rural home transform its look as well as its inhabitants' outlook.

Let Your Fingers Do the Walking. The merchandising idea that helped revolutionize the American home was conceived in 1872 by a traveling dry-goods salesman, Aaron Montgomery Ward, whose travels in rural America taught him the likes, dislikes and desires of farmers. Ward and his brother-in-law, with original capital of $2,400, established a warehouse and drew up their first catalog—which was a single sheet, 8 by 12 inches, listing their goods and how to order them by mail. In two years the sheet had grown to a seventy-two-page booklet, and for a time every item among its seasonally burgeoning pages was illustrated by a woodcut. In 1884 the catalog's 240 pages listed nearly ten thousand items. By 1895 Ward's sales had reached the $4 million mark; its catalog was over six hundred pages. The wish book was in more American homes than the Bible.

What Ward started, Richard Sears, a railroad clerk who became known as the "Barnum of merchandising," and Alvah Roebuck, a watchmaker, perfected to a science. Their "Wondrous Emporium" began fourteen years after Ward's venture, and their catalog, written in a folksy style by Sears himself, reached from Maine to California. It offered everything from the practicality of iceboxes (which made possible the safe storage of perishables) and eyeglasses (which allowed the simple pleasure of reading), to the luxury of an ice-cream maker for "the smoothest and most deliciously mellow cream you ever tasted."

Sears's and Ward's wish books were also pharmacopoeias of "patented" nostrums and cure-alls which, for better or worse, were often country folk's only recourse when doctors were scarce. Most potions were harmless—and ineffective. A farmer's wife learned unblushingly from Sears that city women enlarged their bosoms with "the world famous La Dore's Bust Food," unrivaled for "its purity" and guaranteed to create "a plump, full, rounded bosom." Or, by mailing in a sample of her hair (for "scientific analysis"), she could make over her appearance with the returned package of "puff bangs" or a "Paris wig" in red, gray, gold, or "drab" (a mousy brown). The world was changing, and wish books were speeding the process.

Toys as Fads

Toys are a seasonal wellspring for fads, the richest fad factory in our century. America began to experience a toy explosion in the Oughts that, with time out for the Depression, continues to mushroom. Reasons proffered for America's turn-of-the-century toy boom are many: the discovery of the importance of play for children, the leisure time reality of children working less and playing more, and an immense increase in the number of toy manufacturers. In the 1880s America had 173 toymakers with sales of $3.5 million; by 1910 there were five hundred companies, and sales stood at $40 million. The times were poised for a corresponding explosion of fads.

In 1902 the first successful toy-buying guide for parents advised, "Let toys be simple, strong, and durable . . . Children's instinctive delight in putting their own thought into their playthings . . . explains why the simpler toy is often more pleasing." Another book, *Introduction to Childhood,* emphasized "the need for a great number of new toys that fit different psychological ages." And the influential magazine *Playthings,* founded in 1903, admonished merchants for stocking store shelves only at Christmas (long the practice); toy buying, suggested the magazine, should be a year-round phenomenon. Merchants did not need to be admonished for long; the message was much appreciated and sweepingly implemented.

At the turn of the century the fad toy for boys was the . . .

Daisy Air Rifle

This megahit toy also enriched American colloquialisms with the expression "It's a daisy!" meaning "impressive." Actually the full phrase on everyone's lips in 1900 was "Clarence, it's a Daisy!" referring to a manufacturer of iron windmills, Clarence Hamilton, who conceived the BB-shooting air rifle. More than 43,000 guns sold the first year on the market, each for about 50 cents. That number was astronomical then, as was the toy's advertising budget of $3,000.

Toy air rifles had been made in America since 1884, but the guns were of wood. Hamilton's genius was to create a gun of metal, which even a young boy recognized as being closer to the real thing. When he unveiled the idea to his company's directors, one eager manager exclaimed, "Clarence, it's a daisy!" The rifle had a name.

The trim, authentic-looking weapon was an immediate hit, and probably no toy of that period delighted boys more. Yearly sales of Daisy rifles doubled for a time, and the gun's success prompted Hamilton to change the name of his Plymouth Iron Windmill Company to Daisy Manufacturing—which became the country's number one maker of BB guns. The toy also became a fad plaything in China—though only after an American salesman demonstrated to Chinese officials that the gun was "harmless" by shooting his bare hand at close range; the explosion didn't draw blood, and the pain was numbed by the size of the order. China became the second largest market after the United States for Daisy air rifles.

Not all parents approved of the air-powered BB gun—which eventually was banned in several states. Nor was it the first time a hit toy was viewed as hazardous. The first toy banning occurred in 1746 in France, when the constabulary decreed that any pregnant woman who gazed at the contorted limbs of the country's then most popular toy, jumping jacks, risked giving birth to a misshapen child. Jumping jacks, a string puppet, was of course harmless; other faddish toys of old, though, would never make it to the market by today's standards. During the period when many Americans fought for the exclusion of Chinese laborers from the work force a popular cap pistol, now a prized collectors' item, was titled "The Chinese Must Go Gun."

Since the phenomenal success of the Daisy rifle, toy guns and pistols have been one of the century's recurring hits with boys, sales skyrocketing during every military encounter except one: the Vietnam War, when sales plummeted.

And while boys were playing with their Daisy air rifles, what were young girls clamoring for?

Suckathumb Baby, Tickletoes, and Flossie Flirt

Chatty Cathy, Mattel's megahit, was not the first talking doll. A less loquacious tot was the brainchild of Thomas Edison, inventor of the phonograph. He envisioned one of his early cylinder players inside a doll's chest, and the novelty generated breathless enthusiasm in the press. "Just imagine! Dolls which can truly say 'Mamma' and 'Papa' in a real human voice," forecast a leading magazine in the 1880s. "Dolls that tell fairy-tales and sing songs like real live boys and girls." Hype of the day had Edison sidelining 250 of his phonograph makers to fashion talking dolls, with "about 500 talking dolls ready to be supplied every day."

Premature as the forecast was, Edison did realize that girls were ready for lifelike "action" dolls. Already there were hits on the market: a china-head doll with rolling eyes, and another whose eyes closed "to sleep." Morris Michtom, who launched the teddy bear craze, created Suckathumb Baby, which sucked on its rubber finger; and there was Tickletoes, whose rubber arms and legs supposedly felt like human skin; Flossie Flirt, whose name suggested her batting eyelash action; and **Ducky,** notable for the fact that she was made entirely of rubber—itself then still a trendy material.

Whereas the century's giant doll crazes—like Shirley Temple and Barbie—are examined in other parts of this book, here are the somewhat lesser fad dolls that would appear over the decades—dolls doing things Edison never dreamed of.

In brief: **Saucy Walker** walked; **Baby Coos** cooed (through a clarinet reed in her throat); **Heart Beat** broadcast the sound of a human heart; **Patti Prays** knelt when she prayed; **Blessed Event** sucked like a newborn; **Tiny Tears** cried; **Baby Bubbles** gurgled and blew bubbles; **Baby Heather** matured from an infant to a two-year-old, sprouting teeth; **Saralee** was not a cake but the first black doll with authentic black features.

Betsy Wetsy drank, then in astonishingly short time wet her diapers. This favorite was developed because a friend of Morris Michtom's son worried about the jealousy her three-year-old displayed toward her newborn. Ideal, Michtom's company, came up with a doll that the three-year-old could feed and change, as her mother did to the infant.

Baby Alive was a hit because she dared to go a step further than Betsy Wetsy; she defecated. She ate "solid foods" (red, yellow or green gels; "cherry," "banana," or "lime"), masticated, then after an interval that would infuriate any real parent, performed her touted feat in one of three colors. Though much of the toy industry questioned if a defecating doll was marketable (or tasteful), Baby Alive was the country's number one doll fad of the early Seventies, selling three million tots.

Raggedy Ann was that rarity of a fad that becomes a perennial favorite (despite the fact that she does nothing cute or crude). The oldest of licensed products, created in 1914 by parents John and Myrtle Gruelle, she's been the subject of television shows, comics, and movies. Raggedy Ann was created when the Gruelles' daughter, Marcella, found a faceless rag doll and asked her father, a political cartoonist, to give it features. Her mother restuffed the doll and sewed on a red heart with the words "I love you." Tragically, Marcella died two years later. John Gruelle began composing Raggedy Ann stories as a memorial to his daughter, then created a companion for the doll, Raggedy Andy; both were wildly popular in the early years of the century—and kicked off the product licensing phenomenon that is commonplace today.

Kewpies, a fad among little girls as much as grown women, were probably this century's most popular elfin-doll until the arrival in the Eighties of the Smurfs (see page 440). Puckish, wide-eyed, and fat-cheeked, the tykes—

Rose O'Neill and her Cuddle Kewpies.

produced in models from 2 to 14 inches tall—were modern-day cupids with a topknot in the middle of their hair. A national, then international, craze, Kewpies—or "Kewps" as admirers called them—were the brainchild of illustrator Rose O'Neill, who debuted them as drawings in 1909 in *Woman's Home Companion,* then later as dolls. The naked cherubs spawned a deluge of bestselling spin-offs: stationery, greeting cards, handkerchiefs, table linens, decals, inkwells, mirror handles, rattles, cups, salt shakers, earrings and bracelets—a list worthy of modern marketing.

All Kewps were "male" (except for a female figurine Rose O'Neill issued in the 1920s, when the fad had largely waned), and bore titles like the Chieftain, the Cook, Careful of His Voice, and Plain Kewpie. Kewps were romantic gifts between lovers, they generated fan clubs across America, and legend has it that the British early in World War I lifted their blockade against German ships (the dolls were initially manufactured in Germany) to allow shipments into the country to satisfy their own national mania.

Mechanical Banks

At the turn of the century, amid a thrift-minded Protestant ethic, ingeniously designed mechanical banks were a big business, with various models "must-haves" among children. These iron-cast banks, with animated figures that snatched, swallowed or tossed coins into savings, were a direct byproduct of Civil War craftsmanship in the art of forging weapons. For after the war, there was a surplus of iron and of skilled, unemployed iron casters.

Caster John Hall designed the first patented mechanical bank, named Hall's Excelsior, which was an immediate hit among the parsimonious. The novelty is in the shape of a house, and when the door knocker is pulled, the chimney lifts to reveal a small monkey (a man in some varieties) holding a platter to receive the coin. Toy companies rushed into the business, and between 1870 and the early decades of this century hundreds of mechanical banks filled store shelves. In spite of their clever mechanisms, they sold for about 25 cents to 50 cents. Today, collectors bid up to $10,000 for rare models, while two prized versions—the Girl Skipping Rope and the Bread Winner, both with complicated mechanisms and fragile appendages—are thought to be worth more than $50,000.

At the turn of the century, though, these were favorite Christmas toys. Kids traded models and begged their parents for Educated Pig, or Kicking Mule, or Cat and Mouse. A bank's novel action encouraged play and thus saving. Many actions were highly complex: In the Chinaman, a coin triggers a reclining Oriental figure on a log to salute, revealing a handful of playing cards, while a rat runs out of the log's open end. In the Columbus Bank, one of the most elaborate early models, a coin inserted at Columbus's feet prompts an Indian chief to leap from behind a tree, salute, and offer the discoverer a peace pipe.

Banks also kept up with national crazes: The popularity of stuffed teddy bears was duplicated in a bank of Teddy and the Bear; a famed expedition to the top of the globe was captured in the North Pole Bank; and the amusement wonder of the 1893 Chicago World's Fair was replicated in the Ferris Wheel Bank, which stands 22 inches high with six carriages on the wheel and two figures in each.

Some critics felt banks should not be toys. The *Chicago Tribune* argued at the turn of the century that iron banks are "shamefaced parental impositions . . . that decoy poor, defenseless little children into dropping their hard-begged-for pennies therein to see them work." Truth was, it took a coin (or any similarly shaped object) to activate a bank, and children, as the *Tribune* pointed out, often "cut the buttons off their Mama's clothes to see the bank do tricks." Today, when movable toys are the standard, it's hard to appreciate the hours of fun a child once derived from a mechanical bank.

The Car as a Rich Man's Toy

The first big *male* fad of the century was the automobile; grown men actually hocked their houses for wheels. This section is not about the car as a transpor-

AMERICAN MERCEDES
70 H. P. Demi Limousine Touring Car
$10,000.00

This is the Handsomest Car in the World. Something Entirely New. Immediate Delivery

DAIMLER MFG. CO., Factory, Long Island City, L. I.

SALESROOM, 1777 BROADWAY, NEW YORK

AMERICAN MERCEDES

tation necessity but about an era in which the horseless carriage was a rich man's plaything, when paved roads were nonexistent, when racing at the speed of a horse's gallop was life-threatening; when, in short, "motoring" was the newest and trendiest of men's sports. Being dangerous, dirty, and daring, it was an ideal male sport. Didn't motoring even require a protective lab smock and goggles?

Horseless carriages were at first novelties, and every man of means had to have one. Or two. "So has the race for social supremacy become," reported *Horseless Age* magazine in the Oughts, "that owners of houses are mortgaging them in order to buy as many and as speedy automobiles as their neighbors. Extravagance is reckless and something must be done before utter ruin follows in the wake of folly." The magazine was not alone in its early view of automania as nothing more than a fad. The federal government and Wall Street virtually ignored the car, believing it had no future. Auto shares were not listed on the New York Stock Exchange; manufacturers had to get their financial backing from private individuals. Many were wealthy sportsmen; others were make-a-quick-buck frauds. Consequently, the early car industry was in chaos, and the car buyer often got a costly lemon. Conservative bankers sat out the shakeout of solid auto companies from fly-by-night concerns. All of this uncertainty reinforced the notion of the car as a passing fancy.

In 1900 America had only eight thousand cars. Yet the public was fascinated by these frail, costly, balky contraptions that shook; trembled; clattered; spat oil, fire, and smoke; and smelled. Monied men with a taste for adventure bought up the machines as fast as they were produced (pre–assembly line days), establishing new standards of glamorous consumership. It was not yet certain that the word automobile would triumph as a replacement for the awkward phrase horseless carriage. In a magazine contest for a new name for the wheeled vehicle, first prize went to "motorcycle"—which most people on the street preferred; it being straightforwardly related to the vehicle they rode, a bicycle. Runners-up included "petrocar," "viamote," "autobat," "motorfly," and "mobe"—pronounced "mobee"; the last prompted one newspaper to parody: "To mobe or not to mobe, that is the question."

What to call the driver? A serious contender was "chauffeur," French for "stoker," from the operator of steam-driven cars. In fact, two-thirds of the vehicles featured at the first American auto show, held in New York in 1900, were "steamers" (steam-engine-powered) or "electrics" (battery-powered). Manufacturers displaying their wares included the pioneers Daimler, Benz, Renault, Delanaye, and Peugeot.

The first popular American car debuted in 1901—the curved-dash, gasoline-engine Oldsmobile, produced by Ransom E. Olds. Resembling a surrey without the fringe on top, it cost $650 and inspired a hit song: "In My Merry Oldsmobile." That first year, Ransom Olds sold 425 cars.

In most rural communities, only the town doctor could afford a car. Physicians, using a car to make house calls, played a large role in promoting the benefits of the auto. But since doctors then were viewed with lofty esteem, their ownership of cars reinforced the notion of the automobile as a fad of both the idle rich and the humanitarian rich.

Motoring as Male Sport.   From its inception, the automobile was viewed as a man's possession, the vehicle itself as a "male animal" that had to be cranked by strong masculine arms. Further, the car embodied age-old male cravings for power and exploration. This was not later pop psychologizing, but

the attitude found in 1901 in *Motor World* when the editors (all men) rhapsodized over motoring's hedonistic appeal: "To take control of this materialized energy, to draw the reins over this monster with its steel muscles and fiery heart—there is something in the idea which appeals to an almost universal sense, the love of power." That the vehicles moved with speed also appealed to men. "Add the element of danger," raved *Motor World,* "and the fascination inherent in motor vehiclism as a sport is not difficult to understand."

Five years later, in an article titled "The Automobile in America," its author (a man; Frank Munsey) elaborated on the American male's fascination with the new toy. "It is in the running of a car, the handling of it, and its obedience to one's will, that the keenest enjoyment of automobiling is found." That same year, 1906, another writer (also a man) summed up this fresh male mania when he wrote that "the sensation which arouses enthusiasm for the automobile comes almost solely from the introduction of the superlative degree of speed. The automobile is a vehicle that touches a sympathetic chord in most of us." *Us* of course not including the other half of humanity.

Society took a negative attitude toward women driving from the start; some steering wheels carried the warning "Men and Boys Only." There was some rationale to the sexism: Roads were often muddy ruts and the car's wheels hard to handle; it took muscle to avoid accidents. Women then *were* deadlier drivers; and the association once forged was hard to break.

Speeding as Vogue.   One element that made motoring sport was its dangerous speeds. Wealthy male motorists strenuously resisted speed legislation, arguing that the only criterion should be what is "reasonable and proper" given road conditions. The president of the Long Island Automobile Club, W. Wallace Grant, stated, "The automobilist is always the best judge of his own safe speed. The law should give him the utmost freedom in selecting this speed." The head of the Topeka Automobile Club, James Padget, reassured the frightened public in the Oughts that "an automobile going at a rate of 20 miles per hour is no more dangerous to life than a horse going at the rate of 10 miles per hour." No one was reassured, least the families of those pedestrians who appeared as statistics in the morning papers.

The general public, who could not yet afford the luxury of cars, overwhelmingly favored strict speeding limits for "the swells" and their autos. *Outlook,* a magazine especially concerned about reckless driving, summed up the public sentiment: "It is difficult to persuade the public, who find in almost every morning's paper a report of one or more automobile accidents of a serious nature, that it is as safe to drive an engine twenty to forty miles an hour . . . as to drive a pair of horses eight or ten miles an hour."

There had been early attempts to limit speeding. In England, the Red Flag Act severely limited a motorist to 2 miles per hour in town and 4 miles per hour on the "open road." A horse was faster. As was walking. In fact, an attendant had to walk sixty yards ahead of the car, waving a red flag by day, a red lantern by night. In 1902, Vermont adopted the English law for steam-powered cars.

But for many years most states were without laws about motoring—until around 1906. By that time fifteen states had speed limits of 20 miles per hour, nine states kept drivers on the open highway to 15 miles per hour, while two states had speed limits of under 10 miles per hour: Missouri (9 miles per hour) and Alabama (8 miles per hour). Ironically, the year 1906 marked the zenith of restrictive legislation against the speed of motor vehicles. As cars became safer to drive, and as more ordinary people owned their own cars, speed laws became progressively more lenient. Joe Public was now driving, and he didn't want to be slowed down. As *Outing* explained in 1909: "In the early statutes some antagonism to the automobile perhaps showed itself, but that has all passed away."

Passed away because the car, once a rich man's plaything, had, by the close of the Oughts, begun to become a commonplace, a mass-produced means of transport—due largely, as we'll see in the next chapter, to Henry Ford, who would usher in the next wave of automania with his Tin Lizzie.

FAIRS AND EXPOS

Buffalo's Pan-American Exposition: 1901

With grand fanfare and future shock, America opened the twentieth century with a brilliant rainbow-colored fantasy about the peace, progress, and space travel that lay ahead. At a time when the country's population numbered 76 million, 9 million Americans eagerly shuffled off to Buffalo (the song had yet to be written)—more than the entire population of New York state (7.2 million).

Visitors gasped at the sprawling fair called the Rainbow City of Lights, which featured a 375-foot electric edifice studded with colored lamps and searchlights; additional multicolored beams bathed Niagara Falls, source of the fair's electric power. "Rainbow of colors" was expo's theme, symbolizing the races of people that made up Pan-America. Directors of the exposition—dubbed Pax 1901—also claimed the fair kicked off "an age of American dominance in international affairs." As its name implies, the fair featured countries of the Americas: Mexico, Central America, South America, and the United States, and its possessions in the Philippines and Hawaii.

Spanish Renaissance was the fair's architectural theme, and though Pax 1901 was on a smaller scale than Chicago's 1893 fair, in terms of the magnificence of its Latin American structures it outshone the former. Elaborate fountains and cascades, winding canals, gardens, and caverns glowed under varicolored lights. The chromatic dazzle generated ethnological comments in the press. "The general effect is rich and striking," observed one daily, "suggesting the evolution of man by means of a scheme of color." Reviewing one building's rainbow mantle, the *Buffalo Enquirer* ventured that "the gradual change from an earthy red at the base to an ethereal blue at the top prompts the analogy [with] the ascent of man from savagery to civilization."

To push the color symbolism further, a significant difference could be read into the titles of the 1901 Buffalo fair (the *Rainbow* City of Lights) and the 1893 Chicago fair (the *White* City of Lights). With America still having one foot in the Victorian past, the Chicago fair had been in many ways racist, a white man's resumé of past achievements and his own vision of the future. The Buffalo fair (though still displaying many foreign peoples as primitives) made a stride— albeit a small one—in recognizing that America's future was going to be multira- cial. The press of the day did not miss this comparison, and stressed that the fair's multicolored skyline represented, to borrow a later phrase, a rainbow coalition of races.

To most fairgoers, however, Pax 1901 was just plain fun. One could walk the Streets of Mexico exhibit, witness a "defiance dance" by Iroquois, stroll through the Philippine Village, or take part in Hawaiian hula-hula dances. Whereas the Chicago fair had its Little Egypt, Pax offered the titillations of "Fatima, the Sultan's Favorite." The bewitching, raven-haired, black-eyed hootchy-kootchy beauty drew capacity crowds, and the following year moved her act to Coney Island. Whereas Little Egypt's hip gyrations had scandalized late-Victorian folk and resulted in police raids, Fatima's dancing, less than a decade later, merely delighted audiences. And police; there were no raids. For sheer excitement it was hard to top the fair's disaster shows, such as the devastating Johnstown Flood and the tragic Chicago Fire; the flood and the fire exhibits drew standing-room-only crowds. Americans, it seemed, already had an appetite for sensational misfortune reworked as entertainment. But the most popular event—which stirred nationwide wonder—was the country's first illu- sion ride.

Trip to the Moon Adventure Ride.   Today, any visitor to a Disneyland- type adventure park knows the thrill of an illusion ride. But at the turn of the century the concept was unheard of, the event undreamed of—except, that is, by the architect of the Trip to the Moon, Frederic Thompson. One journalist who took the ride found the special effects so dazzlingly realistic that he exclaimed with gusto, and not a little insight, "There! you see, not satisfied with exhausting the earth, showmen have already begun upon the universe. Behold, the world is a sucked orange." Many people, unprepared for the novelty of special effects, suffered vertigo, motion sickness, and vomiting.

The Trip to the Moon was staged in a commodious, high-ceilinged building and possessed all the wondrous hokum we've come to appreciate in early sci-fi movies. It featured a green and white cigar-shaped flying machine, the airship *Luna,* about the size of a small steamship, which "flew" by flapping its birdlike wings (remember, the Wright brothers would not take off from Kitty Hawk for another two years). Poised on a tower, the *Luna,* containing thirty adventurous passengers, tilted, rocked, and swayed to the imagined motions of spaceflight. Gazing out the craft's portals (at the inner walls of the building), a rider glimpsed the special effects of shooting stars, constellations, and glowing plan- ets, while a "flight lecturer" narrated the journey.

On "takeoff" the *Luna* seemed to soar over the exposition grounds, then the city of Buffalo, on to Niagara Falls (with the roar of water), and finally into space where the Earth appeared as a smaller and smaller ball, then vanished entirely. The special effects of "leaving the atmosphere" consisted of electrical storms, blindingly bright lightning, and deafening thunder. Then darkness. Silence. Riders screamed in excitement, in fear; women fainted, and many of both sexes vomited from motion sickness. At the end of the storm was a "golden dawn" and the face of the Man in the Moon. Literally.

The moon itself was a marvel of imagination and papier-mâché. Soaring stalactites, cavernous crystalline volcanoes, glistening mineral pools—a fairyland no astronomer ever glimpsed. The *Luna* "landed," and those whose legs could carry them disembarked down a gangplank—not onto the moon's surface, but into its richly accessorized interior (located in an extension of the main building). Costumed midgets strolled through grottoes and along sinuous paths, beckoning the Earthlings on to the chamber housing the Man in the Moon himself, who sat on a mother-of-pearl throne, surrounded by Moon Maidens engaged in a rhythmic lunar dance. Picking off chunks from the "walls of cheese," midgets offered the green-tinted snack to anyone who had a stomach for it. All exited over a swaying bridge not back to the spacecraft, but to Earth in the form of the fairgrounds. The illusion of flight was deemed so real that riders argued over whether the plane actually left the building. Amusement architect Thompson went on to assist in the development of Coney Island's famous Luna Park.

Assassination.   If Pax's colored-light theme symbolized the mixture of races of the Americas, and its Trip to the Moon amusement hinted at the space travel that lay decades ahead, another fair event boded tragically for the future: the cold-blooded assassination of a political figure—President William McKinley. Visiting the Buffalo fair, McKinley was greeting visitors when a man in line, Leon Czolgosz, a self-avowed anarchist, stepped forward and shot the president at close range. McKinley died a few days later; that same year Czolgosz sizzled in the century's newest technological invention, the electric chair. McKinley's death brought people in droves to the fairgrounds. One paper editorialized that "The Exposition is recognized now as an enterprise of national importance to a greater extent than it ever was before." Many visitors upon spotting the half-masted American flag in the esplanade burst into tears.

The twentieth century's first American exposition encompassed the goal of racial harmony, the promise of space exploration, and the sickness of political assassination—no one can say the fair did not offer a glimpse of the future.

St. Louis's Louisiana Purchase Exposition: 1904

Twenty million Americans were treated to "a better way of life" coming in the twentieth century through exhibits on air travel, the telephone, and more than one hundred of the latest model automobiles—featuring one car that made the trip between New York City and St. Louis in a record of eighty-one hours and seventeen minutes. This fair, the second such extravaganza in the Oughts, even had a specially composed theme song:

> Meet me in St. Louis, Louis,
> Meet me at the Fair.
> Don't tell me the lights are shining,
> Any place but there.
> We will dance the hootchy-kootchy,
> I will be your tootsie-wootsie,
> If you meet me in St. Louis, Louis,
> Meet me at the fair.

The song was by Andrew Sterling, who months earlier had overheard a bar waiter by the name of Louis receive a shouted order for a popular St. Louis beer: "Another Louis, Louis!" That lyrical ring, coupled with the upcoming fair to celebrate the Louisiana Purchase, moved songwriter Sterling to composition. His song was an immediate hit, sung and played endlessly by bands and entertainers at the fair—which covered 1,240 acres and was officially opened by President Theodore Roosevelt.

Striving for one-upmanship, planners sought to make the St. Louis event more memorable and entertaining than Chicago's Columbian and Buffalo's Pan-American. They imported the Chicago fair's giant Ferris wheel and commissioned a death-defying roller coaster, the Scenic Railway, which attained speeds of 25 miles an hour on the curves and forty in straight drops. And illusion rides, new three years earlier in Buffalo, were now a veritable commonplace: Topping for thrills Pax's Trip to the Moon were an underwater submarine adventure that metamorphosed into a high-flying airplane excursion, and a fanciful experience called the Hereafter. In addition, eight hundred imported wild animals stalked and menaced (from behind steel bars), and the Irish exhibition boasted—no blarney, the press said—an enormous chunk of the original Blarney stone, to be kissed by visitors wishing to avail themselves of the Celtic legend's promise: "Whoever kisses—never misses to grow eloquent."

Olympic Scandal.   The fair also included the first Olympic Games held in the Western Hemisphere. Reflecting the American cult of strenuous living, or "the gospel of muscles" as it was called at the fair, the international Olympic competition vied for spectators with the fair's midway sideshows, resulting in streams of fairgoers racing between sporting events and circus acts. As the games were a first, so too was the scandal of a marathon runner riding a vehicle toward the finish line. As a New York marathoner in the Eighties would secretly ride a subway part of the course distance, at the fair Fred Lorz, a Manhattanite, tired, hailed a lift in a farmer's passing truck, then, less than five miles from the finish line, disembarked refreshed and jogged into the stadium to cheering crowds. Alice Roosevelt, the president's daughter, was posing for a photograph with Lorz and his trophy when officials learned that he'd covered most of the course in a truck.

A rather trivial but delicious item debuted at the St. Louis fair: the **ice-cream cone**. When the supply of dishes ran out at the ice-cream concession, Ernst Hamwi, a Syrian pastry chef operating the adjacent bakery stand, rolled his waferlike waffles (a native treat called zalabias) into cones to help out. Soon the cornucopia-shaped hit was seen throughout the fair. Ironically, the initial capitalization for the Louisiana Purchase Exposition was the exact amount that President Thomas Jefferson had paid France for the Louisiana Territory a hundred years earlier: $15 million. The fair's abundance of exhibits in the arts and sciences moved one commentator to effuse: "If all man's other works were by some unspeakable catastrophe blotted out, the records here offer all necessary standards for the rebuilding of our entire civilization."

The nation was gripped by world's fair fever. After Pax in 1901 and the Louisiana Purchase in 1904, America staged a third event, **Portland's 1905 Lewis and Clark;** then **Norfolk's 1907 Jamestown Tercentenary;** and **Seattle's 1909 Alaska-Yukon.** No decade before or since the Oughts hosted five world's fairs and expositions. And no song lyric better fitted the era than "Meet me at the fair."

DANCE CRAZES

Gotta Animal Dance

With the older generation still waltzing to Strauss and two-stepping to Sousa, a younger, raffish element turned for dance inspiration to animal behavior—an ethology of dance, so to speak, that primitive peoples could easily have appreciated. If adults of one generation have traditionally viewed the teenagers of the next generation as acting something akin to animals, at the end of the Oughts there was literal reason for this. In out-of-the-way nightspots, young people were behaving like bunnies hugging, horses trotting, camels walking, buzzards loping, chickens scratching, and kangaroos dipping.

For the **bunny hug, horse trot, camel walk, buzzard lope, chicken scratch,** and **kangaroo dip** were a few of the vogue steps called animal dances, or, to use a term with more anthropological import, mimic dances. Ancient peoples dressed in the skin of a deer and pranced like the animal as an auspicious act commencing a hunt. Young people in the Oughts were, one might say, anthropologically chic. Of all the animal steps that started with the young and spread quickly throughout society in a new wave of dance fever, one, the first, trotted ahead of the pack.

Turkey Trot

To chicken scratch, you scuff your toes backward against the floor. To buzzard lope, you dive with arms extended as if for carrion. To turkey trot, you bounce up and down on the balls of your feet, craning your neck as gobblers sometimes do; this ballroom romp was done to a ragtime beat, and its spastic movements seemed crude to onlookers accustomed to the smooth glide of a waltz. The appeal that the turkey trot had in common with all later animal dances was that boys and girls moved close together, touched, pawed, and intimately supported each other's perilously off-balance gyrations. That is, opposite-sex proximity.

Parents condemned the turkey trot. Religious groups pressured towns to prohibit all animal mimicry, and teens were arrested and jailed for trotting. Several universities threatened to expel animal mimics. At ballrooms, floor inspectors patrolled the crowds on the lookout for animal behavior. And the influential National Association of Masters of Dance disavowed the turkey trot as graceless; though it was hardly being danced for grace but for jolly good fun. Yet the turkey trot and its animal offspring had an energy and appeal that was infectious. Soon society folk trotted gleefully in resorts like old Orchard Beach, Maine, and Newport, Rhode Island.

In all likelihood, the turkey trot originated in spunky San Francisco night-spots along the Barbary Coast—where Al Jolson is known to have danced it. But its popularity is traced to a 1910 musical revue, *Over the River,* which featured the dance and launched the craze. Similarly, the success of the next animal dance, the grizzly bear, owes much to another musical event, Irving Berlin's "Everybody's Doin' It Now."

Grizzly Bear

The beat of Berlin's song fit both the turkey trot and the grizzly bear, the latter repeatedly emphasized in the song's lyric, "It's a bear." Across America people heard of the tune for the first time and understandably asked, "Everybody's doing what?" The answer helped spread the dance's popularity. In fact, the new syncopated sound of ragtime had ushered in the entire menagerie of scandalous dances: The buzzard lope is thought to have originated in Georgia, while myriad other animal dances, in vogue for only weeks at a time, owe much to one couple's impromptu dance-floor improvisations being copied by other dancers. It was a period in which America began to go mad for dance, and in which social dance was opening itself up to individual creativity. Dance caught the ragged tempo of the times.

If society's moral watchdogs had frowned on the turkey trot, they neared apoplexy over the grizzly bear. From the Vatican, Pope Pius X asked Catholics to forswear the animal mimicry—in fact, all animal dances—and sanely return to dancing the medieval furlana (an Italian step in six-eighths time, long out of vogue). Music historians claim this was a bizarre choice for the pope to recommend since the furlana was once a wild courtship dance for couples, which even Casanova considered violently passionate.

The popular expression "to snuggle up like bears" suggests the dancers' proximity in the grizzly bear. The man's arm is placed tightly around the woman's waist, her head resting on his one shoulder, her arm slung over his other shoulder. She is as secure as a cub, while he drags her through aggressive swooping and rocking gyrations. Never was there to be air space between them. This was heady public intimacy in an era in which women were viewed as fit only for motherhood, in which a wife could not own property in one out of four states, and in which a wife had no claim to her own earnings in several states.

The zoo of animal dances would hold faddish sway until late in 1913 when a young professional dancing couple, Vernon and Irene Castle, pronounced the steps "ungraceful" and, worse, "out-of-fashion," at the same time setting the country ablaze with their own Castle walk and their version of the tango (see page 101).

POPULAR SONGS

Ragtime Beat

Ragtime, the century's first new rhythm, was for a time a young person's vogue, as were rag's animal dances. The sentimental waltz ballad of the Gay Nineties was still popular, though under attack in side-splitting parodies by the blackface comedian Charlie Chase. In his vaudeville act, Chase sang the schmaltzy hits—which required serious emoting if not heartfelt feeling—with a deadpan face, expressionless voice, and waltzless rhythm that made a travesty of the romantic Victorian lyrics. People laughed at lyrics they had previously cried over. The waltz ballad was being nudged aside to make space for ragged and jazzy new tunes.

It was the heyday of Tin Pan Alley, which would last until about 1920. One expert on Alley music estimates that between 1900 and 1910, more than a hundred songs sold a million copies of sheet music. A copy of a song sold for 25 cents at the start of the Oughts, and, due to cutthroat competition, was down to 10 cents a copy by the decade's close. From a music industry standpoint, the era kicked off the phenomenon of a song selling in the millions.

But, truth be told, though the waltz ballad was pronounced moribund in many music quarters, one of the biggest hits of the decade was its most naive, throwback ballad, which all of America was singing at the dawn of the twentieth century.

A Bird in a Gilded Cage: 1900

In 1900 a sofa cost $9.98, a brass bed $3, and a man's shave and a haircut with a bay rum splash did indeed go for two bits (25 cents). At the forefront of music recording technology was the graphophone with its cylinder records, for which the manufacturer, Columbia Records, took the grand prize at the 1900 Paris Universal Exposition (the first of the century's fairs). At the same time, French artist François Barraud painted what would become *the* symbol of the new sound technology—a picture of a dog named Nipper listening at an ear funnel, titled "His Master's Voice." That summer, on July 10, the painting and title were trademarked in the United States Patent Office.

Selling wildly was the sheet music for Harry von Tilzer's "A Bird in a Gilded

Cage." Von Tilzer was already a successful Tin Pan Alley composer when he put the merry lyrics of Arthur Lamb to a sentimental waltz tune. The original words told of a material girl, funded by an older man. Von Tilzer sensed a hit if the free-spending heroine were *married* to the man, not merely living in sin. A little moral editing adjusted a Lamb line to read "She married for wealth, not for love." She was still a gold-digger, but respectably so.

As von Tilzer later told of the music's conception, he'd put the lyrics in his pocket and gone off with male buddies to a roadhouse of ill repute. While his friends were entertained by the girls, the twenty-eight-year-old von Tilzer amused himself at the house piano, picking out a melody for Lamb's text. He turned around from composing and singing the song to find a bevy of unoccupied house girls in tears. Whether they were affected by his melody or empathized with the song heroine's plight, von Tilzer realized he had a hit. "A Bird," he later said, was "the key that opened the door of wealth and fame."

He struck a musical lode two years later with two lilting waltz bestsellers: **In the Sweet Bye and Bye** and **On a Sunday Afternoon**—the latter celebrated a stroll through New York's Central Park and came to the composer *in toto* as he sunned himself on a park bench. In 1902, to give the public more of the sentimentality and artificial bathos that had worked so well in "A Bird," he teamed up with Arthur Lamb for a sequel, **Mansion of Aching Hearts.**

There was also great humor to be found in some bestsellers of 1902—as in the ragtime favorite **Bill Bailey, Won't You Please Come Home?** which belonged to a popular (and pejorative) category of music known then as "coon songs." It displayed music's new catchy syncopation in the opening line of the chorus: "Won't you come home, Bill Bailey, won't you come home?" Perhaps the most joyous hit of 1902 was **In the Good Old Summer Time,** a smash success then and a perennial favorite in that music category once known as gang songs—a term today with dark and violent connotations, but which once meant music to be sung by a group—a church group or a barbershop quartet.

The Innocent Oughts, as we're about to see, produced many hits that became twentieth-century classics.

Sweet Adeline: 1903

In 1903 songwriter Monroe Rosenfield first applied the sobriquet Tin Pan Alley to the cluster of song publishers located on Twenty-eighth Street between Sixth Avenue and Broadway in New York City, and that year's hits were: **Always Leave Them Laughing When You Say Goodbye,** "Sweet Adeline" (the harmonizers' anthem), and **Toyland,** from Victor Herbert's successful stage musical *Babes in Toyland.* (Herbert would close the decade with the greatest operetta hit of his career, *Naughty Marietta,* a work verging on grand opera, and spinning off, so to speak, three hit singles: **I'm Falling in Love With Someone,** the **Italian Street Song,** and the soaring **Ah, Sweet Mystery of Life!** The hits enjoyed a second success when Jeanette MacDonald and Nelson Eddy made a movie of the operetta.)

"Sweet Adeline" was actually written in 1896 by Harry Armstrong, then an eighteen-year-old amateur boxer, pianist, and barbershop quartet harmonizer who earned his living working in a Boston jewelry store. He brought the song, then titled "Down Home in Old New England," with him to New York, where he played honky-tonk piano at Coney Island. After several alterations in lyrics, and an equal number of rejections from Tin Pan Alley publishers, Armstrong and a collaborator spotted a sign announcing the farewell tour of Adeline Patti, one of the great coloratura singers of the nineteenth century. Armstrong's musical ear immediately told him that the triple vowel syllables of "Adeline" could be hauntingly sustained by one voice while surrounded by others in barbershop harmony. Thus, "Down Home in Old New England" became "You're the Flower of my Heart, Sweet Adeline." It was an immediate hit after debuting in a theater revue, and became the campaign song for John Fitzgerald, running for mayor of Boston. A major feature of its popularity throughout the century is the "echo" effect in its title's simple four-note pattern, like that found in the classic Westminster chimes. Harry Armstrong never composed anything that approached the national craze created by "Sweet Adeline."

As we've seen, in the next year, 1904, America was singing the fair's hit "Meet Me in St. Louis"—and Irish performer George M. Cohan (Kohane) opened on Broadway in *Little Johnny Jones,* immortalizing two numbers, **Give My Regards to Broadway** and **(I Am) The Yankee Doodle Boy (Born on the Fourth of July)**—Cohan was actually born on July 3, 1878.

Wait Till the Sun Shines Nellie: 1905

Variety, the country's first serious professional trade paper of show business, began publication in 1905. New York's Hippodrome Theater opened; it had 5,200 seats and a stage 100 feet deep, containing two circus rings housing a swimming tank 14 feet deep with a secret underwater exit so that entire chorus lines could dive in and mysteriously disappear. It was the country's first truly gigantic theater, and one hit show of that first season featured a Civil War battle in which the entire cavalry plunged into the tank.

That year Americans were singing the first automobile song hit, **In My Merry Oldsmobile,** which commemorated the first transcontinental auto race, won by an Olds. The transportation ditty, which launched a fad for car songs, was written by former vaudevillian Gus Edwards, who enjoyed the additional hits **School Days** (1907) and **By the Light of the Silvery Moon** (1909). Edwards, born in Germany and brought to New York by his parents at age nine, was a boy soprano who as a composer knew how to write highly singable tunes.

But perhaps the biggest smash of 1905 was "Wait Till the Sun Shines, Nellie," another hit for Harry von Tilzer and lyricist Andrew Sterling. It was a gang song, immediately adopted by barbershop quartets, and has an interesting origin. The idea for the optimistic ditty came from a newspaper story in which a journalist related how he gave hope to an impoverished East Side New York family by reminding them that "clear weather follows a storm." Von Tilzer saw big bucks in the cliché—and little could he have realized that soon the entire city of San Francisco would be in need of a song of hope and courage following the Great Quake; the hit enjoyed a second success with a one-word substitution for "Nellie": "Wait Till the Sun Shines, Frisco." This tunesmith of the Oughts also wrote one of the first top-sellers of the next decade: **I Want a Girl Just Like the Girl That Married Dear Old Dad.**

The year 1905 can't be discussed without mentioning the first and only song hit with lyrics by a future mayor of New York: **Will You Love Me in December as You Do in May?** by James J. Walker.

Glow Worm: 1907

In 1906, as seven-year-old Fred Astaire made his dance debut with his eight-year-old sister Adele, America was caught up in three patriotic hits: **Anchors Aweigh, You're a Grand Old Flag,** and the **National Emblem March,** a noble song better known today in its parodied version, "And the Monkey Wrapped Its Tail Around the Flagpole." A hit parade success in a different vein was **In Old New York** (or "The Streets of New York").

In 1907 Florenz Ziegfeld staged his first *Ziegfeld Follies,* costing $13,000, on the roof of the New York Theater, and his beauties set a new standard of measurement for American women: bust, 36 inches; waist, 26 inches; hips, 38 inches. That same year, Franz Lehar's operetta *The Merry Widow* created a sensation at the New Amsterdam Theater, leaving the country humming **The Merry Widow Waltz.** But the season's top song hit was the sentimental German import that many called "Glow Little Glow Worm, Glitter, Glitter," but which was "Glühwürmchen" to its composer, Paul Lincke. The song was hastily interpolated into a musical, *The Girl Behind the Counter,* with the sole purpose of giving the leading lady a romantic number for a scene featuring a summer arbor, dusk lighting, and teeming fireflies. The tune had nothing to do with the story, and no one connected with the show thought much of the music. But the public went wild, and sheet music stores could not keep the song in stock. "Glow Worm" made more money that year than just about any other tune.

Take Me Out to the Ball Game; Shine On, Harvest Moon; Cuddle Up a Little Closer, Lovey Mine: 1908–09

In the final two years of the Oughts, Americans were excited over the Columbia Phonograph Company's first two-sided record—"Twice the music per disk!" (which meant something like hearing four minutes instead of two); and they were singing the above-mentioned three hits. Each song would become a classic, and one the theme song of America's national sport. But the outstanding surprise pop number of the period was the exuberant nonsense song **Yip-I-Addy-I-Ay** by Will Cobb and John Flynn. Whereas the Gay Nincties' "Ta-ra-ra-boom-deay" was clearly tuneful gibberish, "Yip-I-Addy-I-Ay" actually sounded as if it meant something—at least people listened to it searching for a message.

For millions, the song's title became a "whoopee" energy release, the cry of excited kids and rowdy cowboys.

In the year Admiral Robert Edwin Peary finally made it to the North Pole (on his sixth attempt), and Henry Ford introduced his Model-T Tin Lizzie, the country was nearing the close of its first decade of the new century. One of the Oughts' final smash songs was **I Wonder Who's Kissing Her Now,** by Joseph Howard a composer who earlier had scored a hit with another kissing number, **When You First Kissed the Last Girl You Loved.** In fact, looking over the list of published tunes, it's apparent that many had "kiss" or "kissing" in the title. Perhaps kissing seemed at once an innocent and daring activity for an American people pulling away from a Victorian sensibility, though it would take World War I for America to truly establish her own unique place in the world—as one historian expressed it: "leaving the Victorians to seem as obsolete as the dinosaurs."

BESTSELLING BOOKS

Happiness Novels

With the concept of a bestseller list having been established in the previous decade, book sales were now being tracked assiduously, readers' tastes for popular fiction discussed, debated (if not yet manipulated), and already criticized from high literary quarters. Women were—and are—the greater readers of fiction, and the Oughts witnessed a cavalcade of hits called "happiness novels" by women, for women, and about women—as well as historical romances, already an established genre. Here's how one male reviewer described the typical happiness novel: "Syrupy pathos, sentiment, and optimism flourish, until the reader is drowned in tears or scorched in the sunshine of gladness." Publishers of happiness novels basked in the sunshine of profit. Books had never made so much money; popular fiction had never been so popular. Seldom had books generated such widespread devotion.

As we'll see in what follows, the young century already had its equivalent of a Barbara Cartland, and more surprisingly still it also had something of a Jacqueline Susann, a tall stately woman who wrote about a sexual theme that shocked England, then America, and sold more books (read in brown paper wrappers) than any of that time. The Oughts "sex" novel was called *Three Weeks.*

We'll start, though, with the early bestsellers of the Oughts.

To Have and to Hold: Number One Fiction, 1900

The twentieth century's first blockbuster, number one for five months in 1900, was the romance *To Have and to Hold* by Mary Johnston. It was a Cartland-like story of a young English lady, a ward of the king, who flees to the American colonies to escape marriage with a nobleman not coincidentally named Lord Carnal. She finds her true love in a heroic Virginian, thus establishing a new theme in the decade's literature, in which a decent European noblewoman is saved from her own continent's royal decadence by an earthy, hardworking American male.

Women went wild for this Houghton Mifflin book. But the developing genre had its critics—such as Upton Sinclair. He himself would make the bestseller list in 1906 with one of the most influential novels ever published in the country, *The Jungle*—a story that awoke the American public to the menace of meat industry abuses, exposed the meat trust, and was instrumental in the passage of the Pure Food and Drugs Act. Sinclair decried women readers' taste for "bourgeois literature" in which a surefire bestseller is any tale "with noble dames and gallant gentlemen dallying with graceful sentiment."

Mrs. Wiggs of the Cabbage Patch: Number Two Fiction, 1902

An early happiness hit that shows how bliss springs from adversity through perseverance was the number two read of 1902—*Mrs. Wiggs of the Cabbage Patch,* a book that actually contains Cabbage Patch kids, flesh-and-blood residents of the town of Cabbage Patch.

Despite its bucolic title, this tale by Alice Hegan Rice unfolds in the suburban slums of Louisville's factory district. The tone avoids bleakness and depression by an unrelenting and hard-hitting emphasis on optimism. The book's opening words, delivered cheerfully by Mrs. Wiggs, constitute both an oxymoron and a philosophy: "My but it's nice and cold this morning! The thermometer's done fell up to zero." Positively basking in the adversity of subfreezing weather, the indigent Mrs. Wiggs never views the thermometer (whose rising and falling is imbued with much symbolism) as dropping, but always ascending from some lower state.

Besides the thermometer as an obvious metaphor for life's vicissitudes, the reader learns on the first page that "the substance of her [Mrs. Wiggs's] philosophy lay in keeping the dust off her rose-colored spectacles." Not surprisingly, thousands of American widows—as Mrs. Wiggs was—empathized with the heroine's fortitude in rearing a family of five children amid hardships and dire poverty.

Never is Mrs. Wiggs despondent, but always gay and courageous, a poor woman who is a shrewd philosopher, dispensing wisdom and practical advice page after bestselling page. In the course of the novel she solves not only her own problems, but the dilemmas of society benefactors who frequently materialize throughout the book to assist her, then to cry on her shoulder over their own personal shortcomings and disappointments. This enables Mrs. Wiggs to point out to the reader that wealthy folk suffer heartache too. At the book's close Mrs. Wiggs neatly ties up the tale: "Looks like ever' thing in the world comes right, if we jes' wait long enough."

Sappy? Yes. Successful? Wildly so. Apparently millions of American women at the turn of the century, faced with personal adversity, craved Alice Rice's uplift. Though initially issued in an edition of two thousand copies, *Mrs. Wiggs of the Cabbage Patch* quickly attracted an enormous following, and at the peak selling frenzy the publisher, Century, was printing forty thousand copies a month—healthy even by today's standards. The novel (really a novelette) remained on the bestseller list for two years, and in a dramatized form ran for seven seasons, sometimes with three road companies playing simultaneously. Had there been television at the time, Alice Rice would have been on "Oprah" and "Sally Jessy Raphael," and explained her success to Larry King.

In real life, the residents of the town that served as Alice Rice's suburban slum experienced good fortune similar to Mrs. Wiggs's. Capitalizing on the book's success, several enterprising real estate developers launched a construction boom, providing jobs and housing, as well as arranging for train stopover tours for the novel's millions of fans who wanted to gawk at Cabbage Patch kids and adults. The phenomenon is not unlike the popularity that descended on the once little-known Boston bar that, after being made famous through a television show, is today called Cheers.

Rebecca of Sunnybrook Farm: Number Eight Fiction, 1904

While *Mrs. Wiggs* was still securely on the bestseller list, the book encountered competition from *Rebecca of Sunnybrook Farm,* a Houghton Mifflin novel by Kate Douglas Wiggin (no relation to Mrs. Wiggs). By this time Alice Hegan Rice had already scored a second hit with a genre sequel, **Lovey Mary,** number four in 1903 (while *Mrs. Wiggs* was number six).

About *Rebecca* writes a contemporary author: "The poor but precocious young heroine carried on her conversations without the homely adages common to Mrs. Wiggs, but she was quite as much an individual in her own right, and almost as beloved by readers, young and old." Kate Wiggin was a kindergarten teacher already famous for her seasonal bestseller *The Birds' Christmas Carol,* and her aptly juvenile tone in *Rebecca* endeared that fiction more to young women of school age, whereas Alice Rice's Cabbage Patch tale drew an older following.

Rebecca was not a Cabbage Patch child of the slums as Mrs. Wiggs's offspring were, but in her own way she embodied the spectrum of adversities that were the times' prevailing vogue: Her mother, for instance, was widowed and poor, hand-in-hand necessities of a happiness fiction centered on parenthood. Rebecca herself lived on a farm, which allowed the character to move among quaint, picturesque country settings. And, as the genre's formula demanded, she touched, amused, and amazed everyone with her spunky spirit and limitless good humor.

As one might expect, many book buyers confused Kate Wiggin's *Rebecca* with Alice Rice's *Mrs. Wiggs,* blurring the line between authorial fact and character fiction. Sales clerks had to repeatedly ask, "You mean Miss Wiggin's novel or the novel about Mrs. Wiggs?" Nonetheless, the audience for each novel was sufficiently different and comparably large to support two bestselling happiness books—as well as to embrace Alice Rice's 1903 hit, *Lovely Mary.* Rice claimed that *Mary* received "the largest advance sale of any book of the year."

The audience for popular books had mushroomed. The country's population—and its literate population—was burgeoning: from 63 million in 1890 up to 100 million at the time America would enter World War I, and reasonably priced books were less a luxury and more a commonplace. In the Oughts it was not uncommon for novels with diversely different themes to rack up sales of nearly a million copies each. As we've seen, merchandise—books, songs, and gadgets—was being measured for the first time in sales of a million. For many manufactured goods, the magic million number had become an attainable goal, if not yet a survival necessity.

If women in the Oughts were reading happiness novels and historical romances, what popular books attracted men in profitable numbers?

The Crisis: Number One Fiction, 1901

Undoubtedly the bestselling author of the Oughts—the James Michener of his decade (even their well-researched books were not all that dissimilar) was Winston Churchill, born in St. Louis, Missouri, November 11, 1871. A graduate at age twenty-three of the U.S. Naval Academy, he wrote historical novels and scored his first success with **Richard Carvel,** number eight in 1900. The tale of Revolutionary Maryland, in which the hero serves as a naval officer under John Paul Jones, sold 420,000 copies within two years of publication, and eventually hit the million mark.

In a Michener-like performance, the next year Churchill's Civil War novel, *The Crisis*—in which the now-familiar heroine is shrewdly a descendant of Richard Carvel—went straight to the top of the bestseller list, establishing the author as one of the leading historical romancers of his period. Set in St. Louis, the patriotic tale pits the hero, fighting for the Union, against the lovely heroine, an ardent Rebel. Many characters from the first book appear in the second.

The Crisis led all other books in sales for four months, and by summer some 320,000 copies were in readers' hands—perhaps many at the beach. The book remained a bestseller the following year and eventually sold more than a million copies.

Winston Churchill (no relation to the later bestselling author and British statesman) again took the number one spot in 1904 with **The Crossing,** a romance of Kentucky pioneers settling the land during the Revolution. If in terms of sales he had begun his career as something of a Michener, in terms of multiple and rapidly successive appearances on the bestseller list, the indefatigable author was now resembling a Stephen King, for Churchill was number one in 1906 with **Coniston,** then at the top of the charts again in 1908 with **Mr. Crewe's Career,** a historical romance with, for a switch, a New Hampshire setting. His *Coniston* was a lightweight novel about reform, but it widely outsold a weightier fiction of that year that actually brought about real reform.

The Jungle: Number Six Fiction, 1906

This was the most significant novel of the Oughts, though it was the kind of "serious" book more talked about than read. People were shocked—many nauseated—by Upton Sinclair's disclosure of the filthy conditions in the meat-packing industry. It seemed that every American in the country, illiterates included, could recount the novel's scene in which a man falls into a vat of lard and is boiled alive. Many readers merely wanted to be told the "good parts" (that is, the gory parts) and not have to search them out from a serious tale of an immigrant worker and his ruminations on socialism. The novel prompted a government investigation, culminating in pure-food legislation. It has been said that Upton Sinclair changed the public mind by turning the public's stomach. Though Churchill's escapist fiction was number one, Sinclair's *The Jungle* became one of the few muckraking novels early in the century to attract a wide readership.

The 1906 bestseller list is notable in that it was the first time that all the authors appearing were Americans. British authors had for once been completely displaced.

Automobile Romances: 1905

As more and more Americans were reading books by American authors, more American authors were beginning to construct their fictional plots around modern technological inventions like the telephone and the automobile. For the first time characters reached out and touched each other over electric lines, and romance was kindled in the back seats of cars. Today we think nothing of a fictional character picking up a telephone or driving through the countryside in a car, but in the Oughts such actions were events. Happenings. Owning a home telephone was a sign that the character was of means, while taking a drive meant that the character could encounter sudden adventure or disaster.

A husband-and-wife writing team, the Williamsons, debuted on the 1905 bestseller list with the first of their many automobile romances. Such stories highlighted a variety of "automobiling adventures" that sound silly to us today. For instance, a pleasant country outing is turned by a downpour and dirt roads into a harrowing tale of hardship and survival; on the final page the riders are rescued. Or, to escape the watchful eyes of their elders, a young man waits in his car in the shadows while his girlfriend finds an excuse to go for a walk; they rendezvous, speed off, then park on the berm and neck. Or, as was the Williamsons' speciality, a wealthy young heroine falls hopelessly in love with her dashing-though-ever-so-common chauffeur to later find that he's actually . . . yes! the scion of a titled British family. Bicycling Americans who could not afford cars wanted desperately to read about the newfangled devices, their dangers, their heady speeds, and what liberties could be celebrated in their back seats. In 1905 the car was still a rich man's plaything and most authors of the day—certainly all of the automobile romance novelists—posed for publicity pictures behind the wheel of a vehicle.

Real Men Read Jack London

Novelist and short story writer Jack London did not make the annual bestseller lists in the Oughts, though he dominated that decade with an outpouring of popular successes in a genre that came to be known as the masculine novel. He was himself a new breed of self-made, turn-of-the-century man.

Deserted as a boy by his father, a roving astrologer, he was raised in Oakland, California, by his mother, a spiritualist. Poor and ill-educated, he traveled the world as a hitchhiking hobo, was arrested for vagrancy, and was won over by Marxist socialism. At nineteen he crammed a four-year high school education into twelve months, tried college and dropped out, pursued the Klondike gold rush and gave up, then turned himself into a writer for men and boys who, from their armchairs, could admire an adventurer's strenuous outdoor life or a social reformer's zeal and zest for change. In the Oughts, real men read Jack London.

His first book, **The Son of the Wolf** (1900) gained a wide audience, and his Alaskan stories, **Call of the Wild** (1903), scored a hit despite his publisher's reservation that the book "is too true to nature and too good a work to be really popular with the sentimental public." American males loved adventures such as that of a dog throwing off its past as a child's pet and responding to the call of nature as the leader of a wolf pack; more than one career-shackled husband or classroom-bound boy envisioned himself as that courageous dog giving in to a masculine yearning for freedom and derring-do.

Most Jack London readers in the Oughts overlooked his Nietzschean doctrines and lost themselves deep in his stories' rugged individualism and adventure. It was for these men and boys that bookstores in 1904 put in advance orders for forty thousand copies of London's new novel, **The Sea Wolf,** featuring a Nietzschean superhero, Wolf Larsen, who, though he goes down to defeat plotwise, survives as a lesson in the power of the human will.

London kept them coming: **White Fang** (1906), more Alaskan stories; **The Iron Heel** (1907), a fantasy of the future that is a terrifying anticipation of fascism; **Martin Eden** (1909), an autobiographical novel; and **Burning Daylight** (1910), more stories. Though his hastily written output was of uneven quality, male readers in the Oughts couldn't get enough of Jack London. He became the highest paid writer in the United States. That his works did not make the industry's annual bestseller lists owes mostly to the fact that they appealed largely to men, who were not as big readers of fiction as women. His death from a drug overdose in 1916 is thought to have been a suicide.

Other memorable bestsellers of The Oughts:

The Virginian: Number One Fiction, 1902

By Owen Wister, this tale of an illiterate cowboy pure in heart, known only as "the Virginian," was set in the Western cattle country that was being made romantically popular by the author's friend, President Teddy Roosevelt. Young men across America sneered out the quotable line, "When you call me that, *smile!*", much as their latter-day counterparts would dare: "Make my day!" The book, which also held the number five spot on the 1903 bestseller list, became a successful play, then a movie starring Gary Cooper, who set off another generation of young men mouthing the threat. Wister dedicated the book to his lifelong friend, Roosevelt.

The Hound of the Baskervilles: Number Seven Fiction, 1902

When Sir Arthur Conan Doyle's story appeared on the bestseller list, it marked the first time a detective story appeared. It was not Doyle's first Sherlock Holmes hit. He'd toured America in 1894, after the success of "A Study in Scarlet," and his popularity had continued to grow through *The Adventures of Sherlock Holmes* and *The Memoirs of Sherlock Holmes.* But the American public came to know him only as the creator of that master of instinctive detectives, Holmes, and his less-astute longtime male companion, Watson. Lacking copyright protection, early Conan Doyle books circulated widely, but it was only through the authorized edition of *The Hound* that he first made the American bestseller list.

But in the decade of the Oughts, one novel more than any other shocked the nation, scandalized readers, and sold so rapidly that bookstores across the country could not keep it in stock.

Three Weeks: 1907

In England, where it was first published, a baffled critic wrote, "An exceedingly difficult work to know how to review," warning, "Not for *jeunes filles.*" In America, the 1907 sensuous romance by forty-three-year-old author Elinor Glyn caused reviewers to recoil in horror; only Mark Twain dared to offer praise. Went a rhyme of the day, hinting at the story's central vice: "Would you like to sin / with Elinor Glyn / on a tiger skin? / Or would you prefer / to err / with her / on some other fur?"

The story, in a pant: The heroine, queen of a mythical Balkan land, holidays for three torrid weeks in the Alps and Venice, forgetting husband and state, reveling on a tiger skin rug with a handsome young innocent. Mind you, there is no explicit sex, just endless suggestion of it, accomplished largely by dashes, ellipses, lacunae, and miry melodrama.

> QUEEN: Paul, you are so young, so young—and I shall hurt you—probably. Won't you go now while there is yet time?

INNOCENT: I may be young, but tonight I know—I want to live! And I will chance the hurt because I know that only you can teach me—just how—

An experienced older woman (a queen, nonetheless) seduces a naive (though eager) young man! The book sold two thousand copies a day on initial release, and more than double that once it was condemned by Boston's Watch and Ward Society and New York's own watch-hound Anthony Comstock. The dazzling, mature femme fatale (a Joan Collins type) sets her sights on young Paul (a Tom Cruise type) from her strategically appointed window. She beckons in a whisper, "Come." He finds her suite choked with roses, tulips, and lilies of the valley; the lights are seductively low, the Balkan royal lolls languorously on a tiger skin. Throughout their trysts in Alps cabins and Swiss inns, he dutifully (and redundantly) calls her "My Queen, My Queen!" and she sighs, "Beautiful, savage Paul!" The breathless dialogue is broken only by more breathless prose: "Oh! glorious, glorious youth! and still more glorious love!"

Many a book had a man seducing a young girl, but Elinor Glyn hit on a new and daring role reversal theme—which apparently ignited a latent fantasy in millions of American women. *Three Weeks* lacked sophistication and good writing but served up a bombshell of a premise. It was still titillating audiences throughout the Twenties, and became a successful 1924 film starring Aileen Pringle as the naughty queen and Conrad Nagel as devoted Paul.

Publicity Tour. Book promotion was relatively new in the Oughts, and Elinor Glyn's arrival in the United States for a publicity tour (called "sightseeing") caused media mania. She descended regally down the gangplank of the *Lusitania* attired head to foot in deep majestic purple: a velvet coat, silk dress, snug toque, chiffon wraparound veil, and the mode in French heels. In her trunks, leaked the press, were sixty pairs of heels. A highborn English woman, Elinor Glyn resented American newspapermen doggedly questioning if her novel was autobiographical. Her silences were interpreted as admission, whereas her explicit denials—"Oh, no! It is the sheerest romance"—were assumed to be polite cover. She was the celebrity of the year, entertained by the likes of Mrs. Frederick Vanderbilt.

Visiting Niagara Falls, she caused a stir by taking notes on the behavior of honeymooning couples—research for a sequel, she said. Lionized by society, she also toured poor regions of the country in the belief, as she told the press, "I am helping to spread the ideals of romance and glamour into the humblest homes." The lady knew how to promote a book. In each city she conducted her own poll among readers to gauge the sensation caused by *Three Weeks,* always informing the press of her conclusions. Interestingly, she found San Francisco in more of a state of shock than any other American city; no one questioned if this was largely aftershock from the Great Quake.

CHAPTER 3

□

The Tender Teens

1910 to 1919

The Over There Decade

The Innocent Oughts opened with America shedding her provincialism; the Tender Teens would close with the country the strongest, richest, and most highly industrialized nation on earth. What happened in between was, of course, a war—one that altered more than the international balance of power: It also trumpeted American popular culture abroad. We sent "over there" not only our bombers and doughboys, but our dance crazes, jazz tunes, fashions, and pop fads, and a veritable dictionary of catchy colloquialisms. World War I put America on more maps than the political ones; it marked the beginning of the exportation of popular culture as a profitable national product.

War, when not fought on home soil, can be immensely profitable, and in gearing up for the world's first global conflict, the United States entered into an era of unprecedented mass production and technological might. We'll examine how the war created many of the decade's fads, hits, and "in" phrases, as families shifted from patriotically singing "Over There," the spirited national theme song glorifying America's role in the war, to "I Didn't Raise My Boy to Be a Soldier," the about-face lament that rang out as the death toll mounted.

As the Teens started, many crazes of the previous decade were still in vogue. Young Americans were, for instance, wilder than ever about animal dances, dreaming up zany steps nightly. Kewpie dolls had yet to reach peak popularity. In women's fashion, the **hobble skirt** was the rage; so named because its narrow tapering to the ankles caused the wearer to shuffle lamely. Radically different from the flouncy traditional skirts of the time, it was destined to be trendy. Then came the more daring **harem skirt,** half skirt, half pantaloons—the pants part causing condemnation in the press, from the pulpit, and from male clubs and boardrooms. Men were not ready for women in pants, even

84

skirt pants. Hemlines inched up as the decade aged, as did women's hairstyles: shoulder-length at the start, bobbed at the close.

Bold as the fashion statements were—including bare arms, peeking decolletage, and a blush of cheek paint—women still could not vote and were arrested for protesting the injustice in public places. Women could, however, "vamp"—in imitation of the silver screen's first sex goddess.

FADS, FOLLIES, AND TRENDS

Theda Bara and Vamping

The 1980s had Madonna and vogueing; the Teens had Theda Bara and vamping, a sexual dance as much as it was a posturing. Complained the original vamp herself near the close of the decade: "Five uninterrupted years of vamping have drawn my nerves taut."

The taxing activity involved wiggling, mouing, seductive slouching, and sexual toying—a vamp's repertory of kittenish titillations, which the century's first femme fatale stamped on an era and bequeathed to a generation of women. "To vamp" entered our language and our sexual foreplay, the verb fittingly

Theda Bara.

from the Tartar noun *ubry* (via German), "witch"—legendary for casting spells.

Theda Bara first cast a spell over the nation with the release of her 1915 film *A Fool There Was.* Billed as the daughter of an Eastern potentate whose name was an anagram for "Arab Death" (Bara Theda), the kohl-eyed Cleopatra (with makeup especially created by Helena Rubinstein) was born Theodosia Goodman, to Jewish parents in Cincinnati, Ohio, on July 20, 1890. A brief stage career under the name Theodosia de Coppet brought her to Hollywood as a film extra, but her portrayal of the irresistible, heartless woman who lived only for sensual pleasure—a vamp—rocketed her to stardom. The motto of millions of women mid-decade was the siren's camp come-on, "Kiss me, my fool."

Whether a role called for vamping or not, Theda Bara brought a pantherlike purring to screen characters in *Romeo and Juliet* (1916), *Camille* (1917), *Cleopatra* (1917), and *Salome* (1918). Her seductiveness was thought to be a grave threat to public morality, yet she sold out movie theaters across the country. The primary fad spin-off was her vamping, a harmless coed coaxing played out at colleges, as well as at society dinner parties and debutante balls. In terms of sexual politics, the vamp stood left of the 1890s Gibson girl and right of the *It* girl, to be popularized by Clara Bow in the next decade. Vamping, all harmless posturings and posings, was old-fashioned coquetry with a bite. It brought sex play out of the chaperoned past and into the spirited new century. Perhaps it was defensive rationalization when Theda Bara argued to critics that her portrayal of calculating, coldhearted women was morally instructive to men: "I will continue doing vampires as long as people sin."

By the end of the Teens, though, the public had tired of silent screen vamping, demanding more of an actress. Theodosia Goodman died in Los Angeles in 1955, at age sixty-four. Her films set the mode for sophisticated sexual themes in motion pictures, as she set the model for the century's sex symbols from vamp to flapper, glamour girl to sweater girl, pin-up to playmate.

Erector Set

"Hello, Boys! Make Lots of Toys!" read the advertising slogan for 1913's hot Christmas gift. And millions of boys across the country took the imperative to heart, constructing towers and bridges from Erector Set's scaled-down girders, nuts, and bolts. The decade of the Teens was a heyday for all sorts of building sets, including, as we'll see, the wooden dowels of Tinkertoy and the rough-hewn Lincoln Logs—all toy classics conceived in the era.

Erector Set, probably America's oldest remaining building toy, was also the first important American toy advertised extensively in national magazines. Spending the then-staggering sum of $12,000 for ads, the Gilbert company kicked off the 1913 Christmas buying season with spreads in the youth-oriented magazines *The American Boy, St. Nicholas,* and *Popular Mechanics,* as well as appealing directly to parents through adult magazines like *Good Housekeeping* and *Saturday Evening Post.* "Hello, Boys!" each ad began, and the salutation became a national marketing catchphrase to grab the attention of millions of youngsters who were eager to "make lots of toys" from the set's multiholed angled girders, wheels, pulleys, gears, sheet panels, and even an electric motor—a great novelty in the Teens.

Origin. Few toy inventors in this century have had a more colorful background than A. C. Gilbert, creator of Erector, and later of children's multipaneled chemistry sets. An Olympic gold medalist in pole vaulting (with two world records), a trained magician, and a Yale-educated doctor, Gilbert also took the lead in founding Toy Manufacturers of America, an industry trade organization and early fad launchpad. One day in the autumn of 1911, Gilbert was visiting New York City in an attempt to increase orders for magic equipment from his successful company Mysto. To him it seemed that all around town girders were going up for buildings and tracks were being laid down for rail cars. "I suppose the idea was germinating in my mind during several trips," he wrote in his autobiography, "but that day everything came together."

At home, he cut out cardboard girders and rectangular sheets. The next day he asked his Mysto craftsmen to duplicate the pieces in tin, then he sat down with a box of nuts and bolts and constructed for himself a simple square from four tin girders. Disappointingly it skewed into a rhombus. It was then that Gilbert devised the locking "lip" along each girder's edge that allowed him to make a rigid square—and a marketable toy.

To his astonishment, none of his colleagues was impressed. Throughout 1912, he perfected his toy, adding clever parts and playing with catchy advertising slogans. The package debuted at the following year's New York Toy Fair. Men attending the annual meeting went wild for Erector, and Gilbert, himself a boy at heart, realized he'd hit on a winner. And just in time for Christmas. Fathers and sons so loved to tinker with Erector Set that Gilbert published a newspaper called *Erector Tips,* a how-to on construction one-upmanship. It was also the time that American psychologists began to discuss seriously the need for toys that teach and toys that challenge—and soon America's boys had another creative toy.

Tinkertoy

Tinkertoy is to wood what Erector Set is to metal. And it debuted a little more than a year after Gilbert's brainstorm. The geometric wonder of angles—right, acute, and obtuse—spoked from multiholed wheels allowed a child to assemble something as simple as a breath-powered windmill or as elaborate as a crank-driven merry-go-round.

Tinkertoy was not a rip-off of Erector Set, but an independent creation by professional tombstone cutter Charles Pajeau. His inspiration came not while chiseling a headstone, but from idly watching a group of children poking pencils into wooden thread spools, assembling them in railroad fashion. Pajeau conceived of shallow spools drilled with holes along the periphery to accept dowels of varying lengths. Handy with his hands, he constructed his own initial Tinkertoy sets.

To attract buyers' attention, Pajeau staged a clever publicity stunt. Hiring midgets, he dressed them like Santa's elves and placed them in store windows in New York and Chicago, where they assembled Tinkertoys with such jolly exuberance and calculated laughter that ogling children dragged their parents into the stores for sets. The Christmas hit of the mid-Teens, Tinkertoy began selling in the millions, and continues to do so—in a version not all that different from Pajeau's original creation.

On the horizon was still another creative assemblage.

Lincoln Logs

This toy was conceived during the Teen's building set heyday by John L. Wright, when he was in Tokyo with his father, Frank Lloyd Wright, who was supervising construction of the Imperial Palace Hotel. The younger Wright could not have been unaware of the success of Erector Set and Tinkertoy— they were already being sold abroad. He claimed that the creative inspiration came to him while watching workers lift timbers into place; he visualized a building toy that would capitalize on America's love of wooden logs and the "lure of the country's pioneering history."

Returning home to Merrill, Wisconsin, John Wright worked out the toy's design. After several manufacturing setbacks and a thoroughly unimaginative name for the timbers, Wright realized that Abraham Lincoln was born in a log cabin, and that the alliteratives "Lincoln" and "logs" had a marketable ring, as well as a built-in patriotic image. The rustic and rugged toy—which assembles into such Americana as log cabins, forts, and covered bridges—became a super hit in the Twenties, and again in the Fifties as a tie-in with the Davy Crockett craze that swept the country (see page 260).

As for A. C. Gilbert, who launched the decade's building set madness, he saved American children from a year in which the federal government became the Grinch that almost stole Christmas: In order to save metal and wood for wartime use, the government encouraged toy manufacturers to cut back on their most popular products—like Erector Set and Tinkertoy—and asked parents to practice wartime self-denial by putting Christmas gift money into war bonds. As a final measure, it considered imposing an embargo on the buying and selling of all Christmas presents. Toymakers quivered at the thought of no Christmas, and Gilbert led a delegation of manufacturers to Washington, D.C. As a weapon, the men took with them many boys' toys, including Erector Sets and Tinkertoys. Cabinet members first listened to the manufacturers' pleas, then assembled tin girders and wooden dowels and announced that they had changed their minds. There would be a Christmas.

Luxury Liners

To ply the Atlantic in a "grand hotel" was an upper-class passion and the dream of millions of other Americans in the Teens. It was more than trendy to travel aboard the great luxury liners; it was, as Thomas Wolfe summed up, "the supreme ecstasy of the modern world." With decks ablaze in lights and promenades as wide as city streets, the floating hotels were christened with names to evoke their epic size and majesty: the *Leviathan,* the *Titanic,* the *Queen Mary.* In the decades prior to jet travel, the Ships of Splendor ruled the Atlantic and captivated the public's imagination.

They were, quite simply, the largest Earth objects that ever moved, awesome machines of a technical complexity that seemed to apotheosize the Industrial Revolution. The public gawked at advertisements in which a ship, to convey its giantism, was juxtaposed against a well-known landmark: the *Mauretania,* for instance, propped up against Egypt's Great Pyramid; the *France* by the Vatican's St. Peter's; the *Aquitania* beside New York's Macy's department store. The liners dwarfed the structures, and onlookers, duly impressed, laid down their life savings for a dream. Destination was irrelevant; getting there was the fantasy. Every nation with any pretension to grandeur flew its flag on at least one great liner.

Floating Hotels.   The craze began in the early years of the century, fueled by a tidal wave of immigration—for the liners' unglamorous lower decks (steerage) were jammed with humanity seeking New World freedoms. The public, though, glimpsed only the vessels' vast and elegant upper decks, reserved for the rich, the royal, the famous, the aspiring. A traveler might, as one brochure touted, have the "privilege of seeing nothing at all that has to do with a ship, not even the sea"—the resemblance to a hotel was that defining. An appraisal of the *Mauretania* ran: "Barring a bridle path for the equestrian, a smooth road for the automobilist and a forest for lovers to walk in, everything else seems to have been provided."

To gauge the opulence that caused ogling: The French Line's *France,* "Chateau of the Atlantic," was an orgy of Louis XIV decor, with sweeping staircases, marble fountains, and stewards in Moorish pantaloons. The Hamburg-American Line's *Amerika* featured an upper-deck restaurant staffed by London's Ritz-Carlton and freshly stocked with the finest oysters, caviar, and truffles—plus mushrooms and strawberries grown in an onboard greenhouse. The Italian Line's sunny *Conte di Savoia* had a Pompeiian pool on deck surrounded by real sand, and marble interiors modeled on the Palazzo Colonna in Rome. The *Aquitania* was designed as a floating museum, with suites named after painters.

With time out for war, the luxury traveling craze resumed—aboard ships like the *Normandie,* the fastest liner of the mid-Thirties, crossing the Atlantic in a record-breaking four days, three hours, and two minutes. By that time, though, air travel—in terms of giant airships and sleeker airplanes—had already begun to catch the traveler's fancy, presaging the end of the golden era of luxury liners.

Two liners of the Teens, though, caused nationwide commotions for reasons other than their grandeur.

Titanic.   The British liner sank on her maiden voyage in one of the greatest sea disasters. At the time, the *Titanic* was (with her sister ship, the *Olympic*), the world's largest passenger vessel at a length of 883 feet. Boasted to be the safest liner afloat, virtually unsinkable, she could carry 2,603 passengers and a crew of 892. Fortunately, the ship was filled to less than capacity when on April 10, 1912, she set out on her maiden voyage to New York amid great acclaim. Four days out she was steaming at 22 knots, 95 miles south of the Grand Banks of Newfoundland, when she struck an iceberg. The time was 11:40 P.M., April 14. The impact ripped a 300-foot gash in her hull low on the starboard side, puncturing six watertight compartments.

There had been no lifeboat drill, and in any event the lifeboats could only hold 1,178 people—on board were 1,316 passengers and a crew of 885. With crew and passengers late to react, believing the ship unsinkable, 1,589 people lost their lives. The decade of the Teens had barely begun, but it had witnessed one of the greatest disasters of modern times. The next in the decade—the war—was also linked to a renowned luxury liner.

Lusitania. With a speed of 24.5 knots, the *Lusitania* consumed 850 tons of coal a day, carrying eighteen hundred passengers and crew from Liverpool to New York, her standard run, begun in 1907.

On her last voyage, May 1, 1915, she was carrying 1,959 passengers and crew, as well as a cargo that included five thousand cases of war munitions. The German embassy in the United States had warned prospective passengers that a war zone existed around the British Isles and that all vessels flying the British flag were subject to attack.

Approaching the Irish coast on May 7, and neglecting warnings to take anti-submarine precautions, she was struck without warning at 2:10 P.M. by two torpedoes from the German submarine *U-20.* With the liner listing 15 degrees to starboard, it was impossible to launch the portside lifeboats. With her sides open to the sea the ship sank, headfirst, in eighteen minutes, with the appalling loss of 1,198 lives, including those of 124 Americans. A wave of indignation ripped across the United States, and the German aggression contributed to America's entry into the war. The *Lusitania* and the *Titanic,* statements of luxury and technological excellence in the Teens, became, through separate disasters, unforgettable symbols of the twentieth century.

Wartime Jargon

Major events leave their imprint on language, and a great war can fire a fusillade of new terms into a vernacular. "The war changed our life and our vocabulary forever," writes Stuart Berg Flexner, a leading lexicographer. "We learned much of our wartime vocabulary from the British via our newspapers." Other jargon we made up as we marched along. Some popular phrases are forgotten; others survive in our everyday speech—though, interestingly, many today have altered meanings. Here, then, according to Flexner, are the trendy expression that in the Teens were on America's lips:

Ace was a pilot who shot down at least five enemy planes. Only after the war did it come to mean an expert in any endeavor.

Bomber came from the British, who experienced German projectiles firsthand. World War I was the world's first real air war, and people on both sides of the Atlantic spoke vehemently against Germany's *ace bomber,* the **Red Baron,** Baron Manfred von Richthofen, whose Albatross biplane was painted bloodred. He scored eighty air victories before being killed in 1918 at age twenty-six.

Big Bertha today is slang for anything behemoth, but it originally was a German long-range gun first used near Liège, Belgium, in 1914, and later to shell Paris from miles away. It was a whopping eponym for Frau Bertha Krupp of the Krupp munitions family, which made the cannon.

Chief of staff was popularized during the war, though it actually dates from 1907, following Secretary of War Elihu Root's reorganization of the army. It replaced "commanding general of the army."

Chow was slang for food during the Civil War, but only became common parlance during World War I, where hungry soldiers, **chowhounds,** queued up at mealtime. The word comes from the Mandarin Chinese *ch'ao,* "to cook." Servicemen almost never used the term food.

Civvies, civilian dress as opposed to a military uniform, originated with the British and was quickly adopted by American servicemen.

Dog tag was a serviceman's metal identification disc, worn around his neck and used to identify him in case of grave injury or death. Its purpose, of course, was precisely that of a dog's identifying collar. In the Civil War a soldier pinned a piece of paper bearing his name on his uniform.

Doughboys is an expression for American soldiers whose origin is unclear. In *I Hear America Talking,* Flexner gives three possibilities: (1) In the 1700s, doughboy was the name of a sweet cornmeal cake, then the name of a biscuit served to soldiers, and in the Civil War it was the term for a circular brass uniform button—then was used to identify the wearer. (2) The word derived from the earth clay, called dough, that soldiers once used to clean their white belts. (3) The word is a corruption from *adobe,* a Spanish term for American soldiers during the mid-1800s, because many men were quartered in adobe buildings, becoming "adobe boys."

Dud, anything that does not live up to expectations, comes from the sixteenth-century English *dudde,* "rags." During World War I, a dud was a bomb that failed to explode; after the war it referred to a person who failed to live up to expectations.

Goldbrick is a word that has been continually devalued. In the early 1800s it was a bar of gold, later a valueless item that only appeared to have worth. By 1914 a goldbrick was an untrained, inexperienced army lieutenant appointed directly from civilian life. After the war a goldbrick was anyone who did less than a fair share of work.

KP became the abbreviation for the army's kitchen police, those assigned to chow chores and cleanup.

Liberty cabbage was what Americans called sauerkraut during the years that anti-German fervor made everything with a German name unappetizing. German measles became **Liberty measles;** dachshund dogs, **Liberty pups;** and hamburgers, **Liberty steaks.**

Red tape, anything that impedes straightforward work, became common-place in wartime, and probably derives from the British practice of sealing government documents with red tape or wax.

Rookie derives from the word recruit, and though it was in use in the Gay Nineties for a new athlete on a sports team, its commonplace usage began in World War I.

Shell shock today means to be overwhelmed to inactivity, and the British used it in wartime for a soldier debilitated from battle.

Sub, the abbreviation for submarine, did not come into common usage until World War I, even though undersea Union and Confederate boats operated in the Civil War.

Torpedo, from the Latin *torpere,* "to numb," originally was the name for a dangerous eellike fish that emits a stinging electrical charge. It became the term for any wartime booby trap of explosives, on land or at sea, and with the adoption of self-propelled torpedoes in World War I, it was restricted to an underwater projectile.

Western Front was the 600-mile expanse from Switzerland to the English Channel during the period of intense trench warfare that began in 1915. Newspapers of the day popularized it through repeated use of the phrase "All Quiet on the Western Front," which became the title of a bestselling novel of the Twenties (see page 145).

Zeppelin today might be a nostalgic reminder of a pop music group, but in the Teens it reminded Americans of Count Ferdinand von Zeppelin, who at the turn of the century perfected his cigar-shaped rigid dirigible, or giant airship, called a zeppelin. During the war, the Germans piloted eighty-eight of the gas balloons to bomb London and other European cities.

Ouija Board

Skeptics claim that you can get a Ouija board to predict any future you wish. Certainly Ouija is a yes-yes game; its name derives from the French and German affirmatives, *oui* and *ja.* The puzzle (or, if you wish, prognosticator) became a national craze during wartime, when the country desperately needed a playful diversion, or hoped for a means of glimpsing the fates of soldiers, their families, and the nation. Sales soared during the war years—as they did again for World War II and the Korean conflict. In 1967, at the height of the Vietnam War, Ouija board sales shot to an all-time high of 2.3 million games, topping sales of Monopoly, the traditional bestseller.

It is the nature of fads that they provide a common experience for millions of people. And for relatives at home, anxious to learn anything about their fighting boys, the alphabetic Ouija board spelled out with its hand-held planchette the health, whereabouts, and homecoming dates of loved ones. Interestingly, following every national conflict, sales of Ouija boards plummet.

Origin. The board predates its vogue. Ouija's occultish origin may have been in Baltimore, Maryland, in the 1880s, where, as one story has it, husband

C. W. Kennard had an eerie experience with a saucer that shuffled around his wife's breadboard with intent. The message appeared to be something like "patent me," for Kennard spent a number of years fighting for legal rights to the game he had named the Witch Board.

As an alternate origin's tale goes: The Fuld brothers, William and Isaac, Baltimore toymakers, received spiritual insight that there had to be a simpler way to contact the occult world than through the elaborate table rapping and tipping of the popular mediums of the late 1800s. Their mechanization of mediumship was to devise a lapboard, adorned with letters and numerals, the words yes and no, and, to sign off, the polite goodbye. Atop the board sat a heart-shaped planchette, and atop this, players placed their fingertips. Pre-Freud, discarnate spirits were imagined to shuttle the planchette to spell out messages; post-Freud, the players' subconscious minds did the maneuvering. Either way, the game made a profit.

"Ouija, the Mystifying Oracle" experienced a slight vogue in the Gay Nineties, when William Fuld applied for a patent, omitting his brother's name from the application and precipitating a lifelong family schism of the sort that should have been predictable. But the dawning of the Great War brought boom times for tea leaf readers and crystal ball gazers, and especially for the do-it-yourself Ouija. As world tensions mounted, William Fuld consulted his oracular board and received the message (in all seriousness) "prepare for big business." He enlarged his manufacturing plant, but sales were even swifter than his spirit contact had forecast—a million games in 1918.

The Model T and America's Car Culture

As the century's manias go, Henry Ford ushered in the first mass consumer-buying spree: the Model T, an item that every family had to have—and most would. From the time of its unveiling in 1908 until production was halted in 1927, Americans bought more than 15 million of Ford's Model Ts. "The Way to make automobiles," swore Ford, "is to make one automobile like another automobile, to make them all alike." As for color: "Let them have any color they want, so long as it's black." Bell's telephone and Edison's light were indispensable conveniences; Ford's mass-produced car was the start of America's automobile culture—an entirely new way of life.

In 1904, when Henry Ford set up his own auto shop, he was a man of forty-one with a singular dream: to produce a "universal car," a sturdy, inexpensive vehicle that would overnight transform the automobile from a rich man's toy into everyman's reality. His Model T cost $850, and was so named because it followed the Model S, which, in a succession of alphabetically named vehicles, had begun four years earlier in a Detroit factory with his Model A. For its dependability and price tag, the Model T was an immediate success. Demand soared to such staggering proportions that the company was forced at intervals to stop accepting orders until the backlog could be reduced. Correspondingly, the price continued to drop: $600 in 1912, $290 in 1924. Ford had done more than find a car for the masses, he'd introduced to the world the miracle of assembly line mass production—what it takes for a potentially hot item to achieve critical popularity.

Before Ford, automobiles were built much the way carpenters construct a house: the entire structure was assembled in one location. Though many men have claimed credit for the moving assembly line, Ford unarguably made it a production reality. By 1914 his Model T could go from bare frame to finished body in ninety-three minutes. And speeds increased. In 1923 a total of 2,011,125 Model T passenger cars and trucks rolled off Ford's line, a record that was to stand for thirty-two years.

Why Tin Lizzie?   The name Tin Lizzie originated with the Model T. Lizzie then was the all-purpose nickname for a family's domestic, a maid for all kinds of work, who on Sunday dressed prettily and strutted off to church with dignity. That also was the routine for the Model T—the family's workhorse on weekdays, used to plow fields, haul fodder, churn butter, pump water, and generate electricity; come Sunday, the car was washed and polished, and it paraded the family to services. Many people believed the car was made of tin, hence Tin Lizzie, but the body was of heavier-gauge sheet metal.

On first sight, Ford's creation looked like something only a father could love: flat-nosed, all angles and bolts and knock-kneed awkwardness. But on the road it ran performance circles around the competition. And given its rudimentary mechanism, any tool-handy male with a wrench, screwdriver, and wire could fix it. Ford even sold do-it-yourself mufflers (25 cents), fenders ($2.50) and assorted parts, encouraging the American male to become his own mechanic. If the ride seemed sluggish, the remedy of the day was to drop a few camphor balls into the gas tank. By the early Teens, more than five million Tin Lizzies, nearly all alike, were rattling around the country, transforming a horse-and-buggy land of isolated villages into a mobile, modern nation. Items with mass appeal often become the butt of jokes, and the all-purpose Tin Lizzie was a prime target: "What shock absorbers do you use on your Ford?" Answer: "The passengers." Or: "What's shaken hell out of more people than evangelist Billy Sunday ever did?" Answer: "A Tin Lizzie." For the decade of the Teens the flood of Ford jokes seemed unstoppable—enriching the repertory of toast-masters and preachers, vaudevillians and doctors attempting to cheer up pa-tients, and college students who pasted labels on their "flivvers" (a pejorative endearment for the Model T, meaning a "worthwhile headache") saying, "Come on, baby, here's your rattle." When a Ford executive canceled car advertisements in a newspaper that had printed Tin Lizzie jokes, Henry repri-manded the man and reinstated the ads, reasoning, "The jokes about my car sure helped to popularize it. I hope they never end."

A song of the decade, "Flivver King," provided a tuneful summation of the popular fascination with the Tin Lizzie: "Henry Ford was a machinist, / He worked both night and day, / To give this world a flivver, / That has made her shiver, / And speeded her on her way." Ford consciously created the nation's Model T mania with philosophies such as: "Every time I lower the price a dollar, we gain a thousand new buyers."

Model T Accessory Crazes.   The nationwide popularity of the Model T launched a series of related fads—from Hammacher Schlemmer car accessories to "automobiling" fashions, clothes as elaborate as those worn by any trendy traveler on, say, an African safari. Saks Fifth Avenue printed a 270-page catalog of trinkets and dress items, and Hammacher Schlemmer promoted an automo-biling "survival kit" of "emergency food supplies" for the hazards of long country trips. Among the items: two two-gallon canvas water bags, four half-pound cans of meat or fish, 2 pounds of sweet chocolate, and two cans of fruit. Actually, the precautions were not such a gimmicky idea considering that roads were still treacherously rutty and roadside restaurants were still a decade away. As faddish car pastimes go, the Teens became known for "automobiling" as the Fifties would be known for "cruisin'."

The Tin Lizzie's fantastic appeal had another side effect: As an item of unprecedented mass consumption, it set a trend of consumer buying for the century. Asked in the Teens what his men were working for, a trade union official replied, "Twenty-five percent are fighting to keep their heads above water; 10 percent want to own their own homes; 65 percent are working to pay for cars." A working-class wife, interviewed by sociologists for a late-Twenties report called *Middletown,* commented, "I'd rather go without food than give up the car." Of twenty-six families in the study without bathrooms, twenty-one proudly displayed their cars. In a little more than a decade, the car had gone from a rich man's toy, to a handyman's hobby, to a family necessity.

A family in the Teens had, of course, more to choose from than Ford's Model T. Here are several of the options that debuted in the decade.

1911.   **Chevrolet** became the first six-cylinder touring car, with the vehicle named after (and designed by) former racing car driver Louis Chevrolet.

1913.   DeSoto was an expensive choice at its introductory price of $2,185. The **Duesenberg** ("It's a doosey!"), introduced by brothers August and Frederick Duesenberg, would become the major American "classic car" of the Twenties, fast (93–135 miles per hour), expensive, and short-lived—disappearing with the stock market crash of 1929.

1914.   Dodge boasted of having the first "all-steel body," and of being the first commercial car with a "hard top."

1918.   Nash was introduced by Charles Nash, after he left General Motors to forge his own auto dynasty.

There was an unexpected benefit to America's automania: The car was environmentally immaculate compared with emissions from its predecessor, the horse. Consider these distasteful statistics: In New York City alone at the turn of the century, horses deposited on the streets, daily, some 2.5 million pounds of manure and 60,000 gallons of urine. Further, carcasses of overworked horses that dropped dead in intense summer heat littered streets and congested traffic. Each year New York City lugged off more than fifteen thousand horse carcasses. The gasoline-powered car seemed, at the time, pollution-free.

Prestige in Your Driveway.   As millions of Americans bought Tin Lizzies, something predictable occurred: Merely owning any kind of automobile was no longer the status symbol to strive for; cachet came from being able to afford (or from going into debt for) a prestige model. The choices were plentiful: Cadillac, Pierce, Buick, Moline, Star, Haynes, Studebaker, Reo, Winton, Packard, Locomobile, Stearns, Case, Maxwell, Auburn—to mention a few of the many that came and went or stayed.

Detroit also learned the faddish appeal in offering consumers an annual new look to whatever cars they owned—often by merely altering a curve or expanding a sideboard. In that sense, the automobile entered the seasonally changing, fickle world of fashion. Indeed, in time we would have vehicles whose exteriors and interiors were "designed by" the likes of St. Laurent, Cardin, and de la Renta.

The mass production and consumption of automobiles in the Teens and the Twenties created a nationwide prosperity, and car ownership resulted in one of the most profound social changes in American history. With more than six million cars on the road, Congress, in 1916, passed the first Federal Aid Road Act to construct a nationwide network of highways. World War I, by disabling European car competitors, was an unexpected boon to the events already under way. And as the war enriched our vocabulary, so too did nationwide acceptance of the automobile. Consider these commonplaces of the Teens and Twenties that would have produced confusion's wrinkled brow on a man or woman at the turn of the century: *blowout, car crash, license plate, road hog, jalopy, traffic cop, speeding ticket, filling station, back seat driver, parking lot, jaywalking, hitchhik-*

ing—the list is long and attests to how quickly Americans warmed to the automobile.

FAIRS AND EXPOS

Panama Canal Celebrations

Americans in the Teens flocked by the millions to the country's West Coast to visit two grand expositions that celebrated the completion of the Panama Canal. The 51-mile-long waterway connecting the Atlantic and Pacific oceans through the Isthmus of Panama had been a three-centuries-old dream realized. As early as the 1700s the Spanish conceived the idea of cutting a canal across the landmass, and in 1846 the United States signed a treaty with Colombia (then New Granada) to allow all nations "free and uninterrupted transit" through the proposed waterway. Begun in 1904, the massive project—the largest structure ever built, costing $7 billion in today's money—opened its locks to traffic on August 15, 1914. The two expos were planned for the following year.

The more regional of the fairs, the Panama-California Exposition of 1915–16, was held in San Diego, whereas San Francisco hosted the Panama-Pacific International Exposition of 1915. The latter city itself was a major attraction, having been rebuilt following the Great Quake of 1906.

The West Coast expos had Americans discussing, and incorporating into their homes, California Spanish-style architecture and marveling at the displays of moving pictures—the first time many visitors had seen movies. Adventurous fairgoers boarded their first airplane for a mile-high ride that was billed as a "breathless amusement." These two festive extravaganzas held in America stood in stark contrast to the escalating conflict in Europe that was making the world seem much smaller and more terrifying.

San Francisco's Panama-Pacific International Exposition: 1915

To celebrate the completion of the multimillion-dollar Panama Canal, the city of San Francisco, itself having undergone a major $300 million rebuilding, seemed a natural site. San Francisco now claimed to be America's most modern city, whereas the canal was billed as the modern world's most impressive single edifice. Also, the city was America's largest port on the Pacific Ocean, which the canal now joined with the Atlantic. Many visitors chose to travel to the fair by ship through the canal, establishing the artificial waterway as the expo's principal attraction.

That year, 1915, nearly nineteen million people visited the "City Loved 'Round the World"—as the new San Francisco was advertised by the fair's promoters—and passed through the turnstiles of the Pan-Pacific festival. Visitors were nearly blinded by expo's central building, the Tower of Jewels, a 435-foot high Trump-like glitterfest, consisting of fifty thousand pieces of glass, each backed with a mirrored surface that dazzled by day and twinkled at night under searing searchlights. On exhibit was an eye-catching, if mystifying, new painting: *Nude Descending a Staircase* by Marcel Duchamp, the controversial French "anti-artist" (so labeled because he "broke down boundaries between works of art and everyday objects"). Today, paintings make news for the million-dollar sums they bring at auction, but in the Teens a picture's content was more newsworthy, and no painting of the day caused a greater sensation than *Nude,* which brought Duchamp worldwide celebrity. Due to the war in Europe, the year the fair opened he took refuge in the United States, eventually becoming a citizen.

The fair had live music: march king John Philip Sousa entertained from one bandshell, while compositions of a more classical nature wafted from the band-shell of the Boston Symphony Orchestra. And the fair had daring feats and death: High above the fairgrounds America's first trick aviators soared, looped, and nosedived in skeletal biplanes, until this premiere air show ended in horror as the leading daredevil, Lincoln Beachy, crashed in a fiery death. Nonetheless, many thrill-seekers boarded their first plane for an aerial view of the fair-grounds. Others—120 people at a time—climbed into the midway's Aeroscope amusement, a massive cage at the end of a 239-foot steel arm (counterbalanced by a giant water tank), which swooped upward 265 feet, then swung out over the fair and San Francisco harbor.

Chorines, Freak Shows, and Films.   The fair and its hosting town Frisco offered many titillations and one or two vices. In addition to slipping into the tented shows featuring belly dancers, a fairgoer could stroll through the re-creation of a '49er gold rush town that was rumored to offer illegal gambling in back rooms. And visitors caught a scandalous eyeful touring the city's infamous Pacific Street, known to sailors for the pleasures it offered as Terrific Street. Men usually left their wives at some wholesome fair attraction to privately take in the street's honkytonk and hootch-kootch and to drink in its tawdry saloons with their flirtatious chorines. A half century earlier, the district, known as the Barbary Coast, had been the hangout of grizzled seamen and gold-seeking miners.

The fair also had its shamefully racist attractions. As with all previous expos, the Pan-Pacific offered walking tours through so-called authentic villages of "primitive" peoples. These events were calculated to give oglers a jolt of cultural shock. "It will amuse you," raved the *San Francisco Examiner* of a Samoan village, "with the primitive ways of its semi-naked citizens. Weird, too, are their dances . . . one gets a glimpse of the life of a race thousands of years behind civilization." More shocking still by today's standards were the mid-way's many freak shows, featuring the deformed and infirm, which in the Teens were still expected attractions at any fair or circus.

Movies, though, were the fair's greatest eye-opener for millions of visitors. "To a degree never seen before," wrote a San Francisco columnist, "the moving picture has taken a place in this exposition as an exhibition." The fairgrounds boasted seventy-seven movie theaters, which bombarded fairgoers with action films, comedies, and shorts on such educational-to-tedious topics as immigration, city planning, canal building, and California state politics. Just to watch pictures in motion was then exciting. Filmmaker D. W. Griffith, who called the fair "the grandest thing the world has known," planned to capture the event in a dramatic epic on the scale of his *The Birth of a Nation,* but the war interrupted that grand dream.

All in all, the fair was a boom to the rebuilt city of San Francisco. It doubled the city's real estate values, brought in scores of industries, and introduced the charms of this modern city to thousands of visitors who stayed on to become residents. "The end of a perfect day," said expo president Charles Moore in his address that closed the fair, "the beginning of an endless memory!" But the paramount memory that would linger from that time was the world's first global war, for even as the fair dimmed its lights, events in Europe were growing more ominous for Americans at home. As a truly international event, the Pan-Pacific Expo had been something of a bust; Americans had attended in record numbers, but Europeans could not focus on entertainment when the issue foremost in their minds was survival.

DANCE CRAZES

Two to Tango

Two dance crazes most epitomized the Teens: the lively fox trot and the sensual tango, and no one did them with more elegance and grace than the dance doyens of their day, Vernon and Irene Castle. The dances themselves caused one mania in the decade; the Castles spawned another. For one public outing, Irene wore a headband to hold down her hair, and it immediately swept the country as a voguish "Castleband." At a wee-hours party, Irene and Vernon clowned a stylish "walk" on the dance floor, and next day New York newspapers heralded the arrival of a new fad, the Castle walk. In instructing America on how to dance they were something of the original Arthur and Katherine Murray, and in setting new standards for elegance and style they were forerunners of Fred Astaire and Ginger Rogers—who would later capture Castlemania in the successful 1939 film, *The Story of Vernon and Irene Castle.*

The Teens has been called the ballroom decade for the same reason that the Seventies is referred to as the disco decade: Each era kicked off not only new dance crazes, but also a new environment in which to dance. Across America couples were enjoying the fox trot, the tango, and the Castle walk, and striving to do them with the same flair as Vernon and Irene. So mad was America for dance that the trendier restaurants installed dance floors where couples strutted between courses.

Fox Trot

The animal dance craze beginning late in the Oughts certainly played into the rapid popularity of the smooth, flowing fox trot—in which dancers stand stylishly erect, elbows akimbo, the woman's right foot intertwining the feet of her partner; all movement to a quick-quick-slow beat. But the origin of this trot, unlike that of bouncy animal mimicry, is well known, undisputed, and only coincidentally bears the name of a fox.

Late in 1913, music hall performer Harry Fox trotted out a jerky two-step routine to ragtime in the *Ziegfeld Follies* that stopped the show—and caught the eye of the show's producers. Realizing the promotional value of a new fad dance, the producers hired dance teacher Oscar Duryea to tame Fox's exhausting trot, mainly by replacing the running the indefatigable comedian did from stage right to stage left by stylishly brisk walking. Duryea, also a nightclub headliner, shrewdly perceived that if Harry Fox's trot was to enjoy a popularity more prolonged than animal mimicry fads, the dance should embody sophistication, simplicity, and a classical smoothness.

Thusly tamed, jerks ironed out, Fox's two-step (related to the Gay Nineties fad dance, and a name today often given to the fox trot) was introduced to the dance-hungry American public. Ballroom dance teachers immediately approved; steps were further polished and standardized by Vernon and Irene Castle; and while tensions in Europe mounted, Americans, hoping to remain isolationists, fox trotted. And when, inextricably, American soldiers joined the global fray, they sparked fox trot mania abroad, dancing the steps in European bars. The fox trot was *the* dance most closely associated with World War I.

Tango

The smooth, suave tango scandalized the country with its Latin sensualness far more than a later dance like the lambada ever could. In the Teens, anything Latin piqued the moral sensors of bluenosed blue bloods. Rumor had it that the New York tango had already been mercifully toned down: "The real Tango," huffed Mrs. Arthur Dodge, organizer of the fashionable Junior Cotillion, "as danced in Argentina, would never be permitted, even in New York." Which said as much for Manhattan as it did for the dance. Coming off the animal dance craze mid-decade, the public was told that to tango they should imitate a panther stealthily stepping through a torrid jungle.

Mrs. Dodge was probably right. In its birthplace, Spain, the tango had erotic overtones and may have been related to a gypsy folk dance of Andalusia. It entered the Western Hemisphere through the bawdy barhouses of Buenos Aires, mixing, it is thought, with the tangano of transported African slaves, after which it resembled a sadistic Apache dance. Its name may come straightforwardly from tangano, or, as some authorities believe, from the Spanish first-person singular *tengo,* "I possess"—and tango is properly pronounced as if spelled "tengo." Certainly a hallmark of an Apache dance—in which a passionate woman attempts to hold the love of a sadistic male—is possessiveness.

Luxury liner–hopping wealthy Argentinians spread the tango in a socially acceptable "genteel" version to Paris late in the Oughts. With its hot-blooded rhythms and suave steps, the dance and its music captivated French society, and by 1913 the craze flourished in England at *thés tango,* or "tango teas"—tea being a dance in late afternoon, often in a restaurant, frequently between courses of a meal. The British tangoed between cups of tea, panther-stepping between tea tables. Vernon and Irene Castle, performing in Paris at the Café de Paris, picked up the tango, dramatized its low dips until couples almost touched the floor, and introduced their sleek version to New Yorkers at an engagement at the Café de l'Opera in 1914.

Dance historians agree that no ballroom dance swept the country faster than the tango. It brought in millions of dollars for dance instructors and tango-music composers, and Rudolph Valentino tangoed his way to fame on the silver screen, causing women in the audience to swoon and faint from worship. It also escalated society's already mad idolization of the Castles. (The Parisian dance master who taught the Castles how to tango, Maurice Walton, was totally eclipsed by their fame and died penniless and in obscurity.) At the dance's peak popularity just prior to World War I, it comprised almost two hundred different steps, though most people stuck to a more basic tango.

Banned.   Despite the Castles' popularity, the dance was banned in Boston. The Massachusetts legislature attempted to enact a law that would fine a tangoing couple $50 for the first offense, and six months in jail if they dared do it again. You could not tango in Cleveland, in Berlin, or, for a time, at the English royal court—though that restriction was scotched after Queen Mary requested a demonstration of the dance at a grand ball. A New York City official, overseeing recreation centers at which dancing was a passion, argued that the tango, fox trot and animal dances "stimulate too much abandon, too much freedom," concluding that "we will stick to the Two-Step, the Waltz, and the Quadrille."

The tango held popular sway until America entered the war, then enjoyed several revivals due to film luminaries such as Ginger Rogers and Fred Astaire, and Carole Lombard and George Raft. To the dance purist, it became the quintessence of high style, a dancer's dance, with a premium on grace and control. And the tango craze offered the public not only a new dance, but also a new Latin rhythm to listen to.

Castlemania

"One of the first things we learned in the dancing business," said Irene Castle, trendsetter extraordinaire, "was never keep the same dance in vogue over a long period of time." Irene and Vernon Castle—she from New Rochelle, New York; he from Norwich, England—exploited the quintessence of faddishness to keep Americans dancing new steps in the Teens. By all measures, Irene Foote (her maiden name) and Vernon Blyth (his real surname; Castle was a stage name) formed the greatest society dance pair that ever trod ballroom parquet.

No one before them—and after them probably only Astaire and Rogers—made dance through imitation a desirable madness. America—and Europe—went Castlewild.

When Irene bobbed her hair (on a whim while recovering from an appendectomy), American women by the thousands cut theirs. When she donned white satin shoes, stores could not keep the items in stock. When she wore a Dutch bonnet, jodhpurs, and a headband (not all at the same time), they became "in" affectations. Men, then less inclined to fashion mimicry, did, though, copy Vernon Castle when he switched from carrying a pocket watch to wearing a *wristwatch;* previously, real men carried pocket watches. By removing the stigma of effeminacy from wearing a "bracelet" watch, Vernon Castle almost single-wristedly opened up the market for men's wristwatches.

The Castles met at a New Rochelle swimming party when she was a stage-struck girl of seventeen and he a stage performer of twenty-three. Unimpressed with his slight (less than 120 pounds), lanky frame, she—a tall, willowy blond of impeccable attire—nonetheless saw stars upon learning he was featured in a Broadway revue. She begged for an audition with his producer, then created a lasting impression with a Spanish-French hodgepodge in which she combined castanets, tambourine, hard-heeled stamping shoes, and can-can kicking. Her first professional part, though, was a three-line walk-on in *The Summer Widowers,* in which she was eclipsed by a show-stopping younger girl with curly hair who had a hopeless crush on Vernon Castle: Helen Hayes. Helen won other roles, while Irene won Vernon Castle, who proposed on Christmas Day 1910.

Castle Walk and the End of an Era.   The Castles' fame began with dancing appearances in Paris. They were already big time upon returning to New York, which was in the grip of ragtime fever. When at a cabaret the Castles improvised steps to the hit tune "The Darktown Strutters' Ball," they invented, as mentioned, the Castle walk, a dance craze as much as a vehicle to their stardom. Throughout the Teens, the Castles were the nation's darlings of dance. Here is how to Castle walk, in the originators' own words: "Walk as in the one-step. Now raise up slightly on your toes, legs a trifle stiff, and breeze along happily . . . now you know all there is to the Castle Walk." They knowingly added in their popular dance book that the dance "sounds silly, and is silly. That's the explanation of its popularity!"

"The Castles are coming!" is how billboards along the East Coast proclaimed their sold-out dance exhibitions. They often played two cities a day, and each performance ended with an audience dance contest, the winning couple taking home a Castle Cup trophy. At the height of their popularity, the couple was earning $31,000 a week. In a lustrous career, they polished the fox trot, defined the tango, invented the Castle walk, and set new standards for elegance and grace in American social dance. Vernon, a wartime aviator, was killed when his plane crashed on a training maneuver at Fort Worth, Texas. A few days later, the *Christian Science Monitor* eulogized: "The Castles showed and taught people of two continents how modern dances ought to be danced. They eliminated vulgarity and replaced it with refinement. They restored poetry to motion." Irene Castle continued to dance, but was no longer a trendsetter.

Castlemania was more than a passing fad, though. For from their widespread popularity, Vernon and Irene Castle influenced social reform in making dance, through refinement and elegance, acceptable to millions of people otherwise inclined. "The Castles," concluded the *Monitor,* "furnished an illustration of the good that may be accomplished in any calling if the effort is rightly and skillfully directed." Ironically, the trendsetting Castles, renowned for their showy pizzazz, were actually the last bulwark of the old sensibility, for the Twenties were about to roar in and America—and social dance—would never again be the same.

POPULAR SONGS

Keep the Home Fires Burning

"Can you dance to it?"

That "American Bandstand"–like question is the great musical divide between popular tunes before and after about 1910. Prior to the start of the Teens, most popular music was meant for singing, solo or in family groups around a piano. But after 1910—when America's mania for dance was already in high gear—publishers of popular tunes grew more insistent that a song be danceable to hit the magic million-selling mark. "In time this became an absolute rule of the industry," writes historian Sigmund Spaeth, "and even if a ballad happened to be printed in the free vocal style, it was immediately supplied with a dance orchestration." Though in the 1950s Dick Clark would make a song's danceability a primary voting criterion among "Bandstand" regulars, the shift from "singable" to "danceable" began in the Teens.

In 1910—when the year's most singable hit was **Let Me Call You Sweetheart,** which would eventually sell five million sheet music copies—parlor pianos were a home commonplace for many, and group singing an evening pastime. That year a minimum of 2 billion copies of sheet music were sold, a high never again to be equaled. For another trend was under way: the consumers' shift away from sheet music toward records.

Also in the Teens, the pace of American life rapidly accelerated, hustled along by luxury liner globe-trotting, earnest talk of airplane travel, and, not the least, automobiling in Tin Lizzies. Speed was a buzzword, and popular music caught the national tempo in ragtime. Ragtime's simple device of syncopation, in which an anticipated accent is shifted to an "off" beat, had already influenced American music, and in the Teens American boys would march to war in ragtime steps. (Only after the war would ragtime's heyday close with the wide acceptance of jazz.) The decade's first immense hit, "Alexander's Ragtime Band," had, appropriately, the word ragtime in its title, though, as we'll see, it actually had little to do with ragtime.

Alexander's Ragtime Band: 1911

Everybody's Doin' It Now was one 1911 hit by a young composer named Izzy Baline, better known professionally as Irving Berlin, America's quintessential songwriter, whose music would dominate the Teens and the Twenties—and resonate throughout the century in such standards as "God Bless America," "Easter Parade," and "White Christmas."

That same year—when Americans were buying sheet music for the season's most singable tune, **I Want a Girl, Just Like the Girl That Married Dear Old Dad**—Berlin published the vigorously danceable "Alexander's Ragtime Band." First performed at New York City's Garden Café by singers Eddie Miller and Helen Vincent, the tune caused an immediate sensation, and soon people turkey trotted and grizzly beared to the rousing march with its so-called black dialect–like lyrics. But the song, erroneously credited with turning America overnight into a syncopated nation, contains hardly a trace of ragtime, except in such verse lines as "Oh, my honey." The chorus is virtually devoid of syncopation's artificial accents. Handel, Beethoven, Brahms, and Tchaikovsky had all made good use of shifting beats, but Irving Berlin claimed, "Syncopation is in the soul of every true American. Ragtime is the best heart-raiser and worry banisher that I know." Ironically, he did not practice what he preached in "Alexander's Ragtime Band."

Nonetheless, the trumpeting "Come on and hear/Come on and hear" called millions of dancers to the floor. And the song made Irving Berlin a celebrity. He could neither read nor write music, knew nothing about musical theory, and lifelong had to compose on a special piano that automatically changed keys, for he only played in F sharp, but from that auspicious success his hits came nonstop. He closed "Alexander's" with a reference to Stephen Foster's "Old Folks at Home"—"if you want to hear the *Swannee River* played in ragtime," which contains a touch of Berlin's syncopation. It was a true march, a surefire hit, and all done by amazing instinct.

Here's how Irving Berlin hits fit in with the decade's other popular songs.

1912.　Now a partner in a major publishing firm, Berlin captured America's love affair with trains—and railroad songs—with **When the Midnight Choo-Choo Leaves for Alabam'.** From the music industry's standpoint, this was also the year in which discs defeated cylinders in the record marketplace (not unlike the modern-day triumph of CDs over LPs).

Non-Berlin hits included the lilting tune **My Melancholy Baby,** the barbershop harmonizer **Moonlight Bay,** and the humorous **Be My Little Baby Bumble Bee** (not "busy" bumble bee, as is often sung). Ragtime combined with bathos in the plaintive bestseller **You Made Me Love You (I Didn't Want to Do It),** and collegians across the country were singing **The Sweetheart of Sigma Chi.**

1913.　Many hit songs have come from Broadway shows, and in 1913 the center of legitimate theater activity shifted to its present area around Broadway and Times Square as Shubert Alley opened that fall. *Billboard* magazine published its first list of sheet music bestsellers, called "Last Week's Ten Best." Among the season's hits was the sentimental ballad **Peg O' My Heart,** which would score a revival on radio's "Your Hit Parade" in the Forties. Sheet music also sold briskly for the dance tune **Ballin' the Jack, The Trail of the Lonesome Pine,** and an adaptation of an old Irish air (the "Londonderry Air") under the title **Danny Boy.**

1914. Irving Berlin scored several successes in this first year of the war in Europe: **This Is the Life, I Want to Go Back to Michigan (Down on the Farm),** and **He's a Devil in His Own Home Town.** But Vernon and Irene Castle so dominated the social scene that many composers hoping for a hit created music around them: the **Castle House Rag,** the waltzlike **Castle Lame Duck,** the **Castle Hesitation Waltz,** and the **Castle Tango,** to name a few. The dancing couple teamed up with Irving Berlin in his first complete musical revue, *Watch Your Step.*

Even folk who couldn't get to the then-trendy Atlantic City beach were singing **By the Sea (By the Beautiful Sea),** which quickly became the resort's theme. Barbershop quartets were still the rage, and the year's related hit was to become a classic: **When You Wore a Tulip and I Wore a Big Red Rose.** And though Bing Crosby later scored a smash with **Too-ra-loo-ra-loo-ra, That's an Irish Lullaby,** the song was high on the charts in 1914, having appeared a year earlier in a revue. The nonsense song of the season, heard everywhere, was **The Aba Daba Honeymoon.**

The year was also musically notable for the formation of ASCAP, the American Society of Composers, Authors and Publishers, which began to enforce song copyright laws rigorously. Previously, despite Victor Herbert's famous battle fought all the way to the Supreme Court (with a historic composer's victory written by Justice Oliver Wendell Holmes), tune stealing had been a profitable way of life.

1915–16. **The Perfect Song** became a hit only because it was included in the elaborate incidental score for D. W. Griffith's silent screen classic of that year, *The Birth of a Nation.* The film, Hollywood's first historical epic, starring Lillian Gish and produced at a cost of $100,000, would eventually gross $20 million, becoming an early motion picture blockbuster. "The Perfect Song" would become the musical signature of the later "Amos 'n' Andy" radio program.

Romantic and sentimental ballads were well represented by Sigmund Romberg's **Auf Wiederseh'n, Fascination,** and the maternal paean **M-O-T-H-E-R (A Word That Means the World to Me).** Tin Pan Alley was caught up in a Hawaiian craze, churning out such hits in 1915 and 1916 as **On the Beach at Waikiki, Song of the Islands, They're Wearing 'Em Higher in Hawaii, Since Maggie Dooley Learned the Hooley Hooley,** and the season's mandatory nonsense songs, **Oh! How She Could Yacki, Hacki**

Wicki, Wacki, Woo, and **Yaacka Hula Hickey Dula.** For piano students, the year was notable for the publication of Felix Arndt's famous **Nola,** a lively composition in which the right hand follows a highly tuneful five-finger exercise; Nola was the name of Arndt's daughter.

Midway through 1916, a young artist by the name of Norman Rockwell painted his first cover for the *Saturday Evening Post.*

1917.   Norman Rockwell illustrated an Army campfire songfest scene for the sheet music cover of George M. Cohan's hit and the war's theme song, "Over There." More on this song later.

One of the year's biggest nonwar hits was **The Bells of St. Mary's,** a British import that would get a second life in the Bing Crosby-Ingrid Bergman film of that title. For harmonizers, there was **For Me and My Gal.** Sigmund Romberg was represented by **Will You Remember?** from his hit show *Maytime.* And **The Darktown Strutters' Ball,** a true ragtime melody, inspired Vernon and Irene Castle to improvise a dance, as mentioned, and start the Castle walk craze.

It was also a year in which black spirituals sold strongly. The hits were **Deep River** (based on an 1875 religious traditional), **Nobody Knows de Trouble I've Seen** (from an 1865 spiritual), and **Swing Low, Sweet Chariot** (from 1872).

The season's nonsense song: **Old MacDonald Had a Farm.** It was not new in 1917, just wildly popular. The melody is British, from the early 1700s; American lyrics were added around Civil War time.

The United States was now engaged in the Great War, and pop music reflected the conflict, the fears, and the sentiments of the nation. But the first wartime hit songs came from England.

It's a Long Way to Tipperary: 1914

Though the global conflict regrettably did not live up to its billing as the war to end all wars, it was an event that ended an innocence, a naiveté, and a simplicity of life never to be recaptured. "It's a Long Way to Tipperary" was written in England in 1912, but it sat on a publisher's shelf until 1914, when British soldiers began marching to the ballad's stimulating rhythm. About an Irishman longing for his beloved County Tipperary in southern Ireland, the lyrics of longing, heartache, and homesickness suited the sentiments of young men who knew they might never again see those sights highlighted in the song's lyrics: "Goodbye, Piccadilly, / Farewell, Leicester Square."

The next year, 1915, another war song came to America from England: the soldier's plea to family, **Keep the Home Fires Burning.** Americans sang the song for its tunefulness, not yet for its heartfelt, home-soil truth. More popular in America that year was the happy-go-lucky English marching song **Pack Your Troubles in Your Old Kit-Bag and Smile, Smile, Smile,** which through its lyrics popularized two British colloquialisms: "lucifer" (match) and "fag" (cigarette).

Home-written war songs—like **I Didn't Raise My Boy to Be a Soldier**—were often anti-war, expressing America's fear of being dragged into that "European conflict." Then the *Lusitania* was torpedoed and Americans found themselves uncomfortably singing **When the Lusitania Went Down.** By 1917, one Tin Pan Alley composer perceived his patriotic duty and executed it grandly with . . .

Over There: 1917

The song that gave its title to the over there decade was written by George M. Cohan on April 6, 1917, after he read the newspaper headline that the United States had entered into the fray; it would win him a Congressional Medal and a personal note from President Woodrow Wilson that the music was "a genuine inspiration to all American manhood." The lyrics said it all:

> Over there, over there
> Send the word, send the word, over there.
> That the Yanks are coming, the Yanks are coming,
> The drums rum-tumming everywhere . . .

The song held out the promise that "the Yanks" would soon put an end to the suffering. First publicly performed at a Red Cross benefit at the New York Hippodrome Theater, the rousing tune—really a bugle call—brought the audience to its feet. The gimmick of repeating buglelike blasts again and again is common to many national and patriotic airs, but given the circumstances in which it was introduced, as well as the determined oath, "We won't come back till it's over over there," the song created in all who heard it an impassioned military fervor. It was the perfect song for a terrible war, and "If George Michael Cohan had created nothing else in his long and active life," writes historian Spaeth, "he would still tower as a giant in the field of popular music on the solid foundation of 'Over There.' "

The war inspired other hits of the decade.

Oh, Johnny, Oh, Johnny asked the question "how can you fight?" and managed to get in the exclamation "how you can love!" Mixing patriotism with passion, it sold more than a million copies of sheet music in 1917.

The most successful of what were called parting songs was **Good-bye, Broadway, Hello, France!** which debuted in a musical revue of 1917.

Irving Berlin made contributions through an all-soldier show, *Yip, Yip, Yaphank,* which contained one of his most famous songs, **Oh! How I Hate to Get Up in the Morning**—which he sang again in his musical dramatization of the Second World War, *This Is the Army.* That same year, 1917, he composed an unblushingly patriotic song—"God Bless America"—but did not publish it (until Armistice Day of 1938) because he felt it was too darkly serious.

Even the war had a nonsense song: the stuttering classic, **K-K-K-Katy,** alliteratively billed in 1918 as "The Sensational Stammering Song Success Sung by Soldiers and Sailors." A contender popular among doughboys was **Made-**

moiselle from Armentieres, Parlay-Voo, also known as **Hinky-Dinky Parlez Vous.** The tune and original words are from a French folk song, "Mademoiselle de Bar-Le-Duc," which a British sergeant and former music hall performer revamped—only to have the verse repeatedly and comically altered by American soldiers.

The war was over by 1919, but it echoed in the year's hit: **How Ya Gonna Keep 'Em Down on the Farm? (After They've Seen Paree).** Jubilant Americans were also singing **I'm Forever Blowing Bubbles,** and **I'm Always Chasing Rainbows,** the latter a melody stolen from Chopin's *Fantasie Impromptu* in C-sharp minor. But the looming threat of nationwide Prohibition was already being lampooned in song: Harry Ruby's **What'll We Do on a Saturday Night When the Town Goes Dry,** and Irving Berlin's contribution from the *Ziegfeld Follies of 1919,* **You Cannot Make Your Shimmy Shake on Tea.** The show also introduced his **A Pretty Girl Is Like a Melody.** The vogue color that year was Alice blue—featured in the hit song **In My Sweet Little Alice Blue Gown.**

Looking over the annual song lists of the Teens, one sees a trend: The word jazz in song titles and lyrics begins to replace ragtime. The music of F. Scott Fitzgerald's jazz age was unleashed, if not yet wildly popular. Jazz music had long been played by live bands in New Orleans, along the Mississippi, and in Chicago, and around 1917 it started to be recorded. It was to be the next major trend in popular music.

BESTSELLING BOOKS

A Nonfiction List

The shot fired at Sarajevo heralded a new kind of nonfiction bestseller—and it also emphasized the need for two separate lists of top ten books: fiction and nonfiction. Previously, fiction and nonfiction were lumped together, the former invariably squeezing out the latter. Only in two years since list-keeping started—1912 and 1913—did *Publishers Weekly* tally nonfiction sales; then it abandoned the concept until 1917.

From the first brief attempts at a nonfiction bestseller list, it is interesting to note the kinds of books that held Americans' attention: self-help, how-to, travel, and biography—recurring themes for the rest of this century. One top-seller of 1912, which engaged American parents and educators in a heated debate, was **The Montessori Method,** by Italian psychiatrist and educator Maria Montessori. Psychiatric jargon like "libido," "Oedipus complex," "neurosis," and "inferiority complex" had already filtered into the vernacular as topics of debate among adults. But Dr. Montessori's bestseller started educators and parents talking another language, one involving terms like "periods of sensitivity" in preschool learning. The psychiatrist linked a child's biological and mental growth, and advocated teaching methods in which children aged three to six maximized their capabilities for acquiring new skills. Essentially she said that certain creative materials can arouse in youngsters an interest not previously thought possible, enabling them to read, write, and count before age six. For a country whose tempo in all things was "fast forward," accelerated learning sounded tailor-made to America's bright future.

War Books

Not long after *The Montessori Method* slipped off the nonfiction bestseller list, the industry's list itself was discontinued, returning only in 1917 as America went to war. In fact, a *third* list was added: war books. The popularity of wartime books had a direct effect on boosting sales of general nonfiction works. In a stroke, it enlarged Americans' reading habits. Whereas the war books list would soon be dropped, the nonfiction list lived on.

Between the sinking of the *Lusitania* and Armistice Day, it seemed that any war-related topic sold well, even patriotic poetry. American aviator Alan Seeger's **Poems** held the number four spot in 1917 and was number ten the next year on the popularity of a single, highly dramatic verse, "I Have a Rendezvous with Death." Another volume of poetry, **In Flanders Fields,** by Canadian Captain John McCrae, scored number five in nonfiction in 1919 on the strength of its title poem alone. Even the prosaically titled **Rhymes of a Red Cross Man** found wide readership, holding number one in general nonfiction for 1917 and 1918. Americans had resisted involvement in the war, had elected a president on the slogan reminder "He kept us out of war," and had shrugged their shoulders at doomsayers' "saber-rattling," but once they went to war their taste in books—and songs, as we've seen—strongly reflected their newfound commitment.

Fiction also benefited from the worldwide conflict.

Mr. Britling Sees It Through: Number One Fiction, 1917

This H. G. Wells novel was the first popular war fiction. The story contrasts the pertinacity of the British to the barbarity of the Germans, and it features an American character who, by observing the courageous Mr. Britling, shifts from neutrality to enlistment in the Canadian army. Though published in 1916, it found a wide readership only after American involvement in the war was inevitable. By this time zeppelin raids were extracting a death toll in England, and American newspapers ran horror stories of innocent European children butchered by the "Huns." Millions of Americans identified with the novel's American character, who really had no moral choice but to side, heart and hand, with the British. The bestseller might well have been instrumental in changing the minds of many American isolationists.

Over the Top: Number Four, 1917

An enormously successful bestseller on the special war books list (it climbed from fourth place in 1917 to third place in 1918), *Over the Top* captured the imagination of Americans at a time when all the country was singing "Over There." Written by an American who actually joined the British army, Arthur Guy Empey, it brought the courage and hardships of a machine gunner in trench warfare home to armchair American readers. The vivid fighting scenes provided the kind of high drama and adrenaline rush appealing to young men of draft age—and supposedly persuaded countless thousands to enlist. Putnam, the publisher, promoted *Over the Top* as the personal account of "an American who WENT"—this at a time when to go or not to go was the question—and claimed that the story told young men "pretty nearly what is awaiting them," though patriotically dramatized. It glorified the doughboy at a time when doughboys were sorely needed.

Draft-age boys particularly liked the book's liberal use of trench-warfare slang; there was so much of it that the publisher printed a thirty-five-page addendum of soldiers' jargon. In its first few months out, *Over the Top* sold 350,000 copies. Empey's lecture tour drew large audiences and boosted sales such that, as James Hart reports in *The Popular Book,* the work "sold 250 copies every working hour over a period of seven months."

Whereas men bought volumes like Captain Ian Hay's **The First Hundred Thousand**—the author's reminiscences "straight from the trenches"; number one on the war books list in 1917—women readers related more to books like May Sinclair's **Tree of Heaven.** It told the story of a courageous English mother whose four children experience the horrors of war; in 1918 it was number two in fiction.

Both men and women made a number four 1918 fiction bestseller of the humorous **Dere Mable** (read: "Dear Mabel"), Edward Streeter's compilation of outrageously misspelled love letters from a rookie enduring barracks life and army chow. It spawned two half-million-selling sequels: **Same Old Bill, eh Mabel!** and **As You Were, Bill!** In truth, many parents were receiving letters from their sons not all that different from Bill's. When the former ambassador to the now much-hated "Fatherland," James W. Gerard, published **My Four Years in Germany,** the book shot to the top of the war books list, selling ninety thousand copies in one week. Americans wanted to know what the kaiser and his fiercely militaristic followers were really like.

The Four Horsemen of the Apocalypse: Number One Fiction, 1919

This was, in the closing year of the Teens, perhaps the decade's most outstanding wartime novel—and a film vehicle for a young dance instructor turned actor, Rudolph Valentino. The publisher, Dutton, set a new standard in spectacular display advertising, as well as in cost for a single copy of a general-appeal book: a steep $1.90 price tag. Many industry insiders felt the public would never pay nearly $2 for a book, but were delighted to be proved so thoroughly wrong.

Though many Americans found *The Four Horsemen*'s author's name—V. Blasco Ibáñez—a tongue-twister, they readily took to his tale, as well as to the biblical tone of the title. Ibáñez "ingeniously combined exotic romance with hatred of the Germans," writes Hart in *The Popular Book*. The formula proved irresistible—in picturesque sketches of "the life of wealthy ranchers in the Argentine and in the art studios of Paris," juxtaposed with descriptions of "German atrocities endorsed by an intellectual Prussian distantly related to the alluring Argentinian hero." The novel held American readers' attention—and bestseller status—for fifteen months, despite the price tag. The story caused a second national sensation in 1921 with the release of the film starring Valentino.

As the Tender Teens drew to a close, a hitherto unknown force—in the form of mass entertainments—was beginning to compete with book readership. It first took the seemingly harmless guise of automobiling amusement, then of motion picture attending, then radio listening, with its most virulent manifestation surfacing in the late 1940s: television watching. Books, at the close of the Teens, were still one of the few major forms of inexpensive, home-fire, mass appeal amusements. Though their days were not numbered, their somewhat exclusive status was.

CHAPTER 4

□

The Soaring Twenties

1920 to 1929

The Self-Expression Era

From boom to bust. From Charleston mania to Wall Street mayhem. Never had a modern people been so recklessly dedicated to trendiness, thrills, and self-amusement. The years between the election of President Warren Harding in 1920 and the catastrophic stock market crash of 1929 seem to us, through nostalgia's lens, a limitless joyride of flappers, dance marathons, transatlantic flights, jazz, sports cars, speakeasies, gangland warfare, and bootleg gin.

The decade merited its catchy and diverse billings: the Dry Era, the Lawless Decade, the Roaring Twenties, the Era of Wonderful Nonsense, the Get-Rich-Quick Decade, and, of course, F. Scott Fitzgerald's Jazz Age. It was even labeled the Plastic Age, fitting for reasons unintended at the time: yes, the fast-paced, thrill-seeking life did seem artificial to many, but, too, the Twenties kicked off America's obsession with synthetic materials: Bakelite, acetate, vinyl, cellophane, and Plexiglas; a *Time* magazine cover in 1924 honored Leo Baekeland, the Father of Plastics. The era was unreal in more ways than one.

The reckless gaiety and commitment to vogue was really only the upside of the story—as we're about to see. For in the wake of the Great War the national character split in two, with puritanical repression and conservatism on one side, and radical self-expression and cynicism on the other—a split yet to close.

The most highly publicized exponent of the new self-expression was the flapper, that modish, short-haired, flat-chested, boyish young girl, daringly outspoken on issues on which she was informed or not. Her appearance, spunk, and verve epitomized the emancipated "new woman," who had finally won not only the right to vote, but to drink and smoke like men—even with men. With her "sheik"—in raccoon coats or stiff yellow slickers, unbuckled galoshes, in a rumble seat, with hip flasks filled with hooch—they were a sight and a phenomenon, which, we'll see, was one of many reactions against the advent of Prohibition in 1920—a legislated folly with disastrous consequences.

For the Dry Era—which would not end until 1933—bred an underworld of big-time gangsters and racketeers. These professional criminals—Capone their rogue model—gunned their way into the bootlegging business, then networked into gambling, loansharking, and sundry other sin ventures. Al Capone's reign of terror in Chicago made that city the most violent in the nation, and many frightened Americans pleaded for the U.S. Marines to come to the rescue. The folly of dryness did more than spawn the Lawless Decade, it created an entire new criminal class in America, which, by the time of Prohibition's repeal, was rich and infamous, organized and permanently ensconced.

In terms of following fads and scoring firsts, the Twenties was a time to *plunge,* not wade into . . . well, anything one desired. It was America's first unabashed era of hype, a time replete with superlatives, a decade defined by deeds of derring-do:

Babe Ruth hit sixty homes runs for the Yankees.
Gertrude Ederle became the first woman to swim the English Channel
    (breaking the men's record by almost two hours).
Charles Lindbergh soloed the Atlantic in *The Spirit of St. Louis.*
Admiral Byrd reached and explored the Antarctic.

Charles Lindbergh.

Margaret Gorman strolled down an Atlantic City runway as the first Miss America.

Rosa Ponselle ruled the Metropolitan Opera stage.

Clara Bow euphemized sex appeal as the big *It.*

Rudolph Valentino set new standards of male chic.

Not to mention **Ty Cobb, Jack Dempsey, Gene Tunney, Rudy Vallee.** And, of course, **The Crash.**

The juxtaposition of two quotes illustrates the apex and the nadir of the Twenties:

> We did as we pleased. We stayed up late. We dressed the way we wanted. I'd whiz down Sunset Boulevard in my open Kissel with seven red chow dogs to match my hair.

—Clara Bow

STOCK PRICES SLUMP $14,000,000,000 IN NATION-WIDE STAMPEDE TO UNLOAD

—*New York Times,* October 29, 1929

FADS, FOLLIES, AND TRENDS

Jazz Age Jargon

With America's identity coming into lush flower, it's not surprising to find that the Twenties is the first nonwar decade to produce its own extensive "in" vocabulary. The period was extraordinarily fertile for the American language. People were doing new things, behaving in unprecedented ways, and each novelty called out for at least one name. Scores of words and expressions sprang into existence, while older ones that had languished in near-disuse were popularized overnight—terms every flapper or sheik had to spout to be trendy.

A cute flapper, whose legs were **gams** (French, *gambe*) was a **beaut,** or the **cat's meow, cat's whiskers,** or **cat's pajamas.** In fact, cat's meow meant anything wonderful, and was synonymous with **bee's knees** and **berries.**

Her boy friend was a **cakeater, jazzbo, jellybean,** or **lounge lizard** (a term then synonymous with ladies' man).

He might be a **big cheese** (important person), or a **flat tire** (thorough bore), either **hard-boiled** (tough, without sentiment) or **peppy** (full of vim and virility). Throughout the course of a **blind date**—which might include **heavy necking**—he could become **ossified** (drunk), having consumed too much **giggle water.**

After a night of **whoopee** (boisterous, convivial fun) at a **gin mill** (speakeasy) he might **upchuck** (vomit). Or he might not.

They could be **stuck on** each other.

Though "petting parties" were popular in the Teens, a frequent boy petter in the Twenties was a **snugglepup,** or a **heavy necker,** who often marked his girlfriend with a proud **hickie.** All of this might occur during a **double date,** and in a **rumble seat,** which gave new meaning to the verb **park.**

If romance soured, perhaps it was because one party was a **two-timer,** soon to become an **ex**—though the wounded might long **carry a torch.**

Flappers to be avoided were **gold-diggers.**

A man and woman who each possessed the alluring **It** were known as a **sheik** and a **sheba.**

Anything a flapper or a jellybean liked was **nifty,** or **the nuts.** Or **swell** or **swanky** or **ritzy.**

Copacetic meant excellent.

Rapture was expressed by **hot diggity dog;** in haste, **hot diggity.**

A stupid girl was a **dumbbell,** or **dumb Dora.**

At a wild party, the flapper who hoisted her skirt high in a wicked Charleston was egged on by cries of **Get hot! Get hot!**

At the close of a date, a flapper might say to her sheik (a Valentino influence), **Thanks for the buggy ride.**

To tell him off she'd snap, **Go fly a kite.**

If her **playboy** (or **sugar daddy**) made her laugh, she'd giggle, **Ooo, you slaughter me!**

A pet expression of disbelief was **It's the bunk.**

Or, **Banana oil.**

Incredulity was conveyed by **For crying out loud!**

Anything strange was **goofy.**

Anyone strange was **a goof.**

Jazz babies never said yes or no, but gave a long, drawn-out **Ab-so-lute-ly,** or **Pos-i-tive-ly.** Other times it was a scramble of both: **Pos-a-loot-ly.**

The **real McCoy** was the genuine article (the derivation is in dispute; it comes either from a Scottish clan leader named MacKay, a boxer named Kid McCoy who had a rival with the same name, or a bootlegger named McCoy who did not adulterate his liquor).

Collegiate Chatter.　The Twenties also saw the heyday of the **Greeks** (fraternities). A young man who survived **hazing** became a **Joe College,** better yet a **Joe Yale;** a failure was aptly a **Joe Zilch.** The campus—where many students had cars—was quickly becoming a center for moral unrest and *the* place to be. College humor and jokes were popular across the country: "She doesn't drink, / She doesn't pet, / She hasn't been / To college yet." Or: FIRST DAD: Do you think your son will soon forget all he learned in college? SECOND DAD: I hope so. He can't make a living necking. A magazine of such witticisms, *College Humor,* had a circulation of 800,000. H. L. Mencken said of the magazine's youthful contributors: "It takes a year or two of pedagogy to iron out a student of genuinely lively mind. By the time he is graduated he is usually ruined, but while he lasts he sometimes contributes something rich and racy to the national humor."

Prohibition Parlance.　Prohibition had failed for the Aztecs, the ancient Chinese, the feudal Japanese, and scores of others. Nonetheless, while thousands of thirsty young men were still overseas and unable to express their opinions, a temperance movement, heady with postwar idealism, rushed into the **noble experiment** by pushing for an Eighteenth Amendment. It was the only time the Constitution had been expanded to *restrict* a freedom, and the amendment, with the Volstead Act as its enforcing strong arm, proved, as the Aztecs could have forecast, an unmitigated disaster. The Volstead Act legally defined intoxicating liquor as "any beverage containing ½ of 1% alcohol," which left off limits even vanilla extract. The doughboys came home and were not pleased. Nor, from the popularity of **bathtub gin, bootleg whiskey, Jake-leg, near beer,** and **home brew,** was anyone really happy with the new law. Mid-Twenties, bootlegging was a $2 billion a year business, employing half a million people. Still, Prohibition left the language with a wealth of colorful expressions.

Any bootleg liquor that came from a tribe of Alaskan Indians known as the Hoochinoo was called **hooch.**

Americans sneaked into **whoopee parlors,** or **speakeasies,** the later word from the nineteenth-century English underworld "speak-softly shop," a smuggler's place of business.

Hospital alcohol was what bootleggers swore they used as a fundamental ingredient, not blinding denatured alcohol, which yielded up **gut rot.**

Red ink was homemade wine. **Virginia Dare** was a "medicinal" tonic, supposedly for anemia, containing 22 percent alcohol and extremely popular among millions who conveniently discovered they were anemic.

The never-ending line of liquor-laden schooners off the East Coast, bringing in the **real stuff** from Canada and Bermuda, was known as **rum row,** whereas anyone working on such a vessel was a **rumrunner.**

Many Americans—**juiced, crocked, fried,** or **polluted**—may have been obsessed with thoughts of **sauce** and **moonshine,** but they were horror-stricken over newspaper accounts of **the mob, syndicates, trigger men, one-way rides to nowhere,** and the **St. Valentine's Day Massacre.**

By the close of the Twenties the noble experiment was clearly a bust— liquor flowed and crime flourished, with the police as guilty as the criminals. It was high time for another amendment (the Twenty-first) to put an end to the Dry Decade.

Flapper: Origin of the Word and the Woman

Hair bobbed, skirt fringed, stockings rolled, style flippant, she was the wild, gin-imbibing, cigarette-puffing, necking, Charleston jazz baby who came to epitomize the Twenties, a free spirit who tossed off restraints to usher in a new American woman. Her figure was defiantly boyish, and by bunching her stockings below the knee she blatantly announced to the world that she wore no corset to hold them up. She wielded a cigarette holder like a weapon, which in the battle of the sexes it was. The woman no longer exists but the archetype thrives—and then some.

During the short epoch that was her heyday, she commingled sex and love, redefining each. She gained entry into the impenetrable male world in the guise of a "boy"—a tomboy—where she played at "men's" behaviors—smoking and drinking and keeping the wee hours—all the while staking out a territory and power base that, when she dropped the flat-chested guise to go back to full-bosom frills, men would never quite win back. On the battlefield of the sexes, the flapper was women's Trojan horse.

If her image resembled that of a French prostitute, there was a fundamental reason for it.

The Noun.   In England in the mid-1700s the word flapper meant a young, wild duck just learning to fly by flapping its wings. It originated from the Middle English echoic *flappe,* "to swing" while making a slapping sound. By the 1880s it meant a young girl who wore her hair long (and flapping in the breeze) rather than in the pinned-up vogue. In France, around the turn of the century, a flapper was a street prostitute, in short skirt, with bobbed hair; a sight familiar to doughboys during World War I. By the close of the Innocent Oughts, any sassy, headstrong woman was a flapper, especially if she espoused women's rights to drink, smoke, or vote. F. Scott Fitzgerald, in his early short stories, remolded the flapper into an image closer to that which became the Twenties style. But the word and the image, in print and pictures, came before women in large numbers actually dressed and acted like jazz babies, a Twenties synonym for flappers.

The media in the Twenties helped fan flappermania. By 1925, newspapers carried endless stories of flapper exploits, as well as how-to articles on achieving the style. *The New Republic,* soberly straitlaced, made space for a flapper feature, defining the new free spirit: "She is frankly, heavily made up, not to imitate nature, but for an altogether artificial effect . . . poisonously scarlet lips, richly ringed eyes." As for the total weight of "Flapper Jane's" clothes: "less than two pounds . . . Jane isn't wearing much this summer." Much titillation was milked from the fact that Jane wore neither petticoat, brassiere, nor corset.

The flapper fascinated millions of Americans because she flaunted respectability—in attire, and by smoking and drinking and descending into speakeasies to kick up her heels till dawn. With her dashing sheik—he packing a hip flask and boasting of his Stutz Bearcat—they left an indelible mark, as is made clear in a mid-Twenties, full-page ad in the *Saturday Evening Post:*

> You may regard the new generation as amusing or pathetic; as a bit tragic, or rather splendid. You may consider their manners crude, their ideals vague, their clothes absurd . . . But it is useless to deny that these youngsters have a definite bearing on the thought, literature and customs of our day. And particularly do they exert a powerful influence on buying habits and the movement of merchandise.

How fitting for today. For any day.

Mah-Jongg

The Asian game of mah-jongg—sort of a combination of dice and dominoes, played with tiles made from the shinbones of calves—was a wealthy man's pastime in China, but a ladies' club fad in America from 1922 to 1925. Shanghai exporters sent 131,400 sets to America in 1922, and 1,505,080 the next year, with deluxe models costing as much as $500. By that time, the game was outselling radios, causing more than 10 million addicted housewives to neglect home, children, and husbands as they assembled midday for marathon playoffs. Government coffers burgeoned from the ten percent tax imposed on the sale of all games.

Whereas a rich Oriental addict might bet the equivalent of a half million dollars in a single evening's search for the perfect hand of fourteen tiles (four sets of three and an odd pair), American women seldom risked heavy wagers. Their addiction lay in owning deluxe games with wonderfully colored tiles, in accessorizing themselves for play in Chinese silk kimonos and embroidered scuff slippers, in shouting trendy game words like "Pung!" and "Chow! and, not least, in getting out of the house for a while. The fad inspired a song, "Since Ma Is Playing Mah-Jongg," popularized by Eddie Cantor. Mah-jongg rule books became bestsellers. Stores could not stock enough Chinese fans, lacquered trays, exotic teas—any authenticity that lent atmosphere to the assembly.

What caused a complex, confusing Oriental game to suddenly catch on in America in the Twenties?

Mah-jongg tiles are engraved with Chinese symbols, one being that of a "mythical bird of a hundred intelligences," resembling a sparrow, which gives its name to the game—thought to be of nineteenth-century origin. The name mah-jongg was coined, then copyrighted, by an American resident of Shanghai, Joseph P. Babcock, who, arriving in California in the early Twenties, introduced his own Americanized version of the Mandarian gambling parlor obsession. To his delight, his handsome sets sold rapidly, mah-jongg first becoming a California fad—perhaps the first California craze to sweep the nation. Several West Coast newspapers carried mah-jongg columns offering playing tips.

The American mania for the game soon caused such a shortage of calf shinbones in China that Chicago slaughterhouses shipped boatloads of these tile precursors to Oriental gamemakers. Boats from Shanghai to California carried not only boxed games, but all Oriental accoutrements for the perfect mah-jongg party—to give the fad its true label. Hotels, to satisfy female guests, converted rooms into mah-jongg parlors.

Mah-jongg mania peaked in 1923. Then, following true fad fashion, cheap cardboard copies of the game began appearing for less than $2. Stores overstocked. Woolworth's offered the game and its accessories; previously hot sellers at Saks. With the game no longer pricey, chic, and exclusive, the bottom fell out of the mah-jongg market. By 1926, sets that once sold for $25 were bargain basement remainders. Game importers sank into bankruptcy. Some social observers thought that the rise of another fad contributed to the demise of mah-jongg.

Crossword Puzzles

Many people blamed the sudden death of mah-jongg on the crossword puzzle fad that swept America in 1924. Conceived in 1913 by journalist Arthur Wynne as a Sunday supplement amusement in the *New York World,* the word games were a newspaper staple by the early Twenties. In 1924 two young publishers, Richard Simon and M. L. Schuster, issued the first crossword puzzle book (with attached Venus number two pencil), which became an immediate bestseller. That year, as mah-jongg mania was rapidly fading, four crossword books became nationwide bestsellers. While it is true that crossword motifs appeared on women's dresses, handbags, shoes, and jewelry; that college teams competed in crossword tournaments; that one minister cast his sermon into a crossword matrix that the congregation solved during the service—indeed, that the nation went so mad for the up-and-down word games that dictionaries became hot sellers—mah-jongg really died because the game's popularity had rested on exclusivity. When every Thelma, Dotty, and Harriet could hold a Woolworth mah-jongg party, the ladies who mah-jongged in silk kimonos with Saks gameboards turned elsewhere for diversion. Whereas the crossword mania of the Twenties mellowed into a passionate pastime for millions of people, mah-jongg party fever vanished as quickly as it had begun—except, for reasons never clearly understood, among middle-aged Jewish women; indeed, mah-jongg became to the synagogue set what bingo was to Catholic congregations (see page 163).

Flagpole Sitting

If mah-jongg was largely a female fad, flagpole sitting, the zaniest of the Twenties self-promoting stunts, was mostly male nonsense. The craze—as well as the next two we'll examine, the Bunion Derby and the dance marathon—comes under the rubric of endurance fads, a phenomenon almost unique to the Twenties, with flagpole sitting perhaps the best representation from the Era of Wonderful Nonsense. Before examining how the outlandishness originated, here, to get a feel for the mania, are some record holders:

LeRoy Haines set a record in Denver with a twelve-day flagpole sit.

H. V. Crouch of New Bedford, Massachusetts, perched for seventeen days and two hours on a flagpole rigged over the floor of a dance marathon— thus highlighting two fads.

Robert Hall, billed as the Phantom of the Flagpole, quickly topped Crouch's record with an eighteen-day stunt.

As for women sitters, in Los Angeles, Bobby Mach, a twenty-one-year-old stunt aviatrix, endured twenty-one days up a pole before the city council passed an ordinance outlawing the craze.

At the height of the zaniness, newspaper reporters attempted to flesh out their stories with "historical precedents" for flagpole sitting—reaching back as far as the fifth century. St. Simeon Stylites, known as the "pillar hermit," as a boy had been a sheep herder in Syria. At age thirteen he entered a monastery, but was eventually expelled for practicing torturous feats of self-denial and penance such as fasting till nearly comatose. He roamed the countryside performing public displays of endurance in the name of enlightenment, and in A.D. 427 found his true calling atop a sixty-foot stone column at Qalat-Serman in Northern Syria. From its lonely heights, he preached to assembled crowds below, his nourishment, bread and water, hoisted aloft in a basket. If this be flagpole sitting, then St. Simeon certainly is the undisputed record-holder: He passed thirty years on his platform, in prayer and meditation. Alvin Kelly, who began the flagpole sitting fad in the Twenties, knew nothing of St. Simeon's perseverance when he climbed his first pole.

Alvin "Shipwreck" Kelly: Origin of an Endurance Fad.   Journalist Damon Runyon labeled people who'd do anything for publicity *Homo saps,* and he forecast that the twentieth century would be overpopulated by the species. Alvin Kelly was perhaps the first of that self-promoting breed.

Billing himself the Luckiest Man Alive, this diminutive Irishman from New York's Hell's Kitchen was about thirty when in 1924 he perched atop his first flagpole in a stunt role for a Hollywood movie. A publicity agent then hired Kelly as a paid shill, to sit atop a pole outside a Los Angeles theater to draw a crowd to drum up business. The ex-sailor enjoyed the modest-paying work and adored the public attention even more. One publicity stunt promoted another, each covered by the press, and soon copycat pole-sitters across the country had created a new fad.

How does one sit, comfortably or not, on a flagpole?

Kelly's own secret was a rubber-covered wooden seat fastened tightly to the pole's round ball top. Other contraptions, to enhance balance and allow for cat naps, had such safety features as anchoring fingerholes in the seat, leg straps, and stirrups. A fastidious groomer, Kelly kept in his pocket a shaving razor and manicure kit, and he downed only fluids—milk, coffee, broth—hoisted up in a bucket. He had acquired the nickname Shipwreck in his days as a boxer, Sailor Kelly, who was knocked out so often that fans took to shouting, "The Sailor's shipwrecked again." In the late Twenties Kelly was the country's number one flagpole sitter, booked by scores of hotels, fairs, amusement parks, and resorts to hook crowds. His best sit: forty-nine days on a flagpole over the boardwalk in Atlantic City; the feat drew more than twenty thousand spectators. One year Kelly spent 145 days atop various flagpoles around the country, pocketing nearly $30,000 in fees. The publicity seeker had become himself a publicity gimmick. And what began as a stunt had spread to a nationwide craze.

Copycats.   Imitators were of all ages. In Baltimore, which became something of the nation's capital for high-up sitting, fifteen-year-old Alvin Foreman kicked off the fad by scaling an eighteen-foot hickory sapling in his backyard. Trees became the amateur's substitute for flagpoles. During one week Baltimore papers featured stories on twenty arboreal balancers (seventeen boys and three girls). The city's mayor, William Broening, proud of Baltimore's lead in the endurance fad, personally visited each pole or tree record-setter, proclaiming that in the "grit and stamina" of their endurance "the old pioneer spirit of early America is being kept alive by the youth of today." Perhaps it's significant that he was running for reelection.

One endurance fad spawned another in the last half of the Twenties. We'll look at the Bunion Derby and dance marathons, but on a smaller scale there was the Madison Square Garden **Noun and Verb Rodeo**—a loquacious logorrhea featuring nonstop talkers, prattling breathlessly for days without end. The press gave it the sexist billing of "a husband's nightmare." Then there was the **Rocking Chair Derby,** in which contestants bobbed back and forth until, fatigued, they literally fell out of their seats.

As for fad-starter Kelly, he came down from his pole long enough to marry one of his admirers, but she soon divorced him, explaining to the judge, "What good's a husband who doesn't come home at night?" His work came between them. His most profitable year was 1929—then came the stock market crash and the Depression, which had everyone up a pole. The fad was dead, and Kelly found himself financially shipwrecked. He did occasional sitting jobs. To promote National Doughnut Week in 1939, he perched atop a Manhattan skyscraper eating doughnuts; he was forty-seven. In 1942 he worked a flagpole at New Jersey's Palisades Amusement Park, but his age was a handicap and he fell and was injured.

On a cold day in October 1952, New York police discovered the body of a homeless man over a street heat grating. He had no identification except for a wad of yellowed newspaper clippings about the feats of Alvin "Shipwreck" Kelly. Across the street was Madison Square Garden, where his name had once graced the marquee.

Bunion Derby: 1928 Transcontinental Foot Race

By 1928 the nation's youth had gone marathon crazy. With boundless energy and enthusiasm, they pushed life to the limit—and sometimes over the edge. Promoters profited by staging endurance contests of every torturous sort—incorporating such modernisms as product tie-ins. One pinnacle of marathon madness was the 1928 transcontinental foot race, a 3,400-mile stamina special from Los Angeles to New York, which, for the toll it took on feet, the press dubbed the Bunion Derby. Dr. William Scholl, a shoemaker turned foot physician, had previously promoted his corn, callus, and bunion pads through the Cinderella Foot Contest, a nationwide search for the most beautiful female foot in America. The Bunion Derby was one natural product tie-in. The faddish event is interesting in itself, but also because it combined the techniques of celebrity tie-ins, product spin-offs, and other such modern-day approaches to profit.

The race was the brainchild of professional promoter C. C. Pyle—whom at the start of the contest sportswriters dubbed Cash and Carry Pyle, and at its conclusion Corns and Callus Pyle. Football great Red Grange would ride in a motorcar ahead of the runners, overseeing media events in each town the race passed through. Pyle contacted manufacturers of shoes, foot salves and pads, suntan oil, and even the U.S. Route 66 Highway Association, which pledged $60,000 toward the contest's cash prizes if Pyle steered his marathoners over the road, bringing it nationwide recognition. The purse: $25,000 for the winner and $23,500 to be split among nine runners-up.

Get Set, Go!   The 421 marathoners who gathered at the starting line in Los Angeles were billed as "new heroes for American boys." Each hero had to pay a $100 entrance fee. Through media hype, the nation was on tenterhooks for "the greatest moment in sports history." Instead, Americans witnessed one sad spectacle. Everything that could go wrong did. Twice.

The first day, 222 runners dropped out from heat exhaustion. Another competitor was the victim of a hit-and-run motorist. The concessionaire hired to feed the athletes as they crossed the sun-baked Mojave Desert reneged. Sunstroke and dehydration took their toll. Host towns backed out as the running field dwindled and disasters mounted. So, too, did the Route 66 Highway Association. The expected crowds failed to materialize. The traveling vaudeville show was unamusing, and worse, unattended.

By Ohio, the field was down to fifty-five runners, the lead held by a nineteen-year-old part-Cherokee Oklahoman, Andy Payne—who was seventeen hours and twenty-eight minutes ahead of his nearest competitor, John Salo, a thirty-five-year-old Finnish shipfitter from Passaic, New Jersey. The Weehawken ferry transported runners across the Hudson River to Manhattan's Forty-second Street pier—where there were no cheering crowds. Nor were there many spectators to egg the racers up Tenth Avenue to the Madison Square Garden finishing line. Indeed, only four thousand people paid to occupy the eighteen-thousand-seat arena. The dehydrated winner, Andy Payne, collected his prize money and keeled over, unconscious. His time: 573 hours, 4 minutes and 34 seconds. John Salo took second prize of $10,000. Canada's famed marathoner, Philip Gravnille, took the $5,000 third prize, while the fourth place pot of $2,500 went to a bartender from Cleveland, Mike Joyce.

C. C. Pyle, who lost money on the "event of the decade," lamented, "There's been a lot of talk about how much the boys suffered. But not one of them suffered more than I did." Pyle maintained until his death in 1939, at age fifty-five, that his race ushered in the "golden age of sports' footwear." Little could he have dreamed of the pricey running shoes of the 1980s (see page 433).

Dance Marathons

> Of all the crazy competitions ever invented, the dancing marathon wins by a considerable margin of lunacy.
>
> *—New York World*

The object of these strange contests, which began in 1923 as part of the marathon mania sweeping the country, was to see which couple could outdance

Dance marathon in Washington, D.C.

all the others. Style meant nothing; endurance was paramount. The phenomenon would reach a second frenzied peak in the Thirties, when record numbers of unemployed men and women desperately danced as much for the modest prize money as to lose themselves in the oblivion of fatigue.

"A pageant of fatigue," said one newspaper. "A macabre modern equivalent of a homicidal Roman gladiatorial spectacle," criticized another. Hearst's *New York American* argued that "no anthropoid ape could possibly have had descendants that could display such hopeless idiocy." The *Literary Digest* concluded, "If such tests of stamina as the marathon dances ever were exacted as punishment, they would be deemed cruel." Every major city in America attempted to ban marathon dancing—often to little avail. In New Jersey, the Society for the Prevention of Cruelty to Animals had a marathon promoter arrested because, as an ASPCA official humanely explained, "We're interested in humans as well as animals."

Nonetheless, all across America young men and women staggered, collapsed, and picked each other up to the tune of fox trots and ballads played by Victrolas or live bands. First prize might be a thousand dollars, but the work was arduous. Spectators crowded dance halls to witness the stay-awake antics of champion marathon couples—who abused each other with smelling salts and ice packs, as well as kicks, pinches, and punches. Equally of interest were the behavioral changes that began to occur on the sixth or seventh day of continual dancing. Women would grow to hate their partners and scream and scratch at them, while men often resorted to more physical violence. The dance marathon did not display humanity at its best. Hallucinations were frequent and fearful, dancers often fleeing the floor, pursued by imaginary villains. The last couple standing won. Seldom were they still on speaking terms. A Chicago marathon ran for 119 days, dancers catnapping in each other's arms, leaving the floor only to use a bathroom.

Why did people do it?

The prize money was often a minor incentive, especially in the Twenties. A major motive was faddishness. It was a young people's wacky vogue, a way to be part of the in crowd, and to rise, through winning, to its top. The dance marathon conferred brief celebrity status on the winners, melded with the national mania for endurance feats, and offered spectators a certain sex appeal lacking in flagpole sitting, chair rocking, and the Bunion Derby.

Rules stipulated that couples simply had to maintain perpetual motion—shuffling, dragging, or dozing—and only the soles of the feet were allowed to touch the dance floor. Some contests permitted brief hourly breaks and time-outs for high-energy snacks, but all sleeping was done on the dance floor, one groggy partner at a time. Waking from nightmares was commonplace, and great spectacle for onlookers. Around the nation there was actually a dance marathon circuit, where couples traveled as if circus acts.

Dance Derby of the Century.   This much-touted Madison Square Garden dancefest began on June 10, 1928, the hare-brainchild of dance marathon promoter Milton Crandall, former newspaperman turned Hollywood press agent. Ninety-one energetic couples commenced dancing to the hit song "Let Me Call You Sweetheart." On the sidelines were shoe salesmen (hawking replacements), and a myriad array of vendors offering food, drink, and foot care salves. Breaks were taken hourly, so couples could be quickly revitalized by sideline Swedish masseurs.

Periodic surveys were taken of the dancers to determine how many former lovers currently hated each other. In the marathon's 131st hour, half the couples still on the dance floor (twenty-eight) could not bear the sight of the partners they clung to. Arguments often got nasty, and onlookers, who paid a $2.20 admission fee, cheered for their favorite "hero" or "heroine." Since there was no such thing as CNN continual coverage, people depended on morning newspapers for a tally of still-standing contestants, as well as flashes on who hated whom, which included verbatim bitching between couples. At the close of the first week of virtual nonstop dancing, the New York Board of Health felt compelled to monitor the physical condition of the remaining thirteen couples with on-the-scene checkups. "They'll be all right," reported one doctor, "if they escape insanity."

During the marathon's 428th hour, it was stopped by the Board of Health commissioner, Louis Harris. Harris had learned that a twenty-one-year-old contestant, who had quit the competition, was hospitalized in critical condition, having collapsed on a Manhattan street corner, vomiting blood. At the marathon's conclusion, there were nine couples on the dance floor, and more than seven thousand spectators on the sidelines. It was hard to say which group was crazier.

As mentioned, the dance marathon craze experienced a revival in the Thirties. It was more frenzied then, with more couples in need of the prize money. That fad would result in numerous reported deaths, and in 1933 the governor of New York signed a bill that made any dancing beyond a seemingly reasonable eight hours a criminal offense. The law may still be on the books.

Miss America Contest

It is fitting that in an era hell-bent on public competitions as a means of gaining individual notoriety, the Miss America contest was created in Atlantic City in 1921. Conceived by the town fathers and local newspapermen, its goal was not only to catapult a milk-fed Miss Nobody into an overnight celebrity, but to promote the seaside resort; specifically to extend tourist season beyond the traditional Labor Day cutoff well into September. And it did keep hotels booked for additional weeks. This premiere pop culture beauty contest, though, has come a long way from the days of its first winner, sixteen-year-old Margaret Gorman (30–25–32), to, say, the success of a Phyllis George (36–24–36).

Today, the televised contest is an annual phenomenon, commanding the attention of nearly half of Saturday night viewers. But the first competition was a modest affair that featured only eight women, with most of the public attention centered on the pre–Bert Parks host, called King Neptune, who was actually Hudson Maxim of the armaments-inventing Maxims. Contestants then represented cities, not states, and qualified by winning a hometown popularity contest. Once in Atlantic City they participated in a "bathing revue," for which even the all-male orchestra donned swimsuits. That was equality.

The hedonism of the Twenties made the contest possible and contributed to its rapidly expanding success—and criticism. In 1922, its second year, fifty-seven cities sent young hopefuls, which the *Atlantic City Daily Press* boldly described as "piquant jazz babies who shook the meanest kind of shoulders, pink-skinned beauties of all types." The "roller chair parade" down the famed Boardwalk, reported the *Press,* showed off "Tanned athletic girls, bare of limb, shapely of figure . . . bejeweled favorites of the harem, stately colonial dames in hoop skirts, with black eyes peeping coyly from behind waving fans." Several girls flaunted the coming vogue of bobbed hair (which was considered by the judges as too radical). A judge that year was the artist Norman Rockwell. Evening gown competition was added in 1924.

In the Twenties the contest already served as a vehicle for the new celebrity-creating mill that was moving pictures. A Motion Picture Ball was held on the Steel Pier in 1922, where film tests were made for each contestant, in search for "a girl who'd 'click' in the pictures." Despite the decade's hedonism, the Miss America contest aroused widespread criticism from several quarters. The Trenton, New Jersey, YWCA worried about the "grave dangers from unscrupulous persons to which the girls were exposed." Before the competition, a spokesperson said, the girls "were splendid examples of innocent and pure womanhood. Afterwards their heads were filled with vicious ideas"—such as money, career, and self. The *New York Times* damned the contest as a "reprehensible way to advertise Atlantic City."

Dumb Doras.   When the first few young winners turned out to be, excuse the bluntness, airheads, contest officials sought out a different type of entrant. "This year the contest will be on a higher plane than ever," promised the *Daily Press* in 1925, "and its fair participants will represent pastors' daughters, school teachers, college girls and femininity generally of the most desirable type." When criticism of the titillating aspects of bathing suit competition refused to be silenced, that revue was dropped—as was the Miss America contest itself in 1927.

The problem was simple: The kind of girl entering the contest was not yet a noble representative of American womanhood, but most often was, in the slang phrase of the day, a dumb Dora. Indeed, when the contest was resumed in 1935, promoters attempted to skirt criticism by instituting a talent competition to convince the public each girl was more than just a body beauty. "In the past," read an official press release, "good looks usually sufficed to win both the coveted trophy and perhaps a stage and screen career. This time there will be no 'beautiful but dumb' Dora."

The caliber of girl was more upscale—that is, she had more education. The next year, 1936, Atlantic City Mayor Charles White opened the pageant with the reminder, "We are past the time when beauty parades are in the nature of floor shows . . . This is a cultural event seeking a high type of beauty." While the Twenties idolized the free-spirited flapper and spawned such liberties as couples' dance marathons, it wanted its representative Miss neither to sport bobbed hair nor to dance the Charleston.

King Tut

Scarab rings and Tut nickel cigars, turquoise Tut bracelets and hieroglyphic-print dresses and handbags, dining chairs in the upright style of Egyptian thrones, and American newborns across the land named Tutter (a boy) and Tuttie (a girl) after, of course, the Egyptian Pharaoh Tutankhamen—these are a sampling from the first wave of Tutmania that swept America from 1923 until the stock market crash. The fad enjoyed an enormous revival in the 1970s, sparked then by an exhibition of Tut treasures at major museums.

The initial fad, fanned by extraordinary newspaper coverage, owed to the discovery in 1922 of the eighteen-year-old pharaoh's intact burial chamber by

Howard Carter with statue from King Tut's tomb.

English Egyptologist Howard Carter. The public quickly learned that inside the tomb the boy king lay within a nest of three coffins, the innermost of solid gold, the outer two of gold hammered over wooden frames. On the king's head was a golden portrait mask, and priceless pieces of jewelry and amulets adorned the mummy and its wrappings. The coffins were surrounded by four shrines of hammered gold, while other rooms were crammed with furniture, statues, clothes, a chariot, and weapons. In life Tut, who reigned from 1361 to 1352 B.C., had little claim to fame, having died in his teens. But through the treasure trove in his tomb he became the most famous of Egypt's male rulers, with, to use a modern measure of celebrity, a Q rating perhaps equal to Cleopatra's. His name was on the lips of millions of Americans.

Many readers of this book probably lived through, if not participated in, the Tut tumult of the Seventies. As some fifty-five priceless tomb treasures toured the country, more than four hundred manufacturers rushed to create and cash in on the pharaoh fad, marketing Tut coffee mugs, wallpaper, needlepoint pillows, and solid gold artifacts; there was even a Tut spoof song, interpreted with funky Egyptian mannerisms by comedian Steve Martin. Department stores like Bloomingdale's and Macy's devoted aisles and cosmetic counters to

Tut paraphernalia, which included exotic kohllike eye paint. But the Seventies madness was nothing compared to the first wave of Tutmania: Tut was the *longest-running* single fad of the Twenties. It was finally calmed only by the crash.

Why such endurance?

Sociologists point to the "intellectual overtones" of a fad based on a scientifically significant archaeological find. The average person, by owning even the most kitsch Tut artifact, became associated with, and participated in, one of the major unearthings of the century. And to be able to talk socially about the tomb and its boy king—Egyptology nonetheless—carried a cachet not applicable to conversations about, say, fads of Frisbees, hula hoops, and the like. In the Twenties, a long-dead Egyptian king was as well known to Americans as such heavyweights as Babe Ruth and Jack Dempsey. Tut was "the top," to paraphrase Porter.

Model Electric Trains

Ninety-five percent of all avid train collectors save Lionel models, with the likes of American Flyer, Marx, and Ives toys coming in a distant second. The passion for Lionel trains first peaked in the Twenties, in the wake of a war that left German toymakers, long dominant in the model train business, smarting from production losses and the worst kind of international press. It was anti-German sentiment, coupled with an extraordinary new line of eye-catching cars by Lionel—in bold colors—that made the perfect Twenties Christmas gift, for fathers as well as sons, a set of electric trains. Trains were *the* boy's toy of the decade.

The Twenties heyday for electric trains was a long time gestating. Trains were one of the first toys "electrified," appearing not long after Edison patented his light bulb—though the lack of such necessities as dry-cell batteries, transformers, and a network of neighborhood power lines long doomed the toys to low sales. Then, electric models were a rich man's luxury. Santa, though, soon appeared in the guise of one Joshua Lionel Cowen.

Lionel and a Christmas Tradition.   Born in New York in 1880, Joshua Lionel Cowen showed a passion for trains by age seven, when he carved a locomotive out of wood and fitted it with a small steam engine—which, unfortunately, exploded. His tinkering over the years produced the first electric doorbell, and a battery-illuminated flower pot that failed as a novelty item but, minus the pot, left a cylinder of batteries that became the start of Eveready Flashlights. In 1903 Joshua Lionel issued his first catalog of toy trains, which included a derrick car, a track switch, and a suspension bridge. His 1908 line offered a cattle car, a boxcar, an oil tank car, a coal car, a day coach, and a Pullman, soon to be followed by cabooses, baggage cars, and elaborate bridges and tunnels. By 1915 Lionel was advertising trains in ten national magazines. But the model train business was dominated by German firms, such familiar names as Marklin and Bing. To Lionel, and to the Chicago company of American Flyer, the war was an unexpected boon; it forever changed the balance of toy train power.

On the eve of war in Europe, Lionel introduced one of the largest, sturdiest, and most brightly colored enameled train sets, measuring almost three feet in length and competitively priced at $10. First it became patriotic to "buy American," then, with German manufacturers locked out of the American market for almost five years, it became essential to buy American if parents wanted to give gifts of electric trains. After the war, American toy manufacturers persuaded the government that the toy industry in the United States, nascent and infinitely promising, should be protected from foreign competition by high protectionist tariffs.

Blue Comet and State Sets. By 1921 a million Lionel sets were chugging around tracks in American homes. Lionel trains were, aficionados agreed, the most realistic models ever manufactured. The company's full-color catalogs highlighted Lionel's standard gauge (a measure of track width) trains, that became the yardstick against which other train manufacturers were judged.

The fad actually hit in 1924. Trains had been strong sellers, but that year Lionel introduced a line of trains that had been specially created for him by an Italian firm, La Precisa. Larger, sturdier, elaborately appointed with brass trim, the set created a new toy aesthetic; and whereas trains previously were drab brown or dark olive green, the new cars shone in brilliant blues, light greens, primary reds and yellows—colors never before seen on American toy trains. Every American boy dreamed of owning the giant Blue Comet or State set. Lionel had turned the electric train into an American toy classic. As fads go, trains were that rarity then and now: a father-son endeavor, a common ground on which the two celebrate boyhood—one for the first time, the other for the second time around.

There is a note of irony to this Twenties craze. With sales soaring, in 1929 one American manufacturer introduced an elaborate gold-colored train, pulled by a giant engine, to celebrate the close of the golden decade—golden in terms of hefty train sales as well as boom times in general. The model, intended to be a Christmas bestseller, debuted just before the October stock market crash and was named the Prosperity Special. The train went the way of prosperity.

Baby Boom Train Craze: A Fad Revisited. On June 5, 1946, the Lionel Company threw a pre–Father's Day open house party for adult males at its Manhattan showroom. To be admitted to this showcase of postwar train innovations, men had to present evidence of fatherhood. Over five hundred fathers showed up, offering children's birth certificates, maternity ward bills, family photographs, crayon drawings in a child's hand, even folded diapers. The marketing gimmick played on the industry fact that fathers bought train sets as much for themselves as for their children. That day, the dads were impressed by the dazzling verisimilitude on display: freight cars with magnetic lifting cranes, ore-dumping cars, conveyors to load coal, oil derricks that bubbled, a water tower that pumped fluids, billowing smokestacks, authentic train whistling, and a refrigerator car in which a man unloads miniature milk churns onto a loading dock.

The war hiatus had been worth the wait. These dads and others were already responsible for the burgeoning baby boom birth rate, and over the next several years the sale of toy trains mirrored that climb. Once again a set of trains became the ideal Christmas gift for boys. Sales at Lionel Company alone hit a record $10 million in 1946, and topped $21 million in 1950. By then, a train set was a symbol of the American family, happy, prosperous, and productive of offspring. Joshua Lionel Cowen was proclaimed a national leisure time hero. *Reader's Digest* titled a biographical article: "He Put Tracks Beneath the Christmas Tree," and *Newsweek*'s December 1952 homage to him appeared in the season when American parents bought a record number of trains as Christmas gifts. The *New York Times* reported that train manufacturers were having a hard time keeping up with orders. Model railroading had reached the proportions of a national mania. Dwight and Mamie Eisenhower posed for White House pictures with a Lionel set under the tree for grandson David.

Though the electric train would remain a Christmas toy staple, the second boom waned by the mid-Fifties, stampeded by a torrent of competing fads, from Davy Crockett hats to Howdy Doody puppets, from Frisbees to hula hoops, from Silly Putty to Wiffle Ball (see Chapter 7). Though these other crazes would bask in a brief glory, then fade (some even from memory), the electric train made that rare transition from a fad item to an American classic toy—and a collector's expensive hobby; early Lionel trains, like the State set, have brought auction prices of over $8,000. The toy train is part of the nation's pastime heritage.

Airplane Travel

Like the first cars, early airplanes had more fad appeal than practical application. To fly in the Twenties was even more daring and dangerous than to motor at the turn of the century. In each case one risked life and limb. Flying—like early automobiling—was a trendy luxury affordable only by the rich few. And following Lindbergh's transatlantic flight to Paris, wealthy Americans took to the skies in increasing numbers.

Today air travel is commonplace. Seven out of every ten American adults have ventured aloft at least once. Couples conduct marriages bicoastally. Politicians stump state to state by plane, often two states a day. Vital transplant organs are rushed from Minnesota to Texas; fresh-caught Maryland crabs are savored that same night in Los Angeles. Air travel has shrunk the globe and contracted time in ways even Lucky Lindy could not have imagined in the Twenties.

But the fact is, most adults in the Twenties, two decades after the Wright brothers flew at Kitty Hawk, probably could not, if pressed, have thought of many practical, everyday uses for flying machines. Of course, World War I had demonstrated that planes added a new dimension to warfare. Then ex–war pilots demonstrated that planes could be used to put on exciting air shows. If in the early Twenties a civilian flew, most likely it was as a five-minute "amusement ride" offered at an air show. A fad.

What transformed aviation from trendy flights for the wealthy into a commercial commonplace?

Air Mail.   More than impressive wartime flying, more than aerial showmanship, it was the transportation of mail by plane that ushered in the age of air travel. In fact, most of the celebrated names in early civil aviation, including Lindbergh, were former mail pilots. In brief: Air flying companies outbid the railroads for transporting the mails, then one by one the new mail carriers merged into major passenger carriers. Western Air Express, a mail ancestor of TWA, began passenger service in 1926.

Air mail did not begin auspiciously. On the first flight, a Washington–New York run, takeoff was aborted because in the excitement the pilot had forgotten to fill the tank. When he did ascend into the clouds, he became lost and was forced down in Maryland. The mail went on by train to New York. Planes as yet had no radios and few navigational instruments, and thirty-one of the first forty air mail pilots on the New York-Chicago run died in crashes. Often the mail burned or was widely scattered. After Congress passed a bill in the early Twenties backing airmail, service improved, and the price of air-postage dropped from 24 cents to a dime for a half-ounce envelope.

Business travelers were among the first to take to the skies. By 1929 "Lindbergh's Line," Transcontinental Air Transport (later TWA), offered scheduled flights from coast to coast. However, you traveled 2,000 miles by air, and 1,000 miles overnight by railroad, since night flights were extremely dangerous. Typically a traveler flew by day, landed before dusk, boarded a train for night passage, then transferred to another plane after daybreak. The enervating experience could take several days. Yet it was also exhilarating, the avant garde way to travel. By the close of the decade, Wall Street believed that air travel might indeed prove to be a profitable endeavor.

Stewardesses.   In 1930, a year after Amelia Earhart flew solo across the Atlantic, United Airlines originated stewardess service: Eight registered nurses were hired for planes on the Chicago to San Francisco route. Why nurses? Cabins were not pressurized, flying was routinely rough, and passengers were frequently sick or stressed out. In those days stewardesses were encouraged to slap a hysterical or hyperventilating flyer. Thus, what began the Twenties decade as a daring five-minute air show fad ended it as the century's newest form of commercial transportation.

Ticker-Tape Parade

Charles A. Lindbergh was the Twenties' greatest hero. The historic arrival of his *Spirit of St. Louis* in France on May 21, 1927, was taken as the ultimate triumph of American rugged individualism, and on his return he received what was probably the greatest outpouring of public adulation in American history.

New Yorkers lined up in the streets ten deep to take part in the biggest ticker-tape parade ever seen; estimates placed the number at 4 million people, more than half the city's population.

But the American pop culture phenomenon of the ticker-tape parade through lower Manhattan began in the decade of the Oughts. The earliest recording of a spontaneous tossing of ticker tape from building windows oc curred on October 28, 1886, when Wall Street revelers celebrated the dedication of the Statue of Liberty. The first official parade was held in 1910 in honor of Teddy Roosevelt, upon his return from a fifteen-month hunting trip to Africa. The parade route, a mile-long stretch up Broadway from Battery Park to City Hall, between skyscrapers, became known as the Canyon of Heroes for all the notables driven along its course. After the parades for Roosevelt and Lindbergh came tons of ticker-tape litter for:

General Dwight D. Eisenhower: 1945. The war hero and future president was celebrated with a record of ticker-tape trash, an estimated 5,438 tons.

John Glenn: 1962. Supposedly the largest parade in New York history, it honored the first American to orbit the Earth. The festivities generated 3,474 tons of paper.

Neil Armstrong, Michael Collins, and Buzz Aldrin: 1969. It was a 300-ton confetti-fest thrown for the first two men on the moon, Armstrong and Aldrin; Collins orbited in the spacecraft.

New York Mets: 1969. After they beat the Baltimore Orioles to win their first World Series, Gil Hodges's baseball team was showered with 578 tons of paper.

American Hostages: 1981. After fifteen months of captivity in Iran, the hostages were welcomed with 971 tons of ticker tape and sundry trash— including endless streams of yellow ribbon.

New York Mets: 1986. More than 2 million fans, tossing 648 tons of trash, cheered the Mets for beating the Boston Red Sox in the World Series. It was the last ticker-tape parade to be held in the Canyon of Heroes.

Nelson Mandela: 1990. New York purchased 150 miles of inch-wide "ticker tape" ribbon to honor the South African. The clean-up required twenty-nine collection trucks, eighteen dump trucks, thirty-nine front-end loaders, and sixty smaller pickup trucks, at a cost of $145,000.

As of this writing, the last parade was for the Persian Gulf troops.

Ticker-tape parades are a uniquely American phenomenon.

DANCE CRAZES

Runnin' Wild, Lost Control

Charleston, shimmy, black bottom, and varsity drag. The boyish flapper wearing her trendy "kiss-proof" lipstick and her dashing sheik with his pocket flask of bootleg gin found no better way to snub their noses at the "drys"—those teetotalers who'd pushed for Prohibition—than to dance with shameless abandon at a speakeasy. Jazz music abounded at parties. Cigarette ads beckoned women to "Reach for a Lucky Instead of a Sweet." And Charlestoning couples flicked their knees open and closed with what was called "peekaboo insouciance." Pastors from the pulpit roared their protest: The jazz belles were nothing but Jezebels; civilization was *really* going to be destroyed this time. One dance came to typify the decade's fun-loving wildness more than any other.

Charleston

All the rage from 1923 to 1926, the Charleston was danced in numerous variations after its high heyday. Perhaps no dance before or after has typified a social period so thoroughly as the Charleston. It was performed by the

Charleston.

decade's "flaming youth" (named after a book and silent film of that title). Swiveling on the balls of their feet, balancing pigeon-toed, swaying the body side to side, and knocking the knees with their hands in a maddening frenzy, the young were "doing it, doing it."

The origin of the Charleston is not completely clear. It's believed to have begun among blacks in South Carolina—or possibly along the levees near New Orleans. What is known is that a principal choreographer of the *Ziegfeld Follies,* Ned Wayburn, saw the steps in the South and introduced them to dance-mad New Yorkers in an October 1923 revue, *Runnin' Wild.* Audience members were seen attempting the footwork as they left the theater. Rechoreographed by two black dancers, Cecil Mack and James Johnson, the Charleston became even wilder as it swept Manhattan clubs, then took the country by storm. By 1925 there were supposed to be at least four hundred different steps to the dance—none dignified.

In fact, the American Society of Dance Teachers attempted to "dignify" the dance by removing its wild kicks and stipulating that the feet not be raised too far off the floor. But without the free-spirited leg gyrations the dance lost its *raison d'etre.*

Not exactly everybody was "doing it." Condemned by waltzers and two-steppers, the Charleston generated intense hostility—more than any previous dance. Whereas animal dances had been "silly," the Charleston was "immoral." "I have no objection to a person dancing their feet off," said a New Jersey mayor, "but it's best to keep away from the Charleston." Many colleges (like William and Mary) banned it on campus, which did much for its popularity.

Abroad, the *London Daily Mail* deemed the dance "reminiscent only of Negro orgies"—until, that is, the Prince of Wales (the future Edward VIII) performed a wicked Charleston. Suddenly all of England was exuberantly kicking up its heels. At the height of the condemnation, forty-four Charlestoners were killed in Boston when the roof of the Pickwick Dance Club collapsed. The tragedy was blamed on the "unnatural stress" that the dance's flailing put on the building. Fear that other dance halls—which had, of course, survived vigorous polkas, pounding square dances, and galloping fox trots—might succumb to the Charleston's swaying allowed a number of establishments to imaginatively ban the dance: "This Building Cannot Withstand the Charleston."

Black Bottom

At the time when the most feverish devotion to the Charleston was waning in 1926, a new dance, employing strong Caribbean-style hip movements, was featured in a Broadway revue, *The George White Scandals of 1926.* In those days, several catchy show-stopping steps were enough to launch a dance craze. The energetic movements included gliding, skipping, leaping, stamping, and, not least, flaunting one's bottom, as do courting baboons.

The dance is thought to have originated among blacks in the Mississippi Delta. And if this is true, the name black bottom seems straightforward enough. Other authorities, however, claim the dance was named after the Black Bottom district in Nashville, Tennessee. The fad's sexually explicit posturing scandalized the older generation, which, in turn, egged young dancers to flaunt their backsides even more exaggeratedly. Other steps included Charleston-like knee swaying, thigh slapping, and heel scooting.

The following year, 1927, a Broadway show spawned another dance craze, the **varsity drag,** performed on stage by Zelma O'Neal in *Good News.* The steps were loosely based on the Charleston.

Shimmy

The shimmy was yet another Charleston spin-off to garner a fad following, and it, too, debuted first on stage. The word shimmy was Twenties jargon for a sheer French chemise, and when performer Gilda Gray extemporaneously began to twist and slither, claiming she was "shaking my shimmy," a new dance was launched. It became Gray's signature step, and to perform it in a tasseled or fringed dress broadcast the height of abandon. Soon America was doing the shimmy, and singing the hit song "I Wish I Could Shimmy Like My Sister Kate." In its turning in of knees and toes the dance resembled the Charleston, while in its vigorous wiggling of the backside it displayed elements of the black bottom. The fad enjoyed a short if passionate life.

Rumba and Son of Rumba

Like the tango of the Teens, the rumba (some spell it rhumba), a Cuban import that fired the dance world in the late Twenties, was, in its original form, highly sexual and born out of exhibitionism in Caribbean brothels. It reached America in a tamed version, called the *son*, which had movements slower, more sentimental, and more coquettish than the original. It's the *son* that was exported around the world and is danced to this day as the rumba. As a dance craze, it is significant because the rumba set the musical taste and welcoming mood for a wave of Latin dance vogues that would follow—like the samba, mambo, calypso, bossa nova, and cha-cha.

Unlike the tango, which is smooth and flowing, the rumba's signature is staccato. The hips are swayed by keeping the feet close together, and all movement is from the waist down; upper torso and shoulders should be held so erect that the dancer could balance a book on his or her head. It became the national dance of Cuba, and style-wise it blends African and Spanish erotic folk elements.

Dance historians believe the steps originally sprang from reenactments of daily farm life among peasants. "The courtship of barnyard fowl," writes one authority, "is suggested in the woman's long ruffled skirt that represents a fowl's tail feathers; the male dancer's ruffled shirt is symbolic of a rooster's neck plumage." In such animal mimicry, the circling of partners around each other is "representative of the circling patterns made by fowl during their courtship procedure."

That certainly would have been news to dancers in the Twenties and

Thirties, who donned ruffled rumba skirts and Ricky Ricardo–like shirts. The craze caught on in ballrooms not only because the dance offered novel steps, but also because it required a special dress-up costume and distinctive musical instruments: maracas (painted gourds), bongo drums, and claves (short wooden sticks that are struck together to create a counterrhythm). For a fad-crazy decade, the dance came with an entire package of novelties. George Raft and Carole Lombard rumbaed their way to silver screen stardom.

POPULAR SONGS

Ain't We Got Fun

"Not much money, oh but honey, / Ain't we got fun?"—crooned the lyrics of the song usually accepted as the credo of the decade of the Twenties. "There's nothing surer, / The rich get richer and the poor get poorer . . ." But the flaming youth weren't complaining, satisfied with speakeasies, bootleg spirits, fad dances, and sex without inhibitions. "We were rude, rough, tough and boisterous," wrote one observer. "The sky was the limit . . . and jazz was the inevitable music of such an unrestrained society."

Though jazz was not an overnight phenomenon, beginning almost two decades earlier in the South, it stamped its rhythms so indelibly on the Twenties that the era would be forever remembered as the Jazz Age. Jazz (or "jass" or "jasz"; our current spelling was first authenticated by the *New York Times* on February 2, 1917) spread something like a cholera epidemic: breaking out in New Orleans, appearing in a strong strain in that "toddlin' town" Chicago, then infecting to various degrees New York, Pittsburgh, Cincinnati, and Atlantic City, finally striking California before being carried abroad to London and Paris.

Serious composers quickly warmed to the syncopated sound. The era had a jazz ballet (by French modernist Darius Milhaud), jazz piano suites (by Paul Hindemith), a jazzy sonata (by Maurice Ravel), and an outstanding piano concerto, "Rhapsody in Blue," by songwriter George Gershwin. None of this "jazz" was, of course, the real stuff, as heard in New Orleans and Chicago, or on one of those trendy excursions by white society folk to Harlem's "in" all-night spots. Harlem was chic. Harlem was hot.

The rage to visit spots like the Cotton Club began in 1921 when a lively musical, *Shuffle Along*—written, produced and performed by blacks—became a smash Broadway hit. Other "black" shows, like *Runnin' Wild* and *Chocolate Dandies,* kept playgoers hopping from Shubert Alley to Harlem dance floors. Harlem in the Twenties had no fewer than eleven night spots that *Variety* called "class white-trade night clubs," plus some five hundred lesser, lowdown jazz speakeasies.

But fitting as jazz was for the tempo of the times, the majority of bestselling pop hits of the Twenties were not even slightly jazzy. They were, as we're about to see, sentimental ballads, old-fashioned waltzes, and nonsense songs.

The decade was so rich with memorable tunes that perhaps it's best to stroll through the era year by year.

Look for the Silver Lining: 1920

As the decade opened, the most famous speakeasy in Manhattan was Jack and Charlie's at 21 West 52nd Street, known to the in crowd (then and now) as 21. Prohibition and women's suffrage became society-shaking realities. And a nascent communication form called radio debuted when KDKA in Pittsburgh broadcast the Harding-Cox presidential election returns. To phone a friend in the year 1920, you no longer had to go through an operator; dial telephones were all the rage.

On stage in the *Ziegfeld Follies,* Fanny Brice introduced **Rose of Washington Square;** it was such a hit that year that the composer wrote for her **Second-Hand Rose,** a smash months later. Americans were also buying sheet music and records to learn **When My Baby Smiles at Me** and the sweetly sentimental **I'll Be with You in Apple Blossom Time.** A musical revue called *Sally* had audiences leaving the theater singing three show-stopping hits: **Wild Rose, Whip-poor-will,** and one of Jerome Kern's best songs, "Look for the Silver Lining."

I'm Just Wild About Harry: 1921

On March 5 of that year the Little Restaurant opened in Manhattan's theater district, later to be relocated and renamed Sardi's, beginning a "first night" dining tradition. The new silent screen star Rudolph Valentino made his first two movies, *The Sheik* and *The Four Horsemen of the Apocalypse,* and, capitalizing on his popularity, a composer scored a hit with **The Sheik of Araby.**

Fanny Brice, in the *Follies of 1921,* not only caused a sensation with "Second-Hand Rose" (as mentioned), but moved audiences to tears with her rendition of **My Man,** a tragic French ballad, "Mon Homme," which Brice made her own.

The all-black show that made Harlem hot, *Shuffle Along,* opened and produced three hits: The title song, **Shuffle Along,** a melodic ballad, **Love Will Find a Way,** and the wildly popular "I'm Just Wild About Harry." In a similar vein, women across the country were singing **Ma—He's Making Eyes at Me**—while Ma might have been humming to herself **There'll Be Some Changes Made.** It was also the year in which the decade's carefree credo scored: "Ain't We Got Fun?" And composer Irving Berlin, who'd had so many hits in the previous decade, began the Twenties with the haunting **All by Myself.** He'd have a hit almost every year.

'Way Down Yonder in New Orleans: 1922

The King Tut fad was about to burst on the world; Egyptologist Howard Carter had opened the boy ruler's tomb, and for a time newspapers highlighted little

Fanny Brice.

else. Gangland violence had not yet peaked in Chicago, and all America was singing **Chicago (That Toddlin' Town);** as well as the jazzy **Toot, Toot, Tootsie! (Good-bye).** Jazz was being celebrated up in Harlem and " 'Way Down Yonder in New Orleans," while flaming youth was **Runnin' Wild,** dancing to **I Wish I Could Shimmy Like My Sister Kate,** staying out till **Three O'Clock in the Morning,** more often than not exchanging a **Kiss in the Dark.** Yet nothing could be finer than the year's top hit: **Carolina in the Morning.** For silliness there was **You Tell Her, I S-t-u-t-t-e-r,** and for sentiment **My Rambler Rose.**

Yes! We Have No Bananas: 1923

No nonsense song of the decade was more popular. Songwriters Frank Silver and Irving Cohn introduced their number in a Long Island club. It was based, they said, on an actual event in which a Greek fruit grocer who had yet to master English spoke in a hilarious mixture of positives and negatives, one day answering the inquiry, "Do you have any bananas?" with "Yes! We have no bananas."

Mirror-image song titles enjoyed a vogue, with **I Won't Say I Will, But I Won't Say I Won't,** causing a moment's reflection; the straightforward **Mamma Loves Papa—Papa Loves Mamma;** and the seemingly vengeful

I Cried for You, Now It's Your Turn to Cry Over Me—this last leaving one to question, **Who's Sorry Now.** Love spats aside, there was the nostalgic **That Old Gang of Mine.**

It was the year that blues artist Bessie Smith, then twenty-nine years old, began to record her hits for Columbia records. *Billboard* later reported: "Following the success of her first blues recording 'Downhearted Blues,' which sold 780,000 copies in less than six months, she will make twelve records a year for Columbia at $125 a side, with an option for twelve more at $150."

California, Here I Come: 1924

Noël Coward, the twenty-five-year-old *enfant terrible* of the British theater, launched two fads (neither songs): wearing turtleneck sweaters and conducting business from bed. Bed was also the perfect place to do the season's biggest craze, crossword puzzles.

Foreign composers scored hits with the show *Rose-Marie* (by Rudolf Friml), which included the popular song **Indian Love Call.** The Sigmund Romberg musical *The Student Prince* produced a string of hit singles: **Deep in My Heart, Dear; Serenade;** and the **Drinking Song,** which was quickly adopted by college Greeks (fraternities).

Couples danced to **Fascinating Rhythm,** pledged **It Had to Be You,** sipped **Tea for Two,** winked **I'll See You in my Dreams,** and dreamed "California, Here I Come." "Tea" appeared in the Chicago musical *No, No, Nanette* (which moved to New York the next year), and the show contained another smash: **I Want to Be Happy.** Gershwin, in addition to his "Fascinating Rhythm," also scored big with **Lady, Be Good** and **The Man I Love.** But George Gershwin's most memorable piece of music from the decade—if not his career—debuted on February 12, 1924, at New York's Aeolian Hall: **Rhapsody in Blue.** Eagerly awaited, the concert resulted in the kind of box-office mob scene associated more with modern rock extravaganzas. Critics either praised the concerto or condemned it, one describing it as "trite," "feeble," "vapid," "fussy" and "futile." Gershwin said the same of the critic.

Irving Berlin could not be overshadowed, producing two of his own hits: **All Alone** and **What'll I Do?** As waltz ballads they went against the trends of ragtime and jazz, but showed that the general public had a strong taste for the old-fashioned.

If You Knew Susie, Like I Know Susie: 1925

Who (Stole my Heart Away) had audiences singing as they poured out of Jerome Kern's show *Sunny,* ready to take to the streets of **Manhattan**—the latter by two young songwriters, Richard Rodgers and Lorenz Hart. It was the year of the Scopes monkey trial, which pitted Clarence Darrow against William Jennings Bryan in the battle between Genesis and Darwin. Bryan could have left the courtroom singing **I'm Sitting on Top of the World,** while the defeated Darrow might have hummed **Jealousy.** John Thomas Scopes, who had dared teach evolution, was not quite **Alabamy Bound,** returning to his native Dayton, Tennessee, though perhaps he was humming **Show Me the Way to Go Home (I'm Tired and I Wanna Go to Bed).** The lyrics for "Alabamy" were by Bud De Sylva, who outdid himself with the year's top hit, "If You Knew Susie, Like I Know Susie," memorably introduced by Al Jolson. Always at the top of the charts with a hit was Irving Berlin, this time with **Always.** Of **Sweet Georgia Brown,** someone, somewhere must have said **Yes, Sir, That's My Baby.**

Are You Lonesome Tonight: 1926

In 1926 Hollywood made an astonishing 750 feature films—some requiring only a few weeks of shooting. The first nonmusical talkie was *Don Juan,* starring John Barrymore. The silver screen lost its sheik to a ruptured appendix: Valentino's funeral in Manhattan caused mob hysteria, with women fans stripping the funeral home of everything but the carpets for souvenirs; "Are You Lonesome Tonight" aptly embodied their sentiments. Downtown on Broadway, the same musical that introduced the black bottom dance craze also produced the song hit, **The Birth of the Blues.**

Birds appeared in two pop numbers: **Bye, Bye, Blackbird** and **When the Red, Red Robin Comes Bob, Bob, Bobbin' Along.** Thematically Berlin was not far off with **Blue Skies,** while flowers were represented in **Tip Toe Through the Tulips,** and they might easily have been **Breezin' Along With the Breeze.**

The brothers Gershwin scored big with **Someone to Watch Over Me** and **Do-Do-Do.** But in saloons, at home pianos, among barbershop quartets, and with all the kids on the corner of the square, the year's sentimental favorite was **The Gang That Sang Heart of My Heart.**

I'm Looking Over a Four Leaf Clover: 1927

With Lucky Lindy having soloed across the Atlantic, songwriters squeezed the name of Charles Lindbergh into an unimaginable number of titles to boost sales. At one point, there were more than a hundred Lindbergh songs, the most popular being **Lucky Lindy,** and **When Lindy Comes Home.** Songwriting mania of this sort probably only occurred on that scale one time in the century.

That year the silent motion picture was slain by the release of Al Jolson's talkie, *The Jazz Singer,* which Jolson introduced with the quip "You ain't heard nothin' yet, folks." The melodrama, in which Jolson performed his blackface vaudeville rendition of **Mammy,** grossed $3.5 million in its first six months and revolutionized the movie industry. Jolson had taken the role for $75,000, refusing a smaller fee plus a share of the profits because he didn't think the talkie would be a hit.

Records were now selling in the millions and none was more popular that year than Gene Austin's rendition of **My Blue Heaven**—called an independent pop since it did not come from the score of a movie or show. Broadway revues, though, did continue to spin off the greatest number of hits: Gershwin's *Funny Face* introduced the fun-to-sing **'Swonderful**; *Good News* contained at least two hits: **The Varsity Drag** and the optimist's serenade, **The Best Things in Life Are Free;** and Rodgers and Hart's *Connecticut Yankee* had everybody singing the British-American slangfest **Thou Swell.** For the superstitious there was "I'm Looking Over a Four Leaf Clover."

Along the **Sidewalks of New York,** a couple walking **Side by Side** passed music stores offering the hits **Bless This House** and **Back in Your Own Back Yard.** The woman might overhear a passerby's compliment **Ain't She Sweet (Just A-walkin' Down the Street),** or catch a true admirer gasp **Girl of My Dreams.** On a dreary day the strolling couple might be advised to **Let a Smile Be Your Umbrella,** and when the sun returned they might glimpse **Me and My Shadow.**

The biggest hit machine of the year was *Show Boat,* which opened at the Ziegfeld Theater on December 27 to unanimous critical acclaim. The collaborative effort of Jerome Kern and Oscar Hammerstein II, based on Edna Ferber's novel, the musical—perhaps America's best opera—ran for 572 performances and had the country singing **Make Believe, Why Do I Love You? Bill, Can't Help Lovin' Dat Man,** and the tune Hammerstein described as "a song of resignation with a protest implied, sung by a character who is a rugged and untutored philosopher": **Ol' Man River.** This last became an "instant American folk classic."

For theater critics the year was unprecedented: 268 opening nights, to be covered by Manhattan's twenty-four daily newspapers. The city never again had so many openings, or so many papers.

Button Up Your Overcoat: 1928

George Gershwin scored a highbrow hit with his tone poem **An American in Paris.** A young man named Walt Disney produced his first animated film, a silent, featuring a nonspeaking mouse named Mickey; later Mickey would speak (Disney's own voice) in *Steamboat Willie.* **I Wanna Be Loved By You (Boop Boop-a-Doop)** became a hit when Helen Kane squealed out the coquettish lyrics in the Broadway show *Good Boy.* She immediately became known as the Boop-a-Doop Girl, and the type was spun off into successful movie and newspaper cartoons (for which Kane sued). The **Betty Boop** character would become a Thirties fad, with shapely Betty in a scanty black dress, with curly pixieish hair, a sexy single garter strap, and a soft, seducing voice. She launched a craze, and as one magazine punned, "She Boops to Conquer."

Far removed from the fictional Betty Boop was the real-life femme fatale Mae West, who in *Diamond Lil* popularized her own steamy version of **Frankie and Johnnie.**

Love was in the air in this year when the stock market was reaching stratospheric heights. In addition to Kane's desire "I Wanna Be Loved," there were couples who promised **I Can't Give You Anything But Love,** who swore **You're the Cream in My Coffee,** who straightforwardly stated **Let's**

Do It (Let's Fall in Love), who were known to be **Makin' Whoopee,** who used metaphor: **You Are Love,** who begged **Wanting You,** who admonished "Button Up Your Overcoat," who gave an ultimatum: **Love Me or Leave Me,** then had second thoughts: **Lover Come Back to Me.** All were hits of 1928.

Happy Days Are Here Again: 1929

The screen in 1929 offered many hit songs—for the first time more hits than the stage. And one movie with a prophetic title, *Chasing Rainbows,* contained a smash song with a sentiment soon to be most inappropriate: "Happy Days Are Here Again." By the end of October the stock market had nosedived into an $18 billion loss and Wall Street executives were said to be diving themselves, out of windows to their deaths. In retrospect, perhaps the most fittingly titled film of the time was *Hit the Deck,* with the most searching song **Why Was I Born?** The year had started off with people **Puttin' on the Ritz,** though it was soon darkened by the St. Valentine's Day massacre. Americans were buying up sheet music and records for **Ain't Misbehavin'** and **More Than You Know.** Cole Porter leaped into prominence with **You Do Something to Me** and **What Is This Thing Called Love?** But the most sensational number was the truly original **Star Dust,** which was written as a fast-paced ragtime piano solo by Hoagy Carmichael, then a recent graduate of Indiana University. Though the piece was popular as ragtime, it became a smash when a friend of Carmichael suggested the tempo be slowed and lyrics added.

Convictions in the Teapot Dome Scandal added to the year's grim side, but any optimist could feel happy singing **With a Song in My Heart,** even while **Singin' in the Rain**—the latter song from the *Hollywood Revue of 1929.* Around **Orange Blossom Time,** somewhere in America a young man must have felt that **Wedding Bells Are Breaking Up That Old Gang of Mine.** By late October 1929, though, many people found themselves **Without a Song, Moanin' Low,** and crying out Ethel Waters's hit of the year, **Am I Blue.**

BESTSELLING BOOKS

Day by Day in Every Way I Am Getting Better and Better

That famous maxim, seemingly so modern, is from a bestseller of the Twenties that typified a new kind of book craze called the "fad for diluted Freud"—which some might say has never subsided. It generated a cataract of self-help nonfiction during the decade, but the Norman Vincent Peale precursor was not the only trendsetting genre of the era. As we'll see, H. G. Wells's *The Outline of History,* published in 1921, kicked off a craze for "outline" books that simplified subjects like philosophy and science into easy-to-digest nuggets. Such bestsellers reflected the fact that more and more Americans were completing high school and going on to college, and everyone felt a need to be educated in a rapidly changing world where people like Freud and Einstein were continually discussed. As we progress through the decade's most popular books, we'll pass by many great books—classics that are read and reread today—that never got to annual bestsellerdom.

Diet and Health: Number One Nonfiction, 1924–25

While Americans were copying the Castles in dance and purchasing their first copy of a new magazine called *Reader's Digest,* Lulu Hunt Peters published a book that would remain on the bestseller list for a remarkable five years. Her *Diet and Health* had American women, striving for the flapper's boyish slimness, endlessly counting calories and measuring their waistlines. Thin was in, and the book climbed the list from number six in 1922, the year it debuted, to number one, selling well in the millions. Three years after publication it was outselling every other nonfiction book. An American obsession with thinness was born, which has never subsided and which continues to create annual bestsellers.

Body consciousness was not the only obsession in the Twenties. An aged French doctor, Emile Coué, launched a mental health fad with the 1923 publication of **Self-Mastery Through Conscious Auto-Suggestion,** which was number seven on the annual bestseller list. The small self-help book, which advocated extraordinary benefits from self-hypnosis (not unlike the modern claims made for subliminal audio cassettes), contained a phrase that was chanted throughout the decade: "Day by day in every way I am getting better and better." Women—and to a lesser extent men—were supposed to repeat that mental health wish as if it were a mantra, or a prayer, drumming the notion into the subconscious. Lectures—such as "How We Reach Our SubConscious Minds"—drew throngs of women at $25 a head for "psychological instruction for gaining and maintaining bodily fitness and mental poise and for building personality." Diluted Freud and pop psychology were all the rage, turning such books as **Outwitting Our Nerves** and **Why We Behave Like Human Beings** into nationwide bestsellers.

Etiquette: The Blue Book of Social Usage: Number One Nonfiction, 1923

The Twenties quest for self-improvement also turned Emily Post's book into the number one non-fiction of 1923. A prize-winning novelist and newspaperwoman from Tuxedo Park, New York, Emily Post wrote the book in the hope of removing "British" snobbishness and elitism from American manners. Her publisher, Funk & Wagnalls, marketed it employing a new trend in advertising: Embarrass people into believing they need a certain product. It had worked successfully with deodorants; now the great American offense was gauche social manners. Ads for the book charged that most Americans not only were ignorant of which fork to use and when, but suffered from slovenliness, halitosis, body odor, and general social ineptitude. This made for a large potential audience—which bought the book in like numbers. Throughout the decade, and beyond, in any social situation people asked, "What would Emily do?" and the book became a bible. Its author achieved such fame that "Post, Emily" became a dictionary entry.

The Outline of History: Number One
Nonfiction, 1921

In the year that Albert Einstein was awarded the Nobel prize in physics, a new bestseller fad began, kicked off by H. G. Wells and his *Outline of History*—the kind of everyman's overview of a subject that academics hated then (and many still do). No one previously had attempted an abridgment of such sweeping scope, and the work initially appeared in England in weekly installments. It was, as one reviewer said, "pure Wells, prejudices and brilliant insights, superficial judgments and intellectual depths all mixed up by no hand other than his." The public adored it; history had never been so fascinating. First issued in two volumes at a pricey $10.50, the book spent two years on the bestseller list, was reissued in one volume at $5, and spawned a craze for outlines.

The following year, 1922, **The Outline of Science,** by J. Arthur Thomson, was number six, while **The Story of Mankind** was Number Two in nonfiction. The trend for sweeping survey books continued, with **The New Decalogue of Science** as a 1924 bestseller, climaxing with the 1926 release of **The Story of Philosophy** by Will Durant. That was also the year for the formation of the Book-of-the-Month Club, which would introduce a novel and extremely successful method of marketing books through the mail.

Reviewers wrote that the reason for the success of outline books in the second decade of the century was that postwar America was attempting to assess its place in the scheme of things historic and scientific. In terms of the decade's penchant for endurance fads and energetic dances the era seemed frivolous, but the public's taste in nonfiction clearly revealed a more serious side, one concerned with self (in both mind and body), and with America's new place in world events. This is not to say that purely escapist books were not bestsellers: Robert Ripley's **Believe It or Not** was an immense success in 1929.

Main Street: Number One Fiction, 1921;
Babbitt: Number Four Fiction, 1923;
Arrowsmith: Number Seven Fiction, 1925;
Elmer Gantry: Number One Fiction, 1927;
Dodsworth: Number Two Fiction, 1929

In bestselling fiction, the Twenties belonged to Sinclair Lewis. While there were other writers of significance—F. Scott Fitzgerald, Ernest Hemingway,

Theodore Dreiser, D. H. Lawrence, James Joyce, Marcel Proust, and T. S. Eliot—not one of them made the *Publishers Weekly* annual bestseller list. If Sinclair Lewis shared the honor of top-sellerdom with anyone, it was Zane Grey, who also had a steady stream of successes: **The Man of the Forest,** number one in 1920; **The Mysterious Rider,** number three in 1921; **To the Last Man,** number nine in 1922; **The Wanderer of the Wasteland,** number eight in 1923; and **The Call of the Canyon,** number six in 1924.

Lewis began his string of bestsellers with the 1921 debunker of normal small-town American life, *Main Street.* It sold 295,000 copies its first year, and brought a new kind of realism into American popular fiction, which had been dominated, as we saw in the previous chapter, by romances and Western adventures (the latter a tradition upheld by Zane Grey). Next, in *Babbitt,* Lewis attacked the average businessman for an inbred crudeness, cussedness, and dearth of culture, enriching the language with the word Babbittry, synonymous with stifling middle-class loutishness. Any pompous bore became a Babbitt. The book was such a shocker abroad that one British reviewer, familiar with America, felt compelled to assure his audience that "America is not so ugly in speech, in background, in thought." In England, a glossary was published to explain the book's Americanisms: *doggone* was "a puritanical euphemism for damn," *ice-cream soda* a "ghastly hot-weather temperance drink," *jeans* meant "trousers," and a *kike* was "a Jew."

Lewis's third novel, *Arrowsmith,* which dealt unflatteringly with the medical profession, confirmed his place both in American literature and bestseller-dom—and it is the book thought to have been pivotal in his being awarded the Nobel prize. As unscrupulousness goes, *Elmer Gantry* did for the ministry what *Babbitt* had done for the business world and *Arrowsmith* for the medical establishment. As a debunker, Lewis was ideally suited for the decade's cynicism, an outgrowth of postwar disillusionment.

Other notable fiction bestsellers:

1921.   The Age of Innocence, Edith Wharton, number four. **The Sheik,** by Edith Hull, number six, was notable in that the popular novel became a movie vehicle for Rudolph Valentino.

1926.   Gentlemen Prefer Blondes, by Anita Loos, told the story of Lorelei Lee, who is "engaged to a gentleman in the button business." Edna Ferber's **Show Boat** was number eight, and in a short time it spawned a long-running musical, and eventually a movie.

1928.   The Bridge of San Luis Rey by Thorton Wilder, number one, with the story set in South America, attracted such immense and immediate fame that, according to *Publishers Weekly,* "the Pulitzer Prize committee departed from its usual custom of giving its award to a story laid in the United States."

1929.   All Quiet on the Western Front, by German-born Erich Maria Remarque, was the great anti-war novel of World War I. It appeared eleven years after the conflict's close and sold 300,000 copies its first year. The book was equally popular in Germany, though thousands of copies were later burned by the Nazis. The phrase "all quiet on the Western front" became a cliché in military communiques and newspaper reports during much of the trench warfare, a rather cynical expression to the troops who were stagnating or dying there, as shown by Remarque's novel.

Among the books published in the Twenties that *didn't* make the industry's annual bestseller list were some classics.

This Side of Paradise, by F. Scott Fitzgerald, was published in 1920. The book made him famous and launched a Fitzgerald cult such that he'd become the spokesman for the Jazz Age, but the public bought only fifty-two thousand copies. The twenty-three-year-old author glibly characterized his own book as "a novel about Flappers written for Philosophers." Even *The Great Gatsby,* published in 1925 and perhaps Fitzgerald's greatest work, did not elevate him to annual bestseller status. In fact, it sold fewer copies than *This Side,* though most critics forecast it would endure, and T. S. Eliot pronounced it "the first step that American fiction has taken since Henry James."

The Sun Also Rises, by Ernest Hemingway, came out in 1926, but his popular reputation did not begin to take off until 1929 with the publication of *A Farewell to Arms*—though neither book made the annual bestseller list in the Twenties.

We'll close this chapter on the Twenties with the decade's most notorious event.

BLACK THURSDAY: OCTOBER 24, 1929

The year Hemingway's *Farewell* appeared was also the year of America's farewell to a decade of unbridled prosperity. The Roaring Twenties ended with the day of reckoning: October 24, 1929, forever after to be known as Black Thursday. Previously, for a few weeks, the stock market had been bobbing, with the Dow Jones averages bouncing up and down and financial headlines alternately optimistic and downright scary. Contrary to popular folklore, the suicide rate among investors was actually higher during this period *before* the crash.

America had been on a wild spending spree, consuming millions of pianos, phonographs, records, and radios largely through credit installment plans. On Wall Street, speculators were literally banking on the country's bright future through "margin buying"—essentially buying shares on credit with very little cash down payment. Thus, the decade's good life was based on the quaggy foundation of debt. A panic that forced debtors to suddenly pay up could, through a chain reaction, sink the prosperity. Contributing to the unsound economy, banks were structurally weak, corporate practices were greedy and often fraudulent, and a large sector of the population—farmers, textile workers, and coal miners—were definitely not partaking in the era's good life; they were at poverty's door. Politicians, pleased that a large segment of voters were content with an upwardly mobile lifestyle, sat on the sidelines—except, that is, to discourage regulatory agencies from meddling in big business, even businesses engaged in highly risky ventures. (Parallels with the 1980s are hard not to acknowledge.)

On October 24, as brokers anxiously waited for prices to rise, a mad stampede of selling began. Brokers were deluged with orders, and the ticker tape was outpaced by the frenzied activity. Panic set in. *Sell!* rang throughout the room. That day nearly 13 million shares were traded. The next day, Friday, there was a slight rise, but from then onward it was down, down, down. On October 29 stocks suffered their worst tumbling. By the end of the year losses had reached almost $40 billion. Thousands of people had lost everything but their lives. Along Wall Street people wailed, "Every wall is wet with tears." The joyride that had been the roaring decade of the Twenties was over. In short time the national tune had changed from "Makin' Whoopee" to "Brother, Can You Spare a Dime?"

CHAPTER 5

□

The Swing Thirties

1930 to 1939

Wrap Your Troubles in Dreams, Dream Your Troubles Away

The Thirties was a period in which people went from surviving the Great Depression to preparing for the Second World War. Yet the troubled decade had no shortage of hits and heydays. If anything, it had more than previous decades, owing in large measure to the golden age of radio. The medium generated overnight sensations in people, products, and songs.

The hard times of the Depression helped create the enormous boom in the entertainment industry—radio and movies. Each week some 85 million movie fans paid about a quarter to watch Fred and Ginger whirling, or Nelson Eddy and Jeanette MacDonald extolling the sweet mystery of life, or the comic antics of the Marx Brothers, W. C. Fields, and Laurel and Hardy. At home, adults laughed with radio's "Fibber McGee and Molly" or "Amos 'n' Andy," and kids cheered the serial adventures of Little Orphan Annie or the medium's "All-American boy," Jack Armstrong.

Radio and movies provided escapism for the almost 3 million people out of work at the opening of the decade—and the more than 10 million unemployed two years later. Americans marched to the pop song imperative "Wrap Your Troubles in Dreams, Dream Your Troubles Away." For a few hours at a time at least.

Hooverisms

President Hoover predicted in the first year of the decade that prosperity would return within two months. "What our country needs is a good big laugh," he said in '31. "If someone could get off a good joke every ten days, I think our

148

A breadline during the Great Depression.

troubles would be over." His blind-eyed optimism exacerbated the economic situation and drove his presidency into ruin. The public's mood was best summed up in a joke about a hitchhiker who crosses the country in record time because of his placard: "Give me a lift or I'll vote for Hoover."

Through his purblindness, Hoover saw his name enter the language as no other president's had: *Hoovervilles* were the proliferating shantytowns of the poor and dispossessed; the yellowed newspapers under which hobos slept were *Hoover blankets;* wild rabbits consumed for food were *Hoover hogs;* footwear with holes in the soles were *Hoover shoes;* and broken-down shells of automobiles pulled along by mules were *Hoover cars.* Even Richard Nixon, the only president forced to resign from office, did not suffer such linguistic derision.

California as Fad Capital

Largely through Hollywood and its dream machine hype, the state of California began to solidify its reputation as the fad-making capital of the country. As early as 1934 *Time* magazine heralded California as "a phenomenon as well as a state." Hollywood was, of course, in the business of creating fantasy, and spinning off fads. From the Thirties onward, as we'll see in this chapter and the remainder of the book, many of our fads arrived with L.A. stamped all over them.

For sheer stupendousness of spectacle, the decade would end with the monumental 1939 World's Fair—which took as its theme the World of Tomorrow, supposedly a dawning new age of "efficiency," "prosperity," and, ironically, "international harmony"; this, despite the scudding storm clouds over

Europe and Asia. At least one visitor to the fair, a member of the British Parliament, tossed a sour note of realism into the gay festivities when he observed: "We shall not be able to enjoy ourselves again until Franco's widow tells Stalin on his deathbed that Hitler has been assassinated at Mussolini's funeral."

FADS, FOLLIES, AND TRENDS

Jive Talk

Each decade has its "in" jargon, and the talk of the Thirties was jive, or swing—swing representing the melodic big-band jazz with its strong dose of improvisation. It was the fast-paced world of swing that gave birth to a lingo called jive, which was as free-spirited and impressionistic as the music. To the uninitiated, both the music swing and the slang jive were equally confusing—so shockingly youth-oriented; as is the trendy talk of each generation. "It don't mean a thing," sang Duke Ellington, "if it ain't got that swing."

A devotee of swing was an **alligator;** a female vocalist of the period a **canary.** In like phraseology, all the musicians in a swing orchestra were **cats,** not least the clarinetist who played a **licorice stick.**

A vocalist who improvised lyrics, substituting nonsense syllables for words, was a **scat singer.**

In this era, a spate of nonsense songs swept the country, with lyrics babyish or intentionally obscure; as in the popular "Three Little Fishes":

> Down in de meddy in a itty bitty poo,
> Fam fee itty fitty and a mama fitty, foo.
> "Fim," fed de mama fitty, "Fim if oo tan,"
> And dey fam and dey fam all over de dam.

Which was followed by repetitions of the nonsense line "Boop boop dit-tem dat-tem what-tem Chu!" Adults thought the younger generation strange.

A dancer limb-flailing to swing music was a **jitterbug,** and to be so totally engrossed in the music as to be oblivious to all else was to be **knocked out. Kicking out** was the behavior of a free-spirited soul who thrived on improvisation in dance, music, or life in general. **In the groove** (a record-and-needle metaphor) meant to be carried away by good swing, an experience unknown to a **long hair,** a person who preferred the classics, or **corn**—schmaltzy ballads meant for sedate dancing.

An **ickie** was a snub for a person who missed the appeal of swing. More damning was to say a person was **dead between the ears;** today's equivalent being "brain-dead."

The opposite was a **hepcat,** who enjoyed **cuttin' the rug**—dancing to swing music. In the Thirties **hep** and **hip** became interchangeable expressions for insiders. Some etymologists believe that "hep" was a later corruption of "hip," which may have come from the opium smoker's slang "on the hip," referring to the reclining body position in which the drug was smoked; it is also possible that hepcat (or hipcat) comes from the African Walof word *hipicat*, meaning "one who has his eyes wide open."

In addition to a swing band—whose informal gatherings for the members' own pleasure were **jam sessions**—all musical instruments carried jive names like the "licorice stick." Drums were **hides** or **skins;** a trumpet, tooted by a **liver-lips,** was the **plumbing;** a piano was an **eighty-eight** or **mothbox;** and music was recorded on a **platter.**

The Depression also enriched the language with a host of acronyms: **FDIC** (Federal Deposit Insurance Corporation, 1933), **FHA** (Federal Housing Administration, 1934), **SEC** (Security and Exchange Commission, 1934), **TVA** (Tennessee Valley Authority, 1933), **WPA** (Works Progress Administration, 1935), and of course **FDR**—the man responsible for the preceding. Roosevelt also enriched the language through his **fireside chats** (radio broadcasts), and his bolstering reminder: **The only thing we have to fear is fear itself.** One term on the lips of hepcats and longhairs alike was **New Deal**—from Roosevelt's acceptance speech at the Democratic National Convention in Chicago on July 2, 1932: "I pledge you, I pledge myself, to a new deal for the American people."

Miniature Golf

What began in the flapper age as one more diversion became the first full-fledged recreational fad of the Thirties. Miniature golf courses sprang up in hotel courtyards, parks, adjoining highway gasoline stations (filling stations then), and at every country fair. The popularity of the pastime is hard to imagine today if you don't play golf, and even harder if you do. Shortly into the decade, the country had some forty thousand miniature golf courses, generating profits of more than $225 million. Cynics viewed the fad as "a doughty attempt by average Americans to enjoy life" through imitating the rich and formerly rich who had access to real golf courses. Most miniature golfers, however, undoubtedly joined the trend as an inexpensive way to spend an afternoon.

Miniature golf, as played in the Thirties, employed a putter to hit a golf ball across a smooth surface (usually crushed cottonseed hulls) and through, over, under, up, and around various baffles, or hazards—abrupt dips or acclivities, sharp turns, curved sections of pipe, and the like—and into a series of holes, nine or eighteen, laid out as a replica of a real course. The game was said to "cure Depression blues," and the number of people who pursued it was correspondingly astronomical.

Origin. The fad actually began two years before the stock market crash, on Lookout Mountain, the Civil War battleground in Tennessee. Garnet Carter, proprietor of Carter's Lookout Mountain Hotel, set up a miniature golf course as a diversion for his guests. Its popularity eclipsed all other hotel recreations, and soon the course was copied by hotels around the country. Carter, who also owned a real estate company, wasted no time in forming the Fairyland Manufacturing Company, which built throughout the South Little Links courses—each for $2,000 and completed in a week.

When the Depression broke out, people joked that the only industry still hiring was miniature golf—which in 1930 employed two hundred thousand people. New York City and Los Angeles alone had more than a thousand courses; and the first minicourse on Long Island almost paid back construction costs in the first day of operation. Not surprisingly, countless people envisioned building their own Tom Thumb golf course as a vehicle out of financial hardship; and for a time courses seemed to materialize overnight in vacant lots across the country (therein lay the death of the fad). Many towns tightened their zoning restrictions to prohibit an infestation of miniature links.

While physicians and pastors debated the pros and cons of the game— outdoor exercise was healthful; playing on the Sabbath was sinful—the courses proliferated. By 1931 the game was deathly overexposed and *Miniature Golf Management,* a year-old periodical, reported that every California course was financially in the red, as was the magazine. The three-year-plus fad was over— having begun in late 1927 and peaking in 1930. No one then could have imagined that a half century later the nation would go almost as crazy for real golf, the miniature version bequeathed to kids.

Pinball as a Pastime

Pinball, an American male passion in the Thirties, traveled to Japan where today it is a national pastime, with profits in 1989 alone at $70 billion—equivalent to half the sales of the Japanese automobile industry. At places like the New Alpha Pachinko Parlor, scores of Japanese youths and adults sit mesmerized in front of machines, amid a deafening roar of bells, buzzers, and rock music, in a haze of cigarette smoke and neon lights. Pachinko, as the game is onomatopoetically known, is a form of gambling. And the nation's fifteen thousand pachinko parlors are scattered throughout almost every commercial area of Japan.

In America during the Depression, unemployed men and boys lost themselves for a penny a game in pinball parlors—which in popularity were not unlike today's video game arcades. Eventually the game of pinball went from a harmless fad in the Thirties, to a "vice" in the Fifties, and reached a modernday level of public awareness in 1975 through The Who's rock opera *Tommy,* about the "deaf, dumb, and blind kid who sure played a mean pinball."

Origin.   Historically, pinball's nearest ancestor is the parlor game of bagatelle, a nineteenth-century fad, and featured in Dickens's *Pickwick Papers.* In that game players used a billiard cue to shoot balls into holes located in the middle of the playing field. A later American version, and closer to modern pinball, was Log Cabin—a tabletop game that featured a large high-value "skill hole," numerous handicap pegs, and several smaller holes that counted for fewer points. A Civil War cartoon depicts the Union Army defeated at Bull Run while President Lincoln plays Log Cabin. (Interestingly, the cartoon also shows rats and slovenly dressed players, suggesting the sleaziness of the game.)

The decade of the Thirties opened with the introduction of the first real pinball machine—an inexpensive tabletop game called Baffle Ball, with seven steel balls driven by a wooden plunger; it cost a penny a round to play. The first year, creator David Gottlieb sold a staggering fifty thousand of these coin-operated games, at $17.50 each. The following year's hit was a more elaborate pinball machine called Bally-Hoo, by a different manufacturer; it had sales of seventy thousand. That year another pinball machine, Whirlwind, became an even bigger seller, convincing manufacturers that American men and boys wanted to play pinball in profitable numbers.

Pinball parlors proliferated. Games now had such standard features as curved loops and spring-activated kickbacks. One of the most significant innovations came in 1933 when Harry Williams, of the Pacific Amusement Company of California, designed a game called Contact, which introduced electric circuitry into pinball wizardry: Four dry-cell batteries in the machine powered colored lights and rang a bell. In rapid succession appeared such features as anti-cheat "tilt" devices, automatic scoring, free games, and thumper-bumpers. It all made for a mean pinball. And, too, spawned a form of psychedelic-type graphics called pinball art, itself a fad in the Thirties and a collector's field today.

The advances in pinball hardware in the Thirties were followed as avidly by players then as innovations today in, say, Nintendo-like software. By the end of the decade, pinball machines were found in bars, cafés, soda fountains, and penny arcades throughout the country.

Pinball as a Vice. Pinball became such a popular entertainment with the nation's youth that it began to suffer criticism from teachers, parents, church groups, decency leagues, and state crime commissions. (Some games in the mid-Thirties rewarded a winning player with a rattle of nickels.) Young men, spending hours in front of pinball machines, were said to be addicted, whereas parlors were supposedly controlled by "the syndicate." Through sinister association, the image of pinball as an amusement was to become seriously tarnished for decades.

Politicians in the 1940s campaigned on the promise to clean up pinball parlors. New York City's Mayor La Guardia waged a veritable war against pinball machines. "One out of every three persons in the pinball business has been arrested at least once," reported the *New York Times* in 1942. "The 11,080 machines now operated in New York bring in a gross 'take' of 20–25 million dollars per year." And that was all in nickels, the only coin the machines accepted; it conveys the passion for pinball. La Guardia condemned pinball as "an evil and a menace to young persons because it develops the gambling urge in children." In police raids on pinball parlors, the machines were axed, as Carrie Nation had axed saloons during the temperance movement.

Innovations continued to appear in the Forties—mainly the flipper, a rubber bat that the player controlled by pushing a button on the side of the machine.

But pinball's heyday had waned, its image sullied. In the Fifties, *Better Homes and Gardens* warned parents of the game's inherent evils (though the machines had long stopped kicking back coins), and quoted "one of the country's leading crime fighters": "Pinball feeds on vast sums siphoned from the worn pockets of those least able to afford the sucker's game of rigged odds. If allowed to get out of hand, it can wreck the civic enterprise and economic well-being of any village, town, or city." Parents believed this to be oh-so-true. It was during this period of pinball approbation that U.S. manufacturers began to sell their colorful machines in Japan—where the fad flourishes as pachinko.

Jukebox

In our era when teenagers bore easily with even quick-edited videos, it's hard to imagine the day when teens dropped a coin into a jukebox and watched the *box*—and, too, the spinning disc. The shimmeringly sensuous jukebox bubbled, glowed, flashed, and was something of the music video of its day. In dazzling art deco design, it was intended to be a feast for the eyes as well as an enchantment for the ears.

Today jukeboxes are collected. A Wurlitzer Model 1015 in restored condition can command more than $10,000—considerably more than the $700 it originally sold for during the golden age of the jukebox, roughly from the mid-Thirties to mid-Forties. The heyday arrived due largely to the innovations of multicolored plastics, amplified sound (which enabled records to compete in volume with a real orchestra), and the so-called internal stage that allowed people to watch records be selected and spun—something they did for hours at a time. The magic machine cast its own spell above and beyond that of the music, making the medium a part of the message. By the close of the Thirties the Wurlitzer Company alone was selling some forty-five thousand jukeboxes a year, and they could be found in virtually every malt shop, diner, and social hall in the country. No one then could have imagined that one day they'd be obsoleted—death by Muzak.

Origin.   Though Thomas Edison invented the phonograph, it was Louis Glass who added a coin slot and introduced the idea that you "pay to play." On November 23, 1889, Glass installed his nickel-in-the-slot marvel in San Francisco's Palais Royale Saloon and the jukebox (of sorts) made its debut. You requested a musical selection and an employee—something like a disc jockey—inserted the record. In the Gay Nineties, "listening parlors"—some featuring as many as ten coin-operated machines and an equal number of "DJs"—sprang up around the country, creating a new industry. Early jukeboxes, though, had little cultural impact on people's lifestyles or musical tastes because they could be heard by only a few people at a time: Each box had several listening tubes that were held to the ear. The jukebox then, without amplification, was like the early moving picture filmstrip without projection: unsuited for mass appeal. Nonetheless, listening parlors are where most people went to hear early recorded music, and they played a pivotal role in creating the record industry.

The word jukebox did not come into popular use until the late Twenties—when the machines were automatic but still without amplification. *Juke* is a word of West African origin meaning "a house of prostitution," which in the American South came to stand for a dance hall, then a dance itself. To juke meant "to dance" (later it would mean to make the rounds of seedy taverns), juke joints were dance halls, and when the music started to be provided by record machines they became jukeboxes.

Golden Age.   Prohibition played a major role in ushering in the golden age of the jukebox. Many of the smaller speakeasies could not afford live bands and thus resorted to records played on automatic phonographs, as the machines were called until around 1930. The Depression also boosted the jukebox industry, since a single nickel could be used to entertain a large gathering of friends—amplification had by then arrived. The bad times proved a boom to the jukebox business.

In addition, the jukebox was a godsend to black musicians attempting to make it in the white-dominated record industry. "The jukebox was often the only way to go," say the authors of *Jukebox: The Golden Age.* "For all practical purposes, there was no place a black musician could have his records heard on a large scale but the jukebox."

Jukebox sales soared during the Depression years. And the jukebox itself never looked flashier in its new bubble-lighted brilliance—or more inviting through its changing bands of colors that flowed inward to hypnotically draw people toward the machine. And by the millions they approached devotedly. The classic jukeboxes produced during this heyday would be purchased for top dollar in the 1980s by the likes of Yoko Ono (as a present for John Lennon), Stephen King, Diana Ross, and Madonna. For the Eighties experienced a wave of nostalgia for the Thirties masterpieces.

The jukebox—as well as the lingering social atmosphere of the diner or malt shop in which it thrived—was gradually done in by the pace of Sixties fast-food restaurants and the disembodied sounds of Muzak. Later, coins that once nourished the jukebox were voraciously gobbled up by the computer-driven likes of Pac-Man.

Not that the jukebox is dead. At the end of the Eighties there were, according to the Amusement and Music Operators Association, 225,000 jukeboxes operating in bars, diners, hotels, and lounges throughout the country. Moreover, modern jukeboxes incorporate one hundred CD albums, offering up to fifteen hundred titles—a far cry from the days when you selected a brief-playing 78 RPM from a menu of twelve choices. But, then, how much of the jukebox's appeal was connected precisely to the limited choice and brevity of each cherished record? You stayed by the machine because you had to keep inserting coins, and because there was the real possibility that you had the leisure time to listen to the jukebox's entire menu.

Goldfish Swallowing

The decade of the Thirties would end with one of the most preposterous of all fads: goldfish swallowing. First in a wave of campus absurdist follies—the harbinger of phone-booth stuffing, piano smashing, panty raids, Frisbeeing, streaking, and the like—this ritual of collegiate lunacy lasted, astonishingly, only through the spring (hormonally, prank season) of 1939, yet it lives in memory as the highest campus madness ever concocted.

As a mania, it began on March 3, 1939, and through newspaper coverage it is better documented than many political decisions made during that eventful prewar period. It certainly must have been more comforting to read about a high prank than about Europe's engulfing quagmire.

The chronology: Harvard freshman Lothrop Withington Jr. became the country's first swallower. Son of the college's 1919 football captain, he boasted during an evening bull session of having once eaten a small, live fish. A dare and a wager ensued, and word spread around campus that the mind-boggling attempt would take place, fittingly, in the freshman dining hall on March 3. Cameras clicked as Withington snared a three-inch goldfish from a small bowl, held it up by the tail, bent backward like a sword-swallower, and lowered the creature into his mouth. He chewed. Then swallowed hard. With flair, he pulled a toothbrush from his pocket and cleaned his teeth; with humor, he remarked, "The scales caught a bit on my throat"; and with irony, he sat down to a dinner of fried filet of sole.

Such an event cannot be kept from other colleges, and by the blossoming of the first crocus, goldfish swallowing was an intercollegiate sport, the spring thing to do. Frank Hope at Franklin and Marshall College in Pennsylvania labeled Withington a "sissy" and outmanned him by downing three goldfish (without chewing, and adding, for effect, salt and pepper). Next day, a classmate, George Raab, upped the record by swallowing six fish. Harvard retaliated through Irving Clark, who gulped down twenty-four small fish (and announced that on demand he'd eat spiders, worms, and beetles). New records were set daily that spring at the University of Michigan (twenty-eight fish), Boston College (twenty-nine), Albright College (thirty-three), MIT (forty-two). A professor of anatomy at one college calculated that an average-sized male could safely consume 150 goldfish; the all-time record would eventually surpass 300 fish at one sitting.

Spin-off Crazes.   The first coed to guzzle goldfish was the University of Missouri's Marie Hansen. Then, to make the fad more palatable to the masses, Boston University's Betty Hines whipped up a fish-shaped sugar cookie with candied golden "scales"—which became a featured dessert at several Boston restaurants. The press instructed on the safest way to swallow a live fish: Let it wiggle until you feel it at the backmost reaches of the throat, then quickly swallow; *do not* attempt to swallow a fish thrashing near the front of the oral cavity. Such advice did not please the medical profession, which warned of choking deaths and disease from worms harbored in raw fish. Nor did it go down well with city animal leagues who sought legislation to preserve goldfish from "cruel and wanton consumption" by college students.

The craze peaked during exam period—with harried students chewing not only fish, but magazines and Victrola records, and biting the heads off live snakes. Then came summer break. Whereas a few trend-following adults might be seen nibbling on goldfish cookies, the campus fad was passé. Students had other things on their minds. Psychologists retrospectively psychoanalyzed the bizarre behavior, seeing in it a need to release exam-time tension, or, as one argued, "The eater takes delight in the repulsiveness of the act." But the act, which lasted about two months, left an indelible impression on the national imagination. Though it would be revived in the Sixties and again in the Seventies, these subsequent outbreaks had to compete with too many other campus events to win over the press as did the first wave of goldfish swallowing.

Supermarket

The newspaper advertisement promised: "You don't carry a cumbersome basket. *You roll a carriage.* And when you have everything you need, you wheel the carriage to a cashier's desk where your order is checked and packed for you." The ad was instructing readers on how to shop at the new kind of store that was causing excitement all across the country: the price-cutting mega-grocers, a Depression-age godsend.

"Pile it high and sell it cheap" was the motto of supermarket innovator Michael Cullen, who launched a Thirties retailing innovation that changed America's food shopping habits as much as the automobile changed its social life. It was the car, in fact, that made the supermarket a reality by allowing families to travel farther distances to bigger stores, and to cart home larger orders in a single trip. Supermarkets, in turn, accommodated shoppers by setting aside vast paved areas for their cars called parking lots—something new in itself.

Further, the Depression—by creating a demand for aggressive price cutting—hurt higher-priced ma-and-pa stores and made the supermarket an idea whose time was decidedly ripe. Michael "King" Cullen opened his first no-frills, self-service store in Jamaica, New York, on August 30, 1930, with the giant banner: "King Kullen, The World's Greatest Price Wrecker—How Does He Do It?" Cullen's brainchild also created boom times for a then little-used invention: the brown, gusseted, flat-bottomed, collapsible paper bag. Never were so many needed so fast.

The mega-grocer was a true American invention. In the late Twenties, Cullen perceived that the American population was expanding too fast for its food needs to be met by small chain stores where a clerk filled your order. The largest downtown grocers were then under 2,000 square feet. Cullen envisioned "a monstrous store . . . away from high-rent districts" with 6,000 square feet, operating on a self-service, cash-and-carry philosophy. Aisles would feature "mass displays of groceries," shoppers would be lured into the store through "newspaper advertising on a major scale," and a hallmark of the entire endeavor was irresistible price-cutting: "I could afford to sell a can of milk at cost," reasoned Cullen, "if I could sell a can of peas and make two cents." From the Piggly Wiggly chain of stores, established in California 1916, Cullen copied the concept of self-service.

Shopping Cart.   The first King Kullen deservedly merited the cliché "overnight success." Within two years Michael Cullen had eight highly profitable supermarkets, and competitors were sprouting up everywhere. And upscaling Cullen's concept. In New Jersey, two businessmen, Robert Otis and Ray Dawson, converted an empty automobile plant into Big Bear, the Price Crusher, a super supermarket with 50,000 square feet of groceries, meat, fruit, and vegetables, as well as radios, coffee percolators, car accessories, and cans of paint. Aisle after aisle, families were able to accumulate their purchases in a wire-and-wheel contraption called a shopping cart. The no-frills Big Bear was followed by the no-frills Giant Tiger, Bull Market, Great Leopard (there was a fad for animal names), and, not least, Humpty Dumpty, whose creator, Sylan N. Goldman, refined the shopping cart to the version we use today. "No frills" became a Depression-era boast.

Not surprisingly, small chain-store grocers and independents complained bitterly of the supermarket's volume price-cutting practices. In groups they petitioned local governments to outlaw price undercutting, and asked newspapers to refuse ads for low-priced national brand products. But for a public in the grips of the country's worst economic downturn, the appeal of bargain prices was unstoppable. In the final three years of the Thirties, the nation's chain-store grocers closed one-third to one-half of their outlets; to survive, others enlarged their stores to nearly supermarket proportions. "Grocer" meant a small store at the start of the decade and a supermarket at its close. Born out of tight times, the supermarket was an American innovation here to stay, and, too, there seemed something appealingly democratic about those banners on the fronts of building that read: "At This Store You May Serve Yourself."

Great Dirigibles

Awesome, lumbering creatures from the past, magnificent in their day, the great dirigibles were inevitable losers in the evolution of speedy transportation. These dinosaurs were for a time the trendy way to traverse the Atlantic. For the wealthy, the spectacular airships were to the Thirties what luxury liners had been to the Teens—an exciting, daring, luxurious mode of transportation. Yet the ephemeral nature of their appeal was almost predictable, for the airplane was already an encroaching reality. "The path followed by the Wright brothers was the true vision," wrote one authority, "and that followed by Count Zeppelin misguided." Even before the *Hindenburg* crashed late in the decade, the demise of the great dirigibles was sealed.

The Thirties opened the much-publicized successes of Germany's magnificent *Graf Zeppelin* airship—including luxury tours of the British Isles and nine "speedy" trips from Germany to resorts in South America. At $2,250 for a round-trip flight, only the rich could afford airship travel, so in 1934 the Zeppelin Company of Germany announced plans for a sort of "average traveler's" airship, still luxurious but offering budget fares of $400. The flagship was to usher in a new era of mass transportation and would be called the *Hindenburg*—a name soon to be synonymous with disaster on a spectacular scale. The maiden voyage took place in early spring of 1936; its fateful last voyage came in the spring of the following year.

For the intervening period, the press heaped superlatives on the *Hindenburg,* and the hoopla was merited. It was twice the size of the *Graf Zeppelin* and more than three city blocks long, but its fuel cost was no more than that of an automobile ($300 worth of crude oil was enough to carry seventy passengers and 13 tons of freight). The airship was easier to steer than a car, and it traveled to inland locations unreachable by ocean liner. Further, it cruised at a speed of just under 80 miles per hour.

Smoking on Board.   Then there was the enticement of luxury. The ship boasted of seventy private cabins, six toilets, a shower, an ornate lounge furnished with lightweight easy chairs and a grand piano (made of aluminum and weighing only 112 pounds), and two long observation decks for those who liked to walk while they "sailed." If the interior resembled that of an ocean liner, the look was intentional. Twenty-five two-berth cabins were electrically heated and equipped with hot and cold running water. On one side of the main corridor lay a spacious dining room, served by a modern, electric galley, while on the other side was a saloon and separate reading-and-writing room.

After a meal—prepared from the ship's stock of turkeys, live lobsters, gallons of ice cream, crates of fruits and cheeses, and cases of American whiskey and German beer—passengers could stroll down either side of the promenade deck and enjoy an unimpeded view of the scudding world below, all through massive windows that inclined steeply outward. And, too, there was a smoking room—for despite the uncomfortable proximity of 7 million cubic feet of flammable hydrogen, Zeppelin engineers had constructed a sealed, double-door chamber, kept at a higher pressure than the rest of the ship, so that any leaking hydrogen could not drift inside. To remove the danger of human carelessness, passengers forfeited cigarette lighters on boarding, and in the smoking room lighters were chained down. Why bother to accommodate smokers on a vehicle that is itself an incendiary device? In the Thirties smoking was not the opprobrium it is today; it was a commonplace among men, and something of a new fad among "liberated" women.

Mass Death and Media Coverage.   The spectacular *Hindenburg* disaster—captured on film and broadcast live on radio, immeasurably dramatizing the event—effectively put an end to the vogue of airship travel on May 6, 1937.

Due to delaying headwinds, the *Hindenburg* arrived above Lakehurst eight hours late, where the press and cameras were assembled. The ship's chief rigger, Ludwig Knorr, confided to a crew member that gas bag number four,

The
Hindenburg
disaster.

near the tail, seemed to be leaking and should be checked. As the ship maneuvered to align with the docking tower, several crew members heard a sound that one of them compared to the "pop" of a gas-stove burner igniting. The chief engineer saw near gas bag number four a sudden and intense glow. Within seconds the giant airship was engulfed in flames as 7 million cubic feet of hydrogen turned a sixth-of-a-mile-long airship into a gigantic blazing torch.

Those aboard were the last to know they were part of an escalating catastrophe. Many gazing from observation windows saw the calamity first as mirrored in the horror-stricken faces on people below. The tail sank toward the ground. The radio commentator, providing an eyewitness account of the *Hindenburg*'s arrival, grew so distraught his sentences became incoherent. As the glowing ship plummeted, cameras captured the horror of human beings racing from the flames. Miraculously, sixty-two of the ninety-seven people aboard survived.

Many people have argued that it was the dramatic film footage, shown in movie theaters around the country, as well as the anguished cries from the radio commentator, Herb Morrison—"It's broken into flames! It's flashing . . . flashing! It's flashing terribly! It's bursting into flames . . ."—that sealed the fate of airship travel in America. Newspaper coverage of a disaster can be disturbing enough, but for millions of people to hear of the tragedy live, to be able to listen again as the anguish is replayed and replayed (as it was), then to *see* human lives extinguished in newsreel after newsreel—it was, in essence, a glimpse of calamity twentieth-century style, and it made an indelible impression on the country and the world. More lives were lost with the sinking of the *Titanic,* but that horror was not broadcast in real time and captured on celluloid.

What caused the leaking hydrogen to ignite is still unknown, though an electrical storm had passed through the area, and electrical disturbances, including lightning, lingered. Whatever the cause, destruction of the *Hindenburg,* vividly captured by the new technologies of radio and film, put an end to intercontinental flights by hydrogen-filled airships. A Thirties vogue had ended.

Shirley Temple Dolls and Polka Dot Dresses

Shirley Temple, for a span of five years in the Thirties, generated a national mania and marketing profits that made all other Hollywood spin-offs before, and for a long time after, pale in comparison. This youngest person ever listed in *Who's Who in America,* little Shirley, from 1934 (when she was five years old) through 1938, reigned as the country's number one box-office attraction, shouldering aside rivals such as Clark Gable, Joan Crawford, and Bing Crosby, amassing fourteen straight smash hit movies and grossing $5 million annually for her studio, which she almost singlehandedly kept solvent in hard times.

Entire industries sprang from her popularity, marketing Shirley Temple polka dot dresses, hair ribbons, hats, underwear, shoes, books, soap, tableware, and mostly dolls. Despite the country's bleak economic straits, more than six million Shirley Temple dolls sold at prices from $3 to $30. In a marketing ploy later used with the Barbie doll, a wardrobe of Shirley outfits often cost more than the doll. For families who could not afford dolls, there were paper cutouts. Even the country's hairdressers profited since thousands of little girls demanded—and got—golden curls like Shirley's.

America had never seen such a sweeping marketing campaign—and the real Shirley Temple was used to aggressively promote it. Her annual movie salary of $300,000 was boosted immeasurably by royalties from swarms of Shirley-

Shirley Temple.

endorsed products. Ever her expressions and mannerisms were copied by adults as well as children—as when she'd clasp her hands to her face and exclaim, "Oh, my goodness!" And, too, young Americans were sipping nonalcoholic Shirley Temples.

Why such a national obsession?

Some say Shirley Temple embodied the innocence, naiveté, and spunk that the Depression had sapped from the country. In *Icons of America,* Phyllis Boring sees Shirley Temple movies as "fairy tale" escapism, in which "poor orphan girls may turn into little princesses, where dead fathers may turn out to be alive after all . . . and where a strong child may in her wisdom lead them all to the inevitable happy end."

Perhaps firsthand observer President Franklin Roosevelt said it best: "When the spirit of the people is lower than at any other time, during this depression, it is a splendid thing that for just fifteen cents an American can go to a movie and look at the smiling face of a baby and forget his troubles." And there were so many movies to go to, including *Curly Top, Little Miss Marker* (the first her parents allowed her to see; she clapped for herself throughout the screening), and *Rebecca of Sunnybrook Farm.* During the filming of each picture, her mother stood on the sidelines shouting, "Sparkle, Shirley! Sparkle!"

The kiddie sparkle lasted, however, only to the end of the Thirties. After two 1940s flops, her parents bought out her studio contract and took her home to sit out her "awkward stage." Sadly, she was a has-been by age twelve. But of course the real life story has a happy ending—a marriage, motherhood, and an ambassadorship. Years later, at a political event, Shirley Temple Black was asked to sing "On the Good Ship Lollipop" and wisely answered: "Nothing could be sadder than a forty-nine-year-old woman singing a child's song. I don't even do that at home."

M-I-C-K-E-Y M-O-U-S-E

In 1929 Walt Disney began the practice of licensing his filmstrip characters, and the phenomenal popularity of merchandise based on one lovable rodent, Mickey Mouse, saved several manufacturing and toy companies during the Depression. Watches featuring the resplendent rodent, selling for about $3, were a $3 million industry. Lionel trains, buckling under hard times, rebounded by issuing Mickey and Minnie Mouse handcars in 1935. The merchandising mania—featuring a host of gadgets that today are collectible—almost equaled that surrounding Shirley Temple.

Mickey (originally cursed with the name Mortimer), first appeared in the silent films *Plane Crazy* and *Gallopin' Gaucho.* But his popularity soared with his talkie debut in the 1928 cartoon *Steamboat Willie* (in which Mickey's squeaky voice was supplied by Walt Disney himself). As a measure of the national mouse mania, in the first two years of the Thirties, Disney made twenty-one Mickey Mouse cartoons, and if one did not precede a feature film, audiences shouted, "What, no Mickey Mouse?"—a phrase that entered our language, meaning the absence of anything humorous or lighthearted.

Our "mouse" vernacular expanded. The phrase Mickey Mouse became an adjective meaning sentimental, corny, or cheaply insincere. During World War II, American servicemen referred to gruesome hand-to-hand combat training films and vivid anti–venereal disease hygiene films as Mickey Mouse movies, striking a much-needed note of irony. And on June 6, 1944, D-Day, when Allied forces began the momentous invasion of Hitler's Europe at Normandy, General Dwight D. Eisenhower's password was Mickey Mouse. What mouse has known more fame?

Mousketeers. Mickey mania would peak again in the mid-Fifties with the start of television's "The Mickey Mouse Club"—spawning a nation of young-sters in mouse-ear hats, in imitation of the show's Mousketeers. Walt Disney's studio conceived the show to enchant America's children, and Mattel, the nascent toy manufacturer that had yet to market Barbie, risked financial ruin to become a sponsor, investing, as the company comptroller estimated, what was their "entire net worth"—such was the magic in the names Disney and Mickey. On air Mattel would be advertising its new **Burp Gun,** a cap gun modeled after World War II jungle fare. The show debuted in November and was an instant smash, kicking off a wave of mouse mania. By Thanksgiving Mattel could not keep up with Burp Gun orders; by Christmas it had shipped more than a million guns, which became the hot boy's toy of the year—all due to commercial time on "The Mickey Mouse Club."

This was no minor event—it had profound implications on the future of toy fads. As the authors of the 1990 book *Toyland* make clear: "Mattel's decision to advertise toys to children on national television fifty-two weeks a year so revolutionized the industry that it is not an exaggeration to divide the history of the American toy business into two eras, before and after television." TV promotion of toys had begun. New fads would materialize faster than ever. "Before television," write the *Toyland* authors, "children generally saw what the buyers chose to stock in the stores. By reaching children directly, the manufacturers not only went over the heads of the wholesalers and large-store buyers, but they also bypassed the children's parents." Mattel's Burp Gun was, metaphorically, a shot heard 'round the world.

Bingo!

If the Twenties game of mah-jongg is largely perceived now as a Jewish pastime, bingo, a product of the Depression, was decidedly a Roman Catholic passion in the Thirties—and its most vocal critics were various Protestant sects.

The bingo craze was begun by Edwin Lowe, an ex–toy salesman who had the misfortune of starting a game business on the eve of the stock market crash. With sales virtually nonexistent, Lowe, in search of business opportunities, was driving one night from Atlanta to Jacksonville, Florida, when he passed a roadside carnival. The most popular event was a game of "beano," in which bettors sat around a table with numbered cards and a veritable succotash of dried beans. As a pitchman shouted out numbers, players shuffled beans until some lucky person filled a card horizontally, vertically, or diagonally. It cost a nickel to play and the prize was a Kewpie doll, an earlier fad that had belatedly reached the South. The pitchman told Lowe that he had first seen the game in Germany, where it was called lotto; beano was his own home-grown variation.

That night Lowe attempted to play beano, but couldn't get near the table—the crowds were so impenetrable. "I watched the people playing," he later recalled, "and I noticed that they were practically addicted to it." In spite of the pitchman's own efforts to end the game, the crowd kept the table open till three o'clock in the morning. A young girl with a filled row of beans, heady with the realization she was about to take home a Kewpie doll, began jumping up and down, shouting not "Beano!" but stuttering "B-B-B-Bingo!" "I cannot describe the strange sense of elation which that girl's shriek brought to me," Lowe wrote. "I was going to come out with this game—and it was going to be called Bingo!"

From that "Aha!" moment Lowe's good fortune grew. A month after he had manufactured bingo, he was visited by a parish priest in Wilkes-Barre, Pennsylvania, whose diocesan coffers were empty. He had learned of the new game from a female parishioner. In a second inspirational "Aha!" Lowe glimpsed the future of the game: It was meant to be a Christian fundraiser. Lowe contacted a mathematics professor at Columbia University, Carl Leffler, and asked him to devise six thousand nonrepeating bingo cards. To abridge this tale that is almost too fanciful to believe: By the mid-Thirties bingo was ensconced as a Roman Catholic pastime, with more than ten thousand games around the country, many supporting cash-short parishes. For years non-Catholics would charge that bingo was gambling, and that "bingo rackets" had Mafia ties, but Catholic ladies played on. Though the game was popular as a fundraiser well into the Sixties, its peak popularity occurred during the Depression years when it served not only to raise much-needed cash, but also to provide an evening's escape from home-fire woes.

As for Edwin Lowe, he had one more brainstorm that he turned into a profitable fad: the dice game of **Yahtzee.**

FAIRS AND EXPOS

The World of Tomorrow

Americans traveled to five U.S. fairs and expositions in the decade of the Thirties, and the Depression had an effect on all of them. Chicago's **Century of Progress Exposition** in 1933, celebrating the city's hundredth anniversary, had people complaining about the practice of selling space to exhibitors instead of donating it, and of selling advance tickets—both monetary innovations necessitated by the times. Once on the fairgrounds, many visitors got their first chill of "conditioned air" (several buildings were air-conditioned), and many viewed with suspicion a demonstration of "tele-vision," a curious, static-plagued, seemingly unpromising medium. In 1935 San Diego hosted the **California-Pacific Expo,** which was followed the next year by Cleveland's **Great Lakes,** and in 1939 by San Francisco's **Golden Gate International.** Successes that they were, they paled in comparison with the fair staged in the final year of the decade on a swampy city dump located 9 miles from Times Square in a region somewhat repugnantly named Flushing Meadow. And the "television" on exhibit there had less static and far more promise.

New York's World's Fair: 1939

"It was good, it was bad; it was the acme of all crazy vulgarity, it was the pinnacle of all inspiration" is how *Harper's* magazine reviewed the fair that had millions of patrons wearing their "I Have Seen the Future" buttons. Its World of Tomorrow exhibits promised that the decades of the Forties and Fifties would deliver not only television, but air-conditioned homes, slum-free cities, cars that could cross the country in under twenty-four hours, and cures for cancer and traffic congestion.

This fair was the grandest, costliest, most ambitious international exposition ever staged, with a price tag of $150 million. Its 1,216-acre fairgrounds in Flushing Meadow, Queens, on the north shore of Long Island, had been created by filling in the entire Queens city dump, then beautifying it with ten thousand mature trees and a million Dutch tulips. The much ballyhooed excuse for the expo was the 150-year commemoration of George Washington's presidential swearing-in. But the underlying reason, as the fair's flamboyant director Grover Aloysius Whalen confided to a group of businessmen, was that "fifty million people would come to New York and spend one billion dollars"—a flow of funds sorely needed during a period known as the Roosevelt Recession.

Forty-five million visitors trekked across the fair's 65 miles of paved streets and footpaths, and marveled at such sights as General Electric's **television studio,** Du Pont's **nylon stockings** (a single pair was rumored to last a lifetime), and General Motors' Futurama, highlighting the future that would be the year 1960. In fact, the fair's World of Tomorrow theme was lavishly exemplified in Futurama's animated scale model of the American landscape in 1960. Each visitor, seated in an armchair on a conveyor belt, drifted over the model on a fifteen-minute tour. Here are several of the predictions that fascinated the 28,000 daily visitors to Futurama; see if you recognize the year 1960.

The Populace. "America in 1960 is full of tanned and vigorous people who in 20 years have learned how to have fun. They camp in the forests and hike along the upcountry roads . . . These people do not care much for possessions."

Express Highways. "A two-way skein consists of four 50-mph lanes on each of the outer edges; two pairs of 75-mph lanes and in the center, two lanes for 100-mph express traffic. Cars change from lane to lane at specified intervals, on signal from spaced control towers . . . Being out of its driver's control, each car is safe against accident . . . The cars, built like raindrops . . . cost as low as $200."

The Environment.   "The land is really greener than it was in 1939. Federal laws forbid the wanton cutting of wooded hillsides. Fewer acres, intensively and chemically cultivated, feed all the citizens of the U.S. More of the surface of the land is in forest and park."

Energy.   "Liquid air is by 1960 a potent, mobile source of power. Atomic energy is being used cautiously. Power is transmitted by radio beams, focused by gold reflectors. The Lanova Cell has made all gasoline motors Diesels."

Medicine.   "Cures for cancer and infantile paralysis have extended man's life span. And his wife's skin is still perfect at the age of 75."

The art of prediction has always been hazardous, if not foolhardy. The fair's time capsule, to be opened at the optimistic date of 6939—fifty centuries hence—contains samples of the technological marvels of plastic cups and asbestos fabrics.

When the fair opened on April 30, 1939, Poland was quaking at Hitler's latest demand and Germany was seeking a military alliance with Italy, but no hint of international tension could be seen on the fairgrounds. Whalen assured investors in the fair: "There'll be no war. That's all newspaper talk. Why, the King of Egypt told me positively that there'll be no war." What was foremost on the minds of Europeans? "A wave of enthusiasm for our New York World's Fair is sweeping Europe," exclaimed Whalen. "That's what Europe is thinking about, not war."

The fair did have enough delights to take one's mind off war or the Depression blues. Billy Rose's Aquacade, perhaps the fair's greatest financial success (it grossed over $4.3 million in its two-year run), starred celebrity swimmers Gertrude Ederle and Johnny Weissmuller in a dazzling water show. For 40 cents, thrill-seekers could experience a free-fall drop on the Parachute Jump— soon to be put to use in armed forces training. Men enjoyed the burlesque bumps and grinds of Sally Rand, a parade of sixteen Lady Godivas on horseback and in G-strings, a Miss Nude Contest, and the titillations of Bubbles Yvonne, Smiles Slane, Pat Paree, Kay Fears, and Rosita Royce—until New York's vice squad moved in. The fairgrounds would later serve as the site for the 1964 New York World's Fair—which would attract more than 50 million visitors, cost a half billion dollars, and turn out to be a financial disaster.

Sadly, the World of Tomorrow turned out to be a world at war. The nightly fireworks displays in the fair's second year seemed less and less dazzling entertainment than dire augury. As one writer later summed it up: "The millions who flocked to Flushing to see the fair's bold vision of the future saw it become the World of Yesterday."

DANCE CRAZES

Swing Time

In the era of the big bands, spirited swing music and jazz dancing took people's minds off the grimness that was the Depression. It was easy to forget hard times, for a while at least, doing the Lindy, big apple, Lambeth walk, and the decade's Latin imports, the samba and paso doble. Music, due to the proliferation of jukeboxes, home phonographs, and radio broadcasts, was never more abundant, night and day. Millions danced to tunes led by Guy Lombardo, the Dorsey Brothers, Harry James, and Benny Goodman. And people both square and hep spoke of Lawrence Welk, Woody Herman, Dizzy Gillespie, and Count Basie. The decade's beat was lively but smooth, and lovingly called swing. Swing dances were even more athletic than the Charleston. Dancers were getting younger, dancing more physical.

Lindy

The Lindy, or Lindy hop, originated in Harlem's Savoy Ballroom. In its frenzied airborne movements, it was a dance rendition of Charles Lindbergh's 1927 solo struggle across the Atlantic. Whereas the Twenties Charleston and black bottom had been wildly acrobatic, dancers stayed close to the floor. In the Lindy—in which boy and girl stood face to face, knees flexed, crooked fingers locked for "coupling"—the woman was tossed in a blizzard of solo turns and supported leaps, simulating, people said, rough flying. After a "landing," she was ready for the next innovative "flight."

"When the Lindy was properly executed," wrote one dance authority, "the young woman looked like a top with her hair flaring out"—an aviatrix in the breeze. With skirts shorter than ever, underwear became a serious dress consideration. As legend has it, the dance began with a group of improvising couples leaping and yelling, "Look, I'm flying like Lindy."

Big Apple

"Cut that apple!" "Shine!" "Polish that honey!" Such were the exhortations white folk heard in Columbia, South Carolina's Big Apple Club. Black folk were doing a jazzy country step that combined swing music with square dancing, caller and all. One onlooker was a young dance instructor named Arthur Murray. Returning North, he revamped the roadhouse romp, incorporating elements of a variety of vogue steps from the shag to the Suzi Q. The time was 1937, and Murray introduced his domesticated Big Apple, in which couples paraded in a circle, hands joined, and a caller indicated which pair was to move to the center and "Shine!" Or "Peel!" Or "Cut the core!" or "Praise Allah!"—this with hands waving above their heads.

The Big Apple turned out to be one of Arthur Murray's greatest dance coups. The **shag,** from which he borrowed, was a rapid hopping dance of the day, involving a small backward kick, and a stomping motion with the front foot. In the **Suzi Q,** a dancer interlaced fingers of both hands at chest height, then with elbows akimbo made a sawing motion across the body while doing crossover footwork. Murray also stole from the time's **truckin'** craze, which involved a rise and sag of the shoulders, and a wagging forefinger high above the head. A couple dancing the big apple might be ordered by the caller to "Go truckin' " or to **hokey-pokey,** in which you then did what the song of that title ordered: "Put your right foot in, put your right foot out, put your right foot in and shake it all about."

Depending on the caller, you might be told to "Paul Revere to the right," or "haul water to the left," and you used your imagination to mime the action. The big apple was an exuberant dance in a tough time, and in the late Thirties everyone was "doin' it"—even the president's son, John, at his engagement party.

Lambeth Walk

The Lambeth walk—in which couples strutted forward, arms linked, strutted back, and jerked their thumbs in the air to the exclamation "Oy!—began in England in 1937 as a musical number featuring Lupino Lane. He sang a cockney song about the country folk of Lambeth and did the so-called cockney strut.

The import hit America during the peak of the big apple's popularity, and during 1938 both dances were the vogue. The Lambeth walk had been seen on stage by wealthy New Yorkers visiting London, and introduced in Manhattan at several society balls that summer. The fad was intense and short-lived. Today the Lambeth walk is remembered best as a featured number in the mid-Eighties Broadway revival of *Me and My Girl.*

Samba

The sensuous samba—characterized by a unique forward and back leaning motion and by a "barrel-roll" effect with partners in intimate proximity—is a Latin American dance, which traveled from Rio de Janeiro to Flushing Meadow, Queens, to debut at the 1939 New York World's Fair. Its immediate popularity prompted songwriters to compose samba-beat music and movie moguls to insist their films have samba spectacles, whether they fit the storyline or not. Carmen Miranda danced the samba to stardom.

The samba is probably a jazzed-up offspring of an old Brazilian folk dance, the batuque. For a time in parts of Brazil, samba was both the name of a dance and the social hall where dances were held. While Americans had adopted earlier Latin-beat dances, like the fox trot and the tango, young dancers went wild over the samba because of its intriguing rhythms and fast pace—the liveliest of the Latin American social dances to sweep the United States.

Samba fever opened the door to other Latin dances, which made American dance schools in the late Thirties and early Forties a profitable business. The samba and rumba (see page 135) were joined by the mambo, the merengue, and the paso doble. To be a trendy social dancer in prewar America meant knowing your Latin dance steps backward and forward, cha-cha-cha—this last being a Fifties fad. The **paso doble** fascinated with its uniquely haughty "matador look," with many steps executed in a controlled marchlike fashion. The **mambo** and **cha-cha** shared similar footwork and flamboyant arm styling that allowed dancers to be highly expressive. The **merengue** was known as a happy dance for its upbeat mood and movements, and its distinctive leg motion (a kind of "limp" step; see page 274). For four decades America had been dance mad, and the Thirties seasoned that mania heavily with Latin flavor—an influence that was to remain with us through the Fifties cha-cha, the Sixties **limbo** and **bossa nova** (a variation of the samba), the Seventies **salsa,** and the Eighties **lambada.**

POPULAR SONGS

Life Is Just a Bowl of Cherries

In the Twenties, we've seen, ragtime was replaced by jazz. In the Thirties, jazz assumed the commercial beat of swing. Bands got bigger and brassier, and a song's popularity depended increasingly on the cleverness of its arranger.

From the standpoint of hits, the decade is conveniently divided in halves: From 1930 to 1935 a hit single was any recently published song that sold in the millions or thereabout. But starting in 1935, Lucky Strike cigarettes sponsored a landmark radio show, "Your Hit Parade." A hit now often meant any of the top ten featured on the show—whether or not a particular song moved strongly in the marketplace—and if a song was not a top-seller before being spotlighted on the show, it was the next week. "Your Hit Parade"—and its later television descendant—*created* hits. As songs were now fashioned by arrangers, they were also commercially marketed like, say, soap. It was a new idea in music, and as profitable for songs as it was for soap.

The following section is divided into two parts: before "Hit Parade" and after it.

1930.   A twenty-one-year-old belter by the name of Ethel zimMERMANn left her $35-a-week secretarial job on Long Island to become a $350-a-week show-stopper in the Gershwin musical *Girl Crazy.* She held the high C in **I Got Rhythm** for sixteen measures and Broadway singing was forever brassier; the show's other hit: **Embraceable You.** That year Americans **On the Sunny Side of the Street** or **Beyond the Blue Horizon** were asking **What Is This Thing Called Love.** Those feeling the Depression's pinch might have been more partial to **Dancing With Tears in My Eyes, But Not for Me,** and **Time on My Hands.**

The movies provided two of the year's biggest hits: the terse **Three Little Words** and the waltzy **Two Hearts in Three-Quarter Time.**

1931–32. The Depression was starting to be featured in song—psychologically as good a way as any to cope with adversity. There was the ironical **Life Is Just a Bowl of Cherries (Don't Take It Serious);** the descriptive **A Shanty in Old Shanty Town;** and the beseeching **Brother, Can You Spare a Dime,** theme song of the early Thirties. Singing a different tune during this period were record company executives—**I've Gotta Right to Sing the Blues**—for sales were down from a high of 107 million in the late Twenties to a mere 6 million by the end of 1932; they might well have been advised to **Wrap Your Troubles in Dreams, and Dream Your Troubles Away.**

Love made the scene in many guises: the proffering **All of Me (Why Not Take All of Me);** the suggestive **Try a Little Tenderness;** the serendipitous **I Found a Million Dollar Baby in a Five and Ten Cent Store;** the rhetorical **Have You Ever Been Lonely;** the expansive **Love Is Sweeping the Country,** which had "waves hugging the shore," ominous for **Love Letters in the Sand.** And songsmith Irving Berlin asked **How Deep Is the Ocean?** and answered **Say It Isn't So.**

A Broadway success, *Of Thee I Sing,* provided a hit of that title, as well as offering **A Hot Time in the Old Town Tonight;** someone was heard to say **I Don't Know Why.** The Great White Way, as it was now called, also had Americans **Dancing in the Dark,** swearing **You're My Everything,** and confiding **I've Told Every Little Star;** all of this, **Night and Day.**

Then there were the famous "when" signature songs: Bing Crosby's **When the Blue of the Night Meets the Gold of the Day,** which would become his trademark, and Kate Smith's **When the Moon Comes Over the Mountain,** which left its mark on radio listeners.

1933. *As Thousands Cheer,* President Franklin D. Roosevelt is inaugurated, Prohibition is repealed, and all of America is singing the Irving Berlin hit from his *Cheer* revue: **Easter Parade.** *Flying Down to Rio,* in **Stormy Weather,** others sing out **We're in the Money.** Still others would **Shuffle Off to Buffalo,** complaining all the way **It's Only a Paper Moon.**

The season's freak hit was the juvenile **Who's Afraid of the Big, Bad Wolf?,** from Walt Disney's successful cartoon, *Three Little Pigs,* a film still **Lovely to Look At.** Two other bestselling pops: **Smoke Gets in Your Eyes** and **I Like the Likes of You.**

1934. President Roosevelt's fireside chats became the nation's most popular radio feature, and radio itself was becoming a force unlike any other in communication history. It created overnight personalities and hit singles. Not all of America got to go to the Cole Porter–Ethel Merman smash *Anything Goes,* but most of America quickly came to know the witty, sophisticated lyrics to **You're the Top; Blow, Gabriel, Blow;** and the cocaine-champagne special, **I Get a Kick Out of You**—the first time drugs were featured in a popular song.

At sophistication's opposite end were the country's two hillbilly hits, the harmonizers' favorite, **Tumbling Tumbleweeds,** and the south-of-the-border folk ditty, **La Cucaracha,** or "The Cockroach"—this, arriving along with **Autumn in New York, All Through the Night,** and **What a Diff'rence a Day Made.**

On radio, a week before Thanksgiving, Eddie Cantor introduced a Christmas song that was soon called an instant classic: **Santa Claus Is Coming to Town.** Stores played the record and parents sang it while tucking in Johnny— **Little Man, You've Had a Busy Day.** Through movies, Shirley Temple became a cottage industry, introducing **On the Good Ship Lollipop,** and her success encouraged parents with daughters to think **You Oughta Be in Pictures** yet wanting them to **Stay as Sweet as You Are.** Down South, **Stars Fell on Alabama** in the **Deep Purple** and under a **Blue Moon.**

Your Hit Parade: Premiere, April 20, 1935

Song ranking changed as a result of the radio success of "Your Hit Parade," sponsored by Lucky Strike cigarettes—which opened with the show's theme (a Twenties hit), "(This Is My) Lucky Day." The Lucky Strike program brought fortune to all it touched: the songs, their singers, and the sponsor, and it spawned a 1937 feature film, *The Hit Parade,* and later a television show. The program's slogan, in its entirety, slipped into everyday speech: "Have you tried a Lucky lately? So round, so firm, so fully packed, so free and easy on the draw," whereas the abridgment "so round, so firm, so fully packed" scored a success as double entendre.

The show was the creation of the American Tobacco Company's president, George W. Hill, whose personal tastes in pop songs so influenced the numbers on "Your Hit Parade" that it could well have been called "His Hit Parade." Often, looking back over the market figures of the Thirties, there is slight correlation between record sales and Hill's hits. Consider these songs that Americans were buying up at record stores but did not make the annual top ten: **Begin the Beguine, Zing Went the Strings of My Heart, Stairway to the Stars, Moon Over Miami, Just One of Those Things, Isn't This a Lovely Day (To Be Caught in the Rain),** or any number from the Gershwin hit of the year, *Porgy and Bess,* including **Bess, You Is My Woman Now; I Got Plenty o' Nuttin', It Ain't Necessarily So,** and the wildly popular **Summertime,** considered by some critics to be one of the finest songs in American music. The Gershwin music was, of course, viewed as "operatic" and "Negro" and perhaps not what George Washington Hill—unflatteringly portrayed in the 1946 movie *The Hucksters* as a tyrant sponsor—wished to be associated with Luckies and tobacco.

The "Hit Parade's" top ten for its first year, 1935:

1. **In a Little Gypsy Tea Room**
2. **Red Sails in the Sunset**
3. **Cheek to Cheek**
4. **On Treasure Island**
5. **I'm in the Mood for Love**
6. **Chasing Shadows**
7. **In the Middle of a Kiss**
8. **Lullaby of Broadway**
9. **East of the Sun and West of the Moon**
10. **You Are My Lucky Star**

In discussing the remaining hits of the Thirties, a "Hit Parade" song is designated by HP.

1936.   I've Got You Under My Skin might well have been on the lips of England's Edward VIII, who had the world abuzz with gossip on his abdication to marry **In the Chapel in the Moonlight** (HP number three) American commoner Wallis Warfield Simpson. He claimed she was **(Oh, So) Easy to Love,** but the palace did not view it as **A Fine Romance.** Demoted to duke, he was nonetheless not short on **Pennies From Heaven** (HP number four). "Hit Parade" ranked **These Foolish Things (Remind Me of You)** as number five; **The Way You Look Tonight** was number two.

1937.   **While Joe Louis won the heavyweight championship of the world and the *Hindenburg* burned, America was singing **Harbor Lights, I'll Take Romance, They Can't Take That Away From Me, and Cole Porter's **In the Still of the Night.** At the top of "Your Hit Parade" were several "water" songs: **September in the Rain** (HP number one), **It Looks Like Rain in Cherry Blossom Lane** (HP number two), and **Boo-Hoo!** (HP number five). A popular Broadway number, which may never experience a revival, was **We're Going to Balance the Budget,** from a political satire by Rodgers and Hart.

1938.   **Walt Disney's first feature-length cartoon, *Snow White,* produced three hits: **Whistle While You Work, Heigh Ho, and **Some Day My Prince Will Come**—the complete musical score actually outsold every hit single of the year, including **You Must Have Been a Beautiful Baby, September Song,** and the slang favorite **Jeepers Creepers (Where'd Ya Get Those Peepers).**

Snow White.

On Broadway, twenty-five-year-old Mary Martin brought audiences to their feet with Cole Porter's **My Heart Belongs to Daddy,** while Hollywood unveiled (in *The Big Broadcast of 1938*) what would become Bob Hope's signature song, **Thanks for the Memory** (HP number ten). Brazilian dance crazes like the samba and rumba helped popularize the ditzy **Chiquita Banana. I'll Be Seeing You** did not make the annual "Hit Parade" top ten, nor did **This Can't Be Love** and **Falling in Love with Love**—all to become standards. Not to be overlooked is the Irving Berlin song composed in 1917 and kept in a trunk until Armistice Day, 1938: **God Bless America,** a signature song for the country as well as for Kate Smith, who introduced it. Berlin voluntarily signed over his royalties to the Boy Scouts and Girl Scouts of America.

1939. The impending war was not mentioned in a single hit song of the year—indeed, the musical mood of the country was almost doggedly light-hearted: The baby-talk smash was **Three Little Fishes; The Beer Barrel Polka** was number nine on the "Hit Parade," **Scatterbrain** ranked number three, and at the top of the chart was the Latin **South of the Border (Down Mexico Way).** In fact, the "roll out the barrel" number gave Tin Pan Alley its first half-million sheet music seller since the Depression began. The Polish folklike song (actually by a Czech composer with an American lyricist) was not only the year's biggest hit in sales, but, during the Second World War, it would become, according to historian Spaeth, "the most popular song in the world," with American soldiers singing it everywhere they went. "Roll out the barrel" became a tavern imperative as much as a song lyric.

As the decade closed and tensions tightened abroad, Americans, still hoping to avoid military involvement, were singing **Stairway to the Stars** (HP number eight), but they were also humming **I'll Never Smile Again.**

BESTSELLING BOOKS

For Whom the Cash Register Tolls

In the world of the popular book, two titles come prominently to the fore: in fiction, *Gone with the Wind* by Margaret Mitchell; in nonfiction, *How to Win Friends and Influence People* by Dale Carnegie. Each was not just a book but a marketplace phenomenon and each influenced its respective genre—the epic, historical romance, and the self-help, how-to, my-way tome.

To be sure, there were other phenomenal bestsellers in the decade— despite the toll the Depression took on the book industry. Sales of books to the general public totaled $22 million in 1933, about half of the high real ized in 1929. Expressed another way, book production decreased from the 214,334,000 copies of new volumes printed in 1929 to 110,790,000 in 1933— with many of these pages languishing in warehouses, unbound.

On the positive side, Americans were actually reading more—getting their books from libraries. During the wicked book-buying slump from 1929 to 1933, library circulation climbed 40 percent, with 4 million new card holders signing up. A borrowed book provided hours of free entertainment.

In one sense, the Depression created millions of new readers. And what did they want to read? Escapist fiction was understandably popular, as was the how-to book. How to survive the hard times. How to make money. How to be happy. In fact, as we're about to see, the Depression created a how-to, self-help craze—one that primed the public to wildly embrace the advice of Dale Carnegie.

Life Begins at Forty: Number One Nonfiction, 1933

Life Begins at Forty, by Walter Pitkin, ranked at the top of the annual bestseller list of 1933, one of the severest years of economic hardship, selling a then-phenomenal 88,897 copies. It remained a top-seller throughout the next year and contributed a new maxim to the language: People continually reassured themselves and others that "life begins at forty"—suggesting "the best" is yet to come—potent positive thinking in a time when "the worst" was the here and now.

On the one hand, Walter Pitkin pitched his book to middle-aged people who had lived the good life of the Twenties and were reduced by the crash to existing on a limited budget. Success was not beyond their grasp. Hope and a fresh start were in fact possible even "at forty." The thin volume of sensible uplift continued to rack up sales well into 1938, by which time it had numerous self-help competitors. *Life Begins* was challenged in 1934 by the imperatively titled **You Must Relax** (number nine for that year), something millions of people who had lost their entire life savings were finding difficult to do. Edmund Jacobson's *You Must Relax* was similar in title to another slim Pitkin self-helper, **Take It Easy!**—imperatives and exclamation marks were big in titles during this sluggish period, as were advice books. Those despondent with Depression blues could also turn in 1936 to Dorothea Brande's **Wake Up and Live** (number two), an exhortation that went beyond the philosophy that life begins at forty to argue through cliché that you had only to "open your eyes," "stand up and be counted," to "reach out and grab the good life." Tens of thousands of down-and-outers reached up and grabbed the self-help manual from bookstore shelves.

Those forced by finances to live alone could take solace in 1936 in the bestseller **Live Alone and Like It** (number eight), by Marjorie Hillis. It sold 100,000 copies in the first year of publication. Actually this entertainingly written book was originally intended for a narrower audience and titled *The Problem of a Single Woman*. The Depression created special problems for women and mothers abandoned by financially ruined husbands and fathers, as well as for young single women who could not find a man willing to take on the financial load of a marriage and children. Marjorie Hillis scored another hit, number five in 1937, with her Depression-conscious **Orchids on Your Budget.**

But the biggest how-to book of the decade—and the most talked about for decades to come—was written by the era's most successful salesman of pop psychology, Dale Carnegie.

How to Win Friends and Influence People: Number One Nonfiction, 1937

With sales of 729,000 in the first year of its publication, Dale Carnegie's bargain-priced $1.96 how-to was a runaway bestseller. And with its subsequent reappearance in paperback at 25 cents it sold well into the millions, such were the number of people who wanted friends and influence. The book's title became a catchphrase well into the Sixties. This book was not about swimming with the sharks and surviving, but about mixing with nice folk and getting your way. In a breezy style, Carnegie numerically summed up the simple truisms to charm associates (six rules), to win over opponents without arousing their ire (nine rules); and to ensure happiness in your home life (seven rules; Carnegie himself later divorced). If you followed the advice, success was simple. And guaranteed.

How to Win Friends presented its arguments in such concise, straightforward form that it was tailor-made for excerption in the Depression-born magazine *The Reader's Digest,* which influenced book sales and won new readers for the magazine. The popular lecturer and head of his own Carnegie Institute of Effective Speaking and Human Relations filled his volume with practical examples. He also used supporting evidence from influential people from ancient times to the present, whose own successes suggested there were hidden, infallible rules to achievement that only needed codification, enumeration, and publication. This last was done by Simon & Schuster, which in two years spent a then-staggering quarter of a million dollars to promote the book. An executive at the publishing house, Leon Shimkin, had attended Carnegie's self-help lectures in 1934 and suggested that a book, in Carnegie's "rapid-fire, talking style" was what Depression-bound Americans sorely needed. Carnegie had been a student of theater in New York, then a performer in the road company of *Polly of the Circus,* and seemed suited to become a bestselling author. That his Institute of Effective Speaking had an impressive list of successful graduates (including Lowell Thomas) meant that he had countless real-life anecdotes to support his rules.

This how-to-of-all-how-tos continued to sell strongly throughout World War II and into the Fifties, becoming the bible for material enrichment. Not even Dale Carnegie's later effort, *How to Stop Worrying,* addressed to the millions who were trying too hard and failing to win friends and influence people, challenged the book's unique spot in pop psychology.

As a closing remark on Thirties' nonfiction books: Number seven on the list in the final year of the decade was **Mein Kampf** by Adolf Hitler, in which he presented his theory of the Germans as the master race and of Jewry as the obstacle to German domination of the world, and his surety that all of Eastern Europe would one day become the soil for a new German *Reich.* It was not fiction, unfortunately, and an abridged English translation had appeared in 1933, but the full text was published in 1939. Apparently not enough people read "My Struggle" or took it seriously, for Hitler's struggle would soon become the world's.

Gone With the Wind: Number One Fiction, 1936–37

"A complete vacation's reading for 3 dollars" is how the ad copy read for the 1,037-page American Civil War narrative *Tomorrow Is Another Day*—as Margaret Mitchell originally titled her book, borrowing from Scarlett O'Hara's closing sigh. Macmillan, her publisher, argued there were already too many novels with "tomorrow" in the title, so the diminutive (under five feet), married-but-childless, thirty-six-year-old author, who had spent ten years writing her first and only novel, renamed the saga *GWTW.* (How many novels in this century, or any other, are known by their acronym?) Before looking at the national mania created by *GWTW,* here are the decade's other top fiction sellers, which the Mitchell book trounced in sales.

1931.　Number one was **The Good Earth,** by Pearl S. Buck, who would win the Nobel prize in literature in 1938 based largely on this epic saga of a Chinese family. It held the top slot throughout the next year, providing millions of Depression-shocked Americans with hours of escape into a foreign setting, and it received the Pulitzer prize in 1932. Number three in 1932 was Pearl Buck's **Sons,** which continued the saga of *The Good Earth*'s Wang family.

1933.　Number one was **Anthony Adverse,** by Hervey Allen, selling a remarkable three hundred thousand copies in its first six months. The historical novel, with no shortage of (tasteful) sex, arrived around the Depression's nadir and provided readers with a romantic flight into the late eighteenth century, following the travels and loves of the novel's picaroon hero. As much travelogue as historical romance, it popularized the big (really big: 1,224 pages) "vacation-reading" novel, and reintroduced Americans to a kind of fiction that had lost favor in the early part of the century. One reader was said to have dropped the tome on his foot and sued the publisher for broken bones. Gags about its heft filled the radio waves and nightclub acts. The author, an English teacher and poet, spent five years writing this first novel, and was virtually penniless when he sent the manuscript off to the publisher. The book continued to sell strongly and in 1936 became a successful Warner Brothers' film starring Frederic March as Anthony. It was still number one in 1934, when the number four slot belonged to **Good-Bye, Mr. Chips,** by James Hilton—the first book to achieve nationwide fame through radio advertising.

1935.　Number three was **Of Time and the River,** by Thomas Wolfe, who had scored literary prominence six years earlier with *Look Homeward, Angel.* Hilton's *Mr. Chips* had dropped to number five, but he was represented by another bestseller: **Lost Horizon,** number eight, a novel that introduced Depression America to the magical word and dreamy world of Shangri-La.

1938.　Aside from still reading *GWTW,* Americans were reading Marjorie Kinnan Rawlings's **The Yearling,** number one; Daphne du Maurier's **Rebecca,** number four; and Kenneth Roberts's **Northwest Passage,** number five. *The Yearling*'s tale of a Florida boy and his beloved fawn captivated American's hearts and opened their pinched pursestrings.

1939.　Number one was **The Grapes of Wrath,** John Steinbeck's tale of the "Okies" dispossessed by the dust storms of 1934. It sold three hundred thousand copies that year, and confirmed that in top-selling fiction the decade belonged to Steinbeck: **Cup of Gold** (1929), **Pastures of Heaven** (1932), **Tortilla Flat** (1935), **In Dubious Battle** (1936), and **Of Mice and Men** (1937). *The Grapes of Wrath* tale of the Joad family, who lose their tenant farm in the Dust Bowl and migrate to California in search of employment as itinerant farm workers, was said to have done "more than any other Depression novel to revise the picture of America as Americans imagined it."

Tara Mania.   In 1939 *GWTW* was still selling, and a much ballyhooed movie search for an on-screen Scarlett had created a second wave of Tara mania.

"Peggy," as the young Margaret Mitchell was called, was the daughter of an Atlanta lawyer who was president of the city's historical society, and who instilled in his child a love of Atlanta's colorful past. Under the byline Peggy Mitchell, the future novelist wrote for the *Atlanta Journal.* She was married to advertising man John Marsh, and in her spare time (and while bedridden with an ankle injury) recorded notes about the fictional adventures of an auburn-haired, green-eyed, tempestuous heroine named Pansy O'Hara . . . "a girl who was somewhat like Atlanta, part of the Old South, part of the new South; how she rose with Atlanta and fell with it and rose again; what Atlanta did to her, what she did to Atlanta and the man who was more than a match for her." But it was apparent early on that Pansy was an ill-suited name for the likes of the fiery Ms. O'Hara; only Scarlett would do.

The book's title would come from a line in Ernest Dowson's lyric poem "Cynara": "I have forgot much, Cynara! gone with the wind."

A Macmillan editor scouting the South for a "southern" novel heard of a

Clark Gable and Vivien Leigh in Gone With the Wind.

behemoth manuscript by a Peggy Mitchell Marsh. As the story goes, the eager editor relentlessly pursued the reticent writer until one morning Peggy Marsh heard a voice in her head whisper, "This is Scarlett's chance" and deposited the manuscript in the lobby of the hotel where the editor, Harold Latham, was about to check out, saying, "There it is, Mr. Latham, take the stuff!" For which he had to purchase a large suitcase to transport the stuff to New York. Next day, Peggy Marsh had second thoughts and wired: "Please send manuscript back, I've changed my mind." The story as yet had no name, was missing the first chapter, and offered three experimental endings. Yet it was riveting.

So, too, thought the critics. "In narrative power, in sheer readability, surpassed by nothing in American fiction," wrote J. Donald Adams in the *New York Times Book Review.* "This is beyond a doubt one of the most remarkable first novels produced by an American writer. It is also one of the best."

Certainly the public agreed, buying up a million copies in just six months—then the fastest-selling book in history. Bookstore windows were smashed and copies stolen (which would not happen again until the publication of *Roots*). Scarlett O'Hara and Rhett Butler were discussed as if they were real people. To get the punchline of countless comedy-act jokes of the day you had to have read the novel. And Margaret Mitchell received such a deluge of fan mail—"Did Scarlett get Rhett back?" "Will you write a sequel?"—she had to hire a staff of secretaries to answer the letters. The book took the 1937 Pulitzer Prize and was translated into twenty-seven languages. Parents across the country named their newborns Scarlett, Rhett, Ashley, and Melanie.

Peggy Mitchell Marsh was traumatized by the snowballing success: "This period of my life has been the unhappiest one." She swore she'd never write another book—and didn't. Ten years after the publication of *GWTW* she was killed by a drunk driver while crossing an Atlanta street on the way to a movie with her husband.

The decade of the Thirties had seen the publication of Fitzgerald's *Tender Is the Night* (1936), Hemingway's *To Have and Have Not* (1937), Faulkner's *Light in August* (1932), O'Hara's *Butterfield 8* (1935), and Caldwell's *God's Little Acre* (1933), but a Civil War romance by a Mrs. Peggy Mitchell Marsh was the publishing phenomenon of the era.

RADIO HITS

Don't Touch That Dial!

Radio dial, that is. For despite a threatening *Variety* headline on April 16, 1930: TELEVISION NEAR READY, the birth announcement was premature; the nation's airwaves for the decade of the Thirties belonged to radio. It was radio's golden age. The promise (or threat) of television was on the horizon at the opening of the decade, but the marketing of TV sets would not begin until 1938—around the time the popular magazine *Radio Mirror* felt a nudging to change its name to *Radio and Television Mirror,* television getting second billing.

How popular was radio in the Thirties? A poll by *Fortune* magazine in 1938 asked Americans which industry best met public demands: Fourth (9.5 percent) was the motion picture industry, third (9.8 percent) was air transportation, second (29.2 percent) was radio, surpassed only by the automobile industry (43.1 percent).

It is impossible for young people today to imagine the tremendous novelty radio was—and the necessity it quickly became in Depression America. It was state-of-the-art communication technology; a twist of the dial and you heard the voices of great entertainers and world leaders. Hit songs, comedies, current affairs came into your living room. Listen and you heard the reassuring welcome of President Franklin D. Roosevelt ("My friend") explaining the New Deal. Or tune in to his wife, Eleanor, on Pond's facial cream's "Variety Fair" to learn how women could best cope with homefront hardship.

All that was required on your part was a commitment of time and a mustering of imagination. Indeed, the aural medium was called the "theater of the mind." *You* conjured the images of scenery and props from words and sound effects, as your mind's eye perceived the faces of, say, Molly Goldberg, Amos and Andy, or Betty Crocker (who was every bit as fictitious as the comedy characters). And for the chills of "Inner Sanctum" or the fright of "The Shadow," you essentially scared yourself, succumbing to the sound of a creaking door, a breathy baritone, a whirring wind. No one living at that time could have imagined that within a few decades we would be a nation obsessed with, and awash in, the visual image, that it would be lights out for the theater of the mind and curtains up for the theater of the eye.

But in the Thirties radio broadcasts were a national passion. What had begun in the Twenties as a ham's hobby had become the country's fourth major industry. And it was largely comedy—specifically that brand we've come to flock to as sitcom—that made broadcasters, sponsors, and actors grin all the way to the bank. Here, then, are the hits that had Depression America laughing.

Amos 'n' Andy: NBC Premiere, August 19, 1929

"I'se regusted with you!" people were going around exclaiming—as later generations would mouth the Gleasonism "One of these days—POW—right to the moon!" the Bunkerism "Aw, chee whiz," the Maudism "God'll get you for that," the Fonzism "A-a-a-a-y," or the Morkism "Nanoo-nanoo."

Americans couldn't get enough of Andy Jones's rumbling, slow baritone when he was "regusted" with his sidekick Amos Brown—as voiced by Freeman Gosden and Charles Correll, who brought their blackface vaudeville characters of Sam and Henry to radio in the sympathetic figures of Amos and Andy. The fifteen-minute serialized program that aired Monday through Saturday at seven P.M. eventually captured 60 percent of all listeners and caused an unprecedented surge in sales of radios (the way "I Love Lucy" would later affect television sales). As celebrities, the fictional Amos and Andy were as big as the real-life Charles Lindbergh and Will Rogers; they were the first of the sitcom's public gods. Sponsors responded immediately to the national clamor for serialized comedy by giving daytime programming its own sitcom in the form of a soap opera, "The Goldbergs." Thus, two entertainment genres—sitcom and soap opera—took root in the first year of the Depression.

"Amos 'n' Andy" perpetuated clichés about blacks, portraying them as less intelligent and less diligent than white radio listeners. But it also sympathetically underscored the difficulties rootless Southern blacks found in entering a Northern metropolis. Comedians Gosden and Correll wanted to record on phonograph discs their Chicago-based "Sam 'n' Henry" series for nationwide syndication but encountered contractual problems with the local station. So they wrote a new script and renamed the leads, first Jim and Charlie, then Amos and Andy. Legend has it that Gosden and Correll met two blacks, an elevator operator and a janitor, named Amos and Andy. In truth, they tested scores of names, searching for two that were short, equal in length, euphonious, and easy to remember. As characters, Amos was trusting, simple, and unsophisticated, whereas Andy was domineering and lazy.

The advertising agency that handled Pepsodent toothpaste thought the show had network potential and contacted America's first national company, NBC (they could as well have gone to the newly formed CBS). Looking for a new show to boost their ratings, NBC hired Gosden and Correll for a staggering $100,000 a year. The first "Brought to you by Pepsodent" network broadcast came on August 19, 1929—just weeks before the stock market crash. The show quickly acquired a following of 42 million listeners—when the country's population was slightly over 100 million.

Depression Humor.   The Depression was often the subject of "Amos 'n' Andy" comedy routines. The first Depression joke occurred on the October 30 broadcast, the day after the market collapsed: Lightnin', an unemployed young man, begs Andy for a job with his Fresh Air Taxi Company of America, Incorpulated.

> ANDY: Is you been keepin' yo' eye on de stock market?
> LIGHTNIN': Nosah, I aint never seed it.
> ANDY: Well, de stock market crashed.
> LIGHTNIN': Anybody git hurt?

While most listeners appreciated the humor in Lightnin's belief that the building had collapsed, the country's editorial writers latched on to a Freudian word from Andy's retort: "Well Lightnin', 'course I would like to give you a job but de bizness repression is not right now." Many found "repression" a better description of the collapse of private enterprise than "depression." Repression became a popular catchword.

Most Americans were baffled by the complexity of factors that contributed to the country's economic demise. "Amos 'n' Andy" simplified things. Four days after the first Depression joke, the two comedians devoted their entire broadcast to the crash, explaining margins, pooling, and stock manipulation through the humorous conflict of "de bulls fightin' de bears." Audiences were laughing and crying at the same time.

Roosevelt's proclamation of a bank holiday and the issuance of scrip terrified most Americans, many of whose life savings were in banks. On the March 7, 1933, broadcast the comedy attempted to restore America's confidence in the government and the banking system. Early on, Lightnin' asks about scrip: "Whut is dat new money?" Andy replies, "New money? I cant even git ahold of none o' de *old* money." The dialogue was funny and informative ("infotainment," as TV executives would say today), and the program closed with support for the president's action: "Mr. Roosevelt means bizness, an' he's gittin' action, so yo' see, dis bank holiday is really a gret thing fo' de country." President Roosevelt, who never missed the show, personally wrote to the comedians thanking them for the broadcast—a high-water mark in the history of sitcom.

"Amos 'n' Andy" did for radio what Milton Berle and his "Texaco Star Theater" would do for television two decades later: It captured the fancy of the nation and overnight gave a burgeoning medium mass appeal. One year after the series made its national debut, the country was rich in Amos and Andy toys, candy bars, comic strips, and phonograph records. Radio sets were selling to people who could barely afford food. Department stores piped in the nightly broadcast to keep shoppers from returning home. Lights on the nation's telephone switchboards went out as people sat rapt in front of their radios. Only Lucymania in the Fifties would cause similar phenomena. George Bernard Shaw, visiting the United States in 1933, exclaimed, "There are three things which I shall never forget about America—the Rocky Mountains, the Statue of Liberty and Amos 'n' Andy."

The Goldbergs: NBC Premiere, November 20, 1929

"Yoo-hoo, Mrs. Bloo-oomm!" yelled Molly Goldberg up the dumbwaiter shaft in a one-way conversation with an unseen neighbor. Or the wise mother figure would advise her Depression-era listeners in her best Yiddish sing-song, "Better a crust of bread and enjoy it than a cake that gives you indigestion."

This first major Jewish comedy of the air—about a poor but loving family living in the Bronx—debuted three weeks after the stock market crash. Such was its appeal that radio's first network soap opera (sponsored not by a soap but a toothpaste) became a full-length Broadway play *(Molly and Me)*, a book and a record *(How to Be a Jewish Mother)*, a feature film *(Molly)*, and in the Fifties a successful television series ("The Goldbergs")—all created by and starring actress Gertrude Berg, based on memories of her Yiddish grandmother. Asked years later why a heavily Jewish sitcom generated such universal appeal, Gertrude Berg answered, "There are surface differences, yes. But the really beautiful thing is that these surface differences only serve to emphasize how much alike most people are underneath."

Adversity lay in the show's conception. Berg, who had studied acting at

Columbia University, turned to writing when her husband's sugar-processing factory burned to the ground in 1929. She created the Goldberg family, with father Jake, children Rosalie and Sammy, and Uncle David. Though the family and its neighbors sounded Yiddish, the show's actors included Joseph Cotten, Van Heflin, and Marjorie Main. Fans visiting the radio studio were often astounded to see Irish actor Paul Kelly, usually in golf knickers, reading the role of a rabbi.

Early on, the use of dialect was heavy, as when Molly chides her son for playing marbles: "For vat is your fadder slaving, for vat I'm esking you? A marble shooter you'll gonna be? A beautiful business for a Jewish boy!" Through the Goldbergs, large parts of the country lacking a Jewish community first learned that a yarmulke was a prayer cap and a cheder a school. As the show's popularity spread through Depression-era America, more and more episodes featured a family getting by on less and less, and the heavy dialect lightened to a unique word placement here, a specialized pronunciation there. Molly, though, continued to dispense household wisdom during the Thirties and to stir up patriotism throughout the years of World War II. The inimitable Gertrude Berg, born in Harlem, died in 1966 at age sixty-seven. She was a media pioneer in her ability to create an image of herself and her travails and have millions of fans see the personal equivalent in themselves and their struggles.

Fibber McGee and Molly: NBC Premiere, April 16, 1935

Featuring radio's most famous liar (later toned down to a grandiose dreamer), Fibber McGee and his best friend, the medium's most pompous windbag, Throckmorton P. Gildersleeve, this hit show had no storyline; situations arose when characters wandered into the McGee home at 79 Wistful Vista, Midwest, U.S.A. In a device that would shock audiences today, the announcer for Johnson Wax, the show's sponsor, doggedly visited the McGees to brag about the shine Glocoat gave their floor and Carnu gave their automobile. The Thirties gimmick was called the integrated commercial, and it created strong sponsor identification—if doing nothing for truth in advertising.

The husband-and-wife team of Jim and Marian Jordan played Fibber and Molly, whose colorful friends included Mayor La Trivia and Mrs. Wearybottom. Radio listeners usually had to conjure only one scene, the McGees' living room, where the sitcom's chatter and gossip took place, and the only door to open besides the front door was the one to the hall closet—the show's running joke. The closet was packed with typical family memorabilia (broken fans, never-used skis, cord-frayed guitars), and the clutter tumbled out in a clanking cascade familiar to all America: *BAM! POW! THUD! SMASH! KER-R-R-RASH! . . . Tinkle . . . Ting!* "Got to clean that hall closet one of these days," Fibber mused—and listeners nodded, reminded of the clutter in their own closets; at least that's how the joke's long-running success was explained over the show's nearly two-decade run.

If Fibber was a dreamer, concocting get-rich-quick schemes, Molly was his anchor to reality—employing her Irish brogue laced with Gaelic wit to cajole him into abandoning nonsense notions. The Jordans had originally done a radio show called "The Smith Family," sort of an all-white "Amos 'n' Andy," then the series "Smackouts," about a garrulous grocer who was always "smackout" of everything. But it was as Fibber and Molly that the couple found an audience of millions, who became tongue-tied trying to imitate Fibber's latest stupefying alliteration—as to his house guest Dr. Gamble: "Hi ya, Arrowsmith. Kick your case of corn cures into a corner and compose your corpulent corpus on a convenient camp chair." As the show's popularity increased, the alliterations— its aural trademark and a national copycat craze—grew mindboggling:

> Punch bowl McGee, pronounced by press and public the pugilistic pixie of the pedigreed paperweight pugs, pummelling pudgy palooka, pulverizing proboscises and paralyzing plug-uglies.

Fans visiting the studio marveled at how Jim Jordan mastered the words in one take. Other Fibber utterances also became Thirties catchphrases: "Take a gander, kiddo," and "What's cooking?"

During the Thirties, approximately one-third of American households with radios followed the "Fibber" series. The Jordans, once starving vaudevillians, earned $3,500 a week. They often played directly to Depression audiences using the comedic device of ego deflation—Fibber continually failed, was the butt of ridicule, was tipsy with delusions of the grandiose, yet was loved throughout it all. The message to struggling husbands and fathers everywhere was simple: bankruptcy, unemployment, and poverty need not cost you the love and respect of family and friends. Jim Jordan believed the show helped families get through the Depression, and at the close of a 1939 broadcast he underscored that philosophy on-air:

> We are not unconscious of the fact that these are serious days. In bringing you a few smiles . . . we hope we are helping to lift your spirits a little bit. The only members of the animal kingdom who are able to laugh are human beings so let's stay human as long as we can.

If, however, you did not wish to laugh along with Amos and Andy or Fibber McGee and Molly, you could cry to the cruel misfortunes that continually befell . . .

Stella Dallas: Premiere, October 25, 1937

Sponsored by Phillips Milk of Magnesia, "Stella Dallas" had as its theme song "How Can I Leave Thee?" and opened with the announcer reminding listeners they were about to hear "the true-to-life story of mother love and sacrifice . . . in which Stella Dallas saw her own beloved daughter, Laurel, marry into wealth and society, and realizing the difference in their tastes and worlds, went out of Laurel's life." Stella had little education, gauchely clipped her "g"s (as in lovin' and cryin'), and with gusto spewed double negatives like "ain't none." Of the sudsy soaps it was peerless.

Frank Hummert, a pioneer producer of several daytime radio soap operas (and of "Stella"), claimed the idea for such programming was prompted by the kind of "teary" fiction American women were reading in books and magazines: "It occurred to me that it might appeal to them in the form of radio dramas." Such female-sided hits included **Girl Alone, Valiant Lady, Manhattan Mother,** and **The Romance of Helen Trent,** this last the story that dared to ask "Can a woman over thirty-five find romance?"—as Helen did indeed find for the next twenty-seven years. By mid-decade the new American art form— soap opera—was buzzing over the nation's airwaves.

"Stella Dallas" had its origins in a turn-of-the-century novel by Olive Higgins Prouty. For daytime radio, the story line became more tragic. "Stella" easily filled its misery-per-episode quota—as when Laurel's wealthy mother-in-law, Mrs. Grosvenor, threatens Stella over a misunderstanding, Laurel says: "Mummy, I can't believe even Mrs. Grosvenor would be mean enough to send you to jail for stealing that Egyptian mummy." (Notice that Stella has not actually gone "out of Laurel's life.") To clear up the mystery of the missing mummy, Stella, in the best tradition of the Iliad of a Greek hero, survives a desert sandstorm, attacks by nomads, and a hair-raising cruise through the Suez Canal in a submarine. All done with sound effects.

First broadcast on October 25, 1937 (the year the long-running **The Guiding Light** first aired), the soap remained popular until 1955, with one actress, Anne Elstner, playing the crude but sharp Stella. It was said that the show was designed originally for mothers who loved to feel miserable over the ingratitude of their children, and for years it played that way. When the hit ended, Anne Elstner opened the Stella Dallas Restaurant in New Jersey, and for the next decade, at a diner's request, she'd bring the tough-talking, wronged mother out of mothballs and to your table.

Edgar Bergen–Charlie McCarthy Show: NBC Premiere, May 9, 1937

Radio being an aural medium, a most unlikely star would be a ventriloquist and his dummy, a voice-throwing act that depends on visual contact with the audience. Thus it is all the more an achievement that *the* top-rated radio program in the country from 1937 until 1940 (and never falling below number seven over the next decade) featured the mild-mannered Edgar Bergen and the loud-mouthed Charlie McCarthy, the dummy—with his monocle, tuxedo, and high-polished patent leathers. Millions of fans bought Charlie McCarthy puppets, alarm clocks, banks, and playing cards, and at Halloween children masqueraded as the sarcastic pipsqueak. Charlie, in many ways, became more famous than his Svengali.

The show premiered in 1937, after Edgar Bergen had been told numerous times that a ventriloquist had no future in radio. Then came hilarious repartee

Edgar Bergen, Charlie McCarthy, and Mae West.

between Bergen and Charlie as guests on Rudy Vallee's "Royal Gelatin Hour"; "Suddenly," said Bergen, "I was a hot number." Charlie McCarthy was perhaps the only ventriloquist's dummy to be the toast of New York's café society, invited to the parties of Noël Coward and Elsa Maxwell, and asked to bring along Edgar Bergen. Few fans ever said, "Let's listen to Edgar Bergen"; it was, "Let's listen to Charlie McCarthy." Why such popularity? Charlie was a blend of rascality, irreverence, and brashness, and Bergen believed that the dummy and the show were a hit because Charlie said things most people dared only think. He flirted outrageously with Mae West, and quarreled with W. C. Fields.

FIELDS: Tell me, Charlie, is it true your father was a gate-leg table?
CHARLIE: If it is—your father was under it.
FIELDS: Why, you stunted spruce—I'll throw a Japanese beetle on you.
CHARLIE: Why, you bar fly—I'll stick a wick in your mouth and use you for an alcohol lamp.

The show became a national pastime. One episode, though, precipitated a countrywide scandal. It involved the smoldering delivery of Mae West as Eve, cajoling Adam (Don Ameche) in the Garden of Paradise—a skit tepid by today's standards. Congress demanded the FCC take punitive action against NBC, executives who approved the script were fired, and Mae West, no stranger to censorship, was, in effect, barred from radio for nearly three decades. In the skit, bored with Paradise (which West calls a "dismal dump"), *she* tempts the snake (who calls her "swivel hips") to hand over the forbidden fruit, then she persuades Adam to eat from her hand "like women are gonna feed men for the rest of time."

ADAM: Eve, it's as if I see you for the first time. You're beautiful.
EVE: Mmmm. And you fascinate me.
ADAM: Your eyes!
EVE: Ahhh. Tell me more.
ADAM: Your, your lips. Come closer. I wanna . . .
EVE: You wanna what? [Their lips meet in a kiss. *Trumpets. Thunder.*]
ADAM: Eve, wha, what was that?
EVE: That was the original kiss!

The religious uproar was immediate. Roman Catholic groups urged a boycott of the sponsor, and the League of Decency expanded its index of forbidden books to include certain radio shows. NBC forbade even her name to be mentioned on the air. "I only gave the lines my characteristic delivery," West explained. "I am Mae West."

"The Charlie McCarthy" show ran for fifteen years. Edgar Bergen opened up an aural medium to voice-throwing acts, leading the way for teams like Paul Winchell and his dummy Jerry Mahoney. Edgar Bergen died in 1978. Charlie McCarthy is propped up in the Smithsonian Institution.

Radio's Battle Creek Boxtop Bonanza

If you were a kid in the Thirties (or Forties) you probably mailed a cereal boxtop to a well-memorized address in Battle Creek, Michigan, then eagerly awaited that morning when the postman delivered a thick, brown envelope containing . . . a Captain Midnight Code-o-graph, or a Green Hornet ring, or a Tom Mix straightshooter, or a Jack Armstrong pedometer so you, like radio-land's all-American boy, could tell how far you had hiked to the Great Elephant Graveyard. Radio premiums were offered by sponsors to sell their products and to keep you tuned in. The freebie gimmick had worked in the past to boost a product's sales, but during the Depression a free offer was doubly appealing, and a free *toy* was enticement enough to finish that cereal box so your mother could buy another. Here are three of the decade's biggest "boxtop" hits:

Little Orphan Annie: NBC Premiere, April 6, 1931. Kids' radio premiums began after the premiere broadcast of the serial about an orphan girl and her dog, Sandy (who went "Arf!"), based on the popular comic strip. ANNOUNCER: Ovaltine presents *Little Orphan Annie!* SINGERS: Who's that little chatterbox? / The one with pretty auburn locks? / Who-oo can it be? / Cute little she. / It's Little Orphan Annie!

The show's extraordinary popularity owed much to the fact that in 1931 it was the only program for young children. It was, in fact, the genesis of the children's serial format, setting a pattern for all the hits that followed. With "leapin' lizards" fidelity to the comic strip, the earliest episodes were lifted directly from newspaper storylines. And the show's opening vocal ditty was one of the best known on the air. By mailing in the seal from the inside of an Ovaltine jar and a dime, you got a Little Orphan Annie Shake-Up Mug or a secret decoder. If you were too old to appreciate Annie and her mug, you could hear about an adolescent's radio premium from: "Wheaties, the breakfast of champions, presents . . ."

Jack Armstrong, the All-American Boy: CBS Premiere, July 31, 1933.   First broadcast in 1933, it became the longest-running juvenile adventure series in radio history. Jack was the super athlete who daringly saved games for Hudson High School, and his famed school ring became a boxtop prize to cherish. Boys around the country knew the theme song better than their schoolwork: "Wave the flag for Hudson High, boys. / Show them how we stand; / Ever shall our team be champions / Known through-out the land!"

The All-American boy soon left Hudson High for exotic adventures in Tibet, the Philippines, the Rockies—wherever all-American boys were needed. Jack and his friends, Billy, Betty, and Uncle Jim, trekked the globe to bring you exciting adventure and to sell Wheaties. Jack Armstrong premiums were must-have-immediately items since they tied directly into the ongoing storyline: How could you help Jack solve a mystery or escape from a bind without a decoder? Or magic ring? Or medallion? Or bombsight? You couldn't, and that's why "Jack Armstrong" reigned on radio for more than seventeen years, and why Wheaties became the "breakfast of champions."

The Tom Mix Ralston Straightshooters: NBC Premiere, September 25, 1933.   Perhaps the biggest boxtop premium promoter of the Thirties was the "Tom Mix" show, the hybrid Western-mystery-thriller that premiered in 1933. The exploits of Tom, "daring crusader for justice" and owner of the T-M Bar Ranch in Dobie Township, were based on the experiences of the Western film star of the silent screen, Tom Mix. The real-life Tom Mix was a true soldier of fortune, serving with Teddy Roosevelt's Rough Riders in the Philippines and later seeing action in the Boer War and in China's Boxer Rebellion.

Ralston cereals, the sponsor, was prominently featured in the show's rousing theme song, which ended with the exhortation: "Take a tip from Tom, / Go and tell your mom, / Shredded Ralston can't be beat!" For a Ralston boxtop and a dime, you could get a rocket parachute, a Sheriff Mike whistling badge, coded comic books, and a photo album "containing highly confidential information every straightshooter should know."

"Tom Mix" enjoyed a long life, thrilling children until the summer of 1950. The real Tom Mix died in an automobile accident in 1940. Today, radio premiums offered on "Tom Mix," "Little Orphan Annie," and "Jack Armstrong" (as well as on "Captain Midnight" and "Sky King") are collectibles, the earliest originals commanding prices that continue to increase with time.

Violence as Entertainment.   Daring action and wild mayhem in juvenile adventure shows—as well as in adult crime series—began in the Thirties and was criticized immediately. Wrote one concerned mother: "Our six-year-old has become gangster-minded this past year since he has been allowed to run the radio at his will." Her son tuned "at will" to the athletic teenage adventurer "Jack Armstrong." "I am greatly opposed to programs for children which employ terrorizing situations."

Thus began the decades-long battle between broadcasters ("only giving viewers what they want") and parents ("this is not want we want"), which would spill over into television. Parents were particularly concerned that a child allowed to "run the radio at his will" would hit upon an evening slugfest like, say, **The Green Hornet,** in which an urban vigilante sought eye-for-an-eye justice through the spice of beatings, shootings, and murder.

The networks, NBC and CBS, announced a new code: "All stories must reflect respect for adult authority, good morals and clean living . . . Disrespect for parental authority must not be glorified or encouraged."

Best intentions stated, mayhem, crime, thrills, horrors, and parental disrespect proliferated, becoming a staple of the industry—as they are today on television. Even the Eighties visceral TV hit "America's Most Wanted" had a Thirties radio counterpart, **True Detective Mysteries,** which in a postscript highlighted a "most wanted" criminal and offered a $1,000 reward for information leading to his arrest and conviction; Charles "Baby Face" Nelson was the first thug featured. And the megahit **Gangbusters** concluded with a chilling description of a "wanted criminal still at large and roaming the streets"—of your neighborhood was implied by the announcer's intoned threat. Despite parents' concerns, in the Thirties crime and "spook" shows drew millions of fans who would not miss an episode of . . .

The Shadow: CBS Premiere, August 1930

ANNOUNCER: Who knows what evil lurks in the hearts of men? The Shadow knows! Ha-ha-ha! [Organ music swells: "Omphale's Spinning Wheel."]

"The Shadow" spawned radio's glamorous detective in the character of Lamont Cranston, a wealthy swell-about-town who secretly (and invisibly) masqueraded as the Shadow, a mysterious do-gooder who champions "the forces law and order." How could the flesh-bodied Lamont Cranston attend a society cocktail party, then suddenly become an ethereal shadow? Each week the announcer reminded you: "Several years ago in the Orient, Cranston learned a strange and mysterious secret . . . the hypnotic power to cloud men's minds so they cannot see him. Cranston's friend and companion, the lovely Margo Lane, is the only person who knows to whom the voice of the invisible

The Shadow.

Shadow belongs." Something of a fast-change Clark Kent with his Lois Lane (the first Margo was Agnes Moorehead), the Shadow was, of course, a made-for-radio hero: a man you could hear but not see.

The thirty-minute series became one of the decade's most enduring mysteries, sending cold tingles down the vertebrae of listeners who succumbed to the phantom avenger's chilling voice—as fiction readers in the nineteenth century had quivered at "a certain shadow which may go into any place, by sunlight, moonlight, starlight, firelight, candlelight . . . and be supposed to be cognizant of everything" (Charles Dickens). All across America, men, women, and children lowered their voices to a melodramatic rumble to copy the show's opening "Who knows what evil lurks . . ." In 1937 the Shadow's voice became that of a twenty-two-year-old actor, Orson Welles—who was forced to abandon the role when his "War of the Worlds" hoax (see page 194) brought him such nationwide vocal recognition that he could no longer anonymously voice the character.

Fans speculated endlessly whether there was something amorous between Cranston and Margo Lane. Only the Shadow knew. The radio hit lasted until 1954, spawning a bestselling magazine and countless fan clubs, and when it was rebroadcast in the Sixties in Chicago, students at Northwestern University formed the Secret Shadow Society, with members made "invisible" by black cloaks and slouch Shadow hats. They, as had Thirties audiences, thrilled to the hokum and melodrama, and mimicked even the announcer's signoff line: "The weed of crime bears bitter fruit. Crime does not pay. The Shadow knows. Ha-ha-ha!"

Inner Sanctum Mysteries: NBC Premiere, January 7, 1941

ANNOUNCER: Goooood eeeeevening friends of the Inner Sanctum. This is your host to welcome you in through the squeaking door for another half-hour of hooooorrooor . . . [Door squeaks open.]

Who cared if the stories were wildly improbable, usually turning on the maddest happenstances? The star of the show was that squeaking door; never has more chilling mileage been wrung from a sound effect. In fact, producer Himan Brown planned it that way. He had been working in a broadcasting studio in which the door to the basement groaned and squeaked when opened or closed. To a friend he remarked, "I'm going to make that door a star."

The show had the nation vowel crazy. The host (sometimes Boris Karloff) was named Raaaay-mouuuuund; who greeeeeeted you with a Hahahahahahaha; told you of that week's story; then, profusely apologizing for the evening's carnage, wished you "Pleasaaaaant dreeeeeams." And the door squeaked shut. "Inner Sanctum" was shameless in its use of melodrama, and audiences loved the show for it. For a time adults and kids spoke like Raaaay-mouuuuund.

"Sanctum" came on the heels of an earlier horror hit, **Lights Out,** first broadcast on NBC in 1935. That sinister show also had throat-clutching sound effects and was a nationwide hit. It employed clock chimes to chillingly tick away a deadline (ANNOUNCER: It . . . is . . . later . . . than . . . you . . . think!), and listeners swore they felt the show's icy wind blow out of their radio receivers as the announcer croaked: "This is the witching hour . . . It is the hour when dogs howl, and evil is let loose on the sleeping world . . . Want to hear about it? . . . Then turn out your lights!" And millions of fans listened in the living room's dark.

"Sanctum" stories—about, say, a sea monster that is killing off sailors but turns out to be the ship's captain—often took second billing to the host's voice and sound effects. A scientist was never merely "mad," but "Maaaad! Maaaad! Stark raving maaad!" Or a gentleman "just like yourself," who did not believe in zombies, was proved "Wrooong! Wrooong! Dead wrooong!" Edgar Allan Poe's stories lent themselves richly to the show's excesses, and in "The Telltale Heart," Boris Karloff's voice had radio fans quaking: "A groan! A groan of mortal terror . . . the low stifled sound that arises from the bottom of the soul . . . I knew the sound well."

The sound effects were among the best on the air. The *thump squiiiish* of a human head bludgeoned was achieved by striking a melon with a sledgehammer. And the show's organist at the Hammond had orders never to play a recognizable tune—just improvised "doom chords," "staccato frenzies" "piercing strings." The ghoulish treatment was even given to commercial sponsors like "Liiiiipton Teeeea and Souuuup." The program, not for the faint- of-heart, thrilled listeners into the early Fifties.

Gangbusters: NBC Premiere, July 20, 1935

For violence and mayhem it had no equal. And, too, for deafening noise: Nonstop machinegun fire, the shrill blast of police whistles, shattering glass, sirens, and screeching tires. Ministers and PTA groups condemned it, yet "Gangbusters" was one of the most popular—and noisiest—shows on radio.

It began with a racket of sound effects: marching feet, machine gun fire, siren wails. Then came an urgent voice, saying, "Calling the police! Calling all Americans! At war, marching against the underworld."

Created by writer-producer Phillips Lord and first broadcast on NBC in 1935, the crime drama grew out of an earlier Lord show called "G-Men" and a dispute Lord had with FBI director J. Edgar Hoover. "G-Men," with Hoover's assistance, dramatized actual case histories of the derring-do of law enforcement agents in their struggle with the underworld. It was violent and bloody, with justice rendered by heavy gun blasts; Hoover had hoped to show his agents as diligent sleuths cleverly tracking down and outwitting underworld gangsters. After twenty-six weeks, he severed association with the show, and Lord merely transformed FBI agents into city policemen and renamed the show "Gangbusters," a more apt title anyway.

A melange of actual police cases and fast-paced melodrama, the show radiated a remarkable aura of authenticity; an actress who played a gun moll continually received marriage proposals from prison inmates. The program dramatized the death of John Dillinger and the exploits of Baby Face Nelson and Willie Sutton, and had the good fortune to air during the golden age of gangsterism. As villains like Bonnie and Clyde glamorized the underworld, "Gangbusters" glamorized the other side of the battle. And it proved irresistible in giving listeners descriptions of criminals at large—"armed and extremely dangerous"—and proffered "clues" as to how you might find them—as if they'd be passing through your neighborhood that week. During a broadcast many terrified listeners checked windows and doors and switched on outside lights. To underscore the imminent threat lurking in your shrubbery, the show closed with the imperative: "If you see this man, notify the FBI, your local law enforcement agency, or *Gangbusters* . . . at once!" In its first three years the show helped capture 110 criminals.

The Lone Ranger: CBS Premiere, January 30, 1933

[MUSIC, "William Tell Overture." Hoofbeats fade in.]
RANGER: Hi-yo Silver! [GUNSHOTS, HOOFBEATS.]
ANNOUNCER: A fiery horse with the speed of light, a cloud of dust and hearty Hi-yo Silver! *The Lone Ranger!* . . . Return with us now to those thrilling days of yesteryear.

With his faithful Indian companion, Tonto, the daring and resourceful masked rider of the plains led the fight for law and order in the early Western United

States. Nowhere in the pages of history can one find a greater champion of justice—or a more popular hero of radio, and movies, and comic books, and television. First heard in 1933, the show was a true product of Depression America, created by lawyer turned producer George Trendle and several friends.

In 1929 Trendle purchased a Detroit radio station, which soon suffered from plummeting profits. To attract listeners and sponsors, he sought to create a bigger-than-life, superwholesome hero with a mystique (which would be provided by a mask) and abundant symbols of "purity" (which would come from a *white* horse with *silver* horseshoes named *Silver,* and a gun that shot *silver* bullets). (Coincidentally, the show's early sponsor was Silvercup Bread.) The hero was to be authoritative, speak intelligently (not in "cowboy" Wild West slang), and command respect and awe—as he indeed did until the show went off radio in 1954. In addition, the spic-and-span hero turned out to be a merchandiser's dream, exploitable through radio premiums, clothes, toys, and guns.

The concept developed piecemeal. The hero's name came about when Trendle mused to a friend, "I see him as a lone operator; he could even be a former Texas Ranger." Exclaimed the friend, "The Lone Ranger!" Another associate, Brace Beemer, suggested silver shoes for the white horse; Beemer himself would for thirteen years play the role of the Masked Man. The Ranger's mask was a direct steal from the popular fictional avenger Zorro in *The Mark of Zorro.*

With these important details decided, Trendle called in a writer, Fran Striker, who, speaking of details, envisioned the Ranger as "being a shade over six feet in height and just under 190 pounds." Recalling a radio series he'd written on Robin Hood, in which he gave the woodsman silver-tipped arrows, Striker typed into his first script: "silver bullets," "silver horseshoes," and "Silver." In having the Masked Man use costly, precious-metal bullets, Striker displayed a stroke of genius: It would be a constant reminder to the Lone Ranger to shoot sparingly, aware of the preciousness of human life. All involved agreed that Rossini's stirring "William Tell Overture" had to be the show's theme.

Tonto and Scout.   Initially, the Ranger did not have a sidekick and spoke to his horse—a device popularized in early Western films. But since radio listeners could not *see* Silver, the Lone Ranger's gab came off as dull monologue. **Tonto** entered the show in the tenth script and, ironically, the actor who voiced Tonto's broken English, John Todd, had won a reputation in Shakespearean plays. Most fans did not realize that the energetic Tonto was actually a man in his sixties when the series began, and over eighty when he read his last script. After 2,956 live broadcasts the show was retired—to reemerge on television—and the Lone Ranger, Silver, Tonto, and Scout (Tonto's horse) became as much a part of American legend as Daniel Boone.

[HOOFBEATS FADE OUT.]
VOICE: Who was that masked man?

SECOND VOICE: You don't know? That was the Lone Ranger! [Music UP FULL, "William Tell Overture."]

Mercury Theatre and War of the Worlds Broadcast: October 30, 1938

ANNOUNCER: [With urgency] Ladies and gentlemen, we interrupt our program of dance music to bring you a special bulletin.

So began the radio dramatization—critics would later say it was radio's moral equivalent of yelling "Fire!" in a crowded theater; fans would call it the ultimate thriller—of H. G. Wells's novel *The War of the Worlds*. It plunged tens of thousands of unsuspecting listeners across the nation into sheer panic, convinced that Martians had invaded Earth—first touching down in New Jersey. "In Newark," reported a newspaper the next morning, "in a single block, more than twenty families rushed out of their houses with wet towels over their faces to flee from what they believed was a gas raid." Reproached the *New York Times:* "The broadcast disrupted households, interrupted religious services, created traffic jams and clogged communications systems . . . [causing] adults to seek medical treatment for shock and hysteria."

The October 30 broadcast was meant by "Mercury Theater" host, Orson Welles, to be a Halloween prank. No one, including Orson Welles, thought radio

Orson Welles, The War of the Worlds.

could have such a devastating impact on listeners who, missing the show's explanatory opening credits, tuned in late and caught urgent "news flashes." No show before or since, on radio or television, sent people from Maine to California racing into the streets, hysterical. The broadcast made the twenty-three-year-old Orson Welles an overnight celebrity, and it remains the most famous single incident in radio history.

Written by Howard Koch, the radio play was titled "Invasion from Mars," and bore only a slight resemblance to H. G. Wells's novel. At a read-through, Koch realized that the initial faithful-to-the-novel adaptation simply did not work. The 1898 British fiction had to be modernized. Thus, Koch sprinkled his script with terms like secretary of the interior, narrative became news bulletins, and the London locale, for backyard believability, was changed to Grover's Mills, New Jersey. Horrific present-tense news flashes ordered people to "get out of town," and updates told of citizens crushed in mad stampedes, and of "seven thousand armed men, pitted against the single fighting machine of the invaders." By the time the show ended, most people were out of their homes, or too hysterical—or phoning police for advice—to hear the prankster Welles chuckle and sign off with: "If your doorbell rings and nobody's there, that was no Martian . . . it's Halloween." Informed of the national panic, CBS immediately flooded the airwaves with reassurances that the play was a Halloween spoof—but it took days before the last vestiges of terror vanished.

Why did so many listeners tune in late, missing the show's opening warning?

Because, say radio historians, at exactly twelve minutes into the Welles broadcast, "The Edgar Bergen–Charlie McCarthy Show," which millions had been following, switched from comedy to introduce a new singer. Listeners went dial-hopping—and caught Welles's "on-scene" reports, intercut with bulletins like: "Red Cross emergency workers dispatched to the scene . . . bridges hopelessly clogged with frantic human traffic . . . Martial law prevails throughout New Jersey and eastern Pennsylvania." The editor of the *Memphis Press* called back his staff to put out a special edition on the Martian invasion. In parts of the West, countless families abandoned their homes and scattered into the hills of the Rockies to hide. Unfortunately, they could not learn of the hoax and eventually had to be tracked down by sheriffs' posses.

Why did the public fall for the invasion? Much has been written about the matter. In 1938 Americans were less informed, more gullible, more trusting of the media, and largely unfamiliar with the notion of a media hoax. And, too, newspapers had been warning of a major war in Europe. Many people later claimed that they thought the invaders were not creatures from Mars, but Nazis from Germany in hideous disguise. Then, too, few actors could read a script as convincingly as Orson Welles.

CHAPTER 6

——————————— ◻ ———————————

The Fantasy Forties

1940 to 1949

The Acne and A-Bomb Decade

ED SULLIVAN PICKS THE STARS OF '40 read a newspaper headline. "Ronald Reagan, former Midwestern sports announcer, has had a solid year of 'B' pictures," columnist Sullivan wrote, suggesting the actor was ripe for big-time stardom. That same year, a young woman named Nancy Davis appeared in a high school play titled *First Lady,* giving a punchy delivery to her one line of dialogue: "They ought to elect the First Lady and then let her husband be President." Sullivan was as right about Reagan as the title of Nancy Davis's play was ironically prophetic: Twenty-nine-year-old Ronald Reagan did become a star in 1940, as dying Notre Dame football player George Gipp, whose coach, Knute Rockne, urged the Fighting Irish to "win just one for the Gipper." And as the later Mrs. Ronald Reagan, Nancy Davis did at times let her husband be president.

Also in that first year of the new decade, a young Richard Nixon lived with his June bride, Pat Ryan, in a rented garage apartment in Whittier, California, while across the country sixteen-year-old George "Poppy" Bush presided over the Greek Fraternal Societies at Phillips Academy in Massachusetts.

In a different vein, advertising, Oldsmobile opened the decade with the breakthrough announcement of Hydra-Matic Drive: "It is here! A car without a clutch pedal . . . a car that never needs shifting . . . the most modern car in the world!" Despite this being the eleventh year of the Depression, one of every five Americans owned a car, one in seven had a phone, and the average middle-class family lived in a $6,500 home bought at 4½ percent interest. Ads assured housewives that happy marriages depended on gleaming bathrooms, dust-free living rooms, and punctual evening meals. And the calypso-beat jingle from another ad had millions of Americans singing, "I'm Chiquita Banana / And

I've come to say / Bananas have to ripen in a certain way"; it ended with the caution that bananas love a tropical climate, "So you should never put bananas in the refrigerator." This was a concern now that more families owned "frosties" like the $99.95 Crosley Shelvador.

Equally new and popular was: "Pepsi-Cola hits the spot, / Twelve full ounces, that's a lot . . ."

So too was Madison Avenue's clever home permanent pitch: "Which twin has the Toni?" Years would pass before the Federal Trade Commission revealed that although one of the women pictured had actually given herself a home wave "at one time," for the photo session both of them had been coiffed by a professional hairdresser.

In the early Forties, housewives bought refrigerators and the likes of the Bendix Home Laundry, the first automatic clothes washer. By the end of the decade the trendy item was a television set. In 1949, Americans bought 100,000 TV sets a week, and nationwide fads had erupted over such "instant" screen stars as Howdy Doody, Milton Berle, and Hopalong Cassidy—all mass appeal phenomena we'll examine in this chapter. The late Forties nationwide buying spree—from kitchen appliances to phonograph players to TV sets; to say nothing of such luxury items as fur coats and diamond rings—was made possible by the booming war economy. World War II gave employment to 7 million unemployed Americans, and provided millions of jobs for women, older folk, and, significantly, teenagers. For the war ushered in the so-called teenage revolution, which in turn provided Madison Avenue with an entire new sector of society easily susceptible to fads and trends.

Bobby-Soxer Fad Mill

The Forties are the acne and A-bomb era for one obvious reason (the dropping of the first atomic bomb) and a not-so-obvious one: Whereas the bomb put an end to the Second World War, acne could as devastatingly end a teenager's social life—something of an equivalent horror in an age when the adolescent emerged as a social phenomenon and marketing target. The teen revolution, which would blossom full flower in the Fifties, was unleashed in the mid-Forties. Adolescence became a cult to be lovingly prolonged, intensely experienced, and profitably catered to as never before. "Teenagers," as adolescents were then popularly labeled, cared little about the bomb: "I think you should have more articles on dates and shyness," a girl wrote to *Seventeen*. "Stories like those on atomic energy are very boring." The magazine itself was launched in 1944 to cater to the new fashions and fantasies of young girls.

The war played a role in creating the cult of the teenager. With men over eighteen in the service, younger boys stepped in as "heads of families," as "big men about town," and picked up easy pocket cash in a labor-scarce work force. Girls, too, earned money to lavish on themselves by baby-sitting for parents on night shifts at war plants. Teens had money, and Madison Avenue moved in to siphon it off by promoting clothing crazes, pop songs, and dances. Saturday nights, swarms of jitterbugging teenagers dropped their hard-earned coins in jukeboxes to listen to the latest 78 or 45 discs. Mid-decade, RCA Victor and Decca were each selling 100 million records annually, and jukeboxes had blossomed into an $80-million industry, with four hundred thousand of the flashing players in soda shops and diners. Home phonograph equipment, as we'll see, became a status symbol, and essential for a teenager's social success.

Seventeen was not alone in addressing the new bobby-soxer market. *Ladies' Home Journal* inaugurated a section titled "Profile of Youth," and newspapers like the *Chicago Daily News* launched widely read columns on "Teen News" and "Teen Views." Unlike their counterparts in later decades, teenagers in the Forties were still largely innocent, sexually naive, uncynical, and uncritical of adults and the world around them. A third of the teens questioned in one study agreed that the most serious problem facing the American teenager was acne. "Zits" became a frequently heard cry; dermatologists were "zits doctors," and advertisers dreamed up salves, astringents, and facial pore cleansers, while teens were advised to avoid chocolate and peanut butter.

In all, the era was the first time adolescents had a separate sense of identity. By the late Forties girls had a uniform: **pleated skirt, baggy sweater, bobby sox,** and **loafers.** On the downside, the absence from the home of a wartime father and working mother, which brought the teenager into the spotlight, also contributed to a new breed of teen who roamed the streets under the rubric juvenile delinquent—a much-used label in newspaper articles and editorials.

As mentioned, after the war prosperous Americans embarked on a spending spree—one that would last nearly two decades. People felt they had earned the right to indulge and enjoy themselves after the privations of the Depression and the battle. Reality had been harsh, and Americans wanted the same thing that Blanche DuBois craved in Tennessee Williams's Forties play, *A Streetcar Named Desire:* "I don't want realism. I want magic! Yes, yes, magic!"

This chapter and the next are devoted to that magic in its many guises.

FADS, FOLLIES, AND TRENDS

Zoot Suit With a Reet Pleat and a Peg Leg

It's been said that the oversized draped shape of the zoot suit became a fad among teenage boys who, with older men at war, wished to step into Dad's role at home and around town by slipping into his size in clothes. The baggy, broad-shouldered look certainly suggested the garment belonged to a larger man, if not a gorilla. The jacket had wide lapels with a long, narrow "reet" pleat, heavily padded shoulders, and multibutton sleeves, and was worn with high-waisted trousers cut full in the thigh and tapering to an ankle-hugging tightness called the peg leg. In many versions the foot opening was so narrow that the trousers needed ankle zippers.

To really "put on the dog," a zoot suiter donned a wide-brimmed fedora hat, a glaringly patterned fish-tail tie, and a lengthy loop of curving key chain that began at the belt, plunged to below the knee, and came to nestle in the gentleman's pocket. His expression "Jeet?" meant "Did you eat?" whereas he called his clothes threads and his girlfriends jills.

Perhaps in his larger-than-life get-up the teenaged boy did feel like a big man, but the fashion fad was as much influenced by gangsters of the period who favored the baggy ensemble for the hidden guns, holsters, cash, and brass knuckles it could easily accommodate. Its popularity spread when the undersized crooning idol Frank Sinatra draped himself in the vogue. Because of its smarmy association with the underworld (and perhaps as well because of its popularity in Harlem among black "hipsters"), the outfit was condemned by many states, while preachers claimed that men in zoot suits appealed only to the pre-repentant Mary Magdalene kind of woman.

Seldom had men's attire caused the kind of riots that broke out in New York and California against zoot suits. In the summer of 1943, a skirmish erupted into a full-scale imbroglio when U.S. servicemen, carousing through the streets of Los Angeles, assaulted any civilian male in a zoot suit. After several days of fighting, servicemen (in part antagonistic to the trendy urban males not serving in the armed forces) were restricted from visiting Los Angeles on pass.

Origin.   There remains dispute over whether the fashion craze was uniquely American, or a British import. Many historians claim that the suit was the invention of a British tailor named F. P. Scholte at the close of the nineteenth century, an adaptation of Guards officers' oversized greatcoats. In London during the early war years a version of the zoot suit enjoyed a vogue among street hawkers, known as "spivs" or "wide boys," who hustled nylons, chocolates, and other niceties in short supply.

The words zoot and reet are believed to come from late Thirties jive talk, with reet meaning "excellent" or "perfect." The origin of "zoot" is assumed to be a jive rhyme pronunciation of "suit." The fashion vogue peaked in the early war years, but went into rapid decline when the WPB (War Production Board) ordered that clothing manufacturers could use only a restricted number of inches of fabric in men's garments. The so-called L-85 restrictions also applied to women's attire and, as we're about to see, influenced what the well-dressed lady wore.

Convertible Suits for Women

Before the war, the American fashion world followed the lead of Paris designers. Though home-grown garment designers and manufacturers ran a $3 billion industry, they trusted the French to tell them what styles to create, what fabrics to use, and where to place buttons, bangles, and hemlines. When Paris fashion oracles were suddenly silenced by a German threat, then an invasion, Americans were forced to make all these crucial decisions themselves. That fact, combined with U.S. government fabric restrictions for civilian garments, produced America's own first fashions.

Initially, the restrictions dictated vogues. A civilian manufacturer, for instance, under the L-85 edict, could produce a dress or skirt with no more than two inches of hem and no more than one patch pocket on each blouse; no top could have an attached hood or shawl. Belts were limited to 2 inches in width, and skirts could be no more than 72 inches around. Cuffs on coats were forbidden. Thus emerged the trend of the "convertible suit"—that is, a three-piece ensemble which, by removal of the daytime jacket, became the evening dining and dancing attire of a soft blouse and short skirt. "It may be a new cutaway suit," advised *Vogue* in 1944, "or an old suit with a new shantung blouse. Whatever you may be doing, short of hoeing your garden, you may be, quite correctly be, wearing a suit." For about four years American women proudly wore their spartan suits, skimpy skirts, and frill-less blouses as their own wartime uniform.

Then, with Paris liberated, the war over, fabric restrictions lifted, Americans again turned to Europe, this time embracing the fresh, bold fashion statement by a Parisian, called the New Look, or the . . .

Dior Look

At ten-thirty A.M. on February 12, 1947, at the salon of Christian Dior at 30 Avenue Montaigne, Paris, the world's fashion editors breathlessly awaited what had been secretly touted as a "couture breakthrough." The doyenne of fashion writers, Carmel Snow of *Harper's Bazaar,* was heard to sigh crossly from her aisle seat, "This had better be good." Two years earlier, the unknown, middle-aged Dior had sketched a handful of dresses outrageously luxuriant in their ample use of rich fabric and bosom and hip padding.

Supposedly the first sound heard at the salon show was the *swiiiish* of petticoats rubbing against yards and yards of skirt fabric hovering a mere 12 inches above the floor. The models had been told to flaunt the cloth, and *Harper's* British writer, Ernestine Carter, reported that the young women delighted in "arrogantly swinging their vast skirts—one had eighty yards of fabric . . . [They] swirled on, contemptuously bowling over the ashtray stands like ninepins . . . This new softness was positively voluptuous." The fashion editors cheered, many wept. "It was like a new love affair," wrote one spectator, "the first sight of Venice; a new chance, in fact a new look at life." That collection, as well as the one that followed it, was dubbed by *Life* as the New Look. After a private showing for England's royal family, Princess Margaret wore a New Look dress for her parents' silver wedding anniversary, and Princess Elizabeth ordered calf-length skirts for her own wedding trousseau.

In America, *Vogue, Harper's Bazaar,* and *Glamour* announced that all of yesterday's wartime clothes were shamefully skimpy and out of date, and henceforth women could only wear the lush, exciting Dior Look—or copy thereof. In advertisements women were encouraged to "throw everything out" and purchase an entire new wardrobe—which meant an outlay of from $20 (for a copy) to $450 per dress. Not all American women liked the idea of accentuating their hips and hiding their legs; in New York City presidential envoy Mrs. Anna Rosenberg proclaimed, "It shows everything you want to hide and hides everything you want to show."

But the first postwar fashion fad had been rhapsodically and unstoppably launched. Dior himself was flabbergasted by the upheaval he had created: "My God, what have I done?" he murmured en route to the bank. The New Look's opulence of fabric was the first truly innovative statement in fashion since the flapper's vogue of the Twenties and, more significantly in terms of trends, it kicked off mass-market demand for designer-named items. The name Dior was on America's lips, paving the way for the fashion and product spin-off vogues later associated with such labels as Ralph Lauren, Oleg Cassini, and Halston. The preeminence of the New Look continued throughout the remainder of the decade of the Forties.

Nylon Stockings

Today the word artificial has a decidedly negative ring, connoting "not the real thing," as in Astroturf, fireproof Christmas trees, polyester leisure suits, and eternally fresh silk flowers. In the Forties, though, artificial was hardly a pejorative tag but the hottest of trendy words. And superpolymer 66, or nylon, seemed to be a substance of limitless promise in products like toothbrush bristles and ladies' stockings, generating nationwide pandemonium in the latter manifestation. Nylon stockings were prized over ones of "natural" silk as the novelty of aluminum dinnerware in Napoleon's day was deemed trendier than gold place settings.

The multichained chemical, a polymer (*poly,* Greek for "many"; *meros,* "parts"), was first hinted at in September 1931 when chemists Julian Hill and Wallace Carothers presented a paper before the American Chemical Society in Buffalo on their studies of polymerization carried out at the E. I. Du Pont Company. It marked the first public announcement of the research program that led to the 1935 perfection of superpolymer 66, later dubbed nylon. First came the late Thirties breakthrough of nylon toothbrush bristles. Then in 1939 nylon stockings were displayed at that year's New York World's Fair and San Francisco's Golden Gate International Exposition. An ensuing avalanche of orders caused more than 36 million pairs to be sold in the following year—even though nylons, at $1.25 a pair, cost more than twice as much as 59-cent silk stockings. And once America entered the war, nylon became such a precious military commodity—for parachutes, rope, and tents—that stockings made of the synthetic could only be purchased on the black market; their rarity then made them even a hotter vogue. After Pearl Harbor, a single pair of nylons cost $10.

Early pairs came with the guarantee that they were unadulterated "100% Virgin Nylon," and the explanatory note: "Shrink proof, moth proof, non-allergic, resists mildew, warm as wool." These promises were major selling points, since moths, mildew, and shrinkage were real concerns with silk stockings. Du Pont slated May 15, 1940, to be "nylon day," the debut of the stockings in department stores across the country, and store stock was limited due to the deluge of retail orders. Test wearers had been quoted in the press as saying the garments endured "unbelievable hours of performance," and rumor had it that a single pair could last a lifetime. Women queued up hours before store doors opened. Hosiery departments were stampeded. In many stores, near riots broke out.

After the war, nylons were in unprecedented demand. To celebrate the industry's rebirth, a two-ton replica of actress Marie Wilson's leg, clothed in nylon, was unveiled in Los Angeles in the late Forties, then the star was hosted aloft beside the giant leg to display her own nylons. Du Pont promised that never again would there be a nylon shortage.

Wash and Wear

Synthetic fabrics—from cellulose, to acetate, to nylon, to acrylic and polyester—were a godsend to housewives in the Forties (and Fifties) who previously had spent up to twenty hours a week ironing skirts and shirts, tablecloths, draperies, and bed linens of natural fibers. Even "magic" blends like "60% acrylic / 40% cotton" shrank laundry drudgery dramatically. In short time, the rage in clothing in postwar America was "wash and wear," a label and a promise, which caused synthetic garments for men, women, and children to outsell natural fiber wear. The trend continued with polyester being a vogue of the Fifties, and nylon pantyhose with spandex tummy control being a hot item in the Sixties. In fact it was the fashion statement of the miniskirt that triggered the switch from stockings to pantyhose around 1966. The circular knitting machines used to make seamless nylon stockings were adapted to knit half the panty at the top of a seamless tube of stocking, then the halves were stitched together to make the finished product. Nylon and its related synthetics soon went into making artificial body parts, and in 1969 Neil Armstrong unfurled a nylon American flag on the moon.

GI Joe

Whereas the First World War produced the image and expression doughboy, the Second World War gave the country no clearer male and female popular icons than GI Joe and Rosie the Riveter.

The term GI Joe seems to have originated in a fashion following that of another American icon, Uncle Sam. Sam Wilson was a New York meat packer who during the War of 1812 provided the military with rations in barrels bearing the initials U.S.—for United States, then still an uncommon expression. The good-natured Wilson was known locally as Uncle Sam, and in time rations stamped U.S. became known to soldiers as bounty from Uncle Sam. Lexicographer Stuart Flexner points out that in the military in the Twenties GI stood for galvanized iron, and that a GI was a sturdy, heavily galvanized army garbage can. By 1935, though, GI was a label stamped or stenciled on every "government issue" from soldiers' underwear to tents to trucks. At the same time, "Joe" was in popular usage in expressions such as Joe College, Joe Blow, and just an ordinary Joe. Not surprisingly, a Joe wearing government issue clothes became GI Joe. "*G.I.* and *Joe* were combined and first appeared as *G.I. Joe* on

June 17, 1942," writes Flexner, "in Lieutenant Dave Gerger's comic strip for *Yank*, the army weekly." The expression quickly became commonplace. In later decades, GI Joe dolls and plastic soldiers would become faddish toys for boys (see page 298).

Rosie the Riveter

At the start of the Forties, a fourth of the nation's work force was female—and had been since the boom liberation years of the Twenties. Women tended dime-store ribbon counters, cotton-mill looms, and, as telephone operators, poked steel-tipped cables into massive switchboards. They also made most of America's shirts and dresses, half of its coats and suits, and a fifth of its cigars. Well over 11 million women went to work, and an uncountable number of others hooked rugs, addressed envelopes, and toiled away at other low-paying jobs from their homes.

The tremendous male labor shortage of World War II drew millions of women into office and factory jobs, especially into defense plants, where they fitted out guns and riveted airplane parts. Working women in the Forties made great strides. The government established a policy of equal pay for equal work for women, and pants (called slacks) became an acceptable part of a woman's attire in the plant, and to a lesser degree at home. Department stores such as Macy's in New York, Filene's in Boston, and Hudson's in Detroit opened slacks shops for women, foreseeing the postwar tend in women's fashions. Through a popular patriotic song, "Rosie the Riveter," all working women in wartime became Rosies. Legend has it that the real-life symbol for the image was a factory worker, Rosie Bonavita, who, with the help of a female co-worker, pounded 3,345 rivets into a fighter plane's wing in a record six hours.

Rosie the Riveter.

Though all GI Joes appreciated the homefront efforts of Rosie the Riveters, the popular female images they hung inside their barracks lockers were of a more glamorous and less attired sort called . . .

Pin-Up Girls

"What ain't we got?" asks the chorus of island-stranded military men in the musical *South Pacific:* "We ain't got dames." Lacking the live article, soldiers substituted pin-ups, plastering them to the doors of their lockers and the walls of their Quonset huts. Even the inside of a helmet was a sure bet to contain a girlie picture. As earlier decades had Gibson girls, vamps, and *It* girls, the female sex symbol of the Forties was the bathing-suit-clad pin-up. It was a separate wartime industry, a male mania. And it made stars out of many a shapely model and Hollywood hopeful.

The phenonemon was also called "Forties girls," and the most famous came from the motion picture industry. Ironically, the most popular pin-up "girl" of

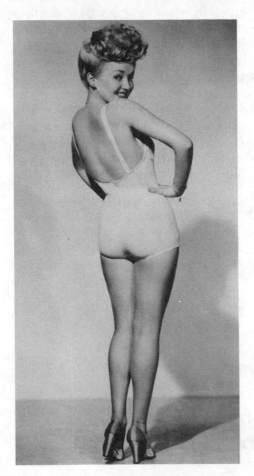

Betty Grable.

the period was the mature, twenty-nine-year-old Betty Grable, glancing back over her shoulder in a tight white swimsuit, which was said to encase the world's "neatest bottom, atop the world's best legs." For that pose of wholesomeness suggesting sex without sin, in poster reproductions and in real-life demonstrations, the star earned $300,000 in one year. The term pin-up girl itself first appeared in the armed forces newspaper *Yank* on April 30, 1943.

Pin-ups popped up everywhere. A popular photo of Rita Hayworth, said to be the most artistic of the genre, was supposedly affixed to the first atomic bomb dropped on Hiroshima in 1945. Hoping to increase circulation, magazines like *Time* and *Life* latched on to the fad, replacing politicians and generals as cover subjects with *cover girls* like Frances Vornes, dubbed "the Shape" and voted Pin-Up Girl of '44. Hollywood released a film called *Cover Girl*, which featured Anita Colby, who simultaneously held the distinctive position of "feminine director" of Selznick Studios. In pin-up photos leggy Jinx Falkenburg (sister of tennis player Bob) was attached to the sides of planes at one air force flight school. Pictures of Chili Williams, famous as the Polka-Dot Girl for the pattern on her swimsuit, were distributed to the armed forces by the tens of thousands.

The busty Diana Dors (born with the risky surname of Fluck) won her first bathing-beauty contest at age thirteen, and within two years had a new name and was labeled "the sultry blonde bombshell with the wiggle." Perhaps her most celebrated pin-up was the pose in a gondola wearing a diamond-studded mink bikini—the **bikini** itself being a Forties innovation by French designer Louis Reard and named after the Pacific Bikini Atoll, site of a 1946 peacetime nuclear test. Two other favorite pin-up beauties were Ava Gardner and Lana Turner.

Esquire and Playboy.   Almost as popular with soldiers as bathing-suited pin-ups were the sultry paintings of women scantly clad in diaphanous costumes that appeared monthly in *Esquire*. So sexy were many of the morale-boosting "girlies" that in 1944 Postmaster General Frank Walker banned them from the mails, causing the magazine to discontinue running the illustrations. "We would like to know who in hell got the bright idea of banning pictures from your most popular magazine," wrote three GIs. "You won't find one barracks overseas that hasn't got an *Esquire* Pin-Up Girl. I, for one, have close to fifteen of them." The soldiers concluded, "Those pictures are very much on the clean and healthy side, and it gives us guys a good idea of what we're fighting for . . . I wish these high-browed monkeys could spend a year overseas without anything but magazines."

Prior to the wave of pin-up girls, sexy pictures of females most often appeared in a publication genre called barbershop magazines. The young women featured were usually burlesque queens and showgirls. There was no nudity, just a bawdy playfulness toward sex. The publications also featured mail-order advertisements on breast and penis enlargement, as well as tips on prolonging orgasm. The wartime pin-up craze is said to have forced the barbershop magazines to offer more skin, while at the same time freeing the covers of staid, serious-minded magazines to print more alluring poses of less-attired women. Pin-ups also made it acceptable for a Hollywood star to unabashedly pose as a sex symbol in a legitimate publication. The pioneering *Esquire* was followed by the trail-blazing *Playboy,* which launched the icon of the monthly centerfold playmate. As the women shed clothing, the camera's focus shifted from the entire body to body parts. According to psychiatrist Karen Horney, pin-ups and playmates are a major cause of modern mental distress. Sexually alluring pictures (1) continually stimulate our desires, (2) frustrate our attempts to satisfy those desires with facsimiles of the pictured women, and (3) set up an atmosphere among men of competition, rivalry, and fear of defeat.

World War II Lingo

As had the First World War, the Second influenced the American vernacular in many colorful ways. It gave us, for instance, the phrase—and the confection—**M&M's,** a war-effort candy developed by Mars company that, unlike a chocolate bar, "melts in your mouth, not in your hand"—an important consideration for a soldier who did not want to have his fingers sticky from chocolate when it came time to fire a gun or toss a grenade. Mars executives Forest Mars and Bruce Murrie lent their surname initials to the candy's name.

Here are many of the popular wartime phrases that permanently entered the language:

Bazooka was used in 1943 by Major Zeb Hastings to name the military's new 5-foot-long, anti-tank rocket gun, which went *bazoooom.* But the name is more than an echoic. In the early years of the century, a bazooka was a harmless two-part stove pipe bomb used by comedian Bob Burns as a laugh-getting stage prop. It's thought the word is from the Dutch *bazuim,* "trumpet," or from bazoo, the mid-1800s slang for loudmouth.

B-girls, short for bar girls, was the term for a saloon's female employees whose job was to mix with male customers, chat, and encourage their purchases of alcohol. She received a commission on drinks and picked up extra cash either upstairs or in a backroom as a prostitute. On the other hand, as lexicographer Flexner points out, a "V-girl" was one who "gave it away" freely to keep up the morale of men in uniform—or who was just partial to men in uniform.

Blitzkrieg (German *Blitz,* "lightning"; *Krieg,* "war") was popularized through Hitler's rapid, devastating armored attacks in 1939 on Poland, which kicked off the war. It became so commonplace that it was shortened to blitz.

Eisenhower jacket was the name of the fitted, belted, waist-length coat favored by General Eisenhower during the war.

Ersatz is German for "replacement," and the English-speaking world borrowed the word early in the war to refer to any artificial item that replaced a natural one due to wartime shortages. Ersatz coffee was made from chicory and ersatz bread from potato peels; and in Germany ersatz hamburgers were often of dog meat. As *Time* disparaged in 1940: "Dog meat has been eaten in every major German crisis, at least since the time of Frederick the Great," adding the epicurean grace note: "Of European dog breeds, the German dachshund is

General Eisenhower in "his" jacket.

considered the most succulent." After the war ersatz came to designate anything fake.

Geronimo, now an explosive exclamation of surprise, was the exuberant shout of American paratroopers on jumping from a plane. "The yell was coined and popularized," says Flexner, "by the many American Indians, especially Yakis and Cherokee, in our paratroop units." The real-life Geronimo, an Apache feared by American troops in the 1800s for his surprise attacks, died in 1909.

Gobbledygook, meaning nonsensical, bureaucratic jargon, was coined in 1944 by Texan Maury Maverick, chairman of the Smaller War Plant Corporation, after he attempted to decipher the obscure "officialese" in a committee memo. He claimed the word was inspired by the gobbling utterances of turkeys.

Kamikaze, Japanese for "divine wind," when combined with the word pilot, came to be the feared expression for Japanese suicide air fighters willing to dive-bomb to their death for the glory of country. After the war the word slipped into everyday speech as a synonym for self-destructive behavior.

Mae West, a canvas and inflatable rubber life vest issued to airmen, straightforwardly derived its name from the entertainer whose chest measurements made her look as through she were wearing an inflated vest.

Penicillin was a new word on America's lips in the early Forties, especially those of soldiers who had watched horrific films that warned of venereal disease and its harsh, pre-antibiotic day treatments. Injected into a wound on the battlefield, the miracle drug saved countless lives and spared thousands of soldiers the trauma of limb amputation from rampant infection.

POW first became the popular abbreviation for prisoner of war in the Forties.

Radar was a new and invaluable technology in the war. Developed by the British, it was called radiolocator, for its use of radio-frequency waves to target an enemy plane. The U.S. Navy popularized the abbreviated word radar.

WAACs and **WAVEs** quickly became familiar acronyms for Women's Army Auxiliary Corps and Women Accepted for Voluntary Emergency Service (in the navy).

Walkie-talkie, the name of a portable two-person receiver and transmitter communication device developed in the Thirties, was popularized during the war. After the conflict, the devices became commonplace among police and campers, and eventually appeared as children's toys.

Popular Forties phrases unrelated to the war effort: **barber,** to gossip; **bucket,** a large, old car; **drugstore cowboy,** a teenager who hung out on Saturday nights at a drugstore soda fountain; **duck soup,** any task easily performed, or a person who was a pushover; a **high pillow,** a big shot; a **Joad,** a migratory worker; a **mothball,** a serious-minded student; and a **pancake turner,** a disc jockey.

Nonsensical talk or baloney was **phendinkus.** To doll up in fancy clothes was to **put on the dog.** A cheap article of clothing was a **reach-me-down.** A party in which guests chipped in cash to help pay for the host's apartment rent was a **rent party.** Food for a beggar was a **lump.** A baseball park was an **orchard.**

Kilroy was Here

Graffiti is ancient, appearing on walls in ancient Egypt, Greece, and Rome. But perhaps the most famous and ubiquitous modern scrawl materialized in the Forties in the many guises of a character named Kilroy, who seemed to be here, there, and everywhere. Pictorially, Kilroy was a wide-eyed, bald-headed face peering over a fence that hid everything below his long paper-clip of a nose, except for his fingers, which gripped the top of the fence. His impish boast, "Kilroy was here," first surfaced during World War II, appearing at countryside rest stops, in city restaurants, and behind the top-secret doors to military boardrooms. The mischievous face and the phrase became a national joke, and a mystery that remains unsolved.

For more than a decade Kilroy was truly everywhere. The outrageousness of the graffiti was not so much what it said, but where it turned up. As on top of the torch of the Statue of Liberty in New York Harbor, on the bullet-scarred base of the Marco Polo Bridge in China, under the Arc de Triomphe in Paris, painted on huts in Polynesia and across a girder of the George Washington

Bridge connecting Manhattan to New Jersey. Contests arose to beat Kilroy to isolated and uninhabited places around the globe. A group of Air Force pilots thought they had preceded Kilroy to an atoll in the Pacific Marshall Islands, only to land and find a freshly painted sign:

NO GRASS ATOLL, NO TREES ATOLL, NO WATER ATOLL.
NO WOMEN ATOLL, NO LIQUOR ATOLL, NO FUN ATOLL.
AND NO KILROY ATOLL . . .
I JUST DIDN'T PAUSE ATOLL: KILROY

Its appearance was not always of GI origin. The phrase or face appeared chalked on the backs of coats of women strolling down Michigan Boulevard in Chicago, and more than one paper reported that a pregnant woman wheeled into the operating room for delivery was unrobed to find "Kilroy was here" scrawled across her belly. Perhaps Kilroy's most daring appearance occurred during the meeting of the Big Three in Potsdam, Germany, in July 1945. VIPs Truman, Attlee, and Stalin had exclusive use of an opulent marble bathroom, off limits to everyone else. On the second day of the summit, an excited Stalin emerged from the bathroom sputtering something in Russian to one of his aides. A translator overheard Stalin demand, "Who is Kilroy?"

Origin.   Much has been written about the origin and proliferation of Kilroy graffiti. It seems first to have appeared on military docks and ships in late 1939, with the phrase "Kilroy was here" prankishly meaning "a U.S. serviceman was here." Soon, though, it acquired a momentum of its own, materializing wherever servicemen traveled, then infecting civilian populations. Some authorities claim it was one big worldwide joke to relieve global tensions.

Others, though, have plumbed deeper subconscious depths, as did Richard Sterma in *American Image,* in 1948: "Cut the name in two and it is 'he who killed the king,' kill *roi."* As Sterma strained to see it, the graffito was a "patricidal striving in ourselves" that swept the globe during a murderous time. "In the unconscious," he concluded, "the enemy in war is identical with the father . . . as the little boy experiences him emotionally in the Oedipus phase of his libido developments."

Whatever the reason for the global joke, it developed a Canadian counterpart in the guise of a character named Clem. In the late Sixties Kilroy-like graffiti mysteriously appeared throughout Los Angeles under the name of Overby, in phrases like "Overby lives," "Overby rules," and "Overby strikes every 7 hours." But no later incarnation ever approached the popularity and ubiquitousness of the original Kilroy, who had no message other than to announce his mysterious presence. Kilroymania peaked during the war, lingered into the early Fifties, then vanished; the joke forgotten as the global conflict was resolved.

Hummel Figurines

A collector's passion that owes its origin to World War II is the Hummel figurine, handmade by the Goebel company of Rodental, Germany, since 1935. The porcelain children in pixielike poses were created in sketches by Sister Maria Innocentia Hummel, a Franciscan nun of the Siessen Convent in the Swabian Alps, who assigned production rights to Goebel. To this day Goebel sculptors derive new hand-painted figurines from Sister Innocentia's artwork, of which there remains an abundance. Since the figurines are handmade, no two Hummels are identical, and fervid fans will collect of the same character—like Daddy's Girls, or Chimney Sweep, or Sings of Spring—which may differ by as little as 5/16 of an inch.

Sister Innocentia was born Berta Hummel in 1909 (she died in 1946 from tuberculosis) to parents who encouraged her artistic talents. After graduating from an art academy in Munich, she joined the convent in 1933 and began to sketch innocent children engaged in play, study, or labor. She used the pictures at first to make elaborate, hand-painted postcards to raise money for her convent. The postcards attracted the attention of the Goebel Art Company, and in 1935 an agreement was reached in which the convent received royalties on the sale of the figurines. Because of the high quality of their craftsmanship, the early Hummels were popular throughout Germany. Each clay figure was (and is) put through a rigid manufacturing process of being fired, hand-painted, glazed, and fired again.

The war disrupted Hummel production, but later American occupation forces began buying the little figurines as gifts for wives and girlfriends back home. By the late Forties Hummels—always bearing the M. I. Hummel signature on the base—were prized collector's items for their rarity as well as their craftsmanship. While Goebel would jump on the instant collectibles bandwagon in the Seventies, producing plates, plaques, and bells, the cherished and pricey items remain the figurines, valued according to their age, which can be determined by various "bee" trademarks stamped on the underside of the base. An original piece from the Forties with a "full bee" trademark is worth several times what its contemporary counterpart is.

Precious Moments.   In many ways, Hummelmania of the Forties is wilder today than ever. Goebel likes to boast that more Americans collect Hummels than any other art form—though Precious Moments, teardrop-eyed figurines based on the artwork of Samuel Butcher and produced by Enesco, is a collectibles' fad fast catching up. The two hundred thousand members of the M. I. Hummel Club, headquartered in Pennington, New Jersey, gather regularly to compare, swap, and buy new Hummels. In the Thirties in Germany, a figurine could be bought for 65 cents, whereas today's prices range from $40 to $1,800, and some scarce older Hummels—like 1935 versions of Silent Night—can fetch $20,000.

Hummel collectors love to hear the news that an original mold is being retired—that is, broken by the company so the figurine can never be cast again.

A quiver of excitement swept through the collectors' world in 1990 when the company announced the retirement of Sings of Spring, its value immediately rising. It remains to be seen if the Precious Moments fad will one day overtake Hummel fever.

TV Frozen Food Dinners

The decade that ushered in television also witnessed the debut of precooked frozen foods that in short time became known as TV dinners. Neither innovation was initially very appealing: early television, as we'll see later in this chapter, suffered from technical problems and the fact that too few people owned sets; the first frozen meals upon defrosting were often tasteless, soggy globs, and most American families did not yet own freezers, only ice boxes, which were not cold enough to keep a store-bought package frozen. Thus a food had to be eaten the day it was purchased.

Nonetheless, as *Consumer Reports* announced in the summer of 1945: "Precooked frozen foods have a brilliant future," conceding that "in their present state of development they vary in both quality and convenience." The next year the watchdog publication predicted that Americans would soon be purchasing food in containers "which can be thrown away when the meal is finished," heralding the multicompartment aluminum TV dinner.

In the early Forties, even families who owned refrigerators were short on precious freezer space, since most appliances had only a small compartment for ice cubes and ice cream. Thus, before World War II, the advantages of frozen foods—promoted by Clarence Birdseye in the Twenties—went largely unappreciated; even freezing compartments in supermarkets had difficulty keeping bulk packages frozen solid.

If you went into a grocery store in 1940, you saw a specialty section containing a large white closed-top freezer with the curious label: "Frosted Foods: Easy to Prepare." Interestingly, much industry consideration went into the decision to call foods frosted; it being, first, a chilled state easier for refrigerators to achieve, and second, a phrase less intimidating in tone to consumers than frozen, which seemed to imply the need for icepicks and hammers to get at the food. On the back of each package were instructions telling the novice how to store, thaw, and cook the item. Among the first frozen foods were raspberries, peas, spinach, and haddock.

Swanson.　What really triggered the consumer trend toward frozen foods, though, was the war, and the subsequent rationing of canned goods for the military use of metal. Frozen food manufacturers even convinced the government to declare their products essential to the war effort. Consequently, food shortages in certain commodities made buying "frozens" both necessary and patriotic; and with a quarter of the nation's housewives working in defense plants, a frozen dinner was a godsend. By the end of the war, Americans were accustomed to frozen foods, and, conveniently, refrigeration technology had greatly improved, with the price of refrigerators continually dropping. These events merged just as the golden age of television dawned. The frozen dinner quickly was dubbed a TV dinner.

By the late Forties, your neighborhood might have been visited by a "Frost-mobile." This was not the Good Humor man, but a "frosting expert" in a converted, refrigerated bus, who demonstrated his company's line of foods and gave curbside instructions on how to thaw and cook items. As television viewership increased, so too did the audience for frozen foods. Swanson Frozen Food Company debuted its extensive line of tasty, aluminum-tray, heat-and-serve dinners in the early Fifties, with the first meal being a festive serving of turkey and whipped sweet potatoes—which was soon followed by roast beef, fried chicken, and ham glazed with raisin sauce.

Boil-in-a-Bag.   In 1965 a new innovation appeared in supermarket freezers, boil-in-a-bag frozen vegetables. The concept won immediate high marks from *Consumer Reports* on convenience, taste, and quality, if not on price.

Frozen foods changed the country's eating habits. In 1920, for instance, the typical American ate (hard as such statistics are to swallow) 110 pounds of "fresh" vegetables a year. Once frozen foods caught on, the poundage started to climb, reaching 220 pounds per capita consumption in 1980, due largely to the year-round availability of all items. Fish is an even larger success story. Prior to the advent of frozen foods and home refrigerators, most Americans simply did not eat fresh (uncanned and unsalted) fish; freezing made the food commonplace.

From a novelty item at the start of the Forties, by the close of the decade frozen foods were a modern convenience. In later decades they would appear in the forms of trendy-sounding gourmet meals (like Swanson's Le Menu line), diet dinners, frozen pizza, croissants, cakes, pies, just about anything that could cut food preparation time for working men and women. Clarence Birdseye— who got his "quick-freezing" brainstorm on a fur-trading expedition in Labrador in the early 1900s, while feasting on thawed caribou and cabbage—changed America's eating habits and launched a multibillion-dollar industry.

Diner

Replaced by McDonald's, Arby's, Blimpie's, Burger King, and the fast-food rest, the diner—an eatery longer than it is wide and always with a counter—was once part of American popular culture, a roadside beacon of stainless steel and hard shiny surfaces for the hungry traveler. Quick, clean, cheap, and completely familiar, the mirrored diner and its menu fare are now more a source of nostalgia for movies like *Diner* and sitcoms like "Alice." Once, though, during its heyday in the Forties, it was the place to come to after school, on a Saturday night, or whenever you were in need of food or conversation. The diner is an American invention.

Origin.   Its origin is in the horse-drawn lunch wagon of the 1870s, which sold sandwiches and coffee to late-night workers, called nighthawks, in an era when restaurants, indeed, towns, closed down after eight P.M. In fact, Walter Scott of Providence, Rhode Island, is credited as the first lunch cart operator, according to the authors of *American Diner.*

As the story goes: One night in 1872 Scott's converted horse-drawn wagon trundled down Westminster Street laden with sandwiches, boiled eggs, pies and coffee. From inside, through a window, Scott served nighthawks, also known as the dude trade. A nickel bought a homemade ham sandwich, or a boiled egg and a slice of buttered bread, or a piece of pie. A plate of sliced, cold chicken cost 30 cents. To avoid waste, Scott invented the unappetizingly named "chewed" sandwich, consisting of leftover bread scraps finely chopped, mixed with butter or mustard and spread between two whole slices of bread. In a short time, Scott had many competitors.

The next step in the evolution of the diner was taken in the mid-1880s by Samuel Messer Jones of Worcester, Massachusetts, who constructed the first horse-drawn lunch wagon that customers entered to be served. The idea came to him when he saw customers standing in the rain, ordering from a lunch wagon through a window. In a later version, Jones's eatery boasted a complete kitchen, stools for customers, and woodworked walls and stained-glass windows. "Its colored windows were a triumph of the glazier's art," ran a newspaper review, "with a bill of fare incorporated in the decorations." The idea was an instant success, and Jones expanded his business by adding more wagons at different locations. Soon, wherever crowds gathered, there appeared a quick-service lunch wagon—first drawn to the location by horse, then by automobile engine.

Lunch wagons became so popular in New England shortly after the turn of the century that in Providence, for example, nearly fifty of the "floating" restaurants were roaming the streets by 1912. Because the wagons got to be so numerous, interfering in their daily comings and goings with daytime traffic, laws were passed in many cities allowing the wagons to remain on the streets from dusk to dawn. Many owners conceived the idea of making their wagons into stationary lunch spots. Diners.

Postwar Razzle Dazzle.   Many diners got fancy in the Twenties, taking on art deco designs, and in the Thirties acquiring the streamlined look that swept the nation. Surfaces and textures were now brushed, polished, rounded or wrapped. Thus began the golden age of the diner. After World War II, the demand for diners increased greatly as tens of thousands of veterans aspired to open their own eateries. With plenty of cash from wartime savings and government GI loans, they generated a diner heyday, installing mirrored walls, stainless steel backbars, and two-tone Formica countertops, the favorite color combinations being pink and beige, turquoise and coral, or tangerine and charcoal. Black and white in checkerboard or stripes was also popular, with highlighting splashes of yellow or orange.

By this time, diners had grown tremendously in popularity and respectability. Families flocked to diners, and the menus altered to suit the tastes of kids—who were offered free balloons and lollipops on the way out. Many diners then could cozily seat up to 150 customers. Though diners would again change in design in future decades, the American classic version had arrived by the late Forties. A favorite architectural flourish of the time was the boomerang (or amoeba) shape, whose curves could be found in diner furniture—as well in home coffee tables, rug designs, and wallpaper; it also dictated the contours of the backyard's kidney-shaped swimming pool. Many called the overall look, which would come to dominate Fifties design, "postwar razzle dazzle."

As a pop cultural institution, the diner even enriched the language of food preparation and service.

Tuna on Whiskey Down Hold the Mayo.   In dinerese, that means a tuna salad sandwich on toasted rye bread with no mayonnaise. On the other hand, if your waitress called to the short-order cook, "A radio, a 51, a stretch, and squeeze it," she'd be requesting a tuna sandwich on toast, hot chocolate, a Coke, and "make it fast."

Dinerese has been steadily disappearing in recent years. But once it was a professional "in" language, as obscure to outsiders as legalese and medicalese are to people not in those professions. When a waiter at a McDonald's can push a cash register button labeled with a food's name (or picture), and the message is electronically communicated to the kitchen, there is no need for the colorful expressions that once filled the atmosphere at American diners. Here are many of the most popular soda fountain, lunch counter, and diner expressions that are part of pop language culture:

A jack, a grilled American cheese; **AC,** an American cheese not grilled. **Jackback,** grilled cheese with bacon. **Full house,** grilled cheese, bacon, and tomato.

Abbott and Costello, franks and beans.

Adam and Eve on a raft, two poached eggs on toast.

All the way, a sandwich with **the works,** that is, every condiment in the kitchen.

Belch water, a glass of seltzer or soda water.

Black and white, a milkshake (or soda) with chocolate syrup and vanilla ice cream.

BLT, bacon, tomato and lettuce sandwich.

Bowl of red, a serving of chili.

Burn it, anything cooked until it's well done; also, **cream it.**

Carfare, I got a tip.

Cowboy with spurs, a Western omelet with french fries; **Cowboy takes LT,** a Western omelet with lettuce and tomato.

Cremate a blue, bikini cut, well-done, toasted blueberry muffin cut not in half but several pieces.

Eve with the lid on, apple pie.

Haystack, strawberry (as straw is like hay) pancakes; **a stack,** pancakes.

High and dry, a sandwich with no condiment on the bread.

Hold the grass, no lettuce. **Hold the hair,** soda without ice.

Murphy carrying a wreath, ham and potatoes with cabbage.

Nervous pudding, Jell-O.

On the hoof, meat rare and bloody.

Put out the lights and cry, liver with onions.

Red lead, ketchup.

Seaboard, any item **to go,** to be eaten out of the diner.

Sissy nut, cream cheese on date-nut bread.

Snow White, a 7-Up.

Suds, a glass of root beer.

Takes a flower, with onion.

Two over with sausage, wheat down two times, two orders, each
   with two eggs over, with sausage and whole-wheat toast.

White cow, a vanilla milkshake; **brown cow,** chocolate milk.

Working, a reminder that an order has been called in and has yet to
   materialize.

Wreck a pair, two scrambled eggs.

5, a large glass of milk; **41,** lemonade; **51,** hot chocolate; **52,** two hot
   chocolates; **55,** root beer; **81,** a glass of water; **86,** nix or disregard a
   previous order; **95,** a customer leaving the diner without paying.

LP Records

The first commercial long-playing record, spinning at 33⅓ RPM, was released
in 1948. It offered twenty-three minutes of music per side, or, expressed
another way, a 15-inch stack of the new LPs played as much music as an
8-foot-high tower of 78s—its forerunner, which had been the industry standard
since before the turn of the century.

LPs were introduced specifically for classical selections, which required
longer playing times than three-to-four-minute pop tunes. No one who heard
the technological marvel could have guessed that in a relatively short time the
LP itself would be obsolete, done in by tape formats and compact discs. "After
declining steadily for years," reported the *New York Times* in April 1990, "sales
of record albums plummeted sharply in 1989," with one interviewed record
executive exclaiming, "There's an entire generation that has never owned a
turntable."

In today's rapidly changing world of audio reproduction, it is hard to imagine
the consumer expectancy and industry hoopla that surrounded the introduction
of long-playing discs. The 78 RPM record had been the unchallenged standard
for nearly a half century. The 78 format was invented by Canadian Emile
Berliner in 1887, and two years later the first commercial discs were released
in two sizes: the 10-inch, which played three minutes of music, and the 12-inch,
which ran for four minutes. By the late Forties hundreds of millions of 78s had
been produced—all to be made obsolete by CBS's 12-inch 33⅓ RPM disc, with
up to three hundred grooves per inch. It represented the first audio innovation
in records in fifty years.

45 RPM.   Long-playing records had been tried in the Thirties, but they never reached the consumer because of the high cost of playback equipment. In April 1948 CBS's innovative genius Dr. Peter Goldmark demonstrated the company's new LP to RCA with the hope of launching a joint venture for the format. But RCA, near perfecting a 7-inch, two-and-a-half-minute 45 RPM format (which it would foolishly promote for short classical music selections), declined the offer. Within a few years, RCA recognized its mistake, relegated the 45 RPM format to popular music, and developed its own library of classicals on LPs. *Consumer Reports* in September 1948 explained to its readers the advantages of the new format: "The ability to play an entire selection uninterruptedly . . . frees the listeners of the annoyance which results with conventional records when the music comes to an end—often abruptly in the middle of a phrase—and the clang of the record changer takes over." That same year, **stereophonic sound** was added to records, and it seemed that audio technology could not possibly get better. The year 1948 was notable for another reason.

High Fidelity.   For years, the long-standing problem in sound reproduction was that radio phonographs were designed as furniture—form followed fashion rather than function.

Eliot Noyes, a prominent industrial designer and Consumers Union's first design consultant, tackled this shortcoming by designing a custom-built radio phonograph especially for Consumers Union's members and subscribers. The unit, described in the June 1948 issue of *Consumer Reports,* was not particularly attractive as an addition to the home living room, but its huge speakers did yield a sound of "high fidelity." This marked the beginning of efforts in the audio industry to concentrate on the perfection of loudspeakers in themselves. The next logical step was the development of component parts systems, where a buyer selected the particular turntable, amplifier, and speakers. With sound so good, people began to refer to their record players as hi-fis. Indeed, hi-fi was a trendy word for the Fifties. No longer did the consumer wish to purchase a "record player," but to "assemble a hi-fi system."

Eight-Track Cartridge: Audio for the Auto.   As trends go, the heyday of the eight-track cartridge was short-lived. The format was developed by jet plane maker Bill Lear, intended to provide a music alternative to the car's radio. Lear persuaded Motorola to manufacture the format, and in 1967 Ford Motor Company agreed to put eight-tracks in its cars. That was the event which made the format familiar to the public. Hundreds of thousands of multitrack cartridges were produced, and many consumers boasted of owning a record library on the format.

Far from ideal, cartridges allowed a listener to switch from track to track, but it was impossible to cue up the beginning of a song because the machines had no fast forward or reverse. And, too, they didn't record. In addition, cuts of prerecorded music would frustratingly fade out in the middle of a song's lyrics, and the tune would reappear after a silence on another track, having lost precious measures of the music. Cartridges were challenged by the welcomed arrival of high-quality cassette recorders, and by the early Seventies Bill Lear's format was in rapid decline. By 1977 manufacturers had stopped making eight-tracks. Across the country cartridges could be had by the boxload at flea markets for giveaway prices.

At the close of the Eighties, for every vinyl LP record album sold, six compact discs and thirteen recorded cassettes were purchased. Most record companies had stopped issuing classical, jazz, and country music on vinyl, and they had cut back on the amount of popular music and rock released in album form. Nationwide, hundreds of chain stores began depleting their "vinyl dinosaurs" stock. If the record—in its many forms as a 78, a 45, and an LP, and under its many names of disc, platter, and wax—were a person, the obituary would say that he died at the age of forty after fighting a long bout with technology.

Levittown as Anywhere, U.S.A.

Suburbia today is the normal habitat of millions of Americans, an integral part of our culture and way of life. That is because in the late Forties one real estate developer, perceiving the post–World War II housing shortage, transformed a vast Long Island, New York, potato field into the country's first mass-produced housing project, redefining the American landscape and reinventing a way of life. William Levitt's solution for inexpensive homes for returning GIs was Levittown, which rapidly became a symbol of an era, a metaphor for suburbia itself, and a catchword of conformity. Opened only to WWII veterans and their families, it democratized the suburbs, which until then were a haven mainly for the rich and upper-middle class.

Shortly after World War II ended, the government estimated that America needed 5 million units of housing immediately. Young men and women returning from military service had begun to raise families and were forced to cram themselves into the homes of their parents and in-laws. A Senate committee reported that across America couples were camped out in "garages, coal sheds, chicken coops, barns, tool sheds, granaries and smokehouses." William Levitt's answer in 1947 was a mass-produced, prefab, Cape Cod–style home that sold for $6,990, and with a federally subsidized mortgage carried a monthly payment of $65.

Like the Joneses. Levittown, which seemed to spring up almost overnight in Island Trees, a Long Island farming community too small to be included in the Forties U.S. census, was more than a housing project, though. In establishing a nationwide building trend that enabled millions of young couples to buy homes more easily than ever before, it spawned the development of suburban supermarkets, malls, and shopping centers, and the new homeowners became major consumers of everything from lawn mowers to matching bedroom suites. Levittown introduced the phrase and philosophy of "keeping up with the Joneses." A decade after America's first tract house was completed, *Newsweek* reported with astonishment, "People buy houses the way they used to buy cars."

In the Forties, the new community of Levittown stunned the nation in many ways. Expanding at the phenomenal rate of one house every fifteen minutes, within four years after ground was broken there were 17,447 homes, a feat that introduced autolike assembly line mass production to the housing industry. Levittown was an entirely new kind of community, a huge, homogeneous, sterile tract of houses, with no center, no charm, and no tradition. Most sociologists declared it a suburban slum in the making. Its architectural uniformity, they predicted, would breed mass human conformity. A novel of the period, *A Crack in the Picture Window,* satirized a young couple named the Drones who move into a "box on a slab." "More insidious and far more dangerous than any other influence is the housing development's destruction of individuality," wrote the author, John Keats. But what the critics saw as a lack of individuality, young GIs and their wives viewed as a community support system. When young couples started to have children—kicking off the century's great baby boom—the state of pregnancy became "the Levittown Look." In the community, laundry had to be hung only on carousel-style drying racks. Lawns had to be mowed every week or a Levitt employee did the job and billed the family. When children reached school age, a school system materialized. The great American dream of owning a home had been codified and sensibly zoned.

Ticky-Tacky Hutches.   Despite the conformity and monotony of the "Levittowns" that soon came to dot the American landscape, they enabled ownership of single-family homes in the United States to grow more in the decade following World War II than in the previous 150 years. Suburban planners laid out suburban malls to be occupied by suburban merchants. America had a new Sunday pastime: "just looking" at new homes. When eight model Levitt homes were completed in a Maryland development, thirty thousand people showed up on opening day, just looking. By 1951 the Census Bureau dubbed a Levittown resident as "the average American." Levittowns became Anywhere, U.S.A.

Today nearly every original Levittown home on Long Island has been expanded, and the average selling price in 1989 was $160,000—far above William Levitt's dream of easy affordability. And provocative rumors occasionally surface that the National Trust for Historic Preservation is considering "ticky-tacky" Levittown as a historic district.

As for the concept of the suburb: Suburbs have sprouted their own suburbs, their own bedroom communities. The phenomenon has been called the suburbanization of the suburb, and the decade of the Nineties, by one forecast, may well be an era in which suburban becomes urban, and the urban city becomes a deserted hovel.

Birth of the American Lawn.   The American lawn, a well-kept plot of green, became perhaps the most famous symbol of America's postwar suburban sprawl. The lawn immediately established a relationship with one's neighbors, the Joneses, and, by extension, with all the country's Joneses across the American landscape. In the Forties, following the creation of Levittowns, mowing the lawn became a civic responsibility. Over the next half century, Americans would roll a green mantle of grass across the continent. The lawn is an American obsession, for nowhere else in the world are private plots of impeccable green as prized as in the United States.

Perhaps no one has written more insightfully of the lawn as a cultural icon than Michael Pollan. Today, America has more than 50,000 square miles of lawn. "Like the interstate highway system, like fast-food chains, like television," claims Pollan, "the lawn has served to unify the American landscape; it is what makes the suburbs of any town in the country look more alike than not alike." Whereas France has its geometric gardens, England its picturesque parks, America has an "unbounded democratic river of manicured lawn along which we array our houses." Whereas in Tudor England the lawn was the setting for games and a backdrop for herbaceous borders, Levittowners in the Forties made the lawn an end in itself.

In America, landscape architect Frank Scott's 1870 book, *The Art of Beautifying Suburban Home Grounds,* is credited with planting the seed for the flawlessly coiffed turf, which Scott envisioned as an upper-middle-class suburbanite's equivalent of a great public park. "A smooth, closely shaven surface of grass," he wrote, "is by far the most essential element of beauty on the grounds of a suburban home." Under the watchful eye of William Levitt in the Forties, that bit of beautifying advice became law.

Since the creation of Levittowns and the compulsion of lawn maintenance, homeowners who commit the sin of not mowing regularly have actually been dragged into court by neighbors. Pollan points out that Americans have traditionally eschewed Old World fences and hedges, and opted for the lawn as an egalitarian conceit, "implying that there is no reason to hide behind a fence or hedge since we all occupy the same middle class." More egotistically, the lawn provides a suitably grand stage for the proud display of one's own home. One landscape writer observed that Americans organize their yards "to capture the admiration of the street," and he attributed the popularity of lawns to Americans' "infantile instinct to cry 'hello!' to the passerby, to lift up our possessions to his gaze."

Rotary Mower and Chemical Fertilizer.   America's love affair with lawns quickly created a new industry. By 1949 lawn mowers were an enormous business. Families shifted from the old-fashioned reel mower to the rotary-blade model. The rotary mower became a status symbol, though its fast-spinning blades caused countless accidents. A survey of physicians found that of 737 mowing accidents reported during 1955 and 1956, nearly 90 percent involved rotary mowers. More than two-thirds of the injuries were caused by contact with the whirling blades. The rest were traced to thrown objects.

Early on, *Consumer Reports* admonished readers to treat a running rotary mower like a gun: "Never allow its discharge opening to point at anyone." Of forty-four rotary models tested, the magazine rated thirty-one unacceptable for a variety of hazards. The rotary mower tamed the suburban lawn. It performed for many the work previously done by a hired hand, a luxury the wealthy in the suburbs could afford, but not the new arrivals. Mowing the lawn became a proud weekly activity.

Milestones in the history of lawn maintenance:

1928. Scott introduces **Turf Builder,** the first fertilizer designed specifically to provide the nutritional requirements of grass.

1947. Scott produces **Weed and Feed,** the first combination of a grass fertilizer and a selective chemical for the control of dicot weeds.

1950. Scott introduces **Scult,** the first dry, easy-to-apply chemical control of the great suburban bugaboo, crabgrass.

Today, to maintain lawns with watering, fertilizing, and chemical weeding, Americans spend about $4 billion a year.

DANCE CRAZES

Jitterbug

The Swing Era that began in the Thirties was interrupted by World War II, which, by siphoning off thousands of men for service, put a crimp in couples' social dancing. At home, in living rooms, to records and radio, women danced with each other; abroad, in bars and canteens, GIs danced with free-spirited girls, with prostitutes, and in a pinch with each other. If there was a common experience, it was the exuberant, gymnastic jitterbug, more a style of frenzied athleticism than a step-assigned craze. Its origin, though, predates the war.

Dance historians trace many jitterbug steps back to such free-wheeling routines of the Twenties as the Charleston and the Lindy, dances that were modified to accommodate the swing music of the Thirties. As a dance in its own right, the jitterbug was recognized as a distinctive style in the mid-Thirties, when it was performed to the big band music of Benny Goodman. The vogue ushered in two dance innovations: the **breakaway** and the **air step.**

The breakaway was a show-off solo for the male. It represented a bit of bragadoccio that harks back to ancient tribal dances and had not been seen in the West since certain European court dances of the seventeenth century. As a spotlight, the male solo had been ousted by a vogue for the so-called closed positions of such dances as the waltz and the square dance.

The air step, as its name implies, involved a dancer literally leaving the floor. Air steps were occasionally executed in the "flying" routines of the Lindy, in mimicry of Lindbergh's flight, but prior to that time they had not appeared in Western dance since the faddishness of the seventeenth century la volta, favored by Queen Elizabeth I. Neither the breakaway nor the air step was new, "but to a generation who showed no interest in or reverence for the past," writes one historian, "they seemed revolutionary."

Name Origin. The jittery, can't-sit-still antics of the jitterbug gave the dance its name. In the Twenties, the tremulous movements from excessive consumption of alcohol were popularly called the *jitters,* following in the tradition of a long line of nomenclature having gone by such previous names as the *shakes* (1850s), the *DTs* (1860s; an abbreviation for *delirium tremens,* Latin for "trembling delirium"), and the *heebie-jeebies* (1910s). In the Thirties, the *jitters,* or just the *jits,* was commonplace for frenzied activity and seemingly a suitable name for the dance; practitioners were vividly called jitterbugs.

Many dancers were injured by the athletics of jitterbugging, and it was definitely a vogue for the young. Parents, teachers, and conservative dance instructors strenuously objected to the boogie-woogie essence of the jitterbug, but the social dance scene in America was undergoing a profound and everlasting change. With older men off to war, dance halls in the early Forties were peopled largely with under-eighteen teenagers, who after the war continued increasingly to exert an influence on dance and danceable music. As we saw in the introduction to this chapter, the Forties was the decade that launched the teen revolution.

The jitterbug was popularized overseas wherever American GIs were stationed. In England, the feverish couples dance was regarded as yet another example of America's progressive attitude toward the sexual emancipation that began in the Roaring Twenties. As a pop culture export, the dance was viewed both benignly and critically as American exhibitionism. Unlike previous vogue dances of the century, the jitterbug, in one variation or another, held popular sway for two decades, paving the way for the zany rock dances of the Sixties. The teen revolution gained snowballing momentum after the war, and the vigorousness of the jitterbug only further helped to displace adults from the dance floor, leaving the space to be used for teen sock hops and proms.

An unrelated dance revolution was simultaneously taking place on Broadway in the 1943 musical *Oklahoma!* Agnes de Mille had choreographed a dream sequence in the show that was not merely a dance interlude between stretches of dialogue but an integral part of the show's story, advancing the plot. The innovation set a trend in Broadway musicals for nearly two decades, in which a show almost had to have a dream sequence.

POPULAR SONGS

I'll Never Smile Again: 1940

As the decade of the Forties opened, from Rome Pope Pius XII chastised women for immodesty of dress, comparing those who "bowed to the tyranny of fashion" to lunatics jumping into a river. Albert Einstein became a citizen of the United States. The country's first superhighway opened in Pennsylvania.

In the world of entertainment, *Billboard* magazine inaugurated "the Billboard Music Popularity Chart," the first published independent national record survey of weekly retail sales; number one for twelve straight weeks was **In the Mood** by Glenn Miller, confirming him as one of the most popular bandleaders of the big band era.

Another was Tommy Dorsey, who, with the young vocalist Frank Sinatra, scored the year's biggest hit, "I'll Never Smile Again," which for the decade's tally would rank in the top ten. Dorsey and his orchestra became part of a bizarre pop music–anthropological experiment in 1940. To test the effect of music on such "savage beasts" as chimpanzees at the Philadelphia Zoo, Dorsey and his band first played a selection of violent, raucous jazz. "The chimpanzees were scared to death," reported *Etude* magazine. "They scampered all over the place, seeking the protection of their keepers and hiding under benches . . . One chimp tried to pull the trombone away from Tommy Dorsey." However, when Dorsey struck up his dreamy theme song, **I'm Getting Sentimental Over You,** the beasts immediately became tranquil, took to their perches, calmly "watching the players with interest." For some, the experiment confirmed that while jazz was a fad, ballads would never go out of fashion. Others said the chimps had no taste.

Walt Disney's film *Pinocchio* contributed the hit song **When You Wish Upon a Star,** number five on radio's "Your Hit Parade." From the Broadway show *Pal Joey* came the enchanting **Bewitched, Bothered and Bewildered,** and the even more popular **The Last Time I Saw Paris** from Oscar Hammerstein II and Jerome Kern. Kern later admitted that this was the only tune in his long career that he ever wrote to an advance text, preferring, as was his custom, to come up with the melody before seeing lyrics. Hammerstein had telephoned him the words, which he put to music. Soon it became a signature song for the incomparable Hildegarde.

The year's hits also included: **All or Nothing at All, All the Things You Are** (number nine on the "Hit Parade"), **Imagination** (HP number six), **It's a Big, Wide, Wonderful World,** and **The Nearness of You.** The comedic twenty-six-year-old Maria do Carmo Miranda da Cunha, better known under her fruit-salad hats as Carmen Miranda, scored a hit with **Down Argentine Way,** from the movie of that title starring the decade's leggy pin-up-queen-to-be, Betty Grable. It was Miranda's first musical film and launched the dance craze of the conga. Songs that would become classics: **Falling Leaves, You Stepped Out of a Dream, Taking a Chance on Love, I've Got No Strings, When the Swallows Come Back to Capistrano,** and the peppy, upbeat **You Are My Sunshine** by Jimmie Davis, who used the tune as a campaign song to win him the governorship of Louisiana.

Chattanooga Choo Choo: 1941

The Glenn Miller novelty song "Chattanooga Choo Choo," which achieved a distinctive sound through the use of a clarinet lead over four saxes, was honored with the first gold record award, officially certifying it as a million-

Carmen Miranda.

seller. It was not the year's only novelty number: there was **Chica Chica Boom Chic,** and the nonsensical **Hut Sut Song,** and a tune made popular by the conga dance craze, **I Came, I Saw, I Conga'd.**

It was the year in which Americans discovered many classical tunes in popular guises. The lush, pounding melody of Tchaikovsky's *Piano Concerto in B-flat minor* appeared in the form of **Tonight We Love.** Still on the "Hit Parade" (as number two) was the classic-derived **Intermezzo,** its theme lifted from Wagner's opera *Tristan and Isolde.* The first movement of Rachmaninoff's *Piano Concerto No. 2* scored a commercial success as **I Think of You;** Tchaikovsky's *Melodie* (op. 24, no. 3) was a smash as **The Things I Love,** and his *Pathetique* Symphony became **(This Is) The Story of a Starry Night.** In this year of melody theft, a traditional Russian folksong became a hit as **Song of the Volga Boatmen.**

Home-soil talent had Americans singing **I Don't Want to Set the World on Fire** (HP number seven), **I Hear a Rhapsody, Deep in the Heart of Texas, How About You,** and **There! I've Said It Again.** Crooner Bing Crosby scored with **Dolores.** And football was immortalized in the satiric **Buckle Down, Winsocki.**

It was the year Disney released *Fantasia,* the first film with a stereo soundtrack, and Americans flocked to theaters to see Mickey as the Sorcerer's Apprentice and the dancing hippos in *La Gioconda*'s "Dance of the Hours."

White Christmas: 1942

With memories of Pearl Harbor acutely fresh, a song hit on everyone's lips was **Remember Pearl Harbor,** as was **This Is the Army** from the Irving Berlin Broadway show of that title, which would be adapted to the screen the next year. With patriotism running high, the radio airwaves were filled with war-related songs from the silly **Good-bye, Mama, I'm Off to Yokohama** to the serious "God Bless America" and numerous versions of the "Star-Spangled Banner." It was, in fact, World War II that launched the enduring tradition of playing the "Banner" before sporting events. Extremely popular in terms of sales of records and sheet music was **There's a Star-Spangled Banner Waving Somewhere** and the sentimental war ballad **(There'll Be Blue Birds Over) The White Cliffs of Dover.**

But the first big wartime hit was Frank Loesser's **Praise the Lord and Pass the Ammunition.** The lyrics were supposedly built on a phrase uttered by a chaplain in the heat of battle, while the melody was "a deliberately sing-song member of the musical family going back to 'The Old Gray Mare,'" according to historian Spaeth.

Because of wartime shortages in raw materials, records were recycled. The industry launched a drive encouraging Americans to turn in their oldies at designated collecting points, and the discs were melted down and reused to record new songs. This wave of patriotism known as the "shellac drive" destroyed thousands of excellent classics, rendering those that survived pricey rarities. Some hits that emerged on shellac: Jimmy Dorsey's **Tangerine, (Theme from the) Warsaw Concerto, I Remember You,** and **Moonlight Becomes You.** Mirroring the new fashion craze among young men was **A Zoot Suit.**

But the most remarkable song of the year, indeed, of the decade, was Bing Crosby's recording of Irving Berlin's "White Christmas." From the musical film *Holiday Inn,* it was called by *Variety* "probably the most valuable song . . . copyright in the world." It broke all records. The longest running song ever on "Your Hit Parade," it sold more than a million copies of sheet music alone in the year it was issued, and by the end of 1976 a total of 108 million records in the United States and Canada, and some 25 million foreign language discs throughout the world. Crosby's recording for Decca sold over 25 million records, and *Billboard* ranked it as the number two song of the Forties.

Other hits of '42: **Don't Sit Under the Apple Tree With Anyone Else But Me** (HP number nine), **Dearly Beloved,** the trendy **Arthur Murray Taught Me Dancing in a Hurry,** the crazy **Conchita, Marquita, Lolita, Pepita, Rosita, Juanita Lopez,** and the war-related **When the Lights Go On Again All Over the World.**

Sinatra Mania

As 1942 drew to a close, the first public demonstration of Sinatra fever erupted at the Mosque Theater in Newark, New Jersey, after Frank Sinatra, following three years of popularity with the Tommy Dorsey orchestra, made his solo bow. Female fans were uncontainable. The seemingly malnourished crooner, who with a punctured eardrum was unfit for military service, later set thirty-five hundred bobby-soxers screaming and fainting at New York's Paramount Theater. Though the hyped king of swoon caused a similar stir at the Hollywood Bowl, his talents remained hidden to millions of Britons; as the London *Times* reported in words it would soon have to eat: "Mr. Sinatra is unknown in this country and likely to remain so."

In the Forties his fortunes were fickle. He temporarily ousted Bing Crosby for popularity, then drew devastatingly bad publicity for palling around in Havana with the likes of Lucky Luciano. The press reported that he "used his fists too frequently," too often experienced "throat trouble," and forecast at the close of the decade that it was not likely he would make a comeback.

Frank Sinatra.

Oh, What a Beautiful Morning; People Will Say We're in Love: 1943

The popular musical phenomenon of the year was the Rodgers and Hammerstein Broadway musical *Oklahoma!* which in addition to producing the above hits had the country singing **The Surrey With the Fringe on Top** and the title song **Oklahoma!** The Decca album, released on 78 RPM, sold over a million copies.

For Oscar Hammerstein II, who had had a run of five Broadway failures and repeated rejections from Hollywood, the new musical, which previewed in New Haven as *Away We Go,* showed every sign of being another disaster. Based on a folk play, *Green Grow the Lilacs,* the collaborative effort with Richard Rodgers was reviewed as "No Girls, No Gags, No Chance." But after almost a month of rewrites and a title change, the show, featuring Alfred Drake and Celeste Holm, opened in New York on March 31 to quickly make theater history. It ran for a then record-breaking 2,212 performances, and Agnes de Mille's daring balletic choreography reshaped dance on the musical stage. Honored with the Pulitzer prize, the show was a true Broadway breakthrough in its unification of story, music, lyrics, and choreography. "People Will Say We're In Love" was voted the best song of 1943, and it made twenty-five appearances on the "Hit Parade."

Novelty Numbers. The novelty song of the year was **Pistol-Packin' Mama,** while the nonsense hit was **Mairzy Doats** ("Mares eat oats . . . and little lambs eat ivy"). This song, played by Spike Jones's City Slickers, a comedy band lovingly dubbed "the King of Corn," was a surprise success, as was the group's parody **Der Fuehrer's Face,** and its 1948 Christmas release **All I Want for Christmas Is My Two Front Teeth.** "Mairzy Doats" quickly sold 350,000 copies of sheet music, and an employee of the United States Embassy in Moscow, Alexander Dolgun, credited the song with having saved his sanity: Arrested and thrown into a cell adjacent to an aeronautical research wind tunnel that made a deafening noise, Dolgun mentally coped with the racket by continually singing the nonsensical lyrics. "The effect on me was fantastic," he later said. "I had discovered an instrument for my survival."

In 1943, the press estimated that about 20 percent of jazz musicians smoked "hay" or "loco weed" (marijuana), which was said to inspire improvisation. The most famous drummer of the period, Gene Krupa, was jailed in California for possessing it.

Other hits of the year included Benny Goodman's **Taking a Chance on Love,** Glenn Miller's **That Old Black Magic, Don't Get Around Much Anymore, I Couldn't Sleep a Wink Last Night, I'll Be Seeing You,** and a song with amusing Frank Loesser lyrics, **They're Either Too Young or Too Old,** introduced by Bette Davis in the film *Thank Your Lucky Stars.* Cole Porter's hit of the year was **You'd Be So Nice to Come Home To.**

Don't Fence Me In: 1944

Cole Porter's atypically corny "Don't Fence Me In" was said to be his stab at going commercial and topical in wartime, but he'd actually written the song in the mid-Thirties. It was sung by the Andrews Sisters in the film *Hollywood Canteen,* and their recording brought it to the top of "Your Hit Parade." Another unexpected success of the year was **Dance With a Dolly (With a Hole in Her Stocking),** which was actually just new words fitted to the old 1840s minstrel song "Buffalo Gals."

The year was more notable for Dinah Shore's **I'll Walk Alone** (HP number five); **Till Then,** and **I'm Making Believe** by the Ink Spots and Ella Fitzgerald. From Hollywood came the film *Meet Me in St. Louis,* which produced **The Trolley Song,** sung on screen by Judy Garland and on record by the Pied Pipers.

Perhaps the most popular song of 1944 was **I'll Be Seeing You.** Recorded by Hildegarde and Frank Sinatra, it appeared twenty-four times on the "Hit Parade," ten times at the top. Though the composer, Irving Hill, did not live to see his creation become a moneymaker, his widow was able to live in comfort from royalties.

If I Loved You: 1945

World War II ended. Roosevelt died. Mussolini was executed. Hitler committed suicide. The troops went from singing the war hit **Lili Marlene** to such appropriately titled favorites as **Ac-Cent-Tchu-Ate the Positive** (HP number ten), **It's a Grand Night for Singing,** and **June Is Bustin' Out All Over.** American soldiers bade their wartime buddies farewell with **Dig You Later (A Hubba-Hubba-Hubba)** and returned home on a **Sentimental Journey**—this a Les Brown and Doris Day hit, number five on the "Hit Parade" that year.

With the end of the war came the end of the big band era. The fad was away from bands and toward star solo vocalists like Sinatra, Crosby, Dinah Shore, and Perry Como—Como scored big with such diverse tunes as "Dig You Later" and "If I Loved You." Within a year Tommy Dorsey, Harry James, Woody Herman, and Les Brown would disband their orchestras. Bands were also crowded out by the popularity among the young of bop. While musicians rejected it, teenagers bought up bop recordings by the millions.

Johnny Mercer had three successes: "Ac-Cent-Tchu-Ate the Positive (with music by Harold Arlen)," **Candy,** and number eight on the "Hit Parade," **On the Atchison, Topeka, and the Santa Fe.**

But the year belonged to Frédéric Chopin. He (played by Cornel Wilde) was popularized in the screen biography *A Song to Remember,* which made a smash hit of the **Polonaise in A-flat,** recorded by Jose Iturbi. Given words, the melody made millions for Perry Como as **Till the End of Time,** number one on the "Hit Parade." *Polonaise* became the title of a stage musical and its theme song. People rushed to music stores for any Chopin recording, especially his

Minute Waltz. There was an immense revival of **I'm Always Chasing Rainbows,** based on his *Fantasie Impromptu in C-sharp minor.* Chopin had never been in such demand.

Carousel.   On Broadway, Rodgers and Hammerstein followed up the success of *Oklahoma!* with the April opening of *Carousel.* The show, based on Ferenc Molnar's enthralling *Liliom,* produced such hits as **Soliloquy,** "If I Loved You," "June Is Bustin' Out All Over," **When I Marry Mr. Snow,** and the million-seller **You'll Never Walk Alone.**

Rodgers and Hammerstein switched Molnar's locale from Budapest to New England in the years between 1875 and 1888. And they took the complex character of Billy Bigelow and, in one unforgettable and joyous soliloquy, made the inner workings of his mind transparent. Sung on stage at the Majestic Theater by John Raitt, the song—about a father-to-be's concern over his worthiness to bring up a boy or a girl—stopped the show.

The freak hit of the year was an import from Trinidad, banned on many radio networks under the argument that it provided free advertising for the products of its title: **Rum and Coca-Cola.** The calypso tune was discovered by Morey Amsterdam and recorded by the Andrews Sisters, and went quickly from the nightclub circuit, where it was introduced, to the "Hit Parade." A Trinidad black, Rupert Grant, claimed to have copyrighted the original words, set to the tune of a Creole lullaby, which satirized the American occupation of his island. He said that the line, "Both the mothers and the daughters / Working for the Yankee dollars" referred to local women selling themselves to American men.

Doin' What Comes Natur'lly: 1946

RCA Victor selected John Philip Sousa's "Stars and Stripes Forever" march to be the company's billionth record. Record sales would quickly be boosted further by the opening on May 16 of Irving Berlin's greatest stage success, *Annie Get Your Gun.* It gave its star Ethel Merman a hit and a signature song in **There's No Business Like Show Business;** Perry Como went to the top of the "Hit Parade" with the show's **They Say It's Wonderful;** Dinah Shore soared up the charts with another tune from the musical, "Doin' What Comes Natur'lly." *Annie* ran for 1,147 performances, and its music dominated radio's "Hit Parade" for ten weeks.

A seasonal standard was born in **Chestnuts Roasting on an Open Fire** (aka "The Christmas Song"), and another in Vaughn Monroe's recording of **Let It Snow, Let It Snow, Let It Snow,** by the successful team of Sammy Cahn and Jule Styne. Also recorded were such classics-to-be as **Come Rain or Come Shine** (Margaret Whiting), **The Girl That I Marry, I Got the Sun in the Morning** (Les Brown and Doris Day), and **It Might as Well be Spring.** The bop song of the year was **Hey-Ba-Ba-Re-Bop.** The year's sentimental favorite: **You Always Hurt the One You Love.**

Ethel Merman and Ray Middleton in Annie Get Your Gun.

How Are Things in Glocca Morra: 1947

On January 10 *Finian's Rainbow* opened at Broadway's Forty-sixth Street Theater. The story of leprechauns, pots of gold, and American racism ran for 725 performances and produced several of the year's hit songs. In addition to "Glocca Morra," it offered the excellent **Old Devil Moon,** the uplifting **Look to the Rainbow,** and the humorous **When I'm Not Near the Girl I Love.** Two months later, on March 13, another hit musical opened at the Ziegfeld Theater: *Brigadoon,* by Alan Jay Lerner and Frederick Loewe. It too enjoyed a long run and produced several of the year's hit songs: **Almost Like Being in Love, The Heather on the Hill,** and **Come to Me, Bend to Me.**

The surprise hit of the year was the bland but wildly popular **Near You,** which put its composer, Francis Craig, much in demand, and the song, according to *Billboard,* became the bestselling single of the decade. Another surprise was radio's Arthur Godfrey's recording of **Too Fat Polka,** which quickly sold a million discs. From Walt Disney came **Zip-A-Dee-Doo-Dah.** Other top-sellers of the year: **Papa Won't You Dance With Me, Sixteen Tons, Time After Time,** and Freddy Martin's rhyming **Managua Nicaragua.**

Buttons and Bows: 1948

For the world of popular entertainment the year was remarkable for two developments: The medium of television began regular programming, producing several landmark shows (which we'll examine in the last section of this chapter); and, as mentioned earlier, long playing records debuted. On the pop music charts, Dinah Shore was riding high with "Buttons and Bows." Peggy Lee recorded her rendition of **Manana (Is Soon Enough for Me).** Nat King Cole scored big with **Nature Boy;** Kaye Kyser with **Woody Woodpecker;** and Margaret Whiting reached the top slot on the "Hit Parade" with **A Tree in the Meadow.** The postwar trend away from the big band and toward the solo vocalist was clearly reflected in the bestseller charts. Another trend was about to burst on the music scene: The 7-inch diameter 45 RPM record was about to become the standard for the release of pop singles.

Other unforgettable hits that year: **A—You're Adorable** by Perry Como and the Fontane Sisters, **It's a Most Unusual Day, (I'd Like To Get You) On a Slow Boat to China** (HP number six), and **Tennessee Waltz.** The season's silly song was **I've Got a Lovely Bunch of Coconuts.**

South Pacific: Opening: April 7, 1949

Based on James Michener's *Tales of the South Pacific,* this Rodgers and Hammerstein musical would run for 1,925 performances and its songs would dominate the "Hit Parade" for the remaining months of the decade. The country was singing along with Mary Martin, Ezio Pinza, and the cast such tunes as the tender **Younger Than Springtime,** the jazzy **I'm Gonna Wash That Man Right Outa My Hair,** the joyous **I'm in Love with a Wonderful Guy,** the rousing male paean to the opposite sex **There Is Nothin' Like a Dame,** the plaintive **This Nearly Was Mine,** the wistful serenade to **Bali Ha'i,** which was number seven on the *Hit Parade,* and the consummately romantic **Some Enchanted Evening,** of which the Perry Como recording held the number one spot for the year. In fact, on a weekly basis, most of the show's tunes scored number one. The original cast album on Columbia quickly sold a staggering million copies. One could not turn on a radio without hearing **Happy Talk, Carefully Taught,** or Mary Martin as Ensign Nellie Forbush defining herself as **A Cockeyed Optimist.** By every measure of success, popular and critical, the musical was a blockbuster.

There were other major hit singles that year: **Diamonds Are a Girl's Best Friend,** Margaret Whiting's **Far Away Places** and **Baby It's Cold Outside,** and Vaughn Monroe held the number nine spot on the "Hit Parade" with **Riders in the Sky.** Sammy Kaye brought back **Lavender Blue (Dilly Dilly),** and Frankie Laine scored a success with **That Lucky Old Sun.** With the approach of Christmas season the hits from *South Pacific* were strongly challenged by a song about the most famous *Rangifer tarandus* of all: **Rudolph, the Red-Nosed Reindeer.** The Gene Autry recording rocketed to the top of the "Hit Parade" as merchandisers across the country sewed red button-noses on any stuffed, plush animal that could be passed off as a reindeer named Rudolph. Not only did the country have a new hit single, but the world had the first new addition to the folklore of Santa Claus in the twentieth century.

BESTSELLING BOOKS

Book Club Mania

The Labor Book Club. The Catholic Children's Book Club. The Aero and Marine Book Club. The Negro Book Club. The Executive Book Club. The Scientific Book Club. The History Book Club. The Non-Fiction Book Club. And, if you felt your reading tastes did not fit into one of those categories, you could take pot luck and join the Surprise Package Book Club.

In the Forties America had at least fifty clubs selling specialty volumes to suit all tastes, in the mail-order vogue begun in 1926 by Book-of-the-Month Club. Then, as now, orders from book clubs could go a long way in making a title a bestseller. Before the advent of mail-order book clubs, about a million readers bought new books annually. By the height of the Forties mail-order heyday, book club membership totaled 3 million "with the average monthly Literary Guild selection being accepted by half of its 1,250,000 members," according to *The Popular Book,* and with "the Book-of-the-Month Club annually distributing almost 11,500,000 books, approximately one and a half times the contents of the Library of Congress."

Paperback Books

Many factors contributed to the surge in numbers of the reading public in the Forties. The decade opened with the appearance of the first inexpensive paperback reprints of hardcover bestsellers, costing a quarter. The 25-cent books could be found in racks in supermarkets, at newsstands, in novelty stores and cigar shops—all new locations for books. Also, World War II helped boost book readership by providing millions of servicemen with well-stocked USO clubs and military libraries—where they acquired the habit of reaching for a book. Postwar prosperity put discretionary money in the pockets of countless Americans, and this, coupled with the realization that the country was now a superpower offering unlimited opportunities for the well-educated, contributed to the surge in library membership enrollments and book purchases. Simply put: America stood at the center of the world stage, and its citizens wanted to come off well-read and well-rounded. *Publishers Weekly* gushed, "Never before have so few titles gone to so many readers ... The major book clubs ... think nothing of printing a half-million copies of a current selection."

The Forties mania for membership in book clubs had positive and negative repercussions for books themselves. On one hand, a title selected by a club experienced a strong burst of sales; on the other, a club's need to continually offer new selections pushed yesterday's hot seller aside to highlight tomorrow's touted release. Books were selling faster than ever, but a typical book's shelf-life was shortening. Some literary critics condemned book clubs, arguing that in choosing selections they imposed a monopoly on literature, and that in signing up only popular books they reduced the reading experience to the lowest common denominator. The *New York Times* assessed the situation and concluded that though clubs "threaten to inflict on American writing the terrible sameness of taste from which the movies and radio suffer, they have taught a lot of people how to read." More Americans than ever were reading. Shortly after the war, the standard estimate was that 49 million people over the age of fifteen read a minimum of one book a month—a high mark relative to population size. In this heady heyday of the written word, a California judge granted a woman a divorce on the grounds that her husband had kept her so preoccupied with housework that she had insufficient time to "keep up with the current best sellers." However, if books were centerstage in the mid-Forties, television, slayer of the written word, was in the wings, poised to make its scene-stealing entrance.

Here, then, by year, are the books America was buying in the Forties, and their ranking on *Publishers Weekly* annual bestseller list.

How Green Was My Valley: Number One Fiction, 1940; For Whom the Bell Tolls: Number Four Fiction, 1940

It was the year in which Hitler attacked England with incessant air power, and in which Franklin D. Roosevelt was elected president for a third term. In London, Agatha Christie published another whodunit, *Ten Little Niggers,* which American readers would come to first know as *And Then There Were None,* and later as **Ten Little Indians.** In America, John Fitzgerald Kennedy published **While England Slept,** stipulating that royalties from British sales go to help cities leveled by Hitler's Luftwaffe bombs.

For Jazz Age great F. Scott Fitzgerald, life had taken a plummeting downturn, due to his bouts of alcoholism, a brush with tuberculosis, his wife's hospitalization for schizophrenia, and the fact that his book royalties for the previous year had totaled a meager $33. "A writer like me must have an utter confidence, an utter faith in his star," he said. "I once had it. But through a series of blows, many of them my own fault, something happened to that sense of immunity and I lost my grip." On December 21, 1940, while reading the *Princeton Alumni Weekly* in the apartment of his mistress, Sheilah Graham, he suffered a fatal heart attack.

The bestselling book of the year, Richard Llewellyn's *How Green Was My Valley,* selling 176,280 copies in the year of its publication, told an emotional tale of Welsh coal miners in magnificently sculpted prose. Not far behind it was Ernest Hemingway's first great commercial success, *For Whom the Bell Tolls,* about an idealist American, Robert Jordan, fighting with the Loyalist forces in the Spanish Civil War. Published on October 21, two days before Hitler met with Spanish leader Francisco Franco in an attempt to enlist Spain's help in an attack on Gibraltar, the novel won high praise from the *New York Times* critic: "The best book Ernest Hemingway has written, the fullest, the deepest, the truest. It will, I think, be one of the major novels in American literature."

Of his own work, Hemingway said, "This one had to be all right or I had to get out of the line [of writing], because my last job, *To Have and Have Not,* was not so good." The swift-moving, action-packed novel about a war sold strongly throughout World War II, hitting the million mark by mid-decade. The 1943 movie version, starring Gary Cooper and Ingrid Bergman, would be nominated for nine Oscars, which further boosted book sales.

On the nonfiction list was **Bet It's a Boy,** by Betty Blunt. A slight cartoon book of line drawing and obstetrical humor, it quickly sold over a hundred thousand copies and is most notable in that it is taken to be the forerunner of what is today called the nonbook, exemplified by volumes like *101 Uses for a Dead Cat.*

Berlin Diary: Number One Nonfiction, 1941; The White Cliffs: Number Two Nonfiction, 1941; Blood, Sweat and Tears: Number Five Nonfiction, 1941

In the first month of the new year James Joyce died of a perforated ulcer; ten weeks later Virginia Woolf threw herself into a Sussex stream; at a cocktail party Sherwood Anderson hastily swallowed an hors d'oeuvre and its accompanying toothpick, which resulted in peritonitis and death. The Japanese bombed Pearl Harbor, America entered the war, and war books predominated the year's nonfiction bestseller list. In fact, WWII, like its predecessor WWI, temporarily shifted the public's reading taste from fiction to fact. Topping the list with bookstore and book club sales of a half million was newspaper correspondent William Shirer's *Berlin Diary,* providing an insider's look at one of the war's two enemies. Alice Duer Miller's *The White Cliffs,* a long, narrative poem of wartime England, struck the hearts of American readers, racking up record sales for a volume of poetry, and becoming the basis for a hit popular song and a 1944 movie, *The White Cliffs of Dover,* starring Irene Dunne, Alan Marshal, and a young Roddy McDowall. It was first brought to the attention of the American public in a dramatic radio-broadcast reading by stage actress Lynn Fontanne.

England's Prime Minister, Winston Churchill, published a book of his speeches, and its title, *Blood, Sweat and Tears,* reflected both the efforts to avert war and the toll the war in Europe had already taken. Months before the Pearl Harbor attack, the Harvard-educated Japanese officer who planned the surprise, Isoroku Yamamoto, and who regarded war with America as suicidal folly, wrote: "To make victory certain, we would have to march into Washington and dictate terms of peace in the White House. I wonder if our politicians, among whom armchair arguments about war are being glibly bandied about . . . have confidence as to the final outcome and are prepared to make the necessary sacrifice."

Americans in 1941 could not get enough war books. In fact, seven of the year's top ten were related in one way or another to war. One, **You Can't Do Business With Hitler,** number six, explained why war had been inevitable.

The Last Time I Saw Paris: Number Three Nonfiction, 1942; The Moon Is Down: Number Two Fiction, 1942

In the first full year of war, war books again dominated the nonfiction list, occupying seven of the top ten spots. Global tensions were also reflected in novels such as John Steinbeck's *The Moon Is Down,* an uplifting tale of social decency defeating inhuman barbarity cast in the setting of Norway under German domination.

War anxiety was also apparent in the public's sudden penchant for inspirational and religious reading. **The Song of Bernadette,** by Franz Werfel, sold nearly a half million copies to become the number one fiction. The following year it would be a smash 20th Century–Fox movie, starring unknown twenty-three-year-old Jennifer Jones as the young French peasant girl Bernadette Soubirous who has a vision of "the Lady." Readers loved the book and viewers adored the film, which the *New York Times* panned as "tedious and repetitious . . . it goes in for dialectic discourse that will clutter and fatigue the average mind." Many average Hollywood minds voted it twelve Academy Award nominations; it won four Oscars.

The Robe, a biblical story set in the time of Christ, soared to the annual number seven spot in 1942, then to number one in 1943. It remained a best-seller into 1945, never falling lower than number five on the *Publishers Weekly* monthly list. In author Lloyd Douglas's use of fanciful Christ-era slang among the Apostles—"Peter has no polish . . . Life wouldn't be worth a punched denarius"—*The Robe* was something new as biblical stories go. The "robe" was Christ's cloak, and the novel described the conversion to Christianity, and eventual martyrdom, of the tribune Marcellus Gallio, who carried out the order to crucify Jesus. "His bodyguard Demetrius," quipped *Time* magazine's reviewer, "is rather like Jeeves." When the government put a wartime restriction on the use of paper, the thick tome was reprinted in a thinner volume, containing the full original text but smaller typeface and less white space. The 1953 film adaptation of the bestseller would star Richard Burton as Gallio, Jean Simmons as Diana, and Victor Mature as Demetrius. It was the first movie in "wide-screen" CinemaScope.

Throughout America's involvement in the war, the sale of Bibles increased more than 25 percent.

The nostalgically titled *The Last Time I Saw Paris,* a glimpse of the city before the grimness of German occupation, inspired a popular song of that name. American readers turned by the tens of thousands to the book for Elliot Paul's sad reminiscences. It became a hit movie in the Fifties.

Forever Amber: Number Four Fiction, 1944

While war books continued to dominate the nonfiction list, three vastly different novels had America avidly reading.

Kathleen Winsor had set out to write a novel of British royalty in the seventeenth century by reading some four hundred books on Restoration England, taking copious notes. After five years of effort, she produced a manuscript of approximately 2.5 million words that totaled 971 pages when it was published by Macmillan in 1944. Weighing in at 2 pounds, *Forever Amber,* banned in Boston, dwelt on the bawdiness of the period, offering pages of tasteful sex, which accounted for its phenomenal sales of a million copies in less than a year.

Macmillan saturated bookstores with 225,000 advance copies. The Boston ban eventually spread throughout the entire state of Massachusetts. The highly photogenic author, formerly a sports writer for California's *Oakland Tribune* and writing under her maiden name, was the wife of All-American football player Robert Herwig—though soon to become Mrs. Artie Shaw. Her racy tale has sixteen-year-old Amber, mistress of Lord Bruce Carlton, by whom she is pregnant, marry the repulsive Channell, who runs off with her money. Thrown into Newgate Prison for debt, she meets a highwayman named Black Jack Mallard, but their romance is cut short because of his appointment with the gallows. She goes on the stage, marries various other men, one of whom is an earl, which makes her a countess, and eventually gains favor in the court of Charles II. Winsor's erotic prose was all her own: "His shirts . . . still carried the male smell of him." *The New Yorker* created a special literary classification for the book and the genre: historico-mammary.

The 1947 movie adaptation, starring Linda Darnell as the quintessential flirt Amber, was, after a private screening, condemned by the Catholic Legion of Decency. Francis Cardinal Spellman, archbishop of New York, cautioned, "Catholics may not see the movie with a safe conscience"—a quote that was to be read at all Sunday Masses throughout the archdiocese. Director Otto Preminger recut the film in accordance with the legion's suggestions, and the organization was grudgingly forced to rescind its condemnation.

Quite different was Betty Smith's tender recollections of days past in **A Tree Grows in Brooklyn,** a story of sensitive childhood published the previous year that was number three in 1944. W. Somerset Maugham's **The Razor's Edge** held the number five spot; it is a wartime tale of a mystical man-of-action who is "something of a combination of Christopher Isherwood and Lawrence of Arabia."

Notable on the 1944 nonfiction list was Margaret Landon's **Anna and the King of Siam,** number eight; the nineteenth-century story of an English governess to the king's children became the basis for a movie and musical titled *The King and I.*

1945. The autobiographical **The Egg and I,** by Betty MacDonald, was number eight in nonfiction in 1945, number one in 1946, and number seven in 1947. It was an earthy, humorous tale of life on a Western chicken ranch, insightfully illustrating the pros and cons of a city-dweller's return to nature. "To city people sitting snug and dry," wrote one reviewer, "Mrs. MacDonald's life in the woods comes as unadulterated fun." The simple nature book apparently held great appeal for millions of war-weary Americans who kept it a bestseller for three years. It was made into a successful 1947 movie starring Claudette Colbert as Betty and Fred MacMurray as her husband Bob. Betty MacDonald followed the success of *The Egg and I* with **The Plague and I,** number ten in 1948.

1946. While Betty MacDonald remained a top-seller in nonfiction, Daphne du Maurier and Taylor Caldwell headed the fiction list with, respectively, **The King's General,** number one, and **This Side of Innocence,** number two. In seventh place was **Arch of Triumph** by Erich Maria Remarque, whose World War I novel, *All Quiet on the Western Front,* was a 1929 bestseller.

1947. Laura Hobson's **Gentleman's Agreement** was number three in fiction. The war and Hitler's atrocities had heightened interest in problems of race relations, especially involving Jews and gentiles, the focus of Hobson's book, which sold more than a million copies.

The Naked and the Dead: Number Two Fiction, 1948; Raintree County: Number Seven Fiction, 1948; The Young Lions: Number Ten Fiction, 1948

"Incredibly beastly," attacked London's *Sunday Times.* "No decent man could leave it about the house." That harsh criticism was for the shocking four-letter words that peppered Norman Mailer's seven-hundred-odd-page wartime novel, *The Naked and the Dead.* Fellow author George Orwell deemed the work, Mailer's first, as "the only war novel of any distinction to appear hitherto," and the book established the author as a new force in American literature. Selling 137,185 copies, the realistic novel of how war brutalizes ordinary men made "the fugging army" out to be as much an enemy of GIs as the Japanese.

Another first novelist on the bestseller list that year was Ross Lockridge, who committed suicide not long after his *Raintree County* achieved critical and popular success. The American Civil War tale became a successful 1957 movie starring Montgomery Clift, Eva Marie Saint, and Elizabeth Taylor, whose portrayal of Clift's ditsy Southern belle wife won her an Oscar.

Yet another first novelist to make the bestseller list in 1948 was playwright and short-story writer Irwin Shaw. His *The Young Lions*—a lengthy wartime tale that depicts its characters, American and German, in peace and in conflict; in Paris, in New York, on the ski slopes of Austria, and in Nazi concentration camps—enjoyed sales of 78,050 books that year.

The nonfiction list was notable for sex researcher A. C. Kinsey's morals-shaking **Sexual Behavior in the Human Male,** number four. It either titillated or incensed readers with its startling findings: 85 percent of all married men have had premarital sex; 50 percent of married men are unfaithful to their wives; semiskilled laborers are the most sexually active group of males, with professional men ranking second, day laborers third, and white collar workers a limp last. If wives wanted to believe that Kinsey exaggerated the figures about married men's infidelity, semiskilled laborers certainly wished the findings about them were true.

But of all the aforementioned books of the Forties, perhaps none had a greater influence on more people than a common sense how-to on bringing up baby, by a little-known doctor named Spock.

Common Sense Book of Baby and Child Care: 1946

Under the guidance of Dr. Benjamin Spock's 1946 manual—which since its publication has sold about a million copies a year—parents began taking a new approach to child rearing. Spock's pathfinding book, which advocated a so-called permissive attitude in child rearing, was one of the first popular medical books in which an acknowledged expert writes for a general audience—setting a trend in itself. He urged parents to replace the sterner methods of older generations with more sympathy and understanding. Asserting that "there's no such thing as a bad boy," he encouraged fathers to become pals with their sons. As no other book of the era, Spock's compendium of pediatric and psychological wisdom was read, reread, and at times misread by millions of young, postwar mothers and fathers.

The book could not have arrived in a more baby-loving era. As a result of World War II, the marriage rate had soared. Three million children were born each year in 1942 and 1943, as opposed to 2 million a year before the war. In postwar America everyone seemed to be planning a large family. Public opinion polls in 1945 reported that the average American woman hoped to have a minimum of four children. Spock's book was born into the baby boom era. Within a few years of its appearance, about 5 million additional children were crowding the nation's classrooms. Novels and other nonfiction of the period were read and enjoyed, but *Common Sense* was carried around the house, from nursery to kitchen to bedroom. When a baby cried, anxious young parents asked "What does Dr. Spock say?" and ran for the helpful how-to.

With translations into twenty-six languages, the manual influenced child-rearing around the world, for better or worse. Later, in the Seventies, critics blamed Spock's "permissiveness" for drugs, student riots, promiscuity and other excesses of the counterculture. But they had misread his 1946 message that the child "needs to feel that his mother and father, however agreeable, still have their own rights, know how to be firm, won't let him be unreasonable or rude . . . The spoiled child is not a happy creature even in his own home."

TELEVISION HITS

Listeners Become Viewers

With the advent of television in the late Forties, audio fell victim to video; listeners became viewers. Whether viewers or critics called the strange new medium "sight radio," "radio moving pictures," or "radiovision," its debut in postwar America was momentous. As Marshall McLuhan would pointedly note, television had "the greatest influence on [people] of all mutations in this century." The transformation of listener to viewer was slow at first, but once a

Imagine Fibber McGee and Molly...
on **TELEVISION**

brought to you by **NBC**

Yes, on NBC Television that crowded closet at Wistful Vista—the foibles of lovable Fibber and the trials of patient Molly, for instance—could all become real visual experiences . . . experiences for you to *watch* as well as hear.

Think what television programs originating in studios of the National Broadcasting Company . . . such programs as the top-notch sound radio which has won NBC the distinction of America's most popular network . . . will add to home entertainment!

Already, plans—within the limitations imposed by wartime—have been placed in operation by NBC . . . plans which with the co-operation of business and government will result in extensive NBC tele-

vision networks . . . chains spreading from Eastern, Mid-Western and Western centers . . . gradually providing television after the war, to all of the nation.

Moderate-priced television receivers will provide your home with sight and sound programs consistent with the highest standards of NBC . . . offer the most popular of the shows in this new, vastly improved field of entertainment. Look forward to other great NBC accomplishments such as FM, noise-free reception . . . faithfulness of tone reproduction.

• • •

Look to NBC to lead in these new branches of broadcasting by the same wide margin that now makes it *"The Network Most People Listen to Most."*

National Broadcasting Company

America's No. 1 Network

A Service of Radio Corporation of America

critical momentum was achieved in numbers of TV sets and devoted fans, the cataract of converts from the theater of the mind to the theater of the eye was unstoppable.

To get an overview of television's arrival:

1939. NBC makes the first regular broadcast at the New York World's Fair, featuring a guest appearance by President Roosevelt. Forecasts the *New York Times:* "The problem with television is that the people must sit and keep their eyes glued on a screen; the average American family hasn't time for it. Therefore, the showmen are convinced that for this reason, if for no other, television will never be a serious competitor of broadcasting."

1941. Technical standards (which remain largely unchanged today) are set by the National Television Systems Committee.

1945. As the war ends only five thousand homes have TV sets, which cost $700 each, the price of a Chevrolet.

1947. Commercial television debuts, with 16 stations this year, soaring to 107 by the end of the decade. A *Variety* headline wonders if television is: RADIO'S FRANKENSTEIN? *Consumer Reports* that year offers its own insightful opinion of commercial TV: "Regrettably, advertising can sink much lower visually than verbally . . . It's one thing to listen to a comedian imploring you to buy a toothpaste . . . but to see him looking at you, sincerity shining in his eyes—well, one has to be steeled to that."

Early reviews of the medium and its fare were mixed:

Eddie Cantor: "What I have seen on my television set . . . has been the worst kind of junk. It seems that the producers of this trivia have only one thing on their minds—Is it cheap!"

Jack Benny: "Hold off television. Science be damned! Long live radio!"

Groucho Marx: "I watch this orgy night after night, bored but nevertheless fascinated by its potentialities. How long can I survive on radio against this new monster?"

The debut of "radio's Frankenstein" had been well planned. As a result of wartime employment, Americans had saved an estimated $100 billion, which television set manufacturers viewed as the financial base for their new empire. Simply put, millions of people—"Levittowners"—could afford TV sets, and the price of sets conveniently dropped as the size of screens widened from 5 inches to 7 to 10. Observed one early TV executive: "Television is about to do to radio what the Sioux did to Custer. There's going to be a massacre." Indeed, in cities reached by the first television programs—which were largely adaptations of successful radio series, featuring the same stars, schtick, and sponsors—radio received less than 15 percent of the evening audience. The choice to listen or to watch was really Hobson's choice.

By the end of the Forties, advertisers were spending $200 million on television, largely to sell cigarettes; cigarettes made broadcasting profitable. The medium's superstars were a red-headed, freckle-faced puppet named Howdy Doody and a failed radio comic named Milton Berle, and in many ways they were not all that different. By the premiere of "I Love Lucy" in 1951, 17 million Americans had bought television sets, and movie theaters across the country had lost up to 40 percent of their audiences.

To begin at the madcap beginning:

Milton Berle's Texaco Star Theater: NBC Premiere, June 8, 1948

Milton Berle had never had a successful radio series. In the decade before he memorably debuted on television, he appeared on such forgettable programs as "Gillette's Community Sing," "If You've Heard This One," and the quiz show "Kiss and Make Up." But on Tuesday night, June 8, 1948, Berle's screwball comedy style propelled him to the kind of national fame that won him the accolade Mr. Television. It is said that he sold more TV sets than any advertising campaign ever devised. People bought "tubes" just to see his much-touted antics, his unscripted quips to the TV audience, and his stable of zany stooges.

Milton Berle.

The joke of the day was by comic Joe E. Lewis: "Berle is responsible for more television sets being sold than anyone else. I sold mine, my father sold his."

Within weeks of his debut, Milton Berlinger, born July 12, 1908, in a New York tenement to a shopkeeper father and a department-store-detective mother, was the most popular entertainer in the nation. His broadcast on October 19, 1948, measured in a "Hooper rating," captured 92 percent of the viewing audience, thought to be the highest rating ever achieved by any radio or television program. *Time* reported that with the show not yet a year old, Berle's "audience in the 24 cities that see him 'live' or on kinescope film two weeks later is reliably estimated at 4,452,000." Observed *Newsweek* that same month, this "radio-stage-screen comic has become not only the country's top-salaried night-club entertainer, but the first and biggest star in the newest and most difficult of all entertainment mediums—television."

Week after week Berle scored an astounding 80 Hooper rating, meaning that 80 percent of TV sets tuned to anything at that hour were receiving him. Expressed another way, no other entertainer in history had ever been seen simultaneously by so many people. Such was the power and the glory bestowed by television.

Nightclubs and restaurants, traditionally closed on Monday nights, now closed on Tuesdays, because doing business opposite Uncle Miltie ceased to pay. For the next few years Tuesday nights belonged to Milton Berle. And Wednesday mornings people around the country laughed again as they related the zany skits and corny jokes to those less fortunate who did not yet own TV sets. So essential was it to see the most talked about show in the nation, families scraped together funds to purchase their first set just to watch "the undisputed No. 1 performer on U.S. TV," as *Time* was quick to label him. "He was the Henry Ford of television," *People* magazine later said, "the one who transformed a rich man's toy into an electronic renaissance."

The Vaudeo Era Begins.   It is no exaggeration to say that Milton Berle became the nation's second uncle, after Sam. Audiences adored his impressive roster of guest stars, his unconcealed devotion to his mother Sandra, his vaudeville slapstick routines, and the surprise getups he'd wear to open each week's show. He was repeatedly hit in the face with cream pies and squirted with soda water from a seltzer bottle, his clothes were torn apart, his wig was pulled off, and he shamelessly resorted to old-time vaudeville stunts like cutting off the tie of a spectator and sticking his fingers in another performer's mouth. He had a penchant for tasteless drag, followed by costumes of clowns, monsters, Superman, Cleopatra, Santa Claus, Sherlock Holmes, the Easter Bunny, Father Time, Charlie Chaplin, and even fellow TV star Howdy Doody. His impersonation of the fruit-laden Carmen Miranda always drew huge laughs.

He blatantly announced that his jokes were stolen from the top comics in the business, as often they were. Entertainment writers realized from the start they were witnessing an unprecedented event, "a phenomenon of massive proportions," wrote Philip Hamburger in the *New Yorker* in 1949. "When the history of the early days of commercial television is eventually written, several chapters will no doubt be devoted to the strange art of Milton Berle."

Uncle Miltie so dominated the airwaves with frantic slapstick humor, corny jokes, and crazy costumes in the tradition of the vaudeville stage that the era of his hegemony, from the late Forties to the mid-Fifties, has been dubbed the medium's "vaudeo era," a combination of old-time vaudeville and the newfangled medium of video.

The extraordinary success of the "Texaco Star Theater" prompted networks to introduce additional comedy and variety programs. "It was something like the Alaskan gold rush," wrote one TV critic. "Every comic . . . who'd ever induced the vaguest snicker from an audience was rushed by his eager agent to attend a top-level meeting with . . . network executives." Rival CBS in 1948 offered viewers Ed Sullivan's **Toast of the Town.** Comedians Sid Caesar and Imogene Coca were featured on the "Admiral Broadway Revue" (1949), a forerunner of their popular **Your Show of Shows** (1950). Comedy began to dominate nighttime scheduling by 1950, the year Jackie Gleason starred on Du Pont's **Cavalcade of Stars.** Groucho Marx appeared in **You Bet Your Life.** The realization that TV was now Americans' favorite home entertainment caused radio comedians to rush into television. Both Bob Hope and Jack Benny had their first specials in 1950. That year TV comedy revues featured Danny Thomas, Jimmy Durante, Dean Martin and Jerry Lewis, Abbott and Costello, and Phil Silvers. If it "wasn't for Berle," Jackie Gleason later admitted, "a lot of us wouldn't have gotten a break either. When he became Mister Television, those network guys began saying: 'We gotta get comics.' " Mr. Television's last regular telecast was in June 1956. By that time viewers' favorite form of programming was the situation comedy.

Sitcoms: Humor the Family Way.   The situation comedy is, has been, and perhaps always will be the bedrock of American television broadcasting. Variety shows have flourished and faded. Dramas have gone in and out of vogue. Bandleaders have been banished; singers silenced; documentaries relegated to public service channels. But the sitcom has endured, indeed thrived, to become the most predictable of prime-time offerings. More than any other program format, the situation comedy has been the television viewer's passion from the first broadcasts of the late Forties until the present—and essentially in an untouched form. What has changed over the years from "I Love Lucy" to "The Mary Tyler Moore Show" to "Roseanne" is a broadening of subject matter; the format, or formula, remains the same.

The sitcom is a cultural icon. It's been called "the art form of today"—which may say more about the state of art than about television. Nonetheless, so passionate is our love of and devotion to the format that a single phrase from a hit show identifies the program for millions of people: "Baby, you're the greatest!" "Kiss mah grits." "God'll get you for that." "Would you believe . . ." Often a single word triggers instant nostalgic recognition: "Meathead!" "Dyn-o-mite!" "Nanoo-nanoo." Many early sitcoms have avid fan clubs. RALPH—the Royal Association for the Longevity and Preservation of "The Honeymooners"—has thousands of members and drew over twenty-five hundred sitcom fanatics to its last convention.

Why such a national mania for the sitcom?

In a word: family. At the heart of every sitcom, virtually without exception, is a family—a biologically related family at home (from the Ward Cleavers to the Archie Bunkers to the Al Bundys) or a family grouping in the workplace, as in "M*A*S*H" or "The Mary Tyler Moore Show." The characters exhibit habits, foibles, and responses to tidings good and bad that are familiar to us from our own friends, family, or neighbors. One definition of a sitcom is "a small hunk of life exaggerated for comic purposes."

Most crucial to the formula in constructing a sitcom is that week after week the characters do not deviate from their habits or foibles; familiarity breeds success. This is true of TV's most wholesome clans from "Father Knows Best" to "The Cosby Show," as well as of the bickering families (the so-called anti-families) of "The Simpsons" and "Married . . . With Children." Whatever the controversial topic treated in a contemporary sitcom—abortion, impotence, menopause, homosexuality—it is addressed through the format of a close-knit, loving or bickering, family-style relationship. It's been suggested that future social historians will look back to each decade's sitcoms to study what each period in history was truly about in terms of the family and its pressing issues. Thus, in this and later chapters we'll look at the sitcom's greatest hits and the spin-off fads and pop phrases that have infused our culture.

It all began with one family.

The Goldbergs: CBS Premiere, January 10, 1949

Sociologically, it is interesting to note that television's first four successful sitcoms involved families that were Jewish ("The Goldbergs"), Swedish ("Mama"), black ("Amos 'n' Andy"), and whiter than white ("The Life of Riley"). All types from America's melting pot peopled the early situation comedies, though in the next decade the white, middle-class majority would surface in abundance through such characters as Lucy, Margie, Ozzie, Joan, the Cleavers, and the Andersons.

Lovable Molly Goldberg, played by series creator Gertrude Berg, brought her warmth, humor, and familiar radio family to television in 1949. In adhering to her radio formula and cast of characters, Berg assured herself a ready-made audience and instant popularity. From the first broadcast the show was a hit. Listeners turned viewers were already familiar with Molly's crazily inverted expressions like "In the pot put the chicken," asides like "So who's to know?" and various malapropisms that were popularly known as Mollypropisms, delivered in a rhythm that made the simplest statement sound like maternal Jewish advice. As with Milton Berle, Molly Goldberg was a hit in metropolitan cities, areas where the density of TV sets was highest and the ethnic humor most appreciated.

"Following the thousand-year tradition of the Wandering Jew," writes Rick Mitz in *The Great TV Sitcom Book,* Gertrude Berg moved her clan to TV, "the Promised Medium." The family's six-room Bronx apartment—Number 3B, at

1030 East Tremont Avenue—was peopled weekly by Molly's gruff husband, Jake, and their well-behaved children, Sammy and Rosalie, who sat on the not-too-prosperous family's shabby furniture. This first cross-over from radio to television took a previously imagined family and suddenly made it *visual.* "Like a long-lost relative, a pen pal finally met in the flesh," says Mitz, "Molly looked like Molly talked. Gertrude Berg—with her sad twinkly eyes, her bassethound face, and her potato sack body—was Molly Goldberg." As Berg herself once said, "I always felt the Goldbergs were a family that needed to be seen." To fans of the radio series, it was instant "sitcamaraderie." As the self-proclaimed "Jewish mother," Molly dispensed more advice in the sitcom format than would be proffered on later hour-long talk shows devoted specifically to that purpose.

Real-Life Tragedy.　While the show was riding high in the rating, disaster struck in the form of a Fifties Red Scare. *Red Channels,* a book about alleged Communist sympathizers, was published in the summer of 1950, and it listed Philip Loeb, who played Molly's husband Jake, as "friendly to Communist causes." Berg told the *New York Times,* "Philip Loeb has stated categorically that he is not and has never been a Communist. I believe him."

But the show's sponsor, General Foods, fearing the effect of adverse publicity on its products, demanded Loeb be fired. When Berg refused, and Loeb turned down $85,000 to quit, General Foods dropped the show as "too controversial." No other sponsor would touch it until a reluctant and crestfallen Gertrude Berg hired another actor to play Jake. For the next two years Berg continued to pay Loeb his full salary out of her own profits, but he was essentially banned from TV and radio work, booed when he appeared in a stage play, and in 1955 killed himself with an overdose of barbiturates. The *Times* obituary scathingly listed the cause of death as: "a sickness commonly called 'The Black List.' " The show's ratings dropped, a new format was attempted— with the Goldberg family moving from New York City to the suburbs, following the real-life lead of the nation's Levittowners—but by the mid-Fifties the show, which had become something of a Jewish "Donna Reed Show," was off the air.

By this time **The Life of Riley**—first telecast on October 4, 1949—was a major hit and Jackie Gleason, the actor who had played Chester A. Riley until 1950, had been replaced by William Bendix. Chester; his wife, Peg; and their children, Babs and Junior, are fondly remembered, as is Chester's catchphrase to every downturn of fate: "What a revoltin' development this is!" If the comic father of television was Milton Berle, the sitcom mother of the medium was Molly Goldberg.

Mama: CBS Premiere, July 1, 1949

With Peggy Wood playing Mama Marta Hansen, this weekly comedy of an immigrant Norwegian family living in San Francisco at the turn of the century could have been titled "Mother Knows Best." Veteran stage actress Wood infused her character with a genuine warmth and advice-giving gentleness that endeared the series to Friday night viewers for seven years.

Each episode opened with daughter Katrin leafing through the family album, reminiscing: "I remember my brother Nels . . . and my little sister Dagmar . . . and of course, Papa. But most of all, I remember Mama." Based on a novelette, *Mama's Bank Account,* by Kathryn Forbes, and a subsequent play, *I Remember Mama,* by John Van Druten (which became an RKO film in 1948), the series was so popular that when CBS canceled it in 1956, public clamor forced the network to resurrect the program as a Sunday afternoon feature.

An example of one of the homey plots is this: "Because Papa is reluctant to go to school to study for his citizenship exam, Mama goes instead, and later teaches Papa, so he can become an American citizen." Overlaying that core premise, weekly episodes concerned Papa's carpentry skills, Dagmar's braces, Mama's efforts to brighten the home furnishings. In one episode, Papa phones at five P.M. to say he's bringing the boss home for dinner *in one hour;* that was the plot. Characters seldom yelled and never insulted each other. Each show ended with that episode's theme neatly and wisely resolved, and with the family seated around a steaming pot of the sponsor's Maxwell House coffee.

The show was an immediate hit. "We had good scripts," explained Peggy Wood. "Such good scripts . . . never maudlin, never sticky. They were really solid, honest things." The show was written by Frank Gabrielson and directed by Ralph Nelson, both with Scandinavian family roots. Nelson would later direct the films *Lilies of the Field, Charly,* and *Requiem for a Heavyweight.* To create a weekly series for seven years, Gabrielson and Nelson were forced to dilute the original source material but never weakened characterization for the sake of a laugh. Like Molly Goldberg, Mama Hansen ran the home and dispensed down-to-earth wisdom. And as "The Goldbergs" brimmed with Yiddishisms, the characters in "Mama" pronounced j's like y's such that Aunt Jenny was known to viewers as "Yenny." Yet ethnic dialect was never used as a comic device, as it was in other sitcoms (for example, Ricky Ricardo's accent in "Lucy"). Humor came from situations.

One classic story, which was repeated each Christmas, involved Papa's telling Dagmar that animals, as a reward for protecting the Christ child in the stable, were granted the gift of speech for a few hours each Christmas Eve. When the family is asleep, a curious Dagmar sneaks into the barn, waits patiently, and falls asleep herself, only to wake and hear the animals talking. A dream or reality? She tells her family but no one believes her—no one, that is, except the home viewer.

It is interesting to note in the fickle world of TV sitcoms the fate of "Mama." When it was first canceled in 1956, after a successful seven-year run, viewers expressed their disappointment in thousands of letters and phone calls. When, a few months later, it was brought back, it flopped; in the interim viewers had forged allegiances with other sitcoms and could barely remember "Mama." Broadcasters learned of the fickleness of fans before there was a market for syndicated reruns. In fact, there can be no reruns, for unlike "The Life of Riley," "Mama" was telecast live rather than filmed. Like Katrin's nostalgic leafing through the family album, we who are old enough can only remember "Mama."

Kiddie TV and Toy Fads

A child is not satisfied merely to watch a favorite TV character, the child wants to touch the creation to enhance its reality. From the dawn of children's television with "Howdy Doody" in 1947 to the cartoon craze among preteens for Ninja Turtles, hit shows have produced a seemingly endless turnover of faddish toys; indeed, Saturday mornings have gone from being a time for children's watching to one of marketers' hawking. Children's television is today synonymous with games, toys, stuffed dolls, and candied cereals. Saturday mornings are fad-fests in the making. Even "Howdy Doody," as we're about to see, generated profitable spin-offs.

From the start of kiddie TV, children turned out to be even more devoted fans than adults, and not nearly so fickle. The three-decade longevity of "Captain Kangaroo" is unprecedented in the realm of children's television. In the Forties and Fifties, children were completely and uncritically fascinated with TV shows for them, and the early shows involved group participation as a dominant theme. Most programs were broadcast live with an adult host, and a gallery of peanut-sized tots. Several of today's stars began in the world of kiddie video: Ed McMahon was a clown in "The Big Top" (1950–57); Don Knotts was Tim Tremble of "Howdy Doody"; and Cliff Robertson was the hero of "Rod Brown, Rocket Ranger" (1953–54).

It's been estimated that more fads have been created on Saturday mornings than all the other days of the year combined. Shows like "The Flintstones," "The Pink Panther," and "Yogi Bear" generated fads through licensing of cartoon characters to appear on products such as lunchboxes, notebooks, and T-shirts. The decade of the Nineties began with Teenage Mutant Ninja Turtles going from a cartoon series to a feature film to a merchandiser's paradise of spin-offs. In this chapter and subsequent ones, we'll look at kidvid hits and the fads they generated. It all began with . . .

The Howdy Doody Show: NBC Premiere, December 27, 1947

BUFFALO BOB SMITH: Say kids, what time is it?
PEANUT GALLERY: It's How-w-w-w-dy Doody Time!
[THEME SONG, TO THE TUNE OF "TA-RA-RA-BOOM-DEAY."]

It's Howdy Doody time.
It's Howdy Doody time.
Bob Smith and Howdy too
Say Howdy-do to you.
Let's give a rousing cheer,
For Howdy Doody's here.
It's time to start the show.
So, kids, let's go!

Howdy Doody and Buffalo Bob Smith.

One of the longest-running and best-remembered children's shows, "Howdy Doody" began on December 27, 1947, and did not vacate its NBC habitat until thirteen years later, on September 24, 1960. It introduced millions of youngsters to the delights of cowboy-marionette Howdy; horn-honking silent Clarabell the Clown (Bob Keeshan; who left the show in 1953 to become **Captain Kangaroo**); Flubberdub (also Flub-a-Dub), part dog, part duck; Chief Thunderthud; Tim Tremble (Don Knotts); a woman for all seasons, Princess Summer-Fall-Winter-Spring; and everyone's comic nemesis, Phineas T. Bluster, an ill-tempered curmudgeon who objected to people having fun.

Set in the colorful town of Doodyville, the series revolved around the antics of a circus troupe led by Buffalo Bob Smith, who dressed in a pioneer outfit and resembled the legendary Buffalo Bill. Smith voiced the freckled-faced (the puppet had exactly seventy-two freckles), puffy-cheeked, wide-grinning Howdy. Keeshan later explained the reason his Clarabell never talked: "I think that NBC had no faith in my acting ability, which was probably well-founded. I was twenty years old and had none." He'd been chosen for the role from among NBC's studio pages.

The show's atmosphere of circus, madhouse, and puppet theater drew children irresistibly to the screen and held them rapt for an hour. *Variety* gave the program a glowing review, not for the antics of its stars, but for the baby-sitting potential of television's first kiddie fare: "In the middle-class home, there is perhaps nothing as welcome to the mother as something that will keep the small fry intently absorbed and out of possible mischief. This program can almost be guaranteed to pin down the squirmiest of the brood." It kept children still—except for their eyelids: The boy puppet continually blinked, and thousands of young viewers picked up the habit. This prompted a deluge of letters from concerned parents and trips to the doctor to see if the practice was harmful.

The show launched a half-dozen fads, and its opening phrase, "It's How-w-w-wdy Doody time!" became a national youth slogan. Howdy's favorite expression, "thingamajigs" (a 1700s British catchall), entered the our everyday vocabulary of inarticulate expression.

Demand for tickets to the live telecast, from children whose fondest dream was to sit in the Peanut Gallery (the bleachers), overwhelmed the NBC staff. The waiting list was so long that a child could have outgrown the show by the time his or her name was selected. *Life* magazine featured a Howdy lookalike contest, which drew thousands of photographs from boys and girls (a boy from Patchogue, Long Island, won). When Howdy appeared at Boston's Jordan Marsh department store, twenty thousand kids stood in line. All of this excitement for a program in which a typical episode included a silent film short, a song or two, and a madcap story involving the comic characters of Doodyville.

Howdy Is Born.   Broadcaster Robert Schmidt became Buffalo Bob Smith for the simple reason that his radio show, "Triple B Ranch," originated from Buffalo, New York, his hometown. His comic sidekick then was an imaginary boy named Elmer, voiced by Smith. "Say, kids, I want you to meet my ranch hand, Elmer," Bob would announce, and Elmer would greet radio listeners with "Well, how-w-w-wdy doody." Kids loved dopy Elmer's dumb delivery of the salutation, so as Robert Schmidt had changed his own name, he rechristened Elmer as Howdy Doody. As yet there was no puppet, just a radio voice.

NBC was attempting to put together an hour-long children's show. Buffalo Bob was hired, and veteran puppeteer Frank Paris oversaw the construction of a wooden Howdy, which was supposed to "resemble" Smith's old Elmer voice. Instead, the doll turned out to look more like a dopey, blond-haired, long-nosed Pinocchio than the later wide-eyed, red-headed, snub-nosed Howdy. In the meantime, Buffalo Bob had softened Elmer's heavy yokel dialect. A revamped puppet could not be ready in time for the December 27 telecast, so for the first show there was only the promise of Howdy Doody. A voice in a drawer said to Buffalo Bob, "Gosh, Ah'm in here, but Ah'm too darned bashful to come out."

Bob coaxed, "C'mon, Howdy boy! The kids wanna see you."

The drawer wouldn't budge, and the voice again said, "Aww gee, I'm just too bashful." The show went on without Howdy, but the dozen kids in the Peanut Gallery, and thousands more at home, were dying to glimpse the reticent puppet.

For the second telecast, a week later—still no Howdy. Anticipation turned into near-hysteria.

Then one show opened with Buffalo Bob standing beside the recalcitrant drawer, which now had suspicious-looking strings protruding outward and upward. Bob knocked and Howdy Doody debuted. Kids across the country screamed, their eyes riveted to the puppet. He wore a vest, bandana, cowboy chaps, and elbow-length work gloves. By any standard he was neither handsome nor cute; rather, big-eared, thick-lipped, and awkward. Kids loved him.

Macy's department store approached Frank Paris about manufacturing the doll; they were receiving hundreds of requests a week. In a legal dispute with NBC over who owned the rights to the puppet, Paris stormed out of the studio: "I literally took my puppet and went home," he later wrote. A former Walt Disney artist, Velma Dawson, was commissioned to construct a different looking Howdy, and in the interim a bandaged-faced puppet appeared on the show, with Buffalo Bob explaining that Howdy was undergoing a facelift to become "the handsomest man in the world." On the West Coast, Dawson produced a freckled boy dressed in a flannel shirt, blue jeans, a kerchief, and a cowboy hat. His mouth moved, his eyes rolled, his eyelids flickered, and he was endearingly cute.

On June 7, 1948, NBC issued a press release: HOWDY DOODY WEARING NEW LOOK AFTER FACE-LIFTING ON COAST, REJOINS BOB SMITH ON NBC TELEVISION SHOW TOMORROW. On June 8 the bandaged dummy was retired, and the new puppet, in bandages, was unwrapped with breathless expectancy. Across the nation, with children and TV critics, the new Howdy garnered glowing reviews. He was cute—and better yet, available for licensing.

Howdy Merchandising Madness.

"Howdy Doody" wakened advertisers to the children's marketplace with a clarion call.

It began in the spring of 1948 when the show was less than a half-year old. As an election year gimmick, Buffalo Bob announced on-air a free giveaway of "Howdy Doody for President" buttons. The show expected to receive requests nationwide for about five thousand buttons. The next day, the New York broadcast station received six thousand beseeching letters; NBC's Philadelphia affiliate got eight thousand; Baltimore six thousand, Washington three thousand. The landslide mushroomed to sixty thousand, then a hundred thousand—approaching the total number of TV sets in the country. The show's producers panicked; where would they get the money for all those buttons?

One NBC executive realized that the money for buttons was peanuts compared to the advertising dollars to be had by telling potential sponsors of the mail inundation. Within a week of NBC's issuance of a press release, makers of Colgate toothpaste, Wonder Bread, Ovaltine, and M&M's had become commercial sponsors of the show. Within a month advertising slots were sold out for a year in advance, with potential new sponsors fighting to get on the waiting list. Madison Avenue learned the selling power of television—before the medium was even out of its infancy. A guest appearance by a little green clay figure named **Gumby** was enough to launch a Gumby doll craze and get the character his own series and an animated film.

A company was formed to merchandise Howdy Doody tie-ins, since it appeared from one estimate that a third of the nation's children were grouping around neighborhood TV sets to watch the puppet. The result was a deluge of licenses for dolls, records, toys, sleeping bags, wallpaper, and wristwatches that carried the impish likeness of the blue-eyed "six-year-old" wonderboy. Toy manufacturers, like Ideal and Marx, literally begged for more commercial slots, as did cereal giants Kellogg's and General Foods, and the confection king Mars. "Howdy Doody" did more than kick off children's television; the show's button mania made the medium a viable marketplace in the eyes of the business community, which previously only had ears for radio. In its thirteen-year run, "Howdy Doody" played 2,343 television performances. The show permanently signed off in 1960 with its daily farewell song to kiddie viewers: "So long, small fry, it's time to say goodbye."

Kukla, Fran and Ollie: NBC Premiere, November 29, 1948.

There was lovable Ollie J. Dragon, a rapscallion brimming with good-natured conceit, a direct descendent of Sir George the Dragon, a graduate of Dragon Prep, perpetually in trouble; he had an enormous velvet mouth and one snaggletooth. There was also gentle, elfin, Kukla, a chronic worrier with a high-pitched voice and bulbous clown nose, victim of Ollie's pranks. And busty, overbearing Madame Ophelia Oglepuss, a grand dame with operatic pretensions and the elusive goal of hitting a high C. And cantankerous, caustic Beulah the Witch, who soared back and forth across the stage on her broom screeching to all, "Hello, dear!" And debonair windbag Colonel Crackie. And last but not least, good-listening friend to all, Fran Allison, a tall, slender ex-schoolteacher from Iowa.

Less familiar to millions of TV viewers was master puppeteer Burr Tillstrom, who created, voiced, and manipulated all the plush, felt, and plastic hand puppets. The ever-worried Kukla, said Tillstrom, was an extension of his own personality, and he derived the glove puppet's name from a Russian ballerina he'd known.

"Kukla, Fran and Ollie" was first seen on a local Chicago television station in 1947, and the following year moved to NBC. By 1950 the show had 6 million viewers. The puppets had been characters in Burr Tillstrom's earlier "Kuklapolitan Players." One of the TV show's most popular features was the enactment—by the zany, conceited, worry-wart clan—of plays and operettas, all overseen by ex-music teacher Fran Allison, straight woman for the comic antics. She and Tillstrom met in Chicago during the Second World War while both were working for the Red Cross and staging shows. Becoming a radio performer, Allison later gained popularity as "Aunt Fanny" and became a much-loved mainstay on the hit "Don McNeill's Breakfast Club."

So popular was the "Kukla" TV show (whose announcer was Hugh Downs), that when NBC canceled it in 1954, overwhelming public demand forced the network to bring it back for an additional five years. Winning a Peabody and an Emmy for consistent high-quality children's entertainment, "Kukla" was finally retired on August 31, 1957. Along with "Howdy Doody," the show was one of television's early "strips," seen Monday through Friday.

To Prime Time. The show was basically unscripted, an improvisational tour de force in which Tillstrom established a basic storyline, and through his characters he carried on humorous chatter with Fran Allison. Ollie, for instance, might blurt out, "Fran, I just love your hair." (He was always complimenting Fran, fishing for return praise.) She'd smile, thank him, then add, "You know, my mother used to wear her hair something like yours. What's your mother's hair like?" And from behind the set's stage, Tillstrom would fabricate some outrageous piece of comic nonsense. Much of the show's magic derived by the spark and spontaneity between Allison and Tillstrom.

Unlike "Howdy Doody," pitched directly to kids, "Kukla" often contained sophisticated adult humor and cultural references beyond the comprehension of children. Thus, Tillstrom was delighted when in the mid-Fifties the program moved to evening prime time, telling the press, "I don't think we ever intended it for kids alone. We've always assumed that *this* family was for the whole family."

In 1969 the show was revived on public television, where it enjoyed a two-year run. Then in 1975 the group appeared in a syndicated half-hour format. On June 13, 1989, Fran Allison died of bone marrow failure at California's Sherman Oaks Community Hospital, at age eighty-one. Tillstrom said of her, "I needed a girl who could talk to a dragon"; a fitting eulogy since Fran Allison seemed particularly fond of the outrageous Ollie. "It may be ironic," observed the *New York Times* in 1952, "but Kukla and Ollie still seem so real that it's always a little disturbing when Burr Tillstrom steps into view." Tillstrom died in 1985 at the age of sixty-eight. Of his creation the *Times* praised: "One of the most imaginative shows ever developed in the electronic medium."

Hopalong Cassidy: NBC Premiere, June 24, 1949

Television is accused of being a derivative medium; it is, and always has been. Its early comedy and variety shows were direct steals from popular radio programs, and its first big Western hit, "Hopalong Cassidy," came from a cultish series of Hollywood films—"horse operas," which were popular Saturday morning fare at theaters across the country.

That Western action genre came thundering across television screens in 1949 due largely to the business sagacity of the movie Hoppy himself, William Boyd. Once a star of Cecil B. De Mille's epic *King of Kings* and *The Volga Boatmen,* Boyd for years had been grinding out low-budget B pictures based on the Hopalong Cassidy stories by writer Clarence E. Mulford. In an era when most feature films were barred from telecasting for fear of loss of profits, Boyd had the foresight to hock all his belongings to purchase the TV rights for the horse operas. With a ready-made following of fans, the Hoppy series became an immediate home-screen hit. He reaped a fortune from endless repeat showings of about a hundred of his Hoppy films. When Boyd finally sold out years later, he reportedly received $70 million.

TV's first cowboy hero was also the springboard for a host of Hoppy fads. Boyd made an additional fortune from royalties on sales to a generation of children of Hoppy hats, cowboy outfits (costing from $4.95 to $75), spurs, and guns and holsters. From the series premiere in 1949 until its termination in 1953, American boys adored Hopalong Cassidy and insisted on dressing like him, riding Hoppy bicycles (as horses), eating Hoppy peanut butter and candy bars, and decorating their bedrooms in Hoppy wallpaper, sheets, and bedspreads. In all, ninety manufacturers shared in the Hoppy selling orgy. In 1951, *Business Week* published an estimate of Boyd's one-year windfall: $350,000 from TV royalties, $600,000 from commercial product tie-ins, $55,000 from Hoppy comic books, $7,000 from Hoppy records, plus an indeterminate amount from personal appearances and foreign rights (Hoppy had fad followings in England, France, Italy, Sweden, and Mexico)—for a gross of more than $2 million.

William Boyd almost missed out on playing Hopalong Cassidy. In 1934, when Hollywood producer Harry Sherman bought the screen rights to six of Clarence Mulford's Western tales, he wanted Boyd to play the dashing cowboy Buck Peters. Boyd, however, preferred the role of Buck's wounded, limping sidekick, who in the novels said spunkily to his companions, "I can hop along with the rest of you." Boyd adopted the name Hopalong, ditched the limp, and turned a minor character into a handsome lead who mounted a white horse named Topper. Over the next twelve years, he made sixty-five low-budget Hoppy horse operas, several filmed in less than ninety hours. In the later films, Indians never bite the proverbial dust, and for largely economic reasons: "The price of Indians went way up," said Boyd. "I use to get a whole tribe for practically nothing. Now they have a union." Boyd parlayed Hoppy from a low-budget Saturday film feature to a cultishly popular television series to an international cottage industry. "Every kid needs a hero," said Cecil B. De Mille. "Hopalong Cassidy takes the place of Buffalo Bill, Babe Ruth, Lindbergh and all the rest."

CHAPTER 7

—————————— ◻ ——————————

The Fabulous Fifties

1950 to 1959

The Do It for the Kids Decade

Kinder, Kirche, Küche: children, church, kitchen. The Fifties have been called the do it for the kids decade, a prosperous time in which baby-boom-breeding parents, who had lived through the privations of a depression and a war, could not, in their newfound economic comfort, do enough and buy enough for their offspring. Sociologists classify American society in the Fifties as a "filiarchy"—ruled not by the willful demands of the young (as later times would be) but by a perception of their needs and wants on the part of their indulging, sacrificing parents.

For the first time kids, as the statistical aggregate known as the baby boom wave, drove the economy. Virtually every poll taken during the decade revealed that parents, flooding into the suburbs, placed children and family life not only as their highest priority but also as their greatest satisfaction. "Children may not have been ruling from their high-chair thrones," writes one social observer, "but their parents were convinced that their own role in life was to make a world for their children that was better than the unstable decades of war and privation in which they had grown up." "Do it for the kids" was the much heard motto; even parents inclined to divorce stuck it out "for the kids."

If you overlook cold war tensions, H-bomb anxieties, stifling conformity, red baiting, and blatant racism (as did many preoccupied parents in the Fifties), the decade was by every other measure fabulous. From the standpoint of nostalgia (defined as remembrance of things favorable) the era is an orgy of fads, hit songs, idealized family sitcoms, and uplifting books like *The Power of Positive Thinking* and the Bible, which in a revised standard version topped the nationwide bestselling list for two years straight. In fact religious books were among the decade's strongest sellers; as top among TV shows were the half-hour weekly chalk-and-blackboard sermons of Monsignor Fulton J. Sheen—dubbed "Uncle Fultie" by the envious "Uncle Miltie" Berle, who had to compete in a ratings war. In the same era, evangelist Billy Graham, with his spellbinding style of preaching, drew nearly 2 million people to Madison Square Garden. All of the preceding being the *Kirche* in the *Kirche, Kinder, Küche* era.

The times were economically prosperous. In the Fifties America witnessed the blossoming of a full-blown consumer culture. In this great American shopping spree (not to be repeated until the decade of the Eighties) more people acquired more goods than ever before—and more goods than anyone actually needed. This fact is evident throughout the present chapter in the sales figures for fad items and trendy fashions, for two-tone cars, ranch-style and split-level homes, pink lawn flamingos, and turquoise bathroom tumblers. Wartime privations had unleashed a peacetime frenzy for possessions.

The Joneses Versus the Beatniks: Emergence of a Counterculture

The nostalgic richness of the Fifties has much to do with the decade being a period of genuine and sustained economic growth. Upward mobility then meant something to every middle-class family. The promise "No down payment for Veterans!" shaped an entirely new housing market. For most of the decade more than 50 percent of houses sold carried government VA (Veterans Administration) or FHA (Federal Housing Administration) mortgages. Thus, GI Joe and his family could move easily out of the overcrowded inner city and into the social-climbing atmosphere of suburbia to compete with the Joneses. On the downside: To own what the Joneses owned implied conformity; and everyone imagining himself to be a Jones bred chauvinism. And, too, the decade's hedonistic chant of acquiring minds—*Buy! Buy! Buy!*—threatened to ensconce material success as the master of all values. It is precisely the herd mentality that makes a fad possible, and the Fabulous Fifties proved to be a vintage decade for items with mass appeal.

Norman Mailer later called the era "one of the worst decades in the history of man"—for all the social ills and injustices people overlooked. Indeed, people traded controversy for conformity. But the decade had its nonconformists in the beatniks—poetry-reading, Eastern-philosophy bohemians, viewed by the establishment with the same disdain as "JDs" (juvenile delinquents), another blight to be glossed over.

As the decade that housed the "beat generation" advanced, though, middle-class conformity and social stability were challenged by the "menace" of Elvis "The Pelvis" Presley, the "corrupting influence" of rock 'n' roll music, and such swaggering anti-establishment idols as James Dean and Marlon Brando. Cults formed around Dean, Brando, and beat writer Jack Kerouac and poet Allen Ginsberg—whose best-known Fifties poem, "Howl," opened with the angry augury: "I saw the best minds of my generation destroyed by madness, / starving hysterical naked, / dragging themselves through the negro streets at dawn / looking for an angry fix."

By the close of the decade, teens were choosing up between two camps: Those with black leather **motorcycle jackets,** two inch-wide tough-guy **garrison belts,** sporting slickly greased hair, pouty lips, and a sneering smile stood in sharp contrast in look and demeanor to the bobby-soxer in her **poodle skirt** and **saddle shoes,** escorted by her Bass Weejun, **penny-loafer** beau. *Newsweek* alarmed parents with a single statistic: "Today, up to 95 percent of females have had petting experience at the age of 18 years."

FADS, FOLLIES, AND TRENDS

California Ranch House: Early Fifties

By the time the Sixties song "Little Boxes" lampooned the "ticky-tacky" Levittown-like homes of suburbia, the trend among the upwardly mobile had long shifted from the boxy Cape Cod to the sprawling one-level California ranch-style house. The vogue in the early Fifties was for the ranch's L-shaped layout, with stone facing, white shutters, and decorative cupola-cum-weather-vane. Whereas the traditional home had for decades been a two-story structure, the *Better Homes and Garden* ideal of the "horizontal" one-level California ranch abode was in demand nationwide in the early Fifties.

The quintessential open-air ranch home originally had been designed in the Midwest by America's most celebrated architect, Frank Lloyd Wright, and his Prairie School. But most Americans called the style available across the country California ranch, for its sunny picture window, spacious patio, and brick barbecue pit. In an effort to impress the Joneses, no architectural feature that might create an impression of affluence was hidden. The expansive picture window, for instance—intended by Wright to frame nature—faced not the tree-filled backyard but the neighbor-lined street, everyone's picture window facing everyone else's. Driveways were prominently featured so that parked cars— trendy **station wagons**—could shout out prosperity. Privacy was willingly sacrificed for the show of material success.

Cold war tensions and H-bomb anxieties made basement and backyard **fallout shelters** seem advisable, but they too became a possession to trumpet prosperity. Then an unexpected reality hit the ever-burgeoning housing market: America's suburbs had become crowded; space was at a premium. One-story ranch-style houses sprawled over too much land. A new, more compact style was needed.

Split Level House: Mid-to-Late Fifties

By the mid-Fifties, the price of suburban lots had climbed. It cost developers and home buyers more money for the luxury of a one-level house spread over several costly lots. At the same time, land was at a premium and families were loath to give up indoor space. In addition, suburban communities began passing legislation that required houses to be constructed a minimum distance from streets and neighbors' property lines. Simply put, developers, to make a profit, had to find a way to cram more house on less land. An FHA study of buyers' preferences revealed that 75 percent did not want to live in the traditional two-story home like their grandparents; they demanded a single-story structure.

For architects, the obvious compromise between the sprawl of the ranch style and buyers' distaste for a two-story was the split level—a two-story house that wasn't traditionally two-story.

The basic idea of the split level was to put part of the family's living quarters—perhaps the kitchen and dining room, or the bedrooms—into what would otherwise be a basement. A short flight of steps above that level sat the rest of the rooms. A sub–living room level might serve as the garage. The advantage of this configuration for the builder was that it made the basement habitable; extra living space was provided without a lot more construction. "Because there was nothing above the living room," writes Fifties observer Thomas Hine in *Populuxe,* "he could shift the gable to the front of the house and let the room go to the roof in the form of a 'cathedral ceiling' "—which quickly became a trendy and highly marketable feature.

"At the beginning of 1954," says Hine, "hardly anyone had heard of the split level. But by the spring of 1955, it was universally understood to be the latest thing in houses." A fad in architecture. A trend in home living. As a come-on, developers advertised, "We Have Split Levels!" and buyers moved in by the thousands, such that the homes remain a prominent fixture of the suburban landscape across America. Observes Hine: "The split level was the most successful new product to come from the housing industry in the mid-1950s."

All the time spent in and around the home suggested a new look in attire:

At Home Wear

Fifties fashions reflected the shifting lifestyles of postwar Americans. To foster the *Kinder, Kirche, Küche* role of the suburban housewife, women's fashions became softer, simpler and more feminine, with women dressing . . . well, like wives and mothers. Whereas Christian Dior's New Look of the Forties had ushered in the first wave of feminine softness—with breasts pushed upward and waists pared down to an anatomical minimum—the massive exodus to the suburbs, in which women stayed home and raised kids, introduced "at home" wear, ranging from comfortable skirts and **lounging pants** to the trendy **car coat,** an accessory to the station wagon, which itself was essential for shopping at malls and supermarkets, and for transporting kids to school.

In the evenings, couples stayed home to watch television, and they invited over friends who were still without their own TV sets. The occasion necessitated a fresh look—like women's floor-length **plaid skirts** or **velveteen pants.** *Life* magazine dubbed the at home leisure wear "semi-public pajamas." Stay-at-home slippers came into vogue: **velvet mules, satin sandals,** and **pancake-soled flats** that were foldable and came tucked in cute little bags.

This comfortable footwear, meant for indoors, soon found itself scuffing across lawns and down pavements as women ventured outdoors in their at home gear.

Television Fashions

Television had a major impact on fashion. The visual medium allowed millions of people to see, with unprecedented intensity and immediacy, what stars and famous personalities were wearing. Previously, ordinary folk turned for guidance to *Life,* fashion magazines, or the movies, but those sources depicted styles already months old.

Television allowed for trendiness in real time. At night you glimpsed the garments preferred by Donna Reed and Dorothy Kilgallen, by "Margie" and Bess Myerson, by "Lucy," "Our Miss Brooks," and Harriet Nelson, and by the mothers heading the idealized families of "Father Knows Best" and "Leave It to Beaver." Next day you went shopping to copy Margaret Anderson and June Cleaver. On the other hand, teenagers copied such "American Bandstand" regulars as Justine and Pat. Thus television shaped a new level of fashion consciousness in what people wore in public and what they wore at home to watch the tube.

Donna Reed and her idealized TV ilk also helped popularize what was called the paper doll style. Take a minimum of two stiff-as-boards **crinolines,** add a **cinch belt,** and you had the silhouette of a "paper doll"—so named by petite New York designer Ann Fogarty, who was her own best advertisement for the Seventh Avenue style. The vogue went that five crinolines were better than four; better yet were five crinolines and a **hoop.** In short time, the fad was for outrageously full skirts, with 4-foot diameter hoops. The fuller the skirt, the more stylish the wearer. Traditional cotton and lace petticoats couldn't fill out a skirt, but stiffer horsehair could, though it itched—a small price to pay for chic. To maneuver aisles, staircases, and wind gusts required an incredible amount of dexterity as well as decorum. For a hoop to flip up was instant mortification for a young woman. Only somewhat less embarrassing was to be accused of having a VHL—that is, a visible hoop line; hoops were never supposed to show.

Poodle skirts were made of felt and bore an appliqué of a fully coiffed French poodle with rhinestones for eyes and additional rhinestones defining a collar. Accessories included **two-tone saddle shoes, white shirt,** a tightly cinched **neck scarf,** and an engraved **ankle bracelet** with links of hearts and pearls. As that teen fad reached its mid-Fifties peak, substitutes for the poodle patch included a bouquet of flowers, a litter of kittens, or a hot-rod car.

For more casual wear, girls again turned to television, imitating the long, loose **dad's shirt** hanging outside of **jeans,** as worn by the younger members of "Father Knows Best" and "The Donna Reed Show." As the decade progressed, and Pat Boone scored hits with songs like "Love Letters in the Sand," saddle shoes were swept aside for the idol's **white bucks,** which were patted clean with a chalk bag.

For men, hair styles in the period went from the clean-cut, collegiate crewcut, to Elvis Presley–length sideburns, to duck tail or DA (duck ass) backs, to the slick combed-back Kookie look, popularized by TV's parking lot attendant on the hit show "77 Sunset Strip." Kookie, played by twenty-five-year-old Edd Byrnes, was obsessively fond of adding the suffix *ville* to nouns— "illsville" for sick, "antsville" for nervous—and of combing his hair. "Kookie, Kookie, Lend Me Your Comb" became a hit song and fad catchphrase in 1959. Tamer than the hip-gyrating Presley, Kookie was the proto-Fonz.

Credit Cards

In the Fifties Americans went on a shopping spree more excessive than any previous spending and one that would not be topped until the Eighties great splurge. A major factor that fueled the shopping then, as later, was, in a word, credit.

In the first wave of shopping, credit came in the form of layaway plans, courtesy cards, and the plastic credit card, a phenomenon born in 1950. On one day that year, business executive Francis Xavier McNamara lunched at a fashionable Manhattan restaurant with several clients. When it came time for him to pay the bill, he realized he'd left his cash at home. After a panic phone call to his wife, and her frenzied rush to the restaurant, McNamara swore he'd never again be embarrassed by being caught short; on the spot, he dreamed up the Diners Club.

Previously, individual stores had allowed favored customers credit. And several oil companies, to entice motorists into their gas stations, had instituted courtesy cards. But McNamara's innovation was the first multipurpose charge account that covered drinking, dining, entertainment, and travel. Even more significantly, it was the first form of credit to be offered not by the seller but by an intermediary, the Diners Club. In a period when the consumption rate in the country averaged a whopping 65 percent of the gross national product, middle-man credit cards seemed like a creation whose time was in arrears. Magazines like *Esquire* and *Gourmet* issued cards to their readers, department store executive Alfred Bloomingdale dreamed up the competing Dine & Sign card, and food writer and cake-mix promoter Duncan Hines launched the Signet Club card.

Many credit ventures failed. Others—notably American Express, debuting in 1958—thrived; by the close of the decade more than a half million people did not leave home without their green American Express plastic. Within the first two years of business, the company was so overwhelmed by requests for cards and by credit paperwork that out of desperation it turned to IBM to computerize its operations; previously, every purchase a consumer made was hand-recorded by a company employee and filed in the cardholder's individual portfolio. The marriage of credit card with computer proved to be a powerful union for the nationwide growth of credit.

3-D Movies

The first three-dimensional movie, in a process called natural vision, was the spear-chucking *Bwana Devil* of 1952, in which sharp, flying weapons seemed to leap from the screen heading straight for the goggle-covered eyes of theater viewers. Film critics panned the November 26 premiere in Los Angeles. But audiences loved the tale of a pair of man-eating lions that attack railroad construction crews in Africa and can only be stopped by countless projectiles hurled at the beasts. In its first week at one Los Angeles theater, the film grossed $95,000, and the manager told the press, "It's the most fabulous thing we've ever seen. They're standing four abreast all the way down to Roosevelt Hotel in Hollywood."

Crowds flocked to see such other "deepies" as the gore-splattering *Creature from the Black Lagoon.* Hollywood, in the midst of a box-office slump due to the popularity of television, geared up for a rebirth of film through the magic of 3-D. The *New York Herald-Tribune* raved that 3-D "made every man a voyager to a brave new world," and predicted that 2-D "flat" films would soon be obsolete. Movie audiences gladly tolerated wearing tinted glasses—one lens red, the other green—to achieve the mind-boggling effect, and the phrase 3-D above a marquee spelled instant success.

For about a year, that is. Fewer costly fads died faster. By 1954 films shot

in the once alluring promise of 3-D had to be released also without the special effect or most theaters across the country would not show them. Suddenly 3-D spelled box-office disaster.

Poor quality killed off the phenomenon. In fact, the first three-dimensional movies were so technologically blurred, defocused, and headache-inducing, they gave the idea of 3-D a bad reputation that persisted for decades.

The process was not new in 1952. The stereoscopic trick had been tried in hand-held photographic viewers at the turn of the century (see page 24), and experimentally applied to silent motion pictures in the Twenties. At that time, the novelty was quickly superseded by the introduction of sound, or talkies. Later, at the New York World's Fair of 1939, visitors donned polarized glasses to view several experimental 3-D films, but the fad never caught the interest of Hollywood executives. Films then were enjoying an unchallenged entertainment heyday. It was the box-office crisis caused by television that forced film producers to search for a gimmick. The industry—which had laid off hundreds of actors, writers, and directors in the greatest shakeout since talkies killed silent pictures—reasoned that it could only survive if it found a way to make the big screen awesomely outdraw the living room intimacy offered by the little screen.

Glamarama. Many wide-screen, wraparound gambits were tried: Cinerama, CinemaScope, VistaVision, Superama, Glamarama, and Todd-A-O. The idea behind the wide screen was to expand the theatergoer's field of view to make a movie more like a live Broadway spectacle. Stereophonic sound was another Hollywood grab to win back the burgeoning TV audience. Ironically, whereas wide screens and stereophonic sound survived to become standards, the gimmick once thought to be the studios' major weapon against television— 3-D—turned out to be a costly joke.

By late 1954 the 3-D fad was dead. The technique has been improved and retried in each subsequent decade, but the critical mass of fans needed to make 3-D a money-making fad has never materialized. Films like Andy Warhol's 1970s *Frankenstein,* the later *Friday the 13th Part III* and *Jaws 3-D* were curiosities, enjoyed for three dimension as a novelty and nothing more. To date, *The Stewardesses,* made in 1969, an R-rated adult film, is reputed to be the biggest-grossing 3-D movie of all time.

Davy Crockett Hats and Haute Cowture

Davy, Davy Crockett, "king of the wild frontier," was rumored to have been born on a mountaintop in Tennessee, and to have killed himself a bear when he was only three. The Wild West legend (played by the ruggedly handsome, 6-foot-5-inch twenty-nine-year-old Fess Parker) came to television on December 15, 1954, in "Disneyland's" hour-long "Davy Crockett, Indian Fighter," the first of a three-part series that Walt Disney himself did not expect to be particularly profitable. He could not have been less astute—and more fortunate. By the time the last episode aired two months later, millions of kids across

Fess Parker in coonskin cap.

America were whipped up in Davy Crockett fervor. Crockett's image appeared on every merchandisable product that would take an impression, from baby shoes to jigsaw puzzles, from lunchboxes to jockey shorts.

But most popular of all imitations was Crockett's coonskin fur cap, with tail. People joked that thousands of Roaring Twenties raccoon coats had been slaughtered to make the caps. This cowboymania was further fired by the popularity of Roy Rogers and Dale Evans, Gene Autry, and Hopalong Cassidy. *Life* magazine carried four full pages of ads for Roy Rogers vests, toy guns, bedspreads, picture frames, clocks, socks, gloves and TV chairs. Dale Evans's outfit of fringed skirt, fancy holster, and spiffy boots topped many a little girl's Christmas list.

The spillover into adult fashion—for example, President Eisenhower's Davy Crockett tie—was dubbed "haute cowture." Publishers rushed out books like *The Story of Davy Crockett,* which alleged to tell the bare truth about the backwoodsman said to have scouted with Andrew Jackson, served three terms in Congress, and died in a heroic last stand at the battle of the Alamo. One estimate of the Western paraphernalia sold in just five years in the Fifties was nearly $300 million.

Western Mambo. Davy the TV legend was often unlike the real-life Crockett. "The historic truth," goaded *Harper's,* "is that Davy Crockett was a juvenile delinquent who ran away from home at the age of thirteen." As to Crockett's self-made claim that he shot 105 bears in nine months, the magazine assured the public that that had to be pure nonsense since "Davy couldn't count

that high." One newspaper pointed out that Crockett, "a drunkard and ca-
rouser" who had deserted his wife, could not have been born in Tennessee
since it was not yet a state at the time of his birth; another claimed that he
actually surrendered at the Alamo and was later executed. *Harper's* went so far
as to claim that Crockett had "weaseled his way out of the Army by hiring a
substitute."

No amount of debunking, though, damped the year-long fad (though experts
would later say that the negative press, in deflating the "hero," damaged his
marketability; more to the point would be that Davy was simply overmarketed).
Woolworth 5 & 10 Cent stores devoted 70 feet of counterspace to hundreds
of Crockett items like telephone sets and reusable plastic ice-cream cones.
Perhaps the most in-demand item of all was Bill Hayes's recording of "The
Ballad of Davy Crockett," number one in the country for five consecutive
weeks according to *Billboard*. It sold 4 million copies and was translated into
sixteen languages; there was even a dance inspired by another single, "Davy
Crockett Mambo." The American alleged to be Crockett's closest living descendant—Mrs. Margie Flowers Cohn of Illinois—simply couldn't understand
all the fuss.

Wiffle Ball

This mid-decade version of old-time stickball was the creation of dad David
Mullany of Fairfield, Connecticut, who in 1953 was watching his baby boom son
and a friend play backyard stickball with one of his own plastic golf balls. The
lightweight golf ball could not be thrown or hit far, minimizing the required
playing field—a feature the father liked. Popular slang for "strike out" was
"whiff," and suddenly David Mullany, a former college and semi-pro baseball
pitcher, had a name for his new game. Aware of the difficulty in trying to throw
curves or sliders with a small, lightweight ball, he used a razor to cut holes in
one hemisphere in several of his plastic golf balls; the pierced "wiffle" balls
curved without a snap of the wrist. Adopting the rules his son used in the
backyard, Mullany launched the Wiffle Ball fad in 1955.

Silly Putty and Slinky

Invented in the late Forties, Silly Putty and Slinky reached fad-buying proportions in the Fifties due largely to the interests of young baby boomers. Since
I've written about their origins in a previous book, here I'll mention them only
briefly. Slinky was developed in 1946 by marine engineer Richard James, who
was attempting to perfect a super-delicate spring as a wave-motion counterbalance for ship instruments. The year James began his company is the one that
sociologists take as the start of the baby boom period. In the Fifties, these kids
were an ideal age to appreciate the clever stealthiness of the walking spring,
and sales of the toy soared.

The same sales phenomenon occurred with bloblike, pinkish-beige Silly
Putty, a failed war effort to develop an inexpensive substitute for synthetic

rubber that first emerged as a toy in 1949. Youngsters in the Fifties loved the way a glob of the pliant goo rebounded higher than a rubber ball, and how its affinity for ink allowed it to lift comic book images off the printed page. More recently, doctors have discovered that Silly Putty's specific gravity is so similar to human flesh that they've used it to align and test CAT scanners. To celebrate the toy's fortieth anniversary in 1989, the manufacturer, Binney & Smith (makers of Crayola crayons), introduced the taffylike silicone toy in four colors: blue, green, yellow, and magenta. The company estimated that over four decades it sold 3,000 tons of indestructible Silly Putty, which prompted environmentalists to ask, "Where is it now?"

Lego

Lego was the 1954 invention of Danish carpenter Ole KirkChristiansen, who discovered that he made more money designing children's toys than building kitchen cabinets. Though children's building blocks had been popular for centuries, Christiansen devised interlocking plastic blocks that young children could assemble and not easily knock down. To name his plastic bricks with extruded knobs that locked into the underside of other bricks, Ole pieced together two Danish words meaning "play well": Lego. His goal of devising an educational toy that taught children a building skill meshed perfectly with that of postwar parents searching for challenging playthings. Within two decades, the Danish manufacturer of Lego was making $50 million a year, and the building blocks represented nearly one percent of Denmark's industrial exports.

Barbie Doll: Fad to Icon

Three years in the making, the most popular doll in history—a long-limbed clotheshorse invariably in the vanguard of fashion—was conceived by Mattel's Ruth Handler and named after her daughter. It is not widely known, and Mattel plays down the connection, but the original model for Barbie was a seductive German doll that (unbeknownst to Ruth Handler at the time) was based on a racy German cartoon character, a prostitute named Lilli. (It's thought that molds of Lilli might have been used to make the shapely Barbie prototypes.)

The 11½-inch toy, promoted as "the only anatomically perfect doll manufactured today," received mixed reviews when she debuted at the industry's annual Toy Fair. Buyers, mostly men, offered opinions from "fashion dolls are dead," to "mothers aren't going to buy a doll with breasts." Sears found Barbie "too sexy" to stock. Convinced she had a potentially hot-selling toy but concerned with the negative reception, Ruth Handler contacted her Japanese supplier and cut back on the number of dolls being manufactured, a mistake she'd soon regret.

Barbie, introduced on March 1, 1959, was more than a hit; she was a marketing phenomenon. The craze for the curvaceous "teenage fashion model" with an enviable wardrobe, hoop earrings, hot red fingernails and toenails, pointed eyebrows, and seductively delineated pouty lips was immediate. Mattel spent the next three years struggling to meet orders because of its initial production cutback.

By the early Sixties, the doll with the "gravity-defying breasts" was selling in the millions and her clothing manufacturer could barely keep up with demands for Barbie dresses, minks, gowns, swimsuits, and sequined bolero jackets. Her chic clothes were never cheap; a complete wedding trousseau cost $35. There was a Barbie magazine and Barbie fan clubs across the United States and Europe, and the shapely figurine was smuggled into several Muslim countries where she was not dressed in a veil.

Material Girl.   Ironically, Barbie's most vocal critics initially were men. One writer found her "a predatory female," another "the perfect bitch" (comments that said far more about the men than the doll). Feminists would later view her as "the perfect bimbo," "an airhead," and fault her for providing young girls with unrealistic goals in physical measurements and perpetual beauty. At Christmas 1964, when the doll was *the* gift for girls, the *Saturday Evening Post* lambasted her as the ultimate material girl: "Anyone looking for deeper values in the world of Barbie is looking in the wrong place. With its emphasis on possessions and its worship of appearances, it is modern America in miniature—a tiny parody of our pursuit of the beautiful, the material, the trivial."

Though Barbie has been many things to many people, she has remained a fad par excellence. The original $3 doll is now a $1,000 collectible. As an American pop culture icon, Barbie was sealed into the 1976 bicentenary time capsule, to be opened a hundred years hence. There is no guessing how she'll be reviewed then: As incidental social memorabilia? Or as our time's standard of feminine shapeliness?

Hula Hoop

Called the "biggest fad in history" and the "granddaddy of American zaniness," the simple, $1.98 plastic hoop, twirled with a hip-moving hula, swept the country in the summer of 1958 faster and more profitably than any fad before it. Within four months after the cheap-to-make poly-plastic tube debuted, 25 million had been sold, and it launched crazes in countries as far away as Japan—where it was called the Huru Hoopu.

Major newspapers and magazines ran features on the phenomenon, offering tips on twirling the hoop and advice on handling back problems. Celebrities twirled hoops on television, and across the country teenagers participated in hoopspinning marathons. U.S. sales eventually topped 100 million. Dozens of manufacturers ripped off Wham-O company's original idea, naming their hoops everything from Hooper-Dooper to Whoope-De-Do. No matter what it was called, for a time it seemed that every man, woman, and child in the country had to spin one. For about four months, after which the hoopla died down, the country was in a "hoopnotic" trance. To this day, the hula hoop remains a standard by which other fads are measured.

Origin. The item came from Wham-O Manufacturing, a concern in the chancy business of creating crazes. Some of their successes: Frisbee, Super Ball, Silly String, and Monster Bubbles. In 1957, Wham-O executives Richard Knerr and Arthur Melin decided to make a plastic version of a bamboo hoop long used by Australian grade-school children in gym class. They were coming off a fad high: 1957's **Frisbee** craze—millions of the 9-inch flying plastic discs had sold for 79 cents, with Frisbeeing become something of a college sport. Desiring a hoop that was sturdy and lightweight, and would float in water games, they approached W. R. Grace chemicals, which concocted a composite plastic called Grex. Melin himself traveled throughout southern California giving demonstrations of the hoops, which had two major selling points: They were fun to play with and inexpensive to purchase. The fad mushroomed in southern California, then spread East through newspaper and television coverage. Wham-O, in fact, spent surprisingly little money on advertising; hula hoop was a word-of-mouth and media-made phenomenon.

Why suddenly a hoop craze?

Psychologists had a Freudian field day: The circular hoop represented the vagina and "entering" it was sexual for some, or a desire to return to the womb for others. Or: The circle was a child's first drawing, a symbol of security, a shape to climb into. Absurdists said the hoop represented God, having no beginning and no end. Tongue-in-cheek, the *Wall Street Journal* argued that the hoop symbolized the circular promises of politicians. Heady from her newfound fame on a TV quiz show, a young Dr. Joyce Brothers saw one-upmanship in kids' obsession with the toys: "They delight in the fact that they can keep the hoops spinning in orbit, while many adults can't." But a fad need have no logical reason for being; it's a manifestation of herd thinking.

The mania proportions of the hula hoop fad faded by October 1958, perhaps because the weather turned cold over much of the country, and twirling hula hoops was preferably an outdoor recreation. In November the *Wall Street Journal* headlined: HOOPS HAVE HAD IT. By Christmas hoops were marked down to 50 cents. The spring-summer craze was a fad at its classic purest.

Scrabble

Scrabble, one of the world's bestselling word games, is a particular enigma among fads. From being a mildly popular game among highbrows in the late Forties, in the fall of 1952 it suddenly became a nationwide craze. The numbers demonstrate the phenomenon: Sales of Scrabble sets in 1949 totaled twenty-five hundred; in 1951, just under nine thousand; in 1952, more than fifty-eight thousand—with most of those selling in the last three months of the year. Like a fall flu, the game, by word of mouth, swept the country. Unlike a flu, Scrabble fever never subsided; in 1954 over 4.5 million games were manufactured, and the game that made the dictionary a bestseller continues to sell strongly itself.

What caused the sudden interest in a game that was invented in 1931 by architect Alfred Butts and originally called Criss Cross?

To backtrack a bit: Left unemployed by the Depression, Alfred Butts amused himself at home by attempting to turn the then national mania for crossword puzzles into a challenging board game. It took him almost a decade to refine Criss Cross, and in 1948 a friend, James Brunot, persuaded him to copyright it as Scrabble and allow Brunot to manufacture it. Until the mania hit, Brunot's small company had no trouble meeting the modest demand for games, producing about sixteen Scrabble sets a day. In fact, Brunot was about to drop out of the nonprofitable Scrabble endeavor when suddenly, in one week of June 1952, orders shot up from the standard of about two hundred to twenty-five hundred.

The jump, thought the manufacturer, was a one-time anomaly. But orders the following week were for three thousand sets, and the demand continued to soar, unabatedly. Department stores were rationed in the number of sets they received. Brunot contacted veteran game-makers Selchow & Righter for manufacturing assistance. The press reported that Scrabble was the favorite pastime of India's Prime Minister Nehru, Broadway's Oscar Hammerstein II, and Hollywood's Darryl Zanuck. Bookstores sold out of dictionaries. What was happening? asked a mystified, but gleeful, Brunot.

The most plausible theory proffered is that a Macy's executive played Scrabble on his summer vacation in 1952, and on returning to the store he discovered the word puzzle was not a standard item in the game department. He prompted Macy's stores across the country to order hundreds of Scrabble sets. Other chain stores followed Macy's lead, kicking off the momentum that would mushroom into a national craze.

Panty Raids

The Twenties decade had its goldfish-swallowing fad. In the Fifties, collegiate nonsense consisted of panty raids, raccoon coats, phone-booth packing, and a squatting fad named hunkerin'. All except the raccoon coat craze were spring-time diversions, which began on one or two campuses and spread by word of mouth and media coverage to colleges across the country. The decade's first craze was the male panty raid on a female dormitory, or "lace riots"—a far more harmless and less socially conscious form of rioting than what would emerge on campuses in the late Sixties.

The fad is thought to have started in late March 1952 at the University of Michigan (some say the University of Missouri) with a shout like "To the girls' dorm!" The game's objective was to return with any article of ladies' lingerie, a trophy to be proudly displayed. The harmlessness of the spirited highjinks was evidenced in the girls' responses: More often than not they, gleeful and squealing, complicitously tossed down stockings, panties, or bras, making the rubric riot all sound and fury. Underwear riots even had a reciprocity: By May 1952, girls were shouting up to men's dormitory windows, demanding jockey shorts and boxer pants.

What drew media attention were the numbers of male students who went on raids: fifteen hundred in one sortie at the University of Illinois; two thousand at the University of Missouri; three thousand in a sweep of sororities at the

University of California at Berkeley—a rampage that turned nasty and destructive, leaving in its wake thousands of dollars of property damage.

Campus police were often called out to quell the more rowdy riots. Editorial writers argued that the students' abundant energy could be better spent fighting the war in Korea. But the undergarment raids flourished, becoming ensconced as a yearly spring ritual—one that lasted into the early Sixties. Searching for historical precedent, sociologists craned back to Roman times and the raucous Saturnalia, a seasonal male chauvinistic feast to the god of plenty. Cloaking the panty raid in ancient precedent gave it an aura of social legitimacy. In spring, hadn't men always gone wild? The activity lost its fun—and thus its reason for being—when anti-Vietnam rioting and sexual permissiveness reduced stealing lace lingerie to an embarrassment.

Raccoon Coats

Perhaps the Fifties popularity of Davy Crockett coonskin hats brought back a campus craze for Twenties raccoon coats, or maybe not. The fact is that mid-decade college men and women, primarily on Eastern campuses, could not get enough of the ratty rags (new furs had no social clout). Part of the reason for the shortage was that thousands of the old coats had been cut up only years before to make Davy Crockett hats. Antique stores and used-fur dealers gladly unloaded their remaining stock, with most garments selling for $25 to $50. A raccoon coat was shabbily chic around campus and especially at stadium football games. Unlike most fads, which die out from overproduction and overexposure, the raccoon coat craze vanished because the number of cheap, used, endearingly moth-eaten garments was severely limited.

Phone-Booth Packing

As the decade drew to a close, the public phone booth became a place of stifling intimacy for collegiate males. As many as two dozen sweating, heavy-breathing undergraduates labored to stuff themselves into the standard square, 7-foot-high Ma Bell booth, where a participant did not have to reach out to touch someone. It gave new meaning to male bonding. The fad came not from California, but, of all unlikely places, from South Africa.

News that twenty-five South African college students had set a "world record" in jamming themselves into a phone booth hit American campuses at the prank-prone time of spring, in 1959. What ensued was a classic case of crazed youth vying for one-upmanship. Chronicled in the pages of *Life*, the fad first involved a sort of willy-nilly packing, with sundry arms and legs protruding from the booth's door. "Clean" packing (all appendages tucked into the booth) was soon deemed the new rule. At schools like MIT, engineering students opted for a scientific approach, resorting to a legitimate mathematical endeavor known as the packing problem—determining the most efficient, space-saving way to fit items of one shape into a nonexpandable container. Tongue-in-cheek, the press labeled the craze as the Fifties version of the jam session. And as goldfish swallowing of the Twenties had branched out into gulping down assorted beetles and biting the heads off snakes, within less than a month phone booth packing had widened into students cramming themselves in record numbers into sports cars, closets, and other undersized containments. It was a short-lived, mostly male fad; women, wisely, did not join men in overcrowded phone booths.

Hunkerin'

Hunker is from the old Norse word *hokra,* meaning "to crouch," or "to squat down" on one's haunches—as it was used in the American South and Northwest. It also means to get in the mood for hard work, as one "hunkers down" to begin a task. In 1959 the phrase was adopted by college men to describe a sort of meditative stance; hundreds of young men squatted on their haunches for hours doing nothing except daydreaming—and, of course, partaking in a new fad.

You could hunker indoors or outside on the campus lawn, in a phone booth while talking, or bare-chested on the roof of a car, sunning. All that was important was that you be seen, and be seen to be hunkerin'. As fads go, it was anemic: sedate, placid, unspectacular, and, not surprisingly, short-lived. Why at exam time in 1959 did thousands of college students suddenly waste hours hunkerin'? Though one social observer later argued that hunkerin' "foreshadowed the Seventies wave of Eastern meditation," it was probably done in the spring of 1959 for the simplest of reasons: to delay studying for exams; any diversion would have done.

Look, Mom—No Cavities!

Medical authorities in the Fifties claimed that adding fluoride to the country's water was a safe means of promoting healthy teeth. The John Birch Society, though, thought the scheme was a diabolical Communist plot, and dozens of concerned mothers marched with placards reading "Don't Poison Our Kids," and "Forced Medication Is Un-American."

The great fluoride debate was conducted in the nation's newspapers and magazines, on radio, and on the new medium of television. Dozens of studies already had shown that people who grew up in towns with naturally occurring fluoride in the water had less than half as many cavities as people from towns without fluoride in the water. Today we know that fluoride bonds with tooth enamel, promotes repair in the early stages of decay, and may even reduce the formation of plaque.

In 1950 the United States Public Health Service recommended that all cities fluoridate their water. Gradually parents' fears were quelled and the chemical— toxic and potentially carcinogenic in high doses—made its way into much of the nation's water supply. And it worked. Fluoridation reduced tooth decay by more than half in communities that had it, saving millions of dollars in dental care costs.

Crest. The idea of lacing toothpaste with fluoride (stannous fluoride, as opposed to sodium fluoride, the compound used in drinking water) occurred to Procter & Gamble. After overcoming several technical hurdles, their new Crest product was tested in clinical studies on residents of Bloomington, Indiana. Families were given unmarked tubes of toothpaste and a brushing regime to follow religiously. So spectacular were the results that in 1956 Procter & Gamble launched a promising new product: "Crest—with Fluoristan." An $18 million advertising campaign—waged in newspapers and magazines and on television, as well as in a memorable series of illustrations by Norman Rockwell—had all the nation quoting P&G's motto: "Look, Mom—no cavities!"

The phrase, however, was more popular than the product until 1960. In that year, the American Dental Association, convinced that fluoride in toothpaste worked, issued its official approval in a statement, which despite its stilted verbosity, achieved nationwide familiarity: Crest "has been shown to be an effective decay-preventive dentifrice that can be of significant value when used in a conscientiously applied program of oral hygiene and regular professional care." It appeared on every tube of Crest and was read by parents and teachers to recalcitrant young brushers. Never had so cumbersome a motto been so widely quoted.

Crest became the first consumer product granted use of the ADA's prestigious name in advertising, and the clout had a huge commercial payoff: By 1963 every third tube of toothpaste sold in the United States was Crest. For a time it seemed that it was impossible to turn on television without catching a commercial of children running home with their dental report cards, exclaiming "Look, Mom—no cavities!" As later decades would have such memorable product catchphrases as "Where's the beef?" and "I can't believe I ate the whole thing," the Crest motto dominated pop ad slogans for more than ten years. It was one instance of truth in advertising.

As of 1990, some 53 percent of Americans drink water containing fluoride; even more use fluoride mouthwashes and toothpastes. The great fluoride debate began anew in the late Eighties, with charges that the undeniable benefits of fluoridation come not without risks (perhaps of bone cancer). Only future research will determine if concerned mothers must once again raise up placards demanding "Don't Medicate Our Kids."

Baseball Cards in Bubble-Gum Packs

Though there exist trading cards for the sports of basketball, football, and hockey, baseball cards outsell all others combined—about 250 million a year are sold. For a new round of releases, players are photographed in the spring, with and without team hats, to allow for players being traded before the cards appear in packs of bubble gum.

Old Judge Cigarettes, in the 1880s, was the first product to carry baseball cards. Other tobacco companies soon offered the freebies, and by 1910 young boys had a preferential taste for Tip Top Bread and Cracker Jack, which offered sports cards. For decades, collecting and trading baseball cards was kid stuff.

But a passion for the pastime began to build in the Fifties—baseball cards' golden age—until today adult men subscribe to *Baseball Card News,* attend baseball card conventions, and sign up for organizations like the Baseball Card Society, a kind of card-of-the-month club for collectors. When did the baseball card go from inside a cigarette pack to under a bubble gum wrapper?

Though the fad for full-color, 2½-inch by 3½-inch baseball cards, with a photo of the player on the front and his statistics on the back, began in the Fifties, cardboard cards, as mentioned, had already been around for more than a half century. The first ones, in black and white and about a third the size of today's cards, were issued in 1886 by the manufacturers of Old Judge, Gypsy Queen, and Dog's Head cigarettes. Poses were formal, backgrounds were artificial, and baseballs were suspended on strings to simulate action. The promotion gimmick worked—for almost two decades. In the early part of this century, cigarette companies started to discontinue the practice, feeling that the miniature cards were no longer serving as an inducement to buyers, and other companies began to take over the practice. Cards were elaborate, some embossed and inked in gold.

Honus Wagner.   This period saw the release of what is called the king of baseball cards. Featuring Honus Wagner, the great shortstop for the Pittsburgh Pirates, the cards are major collectibles. At a Sotheby auction in 1991, one in mint condition was bought by hockey great Wayne Gretzky for $451,000—the highest price paid at auction for sporting memorabilia, about four times the previous record, set in 1989 for another Honus Wagner card.

The association of bubble gum and baseball cards is a phenomenon of only the past half century. In the Thirties, when gum was perfected for blowing bubbles, the preferred method of selling a slab of the taffy was in a colorful waxed wrapper containing a baseball card. Most cards in the Thirties were approximately square, with players depicted in colorful paintings. For the first time, considerable attention was paid to the backs of cards, presenting biographical details, career highlights, and past season statistics. In 1952 Topps, based in Brooklyn, introduced the largest cards ever offered—and the largest single-year issue: 407 different cards. The following year Bowman, a major postwar competitor, introduced the first high-quality color photographs of players in its 160-card series. For several years each company vied for exclusive contracts with players, with Topps emerging as the victor. By 1957 Topps enjoyed a virtual monopoly, which it would hold for the next twenty-five years, and the modern baseball card had been born. The production of high-quality cards coincided with the arrival of a tidal wave of postwar baby boom boys (ages six to twelve), and the two events transformed collecting and trading baseball cards into a fad of unprecedented proportions.

Drive-In Movie Theater

The concept of the drive-in movie theater was the brainchild of Richard Hollingshead of Riverton, New Jersey; on May 16, 1933, he was granted a patent

Drive-in.

for his "ramp drive-in system." He'd experimented with projecting outdoor movies at night on a screen hanging from the front of his garage. On June 6, 1933, he opened his first public drive-in, which accommodated four hundred cars and was located on Wilson Boulevard in Camden, New Jersey.

But the semi-al-fresco concept did not mushroom into a pop culture phenomenon until after the blossoming of suburbia in the late Forties and early Fifties. To oversimplify the situation slightly: Movie theaters were in cities, drive-ins in the suburbs. The new suburban family—Mom, Dad, and three kids—found watching a movie from the privacy of their car an appealing alternative in cost, comfort, and all-around convenience to trekking the brood to a sit-down theater. Hollingshead had had the right idea, if a hair ahead of its time. The teenage generation of the Fifties found in the drive-in's darkened privacy a place to experiment sexually and occasionally to watch the movie.

Horror Movie Heyday.   The drive-in was also responsible for a cult of grade-B horror films of the decade. Cheap to make, they drew in carloads of teenagers seeking a Saturday night thrill by way of an adrenaline rush. *I Was a Teen-Age Werewolf* (1957; starring a twenty-year-old Michael Landon, in khakis, basketball jacket, and fanged werewolf mask) had a production budget of $82,000, but grossed several million dollars. In terms of stock shocks, it was the granddaddy of such violent later thrillers as *Nightmare on Elm Street* and *Halloween.*

Catering to the new teenage audience, Hollywood released a rash of gory, gross thrillers whose titles shamelessly pitched the film to the teenage viewer: *I Was a Teen-Age Frankenstein* (1957), or *Teen-Age Cave Man* (1958; starring a boyish Robert Vaughn). And there were teenage zombies, she-wolves, brain eaters, and creatures from outer space. Other "trash" classics featured adults: *How to Make a Monster* (1958), *Horrors of the Black Museum* (1959), *It Conquered The World* (1956), *Attack of the Giant Leeches* (1959), *Invasion of the Saucer-Men* (1957), *The Amazing Colossal Man* (1957), *War of The Colossal Beast* (1958), and ghoulish others. Hollywood took to heart the Fifties parental motto "Do it for the kids," catering to teens as the movie industry had never done before.

Cruisin' and the Teen Car Culture

As crude, fatuous, and inept as many of the grade-B horror films were, they revealed a salient aspect of the times: teenagers with wheels, pocket cash, and a penchant for drive-ins, who reveled in the birth of their own music, rock 'n' roll. The era marked the emergence of the autonomous teenage car culture. Cruising' became a catchphrase, a passionate Saturday night pastime, and found its way into the lyrics of popular songs. Teenagers cruised in sleek, gas-guzzling monsters, with mean-looking tail fins, grinning front grilles, and wraparound windshields, bodies lashed with chrome highlights.

America's deification of the car became more pronounced than ever with the blossoming of the teenage car culture. Designers attempted to create "sexy," bullet-shaped cars whose phallic lines were as obvious to psychologists as they were subliminal to teenage drivers. As earlier decades had the faddish pastimes of motoring and automobiling, the Fifties introduced the variant called cruisin'; the word itself implied a search for sinful pleasures. And, too, the use of the word teenager in numerous movie and song titles of the era clearly revealed the free-spirited connotations of that term when it was first widely applied to popular culture in the Fifties.

Saturday Night Out

The Fifties was also the decade in which Saturday, the "loneliest night in the week" (as the 1944 song by Sammy Cahn expressed it), acquired an almost oppressive peer-pressure significance. Saturday has always been special (even in Christ's time, when Saturday was sacred, and the other six days profane). But with the arrival of postwar affluence, easy credit, a burgeoning middle class, and a teenage car culture, weekend recreation became an end in itself. You *had* to have a good time on Saturday night or there was something pathologic at your core.

"The satisfying life after the war," writes Susan Orlean in *Saturday Night,* a history of the evening, "included an imperative to have fun, and Saturday night was the center of it." By the Fifties Americans were leisure time slaves to what Orlean calls "the Fun Imperative"—"the sensation that a Saturday night not devoted to having a good time is a major human failure and possible evidence of a character flaw." The acute, aching loneliness one can feel only on Saturday night, argues Olean, "is the Fun Imperative unrequited."

The sixth night of the week took on new and unexpected dimensions. The cheap handguns known as Saturday night specials got their nickname in Detroit in the Fifties because through loose local gun laws they were available in the city's convenience stores and bought (and used) on Saturday night. Perhaps coincidentally, more people are killed on Saturday nights than any other night. Also, the nation's telephone operators are besieged on Saturday nights by lonely callers simply wanting to talk. Toll-free 800 numbers for advertised products are dialed by thousands of people on Saturday nights who express only a passing interest in the merchandise, then launch into a chatty conversation with the operator. On Saturday night, writes Orlean, "People get together, go dancing, go bowling, go drinking, get drunk, get killed, and kill other people." In the second half of the twentieth century, Saturday night changed, perhaps forever—it became synonymous with leisure time and the myriad play that encompasses.

One cruisin' Saturday night car of the Fifties, though, was decidedly not sexy. In fact, it was downright stodgy, yet cultishly popular.

Volkswagen Beetle

In an age of tail fins, swaths of chrome, and general gargantuanism in American cars, the German *wagen* designed for the *volks* (the "people's car") was an anomaly if not an eyesore. In size and fuel economy, it was also a prophet before its time. The Beetle, conceived by electrical-engineer-turned-car-designer Ferdinand Porsche (father of the sports car that bears his name), inspired fierce loyalty or open ridicule. Volkswagen became the world's largest selling single make of car, the Beetle so "unimprovable" that in 1981, when the 20 millionth Bug rolled off the assembly line, the car differed only in slight details from Porsche's first 1934 drawings. The VW Beetle developed a cult following for the simple reason that it was a reliable, cheap car in an age of expansive, temperamental monsters.

In *Small Wonder: The Amazing Story of the Volkswagen,* Walter Nelson details Porsche's dream of a "people's car," an update of Henry Ford's Model T for the European masses. He examines Stalin's particular interest in a utilitarian vehicle for the German population, Hitler's financial involvement in the construction of auto plants (Hitler referred to the VW as the "strength through joy car"), and finally Madison Avenue's revolutionary new advertising efforts—humorous, self-effacing mottos like "Ugly is only skin deep"—to introduce the "car nobody wanted" into the gaudy, glitzy, oversized American market of 1949. A year later, only 330 Americans owned Beetles. The car—with a rear-mounted engine, a top speed of 60 miles per hour, no fuel gauge (one peered into the gas tank or used a dipstick), costing a reasonable $1,280—was not an overnight success. A Detroit auto scout reported back to Henry Ford, "I don't think it's worth a damn."

What really made the Bug a cult classic was the clever advertising of the firm of Doyle Dane and Bernbach—"They deliberately decided to play up the Beetle's quirky cussedness against the flash chrome of its competitors," writes

Deyan Sudjic in *Cult Objects*. While Detroit layered each year's new models with more and more chrome, VW boasted of keeping the Beetle virtually unchanged. "It was a tactic that quickly made the Beetle the smart, Eastern establishment car to drive," says Sudjic, "a protest against built-in obsolescence and superfluous gimmickry."

In the end, the Beetle was unable to compete effectively with the wave of Japanese cars that poured into the United States starting in the Sixties. Thanks in part to the Bug, the idea of a practical, inexpensive, reliable car took root among consumers—clearing the way for Toyotas, Hondas, Nissans and the like. In the movie *Sleeper,* Woody Allen paid the VW the ultimate compliment: A Beetle that had sat unused for hundreds of years is cranked—and starts up instantly.

DANCE CRAZES

Cha-Cha

With elbows bent at right angles, chest puffed, feet shuffling snugly side by side, those who danced the cha-cha, an outgrowth of the Cuban mambo, instinctively spoke of the craze using an extra "cha"—for cha-cha-cha embodied the dance's triple-step "quick-quick-quick" rhythm: One, two, cha-cha-cha. The dance originated in Cuba in the early Fifties, a variation of the double-step mambo, which had been fashionable in the previous decade. Musicians, desiring a more complex beat, began to alter the mambo's rhythmic pattern, eventually producing a "triple" mambo that arrived in the United States as the three-beat cha-cha-cha; which, in turn, paved the way for a lesser Latin dance craze revival: the merengue. The name cha-cha is thought to be an echoic, deriving from the scuffing sound made by a kind of heelless slipper favored by Cuban women doing the dance. "A curious combination of sexy come-on and staid standoff-ishness," assessed one dance critic in 1956, a year after the craze hit America. "The couples make only occasional and fleeting contact. For the most part, each works intently on his own [footwork]." The dance was popular among teenagers because in part it encouraged individual innovation and self-display, and it appealed to older folks who were already acquainted with the mambo and rumba.

The **merengue,** originating in the Dominican Republic, incorporated what is called a "limp" step; that is, a loose-leg movement that suggests the dancer suffers from a limp. Legend has it that the Latin dance, done to samba music, was first performed by a crippled Dominican general whose fellow guests respectfully imitated his every move as he dragged his lame right leg across the dance floor. The affectation was stylized to become a distinctive feature of an otherwise vigorous dance.

Calypso

The West Indian calypso dance became an American craze following Harry Belafonte's recording of an all-Latin album, "Calypso." The young singer, born in New York City but of West Indian extraction, helped launch not only the Trinidadian dance, but also a passing passion for bongo drums and maracas, as well as a wave of Hollywood film spin-offs such as *Bop Girl Goes Calypso.* The late Fifties was not the first time Americans had danced to a calypso beat, but that particular wave of the fad was the strongest. Etymologists are at a loss to account for the Trinidadian use of the ancient word calypso, though they are certain it has nothing to do the sea nymph Calypso (Greek *Kalypso*) in Homer's *Odyssey,* who kept Odysseus on her island for seven years; nor is it related to the white-purple-and-yellow orchid *Calypso bulbosa,* which grows in boggy regions of the Northern Hemisphere.

In the Fifties, teenage dancers on the then-new television show "American Bandstand" combined the cha-cha with the calypso to create their own fad dance, the **cha-lypso.** The dance inspired the singing group of Billy Duke and the Dukes, after a visit to the show, to write a hit song titled "Cha-lypso."

As we're about to see, "American Bandstand" had a profound effect on social dance, introducing a nation of teenagers to such crazes as the bunny hop, the bop, the stroll, the **walk,** the slop, the pony, the chicken, the monkey, and the **circle dance**—all of these debuting in only the last few years of the Fifties. Never before had dances gone in and out of style so rapidly; such is the fickleness mass communications affords.

American Bandstand: ABC Premiere, August 5, 1957

The boys wore suits, or sports coats and dress slacks, and ties were mandatory; a V-neck sweater could be worn under a jacket but never alone, nor with an open-necked shirt. Their short hair was often slicked back in a DA with a pompadour held high with Brylcreem. The girls favored hairdos that required bobby pins or headbands, and they wore cardigan or crewneck sweaters, rabbit-fur belts, a blouse with a "Philadelphia collar" (a variation of the classic Peter Pan collar) and mid-calf-length skirts; the ensemble was often accessorized with brooches, strings of pearls, and voguish pins of mink cats and felt poodles; footwear ranged from bobby sox with saddle shoes, to penny loafers, to flimsy ballerina pumps. The outfits were as important as the dances, though dancing was the heart and soul of "American Bandstand."

As a local Philadelphia program, the show, then titled "Bandstand," debuted in September 1952, with radio disc jockey Bob Horn as host. Ironically, the telecast in those days was more like MTV, previewing short musical performance films of pop stars like Patti Page and Perry Como, who'd typically, on film, stroll along a sun-drenched beach or through a sun-dappled, tree-lined park, accompanied by primitive special effects that were intended to enhance a song's "atmosphere." To express this innovation anachronistically: The original version of "Bandstand" showed music videos. There was no audience of dancers as yet. However, in an attempt to boost rating, the show's producer began to invite local teenagers into the studio to dance to the latest record releases. Almost immediately viewers swamped the station's switchboard with calls to say they loved to watch the dancing. The show, which would soon be a nation-wide trendsetter, made two other innovations in its pre-network days.

Lip-Synching and Rate-a-Record.   The idea of having a singer, during a live telecast, mouth the words of his or her hit single seemed a risky venture. Indeed, as Dick Clark later stated, during the show's first network week on ABC guest Paul Anka was lip-synching his first hit, "Diana," when the needle stuck in a groove of the 45: "It happened right in the middle of the chorus," relates Clark, "as Paul's voice was launching into that long, heartfelt 'Oh' that precedes 'Please stay with me, Diana.'" Bluffing, the young singer attempted to actually hold the unnaturally long note until the skipping sound of the stubborn needle became decidedly pronounced. "Nobody who saw that," said Clark, "ever forgot it." Despite its inauspicious network debut, lip-synching became a prime feature of the show.

Another feature was Rate-a-Record, in which four of the show's regulars scored a new single release for its "danceability." As the system was set up, a song's tally could be no lower than thirty-five and no higher than ninety-eight, a range Dick Clark favored because it eliminated the extremes of total failure or perfection.

In a relatively short time after its local debut, the show's format was fixed—and the broadcast studio on Philadelphia's Market Street (now American Bandstand Boulevard) had a daily line of hopefuls waiting eagerly to be admit-ted. Though nostalgically we think of "Bandstand" as being synonymous with rock 'n' roll, the music did not exist in mainstream America during the show's early years. Its popular acceptance cross-country coincided closely to the ar-rival of . . .

Dick Clark as Host.   America's perennial teenager—born in Mount Ver-non, New York, on November 30, 1929—came to the TV show from radio, where he'd headed a radio spin-off program titled "Bandstand." His first official day as host was Monday, July 9, 1956, and the number one tune that week was "Stranded in the Jungle" by the Jayhawks. As Clark later admitted in *Rock, Roll and Remember,* at first he himself did not appreciate the new beat: "I really didn't understand the music"—which was being denounced in the press and by parents' groups as the "devil's rhythm."

But as the clean-cut Dick Clark played one rock 'n' roll number after another, he turned into a champion for the music and parents began to soften their objections. When, on August 5, 1957, the show went national (in sixty-seven markets coast to coast, with 20 million viewers), an unexpected phenom-enon occurred: Its regular teenage dancers began to receive bags of fan mail; they became overnight celebrities with their own fan clubs.

And host Dick Clark became a household name. Whereas "Your Hit Parade"

Dick Clark hosting "American Bandstand."

was television's first song show, "American Bandstand" was its first dance show, and its popularity was such that the program became a springboard for records, pop artists, and fad dances—the dances often dreamed up by the show's regulars. One of the first dance crazes to spring from *Bandstand* was the . . .

Bunny Hop

This conga line dance—in which each participant holds on to the hips of the person in front and executes left-right foot movements, interspersed with forward and backward hops—sprang from the hit record "Bunny Hop" by bandleader Ray Anthony. The dance came on the heels of the jitterbug, the fast dance favorite in the early, pre-network days of "Bandstand." While the bunny hop was enjoying its short vogue, "Bandstand" regulars helped popularize a dance of more significance in that it presaged a trend for the Sixties in which dancing couples never touched.

Bop

Anyone who bought Ray Coniff's record "Dance the Bop" received a sheet of instructions on how to do the vigorously athletic pogo-style dance. The steps emphasized the music's up-beat, and the dance was said by one critic to be something like "marching in place." Partners faced each other, jumped up and down, and on landing furiously ground their heels into the floor.

Unrelated to the jazz form known as bebop, pioneered by Charlie Parker, the bop began on the West Coast and was "discovered" by Dick Clark when several teens visiting his show from Southern California were spotted doing it in a corner, off camera. Clark asked the Californians to teach the steps to his show's regulars, who in turn proceeded to teach it to 20 million teenage viewers. One bopped to such hit songs as "Be-Bop-a-Lula" or "At the Hop." A laid-back, sloppy version of the bop became known as the **slop.** To bop while skipping in place became the **pony,** whereas doing the bop to other animal mimicry produced the **chicken** and the **monkey,** as well as the only two dances ever banned from "American Bandstand" for being too risque: the **dog** and the **alligator.** The next entirely different dance craze was the . . .

Stroll

A line dance reminiscent of the old-fashioned Virginia reel, the stroll was executed not with carefree country merriment but calculated city cool. Several couples faced each other, boys in one line, girls in the other. In unison, the dancers crossed one foot in front of the other while stepping sideways, advancing a number of steps in one direction, then crossing the other foot in back and returning to the starting point. One couple, holding hands, sashayed down the aisle, executing turns, half turns, or their own imaginative variations. When that couple returned to the line, a second pair sauntered their stylish steps. Everyone got a turn to parade. One strolled to the hits "C. C. Rider," "Silhouettes," or the dance's anthem, "The Stroll," by the Diamonds. The Canadian quartet recorded their hit single after they'd first seen the dance during a guest spot on "Bandstand."

The effect of "Bandstand" on social dance in the late Fifties and early Sixties is inestimable. It brought audience and home viewer participation in a television show to unprecedented heights. One did not have to go to a trendy night spot or a dancing school to learn the latest fad steps. They could be seen—and copied—weekdays during the hour-and-a-half show.

POPULAR SONGS

Bop to Rock

In terms of popular music, the Fifties can be conveniently divided down the middle: The week of July 9, 1955, the lilting "Cherry Pink and Apple Blossom

White" slipped from its number one spot on *Billboard*'s chart of hits to be replaced by Bill Haley and the Comets' "(We're Gonna) Rock Around the Clock." "It's only from our perspective three decades later," wrote music chronicler Fred Bronson, "that we can see the impact this song had on our culture. It was the beginning of the rock era." As we'll see, "Rock Around the Clock" was not the first rock 'n' roll song, but from the standpoint of popular tastes and record sales it catapulted the music, with its pounding rhythms and raucous lyrics, to the mass consciousness of America.

Reactions were mixed, to say the least. Crooner Frank Sinatra was quoted in the *New York Times* as saying that only cretinous goons wrote and performed rock music. Dinah Shore told *Dance* magazine, "I feel Rock 'n' Roll can be healthy and stimulating. It has certainly brought back dancing of an athletic variety." *Time* reported that in many cities the vigorous music was banned from jukeboxes because "its primitive beat attracted 'undesirable elements' " who delighted in "spastic gyrations." Despite the disparate notices, a music revolution was launched, a rock 'n' roll generation born. "Rock Around the Clock" was, argues Bronson, "a brilliant signal flare that all that followed would be different from all that came before. It was the musical harbinger that preceded Elvis Presley, the Supremes and the Beatles."

In the Fifties there was the "white" rock of Pat Boone, Bobby Darin, and Frankie Avalon, and the "black" rock (and rhythm and blues) of Fats Domino and Little Richard. But there were also the phenomenally popular ballads of, say, Patti Page, Rosemary Clooney, and Nat "King" Cole. Hits by the year:

TV's Hit Parade Debuts: 1950

In 1950, American folk music reached its widest audience ever as **Goodnight, Irene** by Gordon Jenkins and the Weavers broke the 2 million selling mark. In that year of America's first "undeclared war," in which President Truman sent combat forces to defend South Korea from a Communist takeover, Christmas homeside could not have been more tuneful: Selling strongly were **Silver Bells, All I Want for Christmas Is My Two Front Teeth, Christmas in Killarney,** and **Frosty the Snowman.** Number ten on the "Hit Parade" was **If I Knew You Were Comin' I'd've Baked a Cake;** number five, **Dear Hearts and Gentle People.** But then the Lucky Strike radio show, a pop music staple since the Thirties, was retired—to be reincarnated on July 10, 1950, as a successful NBC-TV program. A regular cast of singers, the Lucky Strike Gang, entertained viewers with "the songs most heard on the air and most played on the automatic coin machines," which the TV audience was assured represented "an accurate, authentic tabulation of America's taste in popular music"—though no explanation was ever given as to how the show's hits were chosen, nor did anyone inquire. The decisions were made in great secrecy at the offices of Lucky Strike's advertising agency, Batten, Barton, Durstine & Osborne.

The emergence of rock 'n' roll mid-decade would create headaches for the show—not only was the new music "wild," but teenagers who bought hit songs wanted to see them performed by the original singers, not by *Hit Parade* regulars like Gisele MacKenzie or Snooky Lanson. Lanson's weekly rendition of Elvis Presley's "Hound Dog," always in a varied stage setting, was sadly ludicrous. In 1959 the Lucky Strike Gang would sway back and forth singing their familiar "So long for a while . . . that's all the songs for a while"—which on that particular evening would be their swan song.

Mona Lisa: 1950

Throughout the Forties Nat "King" Cole had had a string of hits: **Straighten Up and Fly Right** (1944), **Chestnuts Roasting on an Open Fire** (or "The Christmas Song," 1946), and **Nature Boy** (1948). He almost missed recording his biggest single, "Mona Lisa." Paramount Pictures, eager to promote its film *Captain Carey U.S.A.,* asked Cole to record one of the movie's songs. "What kind of song title is that?" responded the singer—who grew fond of the tune once he heard it played. Capitol Records thought the song would be a flop so the company put it on the flip side of what it felt was a surefire hit, "The Greatest Inventor of Them All." The nation's disc jockeys, however, loved "Mona Lisa," and on June 10, 1950, it reached number one on the *Billboard* chart. Soon the singer—born Nathaniel Adams Coles in 1919 to a poor, religious family in Alabama—was sipping champagne with royalty and appearing in a command performance for the king and queen of England. The landmark sales figures for "Mona Lisa" would later be challenged by such Cole hits as the country-western singalong **Ramblin' Rose;** the not-to-be-forgotten **Unforgettable;** and the upbeat, nostalgic **Those Lazy, Hazy, Crazy Days of Summer,** which for Cole turned out to be a posthumous hit.

1951. In this year when Johnnie Ray had the country's number one single, **Cry**—written years earlier by a security guard at a Pittsburgh dry-cleaning store, it eventually sold 2 million copies and its flip side, **The Little White Cloud That Cried,** was also be a hit—a major precursor to rock 'n' roll was heard in the Dominoes' rhythm and blues hit **Sixty Minute Man.** On the lighter side, Bing Crosby and Jane Wyman had **In the Cool, Cool, Cool of the Evening,** Mario Lanza sang **Be My Love,** and Rosemary Clooney performed **Come on-a My House.** And a Broadway show, Rodgers and Hammerstein's *The King and I,* produced a run of hits for a variety of singers: **Hello Young Lovers, Whistle a Happy Tune, Shall We Dance, Getting to Know You,** and **We Kiss in a Shadow**—all ballads ideally suited to the kind of staged presentation favored by TV's "Hit Parade." The year was also notable for Jo Stafford's **Shrimp Boats,** Tony Bennett's **Because of You,** and the Weavers' **On Top of Old Smoky.**

1952. **I Like Ike** became the highly effective campaign song for General Dwight D. Eisenhower. Derived from the tune "They Like Ike" in Irving Berlin's Broadway success of 1950, *Call Me Madam,* the song is thought to have substantially helped elect Eisenhower president. The movie *High Noon* produced the hit **Do Not Forsake Me,** and at Christmas time much of the country was singing **I Saw Mommy Kissing Santa Claus,** while detractors claimed the lyrics were scandalously suggestive for children who had yet to equate Santa with Daddy.

1953. Vaya Con Dios was a hit for Les Paul and Mary Ford, Tony Bennett scored with **Rags to Riches,** Frankie Lane with **I Believe,** and Eddie Fisher with **O Mein Papa.** Patti Page went to the top of the charts with **(How Much Is That) Doggie in the Window,** challenging Perry Como's lingering hit from 1952, **Don't Let the Stars Get in Your Eyes.**

Rock 'n' Roll Emerges: 1954

New York disc jockey Alan Freed popularized the phrase rock 'n' roll in this year when the country was caught up in a mambo dance and song craze: **Mambo Italiano, Papa Loves Mambo,** and **They Were Doing the Mambo** were all hit singles. And the same year that Americans were singing **Three Coins in the Fountain** and **Mister Sandman,** a young man named Elvis Presley had his first Sun Records release, **That's All Right,** which in no way competed in sales with the Crew-Cuts' **Sh-Boom,** Rosemary Clooney's **This Ole House,** or her other hit of the year, **Hey There.** Quickly, though, Presley would come to dominate the pop music scene.

Alan Freed used the phrase rock 'n' roll as the theme of his popular radio show, "The Beat Beat." However, there exists disagreement as to its exact derivation. It may come from the then-contemporary song "Rock with Me, Henry, Roll with Me, Henry." Or from a 1934 Jack Benny film, *Transatlantic Merry-Go-Round,* which contains a song titled "Rock and Roll." Or from an abbreviation (supposedly used by Freed) of a 1947 rhythm and blues hit, "We're Gonna Rock, We're Gonna Roll," by Wild Bill Moore.

Called "one of the most significant art forms to rise out of recent American culture," rock music was more than an expression of youthful rebellion—though not to parents in the late Fifties. To them the music of Chuck Berry, Little Richard, Jerry Lee Lewis, and Elvis Presley was disturbingly chaotic and sexual, the antithesis of life in the first years of the do it for the kids decade. The indulged ingrates were now out of control. Indeed, the deterioration of genteel society seemed apparent everywhere: in the French "art" films of Brigitte Bardot, in the glossy centerfolds of *Playboy,* and in Alfred Kinsey's alarming report of premarital (and extramarital) sexual shenanigans.

What passed for rock in the early Fifties was wistfully mild compared to what was to follow in the Sixties counterculture. In fact, few parents in 1954—singing along to the year's hits such as **Misty, All of You,** and **Count Your Blessings (Instead of Sheep)**—knew what rock 'n' roll was, though Bill Haley was about to change that.

We're Gonna Rock Around the Clock: 1955

It was the year Chuck Berry kicked off his career with the hit **Maybellene;** Pat Boone scored big with **Ain't That a Shame;** TV personality Tennessee Ernie Ford had a seven-week hit with **Sixteen Tons,** then the fastest-selling single in the history of the record industry; Roger Williams scored an instrumental smash with **Autumn Leaves;** the Four Aces were at the top of the charts with **Love Is a Many Splendored Thing,** the title song from a successful film; and Mitch Miller, who would become a long-time critic of rock and roll, was leading his band in **The Yellow Rose of Texas,** a Civil War marching song once popularized by traveling minstrel shows.

Initially enjoying comparatively mild success for all that it portended was Bill Haley's "Rock Around the Clock," a song that did not propel him to national stardom; *that* would come from his hit **Shake, Rattle and Roll.** Though, as mentioned, "Rock Around the Clock" was not the first rock song—perhaps that distinction goes to a 1951 recording, "Rocket 88," by saxophonist Jackie Bren-

Bill Haley and the Comets.

ston and the Ike Turner Band—Bill Haley's rock venture made money. And when the song was incorporated into the year's most shocking movie, *The Blackboard Jungle*, about a high school teacher struggling against student violence, the song suddenly reached a larger audience and had a greater impact. Whereas the film caused riots in theaters and was banned from the Venice Film Festival, the song (rereleased) shot to number one, remained there for eight weeks, and awakened the country to the age of rock 'n' roll. Producers and artists immediately realized there was a huge market for raucous, rebellious music. Perhaps Frank Sinatra's slur that only cretinous goons perform rock music had something to do with the fact that in the summer of 1955 Bill Haley's "Rock" displaced Sinatra **Learnin' the Blues** as number five on *Billboard*'s chart.

Also notable that year: **The Great Pretender; The Bible Tells Me So; Unchained Melody;** perhaps the era's most cherished golden oldie, **Earth Angel (Will You Be Mine);** and singer Joan Weber's **Let Me Go Lover**—a song that had bombed the previous year under the title "Let Me Go, Devil," the demon being rum. By changing a man's alcoholic addiction to a woman's romantic entanglement, the publishing house of Hill & Range Songs created a million seller. Painfully ironic for Joan Weber, shortly after "Let Me Go Lover" hit the top of the charts, her marriage ended in divorce and her recording contract was terminated. Twice let go, she sank into depression and was rumored to be in a mental hospital; later, a royalty check for the song was returned with the envelope stamped "address unknown." She died on May 13, 1981.

Heartbreak Hotel; Love Me Tender; Hound Dog; Don't Be Cruel; I Want You, I Need You, I Love You: 1956

The phenomenon of Elvis Presley as the first superstar of rock emerged in 1956, with his "Heartbreak Hotel" rising to the nation's number one record in February. The year, and the age of rock, had barely dawned when the TV-censored, swivel-hipped twenty-one-year-old singer released another, then another hit, for a total of *nineteen* songs in twelve months, three soaring to number one.

Elvis Aron Presley, ex-truck driver for the Crown Electric Company of Memphis, Tennessee, also appeared that year in his first movie, *Love Me Tender.* For his much-anticipated September 9 TV appearance on Ed Sullivan's "Toast of the Town," cameras shot him from the waist up in an attempt to mollify persistent cries of impropriety—though papers like the *New York Times* still decried his behavior as "burlesque," and *Music Journal* later condemned his "filthy" performances with their "whining, moaning and suggestive lyrics" which "blandly offered a vicarious sexual experience." Jackie Gleason, who booked Presley for a television show in 1956, appreciated his rebellike appeal to Fifties teenagers in labeling him "a guitar-playing Marlon Brando."

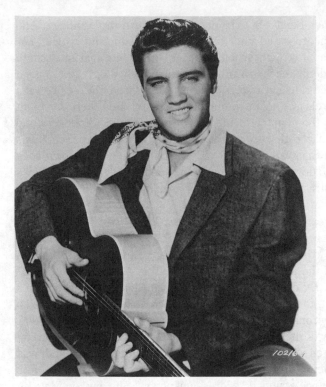

Elvis Presley.

The first white performer to expose a national audience to rock 'n' roll later said of himself: "I never thought of my performing style as wicked. *Wicked?* I don't even smoke or drink!" Within his first two years on the pop scene, Elvis Presley sold a staggering 28 million records and appeared on bestseller charts fifty-five times, earning him a fortune, the status of legend, and the sobriquet of "the King." Popular music would never again be the same.

I Could Have Danced All Night; On The Street Where You Live: 1956

While teenagers in 1956 shrieked and squirmed to Elvis's latest hits (like **Blue Suede Shoes**), their elders enjoyed the incomparable score from Alan Jay Lerner and Frederick Loewe's Broadway play *My Fair Lady,* starring Julie Andrews as Eliza and Rex Harrison as Professor Higgins. Opening at the Mark Hellinger Theater on March 15, it would go on to break all records in New York (and London), running for 2,717 performances on Broadway, and yield an original cast album that sold 5 million copies. Few people had thought that George Bernard Shaw's play *Pygmalion* could be transformed into a musical, but it grossed $80 million in its theater run, and sold to Hollywood for $5.5 million.

In addition to the popularity of the play's ballads, several other "slow" songs competed on the charts with rock 'n' roll's "fast" music. Patti Page scored with **Allegheny Moon;** Doris Day had **Whatever Will Be Will Be (Que Sera, Sera);** and Gale Storm played with the lyrics of **I Hear You Knockin' (But You Can't Come In).**

Thirty-nine-year-old Dean Martin began the year at the top of the charts with **Memories Are Made of This,** a hit for five straight weeks. Dino, a one-time boxer under the name Kid Crochet, had already teamed up with comic Jerry Lewis to produce more than a dozen movies, and had scored a pop music hit with **That's Amore.** "Memories," though, would be his greatest hit ever, and a few months after it became the nation's top song, Martin shocked movie fans with the announcement that he and Jerry Lewis were going their separate ways.

The Wayward Wind: 1956

Two big hits in the summer of 1956 were Gogi Grant's **The Wayward Wind** (number one in June) and the Platters' **My Prayer** (number one in August), the latter an English version of a French song titled "Avant de Mourir." Grant (born Audrey Arinsberg) had been performing in the Borscht Belt under the name Audrey Grant when record executive Dave Kapp claimed that the inspired name of Gogi came to him in a dream (perhaps because he regularly lunched at New York's Gogi's La Rue Restaurant). She had gone to a studio to record "Who Are We" in a three-hour session; with fifteen minutes of studio time left over she begged to record a song she'd been shown, written for a male singer. After adapting the lyrics to a woman's viewpoint, she rushed through "The Wayward Wind." "Who Are We" never climbed higher than number sixty-two; five weeks after "The Wayward Wind" was released it displaced Elvis Presley's "Heartbreak Hotel" from number one. The Platters' "My Prayer" held Elvis's "I Want You, I Need You" to the number two spot on the late summer charts.

Other notables from 1956: **See You Later Alligator, This Could Be the Start of Something Big, Friendly Persuasion, Band of Gold, Why Do Fools Fall in Love,** and **Standing on the Corner (Watchin' All the Girls Go By).**

Love Letters in the Sand; April Love: 1957

Second only to Elvis Presley, boyish-looking Charles Eugene "Pat" Boone was the most successful pop singing artist of the last half of the Fifties. In the year when Johnny Mathis began his career with the hits **Wonderful Wonderful** and **It's Not for Me to Say,** and Leonard Bernstein retold Shakespeare's *Romeo and Juliet* as the gangland *West Side Story,* cheery, cherub-faced twenty-three-year-old Pat Boone, alleged to be the great-great-great-great-grandson of frontiersman Daniel Boone, rode to the top of the *Billboard* chart with "Love Letters in the Sand" (in June) and "April Love" (in December).

"Love Letters" was not Pat Boone's first hit. He'd scored "white" rock successes with his own unique versions of Fats Domino's **Ain't That a Shame** and Little Richard's **Long Tall Sally** in an era when most of the country's radio stations wouldn't play black artists' rhythm and blues releases. But "Love Letters," a 1931 song (previously recorded by Rudy Vallee and Bing Crosby) added at the last minute to Boone's first Hollywood film, *Bernardine,* to give him a vocal spotlight in the nonmusical movie, became the most successful single of his career, twenty-three weeks on the bestseller chart, five at number one. In the summer of 1957 more teenagers slow-danced to "Love Letters" than rocked to Elvis Presley's **All Shook Up** and Ricky Nelson's **I'm Walkin'.**

The formula of having Boone sing a ballad in a film to guarantee the song's success was tried again in the year-end movie *April Love.* Written for him by specialists in "love" songs (by the composers of "Love Is a Many Splendored Thing" and "Secret Love"), "April Love" was the country's top-selling song at Christmas time, beating Danny and the Juniors' **At the Hop,** Sam Cooke's **You Send Me,** and Elvis Presley's **Jailhouse Rock.** Boone had such affection for the song that he later had a car horn made that played the melody.

School Day: 1957

Parents who approved of their teenagers listening to Pat Boone most likely disapproved of the lyrics of Chuck Berry's 1957 seminal hit, "School Day." (It followed his success in 1955 with "Maybellene" and in 1956 with "Roll Over Beethoven.") Berry, more than Boone, captured the social dynamics of the times and the direction in which pop music was heading. The song told of the humdrum of a typical school day, of the welcome ring of the three o'clock liberation bell, when students shed responsibilities and inhibitions in front of the local jukebox, freely expressing their inner yearnings by "Feelin' the music from head to toe." The song's lyrics combined the desire "Deliver me from the days of old" and the promise "Long live rock 'n' roll." It was a paean to a new culture. Berry's music, which portrayed teen life revolving around rock 'n' roll, influenced the Beatles, the Rolling Stones, and the Beach Boys, and, as augury, it spoke of a new teen-oriented society.

February to June 1957.   The decade's calypso fad was perfectly mirrored in the "day-o" tune **The Banana Boat Song,** recorded by Harry Belafonte, and by the group the Tarriers—one member of the three-man team was Alan Arkin, who'd soon pursue an acting career on Broadway and in movies. For teens who preferred to slow dance there was **Young Love** by a twenty-six-year-old U.S. Coast Guardsman turned blond screen idol, Arthur Andrew Kelm, adored under the name Tab Hunter. Though his singing career was pointedly brief, for a few weeks in the winter of 1957 his record outsold Elvis Presley's **Too Much** and Pat Boone's **Don't Forbid Me.**

Mickey (Baker) and Sylvia (Vanderpool) had a mammoth hit in their sexually suggestive **Love Is Strange,** written by Bo Diddley—who did not want to record the song himself because of a dispute with his publisher. Two years later Mickey and Sylvia split, he going off to perform in Europe, she to marry and become Sylvia Robinson who, in a breathy bedroom voice, had the disco-era hit **Pillow Talk.**

The same month that teens were "All Shook Up" over Elvis, The Diamonds scored big with their doo-wop classic **Little Darlin',** and Buddy Knox enjoyed the number one single, **Party Doll.** Knox wrote the song himself in 1948 (in a haystack behind a barn), and he was one of the innovators of the Western "rockabilly" style that became known as Tex-Mex music. Twenty-four-year-old Knox had been working on a master's degree in business, but quit school to tour when the record hit the top-selling charts.

July to September 1957.   As an expression of brokenhearted self-pity, the Everly Brothers' summer smash **Bye, Bye Love** is hard to top. The singers bade farewell to love and to happiness, and with a heartfelt "hello" welcomed loneliness, admitting they're "about to cry." Despite the crybaby lyrics, the song's spunky melody suggests the brokenhearted lover might yet muddle through. The tune competed for *Billboard*'s number one spot with Presley's **(Let Me Be Your) Teddy Bear,** a song prompted by a rumor that Elvis collected plushes. He didn't at the time, but thousands of fans sent him stuffed bears, which he donated that Christmas to children afflicted with polio.

Over the Mountain, Across the Sea was a summer winner for Johnnie & Joe, at the same time that a young Debbie Reynolds trounced the virtually all-male roster of pop singers with **Tammy.** From her film *Tammy and the Bachelor*—the tale of a teenager who nurses an injured pilot back to health— the song shot to number one, boosted attendance at the movie, and was performed by Debbie Reynolds at the following year's Academy Awards ceremony.

The young singer who soon displaced "Tammy" to number two was sixteen-year-old Paul Anka, with his "I'm so young, You're so old" love poem, **Diana.** A year earlier Anka, infatuated with his sister's eighteen-year-old baby-sitter Diana and frustrated that she'd have nothing to do with him, sent her a poem. Her further rejection prompted him to commit the stanzas to music. When the song became a nationwide hit, the real-life Diana experienced a change of heart. But by that time the youthful star was more interested in his thousands of worshipping female fans.

As teens returned to school in September 1957, they could rock to Jimmy Rodgers's **Honeycomb,** Buddy Holly and the Crickets' **That'll Be the Day,** Jerry Lee Lewis's **Whole Lotta Shakin' Goin' On,** and **Mr. Lee** by the Bobbettes, a group of five young singers who'd shared their Harlem High School stage as part of the school's glee club. The song's real-life Mr. Lee was a fifth grade teacher the group remembered less than fondly; in fact, many of the lyrics' unflattering lines were toned down before Atlantic Records allowed them to record the song. No one thought the disc would be a hit, but it quickly sold 2 million copies.

Wake Up Little Susie: 1957

The Everly Brothers scored another hit late in 1957 with "Wake Up Little Susie." The song tells of the plight of a young couple at the movies who "fell asleep." Waking at four o'clock in the morning, the boy attempts to rouse his Little Susie, while fretting over what to tell her parents and her straitlaced friends who are sure to scold "ooo-la-la." The phrase "ooo-la-la" received much social analysis as a statement of mocking hypocrisy: The teens, you see, had done nothing wrong, but they realized, by the standards of the time, that the mere appearance of returning home in the wee hours was enough to blemish their reputations. Brothers Don and Phil Everly did not find the song racy, but many radio stations refused to play the record because of the possibility that the fictional couple just might have "fooled around." Despite the ban, the record soared to the top of *Billboard*'s chart—for a time surpassing Johnny Mathis's **Chances Are.**

Happy, Happy Birthday Baby by the Tune Weavers, an a cappella singing group, was a surprise 2-million-seller in October. The group was discovered in a club singing the song that two members had recently written; a record executive in the audience jumped up shouting, "That's it! That's it! That's the one we're going to record."

Around the time this occurred, the stroll was the fad dance, and a favorite tune to stroll to was the Rays' **Silhouettes (On the Shade).** The song originated from an actual incident. One evening while riding a Philadelphia train, Bob Crewe, the song's co-writer, caught sight of a silhouette on a bedroom window shade of two lovers in a passionate embrace. Unable to shake the imagery from his mind, he related the incident to his co-writer, Frank Slay, and the two concocted the song—which was an immediate sensation. As the year of 1957 drew to a close, "Silhouettes" was number four, "Wake Up Little Susie" number three, Presley's "Jailhouse Rock" number two, and at the top of the chart was Sam Cooke's rendition of "You Send Me."

Witch Doctor; The Chipmunk Song: 1958

Consider these memorable lines from two 1958 hits: "Oo-ee, oo-an-ah, ting-tang, walla walla bing-bang" ("Witch Doctor"). "Sha na na na . . . yip, yip, yip, yip, yip, yip, yip, yip, boom, boom, boom, boom, boom" ("Get a Job"). The year was rich with nonsense rhymes, speeded up voices, and novelty songs; in fact, three novelty tunes soared to number one, a record for the gimmickry genre.

Two of those unlikely successes were from the fertile brain of a failed grape farmer turned songwriter, David Seville (born Ross Bagdasarian), cousin of famed novelist William Saroyan. One day at home while reading a book titled *Duel with the Witch Doctor,* Seville got the bizarre but profitable notion of creating a song about a witch doctor in which the voice of the character would be recorded at twice the speed of the musical accompaniment—a trick that within a few months would suggest to him creating a group of squeaky-voiced singing rodents named Simon, Alvin, and Theodore.

In April 1958 "Witch Doctor" topped the *Billboard* chart, outselling The Platters' "Twilight Time" and Elvis Presley's **Wear My Ring Around Your Neck.** It was not Seville's first success; he and his cousin Saroyan had written an ethnic-sounding ditty, **Come On-a My House,** which Rosemary Clooney sang in the summer of 1951. Seville (a name he adopted from the Spanish town where he'd been stationed during World War II) conceived "The Chipmunk Song" after he almost struck a squirrel on a country road; he named the characters after three record executives, Si, Al, and Ted. The song became the year's fastest-selling record, captured three Grammys (best comedy performance, best engineered record, best recording for children), and launched an animated television series, as well as a fad for Alvin, Simon and Theodore dolls. It was one of those rare records that becomes a pop culture cottage industry.

The Purple People Eater; Dinner With Drac: 1958

In the year that the Lerner-Loewe musical film *Gigi* had serious-minded adults singing **Thank Heaven for Little Girls, I Remember It Well,** and **The Night They Invented Champagne,** serious-minded teens were rapt over "The Purple People Eater." The novelty number by Sheb Wooley was inspired by a genre of joke popular in the Fifties: "What has one eye, one horn, flies, and eats people?" The formulaic answer: "A one-eyed, one-horned, flying people eater." In lesser hands this joke would not have become the early summer's bestselling record—which in turn launched a fad for "people eater" T-shirts, mugs, plastic horns, a purple-tinted ice cream, and other pop paraphernalia, as well as a rip-off song, **The Purple People Eater Meets the Witch Doctor.** On the record, Wooley, an actor (in the Liz Taylor-Rock Hudson 1956 hit *Giant*), made use of the speeded-up voice gimmick popularized by David Seville, and the song sold 3 million copies.

John Zacherle, a former U.S. Army major with a bachelor's degree in English literature, was more popularly known in the Fifties as Roland, "the Cool Ghoul," the host of a TV show called "Shock Theatre." So popular was the late-night telecast that a record executive calculated that "the Ghoul" was a guarantee for a novelty song hit. The hastily written "Dinner With Drac," in which Zacherle did a Dracula impersonation, quickly climbed the pop charts and won its hobgoblin singer a regular guest-host spot on "American Bandstand's" annual Halloween party.

In addition to novelty numbers, the year was also rich in songs that would become classics.

January to June 1958.   The year opened with Danny and the Juniors at the top of the *Billboard* chart with **At the Hop,** a song originally titled "Do the Bop." On the advice of Dick Clark, who claimed the bop craze was nearing saturation, the song's composers altered "bop" to the rhyming "hop" and had what Clark predicted: a hit. In its turn at number one it outsold Jerry Lee Lewis's **Great Balls of Fire** and Buddy Holly's **Peggy Sue.** Though the group's next release, **Rock and Roll Is Here to Stay,** was also a hit, its popularity could not match that of "At the Hop."

Singer Rick Lewis wrote **Get a Job** (number one in February) while in the army, stationed in Germany. After returning to the States he joined a Philadelphia gospel group, the Gospel Tornados, which evolved from sacred to secular singers, changing their name along the way to the Silhouettes (after the hit song of that title). Lewis's song of social protest—the lyrics tell of a man rising from bed, searching the help wanted ads, and being harassed by friends for being a failure—was actually the flipside of the record (the A side was "I'm Lonely"), but its wonderful nonsense syllables mesmerized the ears of radio DJs and teens. One of the group's singers came up with the gunshot "yip, yip . . . boom, boom" phrase, while a record company song arranger added the softer "sha na na na." The song sold over a million copies, became one of the first rhythm and blues singles to cross over into the realm of pop rock, and is regarded today as among the most memorable of golden oldies.

Twilight Time: 1958

Topping the charts in April were the Platters' hauntingly romantic "Twilight Time" and the revival of a 1927 gospel favorite, **He's Got the Whole World in His Hands,** by a thirteen-year-old British male singer with a high-pitched voice, named Laurie London. He'd recorded the song in England where it enjoyed only modest sales, but, for reasons mysterious, it was a flash success in the United States, the country's number one single mid-April. It was soon shoved to number two by "Twilight Time."

Songwriter Sam Buck Ram composed the "Twilight" lyrics as a poem when he was in college in the Forties; and when put to music the song was a bestseller in 1946. The Platters—already scoring with such hits as "Only You" and "The Great Pretender"—played their version for Dick Clark, who immediately forecast it would be a million seller. In addition to becoming a classic, the record holds another distinction: It was released as both a 78 RPM and a 45 RPM, and its enormous sales on the smaller disc (98 percent) sounded the death knell for pop singles on the larger format. Henceforth, single was synonymous with 45.

That same month, April, teens were dancing to **Lollipop** (number twenty), and the Monotones' **Book of Love** (number five). As industry legend has it, one of the Monotones, Charles Patrick, heard a radio commercial: "You'll wonder where the yellow went / When you brush your teeth with Pepsodent." The jingle, and its word "wonder" stuck in his mind, evolving into the line "I wonder, wonder, who / Who wrote the book of love." From a banal jingle came an unforgettable classic.

In May the music scene was dominated largely by the Everly Brothers and **All I Have to Do Is Dream,** a tune of vocal hesitations, musical syncopations, and such unlikely rhymes as "Only trouble is / Gee whiz." Written in fifteen minutes, the song was the Everly Brothers' bestselling single, though they had a string of hit follow-ups such as **Devoted to You** and **Bird Dog**—as in "Heeez a burd / Heeez a dawg . . . Heez a burd dawg." The brothers' nasal twang came from their rhythm-and-blues training, and by effectively marketing it they crossed over into pop rock. As summer began, teens were dancing cheek-to-cheek to Ed Townsend's romantic ballad **For Your Love.**

July to December 1958.   Under the nonsense title **Yakety Yak (Don't Talk Back),** the Coasters scored a hit (number two) with a tune that's been called a "parental lecture with saxophone." An equally alliteratively rhyming title occupied the number four spot in late July: Bobby Darin's **Splish Splash (I Was Takin' a Bath),** which beat by a breath Ricky Nelson's **Poor Little Fool.** For making out, the Danleers produced what would become a young lovers' perennial classic: **One Summer Night.**

For fast-dancing there was Elvis Presley's tenth number one hit, **Hard Headed Woman,** secure at the top of the charts while the idol, now a GI, was in basic training in Fort Hood, Texas. It was a sad time for the singer: His mother, Gladys, had fallen ill, and he'd repeatedly been denied requests for leave to see her, the army fearing it would come under criticism for giving the celebrity preferential treatment. He eventually was granted a week's leave. She died on August 14, and a grief-stricken Elvis collapsed several times at her funeral.

Volare (Nel Blu Dipinto di Blu): 1958

During a hot August, while **Willie and the Hand Jive** had teens rocking to a "shave-and-a-haircut, two-bits" beat, the country's number one record was an unlikely Italian import: "Volare (Nel Blu Dipinto di Blu)," by Domenico Modugno. The dreamlike story tells of a man with hands painted blue who flies through a blue sky; "blue painted in blue," *blu dipinto di blu;* though most Americans, who bought the record in the millions, hadn't the slightest idea what it was about; they liked its sound. "Volare" won Grammys for best song of the year, best male vocal performance, and record of the year. Dean Martin's version of the tune climbed the charts no higher than number twelve. Modugno's "Volare" was soon overtaken by Eric Hilliard "Ricky" Nelson's "Poor Little Fool," the teen idol's sixth hit single.

As teens returned to high school in September, they bought up 45 RPMs of the Quin-Tones' "ladies' choice" **Down the Aisle of Love,** and of the Poni-Tails' female lament **Born Too Late,** about the frustration of falling for an older boy.

In terms of composers, the unique hit of the season was **It's All in the Game,** with a melody written earlier by a former vice president of the United States (in Calvin Coolidge's second administration), Charles Gates Dawes. Unless a future vice president writes a number one hit, Dawes, a banker and amateur flutist before entering politics, will retain that singular achievement.

Climbing the charts in October were Bobby Day's "tweedlee-dee-dee /

tweet tweet" harmonies in **Rockin' Robin,** and the Shields' **You Cheated,** which from the fast pace of sales seemed to have struck a sympathetic chord in many lovers. A Presley-like ballad, **It's Only Make Believe,** became a number one hit for Harold Lloyd Jenkins, a singer who renamed himself by borrowing from the southern towns of Conway, Arkansas, and Twitty, Texas. Conway Twitty was the model for the character Conrad Birdie in the Broadway musical *Bye Bye Birdie.* In November his song was displaced from the top of the charts by the Kingston Trio's version of an old American folk tune ("Tom Dula"), **Tom Dooley;** Dula was a real-life mountaineer hanged for murder in the 1860s. The hit single caused a surge of interest in Dula's story, and his long-abandoned, weed-strewn grave in North Carolina was spruced up and photographed by national magazines.

As Christmas season approached, another song based on a real-life fact became the country's bestselling single: **To Know Him Is to Love Him,** by the Teddy Bears. The group, including singer-writer Phil Spector, took its name from Presley's hit "Teddy Bear," and Spector conceived the song from the epitaph on his father's tombstone: To Know Him Was to Love Him; his father had committed suicide when Spector was nine.

Raining in My Heart: 1959

The year 1959 has been called the year the music died for a number of reasons. The burst of creative energy released throughout the last half of the decade, which produced a pantheon of classics, petered out, replaced by, as one authority states it, "an era of schmaltz and pimple cream" tunes. At the close of the decade such clean-cut, straitlaced idols as Paul Anka, Fabian, Connie Francis, Frankie Avalon, Ricky Nelson, and Bobby Vee dominated the charts. "They homogenized, bastardized, and sterilized the original rock 'n' roll sound. They overrode the music of the previous five years and transformed rock 'n' roll into pop music for teenagers."

Another mark that an era had ended was the tragic death in a plane crash on February 3, 1959, of twenty-two-year-old Charles Hardin Holly, known professional as Buddy Holly. From his 1957 hit **That'll Be the Day,** to **Peggy Sue,** to **Maybe Baby,** to his posthumous success in 1959, "Raining in My Heart," he'd produced, in three years, a body of work that would influence artists from the Beatles to Elton John, from the Rolling Stones to Linda Ronstadt. He became a cult figure, the focus of a 1978 movie, *The Buddy Holly Story,* and a 1990 Broadway musical, *Buddy*—a remarkable achievement for any artist, and even more so for one affectionately called "a four-eyed, skinny geek" from Lubbock, Texas. Today, the overnight bag he carried on the prop plane that crashed—containing suntan oil, throat medicine, a hairbrush, comb, and lint remover—is one of many priceless Buddy Holly relics cherished by his legions of fans. In his lifetime, he never enjoyed the celebrity status that haloed him in death.

Buddy Holly.

From the standpoint of popular music, the year 1959 was also memorable for the hits from two Broadway shows. In May Ethel Merman starred as Gypsy Rose Lee's mother in the Stephen Sondheim/Jule Styne musical *Gypsy,* introducing **Small World, Some People, Together Wherever We Go,** and **Everything's Coming Up Roses.** In November Mary Martin opened in Rodgers and Hammerstein's *The Sound of Music,* from which virtually every musical number became a hit for one recording artist or another. Particularly popular were the show's title song, **The Sound of Music, Climb Every Mountain,** and **Edelweiss.**

In this year when Alaska and Hawaii became part of the United States (the forty-ninth and fiftieth states, on January 3 and August 21, respectively), here's how the other pop songs stacked up:

January to June 1959.   The year opened with the Platters, the Fifties' most popular group, at the top of the *Billboard* chart with **Smoke Gets in Your Eyes,** their priceless version of a 1933 Jerome Kern tune from the Broadway musical *Roberta*. Sadly, at the height of their careers, they were arrested in August 1959, and charged with drug possession and soliciting prostitutes (the case against them was eventually dismissed). Many radio stations refused to air their records. "Had the Four Platters been four itinerant businessmen," criticized *Billboard,* "and had an issue of race not been involved, the matter would not have become a subject of scrutiny." Their stellar career abruptly dimmed. Thus, in yet another sense, 1959 marked the year the music died.

Number one in February—when "The night was clear and the moon was yellow / And the leaves came tumbling down"—was a rock version of a hundred-year-old folk tune, "Stack-O-Lee," about a real-life Memphis gambler named James "Stacker" Lee. As **Stagger Lee,** the song told of an urban badman to be respectfully feared. Black Panther Bobby Seale later named his son after the tough character, claiming Stagger Lee was a positive role model for black males before Malcolm X arrived on the scene. In its original uncensored version (the song was later rewritten) Dick Clark refused to play it on "American Bandstand," banning a song about a criminal celebrated for gambling and murder. Lloyd Price's single topped the charts for four weeks, beating the Crests' quite different **Sixteen Candles.**

In March, nineteen-year-old Francis Thomas Avallone—Frankie Avalon— had the nation's top pop record in **Venus,** which eventually relinquished its number one spot to the Fleetwoods' **Come Softly to Me.** In fact, when the group arrived to appear on "The Dick Clark Saturday Night Beechwood Show," they were greeted by another guest, Frankie Avalon, who good-naturedly broke the news to them that "Come Softly" had just passed his "Venus" as the top record.

In May, when Edd Byrnes as the comb-wielding character Kookie (full name: Gerald Lloyd Kookson III) on TV's "77 Sunset Strip" was all the rage, his single, **Kookie, Kookie (Lend Me Your Comb),** climbed the charts to number four. Born Edward Breitenberger, the actor turned singer never again enjoyed a hit record, or the success he'd achieved as Kookie. As summer began, teens across the country were dancing to the Mystics' first record, **Hushabye.**

The Battle of New Orleans: 1959

An unlikely hit in July was this eighteenth-century folk melody, later played by fiddlers and drummers to celebrate the defeat of British forces at New Orleans and the end of the War of 1812. Given new lyrics and a new title, "The Battle of New Orleans" climbed the *Billboard* chart to number one, becoming the first hit for fisherman turned singer Johnny Horton. The record took Grammys for best song of the year and best country and western recording. It was pushed to number two by Paul Anka's **(I'm Just a) Lonely Boy,** a heartfelt, highly personal ballad written by the young singer-composer after the untimely death of his mother at age thirty-nine. Later in the year he'd enjoy another hit with **Put Your Head on My Shoulder**—at that time Connie Francis was singing **Lipstick on Your Collar.**

As the year, and the decade, drew to a close, Bobby Darin had a hit (number two) in **Mack the Knife,** while the Fleetwoods took the number one spot with **Mr. Blue,** a song its composer, Dewayne Blackwell, had written with the hope that the Platters would record it. The group might well have accepted the song, but Blackwell met with repeated failure in his attempts to win an introduction to the famous singers; then he met the Fleetwoods. Fate stepped in and the Fleetwoods had their second smash hit following "Come Softly to Me."

BESTSELLING BOOKS

The Search for Bridey Murphy: Number Six Nonfiction, 1956

The decade had more important nonfiction books: **Betty Crocker's Picture Cook Book** (number one, 1950), Thor Heyerdahl's adventurous **Kon-Tiki** (number nine, 1951), Rachel Carson's pre-environmental alarm **The Sea Around Us** (number four, 1952), Reverend Fulton J. Sheen's optimistic **Life Is Worth Living** (number five, 1953), and a book that stated a social concern, **Why Johnny Can't Read** (number eight, 1955).

But the hot read in 1956, setting off a national obsession for the subject of reincarnation and past lives, was Morey Bernstein's search on two continents for a long-dead, red-haired lass named Bridey Murphy. Bernstein, a Pueblo, Colorado, businessman turned hypnotist, had through trance elicited from the subconscious of a petite, brown-haired housewife, Virginia Tighe, a tale, told in an Irish brogue, of her nineteenth-century life as one Bridey Murphy of County Cork, Ireland. The book climbed to the top of the country's bestseller lists, was serialized in more than thirty-five newspapers and magazines, and was translated into several languages. It ranked as the number six bestseller for the year 1956, and a tape recording of Virginia Tighe in trance as Bridey became a bestselling LP record. As science writer Martin Gardner points out in a critical analysis of the phenomenon, society hostesses in 1956 threw chic "Come as you *were*" parties, jukeboxes blared out the rollicking "Do You Believe in Reincarnation?" the schmaltzy "The Love of Bridey Murphy," and the hip "Bridey Murphy Rock and Roll." Suddenly nightclub hypnotists drew standing-room-only crowds.

Many people felt author Bernstein, through "hypnotic regression," had hit upon an irrefutable "scientific" method for proof of reincarnation and the existence of an afterlife. Others were harshly skeptical. And whereas Bernstein searched in Ireland for evidence of a historical Bridey Murphy (turning up little of significance), a newspaper, the *Chicago American,* commenced its own investigation closer to home—or, more specifically, in Virginia Tighe's early childhood neighborhoods. An embarrassment of coincidences surfaced, which shocked believers and delighted skeptics. Virginia had been born in a house exactly like the one Bridey described. Virginia's mother's name was Katherine; Bridey's was Kathleen. Virginia's sister had suffered a severe fall down a flight of stairs; Bridey had died in just such a tumble. Bridey claimed to have lived in Cork; Virginia had spent many hours with a neighborhood lady named Mrs. Corkell—who had a son Kevin, also the name of one of Bridey's nineteenth-century friends. Most damaging of all: Mrs. Corkell's maiden name was . . .

Bridie Murphy. Book sales plummeted. LP records of the trance session were returned to stores in hopes of refunds. In a trance, Virginia Tighe had simply dredged up recollections of childhood, recasting them in a profitable light.

Other nonfiction bestsellers of the Fifties had a considerably longer shelf-life:

Look Younger, Live Longer: Number One Nonfiction 1951

Published a year earlier, where it rose to the number three spot on the *Publishers Weekly* annual list, this forerunner of modern nutrition books, by Gayelord Hauser, the health guru to Hollywood's biggest stars, had a simple premise: "you are what you eat." Though the science of nutrition was still in its infancy, Hauser proffered much advice that later studies would verify as sensible, and a good amount of nonsense.

The Power of Positive Thinking: Number Two Nonfiction, 1953–55

Whereas Gayelord Hauser espoused "you are what you eat," preacher Norman Vincent Peale spread the word that "you feel what you think"; negative thoughts are self-defeating, positive ones provide the power to achieve your most cherished goals. Published in 1952, the number six bestseller of that year, it enjoyed four consecutive years on *PW*'s list, selling nearly 2 million copies.

Kids Say the Darndest Things! Number One Nonfiction, 1957

Assembling humorous material from his popular radio and television shows, host Art Linkletter scored a hit with his lightweight book, amusingly illustrated by cartoonist Charles M. Schulz, creator of the "Peanuts" series.

Twixt Twelve and Twenty: Number One Nonfiction, 1959

At the pinnacle of teen idolatry, supported by a decade of solid pop single hits, boyish Pat Boone shared his conservative do's and don't's with his fans in a book published in 1958, and number two in sales for that year. His volume of gentle admonishments to his admirers between the ages of twelve and twenty trounced Abigail Van Buren's **Dear Abby,** number nine in 1958. Making a strong showing in 1959 was Vance Packard's **The Status Seekers** (number four), a commentary at once amusing and acerbic on class status symbols in American life and the Fifties obsession of keeping up with the Joneses.

The Affluent Society: 1958.

In this groundbreaking and controversial book, economist John Kenneth Galbraith addressed consumerism squarely. He pointed out that even after the majority of American families satisfied their desires for television sets, automobiles, refrigerators, and other "durables," they must be convinced through advertising to continue buying—another TV set, another car, another refrigerator—or recession sets in, profits fall, and unemployment rises. He described a pathologic "dependence effect" in which prosperity can only be maintained through buying of goods needed, then of goods for which needs are artificially created through advertising. And the cost of continually stimulating the consumer to buy, buy, buy grows enormously as the consumer has all that is truly required and more.

The net result: consumers obsessed with satisfying their own personal wants and instantaneous whims while neglecting to provide decent schools and housing, adequate public transportation, parks, efficient police protection, and even research and development programs for the nation's security and the next generation's future. He asks scathingly, "Is this the American dream?" And he states that no society whose central figure is the bill collector can be truly "good." The title of the book became incorporated in popular speech, though its salient message seemed to be lost in the unabated rush to buy, buy, buy.

And what fictions were adults reading in the Fifties?

1950.   Henry Morton Robinson's **The Cardinal** (number one), and Ernest Hemingway's **Across the River and Into the Trees** (number three).

1951.   James Jones's **From Here to Eternity** (number one), and Herman Wouk's **The Caine Mutiny** (number two).

1952.   Daphne du Maurier's **My Cousin Rachel** (number four), and Hemingway's **The Old Man and the Sea** (number seven).

1953.   The $1.98 movie edition of Lloyd C. Douglas's **The Robe,** the biblical bestseller of 1942 through 1945.

1954.   **Not As a Stranger** (number one), **No Time for Sergeants** (number six), and John Steinbeck's **Sweet Thursday** (number seven).

1955.   Herman Wouk's **Marjorie Morningstar** (number one), Patrick Dennis's **Auntie Mame** (number two), and Sloan Wilson's **The Man in the Gray Flannel Suit** (number five).

1956.   One of the top-selling novels of all time: Grace Metalious's **Peyton Place** (number three; number two in 1957), which launched a movie and the long-running television serial—which in turn boosted sales of the novel.

1957.   Nevil Shute's **On the Beach** (number eight), and Ayn Rand's **Atlas Shrugged** (number ten).

1958.   Boris Pasternak's tale of a Russian doctor-poet during the tumult of the Russian Revolution, **Doctor Zhivago** (number one; number two in 1959); Robert Traver's **Anatomy of a Murder** (number two); and Vladimir Nabokov's scandalously sexy **Lolita** (number three).

1959.   Leon Uris's story of the making of modern Israel, **Exodus;** James Michener's tale of the making of a chain of Pacific islands, **Hawaii** (number three); Allen Drury's politically hot **Advise and Consent** (number four); and D. H. Lawrence's hot-under-the-collar **Lady Chatterley's Lover** (number five).

TELEVISION HITS

Color TV

In the closing year of the Forties, *Newsweek* reported: "There are still those to whom television itself, with its fledgling productions and unsure reception, is something like the Zeppelin: a great modern invention that doesn't quite work." Rapid progress soon forced the magazine to eat its assessment. Reception improved, programming stabilized, and to the black and white picture was added a rainbow of color—if not always of the most natural hues.

CBS broadcast the first color picture in 1951, with images of a trip to a zoo, a football game, and an "artistic" scan of a Picasso painting. Until an industry standard was adopted, the color of your favorite star could vary from week to week, from TV set to TV set. The joke in the industry was that the acronym for the organization striving for color standards—NTSC (the National Television System Committee)—actually stood for "Never the Same Color." Nonetheless, viewers loved color, any color, and in the Fifties those who could not afford a pricey color set ($1,000 for an RCA) bought a rectangle of rainbow-hued plastic and taped it over the screen. Green (for grass) was the bottom-most shade; blue (for sky) was the uppermost band; the swatch of red roughly corresponded to the height a character's face might fall, if standing. If the character was seated, or the scene was indoors, the effect could be said at best to be surrealistic.

Two other innovations of the Fifties:

Canned Laughter

Television's first sitcom to employ a taped track of human voices chuckling, cackling, and caterwauling—to let the home viewer know that an incident was supposed to be funny—was the much-forgotten 1950 "Hank McCune Show." "There are chuckles and yuks dubbed in," reviewed *Variety,* informing TV owners that in truth "the show is lensed on film *without* a studio audience."

Still, the entertainment paper forecast a bright future for faked merriment: "Whether this induces a jovial mood in home viewers is still to be determined, but the practice may have unlimited possibilities if it's spread to include canned peals of hilarity, thunderous ovations and gasps of sympathy." TV writers, groping into history for a precedent to canned laughter, came up with the Greek chorus. Thus, the practice was not kitsch but a variant on a venerable tradition.

Nielsen Ratings

While audiences heard canned laughter, television advertisers listened to the compiled statistics of the Arthur Charles Nielsen Company. In 1923 Arthur Charles Nielsen had founded a market research company to investigate consumer tastes and appreciation of products. From measuring sales at supermarkets, he branched out in 1952 to surveying TV viewers on their favorite weekly fare. The sampled population was small, the statistical methods questionable, the results probably not truly representative of national tastes. Nonetheless, TV executives and sponsors needed some quantitative measure of a show's success and Nielsen, with his ratings, amassed power and an empire.

Years later, when the weaknesses in the polling system were pointed out, the Nielsen ratings were so ensconced that complaints fell on stone-deaf ears. Invariably, popular shows, with high ratings, praised the rating system; unpopular programs, with lower ratings damned the numbers. But, as the cliché goes, history is written by the victors, and every season there was a cheering of victors to champion the rating system. Two years after the Nielsen ratings were unleashed, futuristic writer H. G. Wells watched the new medium and predicted of its future fare: "Nothing but parades; an endless newsreel of parades and sports." Sports, yes; and parades, too. But what he did not envision was that the most consistently popular kind of TV fare would be the sitcom.

But first, in brief, here's how the decade opened:

Garroway at Large, starring the easy-mannered Dave Garroway, was one of NBC's most popular programs in 1950. The host introduced songs, skits, and guest stars, then became a fixture on the station's "Today" show, which launched the early morning news and special features genre of program.

What's My Line? the granddaddy of television's quiz panel shows, a staple of the Fifties, debuted in 1950 with host John Daly, and columnist Dorothy Kilgallen and actress Arlene Francis as panelists. They were eventually joined by Bennett Cerf and Steve Allen.

The Jack Benny Show debuted in October 1950, bringing from radio the deadpan comedian himself, plus his familiar cast of characters: sidekick Rochester, vocalist Dennis Day, and wife Mary Livingston. Marilyn Monroe made her TV debut on the show.

You Bet Your Life, premiering in October 1950 and hosted by Groucho Marx, was the first show of the comedy-quiz format, with good-natured announcer George Fenneman, the butt of Groucho's comic jibes. Home viewers eagerly waited to see if a contestant might utter the "secret word," prompting a Groucho-looking duck to descend from the ceiling with a billful of cash. So a losing contestant would not go home broke, Groucho resorted to his easy question: "Who's buried in Grant's Tomb?" Typical of the exchanges between host and contestant:

GROUCHO: Are you married, Georgette?
CONTESTANT: Yes, I've been married for thirty-one years to the same man.
GROUCHO: Well, if he's been married for thirty-one years, he's not the same man.

The Kate Smith Hour brought to television in 1950 the country's most popular full-voiced singer, as well as her trademark song, "When the Moon Comes Over The Mountain."

The Roy Rogers Show, 1950, introduced the cowboy, his wife Dale Evans, his horse Trigger, and his dog Bullet, to television's first generation of kiddie viewers. For somewhat different fare, children in 1950 could switch dials to catch the opening line—"It's a bird . . . it's a plane . . . it's Superman!"—of **The Adventures of Superman,** starring George Reeves in the dual role of Clark Kent and the man from the planet Krypton.

The following year children were introduced to **Mr. Wizard,** one of the medium's most successful educational programs. Mr. Wizard (Don Herbert) dramatically demonstrated simple scientific principles, amusing and educating kids, and earning for the show two Emmy nominations in its fourteen-year run; it spawned more than five thousand "Mr. Wizard" science clubs across the United States and Canada. For the preschool toddler audience, there was Miss Frances (Dr. Frances Horwich), who presided over the **Ding Dong School** in grandmotherly fashion. Mothers across America got a breather when the school bell rang and Miss Frances entertained home tots with singalongs, stories, games, and instructions on drawing and coloring.

The George Burns and Gracie Allen Show: CBS Premiere, October 12, 1950

GEORGE: Gracie, what do you think of television?
GRACIE: I think it's wonderful—I hardly ever watch radio anymore.

With their own blend of zany humor, the vaudeville team of Burns and Allen debuted in a long-running, weekly television series that opened with the cigar-wielding George Burns delivering a monologue, usually about his muddle-headed wife and her cockamamie logic: "Gracie's the kind of girl who shortens the cord on the electric iron to save electricity." The cast regulars included the perpetually perplexed next-door neighbors Blanche (Bea Benadaret) and Harry Morton (Hal March), the Burns's real-life son, Ronnie, and announcer Harry Von Zell.

More unconventional than Gracie's humor was the show's clever device of

George Burns and Gracie Allen.

having George Burns suddenly step out of his sitcom character to deliver a private aside to the home audience. Or to predict what was about to happen—as when George winked at viewers and said: "According to my calculations, Harry Von Zell should be over at the Mortons' and by now Gracie should have him mixed up in this too. Let's take a look." The gimmick of George Burns being on television at the same time he was watching himself on television, as was the audience, took getting used to, but proved highly effective. Equally surreal was to have the show's announcer, Von Zell, also be a sitcom character.

If the show had one star it was Gracie Allen. The program's producer, Ralph Levy, felt her success derived from the fact that she was first an actress, then a comedienne. "Gracie was one of the finest actresses that ever lived . . . the word actress is crucial. True, she played the silliest woman you could ever meet, but she never thought of herself as a comedienne, and George never treated her as one." Much of her character's humor stemmed from taking statements literally, as when Harry Von Zell recommended a doctor who had "hundreds of nervous patients." Gracie responds: "He can't be so good if he makes all his patients nervous."

In 1958 Gracie Allen decided to leave the series, retiring from a lifetime in show business. Though the program played for another year with all of its other characters, things were not the wacky same without the goofball goings on of Gracie. And, too, the audience missed George Burns's sign-off line: "Say good night, Gracie," and Gracie's wide-eyed, innocent "Good night," delivered as if the previous half hour of frustrations and misunderstandings had never occurred; as they had not by her own logic.

I Love Lucy: CBS Premiere, October 15, 1951

For comedy, the 1951–52 television season was notable for the debut of **The Red Skelton Show** (two of Skelton's favorite expressions were: "I dood it!" and his signoff, "God bless"), of Wally Cox as the timid **Mr. Peepers,** and of Gale Storm as the perky **My Little Margie.** But the season also contained the most successful situation comedy in the history of television—revolving around bandleader Ricky Ricardo (Desi Arnaz) of the Tropicana Club, and his zany, accident-prone wife, Lucy MacGillicuddy Ricardo (Lucille Ball), bent on breaking into show business given the slightest opportunity. Their neighbors-as-accomplices-in-mayhem were Fred and Ethel Mertz (William Frawley and Vivian Vance).

Based in part on Lucille Ball's radio show "My Favorite Husband," "I Love Lucy" quickly became a national mania. President Eisenhower delayed an address to the nation rather than run against the show, and department stores installed TV sets to keep shoppers from staying home on Monday nights to watch their favorite program. When Lucille Ball became pregnant with her second child in 1952, the nation followed the comic travails of the gestation and birth of "little Ricky" in the character of Lucy Ricardo. And a new television magazine, *TV Guide,* debuting in 1953, chose for its first cover the baby, Desiderio Alberto Arnaz IV, and placed Lucy's familiar face in the upper right-hand corner. During its six years in originals, "Lucy" never ranked lower than third in ratings among all TV programs—ending up as the highest-rated TV show of the Fifties.

In her radio character of Liz Cooper, Lucille Ball had already honed the scatterbrained logic, vocal intonations, and crying fits ("Wah-h-h-h") that would become hallmarks of Lucy Ricardo. In her desire to make the move to television (as well as to mend her troubled marriage), she insisted that her TV husband be her real-life spouse, Desi Arnaz—despite his thick Cuban accent, which TV executives thought might be unintelligible to middle America. Instead, Arnaz's broken English became a comedy gimmick, especially when he lost his temper at "Loo-o-o-cy" and unleashed a stream of truly unintelligible Spanish epithets. And Lucy loved to mock him.

RICKY: Loo-o-o-cy, you get rid of that thin'.
LUCY: Oh, yeah? What thin' do you mean?

To prove the appeal of Desi as the TV husband, the team went on tour in 1950, performing before live audiences, then with $5,000 of their own money produced a film pilot for the series. A hit was born instantly.

From the show in which Lucy attempted to bake her own bread (only to be pinned to the kitchen wall by an overly yeasted leviathan loaf), to the episode in which she rehearsed a cough medicine commercial so many times that she got drunk from the medicine's alcoholic content, every fan had, and has, a favorite program. In fact, in 1958 when CBS brass attempted to assemble a collection of reruns titled "The Top Ten Lucy Shows," try as they did, they could not winnow their own favorites to fewer than thirteen programs.

Syndication and Fan Clubs.   The end came to "I Love Lucy" in 1957 not because the show declined in ratings (it was number one), but because Lucille Ball and Desi Arnaz were exhausted from the grind of filming weekly before a live audience. In fact, the end never really came to the series, for in one country or another it continues to live in syndicated reruns—and now is available on VHS tapes. The success of the syndication in America and abroad set the pattern for all of television's later sitcoms.

It's been written that "I Love Lucy" had an impact on "everything from attitudes toward American humor to American pregnancy to Cuban immigration to the U.S." And it's become a trivia buff's delight:

The Ricardos lived at: 623 East 68th Street, Apartment 4A, Manhattan. Little Ricky's babysitter was: Upstairs neighbor Mrs. Trumbull. Little Ricky was initially played by: The Mayer twins, and later by child actor Richard Keith (whose real name was Keith Thibodeaux). As bandleader at the Tropicana, Ricky's salary was: $150 a week. Lucille Ball's first choices to play Fred and Ethel Mertz were: Gale Gordon, school principal on radio's "Our Miss Brooks," and Bea Benadaret, who was playing Blanche Morton on "The Burns and Allen Show." The first "Lucy" episode: "The Girls Want to Go to a Nightclub."

The trivia alone could fill a book—and has. Several books, to which I'm indebted. Perhaps no show in the history of television has prompted more analysis and provided more enjoyment.

Our Miss Brooks: CBS Premiere, October 3, 1952

The sitcom season after "Lucy" was rich with viewer hits. Ann Sothern bowed in as the well-intentioned but meddling Susie McNamara in **Private Secretary;** viewers loved the show in which her boss, Mr. Sands, impatiently called "Misssss McNamara!" but the critics were harsh. Said the *New York Times:* "It's all situation and no comedy." And that was a *good* review.

Equally labeled as a "featherweight comedy" was **My Friend Irma,** starring Marie Wilson, fresh from playing radio's dumb blond Irma Peterson. Another sitcom more popular with viewers than with critics was **I Married Joan,** with radio comedienne Joan Davis and TV husband Jim Backus.

A more critical success of the season was "Our Miss Brooks," starring Eve Arden as the tart-tongued, man-hungry schoolmarm Connie Brooks, out to land the dense bachelor biology teacher of Madison High School, Philip Boynton (Richard Rockwell). In one episode she invites him to dinner at her house:

MISS BROOKS: Anything special you want for dinner?
MR. BOYNTON: I'm not fussy. I'll love whatever you put on my plate.
MISS BROOKS: Fine—I'll be on your plate.

If anyone in the country complained about the show it was America's school-teachers, who felt that the undignified, wisecracking, husband-hunting Miss Brooks "set the teaching profession back 100 years." Also offensive to teachers were the bullying tactics of the show's principal Osgood Conklin (Gale Gordon), and the talking back from problem student Walter Denton (Richard Crenna).

The Adventures of Ozzie and Harriet: ABC Premiere, October 10, 1952

This family sitcom featured radio stars Ozzie and Harriet Nelson, and their real-life sons David (age sixteen) and Ricky (then a twelve-year-old eighth-grader at Bancroft Junior High in Hollywood, soon to be a pop music phenome-non of the Fifties). The Nelsons played themselves, and in the fourteen years the show was telecast, the nation watched Ricky go from a young boy with a crewcut to a top-record-selling teen idol and young adult crooner. The show began on radio in 1944 as a straightforward treatment of the family's home life. "The pattern of the TV show," explained the *New York Times* in 1952, "is the same as that the Nelsons used on radio, and that in turn is inspired to large degree by incidents they or their friends have experienced in real home life." The paper concluded: "fine family fun."

Ozzie and Harriet Nelson, cognizant of the wholesome image they wanted the show to project, began the series by making all the scenes involving their

"The Adventures of Ozzie and Harriet."

school-age boys take place on Saturdays so viewers would not think the children were missing classes. From the start, the impish, playful Ricky stood out in the mellow sitcom; he scored an immediate hit with young viewers.

Then came the show of April 10, 1957, an episode titled "Ricky the Drummer," in which the seventeen-year-old actor, after begging his father to allow him to sing on the program, cut loose with the Fats Domino hit "I'm Walkin'." Overnight he became a rock 'n' roll star. The song shot to the top of the charts. Fan clubs sprang up around the country. Whereas Ricky the rock star gyrated in his live stage performances, on the sitcom his singing was calculatedly sexless (at least through the Fifties). "Mr. and Mrs. Nelson just wouldn't stand for that kind of conduct," the *Times* once said about the parents' strictness with their sons. The show went off the air in the mid-Sixties.

Other hits premiering from 1953 to 1955:

Topper. The 1953–54 season brought to television the first "spirit" sitcom (like the later "Bewitched" and "I Dream of Jeannie") featuring ghosts of a couple and their dog Neil (killed in an avalanche), starring the real-life team of Anne Jeffreys and Robert Sterling as the ghosts, and Leo G. Carroll as the "live" cast member, Topper.

Make Room for Daddy. A season alternative to the ghost couple was the solidly down-to-earth family of nightclub comedian Danny Williams, played by Danny Thomas in his CBS series. The family consisted of his sharp-tongued wife Margaret (Jean Hagen), feisty son Rusty (Rusty Hamer), and sarcastic daughter Terry (Sherry Jackson). It was the first TV sitcom in which the father of a family was not dense, bumbling, or just plain stupid. Danny Thomas, largely as himself, was warm and witty, sarcastic but also self-deprecating. It was also the only sitcom in which the mother was quickly killed off: Jean Hagen hated playing last fiddle to Danny Thomas and the kids and pleaded to get out of the show. Divorce was taboo, so the producers arranged her "death" and had a teary-eyed Danny Thomas explain to the children, "Mommy has gone to heaven." For a while Williams was a widower, and the show became known as "The Danny Thomas Show." But in 1957 he married Kathy (Marjorie Lord) and the children adjusted to their new stepmother and her daughter, Linda, played by the impish Angela Cartwright.

December Bride. In the 1954–55 season, Spring Byington starred as "the widow Lily Ruskin," who made believable the comedic situation in which a mother-in-law lives with, and in harmony with, her adoring son-in-law Matt—who tries desperately to find her a husband—not to get her out of the house, but for her own happiness.

Lassie. Equally unusual for a sitcom was the adaptation of the Metro-Goldwyn-Mayer "Lassie" stories. The star of the show was the farm-dog-as-hero Lassie, a brave, loyal and remarkably intelligent collie owned by the young Jeff (Tommy Rettig), his widowed mother Ellen (Jan Clayton), and his grandfather (George Cleveland). Cast changes were rapid and confusing. Gramps dies (because actor George Cleveland actually did die), Lassie brings home an orphan boy named Timmy, mother Ellen decides that farm life is too hard and moves with son Jess to the city, selling the farm to a childless couple, the Martins, who inherit both Timmy and Lassie. Audiences did not seem to mind the shuffling (which continued), nor did many child viewers realize that over the years many lookalike collies played the intrepid Lassie. Not only did the show's characters undergo cast reincarnation; the series itself originated with a 1940 bestselling novel *Lassie Come Home,* which became a 1943 movie with Roddy McDowall and Elizabeth Taylor, then a series of popular movies, then a successful radio program, and finally made its way to television—exemplifying the kind of dogged perseverance characteristic of its canine star.

Kids that season also enjoyed **The Soupy Sales Show** (premiere, July 4, 1955), which became famous for the countless number of cream pies slammed into the faces of famous guest stars; the zany **The Pinky Lee Show** (premiere, January 4, 1954); the educational **Children's Corner** (premiere, August 20, 1955); Walt Disney's **The Mickey Mouse Club** (premiere, October 3, 1955); and last but longest-lived of the lot: **Captain Kangaroo** (premiere, October 3, 1955), starring Bob Keeshan as the gentle, kindhearted captain whose trademark jacket had baggy pockets stuffed with as many surprise goodies as Santa's satchel. It was a landmark in children's programming, running well into the Eighties, making it the longest-running kiddies' show in TV history.

Father Knows Best: CBS Premiere, October 3, 1954

Jim, Margaret, Betty (Princess to her father), Bud, and Kathy (called Kitten)— the Andersons, as millions of fans knew the idealized family that all Americans in the Fifties wished was a model of their own. This was a sitcom unlike any before, and few after it. Never had a TV family's life (or anyone's real life) been so tranquil; never had there been parents so patiently loving, continually well-dressed, and totally understanding of their children's growing-up problems. Never had a family had more perfect children than those who lived at 607 South Maple Street, Springfield, U.S.A. The U.S. government felt the Andersons were so typical of the American family (as it wished families to be) that it oversaw the production of an episode as a half-hour commercial to promote U.S. savings bonds—which was not shown on TV but was distributed to the nation's churches, schools, and civic organizations. The episode's messages were: Buy savings bonds; try to get along like the Andersons; housewives, vacuum in pearls.

In fact, Margaret Anderson (Jane Wyatt) did all of her housework in a tasteful dress, high heels, button earrings, and a string of pearls. In one episode, when she's vacuuming (attired as mentioned), Jim, mail in hand, arrives home from his insurance job and asks with the slightest edge to his smooth baritone: "Doesn't anyone bring in the mail anymore?" Margaret, who despite her impeccable appearance claims she's had a "bad day," answers, "Who has the time? By the time I've finished the dishes and picked up after all of you, and repaired the vacuum cleaner . . ." None of this seemed incongruous to viewers in the Fifties. In 1955 the show won an award "for constructive portrayal of American family life." The era was, after all, the do it for the kids decade, a family-oriented span of years in which Eisenhower was the country's president and Jim Anderson was its father.

Original episodes ended in 1960, though not because of a drop in ratings (it was still in the top ten), but because "father" Robert ("Marcus Welby, M.D.") Young had tired of the role and wanted to move on to other things.

What most viewers never knew was that in its initial (radio) conception the show's title ended with a question mark: "Father Knows Best?" that is, punctuation as sarcasm, suggesting that Father Anderson was as confused about raising children as most American dads. The skillful acting of Robert Young, however, made it entirely believable that Jim Anderson really did know best; the question mark was dropped. In doing so, what might have been a sarcastic sitcom with a dense and confused Father (typical of what was then on the air) became an American gothic classic. Jim Anderson was television's first Superdad. Reviewed the *New York Times:* "Robert Young and Jane Wyatt have restored parental prestige on TV."

The Honeymooners: CBS Premiere, October 1, 1955

RALPH KRAMDEN: One of these days, Alice—POW—right to the moon!
RALPH KRAMDEN: Baby, you're the greatest!
ALICE KRAMDEN: Forget it, Ralph.
ED NORTON: Hi ya, Ralphie-boy!

Perhaps no other TV sitcom has produced such a fanatically devoted set of fans or so many lines with such nostalgic impact.

Ralph (Jackie Gleason) drove a bus through the grimy streets of New York. He and his wife Alice (Audrey Meadows) shared a two-room walk-up—at 328 Chauncey Street, in the Bensonhurst section of Brooklyn—in which the only pieces of furniture were a dinner table and chairs, a chest of drawers, and an ice box that continually broke down. Typical of their exchanges:

RALPH: Before I'd let you go to work, I'd rather see you starve. We'll just
   have to live on our savings.
ALICE: That'll carry us through the night, but what'll we do in the morning?

Upstairs lived Ed Norton (Art Carney), who worked in the sewers, and his wife, Trixie (Joyce Randolph). Ed loved Ralph and good-naturedly took endless abuse, but he also continually ribbed "The Great One" about his weight:

"The Honeymooners."

RALPH: Norton, I'm gonna learn from here on in how to swallow my pride.
ED: That ought not be too hard. You've learned how to swallow everything else.

Ed Norton, who saw himself as an "underground engineer," adored his job and delighted in telling Ralph about the intricacies of New York's sewer system—which could take a person anywhere:

RALPH: It's rush hour. We'll never be able to get across town in this traffic.
ED: Trust me. We'll go by sewer.

Origin.   Jackie Gleason scored big on television in 1952 with a CBS comedy variety hour, "The Jackie Gleason Show," performed live from New York. His comedic sidekick was Art Carney, and the show featured the June Taylor Dancers and Ray ("the Flower of the Musical World") Block's Orchestra. He created the unforgettable characters of the Poor Soul, Joe the Bartender, the Loudmouth, and Reggie Van Gleason II. But his most enduring creation (first seen in 1951 on "Cavalcade of Stars") was Ralph Kramden, in a comedy skit called "The Honeymooners." "I had this idea for a long time," Gleason later said. "I knew a thousand couples like these in Brooklyn. It was the loudmouth husband . . . with a wife who is a hell of a lot smarter than her husband. My neighborhood was filled with them." The hour variety show was a huge success and his tag lines, "And awa-a-aaay we go" and "How sweet it is!" were repeated by fans across the country.

But there existed a special chemistry among the characters in the Honeymooners skits. And in 1955 the skit became a half-hour series—and Jackie Gleason received one of the biggest contracts in television history—a $7 million deal. Gleason liked to keep rehearsals to a minimum. "Once our cameraman said he absolutely needed a rehearsal," wrote the comedian. "I told him: 'Just have the damn camera follow me.' Where the hell am I going to go? Out the door?"

After thirty-nine episodes of "The Honeymooners" had been filmed in 1955–56, Gleason refused to film the second year; which is why series fans have only thirty-nine shows to watch in reruns. He was offered another $7 million but argued, "I said we couldn't come up with the same high quality of scripts that second year. It was that simple."

Leave It to Beaver: CBS Premiere, October 4, 1957

Ward, June, Wally, and Theodore "Beaver" Cleaver lived at 211 Pine Street, Mayfield, U.S.A. Unlike Jim ("Father Knows Best") Anderson, dad Ward (Hugh

"Leave It to Beaver."

Beaumont) did not always know best. In fact, the parental advice he gave sons Wally (Tony Dow) and Beaver (Jerry Mathers) often backfired. Mother June (Barbara Billingsley) usually avoided dispensing wisdom, preferring to dish out milk and cookies.

Unlike other sitcom kids, the older Wally and the younger, denser Beaver experienced real-world problems and thorny growing-up uncertainties. What's more, as boys are *supposed* to do, they delighted in tossing worn clothes on the floor and leaving bureau drawers open, and took a boy's pride in not wanting to take regular baths. And they openly despised homework. Not quite Bart Simpsons, they were television's early underachievers. There was even a meanness in Wally's pal, smarmy Eddie Haskell, and his bullying of the Beaver and stinging him with the slur "squirt." In an era of idealized sitcom families, the Cleavers were a bit more realistic than their TV competitors.

June Cleaver, however, like Margaret Anderson of "Father Knows Best," did housework in heels, pearls, and going-shopping makeup. (Pearls were obligatory for a Fifties' sitcom mom: Even as the decade closed, Donna Reed, in **The Donna Reed Show,** as yet another idealized mother, Donna Stone, would have been naked without a double strand.) Still, "Beaver" fans like to point out that in terms of realism the sitcom was the first to show . . . a bathroom. The Cleavers *were* real people.

Origin.　　The birth of the show lay in the desire of writers Bob Mosher and Joe Connelly (who'd written over a thousand "Amos 'n' Andy" radio and TV scripts) to create a sitcom centered not on parents, but on kids and their neighborhood friends. Originally it was titled "Wally and Beaver"—to emphasize the focus on its young characters. But the writers felt that might suggest to some viewers a story about a boy and his pet, and last minute they changed the title. The wide-eyed Beaver was forever saying, "Gee Wally," and Wally liked to warn, "Boy, Beave, are you gonna get it." Eight-year-old Jerry Mathers, already a veteran actor in television and movies, landed the role of the Beaver when after reading for the part he abruptly announced, "I gotta go now, I got a Cub Scout meeting"—something the Beaver himself would blurt out. Polite to his elders, Beaver always answered with a "Yes, sir" or "Yes, ma'am," and his prepubescent distaste for the opposite sex was expressed in comments like "I'd rather look at a skunk than look at a girl." Throughout its six-season run and 234 episodes the show never placed in the annual top ten, though it was highly successful and acquired a passionate cult following. The last show was telecast on September 12, 1963.

The Many Loves of Dobie Gillis: CBS Premiere, September 29, 1959

Whereas "Beaver" was the first sitcom to focus on young kids, "Dobie Gillis" was the first to deal with a modern teenager from a teen's point of view—it even offered viewers the first prime-time beatnik in the character Maynard G. Krebs, who dressed shabbily, shunned work, and prefaced his every remark with the word *like*. As the confused Dobie—who has trouble getting dates because he woos girls to the point of nausea ("You are the sun, the moon, the stars, all miracles and legends incarnate. Your eyes are peekholes in the walls of heaven")—Dwayne Hickman watched his hair turn quickly from blond to brown because producers wanted him to look different from how he'd appeared on an earlier TV show.

Poor and not the least bit ambitious, Dobie had one overriding goal in life: to marry the lusciously well-built, totally unattainable Thalia Meninger (Tuesday Weld)—whose dream, in turn, was to marry a millionaire. When Dobie first sees Thalia at the movies, he walks up to her and announces, "I'm Dobie Gillis. I think I love you." Thalia answers, "I'm getting nauseous." Thus, a long-running theme was struck. Dobie summed up his impossible dream in the first episode (as well as the course the series would take) by confessing to the audience: "I love girls. I'm not a wolf, mind you. A wolf wants lots of girls. I just want one—one beautiful, gorgeous, soft, round, creamy girl for my own—one lousy girl! But to get a girl you need money." The show's gimmick to express Dobie's inner frustrations was to let him grouse in front of a statue of Rodin's *The Thinker* in a park, and he often struck the statue's crouched, elbow-on-knee pose. The final show was telecast on September 18, 1963.

CHAPTER 8

———————— □ ————————

The Schizophrenic Sixties

1960 to 1969

The Do It by the Kids Decade

The *Kinder, Kirche, Küche* atmosphere of the Fifties, which made it the do it *for* the kids decade, was gone. The spotlight for the Sixties shone on just the *Kinder,* who were coming of age with revolutionary fervor. If decisions in the Fifties were made *for* the kids, in the Sixties those same kids were calling the pop culture shots. The keynote of the decade was youth; the country even had a young president in John F. Kennedy, who asked the now-teenaged *Kinder* to join the Peace Corps and the Volunteers in Service to America (VISTA).

The decade, though, was decidedly schizophrenic—of two minds and two voices. The idealistic youth of the first half of the era gave way to an alienated uprising of hippies, yippies, and war protesters, assortedly cynical, spaced out, committed to social change, or obsessed with self in its myriad infatuations. Confusion and disenchantment were in the air and everywhere on the airwaves. An incomprehensible war raged in Vietnam, and at home assassins took the lives of three of the country's most charismatic leaders: Kennedy, King, and another Kennedy—men who were symbols of a more humane future. As a country, we lost our naiveté, and cynicism was settling in for a long stay. The Schizophrenic Sixties encompassed Camelot's hope at one end and Vietnam's horror at the other. Anyone who lived through the tumult cannot forget its diverse benchmarks:

Andy Warhol and **soupcan art** . . . the **Age of Aquarius** and of **Timothy Leary, Ken Kesey, LSD,** the **drug culture,** and slogans like **"Due to a lack of interest, tomorrow has been cancelled"** . . . the **twist, watusi,** and **jerk,** and **Jimi Hendrix, Janis Joplin,** and **The Grateful Dead** . . . the **Beatles** and **Jackie Kennedy** fashions . . . **Dick Clark** and **acid rock** . . . **Nehru jackets** and **bell-bottom pants** . . . **love beads** and **long hair**

for men . . . **Quotations From Chairman Mao Tse-tung** as a nationwide bestseller, catapulting revolutionary Chinese rhetoric to chic cocktail party chatter . . **communes, flower children,** and the summer of 1969: in which America landed two men on the moon and a celebration of a half-million peace lovers inundated the environs of Woodstock, New York, for an unprecedented act of theater al fresco in which the audience eclipsed the performers. The *Kinder* became The Event. But first, a statistical glimpse of . . .

American Life in 1960

From the dawning of the American century to the start of the Schizophrenic Sixties, the country had come a long way.

The turn-of-the-century population of 76 million Americans had baby boomed by 1960 to 179.3 million—more than a doubling. No longer did 60 percent of the nation's people live in rural areas; only 37 percent did. New York, the most populous state in 1900 (population 7,268,894), still held that title with a total of 16,782,304 inhabitants. California, though, number twenty-one in 1900 (population 1,485,053), had climbed to number two with 15,717,204 potential fad-starting trendmakers. (Nevada, least populous in 1900, was still that way in 1960.)

Whereas average male life expectancy was a mere 46.3 years in 1900, it stood at 66.6 years in 1960. For women, the improvement was even greater: from 48.3 to 73.1 years. The leading causes of death for the Gibson girl and the Gibson man—ailments of the heart and arteries—were still taking more lives than other diseases. However, whereas tuberculosis claimed 202.2 people out of every 100,000 at the turn of the century, TB deaths had plummeted to 6.1 per 100,000 in 1960. On the other hand, nationwide motor vehicle deaths in 1900 were fewer than 100; in 1960 a total of 38,137 Americans died in or under a car.

Women had made great strides in entering the work force (if not in receiving equal pay). There were 23.7 million working women in 1900, 47 million in 1960. The country's major industry had shifted from agriculture (1900) to manufacturing (1960). The nation's dressmakers had decreased by two-thirds, blacksmiths by sixth-sevenths, while the number of the nation's physicians had about doubled, as had the number of bartenders. Telephone operators (19,000 in 1900) and electricians (51,000), relatively new fields at the turn of the century, had mushroomed by the mid-Sixties: 357,000 and 337,000 respectively. The average work week had shrunk from 59 hours to 39.7, while the average weekly pay increased from $12.74 to $89.72.

In 1900, some 4,490 new books were published; the number stood at 12,069 in 1960. Radio and television had cut into the newspaper business: The total number of the nation's daily newspapers had dropped from 2,226 to 1,763, a trend that would continue.

As for the American family, the size of the average household had decreased from 4.7 to 3.7 persons, while the total number of families in the country climbed from 16 million to 45 million. Climbing too was the number of divorces:

56,000 to 393,000—another trend that would continue. On the positive side, lynchings had gone from 115 in 1900 to none in 1960—at least none were recorded.

FADS, FOLLIES, AND TRENDS

The Jackie Kennedy Look

An obsessive love affair began in 1961 with the inauguration of the boyish John F. Kennedy as president; the love interest was the country's First Lady, Jackie. From almost the moment she ascended the White House steps, millions of American women primped, preened and dieted to approximate the Jackie look. Not since the Gibson girl of the Gay Nineties had women had a model of such poise, elegance, and tasteful understatement. No other personality to emerge from this decade of famous faces was so closely copied, so trendsetting in manner and dress. Her appearance at a social function automatically telegraphed a "fashion flash": "Mrs. Kennedy was wearing a . . ."

Pillbox Hat.   The craze for the hat that resembled a box for carrying pills began at the presidential inaugural ceremonies, when the First Lady's modest hat seemed ultra chic in contrast with the traditional millinery sported by Pat Nixon and Mamie Eisenhower. Jackie's was not the first pillbox. Photographs

Jacqueline Kennedy.

were later published to prove that the wife of the president of Mexico had worn a pillbox hat earlier, and that a variant of the vogue had surfaced briefly in the Thirties. But on the stylishly coiffed head of American's young first lady the design carried social cachet. As did the **two-piece suit** with a semifitted top ending just below the waist though atop the hipbone; the **overblouse** that was loose-fitting but never blousy; the **oval neckline** often lacking a collar; **bare arms** or **three-quarter-length sleeves** (never full length); the slim **A-line skirt** to mid-knee or just a kneecap longer; and on the feet **low-slung, sensible pumps.** For evening dress, only the French **Empire** style would do. Never had so many people with such little knowledge of French pronounced "om-peer" (never "em'-pyre"). **Big buttons**—huge ones, 2 inches in diameter—became a Jackie trademark. And whereas a woman's jacket had always buttoned from waist to neck, the First Lady made it chic to have only one button—not at the waist, but near the neck. This was a minor fashion revolution copied on a major scale.

The pillbox hat had its detractors. A fad game, Pin-the-Pillbox-Hat, lampooned the style, as did Bob Dylan's song "Leopard Skin Pillbox Hat." But the jibes abruptly stopped on that day in November 1963 when, wearing a pink pillbox hat, the First Lady cradled the bloodied head of her husband as their open-topped car raced through the streets of Dallas to Parkland Hospital. The pillbox hat—the entire Jackie ensemble—came to represent to the American people an ineffable sadness, the violent end to an era that may or may not have produced a Camelot. Jackie's pillbox was the last of the serious hats.

Bouffant Hair.   The pillbox hat and the simple oval neckline focused attention on the head—thus the hairdo assumed crucial importance. As the First Lady wore the bouffant style, it was sculpturally rounded and lifted only slightly from the scalp—like a regal, full-headed crown. As copied throughout the country, though, the bouffant was inflated until it resembled a hot-air balloon, anchored down to the cheeks by two lacquered guiche curls in the shape of the letter C, which to hold their stiffness were often taped to the wearer's cheeks. Unattractively monolithic, the hairdo had the hair-spray consistency of cotton candy.

The renaissance of the bouffant in America goes back to 1957 when *Life* magazine published a series of stylish photographs of women in bouffants that were adorned in jewels and feathers. The article gave tips on how to achieve the look through the use of giant curlers, dedication, and a can of superhold hairspray. The next year all of designer Givenchy's mannequins sported the full-head halo. Known in variations as **the bubble** and **the beehive,** the style was exaggerated until it interfered with a good night's sleep—and entered the realm of urban legend: Roaches and mice nested in bubbles that weren't washed, insidiously eating away at the wearer's brain; bad girls concealed knives and brass knuckles in their varnished domes; rumor had it that a dense bubble could shatter, hair chips falling to the ground like broken china, leaving the wearer bald. The look, which had become a parody of the elegance it once espoused, would have gone the way of the Fifties had not the First Lady, with the help of her skilled hairdresser Kenneth, reined in the style and made it a statement of chic.

Wraparound Sunglasses.   Two years before the Foster Grant company made wearing sunglasses ultra trendy with its "Sunglasses of the Stars" campaign—with its catchphrase: "Isn't that [celebrity's name] behind those Foster Grants?"—Jackie Kennedy had launched a craze for wraparound shades: wide-framed glasses curved around the face from the bridge of the nose to the temples.

The glasses, in extremis, were not that dissimilar from those preferred by early automobilists protecting their eyes from uptossed dirt and stones. Purdy Opticians in Manhattan offered a plastic-frame type (made in Italy) for $15 and a rimless version (from France) for $17.50, and claimed to have sold the First Lady her wraparounds. When the store ran an advertisement featuring Jackie in their sunshades, the White House protested to the New York Better Business Bureau, arguing that likenesses of the country's First Family cannot be used to endorse a product. Though Purdy withdrew the ad, Jackie herself, by wearing the wraparounds, had already set off a craze for wearing sunshades— even in the absence of solar glare.

As millions of Americans were purchasing cheap plastic wraparounds, Foster Grant, searching for a way to boost profits, gambled that there existed (or could be created) a market for brand-name sunglasses. "We chose to put the emphasis on *glamour,*" said advertising director Mauri Edwards, whose early advertisements featured Peter Sellers, Elke Sommer, and Anita Ekberg discreetly camouflaged behind Foster Grants. Suddenly sunglasses, made stylish by the First Lady, made costly by Madison Avenue, were a status symbol. By the end of the decade the name Foster Grant was part of the American idiom, a trendy synonym for sunglasses regardless of the manufacturer.

Nehru Jacket

Jawaharlal Nehru was the first prime minister of independent India, from 1947 until his death in 1964. He established parliamentary government, was idolized by his countrymen, and for his peaceful resistance to British rule became an icon for young American pacifists early in the Vietnam era. In fact, everything Indian was exalted by the Sixties counterculture—**patchouli oil, incense, paisley-printed fabrics, weighty mandala medallions hanging from the neck**—which cherished Eastern philosophy for its de-emphasis on materialism and emphasis on peaceful resistance to oppression. Nehru favored a lapel-less jacket with a small stand-up collar, never imagining the garment would launch an American fashion craze three years after his death.

As pop culture legend has it, entertainer Sammy Davis Jr., performing in London, purchased the kind of lapel-less jacket then worn by the Beatles and hippies and dressed it up with a turtleneck shirt and a heavy gold chain and medallion. He called it his "guru coat." The Indian garment might never have made the transition from the hippie subculture to the world of mainstream fashion had French designer Pierre Cardin not been present at a party for Sammy Davis. Cardin modified the button-down-the-front jacket, and his name gave the style cachet. For the brief period from 1967 to 1968 major retailers across America featured Cardin-styled Nehru jackets, often in Sixties colors and trendy bold prints.

Sports figures helped popularize the garment among men not usually given to trendiness. New York Jets quarterback Joe Namath wore a Nehru, accessorized with love beads, as he prowled the Manhattan nightclub scene; Boston Red Sox slugger Ken Harrelson owned a powder-blue Nehru; Detroit Tiger pitcher Denny McLain boasted a $3,000 white broadtail Nehru made from the pelts of prematurely born Asia Minor lambs. Sammy Davis claimed to have a closet full of pastel-colored "guru coats," though he wore a tasteful tweed Nehru to the 1968 funeral of Martin Luther King Jr. The cover of Sears's 1969 summer catalog featured a "Perma-Prest" Nehru for children from its Winnie-the-Pooh collection—a clear sign that the trendy garment was by then terminally overexposed.

Edwardian Look.   In fact, that summer, the simplicity of the Nehru look was already being supplanted by the richness of the ersatz Edwardian style. Stockrooms began to pile up with unsold Nehrus, and one menswear chain, Harris and Frank, tried to cut their losses by sewing collars and lapels on the jackets, converting them into Edwardian suits.

Short-lived as the Nehru style was, it influenced men's fashions for the next decade. The Nehru jacket convinced fashion designers that the times were sufficiently ripe with revolution that American men by the millions were willing, if not eager, to abandon conventional attire for styles that made statements. Expressed in economic terms, the love generation was discovered to have commercial clout. The Nehru is said to have paved the way for acceptance of wide-lapeled jackets, acid-colored neckties, colored and patterned dress shirts, and . . .

Bell-Bottom Pants

The pants, which flared out at the bottom like a bell, were a fashion steal from the traditional navy uniform. For a time the attire was called sailor's pants—and worn with a sailor's navy-blue peacoat. The bohemian counterculture statement became a trendy fashion among adults wishing to ditch the "square" Ivy League look of chinos for the low-on-the-hip, broad-belted bells. If Sammy Davis Jr. became the celebrity champion of the Nehru jacket, Sonny and Cher took bell-bottoms to fashion's far-flung extreme with fancy ruffled cuffs. The style, called elephant bells—because the flare-out from the knee down could accommodate the leg of a pachyderm—carried over into the Seventies, giving men and women in silhouette a shape that would in time be an embarrassment even to remember. The vogue of gigantic bell-bottoms died slowly, a form of cultural extremism favored by Elvis Presley right up to his final stage performances.

Tie-Dye Fabrics

The fabric coloring process known as tie-dye originated in China in the sixth century, and many of the world's museums display examples of the art from ancient times. The Chinese twisted and knotted silk and cotton cloth into intricate folds such that during the dyeing process various parts of the fabric absorbed different intensities of color. Tie-dye garments were worn only by priests and the wealthy, and certain patterns and colors indicated the wearer's social rank.

The process existed in virtual obscurity in the Western world until hippies in San Francisco's Haight-Ashbury district began to tie-dye every garment that would absorb color. Tie-dyed clothes, in swirling collages of hues and "exploding" designs, first became the hippie's uniform, then a mass cultural fashion phenomenon. At the height of the craze in the late Sixties, major manufacturers offered lines of tie-dyed bedsheets, throw rugs, and curtains, as well as T-shirts and tank tops. Fashion designer Halston dressed a host of celebrities in expensive tie-dyed blouses and scarves, and Liza Minnelli was clad in Halston tie-dyes when she opened her 1970 show at the Waldorf.

Tie-dye was an eye-catching statement inexorably linked to the popularity of hallucinogenic drugs, the two sharing a sensory imagery. Because the coloring process was easy and inexpensive to execute, tie-dyed fashions became the hippie's trademark, and a large part of the vogue's pleasure was in creating one's own vibrant designs. When lengths of fabric were knotted off at intervals, the bunched area would not absorb colors when dipped into kitchen pots of boiling dye. The end result was radially streaming bands of color interspersed with milky white streaks. Items were repeatedly dipped in different colors to create more hallucinogenic garments.

It is said that there were more tie-dyed clothes at the 1969 Woodstock "happening" than were produced throughout the ancient Chinese dynasties. A centuries-old statement of social status had been turned on its head to symbolize discontent with a society engaged in a questionable war and caught up in what was touted to be the dawning of an "Aquarian" culture. By then, though, Burlington Industries was mass-producing tie-dyes for mainstream America, Macy's devoted aisles to the multicolored garments, and *Newsweek* columnist Stewart Alsop ribbed the fashion and what it once stood for: "It costs a bit more, but the more affluent young revolutionaries can now buy their pants pre–tie-dyed . . . These pants—and much else besides—make it a little difficult to take the youth revolution so solemnly as it was once taken."

Go-Go Boots

One indelible image of the Sixties is that of the go-go girl dancing in a suspended cage at a chic nightclub, scantily clad in a miniskirt and gleaming white leather mid-calf boots. The boots were a French import, created specifically to be worn with a miniskirt, but the broad-heeled footwear in virgin vinyl became a separate craze, outliving the short skirt.

The first French boots—some fur-lined, others fringed at the top—arrived in the United States mid-decade and were immediately labeled hot. At first they were most visible at West Coast discotheques like Los Angeles's trendy Whiskey A Go-Go, ranked by *Esquire* magazine in 1965 as the hottest club in the country. While the club featured performances by the likes of Johnny Rivers and the Doors, men of all ages shoved their way inside to see the dancing go-go girls, protectively caged in glass-walled booths. Look but don't touch was the message, and soon, with the assistance of an NBC prime-time hit called "Hullabaloo," which highlighted go-go girls, the mid-calf footwear caught on with women around the country.

What Sammy Davis was to the Nehru jacket, what Sonny and Cher were to bell-bottom pants, pop singer Nancy Sinatra was to the vinyl footwear. Through her smash single, "These Boots Are Made for Walkin'," which sold nearly 4 million copies and was the nation's number one single in late February 1966, she became synonymous with the fad. Touring to promote the record, she carried 250 pairs of go-go boots—and, believe it or not, she had a significant influence on current pop star Madonna: "My first pop idol was Nancy Sinatra," the material girl confessed to *Spin* magazine in a 1985 interview. "Nancy Sinatra with go-go boots, miniskirt, and fake eyelashes. She was cool."

Granny Dresses

Long dresses dowdy enough for a grandmother to favor became the unlikely fad for a generation of American teenaged girls bent on being different. The granny dress craze is said to have originated on a popular Los Angeles teen dance show, begun by a group of girls rebelling against the miniskirt. The young dancers rummaged in their parents' attics for "granny" wear, or made their own fuddy-duddy garments, never thinking that what was intended as a one-time statement would turn into a counterculture costume. A week after the TV show aired, girls throughout California, then beyond, had become their own seamstresses, stitching up one garment more dowdy than the next. When *Teen* magazine touted the dresses as hip and offered instructions on how to make them, designers saw profit in the decidedly anti-fashion fashion. Thus at the hands of Seventh Avenue dress makers, the American fashion scene was revisited by the Gibson girl look of the Gay Nineties. The granny dresses that hung on the racks of the nation's retailers were more stylish than the first crude versions, but they too were offered as an alternative to the miniskirt look, which simply did not look good on every woman. For a time mid-decade the two fashions hotly competed. But ultimately the allure of bare leg won out; the mini survived, and even enjoyed a renaissance.

Ben Franklin Specs

At the same time young women were wearing granny dresses, American teens of both sexes became enamored with granny spectacles, also called Ben Franklin specs after the statesman who popularized wire-rimmed bifocals. The fad for half-frame glasses, whether one's vision needed correction or not, originated not as part of London's mod scene led by the Beatles, as is commonly believed, but with a popular California rock band called the Byrds. Though Beatle John Lennon is best remembered as a wearer of granny glasses, the Byrds, whose music combined folk lyrics with electric rock, had a large West Coast following.

The group scored a number one hit, "Mr. Tambourine Man," in June 1965; it was a seminal record. "Before the Byrds recorded Bob Dylan's song," writes pop music chronicler Fred Bronson, "there was folk music and rock music. Electrifying Dylan's song, the Byrds created an amalgam of folk rock music that influenced and spawned a generation of musicians." The band's lead guitarist and singer, Roger McGuinn, took to wearing small, rectangular, dark-lens glasses in performance for the practical reason of protecting his eyes from the glare of stage lights. His California fans adopted the eyewear as an affectation. When McGuinn appeared on the coast-to-coast "Ed Sullivan Show" in the tiny frames, as well as on the cover of his hit record album "Turn, Turn, Turn," a nationwide teen craze was hatched. McGuinn's idea was copied by John Lennon and Bob Dylan. At the height of the short-lived craze, *Newsweek* featured a photograph of a girl in granny glasses in an article claiming that America was in the grip of a teen culture that showed no sign of abating in the near future.

Super Ball

In 1965 McGeorge Bundy, special assistant to President Lyndon B. Johnson for national security affairs, would retire to the basement of his Washington, D.C., home after a taxing day at the office and bounce a small, dense ball—that in size and color resembled a plum—against the walls to relieve tension. In the streets of the capital, as well as those across the nation, millions of children bounced the same "physics-defying" Super Balls, which, remarkably, rebounded almost 100 percent; that is, dropped to the ground from shoulder height, the high-potency plaything nearly returned to its starting point. The super-sensitive sphere, manufactured by Wham-O of San Gabriel, California (producers of the hula hoop and the Frisbee), could ricochet at highly unpredictable angles. McGeorge Bundy was not the first Washington official to be enthralled with a season's hottest toy: In the Gay Nineties, senators retired from their chamber to play the then-trendy game of Pigs in Clover (see page 27).

The creator of Super Ball was chemist Norman Stingley of the Bettis Rubber Company of Whittier, California. Experimenting with high-resiliency synthetics, Stingley concocted a compound he called Zectron (primarily polybutadiene, with sulfur as a vulcanizing agent), which when molded into a sphere under high pressure outbounced in height and duration more conventional balls. Dropped from five feet, a tennis ball bounces for only about ten seconds. A Super Ball bounces for about sixty seconds. Wham-O sold the toy mid-decade for 98 cents, from which Stingley earned a penny royalty on each ball—and the pennies quickly piled up.

At the fad's height, Wham-O's factories were molding 170,000 Super Balls a day. Adults as much as children became addicted to the ball's remarkable bounce. Psychologists claimed that the ball's high coefficiency for rebound, which let it return to the thrower with a vengeance, allowed for a tension-releasing "war" between the ball and the thrower. So convinced of the benefits of Super Ball bashing, McGeorge Bundy bought sixty of the toys for White House staffers. Floor traders at the country's leading stock exchanges also took their frustrations out on the Wham-O toy. Within six months, the company sold 7 million balls, and the craze lasted well into 1966 before losing its faddish bounce.

Troll Dolls

In 1963 college professors around the country noticed a strange ritual during exam time: Sitting on the desks of understandably anxious students were tiny, pudgy, naked, glassy-eyed imps, with shocks of white sheep's wool hair, flared nostrils and jutting ears; gnomes comical in their ugliness. The troll dolls—originally known as Dammit Dolls after their creator, Danish woodcarver Thomas Dam—were said to bring their owners good luck. Indeed, the press had recently reported that daredevil pilot Betty Miller, who had replicated Amelia Earhart's 1935 solo flight of 7,400 miles, had as her "co-pilot" a troll doll. The country's First Lady, Lady Bird Johnson, let it be known that she owned a troll doll. By the end of the Sixties, the small elves were the second bestselling doll in the country—topped only by their comely antithesis, Barbie.

In the fad's early years, troll dolls were largely the heartthrobs of college and high school girls, who carried them as much for their impish cuteness as for their promise of good luck. As the craze spread, trolls in various sizes became the mascots of sports teams, and the gift to give if adorability was one's goal.

The elf actually underwent a transformation as it passed from being Thomas Dam's humble birthday gift to his daughter to being an icon of profitable sentimentality. Dam's original wooden doll, for instance, was naked and embodied as close as he could carve the cute-ugliness of the mythic forest elves of Scandinavian folklore, which served as his model. The gift caught the attention of a Danish toy shop owner, and soon indigent Thomas Dam, who'd carved the doll because he couldn't afford to buy his daughter a present, was in the toy business—convinced that elves really did bring good fortune.

When Dammit Dolls first arrived in the United States in the early Sixties, they were faithful replicas of Dam's original. But as their popularity spread, their cuteness became increasingly more calculated. Available as "adult" trolls ($5.95) or diminutive "baby" trolls ($1.95), they and their nakedness were clothed in diapers, dresses, and even formal wear; their white hair was dyed trendy psychedelic colors; and they were accessorized with miniature props such as ironing boards and motorcycles. Eventually they could be purchased at truckstops and greeting card shops in a stance with arms outstretched and mounted on a pedestal bearing the come-on "I Love You This Much." Or "Forgive Me." Thomas Dam's Dammit Dolls had become, as Bette Davis once said in a different context, cheap sentiment. To collectors, Dam's simple originals are the only genuine troll dolls. And true to their good luck legend, they are currently worth $100 each, with the price rising.

Slot Cars

The hobby of racing mini plastic vehicles called slot cars, which can achieve speeds of 600 miles an hour *at scale,* took the country by thundering storm in the early Sixties, suggesting at the height of the craze that slot car racing— performed on platforms not unlike those set up for model trains—might surpass bowling as the nation's favorite family sport.

By mid-decade an estimated 3.5 million Americans were slot car racers. The country had more than five thousand racing clubs and a score of slot car newsletters, and the toys were a multimillion-dollar industry. Adult males were reveling in a second boyhood. Slot car racing teams formed at many of the country's leading universities, including Princeton, Yale, and Penn State, and, as fads go, the mini cars drew unprecedented press when newsman Walter Cronkite admitted being a slot car fan, and Attorney General Robert Kennedy raced a model car on its slot track during dedication ceremonies of the John F. Kennedy Park in Washington, D.C. Slot cars were a fad with a diverse following.

Origin.   Model car racing dates from turn-of-the-century England. British cars then were larger and slower than the lightweight plastic slot versions later developed in America—which sold for from $3 to $8 a model. Nearly exact replicas of actual racing cars, the slots derived their name from the small projection under the car's nose that was inserted into a groove, or slot, of the racing track. The cars were electrically powered by brushes that made contact with metal strips on the course. A hand-held rheostat allowed a racer to "up" the current, and correspondingly the vehicle's speed. Operating the models at high speeds around hair-raising curves required a degree of skill, since a car could easily slip from its slot and careen into a wall. Aurora Plastics Corporation introduced the first tabletop racing kits around 1959, which included 2-inch cars on HO-scale track, selling from $20 to $40. By 1963 slot cars were a $100 million business, having overtaken electric trains in sales.

Fans paid painstaking attention to the detailing of their racing cars. Many slot car buffs drilled holes in the chassis of their models to lighten the vehicle and achieve even greater speeds. Whereas a platform track in one's basement was limited in size, those set up at special slot car centers offered courses more than 225 feet long, sporting figure eight and clover leaf track designs. You could rent an hour of track time in the Sixties for about $1.50, and if you did not own a slot car, you could rent one for 50 cents.

Occasionally special deals were struck between slot car manufacturers and real car companies. When the Ford Mustang was introduced in 1964, Aurora realeased its own plastic replica, which with sales exceeding a million in 1965 became the company's biggest selling model ever. As a nationwide craze, slot cars were derailed around 1967 by competing fads of that period. But as a hobby, the racing sport still exists.

Skateboards

To present the full evolutionary picture: Roller skates date back to the 1700s, the "wheeled feet" being the novel idea of Belgian musical instrument maker Joseph Merlin. Skateboxes arrived about fifty years later, when clamp-on style roller skates were attached to a wooden orange crate to make a scooter. The modern phenomenon of skateboards has its roots in California in the early Sixties, when ocean-wave surfers, wishing to stay fit and maintain a competitive edge while not riding frothy white crests, attached skate wheels to surf boards to become "asphalt surfers."

As a complementary aside: Wave surfacing itself was first reported in 1771 by British explorer Captain James Cook, who to his amazement witnessed Polynesians riding waves on slats of wood: "Most perilous and extraordinary," he scribbled in his ship's log, "astonishing, and scarcely to be credited"— something that could certainly be said of the acrobatics of skateboarding.

The California surfing set held a monopoly on skateboards until around 1963. By then, several entrepreneurs had realized that millions of young people landlocked from coastal areas, or driven from the ocean by winter weather, were potential asphalt surfers. The first mass-market skateboards were about two feet long, composed of wood or hard plastic, and with a track of wheels on the underside that allowed the rider to use knees and body weight to steer, re-creating the surfing experience. In 1965 manufacturers sold more than $30 million worth of asphalt surfboards.

The singing duo of Jan and Dean enjoyed a smash single that advised, "Grab your board and go sidewalk surfin' with me." Another line of the million-seller song popularized the phrase "asphalt athlete": "Get your girl and take her tandem down the street / Don't you know you're an asphalt athlete?"

Safety. From the start it became apparent that the greatest drawback to asphalt surfing was injury by way of bruises, broken bones, and concussions — something Captain James Cook could certainly have appreciated. After more than a score of serious accidents, and two deaths resulting from the collision of California skateboarders with California motorists, the state's medical association officially proclaimed the nascent sport "a new medical menace." (A few years earlier the same group had issued a less severe warning about the fad of spinning hula hoops.) As the skateboard craze spread eastward, accompanied by casualty statistics, the National Safety Council alerted parents of the frequency with which young skateboarders were colliding with trees, cars, bicyclists, and pedestrians. New Jersey, New York, and Massachusetts banned skateboards from major thoroughfares, and legislation was considered that would force skateboarders to wear protective helmets. By the late Sixties it was apparent that passion for the sport was not about to abate, and manufacturers, keeping a pulse on profit, began to design safer boards.

An Olympic Sport?   A breakthrough came in 1973 with the introduction of urethane wheels; earlier, harder wheels offered poor traction, and a pebble could suddenly turn a high-speed rider into an airborne projectile. The new wheels, credited to California inventor Frank Nasworthy, allowed a rider to skirt corners at breakneck speeds, cut sudden sharp angles, and scale walls using centrifugal force as a booster. The use of fiberglass also made boards lighter and more manageable, improving safety.

As skateboards moved out of toy stores and into sporting goods shops, their prices rose to as much as $200. Simultaneously, a new breed of asphalt surfer emerged, one more daring in execution of stunts, and willing to don a helmet, knee pads, and elbow protectors. The safety paraphernalia alone created a multimillion-dollar industry. A decade after mass-market skateboards were introduced, the hobby-turned-sport was a half-billion-dollar business. Champion skateboarders—having dreamed up stunts such as the "Gorilla Jump," "Flip Kick," "Coffin" (executed flat on one's back, arms crisscrossing the chest), and the "One-wheel Peripheral Commitment" (to which one is inextricably committed once the feat is begun)—had their own skateboard parks, with high, arching obstacle courses on which to perform daredevil feats "scarcely to be credited." The fad of the Sixties and the Seventies died down in the Eighties, but across the nation there exist adherents of the sport who are arguing for its acceptance into the Olympic Games.

GI Joe Doll

As shocking as many men may find this fact, the macho military toy beloved as GI Joe was developed in the early Sixties, by Stanley Weston, as a boy's substitute for the then-popular Barbie doll, which Weston believed little boys across the country were playing with surreptitiously—not so much for Barbie's fabulous furs and heels, but because of her all-too-adult-shaped body. Simply put: Weston felt that the only thing guaranteed to wean boys off Barbie's breasts was a war toy. Debuting at the 1964 Toy Fair, the soldier GI Joe—then a foot-tall infantryman dressed in World War II fatigues and accessorized with rifle, flamethrower, and demolition gear; he could also be dressed as a sailor, a marine, or a pilot—intrigued male buyers. In its first year on the market, the military doll (later reintroduced as a series of smaller flexible arm-and-leg combat figures with names like Hot-Shot and Recoil) generated sales of $17.5 million.

From the numbers, one would have to assume that Stanley Weston (licenser for such later fad items as Alf, Couch Potatoes, and Nintendo) had grasped the dynamics of the young male psyche. Weston also turned on its head the toy industry maxim that boys would not play with dolls. The original GI Joe, made in Hong Kong, was definitely a doll, a fact recognized by the U.S. Customs

Service when it insisted the American distributor, Hasbro, pay the 12 percent tariff on "dolls" as opposed to the cheaper 6.8 percent duty on "toys."

In the minds of many, though, Hasbro had turned boys' thoughts away from sex (Barbie) and toward violence (Joe). "The doll's appeal," admitted one Hasbro marketing executive, "was violence . . . It was evident that the most popular G.I. Joes were the more militant ones. The marine sold best, and after him, the soldier." As the Vietnam War escalated in the Sixties, all war toys came under public attack, and a new edition of Benjamin Spock's *Baby and Child Care* condemned toy guns and dolls like GI Joe. By 1967 toy store orders for GI Joe had halved, and inventory piled up at Hasbro's Pawtucket, Rhode Island, factory.

Desperate, Hasbro redesigned Joe in 1969 as a "global adventurer" hunting for lost treasure and exotic wild animals. Despite the fact that the doll still bore the unmistakably military name of GI Joe, its new nonwar image, achieved through a change in costume and accessories, was enough to cause a modest upswing in sales. The new Joe no longer blew the head off a native but offered him a handshake. Ironically, docile Joe, despite his macho GI sobriquet, was far too mild-mannered to please many fathers who, as a Hasbro executive lamented, "grumble that they will 'never let my kid play with a doll.' " It seemed that in the minds of many fathers, Hasbro, by stripping Joe of his bayonet, had turned a hero into a wimp.

Buttons and Bumper Stickers

"Make love, not war." "Draft beer, not boys." "Tune in, turn on, drop out." Many of the most nostalgic slogans of the Sixties came not from the era's radical leaders but from the lapel buttons worn by their millions of followers. "Hire the morally handicapped." "America has gone to pot." "Kill a Commie for Christ." The human chest became a billboard for ideas radical and revolutionary, and young people festooned with buttons became "walking graffiti." It was the protesters' way of wearing their hearts on their sleeves.

The button craze followed on the heels of the early Sixties mania for car bumper stickers—which, because older people owned cars, were usually more conservative: "God bless America." "Support your local police." The button was the hippie's equivalent of the bumper sticker. Buttons cost pennies, and were passed around as often as a marijuana joint. If the slogan was not against war, it was in favor of sex: "Cure virginity." "If it feels good, do it." "Lay, don't slay." "If it moves, fondle it." And there was the out-of-the-closet homosexual's button: "Love is a many-gendered thing."

As the craze spread into the Seventies, and across middle America, one wore buttons not so much for the espousal of a cause but because it became the in thing to do. Consequently, slogans got sillier: "J. Edgar Hoover sleeps with a nightlight." "Mary Poppins is a junkie." Later, sex teamed up with environmentalism: "Save water, shower with a friend." In June 1970, California's Zodiac Killer, who claimed to have killed ten people, wrote to newspapers that he'd blow up a school bus unless city officials distributed "zodiac buttons" about him: "If you don't want me to have this blast . . . I would like to see some nice zodiac buttons wandering about town . . . It would cheer me up considerably . . . Thank you."

Origin. Buttons were not new in the Sixties. In 1896 the first celluloid buttons appeared as part of the year's presidential campaign between McKinley and Bryan. Celluloid was a relatively new material, and laying it over a printed piece of paper atop a metal disc made for a novel and durable memento—and it was an effective way of showing one's political affiliation. During the Twenties, tin lithographed buttons were the rage in political campaigns.

But it took the turbulent times of the Sixties to transform campaign buttons into badges for all kinds of laurels and laments. A New York store owner was arrested for selling obscene buttons, of which the most printable read "Pornography is fun." Many high schools in the country banned the wearing of buttons. As the button craze was dying out in the mid-Seventies, President Gerald Ford had tens of thousands of red "WIN" buttons printed to support his Whip Inflation Now program—he'd have done better having the slogan printed on **T-shirts,** because, at the time, they were the newest manifestation of walking graffiti.

Water Beds

In 1968 California furniture designer Charles Prior Hall was attempting to construct a supercomfortable chair, filled with liquid starch, that would conform to a body of any shape. Popular at the time was **vinyl bean-bag furniture** (which Hall found too stiff for his liking) and **air-inflated balloon chairs** (which Hall felt were *too* soft). His own Incredible Creeping Chair—so named because it was supposed to slowly envelop and caress the sitter—was made of vinyl and filled with 300 pounds of liquid starch. As he sat in his creation, he was not so much caressed as devoured by the wraparound blob. It wasn't until Hall literally lay down on the job that he realized liquid-filled furniture ideally should be in the flat shape of a bed.

After a few nights' sleep on an experimental water bed, Hall concluded that water got uncomfortably cold. The mattress became an ice pack. So he designed a heater for the bed. Then a patch kit for repairing leaks. By 1970 he had perfected, to his own standards, what would become known as the water bed.

With the dawning of the Age of Aquarius (Latin, "the water carrier"), a bed of water seemed suitably in tune with the times. The beds first appealed to two diverse sectors of society: members of the counterculture and the jet-setting superrich. *Playboy* publisher Hugh Hefner installed a lavish king-sized model in his Chicago mansion. Las Vegas hotels made them features of their luxury suites.

Most of middle America, though, worried about the potential problems of having two tons of water in a second-floor bedroom. Indeed, *Good Housekeeping* did not give its seal of approval to the beds; instead, it related nightmares of owners whose floors had collapsed under the weighty beds, and whose electrical circuitry had shorted out because of leaks. These fears were further fanned by popular accounts in newspapers which focused on horrors Charles Hall never imagined: A balcony holding a water bed and two coupled lovers collapsed, crushing the pair fatally close; a water bed being filled in a Californian's terraced backyard broke away and under its own momentum careened down the lawn like a run-amok steam roller flattening . . . Well, the stories, tragic truth or amusing fiction, entered the realm of urban legends.

Charles Hall was lucky that counterculture followers, who on the average could not afford water beds, were on the wane when he patented his invention in 1971. On the rise were Seventies singles, who had both the money and the free-wheeling lifestyle to make the most of a bed called "Pleasure Island" that responded to your every movement. Ironically, Hall's quest for a comfortable easy chair to snooze in produced the preeminent sex symbol of the swinging singles era, a bed to do everything in except sleep. Advertising slogans like "Love in Liquid Luxury" and "The Ultimate Wet Dream" did not trouble Charles Hall; he'd become a multimillionaire.

Disposable Diapers

"Here today, still here tomorrow" is the modern environmentalist's slogan for the kind of disposable diaper Procter & Gamble introduced in 1961 under the name Pampers. That year, disposables captured only one percent of the market; in 1990 they accounted for 85 percent of the $3.5 billion diaper industry. Expressed another way, about 8 million American babies under the age of thirty months wear disposables, accounting for the 15.8 billion diapers tossed in the garbage each year. In the Sixties, though, no one dreamed that one day diapers would be overrunning landfills, a bane of the environment.

Pampers and its competitors seemed like Mom's way to join in the decade's cultural revolution. Teens were being told by Timothy Leary to "turn on, tune in, and drop out," clothing styles were changing yearly, hair was growing longer, social concepts became more radical, music headed toward acid rock, and where was the American mom? Changing diapers, soaking diapers in bleach, hanging diapers on the clothesline to air dry. It was a tedious, hated, thankless task, and Pampers seemed a welcome solution. *Consumer Reports,* surveying the competition—which included Sears's Honeysuckle Disposables, Montgomery Ward's Tiny World, Johnson & Johnson's Chux (rated as a "best buy Christmas gift" for the infant who has everything), Curity, and Perma Throwaway Diaper—advised its readers, "You probably won't want to use them regularly, but there are times you won't want to be without them."

The postwar baby boom had produced a diaper problem. In many suburban neighborhoods, diaper services sprang up in the Fifties, offering mothers one alternative to coping with the sixty to one hundred diapers dirtied weekly by an infant in the first year of life. The services were expensive, as were early disposable diapers: about a dime a diaper—though by 1966 a Pampers diaper was down to 6 cents. Early disposables were not perfectly absorbent or leakproof. Yet they filled a need. What's more—though the cost of diaper services also dropped—disposable diapers became the trendy, modern way to treat an age-old problem. By the Seventies, when Pampers were worn by almost half the babies in America, image-conscious parents automatically reached for Pampers; a cloth diaper seemed not only inconvenient but stodgily old-fashioned.

In the late Eighties, concerns about solid wastes and the environment—and the fact that a disposable diaper takes about four hundred years to decompose—would cause a rebirth in cloth diapers. Diaper services that managed not to go bankrupt in the Sixties and Seventies had waiting lists of families begging for their door-to-door service. Today a diaper service typically costs $11 a week, in contrast to about $15 for disposables. An idea of the Fifties, nearly killed off by a trend for anything throwaway, is making a strong comeback.

Lava Lites

At a 1965 home furnishings show in Hamburg, Germany, Chicago businessman Adolf Wertheimer stood in awe as he watched the eerie bubbling of colored wax inside a new lamp designed by Englishman Craven Walker. Then called an Astrolight, it was unlike any other lamp in the show; unlike any lamp Wertheimer had ever seen. Within its long, cylindrical, vaselike shape, a bright yellow, semisolid wax (heated by a coil) slowly erupted upward in bulbous bursts, hovered at the top like a psychedelic cloud, then, cooling, drifted downward to the lamp's base, which contained a concealed 40-watt bulb. The cycle continually repeated.

The phlegmatic Astrolight did not throw off enough illumination to read by; it was intended to be Sixties decorative— providing a "meditative" atmosphere in an otherwise darkened room. Wertheimer thought the oozing wax resembled lava, and he envisioned the light as a lucrative fad in America. Under an agreement with Astrolights, he formed Lava-Simplex Internationale and began to market the product as Lava Lite. The lamp that had "a motion for every emotion" held particular appeal for a culture engaged in sit-ins, love-ins, and interpersonal encounters of the closest kind. By the end of the decade, 2 million Lava Lites decorated college dormitories—and American living rooms; for watching a giant glob of canary yellow or electric blue "lava" burst into dancing globulettes became an amusement to be enjoyed stoned or straight. Or as a Sixties architect expressed the lamp's appeal: "Its kinetic sculptural elements constitute an intriguing relief from hard-edged rectilinearity."

The hard-edged reality of trendiness reared its head by 1975. Lava Lite sales had plummeted, and the artifacts could be had for a few dollars at flea markets across the country. Though sales picked up in 1985, the year pop technology's bubbling masterpiece celebrated its twentieth anniversary, the Lava Lite seems destined to be no more—or no less—than a nostalgic *objet d'art* from the Age of Aquarius.

Black Lights

In the LSD atmosphere of the Sixties, many attempts were made to visually re-create (or reinforce) the phantasmagoric splendor, or horror, of a drug trip. Phosphorescent posters, which revealed their cryptic images only when exposed to ultraviolet light, proved to be one enhancer of the psychedelic experience. That fad kicked off a craze for fluorescent "black light" bulbs, which by the late Sixties were casting their eerie glow in dormitory rooms around the country.

Black lights became an essential accessory of hippie decor. And they were necessary to reveal the fluorescent-painted pop posters of San Francisco artists like Wess Eilson and Stanley Mouse. Clothes washed in detergents containing fluorescent phosphates glowed ghoulishly under black lights, and a simple white T-shirt or white dress, under a black light, assumed a pearly-white iridescence of the kind Francisco de Goya spent a lifetime trying maddeningly to capture on canvas. Teeth brushed with toothpastes containing monofluorophosphate radiated an radiumlike luminescence, the envy of any Dracula.

You bought black light bulbs in "headshops," along with fluorescent paints, dyes, and crayons. Trendy nightclubs and restaurants installed black light motifs to satisfy patrons who worshipped druglike effects (for the eerie glow did nothing to enhance the look of food, and it annoyingly highlighted specks of white lint on dark clothes). Discos in the next decade popularized flashing black light strobes both to approximate the LSD experience and to provide an atmosphere for whatever drug-of-the-month the dancers had swallowed. Black lights are still sold in many poster stores, but from the standpoint of faddishness their glow long ago dimmed.

Day-Glo Colors

In the Thirties, two Cleveland chemists, brothers Joe and Bob Switzer, experimenting with fluorescent dyes and resins, concocted pigments of incandescent-like color, in shades of orange, yellow, and red. An object painted with the pigments glowed in ordinary daylight as if it contained its own hidden source of illumination—hence the name Day-Glo.

The Switzers' paints were first used to create the illusion of luminescence under conventional stage lights in magic shows. Largely a stage special effect in the Forties, in the next decade Day-Glo colors became a gimmick for marketing laundry detergents by creating a package design that seemed to luminously shimmy on supermarket shelves. Not until the pop art/op art of the Sixties and Seventies did Day-Glo colors become a fad to be painted on everything from ties to guitars, from posters to the side panels of vans. In an era when art was meant to scream out its intent, Day-Glo paints became *the* medium for the message. Since then, Day-Glo–like dyes have become a standard in ski wear and brightly colored summer swimsuits, in addition to being found in all sorts of plastics, writing inks, and, of course, highlighting Magic Markers. Day-Glo was a fad of the Sixties that did not fade away, but became commonplace through its ubiquitousness.

Woodstock Music and Art Festival

In the year 1969—which witnessed the landing of Neil Armstrong and Buzz Aldrin on the moon, the rise in sports of the Miracle Mets, the watershed of gay liberation with riots at the Greenwich Village club of the Stonewall, and the death at Chappaquiddick of Ted Kennedy's passenger Mary Jo Kopechne—the event that came to label a decade and a generation was the wacky musical gathering of four hundred thousand hippies, on August 15, 16, and 17, on a farm 40 miles from Woodstock, New York. It's been said that the success behind the Woodstock happening was its spontaneity, which created a mania akin to magic.

It was a miracle that the happening even happened. As planned by its organizers, the three-day concert, billed as "Three Days of Peace and Music"—featuring performances by the Who; the Grateful Dead; Janis Joplin; the Jefferson Airplane; Crosby, Stills & Nash; Jimi Hendrix; and others—was to raise money for a recording studio in Woodstock, New York. By the time tickets were printed for the Woodstock Music and Art Festival (yes, it was also to be about arts and crafts), backstage bickering and financial hardships had forced the gathering to accept the offer of Max Yasgur to hold the concert on his farm in White Lake for a fee of $50,000.

Woodstock, though, was more than music. Despite the outstanding performances by super groups, the real star of the show was the free-wheeling, drug-taking audience of scruffy, half-naked, "tripping" teenagers. There were so many bad LSD experiences that "acid tents" were erected to assist "brothers and sisters" through their hallucinogenic travail. A memorable, often-quoted line from the event is: "That brown acid now circulating among us is not specifically too good." Amid the deafening music and drug-induced confusion, hippies deputized themselves into the "Please Force," marked with armbands bearing a winged pig.

The true miracle of Woodstock was that in a mob of four hundred thousand long-haired, often-naked people, swallowing acid and policing themselves, not a single violent incident erupted. One person died of a drug overdose, another was hit by a tractor, but supposedly not one hippie raised an unwashed hand against another. And when local folk heard that the hippies were running out of food—mostly peanut butter and jelly sandwiches—they boiled farm eggs and made sandwiches, which were flown in by helicopter. The event that labeled the Woodstock generation has been called, in earnest and out of sarcasm, "the greatest outdoor party since the miracle of the loaves and fishes."

Why, under such adverse conditions as too little food, excessive drugs, overcrowding, and underwashing, was there no violence?

Champions of the Woodstock experience claim that the attendees were deeply peace-loving flower children. Critics, on the other hand, point to the mind-altering drugs, arguing that it is hard to riot when you can't determine whether you're staring down at your own wiggling toes or a nest of vipers. More than twenty years after the festival, a sign by the roadside marks the acres of field that were the site of communal living on a monumental scale. The 300-foot long stone wall that once separated the field from the road is gone, dismantled piecemeal over the years by tourists and visitors making pilgrimages to the Aquarian Age shrine. Woodstock never made a profit for its promoters, but it assumed a permanent place in the social history of the century.

DANCE CRAZES

The Solo Era Is Born

As the phenomenon called the generation gap burgeoned in the Sixties, "oldsters" (over age thirty) were pitted against youngsters in the arenas of politics, sexual freedom, popular music, and dance. If "Do your own thing" was a motto of the youth movement, in dance it assumed the additional meaning of "going solo," a shift from *pas de deux* to *pas de un*. Partners never touched in dance crazes like the twist, mashed potato, watusi, Bristol stomp, frug, swim, monkey, pony, jerk, cool jerk, shaggy dog, skate, funkie, boogaloo, and hitchhiker—such a welter of weird and wacky steps that in the Sixties America was called "the land of a thousand dances."

The dance that touched off the solo era—and opened the decade of the Sixties—actually started in 1959, when groups of black teens dreamed up torso-twisting steps to a record, "The Twist," by the Detroit group of Hank Ballard and the Midnighters. It would take another year for an ex-chicken plucker named Ernest Evans to rerecord the hit under the name Chubby Checker (he took the name Chubby because his hero was Fats Domino), and for the song to debut on "American Bandstand," where it was introduced to the white audience through regulars Justine and Bob and Kenny and Arlene. Twisting time was here.

Twist

As Chubby Checker himself explained the dance revolution inspired by the twist: "Before the Twist came, everyone danced together. I'm the guy that started people dancing apart. I taught the world how to dance as they knew it today."

Checker also offered a description on how to twist: "It's like putting out a cigarette with both of your feet, and coming out of a shower and wiping your bottom with a towel to the beat of the music. It's that simple."

While Chubby Checker started teens twisting, he graciously acknowledged, "I couldn't have done it without Dick Clark and *American Bandstand*. That show was just *it* in those days." From being performed on television and by teens, the twist quickly swept the country. "As anyone knows who has seen a magazine or newspaper or television set lately," said *TV Guide*, "there is a dance craze—a torturing, dervishlike tribal rite—rampant in the nation." At Manhattan's posh Four Seasons restaurant, 250 prominent New Yorkers gyrated the night away at a benefit "twist party." In October 1961, Ed Sullivan invited Chubby Checker to sing and dance "The Twist" on his nationwide TV show. Dance historians searching for roots of the Twist in past crazes offered the shimmy and the black bottom (see pages 134 and 135), and pointed out that a song popular in the first decade of the century included the line "Mama, mama, where is sis? / Down on the levee doin' the double twis'." That might be twisting history a bit.

Peppermint Lounge and Peppermint Twist. The twist became a dance craze with adults due primarily to its acceptance by the jet set. And it happened in a once-seedy, hole-in-the-wall hangout of pimps and prostitutes reincarnated through a cheery coat of paint and countless lights as the Peppermint Lounge. What "Bandstand" was to teens, the Peppermint Lounge, on Manhattan's West 45th Street, was to the likes of Elizabeth Taylor and Richard Burton, Jayne Mansfield and Judy Garland, debutante Charlotte Ford and international playboy Porfirio Rubirosa. Garbo got in but didn't dance. The Arthur Murrays endured the deafening music and sweating crowds "to learn and not to teach" the dance; weeks later their nationwide chain of dance schools advertised "Six easy Twist lessons for $25." Writer Truman Capote twisted, as did composer Leonard Bernstein.

The Peppermint Lounge was the Studio 54 of the Sixties. Hopeful dancers were even insulted at the door and turned away. A hit song, "The Peppermint Twist," by Joey Dee and the Starliters—for three weeks in January 1962 the country's number one single—celebrated the lounge and the dance craze. *Saturday Review* claimed the twist was "a valid manifestation of the Age of Anxiety"; *Time* found it to be "a replica of some ancient tribal puberty rite." But from the standpoint of social dance it was important for two reasons: It was the first dance strictly for the individual and not the couple, and it was the first dance of the rock era to cross the generation gap from teen to trendy adult.

The dance craze spawned song and movie spin-offs. The Isley Brothers released **Twist and Shout,** Gary "U.S." Bonds had a hit in **Dear Lady Twist,** Sam Cooke had a bigger hit in **Twistin' the Night Away,** and Elvis Presley got in on the mania with **Rock-a-Hula Baby.** Columbia Pictures rushed out *Twist Around the Clock,* while Paramount competed with *Hey Let's Twist.* For a time it seemed everyone was "twisting the night away"—except twist detractor former President Dwight D. Eisenhower, who, at the dedication of the Eisenhower Library in May 1962, asked the assembled crowd, "What has happened to our concept of beauty and decency and morality?"

Once unleashed, though, the twist was like a twister that could not be stopped, sweeping not only across the country as a dance craze, but ripping through the decade as a revolutionary force in dance. The solo, hip-swiveling dance is credited with being the progenitor of such kindred fads as the mashed potato, pony, mess around, majestic slop, jerk, swim, mule, fly, Philly dog, watusi, and hully gully—as we're about to see. Like the twist, these other dances involved pantomime—and in that sense they were not unlike the wave of mimic animal dances of the Teens and the Twenties.

Mashed Potato

Popular in 1961 and 1962, the mashed potato was a variation of the twist, and like that dance it also contained the so-called lasso movement; as a social dance manual explains: "Stand with one foot in front of the other about 6 inches apart and transfer weight from one foot to the other with basic Twist step; at the same time circle right hand overhead with pantomine of a lasso." The "mashed" part of the dance involved alternating swiveling ball-of-foot movements, as if you were mashing potatoes. The dance inspired several songs, including the country's number one single for two weeks in October 1962, "Monster Mash," by Bobby "Boris" Pickett and the Cryptic Kickers. Interestingly, Pickett first titled the song "Monster Twist," but by the time he got around to recording it the mashed potato was more *au courant* than the twist, so he made the title trendier.

Swim

Popular in 1964, the swim reflected the growing interest in the sport of surfing, which had already spread eastward from Southern California. Surfing was performed on ocean waves, later on skateboards, then on the dance floor in the form of the swim—with feet largely stationary and arms pantomiming a breast-stroke, backstroke, crawl, or dog paddle, or outstretched to simulate floating. It was popularized by Bobby Freeman's "swim" songs, in which a dancer boogalooed while doing the above, and pantomimed submerging the body underwater while pinching the nostrils closed.

Watusi

As in the swim, the stance of the watusi dancer is that of a surfer balanced on a moving surfboard. A springing action of the knees, together with a half-arc hip sway, creates an illusion of the ocean's ups and downs a surfer would experience while riding a wave. The dancer's hands and arms are free to imaginatively perform any action associated with, in any way, the surf; as a dance manual lists: "Picking up a sea shell and listening to it; looking around and beckoning for other surfers or swimmers; fishing; shaking water out of an ear; losing balance." The actions are limited only by one's imagination. The dance was popularized by the Orlons' hit single "Wah-Watusi."

Monkey

Popular in 1963 and 1964, this mimic dance was characterized by its tugging hand motions, as if hauling oneself, hand over hand, up a rope—or climbing, monkeylike, up a coconut tree. A monkeying purist, when reaching the top of the tree, shakes free a coconut that hits the dancer's head, then the dancer shrugs and drinks coconut milk. Next, the dancer locates a banana tree, climbs it, peels a banana, and eats it. The steps are as diverse as one's familiarity with wildlife series. A hit single in 1963, based on the dance, was "The Monkey Time," by Major Lance.

Freddie

In England, a former milkman, Freddie Garrity, with several friends formed a band called Freddie and the Dreamers. When Freddie performed on stage, he had a habit of jumping wildly up and down—thus, with imitation the sincerest form of flattery, teens immortalized the antsy singer with a dance. Freddie's own instructions on doing his dance: "You have to lift up your feet like a farmer in boots coming out of a muddy field." Few Americans teens shared that rural experience, but they proved to be proficient imitators. As a dance craze, its popularity was more fleeting than most.

Jerk

Popular mid-decade, the dance was not recommended for anyone suffering from a back problem, for it involved snapping your upper body forward with a jerking motion while the lower portion remained relatively stationary. Unlike the mimic dances of the decade, the jerk was a radical departure in that it became the individual dancer's spastic response to the rhythmic beat of the accompanying music. It could be danced, according to an instruction manual, "while moving forward and backward in a basic pattern lifted from the Charleston of the Twenties"—though one doubts that teens in the Sixties realized this is what they were doing. It was danced to the Capitols' hit single "Cool Jerk."

Frug

The frug of the mid-Sixties is thought to have originated among college students at Syracuse University in upstate New York. Like the twist, it was predominately a hip-swiveling dance, but with one defining hand motion: the thrusting of a wagging index finger above the head, high into the air, as in a scolding gesture. The action was strongly reminiscent of the finger thrusting done in the Thirties fad dance the Lambeth Walk (see page 156). By adopting, instead, a thumb-out hitchhiking gesture, one did the **hitchhiker.**

Shaggy Dog

Also called the **skate,** this dance of 1966 involved continuously shaking your head from side to side as if seized with Parkinson's palsy. The foot movements were those of skating in place. "The entire dance," writes one authority, "was strongly reminiscent of Little Eva crossing the ice in the main ballet sequence of *The King and I.*"

As Dick Clark points out in *Rock, Roll and Remember,* in the late Sixties, as the hippie movement gained momentum nationwide, dances ceased to have faddish names. Many teens, stoned, simply moved to music impressionistically, or exhibitionistically, as the drug they were on inspired them. Comments one historian: "Dancers swayed, swooped, and twirled in a formless expression of ecstasy or sometimes despair." Not until the popularity of disco music in the Seventies did dances again have catchy names—but by then the era of a thousand dances had ended.

POPULAR SONGS

Land of a Thousand Tastes: From the Beatles, to the Beach Boys, to Motown, to Folk, to Acid Rock

If in the Sixties America was a land of a thousand dances, it was also a land of diverse musical tastes. Never had popular music been so popular, and, more significantly, never had a decade's music (like the decade itself) been so schizophrenic: Opening with solo voices from the Fifties of Connie Francis, Pat Boone, Ricky Nelson, as well as the mellow "surfin'" sounds of the Beach Boys; visited mid-decade by rock groups from a foreign shore (the Beatles, the Rolling Stones, Herman's Hermits), as well as from the Supremes with their Motown sound; awakened by the "folk" songs of Simon and Garfunkel, Joan Baez, and Bob Dylan; shaken by the acid rock of the counterculture's the Grateful Dead, the Jefferson Airplane, the Who, Janis Joplin, Jimi Hendrix, and all the unconventionality that blossomed from the Haight-Ashbury district in San Francisco and the Fillmore East in New York. By the end of the decade, with the opening of the musical *Hair*—with its hints of nudity and promise of the Age of Aquarius—rock music, an enigma to many a few years earlier, had made it big in establishment theater.

The fact that the Sixties was a period that bridged relative tranquillity and profound unrest was clearly reflected in its popular songs. As a people, Americans were shaken by a plague of political assassinations (of John Kennedy, Martin Luther King, Robert Kennedy, Medgar Evers), and an out-of-control conflict in Vietnam, the first war in modern American history to meet with widespread domestic hostility. From the standpoint of popular music, no other decade in this century experienced such extremes in popular tastes. In a period of a little more than ten years, popular music went from doo-wop and bee-bop, to the "good vibrations" of the California surfin' sound, to Detroit's sleek Motown beat, to Beatlemania, to Rolling Stones mayhem, then into a shrill, manic acid scream. More astonishing still, much of this dramatic diversity co-existed, proving that American had become a land of a thousand tastes.

Hits by the year:

It's Now or Never: 1960

As the decade opened, black music producer Berry Gordy created his Motown music factory in Detroit, Michigan, and a star-making factory it would be: Smokey Robinson and the Miracles (1960), the Marvellettes (1961), the Supremes and Dionne Warwick (1962), Martha and the Vandellas and Stevie Wonder (1963), the Temptations and the Four Tops (1964), a solo Diana Ross (1967), the Jackson Five (1969). But high on the charts that first year of the decade were names familiar from the Fifties.

Elvis Presley had at least four hits: **Stuck on You,** "It's Now or Never," **Surrender,** and his inimitable version of a 1926 Al Jolson success, **Are You Lonesome Tonight?** This last, a sentimental ballad (a hit in 1959 for Jaye P. Morgan), was Presley's fourteenth number one single, and he recorded it in a marathon two-day session, which also produced "It's Now or Never," a song with a melody based on the 1899 Neapolitan tune "O Sole Mio." Older Americans were acquainted with Jolson's and Morgan's "Are You Lonesome," and with versions of "Now or Never" by Mario Lanza (as "O Sole Mio") and Tony Martin (as "There's No Tomorrow," 1949), and these two Presley records helped broaden the King's appeal across America.

Easy-listening radio stations continually played "It's Now or Never." It became, according to *The Guinness Book of Music,* Presley's biggest-selling single, with more than 20 million in sales in America and abroad. Presley later admitted that "It's Now or Never" was also his own personal favorite. During its eight weeks at the top of the charts, it outsold the season's novelty hit **Itsy Bitsy Teenie Weenie Yellow Polka Dot Bikini;** fifteen-year-old Brenda Lee's tearful **I'm Sorry,** a tale of unrequited love; Roy Orbison's hauntingly beautiful **Only the Lonely;** and **Alley-Oop** by the Hollywood Argyles, a group that would never again score a major hit.

Cathy's Clown: 1960

Though Don and Phil Everly had already had nine consecutive hits, "Cathy's Clown," number one in the spring of 1960, proved to be their biggest seller ever, a smash simultaneously in America and England. The brothers had recently signed with a new record label, Warner Brothers, and were under pressure to come up with a hit. At home in Nashville, Tennessee, Don wrote the song about his high school girlfriend and their traumatic breakup, which left him feeling "like Cathy's clown"—an incident that had happened five years earlier. In record store sales, the single received strong competition from Johnny Horton's **Sink the Bismarck,** Connie Francis's **Everybody's Somebody's Fool,** and the most successful instrumental single of the rock era, **Theme from A Summer Place,** by Percy Faith.

"Theme" had been at the top of the charts itself for nine straight weeks. The music was composed for the 1959 film *A Summer Place,* which starred teen heartthrobs Troy Donahue and Sandra Dee. It would again become a hit in a 1976 disco version. For 1960, *Billboard* voted "Theme" as the year's number one single.

Off-Broadway, a small-scale musical with a score by Tom Jones and Harvey Schmidt opened; it would prove to be the longest running production in American theater history: *The Fantasticks.* It produced two hit singles: **Try to Remember** and **Soon It's Gonna Rain.**

Runaway; Running Scared; Runaround Sue; Run to Him: 1961

In this year when the movie *West Side Story* opened with Natalie Wood and Richard Beymer, and when surfing caught on as the newest California craze, the word run seemed to dominate the musical charts. Roy Orbison claimed to have written his "Running Scared" in five minutes; one writer called the song a "paranoid bolero with Mexican strings." Del Shannon (born Charles Westover) wrote his strange-sounding "Runaway" after hearing another musician play an "unusual chord change" (from A-minor to G) on an organ. Dion DiMucci based his "Runaround Sue" on a real-life runaround named Roberta, though, coincidentally, he married a woman named Sue. It shot to the top of the charts in early winter, displacing the dance-craze hit single, **Bristol Stomp,** by the Dovells. And Bobby Vee had a hit with "Run to Him." All of these "run" songs came on the heels of Johnny Preston's 1960 hit, **Running Bear,** about an Indian of that name in love with Little White Dove.

Fifties teen idol Pat Boone had a comeback hit in **Moody River,** and Ricky Nelson, also big on Fifties charts, made a comeback with **Travelin' Man** (which he'd introduced on his family's TV show, "The Adventures of Ozzie and Harriet")—it followed a string of four singles that had failed to make it into the top ten. As it turned out, the record's flip side, **Hello Mary Lou,** also became a hit. Climbing the charts to number one in the spring, "Travelin' Man" passed the Shirelles' **Mama Said** (number four). The Shirelles, the recording industry's first female rock group to enjoy a hit single, had begun 1961 with the country's top popular song, **Will You Love Me Tomorrow,** which would become a classic oldie but goodie—in fact, that phrase was in the title of one of the summer's most popular ballads, **Those Oldies But Goodies (Remind Me of You),** by Little Caesar and the Romans. Two hits of a different nature were Lawrence Welk's plucky harpsichord rendition of **Calcutta** (originally written in 1958 and titled "Tivoli Melody"), and duo-pianists Ferrante and Teicher's version of **Exodus,** from the score of the successful movie.

Other hits of '61:

Neil Sedaka's **Calendar Girl;** Connie Francis's **Where the Boys Are,** from the classic teen film that made Fort Lauderdale, Florida, a mecca for college students and a nightmare for locals; the Shirelles' **Dedicated to the One I Love;** a 1934 Rodgers and Hart tune, **Blue Moon,** which the Marcels spiced up to "Dang-a-dang-dang, ding-a-dong-ding, Blue Moon"; Dee Clark's **Raindrops;** two twisting favorites: Gary "U.S." Bonds's **Quarter to Three** and Bobby Lewis's **Tossin' and Turnin';** Ray Charles's **Hit the Road Jack;**

Jimmy Dean's **Big Bad John;** and, out of the Motown factory the Marvelettes' **Please Mr. Postman,** the first number one single for the Detroit label. To the pop music scene, it was a sure sign that the Motown sound was here to stay.

The year's bestselling novelty song was The Tokens' **The Lion Sleeps Tonight,** number one in the country at Christmastime. The group took a South African folk song, "Wimoweh," which had been a hit for Miriam Makeba in Zulu a decade earlier, and added English nonsense lyrics. After listening to the playback at the recording session, the five male singers were so embarrassed with their novelty song that they considered not releasing it. In fact, they put a Portuguese folk song on the flip side, thinking *it* would have greater success. "The Lion" enjoyed three weeks at the top of the charts.

Sherry; Big Girls Don't Cry: 1962

The year was notable for the introduction of the first practical electronic keyboard for synthesizing music: the Moog, invented by Robert Moog—the nonacoustical music maker kicked off a new era in sound and composition. In England, a group that had changed its name from the Quarrymen, to the Moondogs, to the Moonshiners, to the Silver Beatles, was performing at a jazz club as the Beatles; John Lennon and Ringo Starr were twenty-two years old, Paul McCartney twenty, and George Harrison nineteen. In America, **The Peppermint Twist,** by Joey Dee and the Starliters, supported one dance craze; Dee Dee Sharp's **Mashed Potato Time** supported another, as did Chubby Checker's **Limbo Rock** and Little Eva's **The Loco-Motion**—America was then, as we've seen, the land of a thousand dances.

The Four Seasons, featuring the stratospheric falsetto lead vocals of Frankie Valli (born Francis Castelluccio), began a remarkable string of eleven top ten records between August 1962 and November 1965 with "Sherry," a song that took its composer, Bob Gaudio, only fifteen minutes to write: "Some songs take forever. 'Sherry' was a quickie," he admitted. On the charts, it shot ahead of Neil Sedaka's **Breaking Up Is Hard to Do,** and remained number one for five weeks, finally pushed to second place by Bobby "Boris" Pickett's eerie-sounding **Monster Mash.** Two months later, the Four Seasons had another number one hit with "Big Girls Don't Cry," a title taken from a line uttered by Clark Gable in a movie. Both "Big Girls" and "Sherry" had been recorded at the same studio session, released just weeks apart. In November 1962, "Big Girls" beat out Elvis Presley's **Return to Sender** and the Crystals' **He's a Rebel.**

The Four Seasons would start off the new year of 1963 with another hit, **Walk Like a Man,** making them the first group to have three consecutive number one singles. As one of their critics wrote, "The group used the production techniques of the uptown rhythm and blues formula in an uninspired, if not awkward manner. Their widespread success reflected the state of the early 1960s market." And partly because the Four Seasons' songs so perfectly reflected the pop tone of the early Sixties, all are nostalgic classics today.

Other hits of '62:

Doo-wopping Gene Chandler began the year by turning his musical obsession for a scale-climbing "duke, duke, duke" phrase (initially conceived as "doo, doo, doo") into the top-selling **Duke of Earl,** which beat Dion's **The Wanderer.** The young daughter (Shelley Fabares) on the popular TV sitcom "The Donna Reed Show" surprised viewers with her number one single **Johnny Angel,** which for two weeks in April outsold Elvis Presley's **Good Luck Charm** and Roy Orbison's **Dream Baby.** Mid-spring, the Shirelles were at the top of the charts with their pleading **Soldier Boy:** "In this whole world, you can love but one girl / Let me be that one girl / For I'll be true to you." The hit was hastily written in the studio and recorded in the final minutes of a session. For a time it outsold Ray Charles's **I Can't Stop Loving You,** which became a summer ballad favorite, along with Bobby Vinton's **Roses Are Red.**

That summer of 1962, the United States launched the world's first communication satellite, Telstar, and British composer/recording engineer Joe Meek turned the event into a number one Christmastime record, **Telstar,** a commemorative instrumental by the Tornadoes that featured otherworldly-sounding special effects. It was the top-selling record as the year closed, beating Marcie Blane's **Bobby's Girl.** The Tornadoes became the first British group to have a number one hit in the United States—a phenomenon that was soon to become commonplace.

Deep Purple; Blue Velvet: 1963

The fall of 1963 saw two old standards climb to the top of the pop charts: "Blue Velvet" (a hit in 1951), by Bobby Vinton, and "Deep Purple" (from 1934), by Nino Temp and April Stevens. In fact, the latter song was number one that tragic week in November when President John F. Kennedy was assassinated in Dallas, plunging the nation into deep mourning.

For Bobby "Roses are Red" Vinton, "Blue Velvet" came four months after his hit **Blue on Blue,** causing people to refer to early 1963 as his "blue period"—the singer actually recorded an album of all "blue" songs, including "Blue Moon," "Blue Hawaii," and "Am I Blue."

The year had begun with Sidney Leibowitz (professional name, Steve Lawrence) scoring a number one hit with **Go Away Little Girl**—which was soon displaced by the Rooftop Singers' **Walk Right In,** a tune from the Thirties. Peter, Paul, and Mary had a 2-million-selling record in Bob Dylan's **Blowin' in the Wind** (a hymn for the rebellious anti-war, social-protesting generation), while another Paul teamed up with a woman named Paula for their smash duet **Hey Paula**—for a time the song outsold the Drifters' **Up on the Roof.**

In late winter, teens were dancing to Ruby and the Romantics' **Our Day Will Come** and the Chiffons' **He's So Fine.** Come spring, Lesley Gore proclaimed **It's My Party (and I'll Cry If I Want To),** Little Peggy March swore **I Will Follow Him,** Andy Williams confessed **Can't Get Used to Losing You,** and Peter, Paul and Mary scored a hit with **Puff (The Magic Dragon).**

Surfin' Singles.   Surfing was a summer fad, and riding the waves was glorified in the Beach Boys' **Surfin' USA** and Jan and Dean's **Surf City.** The idyllic sound called surf music was big from coast to coast—and inland. "The Beach Boys," wrote one critic, "spoke directly from adolescent experience . . . unlike the contrived teen idols [of the Fifties]. Their songs flowed from the life around them. They presented plausible visions of surfing, cars, dating, the beach, the drive-ins and rock 'n' roll." Within less than two years, the group scored with seven smash albums of smooth harmony and surf-riding rhythm. From **I Get Around** (1964), to **Help Me Rhonda** (1965), to **Good Vibrations** (1966), their music, writes one reviewer, "presented adolescent summertime freedom in an affluent, consumer society," and within "their vision of carefree bounty lay optimistic *joie de vivre* which became the foundation for the love generation." As a group on the pop music scene, though, they (and practically everyone else) would soon be eclipsed the arrival of the Beatles.

Other 1963 hits included **So Much in Love, Easier Said Than Done,** Elvis Presley's **(You're the) Devil in Disguise,** and **Fingertips—Pt. II,** by twelve-year-old Little Stevie Wonder, who'd blossom into a major recording artist of the next decade.

As Christmas approached, an unlikely pop performer named Sister Luc-Gabrielle from Belgium's Fichermont Monastery recorded an album of modest songs loved by her order. One, **Dominique,** released in America, eulogizing the founder of the Dominican order, Saint Dominic, climbed to the top of the charts and made "the Singing Nun" an overnight sensation. She appeared on the "Ed Sullivan Show," and Hollywood rushed out a movie of her life starring Debbie Reynolds. By that time, Sister Luc-Gabrielle had left the convent and returned to private life, a well-to-do secular woman.

I Want to Hold Your Hand; She Loves You; Can't Buy Me Love; Love Me Do; A Hard Day's Night; I Feel Fine: 1964

The year 1964 belonged to the Beatles, from the January release of "I Want to Hold Your Hand" to the December hit of "I Feel Fine"—the group had six top-selling records in twelve months. There were other number one singles: Bobby Vinton's **There! I've Said It Again,** the Kingsmen's **Louie Louie,** the Dixie Cups' **Chapel of Love,** Barbara Streisand's **People** and Dean Martin's **Everybody Loves Somebody,** the Four Seasons' **Rag Doll,** Roy Orbison's **Oh, Pretty Woman,** and the Shangri-Las' **Leader of the Pack.** But no group stirred up such passionate fan pandemonium as the Beatles, stars overnight gone supernovae.

The only group to approach the Beatles in multiple hits in 1964 was The Supremes: **Where Did Our Love Go** (number one in August), **Baby Love** (number one in October), and **Come See About Me** (number one in December).

The Beatles with Ed Sullivan.

Beatlemania.   The pop musical milestone began on Friday, January 14, 1964, with the release of "I Want to Hold Your Hand." It shot from number forty-five to number one in two weeks, and remained at the top of the charts until March 21, only to be replaced by "She Loves You." The Beatles' February appearance on the "Ed Sullivan Show" yielded one of the highest Nielsen ratings in television history, with an audience of 73 million people.

By April the group claimed five top spots on the singles charts (with "Can't Buy Me Love," "Twist and Shout," "She Loves You," "I Want to Hold Your hand," and "Please, Please Me"), in addition to scoring with two albums: "Meet the Beatles," the bestselling album in music history up to its time, and "The Beatles' Second Album," which soared to the number one position in two weeks. Before the start of summer in 1964, *fourteen* Beatles songs appeared in *Billboard*'s "Hot 100," and the lads from Liverpool accounted for *60 percent* of the industry's single sales. With unparalleled frenzied fanaticism, Beatlemania had swept the nation.

Not that the mania had been entirely predictable. A little more than a half year earlier, Dick Clark, at the behest of a friend, had "tested" a British hit, "She Loves You," on "Bandstand's" Rate-a-Record. The first teen reviewer said, "It's all right, sort of Chuck Berry and the Everly Brothers mixed together. I give it a 77." As Clark himself later related: "The second grumbled, 'It's not that easy to dance to—I give it a 65.' The third said, 'It doesn't seem to have anything special, but it is kind of catchy. The best I can give it is a 70.' " The single that would help usher in a new era in popular music—as well an invasion of British performers—scored an average of seventy-one. "Score a miss for Rate-a-Record," Clark later cracked.

Following the Fab Four's stupendous debut on the Sullivan show, "Bandstand" moved quickly to telecast a "Beatles tribute" program. Across the nation teens copied the Beatles' monkishly long hairstyle, their collarless jackets, and their leather boots called Beatle boots. "The importance of 'I Want to Hold Your Hand' cannot be overestimated," says Fred Bronson in *The Billboard Book of Number One Hits.* "Next to [Bill Haley's] 'We're Gonna Rock Around the Clock' (which ushered in the era of mainstream rock and roll in 1955), it is the most significant single of the rock era, permanently changing the course of music. The influence of the Beatles has been felt by every artist who has followed them." Rebels or heroes, they became overnight pop culture icons. As John Lennon humbly perceived, "Yeah, well, if there is a God, we're all it."

Adults who found Beatle music hard on the ears, could, in 1964, buy the cast album of Broadway's two newest musicals: *Fiddler on the Roof,* starring Zero Mostel, which would run for 3,242 performances, and *Hello, Dolly!,* with Carol Channing as the matchmaking Dolly Gallagher Levi, which by the time it closed after 2,844 performances had featured an all-black company starring Pearl Bailey.

(I Can't Get No) Satisfaction: 1965

The Beatles weren't any less of a phenomenon in 1965—with such smash hits as **Eight Days a Week, Ticket to Ride,** and **Yesterday.** They were joined on America's shores by Herman's Hermits with **Mrs. Brown, You've Got a Lovely Daughter** and **I'm Henry VIII, I Am,** and Petula Clark with **Downtown.** The Supremes, too, scored big with **Stop! In the Name of Love, Back in My Arms Again,** and **I Hear a Symphony.** But an emerging new phenomenon—also part of the British invasion—was the Rolling Stones.

With Mick Jagger in the lead, the group scored an American hit with the sexually suggestive "(I Can't Get No) Satisfaction," number one in July 1965. Four months later they were again at the top of the charts with the belligerent **Get Off My Cloud.** "The Rolling Stones is not a bunch of cleancut youngsters out to make a buck from innocent kids," reviewed *Variety.* "The group is tapping on the Freudian vein of savagery in their parlay of frantic guitars and drums, wild vocals, bumps, grinds and twitches." Hardly a parent disagreed. The Rolling Stones moved rock closer to the realm of social protest that was then familiar in the folk music of Joan Baez, Bob Dylan, and Peter, Paul, and Mary—though doing so through radical rebellion rather than folk's peaceful political activism.

I Got You Babe: 1965

Salvatore Phillip Bono and Cherilyn Sakisian LaPierre were a Sixties music phenomenon of another sort entirely. A "doltish Sonny" and a "cloddish Cher" is how one writer described the early duo, who were at the top of the charts in August 1965 with "I Got You Babe," a funky love song in the form of mutual pledges of allegiance that introduced the pair of flower children to nationwide fame. Much to the astonishment of everyone associated with the record (except the writer, Sonny Bono), it sold 3 million copies and became an anthem for the emerging love generation.

The couple met in a Hollywood coffee shop when Cher was only sixteen. They quickly parlayed their hit single into a string of bestselling records, two films (*Good Times,* 1967; *Chastity,* 1969), and a top ten network TV series before they split up to pursue separate careers—Cher, of course, to emerge as a multitalented pop entertainment icon. In 1990, *Premiere* magazine named Cher—who dropped out of high school in 1962 and moved in with Sonny, eleven years her senior and married to another woman—"the most powerful actress in Hollywood," commanding $5 million a film. Sonny had aggressively pushed "I Got You Babe," which Atlantic Records executives felt was "a piece of fluff," with one thought in mind. "From the day I met Cher," he later

Sonny and Cher.

confessed, "she wanted to be a star. And I wanted to make her a star. I knew that song was going to do it." Cher herself later admitted that in the Sixties, "Hippies thought we were square; squares thought we were hippies."

Writer Stephen Farber sums up America's obsession with Sonny and Cher in the late Sixties and early Seventies: "Their appeal seemed to lie in domesticating the hippie movement for middle America. With their bell bottoms and paisley outfits, not to mention their reputation for casual living arrangements, they embodied the freewheeling style of the Flower Power generation." Yet— and this is a vital difference: "They neither took drugs nor endorsed radical politics. They were nonthreatening, easier for middle America to embrace than farther-out artists like Janis Joplin or Jim Morrison." In a nutshell: Sonny and Cher packaged the radical Sixties as showbiz.

The Sounds of Silence; Monday Monday; Mellow Yellow; Cherish: 1966

It was the year that soft rock (later known as MOR—for middle-of-the-road) emerged as a top-selling brand of popular music. Protest without harshness. Lyrics were "meaningful." Once protest music began to receive widespread attention, it underwent a mellowing to make it more palatable to urban audiences and thus render it more commercial. This softening and melding into rock, writes one critic, "freed folkies from the concerns of authenticity and liberal expectations . . . which, in turn, reoriented the rock genre as well."

The new sound first appeared on the charts in January 1966 with Paul Simon and Art Garfunkel's "The Sounds of Silence," an event that astounded everyone associated with the making of the record, especially writer Paul Simon. The duo—who had first appeared on the stage together in a sixth grade production of *Alice in Wonderland,* Simon as the white rabbit, Garfunkel as the Cheshire cat—were already popular on the Greenwich Village coffee house circuit. For a time their first blockbuster single beat James Brown's **I Got You (I Feel Good)** and the Byrds **Turn! Turn! Turn!.** The Mamas and the Papas were at the top of the charts with "Monday, Monday" in May, Donovan in September with "Mellow Yellow" and **Sunshine Superman,** and the Association in October with "Cherish."

Aside from soft rock, Nancy Sinatra scored a single's hit and started a footwear fad with **These Boots Are Made for Walkin'** (number one in February), while her father, Frank, enjoyed a number one single in July: **Strangers in the Night.** The following year father and daughter teamed up for **Somethin' Stupid.**

Popular music of still a different vein came in a cascade of hits from two Broadway successes of the year: *Cabaret,* yielding **Willkommen** and **Why Should I Wake Up?,** and *Man of La Mancha,* with **The Impossible Dream** providing hit singles for Jack Jones and Roger Williams.

Other hits of 1966: **Georgy Girl, A Groovy Kind of Love, Lara's Theme** ("Somewhere My Love"), **96 Tears, Summer in the City, Wild Thing,** the Rolling Stones' **Paint It Black,** the Supremes' **You Can't Hurry**

Love and You Keep Me Hangin' On, and the Four Tops' Reach Out, I'll Be There.

Ode to Billie Joe: 1967

If rock softened and went mainstream in 1966, it journeyed to off-Broadway the following year in the granddaddy of rock musicals, *Hair.* So successful was the production at the New York Shakespeare Festival Public Theater that within a few months the musical about flower power and the dawning of the Age of Aquarius opened uptown at the Biltmore Theater—then blossomed into fourteen touring companies of this landmark show. This was also the year that Aretha Franklin scored a number one hit with her hard-driving Respect, Lulu with the schmaltzy To Sir With Love, and Bobbie Gentry with the enigmatic tale of the "Ode to Billie Joe."

Fans who bought this last hit single puzzled over what Billie Joe McAllister and his girlfriend tossed off the Tallahatchee Bridge. And why the next day he jumped to his death. Radio DJs asked listeners to solve the mystery—which had no answer; though in a 1976 movie based on the song, viewers discover that Billie Joe had thrown his girlfriend's rag doll into the water and jumped because of uncertainty about his heterosexuality. Fans of the record preferred the mystery to Hollywood's solution.

In March of that year Dick Clark introduced two of the first "music videos": the Beatles' films of Strawberry Fields Forever and Penny Lane—never guessing that one day a song video would be as commercially important as the disc itself.

I Heard It Through the Grapevine: 1968

The pop charts were filled with the decade's "regulars" in 1968: Simon and Garfunkel had Mrs. Robinson; Herb Alpert, This Guy's in Love With You; Otis Redding, (Sittin' on) The Dock of the Bay; the Beatles, Hey Jude. Performing on Broadway in *Fiddler on the Roof* was the soon-to-be "Divine Miss M," Bette Midler. Hugo Montenegro had a hit in The Good, the Bad and the Ugly, as did the Lemon Pipers in Green Tambourine, and Jeannie Riley in Harper Valley P.T.A., which made the biggest one-week leap in singles record history: from number eighty-one on the "Hot 100" to number seven—a week later it was the country's number one pop single.

One of the year's biggest hits—and a favorite from the decade of the Sixties—was Marvin Gaye's "I Heard It Through the Grapevine," which one critic claimed is not about saving a love affair but is an "essay on salvaging the human spirit." "The record distills four hundred years of paranoia and talking drum gossip into three minutes and fifteen seconds of anguished soul-searching," says Dave Marsh in *The Heart of Rock and Soul.* Seven weeks at number one, it is the second longest running hit for a Motown single (to be topped only by Diana Ross and Lionel Ritchie's "Endless Love," with nine weeks at the top of the charts). Whereas the dramatic song was known as a Marvin Gaye hit in the Sixties, and a reworked success for Creedence Clearwater Revival in the Seventies, a more recent generation recognizes it from a TV commercial for California Raisins. For Motown in 1968, it was a commercial godsend, becoming part of the company's rich history.

Aquarius / Let the Sunshine In: 1969

In this year when John Lennon married Yoko Ono, the Fifth Dimension enjoyed a smash success with a song from the rock musical *Hair.* "Aquarius / Let the Sunshine In" was only one of four show numbers to climb the charts; the others: **Hair,** an ode to long, beautiful locks; the perky **Good Morning Starshine;** and **Easy to Be Hard.** The play would run for 1,742 performances and spawn a successful 1979 motion picture, and "Aquarius / Let the Sunshine In" became *Billboard*'s second biggest single of 1969.

Other hits from the final year of the Sixties: Creedence Clearwater Revival's **Bad Moon Rising,** the intriguingly titled **A Boy Named Sue,** Eddie Holman's **Hey There Lonely Girl,** Peter, Paul and Mary's **Leaving on a Jet Plane,** and Henry Mancini's **Love Theme From Romeo and Juliet** ("A Time for Us").

BESTSELLING BOOKS

Valley of the Dolls: Number One Fiction, 1966; The Love Machine: Number Three Fiction, 1969

The decade of the Sixties of course had numerous novels more significant than Jacqueline Susann's *Valley of the Dolls* and *The Love Machine* Two carryovers from the late Fifties, Allen Drury's **Advise and Consent** and James Michener's **Hawaii,** the number one and number two bestsellers for 1960. The next year the top three spots were occupied by Irving Stone's novel of the life of Michelangelo, **The Agony and the Ecstasy,** J. D. Salinger's second novel, **Franny and Zooey,** and Harper Lee's Pulitzer prize–winning **To Kill a Mockingbird.** And there were Mary McCarthy's tongue-wagging tale of Vassar alumnae, **The Group** (number two, 1963), John Le Carre's thriller, **The Spy Who Came in From the Cold** (number one, 1964), and Michener's archaeological dig into Israel's past, **The Source** (number one, 1965).

But in terms of media hype and aggressive author publicity, Jacqueline Susann was a new publishing phenomenon—and a harbinger of things to come for turning a glamorously trashy book into a profitable three-ring circus.

Her media blitz for the pill-popping saga of three glamorous women in show biz, *Valley of the Dolls,* prompted even her publisher to remark, "the only thing you could turn on without getting Jacqueline Susann was the water faucet." TV show hosts, usually reluctant to invite novelists for fear they'd ramble on about fiction plots, found Jacqueline Susann's racy talk of real-life scandals (supposedly unrelated to her fictional events) irresistible. "She prowled the media," wrote one observer, "shunning no exposure, however small the station or inconsequential its location." Her trekking paid off: In hardback, *Valley* sold 350,000 copies; in paperback, 22 million. The film version of the book—though savaged by critics (and Jacqueline Susann herself, who said, "The picture's a piece of shit")—grossed $80 million.

For Jacqueline Susann, self-promotion came naturally. She'd begun her professional life as an actress in Clare Booth Luce's play *The Women,* later moved to television with appearances on the "Milton Berle Show" and in a soap opera called "Hearts in Harmony," and at one point hosted her own talk show. But she pined for stardom of the widest sort. Her 1962 "biography" of her French poodle, **Every Night, Josephine!** a commercial success, revealed two things: She could write and, even better, she could promote a book. With *Valley,* four years later, she honed her promotional skills. For her next bestseller, *The Love Machine,* an erotic tale about the behind-the-scenes world of television (of television she said, "You turn it on and it loves you endlessly"), she jetted from talk show to talk show in her private Grumman plane that had "Love Machine" emblazoned on each side. She was something of a book herself: a how-to in the profitable art of self-promotion.

Before her death from cancer in 1974, she enjoyed success with another suggestively titled bestseller, **Once Is Not Enough.** At her funeral a friend eulogized, "She had more imitators in concept and style than any writer I know. But she had no equals"—an assessment hard to fault. In fact, she and her writing style became the basis of the decade's most famous literary hoax.

Naked Came the Stranger: Number Seven Fiction, 1969

The bestseller fiction list was most notable in 1969 not for literary quality but for eroticism: number one, Philip Roth's sex-obsessed comedy, **Portnoy's Complaint;** number three, Jacqueline Susann's *The Love Machine;* number four, Harold Robbins's heavy-breathing **The Inheritors;** and number seven, *Naked Came the Stranger,* a sex-riddled novel supposedly penned by a young Long Island housewife named Penelope Ashe. The book about sex in suburbia sold ninety-eight thousand copies, twenty thousand before the public learned that the novel was the collective effort of two dozen *Newsday* journalists working under the guidance of columnist Mike McGrady, who felt that "inept writing held the key to success."

"I was fed up with people like Harold Robbins and Jacqueline Susann," he later confessed. "I saw the writing that was being accepted and it seemed absurd." So he set out to spoof the genre.

In June 1966 McGrady sent a memo to twenty-four *Newsday* colleagues: "You are hereby invited to become the co-author of a best-selling novel." Following a loose outline conceived by McGrady—about a wife's discovery of her husband's infidelity and her tireless exploits to even the score—each writer was to submit one chapter. "There will be an unremitting emphasis on sex," the memo stated, "and true excellence in writing will be quickly blue-penciled into oblivion."

Crime reporter Bob Greene contributed a chapter about the heroine's involvement with a suburban ganglord. Sportswriter Bob Waters centered his chapter around the heroine and a prizefighter. With the manuscript of purple prose assembled, McGrady persuaded his sister-in-law to pose as housewife-turned-author Penelope Ashe. "I figured if Jacqueline Susann can do it," Penelope told her publisher at their first meeting, "I can do it." With reviews stressing the book's nonstop sex, the hoaxers felt confident they had a bestseller—and for many weeks *Naked Came the Stranger* outsold Susann's *The Love Machine.* It rose to fourth place on the *New York Times* bestseller list, was ranked by *Publishers Weekly* as the seventh bestselling novel of 1969, and became the basis of a successful Hollywood film.

Other highly popular novels of the Sixties: Harold Robbins, **The Carpetbaggers** (number five for 1961) and **The Adventurers** (number two for 1966); Irving Wallace, **The Prize** (number eight for 1962) and **The Plot** (number eight for 1967); Arthur Hailey, **Hotel** (number eight for 1965) and **Airport** (number one for 1968); James Clavell, **Tai-Pan** (number eight for 1966); Ira Levin, **Rosemary's Baby** (number seven for 1967); and Mario Puzo, **The Godfather** (number two for 1969).

Happiness Is a Warm Puppy: Number One Nonfiction, 1963; Security Is a Thumb and a Blanket: Number Two Nonfiction, 1963

In 1962, as a breath of lighthearted relief to such tensions as the Cuban missile crisis and the resumption of atmospheric nuclear tests by both the United States and the Soviet Union, popular "Peanuts" cartoonist Charles Schulz published a Christmastime bestseller, *Happiness Is a Warm Puppy,* which sold 175,000 copies and, more significantly, kicked off a mania for Schulz's spunky characters that would in time spawn a cottage industry. The following year, while *Happiness* rose from number five to number one (selling over a million copies), Charles Schulz published a "Charlie Brown" sequel, *Security Is a Thumb and a Blanket.* Then in 1964 Schulz's cartoon characters were the subjects of two bestsellers, **I Need All the Friends I Can Get** and **Christmas Is Together-Time.** Schulz's titles prompted imitation. "Tonight Show" host Johnny Carson published two books of one-liners with illustrations, titled **Happiness Is a Dry Martini** (number five for 1965) and **Misery Is a Blind Date** (number two for 1967).

There were more significant nonfictions of the decade: William Shirer's **The Rise and Fall of the Third Reich** (number two for 1961); Helen Gurley Brown's liberating **Sex and the Single Girl** (number nine for 1962); Eric Berne's psychologically revealing **Games People Play** (number three for 1965); Masters and Johnson's popular medical work, **Human Sexual Response** (Number two for 1966); and Laurence Peter's witty advice on achieving business success, **The Peter Principle** (number three for 1969). But one nonfiction from the decade was more than a book—it was a frightening warning of encroaching global disaster, which, unfortunately, sold better in the Sixties as a book than as a call for definitive action:

Silent Spring: 1962

Three Sixties bestsellers had a direct impact on current events: Ralph Nader's **Unsafe at Any Speed** forced the automobile industry to begin producing safer cars; Jessica Mitford's darkly satirical **The American Way of Death** lampooned the funeral business in America and compelled it to make changes; and Rachel Carson's ominous *Silent Spring* called dramatic attention to the perils of indiscriminate use of toxic chemicals in agriculture and industry. Carson's book marked the beginning of an environmental consciousness that would not fully blossom until the devastation of the environment became more extensive than any single book, or books, could justly accommodate.

What was silencing the voice of spring, wrote Carson, an eminent marine biologist, was the blanket airplane spraying of vast areas of the country, as well as countless misuses of insecticides and herbicides. The devastation began, she said, following the success of chemical agents on insect control during World War II. By the late Forties, chemical manufacturers and government agricultural agencies were aggressively promoting the use of toxic compounds to exterminate pests and undesirable plants—with little or no understanding, or concern, for the consequences.

For thousands of years people had controlled pests and weeds with nature's own means—compounds such as nicotine and vegetable derivatives lethal to certain insects. In postwar America, though, there suddenly was an arsenal of man-made toxins, such as DDT. This kind of poisoning was unprecedented, as Carson made clear:

> For the first time in the history of the world, every human being is now subjected to contact with dangerous chemicals, from the moment of conception until death. In less than two decades of their use, synthetic pesticides have been used around the world. They have been recovered from most of the major river systems. They have entered and lodged in the bodies of fish, birds, reptiles, and domestic and wild animals so universally that scientists . . . find it almost impossible to locate subjects free from such contamination.

And she sounded the ultimate alarm: "These chemicals are now stored in the bodies of the vast majority of human beings, regardless of age. They occur in the mother's milk, and probably in the tissues of the unborn."

Though her dark picture was primarily about pesticides, explains Robert Downs in *Books That Changed America,* it was part of a larger canvas of environmental pollution from auto exhausts, aerosol sprays, refrigerant gases, and the noxious byproducts from the burning of synthetics. A gentle scientist, she also possessed biting wit: Of the poisons we were spreading unrestrainedly around us she said, "As matters stand, we are in little better position than the guests of the Borgias."

People started to pay attention. Shortly after the publication of *Silent Spring,* the U.S. Public Health Service concluded that pesticides in farm runoffs released into the Mississippi River had killed 10 million fish. Magazines like *Newsweek* and *Time* began to report on environmental damage occurring around the world. *Silent Spring* was an instant bestseller, and it remained on the *New York Times* list for thirty-one weeks, selling a half million copies in hardcover before being issued in paperback.

The book had its critics—the chemical industry. Carson's claim that the industry pushed chemicals on the basis of profit rather than need was vigorously denounced, though not disproved. Chemical executives from Dow to American Cyanamid accused her of gross factual distortions and of whipping up mindless hysteria. To say time has vindicated her vision is more than an understatement.

Her urgent message that carcinogenic chemicals were now everywhere, poisoning the planet and all its inhabitants, was dramatically underscored when, two years after the appearance of *Silent Spring,* Rachel Carson herself died of cancer. She was fifty-six. In a front-page obituary, the *New York Times* called her "one of the most influential women of her time."

TELEVISION HITS

Color Sweeps the Country

Since black and white TV can rarely be seen anymore, it's something of a shock to recall (still more of a shock to learn for the first time) that color telecasts were not commonplace until the mid-Sixties. In fact, in 1965 color exploded all over prime-time viewing hours. Slow to start in the Fifties, color telecasts accounted for only about a thousand hours on NBC in 1960. This doubled to two thousand hours in 1962—which one authority counted as "more than the total of American color motion pictures produced in the previous decade."

At mid-decade, ABC upped its color broadcasts 50 percent; CBS reserved color for specials, and NBC could be thought of as the "peacock" station when it began to boast of being "the full color network." By the end of 1965, 96 percent of NBC's nighttime schedule, as well as all its sports events and specials, were in lavish color—encouraging about 3 million Americans to lay out $500 for a color set, half the price of a color TV a little more than a decade earlier.

By year, here are the decade's most popular shows:

The Andy Griffith Show: CBS Premiere, October 3, 1960

Starring Andy Griffith (as Sheriff Andy Taylor, a widower), six-year-old Ronny Howard (as his son, Opie Taylor), and fidgety Don Knotts (as television's most inept, hypertense, nervous-Nellie deputy, Barney Fife), the homespun rural sitcom took place in the peaceful, crimeless town of Mayberry, North Carolina—that there was a crimeless town anywhere in the country was still credible in the "I Like Ike" innocence that was 1960. Affectionately called "television's most sophisticated rural sitcom ever" (as compared with the cornpone likes of "The Beverly Hillbillies" or "Green Acres"), the show won six Emmys and remained on the air until September 16, 1968—always in the top ten.

The show's strength was in the gentle, understanding, philosophical outlook of its lead, Sheriff Andy. "Though he had a drawl and a down-home manner," writes fan John Javna in *Cult TV,* "he was no hayseed. He was a bright humanist with a badge, enforcing the law by bringing out the best in everybody." With Mayberry (town speed limit: 20 miles per hour) crimeless, the jail never had real prisoners. Its single cell resembled a comfortable living room, in which a temporarily inebriated or rowdy local was more the sheriff's guest. Fidgety Barney saw trouble where it didn't exist, and was forever advising Sheriff Andy to "Nip it in the bud!"—fans of the show counted the number of utterances of the phrase per episode. Episodes centered on the relationships of the sheriff, his deputy, and his son with the cast of citizens of Mayberry—such as Andy's girlfriend, schoolteacher Helen Crump, and Barney's girlfriend Thelma Lou.

Actor Jim Nabors joined the successful sitcom in the spring of 1963 in the role a naive, goofy, lovable gas station attendant, Gomer Pyle. He worked at Wally's Filling Station, and uttered deep-voiced exclamations like "Gaaaw-lee!" and "Shaazam!" and bade everyone a big-grinned goodbye: "Lots of luck to you and yours."

Nabors soon left the program for his own 1964 sitcom, **Gomer Pyle, U.S.M.C.,** as did Don Knotts a year later for his own variety series, **The Don Knotts Show.**

The Griffith show had been created in 1960 specifically for then–movie actor Andy Griffith, who wanted to break into television—and it was conceived by Sheldon Leonard, executive producer of the successful "The Danny Thomas Show." In fact, TV viewers first met Sheriff Andy in a pilot that was telecast as an episode of the Thomas show: "Danny Meets Andy Griffith." Six months later actor Griffith became a TV regular. When he decided to quit the show in 1968, it was rated number one.

Rocky and His Friends: ABC Premiere, September 29, 1959; The Flintstones: ABC Premiere, September 30, 1960

Television executives in 1990 would daringly pit the cartoon "The Simpsons" against the wildly popular "Cosby Show." Three decades earlier, adult and

© 1987 Jay Ward Productions, Inc.
© 1960 Filmtel International Corp.

"Rocky and His Friends."

prime-time cartoons were a new feature on television, the most notable involving the adventures of an impish flying squirrel, Rocky, who sported a pilot's helmet and an elf's grin, and his devoted sidekick, Bullwinkle the moose. "Rocky and His Friends" premiered in late 1959 and was soon retitled "The Bullwinkle Show." Episodes pitted the squirrel and the moose against evil Russian agents Boris Badenov (bad enough for any occasion) and the fatal femme Natasha Fataly. They were in cahoots with Mr. Big, a tiny midget with grand designs.

Another cartoon segment that appeared regularly on the show featured a polite and scholarly dog, Peabody, and his young student friend, Sherman—the two characters time-traveled in their "Way-Back Machine," in clips called "Peabody's Improbable History." Adults loved the show as much as, or more than, children—a signal to producers.

The fall of 1960 saw the second cartoon in prime time, Friday night's "The Flintstones," Stone Age "honeymooners" deliberately patterned on Jackie Gleason's successful "Honeymooners" characters. Fred and Wilma Flintstone were the equivalent of Ralph and Alice Kramden, while their neighbors, Barney and Betty Rubble, were inspired by Ed and Trixie Norton—more or less. The show's gimmick was to feature modern technology in a prehistoric setting, and the Stone Age suburbanites were a huge hit with adult viewers; the award-winning show ran for five year.

Other prime-time cartoons were rushed onto the airwaves: **Alvin and the Chipmunks, Top Cat, Beany and Cecil,** and a takeoff on "Amos 'n' Andy" called **Calvin and the Colonel**—all debuting in 1961.

"The Flintstones."

The next season introduced adult viewers to **The Jetsons,** cartoon cousins to "The Flintstones" who lived in the future. The animated series followed the wacky adventures of "a typical space-age family." The fad for prime-time cartoons soon yielded shows for Mr. Magoo and Bugs Bunny.

Mr. Ed.   A step away from the prime-time cartoon was the 1960 sitcom featuring television's first talking—and wisecracking—horse (voiced by former movie cowboy Rocky Lane). Mr. Ed addressed his wimp-of-an-owner Wilbur in a breathy "Well, come on, Wilbur. Let's go," and he was based on a series of popular films in the Fifties that featured Francis the Talking Mule. The show opened each week with the palomino who played the horse sticking his head through a barn door and greeting viewers with "Hello, I'm Mr. Ed."

Dr. Kildare: NBC Premiere, September 28, 1961; and Ben Casey: ABC Premiere, October 2, 1961

A second vogue in the early Sixties was prompted by the discovery that viewers loved doctor shows. "Dr. Kildare" and "Ben Casey" began in the fall of 1961, airing within days of each other. Dr. James Kildare, played by Richard Chamberlain, became a TV hero, symbolizing President Kennedy's New Frontier philosophy, which called on youth to get involved in shaping the future of the country. Kildare cared. And some critics claimed that the tremendous success of the show was not unrelated to the atmosphere of caring embodied in organizations like Kennedy's Peace Corps.

"Dr. Kildare" came to television after having been an extremely successful series of movies in the Forties. It made Richard Chamberlain the hottest TV idol of the early Sixties. Fan-loving facts that John Javna points out: Richard Chamberlain got more fan mail than Clark Gable did in his prime; the show's theme song became a top ten hit; "Dr. Kildare" comic books sold over 500,000 copies in six months after the show debuted; and the program was so popular behind the Iron Curtain that the Polish Communist party rescheduled its meetings from Wednesday to Thursday so as not to conflict with the Wednesday night telecast.

Whereas Dr. Kildare was a mild-mannered internist at Blair General Hospital, Dr. Ben Casey, played by Vince Edwards, was a brusque and burly neurosurgeon at County General Hospital. Casey "was a MACHO doctor," writes Javna. "His shirt was always open, revealing a thick mat of chest hair." Half humane hero, half sexy truckdriver, Casey would violate any hospital rule to save the life of patient—and plots often revolved around such infractions. For a while, Vince Edwards and Richard Chamberlain vied for TV's biggest sex symbol. Female fans, torn between the gentle Kildare and the gruff Casey, wore oversize buttons to proclaim their devotion.

The Dick Van Dyke Show: CBS Premiere, October 3, 1961

Can you match the catchphrase with the sitcom character: "Oh, Rooob!" "Shut up, Mel!" "Yeccch!" "My Aunt Agnes always says . . ."?

Whenever Laura Petrie (Mary Tyler Moore) was upset at her husband, played by Dick Van Dyke, she'd sigh, "Oh, Rooob!" in this highly successful series, viewed as one of television's classic sitcoms because of its first-rate scripts and actors. The show's setting, fittingly, was behind the scenes of a fictitious TV comedy program ("The Alan Brady Show"), and working with head writer Rob Petrie were writers loudmouth Buddy (Morey Amsterdam) and man-hungry Sally (Rose Marie)—she always introduced homilies with the phrase, "My Aunt Agnes always says . . ." Their office nemesis, and the butt of many jokes, was the producer of the fictitious comedy program, balding and pompous Mel (Richard Deacon), whose reaction to just about anything Buddy did was "Yeccch!" and who endlessly prompted the put-down "Shut up, Mel!" The real show's writer (and director), Carl Reiner, occasionally played the role of Alan Brady.

It was the first television sitcom about people who worked in television, and Carl Reiner, coming off his long association with Sid Caesar, created the series as a vehicle for himself. His producer, however, convinced him that Reiner should be the writer and hand over the on-camera lead to another actor—Dick Van Dyke—so the show's original title, "Head of the Family," was changed to highlight Van Dyke.

The advice, hard to accept, proved to be wise. Once established, the show never fell from the top twenty. The *New York Post* reviewed it as "the best situation comedy on television." The humor grew out of its characters, and the cast performed before a live audience. After 157 episodes, and winning fifteen Emmys, it went off the air in 1966 because the actors wished to pursue other projects—perky Mary Tyler Moore going on to even greater success with her own sitcom in the Seventies (see page 418).

The Beverly Hillbillies: CBS Premiere, September 26, 1962

To the supreme delight of viewers and the august horror of critics, the sitcom about a family of local-yokels, the Clampetts—fresh from their ancestral cabin in the Ozarks, flagrantly resettling in posh Beverly Hills—debuted to foul reviews but high-on-the-hog ratings. The Clampett clan—headed by father Jed (Buddy Ebsen) and Granny Daisy Moses (Irene Ryan)—had struck oodles of oil in the Ozarks, and moved to a mansion at 518 Crestview Drive, Beverly Hills, in a dilapidated flatbed truck with their rickety furnishing, jugs of home-brewed hardstuff, and pocket cash of about 25 million brand new dollars.

The characters were crass and uneducated. They called gourmet food vittles, hung laundry to dry on outdoor clotheslines, called the crystal-blue swimming pool their "cement pond" and allowed the family's barnyard "crit-

"The Beverly Hillbillies."

ters" to use it as a watering trough. Yet they seemed to possess more innate wisdom and common sense than their more conventionally well-to-do neighbors.

The show's immense popularity was due precisely to this clash of cultures: the classic wise-fools and common-sense philosophers pitted against a neighborhood of unprincipled scoundrels and pretentious snobs. The simple folk *were* better, happier people. The hillbilly sitcom also reinforced such appealing homilies as "money can't buy happiness," "money comes with its own kinds of problems," and "innocence triumphs over corruption." "The Beverly Hillbillies" was biblical parable made entertainingly palatable for network profit. And it was funny—throughout its record-breaking nine-year run.

The show's specially composed theme song, "The Ballad of Jed Clampett," made the national charts, while the program itself ranked number one for two consecutive seasons, attracting about 60 million viewers a week. In addition to patriarch Jed and potion-concocting Granny, the clan featured a curvaceous daughter, Elly May (Donna Douglas), the hulking giant of a cousin, Jethro Bodine (Max Baer Jr.), and local banker Mr. Drysdale (Raymond Dailey), who gave his bank's biggest depositors special treatment. The Drysdales and the Clampetts were, in the best of sitcom tradition, next-door neighbors. The show, pure corn (and sponsored by Kellogg's), was so astonishingly successful that it ushered in a wave of country cousin copycats, like "Green Acres" and "Petticoat Junction." The show was last telecast in originals on September 7, 1971.

My Favorite Martian: CBS Premiere, September 29, 1963

If an Ozark clan could find ratings success with the one-joke premise of moving to Beverly Hills, what about a Martian—with alien antennae on his head, and powers of telepathy, clairvoyance, and astral projection—moving from Mars to Earth? Thus debuted in 1963 "My Favorite Martian," starring Ray Walston as Uncle Martin, who in the first episode finds a reporter staring at him and asks, "What are you waiting for me to say—take me to your leader?"

Critics thought the show unendurably silly, but it was a huge success with viewers for three years. Uncle Martin the Martian had always hated Earth, criticizing the planet and its people from episode to episode, and on September 4, 1966, the show's producers let him return to Mars—and commenced reruns.

Bewitched: ABC Premiere, September 17, 1964

Four years into the decade of the Sixties, viewers had seen a hillbilly clan move to Beverly Hills, a Martian come to live on planet Earth, and two witches, benign Samantha Stephens (Elizabeth Montgomery) and her less-benign, witch/bitch mother, Endora (Agnes Moorhead), move into an otherwise normal neighborhood. With the twitch of her nose Sam could do anything, and her doting, goofball husband, Darren (originally played by Dick York), a human advertising executive (no insult intended), was forever beseeching her to forsake the conveniences of witchcraft (like cleaning the house in a nose-twitching instant) for the humdrum life of a hardworking wife. In the course of the show's seven-year run—during which it won three Emmys—Sam and Darren had two children, a witch and a warlock, but what made the high-rated show truly bewitching (for male viewers, at least) was the playful, slow-smoldering sexuality of Elizabeth Montgomery's Samantha.

Viewers also adored Endora. Never approving of her daughter's marriage to a mortal, and especially a bungling one like Darren, she infuriatingly calls him everything but his real name: Dumbo, Darwin, Dum-Dum, Daurwood, Donald—in fact, only once during the show's long run did Endora say Darren, when placed under a spell to be nice to him. Endora never understood how her daughter could carry on a relationship with "something that is ninety percent water, six percent potash, and four percent mohair." So beloved was the character of Endora—who would teleport herself in for tea—that Agnes Moorehead was invited by NASA as a "technical consultant" to witness the 1969 launching of the historic Apollo flight to the moon, since as a broom-flying witch she was intimately familiar with lunar terrain.

The part of Sam had been offered to actress Tammy Grimes, then starring in Broadway's *The Unsinkable Molly Brown,* but she found the show's concept silly. The sitcom made Elizabeth Montgomery a star. It was last telecast on July 1, 1972.

The Addams Family: ABC Premiere, September 18, 1964; The Munsters: CBS Premiere, September 29, 1964

Martians and witches were not the only nonhumans to have family sitcoms in the mid-Sixties. It was a fertile time for two close-knit families of suburban ghouls. In "The Munsters," 6-foot-7-inch-tall actor Fred Gwynne as Herman Munster was a dead ringer, so to speak, for Frankenstein's monster. He had a wife named Lily (Yvonne DeCarlo), a vampire; and a line of blood relatives like their ten-year-old, pointed-eared son Eddie Wolfgang, a werewolf; and 378-year-old Grandpa, akin to Count Dracula but infinitely kinder; plus family pets Igor the Bat, a raven with the annoying habit of repeating "Nevermore," and a prehistoric mongrel named Spot. In their spiderweb-covered mansion at 1313 Mockingbird Lane, Lily cooked in a caldron and served her clan bat's milk.

That same season, 1964–65, the bizarre cartoon characters of Charles Addams traveled successfully from the pages of *The New Yorker* magazine to television as "The Addams Family." The demented clan was headed by father Gomez (John Astin), a smarmy lawyer with destructive urges, and his eerie wife Morticia (Carolyn Jones), a fiend with a penchant for black wedding gowns for herself, headless dolls for her daughter, and real ray guns for her son. Lurch (Ted Cassidy) was a zombielike butler, Thing was a servant who was literally

"The Addams Family."

the family's right-hand man (a disembodied human hand), and pets included an octopus, a black widow spider, and a man-eating plant named Cleopatra. Uncle Fester, Morticia's relative, was toothless, hairless, and liked to fish with sticks of dynamite. They lived in a funereal world, and entertained relatives like Cousin Itt (Felix Silla), an entity covered entirely in blond hair. Given all of the this, the Addamses could never understand why neighbors stared at them. They thought themselves a normal, average clan, if anything a bit boring—therein lay the sitcom's central joke.

How did television get two monster sitcoms the same season? Behind the scenes, ABC (then ranked number three) learned in early 1964 that the top-rated network, CBS, planned to debut a sitcom based on a family of kindhearted ghouls—"The Munsters." Not to be outdone, ABC executives searched around for their own monster project and found it in a recently published collection of Charles Addams's cartoons, which enjoyed a large cult following. Spookily, the two shows debuted the very same week in 1964, and, more eerie still, both disappeared from the airwaves the same week in 1966.

Gilligan's Island: CBS Premiere, September 26, 1964

Also debuting in the 1964–65 season was the improbable tale of eight people stranded on an island in the Pacific Ocean when their sightseeing launch gets beached. Neither the cast of castaways nor CBS executives thought the sitcom would survive more than a season. Critics tried to kill it even sooner. Nonetheless, in its three years of original shows, it developed a huge cult following and remained popular in reruns for more than two decades. It holds the unique distinction of being the sitcom critics most single out as television at its pathetic worst. In some circles, writes John Javna, it's held up as "a symbol of the bankruptcy of the American TV culture." Ironically, the sitcom was inspired by a literary classic, Defoe's *Robinson Crusoe.* How it became the highly improbable, cliché-ridden tale of castaways familiar as "Gilligan's Island" is something that could only happen in the world of television.

Get Smart: NBC Premiere, September 18, 1965

Agent 86, Maxwell Smart (Don Adams), was forever saying to his sidekick, Agent 99 (Barbara Feldon), "If you don't mind, 99, I'd like to handle this myself"—then he'd bungle the task. A spoof of James Bond-like spy stories, the show had Agents 86 and 99 employed by the secret government agency CONTROL, which sought to stamp out the criminal activities of an outlaw organization named KAOS.

Despite his phenomenal ineptness, Maxwell Smart always caught the week's criminal, while uttering such catchphrases as "Sorry about that, Chief" (when he'd blunder), and "Would you believe . . . ?" (when he tried to cover up one of his transparent fabrications). The last phrase caught fire with young people around the country—as did the sophomoric, but highly successful, spoof. James Bond movies were extremely popular in the decade, and "Get Smart" benefited from comic association. Typical dialogue between Max and bad-guy Mr. Big:

> MAX: At the moment, seven coast guard cutters are converging on us. Would you believe it?
> MR. BIG: I find that hard to believe.
> MAX: Hmmm . . . would you believe *six?*
> MR. BIG: I don't think so.
> MAX: How about two cops in a rowboat?

It was formulaic, but for five years the formula entertained millions of viewers as a classic example of screwball comedy. The show was a spoof that laughed at the James Bond genre, but also had the wisdom to laugh at itself. In its penultimate season, Agents 86 and 99 married, and in the final season they produced a baby boy. But the sitcom had had its successful run and had begun to lose viewers, and no romance or tot could save it.

Also debuting in the 1965–66 season:

Green Acres was the converse of "The Beverly Hillbillies," in which a successful Manhattan lawyer, Oliver Wendell Douglas (Eddie Albert), and his glamorous socialite wife, Lisa (Eva Gabor), in order to "get closer to nature," chuck their Park Avenue penthouse and move into a ramshackle house on a 160-acre farm near Hooterville. Thus, the premise was set for six successful years of situation comedy.

Hogan's Heroes featured Colonels Robert Hogan (Bob Crane) and Wilhelm Klink (Werner Klemperer) as American and German adversaries in a sitcom based on life in a Nazi POW camp during World War II. Executives initially doubted if the unorthodox theme would work. But the combination of a barbed-wired prison camp with sadistic but incompetent German guards, a French chef secretly preparing gourmet meals for the POWs, and such camp conveniences as a barber shop and steam room all proved to be an irresistible blend of contradictions with limitless comic possibilities. The show had a successful run of six years.

I Dream of Jeannie starred Larry Hagman as astronaut Tony Nelson and Barbara Eden as his uncorked genie in a bottle, Jeannie, ever ready to do her master's bidding: "Thou may ask anything of thy slave, Master." Crossing her

"I Dream of Jeannie."

hands over her chest, she blinked, and his wish came true. For five years Jeannie—born in 64 B.C. in Baghdad—continually misunderstood her master's wishes, turning a favor into a disaster or a professional embarrassment for the NASA astronaut who was at a loss to explain countless mysterious disappearances and materializations in his life.

The following season, viewers got their first glimpse of Sally Field as Sister Bertrille, **The Flying Nun,** a cleric in the habit of hang gliding because of the peculiar aerodynamics of her cornette.

But the Sixties was notable for more than its lightweight sitcoms. It was the decade that heavyweight science fiction came to the small screen. The Sixties was TV's sci-fi decade.

The Twilight Zone: CBS Premiere, October 2, 1959

You're traveling through another dimension, a dimension not only of sight and sound, but of mind; a journey into a wondrous land whose boundaries are that of the imagination. That's the signpost up ahead! Your next stop . . . the Twilight Zone!

Writer Rod Serling created television's granddaddy of sci-fi thrillers because of his frustration with sponsors tampering with his scripts for the esteemed dramatic series "Playhouse 90." "One sponsor (an auto maker) de-

Rod Sterling.

manded that the Chrysler building be painted out of a scene," explains John Javna. "Another (a tobacco company) deleted the word 'lucky' from a script because Lucky Strikes weren't their brand. And when an insurance company refused to allow a central character to commit suicide, Serling quit." He created a fantasy thriller that was not a smash hit in the six years it ran in originals, but that acquired a cult following and became a classic of its genre.

Serling began writing after World War II, and in the Fifties he won three Emmys: one for his 1955 play *Patterns,* about dogged ambition in big business; a second a year later for *Requiem for a Heavyweight;* and a third in 1957 for *The Comedian*—and he would win three more for "Twilight Zone." Listeners hung on his resonant voice, which opened each episode with a chilling promise of the unexpected eeriness to come: "There is a sixth dimension beyond that which is known to man . . . It is the middle ground between light and shadow— between science and superstition; between the pit of man's fears and the sunlight of his knowledge."

The scripts were as literate as the openings, and of his writing Serling once said, "Style is something you develop by copying the style of someone who writes well. For a while you're a cheap imitation. I was a Hemingway imitator"—though not for long; soon others were copying the Serling style. Each show's ending was a guaranteed shocker. In "People Are Alike All Over," the first Earthman to visit Mars (Roddy McDowall) discovers that Martians are even more hospitable than Earthlings. They build him an exact replica of his Earth home, furnish it in the same style, feed him well. Then he discovers the doors are locked. Parting the curtains, he sees a crowd of Martians gazing at him, then he glimpses a sign: "Earth Creature in Native Habitat."

In addition to the series acquiring a cult following, its title slipped into the American idiom—the phrase twilight zone became synonymous with a state of the unknown. In the early Sixties, then Secretary of State Dean Rusk spoke of the "twilight zone of international relations"; renowned boxer Archie Moore said of a punch that flattened him, "Man, I was in the twilight zone"; and in the next decade, following the death of Mao Tse-tung, editorialists wrote of the twilight zone of Chinese-American relations.

Serling often boasted of writing an original "Twilight Zone" script in under thirty-five hours. And he rarely used a typewriter, preferring to dictate the contents of his imagination into a tape recorder. When "Twilight Zone" went off the air in 1964, Serling wrote screenplays for movies like *Planet of the Apes,* and in the fall of 1970 introduced a new TV series, "Rod Serling's Night Gallery," which dealt more with the occult than with science fiction. Five years later, at age fifty, he died from complications following open-heart surgery, entering, as he himself liked to say, the ultimate twilight zone. The series remains the best science fiction anthology ever created for television.

The Outer Limits: ABC Premiere, September 16, 1963

In the Eighties television would be criticized for its "disease of the week" programming. In the Sixties it was adored by fans for its monster of the week, most notably found in ABC's high-budget, imaginative special-effects, hour-long sci-fi thriller "The Outer Limits."

The show began with the image on your television screen suddenly going haywire and a firm voice stating:

> There is nothing wrong with your television set. Do not attempt to adjust the picture. We are controlling transmission. We will control the horizontal, we will control the vertical. For the next hour, sit quietly and we will control all you see and hear. You are about to experience the awe and mystery that leads you from the inner mind to . . . *the Outer Limits*.

The show and its weekly roster of creatures debuted just as television viewers were about to go crazy over sitcom monster families like "The Addams Family" and "The Munsters." Mid-decade, monsters were big business. They were even featured in pop songs and dance crazes like "The Monster Mash."

"The Outer Limits" was originally titled "Please Stand By." But with its scrambled-picture opening and Big Brother voiceover, TV executives thought (especially following tensions created by the Cuban missile crisis and the threat of World War III) that unsuspecting viewers might flip to the channel and react in an Orson Welles–"War of the Worlds" kind of panic. In fact, the show's creator, Leslie Stevens, as a high school student had sold a play to Welles's "Mercury Theater" and talked himself into a job with the company. The show's co-writer, Joseph Stefano, had written the screenplay for Alfred Hitchcock's thriller *Psycho*. The talent behind "The Outer Limits" was abundant, the scripts were highly original and literate, and the monster of the week really served as a metaphor for human foibles. Whereas "The Twilight Zone" elicited from viewers a shudder and a smile, its ABC competitor strived for hair-raising terror. No "Outer Limits" episode was filmed for less than $150,000, and special effects were often state-of-the-art scary.

Many of the most memorable of the show's forty-nine episodes were by Stefano. In "The Invisibles," a group of supremely intelligent extraterrestrials, resembling slimy slugs, attach themselves to humans by eating into the hosts' spinal cords—an operation filmed in shudderingly graphic detail. No expense was spared for gore. "Outer Limits" scored high viewer ratings until TV executives foolishly moved it from Mondays to Saturdays, where it fell opposite the popular Jackie Gleason show. It lost its following and was subsequently telecast for the last time on January 16, 1965. It remains a landmark in television for cinematography and special effects that approach those typically found in high-budget feature films of that day.

As the Sixties obsession for science fiction progressed, undoubtedly the preeminent example of the genre debuted in 1966.

Star Trek: NBC Premiere, September 8, 1966

In a scholarly essay, "Science Fiction and Fantasy TV," Mark Siegel argues that in Gene Roddenberry's "Star Trek," humans often encounter races technologically superior to themselves, but "they prove victorious because their values are well adapted to life on the frontier. Like their American pioneer forebears, they are scrappy, persistent, resourceful, and quick to adapt. While the crew is a mixture of races, its character is obviously American."

Roddenberry, in the early Sixties, also saw strong similarities between America's space exploration and the experiences of the country's pioneers. And he based his idea for a sci-fi trek to the stars on a western called "Wagon Train" and referred to the idea as "a wagon train to the stars."

The pilot episode, titled "The Cage," cost an extraordinary $630,000 to film and featured only two members of the final cast, Leonard Nimoy and Majel Barret. NBC hated it and requested a second pilot—which was auspiciously titled "Where No Man Has Gone Before," and which included such characters as American Captain James Kirk, half-Vulcan/half-human Mr. Spock (with a charming logic all his own), British Commonwealth systems engineer Scotty, and Japanese navigator Sulu. NBC moved it into its fall schedule—and the "number one cult TV show of all time" was born, as any Trekkie would vouch.

"Star Trek."

Nelson Rockefeller, governor of New York, admitted it was his favorite show. Writer Isaac Asimov said it was the *only* TV show he watched. Fan clubs formed across the nation. Trekkies gathered (and still do) for conventions; they circulate newsletters—even though in original episodes (of which there are seventy-eight) the series has been off the air since September 2, 1969. President Gerald Ford in 1976 named the country's first reusable orbiting space shuttle the *Enterprise* in honor of the spaceship on the show. A stickler for scientific accuracy, Roddenberry consulted experts in space science and medicine to make certain that every aspect of the *Enterprise* was credible. Indeed, the creation was so good that the navy later expressed interest in plans for the spaceship's landing deck, and NASA doctors were interested in the craft's diagnostic beds in sick bay.

Fad and Movie Spin-offs. Roddenberry's creation spawned a cottage industry of "Star Trek" products: faddish Spock ears, "phaser guns," bubblegum cards, school lunchboxes, and the like, and feature films. Not bad for a show that was canceled after only three seasons—an NBC decision that resulted in network offices being deluged with over a million pieces of protest mail, many threatening executives with bodily harm if they did not reconsider. Truth was, the program of Earth heroes battling futuristic Huns like Klingons and Romulans never ranked in the top twenty-five shows of a year. Though the show had its zealous fans in the late Sixties, it became a true cult phenomenon in reruns.

"Historically," ventures Siegel, "it is tempting to suggest that *Star Trek* reflects not merely the general precepts of American culture, but also the particular issues that predominated in the last four years of the 1960s when it originally ran." One of those issues was the genuine fear that emerging technology was going to obsolete ordinary working people. "The show," says Siegel, "reassured the working American that, however much he might fear the encroachment of technology on his home and his workplace, man would always triumph because of his particularly human qualities."

Creator Gene Roddenberry said his show suggested "that there is a tomorrow, that there is challenge and romance in the world." But it also said more: "It goes rather like this," he wrote. "You human biped thing called Man, you strange creature, still in a sort of a violent childhood of your evolution, you're awkward and often illogical, you're weak, vain, but damn it, you're also gorgeous!"

CHAPTER 9

□

The Self-Seeking Seventies

1970 to 1979

The Me Decade

Tom Wolfe called the Seventies the Me Decade for the emergence of "the first common man . . . with the much dreamed-of combination of money, free time, and personal freedom"—not unlike our *Homo ludens,* the liberated leisure time man discussed in the introduction. Wolfe might well have singled out "the first common woman" for it was also the decade of women's liberation, sexual liberation, and gay liberation, as well as the liberation of animals from laboratory experimentation. Indeed, liberation was everywhere. The decade's motto could have come from the Clairol ad: "If I've only one life, let me live it as . . ." *me.*

The new man and woman embarked on a search, trenchantly trendy, for *self*-mastery, *self*-knowledge, and *self*-actualization of "potential as a whole human being." For a few hundred dollars this could be done at the Esalen Institute at Big Sur, or in "group encounters" around the country where you painfully bared your peccadillos to "get in touch with your inner *self.*" Self was the star of the me decade.

At the start of the decade there were more than two thousand communes around the country for personal soul-searching. Celebrities included such unlikely foreigners as Maharishi Mahesh Yogi and Swami Prabhupada, gurus to the stars. The search for self was evident in fads like the mood ring and the emergence of a spectrum of born-again Christians like Watergate criminal Charles Colson, pornographer Larry Flynt, and President Jimmy Carter.

Religions—Eastern and Western—became confusingly crossed and entertainingly chic. On Broadway was the boldly revisionist and musically influential *Jesus Christ Superstar,* and on the nation's streets were "Jesus freaks" and the Reverend Sun Myung Moon's proselytizing Moonies. Sixties flower power had teemed up with Seventies search for self to unleash a Pandora's box of cults,

366

clown-Christ musicals like *Godspell*, and gurus like the fifteen-year-old "perfect master," Mararaj-ji, who through his American followers sold enlightenment while enriching himself and amassing a collection of Rolls-Royces, Jaguars, and Mercedes.

More dangerous was the messianic preacher Jim Jones, who took his San Francisco-based People's Temple to "Jonestown," Guyana, to found an earth-bound nirvana, only to lead nearly a thousand of his followers to mass suicide with poisoned Kool-Aid.

Human Potential Movement and est

Former used car salesman John Paul Rosenberg of Philadelphia, reincarnated under the stand-up-and-salute moniker of Werner Erhard, merchandised enlightenment to a generation through something called est (for Erhard Seminars Training). In its catchy lowercase e. e. cummings–like come-on, est was the success story of the human potential movement—the blanket movement to maximize self. At an emotionally charged weekend seminar, a few hundred dollars bought you heaps of verbal abuse and discomforting physical deprivation—with the claim that this was a "transforming experience" designed to "get rid of old baggage."

"You are the architect of everything you do," preached Erhard, "and the sole cause of *everything* that happens to you"—a philosophy that left little room for the niceties of compassion and social responsibility. If you smiled, Erhard was known to shout, "Wipe that stupid smile off your face." An estimated seven hundred thousand customers signed up for est, including Cher and former astronaut Buzz Aldrin. In time John Paul Rosenberg's success story would give a new twist to the quip, "Would you buy a used car from this man?" (For the Eighties, Erhard "yuppified" est, renamed it the Forum, and pitched it to corporate clientele until he sold out under a cloud of controversy.)

More medically respectable was . . .

Transcendental Meditation

TM, as the craze was called, was at once a legitimate form of meditation and relaxation and a much-hyped route to lower blood pressure and diminished executive stress. Books on TM topped the bestseller lists. TM centers sprang up throughout the country. The twenty-minutes-a-day form of meditation "my way" was the subject of *Time* and *Newsweek* cover stories, the hot topic on TV talk shows, and, too, the focus of serious medical research. "TM was a pantheistic grab bag," write Andrew Edelstein and Kevin McDonough in *The Seventies*, "the turn-on of the 70's, a drugless high even the narc squad might enjoy." Rock stars and congressmen TM'ed. And the relaxation technique was "adopted and subsidized by such diverse corporations as AT&T, General Foods, Blue Cross/Blue Shield of Chicago, and Folsom Prison." TM was another example of the search for self gone mainstream.

On the other hand, a quest for mastery of physical self gave birth to such

Seventies pursuits as *jogging, cycling,* and *fast walking.* In the Me Decade, Americans for the first time in the century began to take an almost obsessive concern for the fitness of their bodies—a concern that would spill over into the Eighties. A staple of attire was the **jogging suit,** a sweatshirt and sweatpants ensemble that in time would become an all-purpose costume, suitable for lounging around the house or shopping in malls.

What's Your Sign? / Your Place or Mine?

Many of the decade's fads and trends, as we'll see, came from a meeting of East and West. There was the Chinese needle medicine of **acupuncture,** and the occult wisdom to be gleaned from **Tarot cards,** the **I Ching,** and **Linda Goodman's Sun Signs**—with astrology providing arguably the century's most annoying boy-meets-girl opener: "What's your sign?" Spilling over from the hippie Sixties were vogues for **herbal teas** (Red Zinger, Morning Thunder, chamomile, Sleepy Time), and a cornucopia of natural foods: **tofu, tahini, brown rice, banana bread, lentil loaf, alfalfa sprouts, zucchini bread, avocados, carob** as a chic stand-in for chocolate, and **honey** instead of processed sugar.

Synonymous with the first person singular in the Me Decade was the word singles—as in **singles' bars** and **singles' pads.** And, too, as in **swinging singles,** like Seventies archetypes *Bob and Carol and Ted and Alice.* Following the opener of "What's your sign?" and the passage of a modest period of time came the punchline, "Your place or mine?"

We begin this chapter with a look at faddish Seventies clothes.

FADS, FOLLIES, AND TRENDS

Ours has been a century of synthetics. The Gay Nineties had celluloid; the Teens cellophane; the Roaring Twenties vinyl and acetate; the Thirties acrylics and Melmac; the Forties nylon; the Fifties styrene and Formica; the Sixties polyester and Teflon. For the Seventies the hip synthetics were **Lycra** and **Spandex**—for stretch disco pants, swimwear, and brightly colored jogging attire—as well as fake leather and faux furs. "Seventies' style began with the confluence of two mighty movements," write the authors of *The Seventies.* "The sexual and the synthetic revolutions combined forces to produce some of the ugliest and most outrageous clothes ever seen." To start at the feet:

Earth Shoes

Environmentalism had been launched by Rachel Carson in the previous decade. But it got a giant media boost when April 22, 1970, was declared Earth Day, a time for mass recycling and consciousness-raising. Ecology became an in word, and the decade's back to nature movement was reflected in things as diverse as the creation of the Environmental Protection Agency, the passage of the Clean Air Act, and the consumption of sprouts and grains and organically grown fruits and vegetables. On that April day a fad was, to pun, afoot.

The earth shoe had a patented "negative heel" that allowed the wearer to "walk the way nature intended." Designed by Anne Nalso, a Danish yoga instructor, "to simulate the print of a bare foot in soft earth, with the heel placed lower than the toes to relieve forward pressure and promote better posture," the shoes were introduced in the United States on Earth Day (the origin of their name), and cost from $24 to $50. The footwear became a runaway fad, spawning more than eighty-five imitations, with more than 2 million Kalso pairs alone sold by 1975. Dr. Paul Scherer of the California College of Podiatric Medicine in San Francisco studied the shoe and determined that 70 percent of wearers developed heel and calf pain in the first two weeks (though it soon subsided). The shoe did seem to alleviate the annoyance of bunions. He cautioned diabetics against wearing the shoe because the unaccustomed pressure on the feet could cause skin problems and bleeding. The dowdy Earth shoe had a glitzy rival.

Platform Shoes

The elevated orthopedic nightmare began in the Sixties with an inch or two added to the sole. A wedgie heel was not new, but the platform toe was an innovation introduced to "balance the sexy mini-skirt look," said one fashion authority. "It cut the seduction aspect of the mini drastically to see a sweet young thing in these clunkers. And, too, the shoes eliminated the wiggle in the walk." Entertainers like Elton John helped exaggerate the platform to ludicrous and dangerous heights, while decorating the funky pumps with gold glitter, sequins, and popular polka dots. So far removed from conventional high heels, the platform appealed to both sexes, conferring on the wearer an androgyny that itself was trendy. "It kept the foot rigid and made the wearer clomp along gracelessly," wrote one observer.

Hot Pants

The scandalously short shorts, not unknown to European prostitutes in decades prior to the Seventies, arrived on the American fashion scene in 1970. *Women's Wear Daily* christened them hot pants. In leather, lace, ranch mink, velvet, satin, or denim, the pants were a fashion rebellion against the mid-calf midi hemline favored by Paris designers the previous year—itself a replacement for the Sixties miniskirt.

Hot pants, though, revealed more leg and lower cheek than the shortest mini ever had. They appealed to women at all levels of society. Jane Fonda wore them in *Klute*. Ursula Andress wore a bronze velvet pair to a fashionable New York restaurant. Jackie Kennedy Onassis bought Halston hot pants for sunning on her husband's yacht. James Brown extolled hot pants in song. David Bowie dared to don them on his first U.S. tour, as did Sammy Davis, Jr., in his Las Vegas show. Liberace entertained at the keyboard in a patriotic red-white-and-blue pair. California brides married in white lace hot pants, designer Valentino debuted all-sequin short-shorts, and debutantes donned black formal tuxedo hot pants for charity balls.

Hot pants became acceptable attire for everything from supermarket shopping to black-tie dining. And in winter, despite intense cold, women wore them to malls, theaters, and dinners beneath long overcoats and minks. Though originally targeted for the spring fashion market, the vogue raged on throughout the following winter. So widespread was the fad that the conservative-minded Miss America pageant allowed contestants to wear hot pants during their talent competition. At the height of the vogue Alexander's in New York was selling fifteen hundred pairs a week. A Seventh Avenue fashion executive who had banked on the mid-calf midi told *Newsweek,* "We don't control the ladies. They control us now." When the fad passed, before its second winter, the fashion reverted to streetwalkers and, in polite society, to cheerleaders like the Dallas Cowgirls.

String Bikini

What hot pants were to slacks, the 1974 string bikini was to female swimwear. Consisting of three triangles of cloth draped over the upper and lower erogenous zones of the female body (held on with strings), the micro-swimsuit, costing from $35 to $45, sold out at New York's Bloomingdale's two weeks after it was introduced. From the French Riviera to Long Island's Jones Beach, the sexy string was all the summertime rage—though decidedly among slender, younger women.

The fashion is thought to have begun on Ipanema Beach in Rio de Janeiro. It was patterned on the skimpy loincloths once worn by coastal Brazilian natives. Though it captured the bare essence of the decade's swinging singles theme, the vogue enjoyed only one summer in the sun—perhaps because it was quickly spoofed by designer Rudi Gernreich in his boldly bottomless bikini known as the **thong**—worn by both men and women. Given considerable if discreet press coverage, the thong made a joke of the string, and before the first blush of fall both fads were forgotten.

Tank Tops

The fad of the sleeveless T-shirt, the tank top, peaked around 1973, the garment becoming the symbol of informal dress for the country's youth. The design is thought to have originated in Europe among women in the experimental years of the early Sixties when going bra-less was a brazen statement. At that time, the tank top was an alternative to the tube top and the halter.

In America, though, it quickly became a unisex top. And following gay liberation, it became a summer costume of the Village Clone, one of several gay stereotypes (including the Leather Man, the Construction Worker, and the Biker) made recognizably mainstream by the band called the Village People. When the California "muscle culture" emerged mid-decade, the tank top became the respectable way to showcase bulging biceps, leviathan lats, petrous pecs, and other alliterative muscle groups. Whereas other fashion fads died out, the unpretentious, inexpensive, practical tank top eventually became a quiet undershirt.

Jazzed-Up Jeans and Designer Labels

Blue jeans were the 1800s brainchild of immigrant tailor Levi Strauss, made from heavy-duty tent canvas and sold to California panhandlers during the gold rush boom. But from the start jeans underwent alterations. Cowboys, preferring snug-fitting pants, sat in water troughs to soak their jeans, then lay out in the sun to shrink them. Miners, unencumbered by the etiquette of underwear, found that squatting too near a campfire heated the copper crotch rivet to give a painful burn; it was abandoned. In the Thirties, American schoolteachers complained that back-pocket rivets on the jeans of children were gouging wooden desk seats; pocket rivets were abandoned.

In that same decade, the strictly utilitarian garment became a hot fashion item when an advertisement appeared in *Vogue* featuring two society women in tight-fitting jeans, in a look called **western chic.** Several jeans fads followed: the Forties vogue for **denim jeans with saddle oxfords and a sloppy out-of-pants shirttail;** the Fifties look of **jeans rolled up to the knees, tight sweater, dark sunglasses, cigarette holder, and highball glass.** Those fads, though, were minor compared to the one that erupted in the Seventies.

The phenomenon of jazzed-up jeans began when counterculture youths began to personalize their faded, tattered pants with patches, creative stitchwork, painted messages and studded designs. The decorative jean arrived at a time when teens were searching for their own code of dress and means of self-expression. Levi Strauss's tent-canvas pants became a personal billboard. Seventh Avenue, spotting a new market, introduced tight-fitting jeans embellished with rhinestones, sequins, silk applique, frills, and lace, intended for a more upscale audience. At Vassar, to wear a full-length mink coat over a pair of jeans became the height of devil-may-care chic.

But when big-name designers—like Calvin Klein and Gloria Vanderbilt—entered the jeans market, out went the decorative appliques, in came the costly designer label (for the label is what one paid for), usually stitched across the upper right buttock. **Jordache, Sasson,** and **Sergio** became synonyms for trendy jeans. And at the close of the decade, when Calvin Klein introduced TV viewers to a young Brooke Shields wiggling into her **Calvins** and purring "Know what comes between me and my Calvins? Nothing," the pants once intended for hard work became the ultimate costume of serious play. At the height of the designer jeans wars, Calvin Klein jeans, despite their high price of $50 (or because of it), were selling at the rate of 250,000 pairs a week. No doubt Levi Strauss himself would have been flattered.

Annie Hall, Saturday Night Fever, and Urban Cowboy Looks

Several fashion statements were inspired by movies. Diane Keaton's crazily lovable character in the 1977 Woody Allen movie *Annie Hall* spawned an "anti-style," which in its oversized men's shirts, long skirts, cloddish shoes, and baggy khakis allowed women to be at once funkily chic and safely conservative. John Travolta's energetic portrayal of Italian stallion Tony Manero in *Saturday Night Fever* introduced a generation of young men to the passing fad of the three-piece white suit; the attire was almost mandatory at certain nightspots and all senior proms. Western wear was already popular when the movie *Urban Cowboy* premiered. But the film created an unprecedented demand for Wild West apparel, which included shoestring ties, fancy hats with feather bands, glittery silk shirts with mother-of-pearl buttons; and especially high-priced ostrich, python, and lizard-skin boots. By late 1981, reported the *New York Times,* "Western apparel created a $5 billion industry." Though the galloping success of the fad would wane the next year, the most gung-ho designer of Western paraphernalia, Ralph Lauren, would make it his signature.

Polyester Leisure Suits

First, a bit of background: The men's three-piece wool suit originated in Europe in the eighteenth century, not as business wear, but as more leisurely country horseback-riding attire. Appropriately, the cut was loose, bordering on baggy, and the coat-vest-trousers ensemble was called a lounge suit. The jacket's back slit accommodated the horse's back, and the lapel hole was intended not for a carnation but so that on a cold day a man could turn up his collar and button it snugly. Gentlemen found lounge suits so comfortable, they began wearing them in the city as well—and a business tradition was born.

The early Seventies after-hours leisure suit, a fashion nadir, was something of a return to the lounge suit—worn not by country gentlemen, but by that swinging singles predator, the lounge lizard. Hardy wools, Harris tweeds, and earth-tone colors—staples of the traditional suit—were replaced by indestructible polyester, welting pattern weaves, and an array of pastel colors that would make the Easter Bunny blush. As the eighteenth-century lounge suit was designed to be a casual alternative to tailored business and formal wear, so too was the leisure suit—often without lapels, given boxy hip pockets, and cut along the lines of a loosely belted tunic; all features to emphasize its recreational intent. To maximize profit, it was promoted as acceptable office attire.

The leisure suit was not new in the Seventies. It had been favored for more than a decade by golfers on the courses in Miami and Palm Springs. But now it was priced down and promoted as what the groovy single wore to relax or prowl; it never did catch on as an executive's office attire. Favored by sports figures and entertainers, by the end of the decade a leisure suit in one's closet was an embarrassment—evidence of being, or having been, a lounge lizard.

Elegant restaurants, like New York's Lutèce, posted signs: "No Leisure Suits." As hot pants were bequeathed to prostitutes, leisure suits, upon the fad's demise, went to pimps.

Campus Toga Parties

In the summer of 1978, to the surprise of Hollywood executives, *National Lampoon's Animal House* had moviegoers standing in long lines to view the grossly humorous shenanigans of "Saturday Night Live's" John Belushi and his fellow boys of Delta House at fictional Farber College. The beer-swilling, barfing, underachieving Delta boys were unsavory as role models, but their obscenely funny antics—inspired by *National Lampoon* founder Doug Kenney and contributor Chris Miller—created a fall campus fad reminiscent of earlier crazes like goldfish swallowing and phone-booth packing.

The blockbuster movie, set in the early Sixties, contained a brief, wild toga party (called a Greek party in the Sixties), in which fraternity boys, donning bedsheets and laurel wreaths, dance lasciviously while drinking themselves into oblivion. One month after the nation's colleges had resumed fall classes, *Newsweek* reported that more than a hundred campuses were hosting weekend toga parties. Ten thousand partying undergraduates at the University of Wisconsin attempted to get their toga party into the *Guinness Book of World Records* by creating and consuming the world's largest mixed drink: a vat of sundry BYO booze.

Animal House.

Why did the Greek toga party amass such a devoted following in the late Seventies?

Sociologists argued that after the Sixties radicalism, American college students had grown more conservative, their campus pranks more measured in zaniness and irresponsibility. In a nutshell, they were bored and thus primed for the kind of "good ol' red-blooded American mischievousness" depicted in *Animal House,* explained one observer at the height of the winter of 1978 toga mania.

Unfortunately, showings of the unreservedly rowdy movie around the country left a wake of student vandalism. Numerous campuses reported an increase in the incidents of cafeteria food fights, in pranks played on teachers and administrators, and costly damage to school property—all highlights of the film. Belushi's egging cry of "Toga! Toga! Toga!" became a much-feared call to prankishness on campuses around the country.

For the folks at Universal, the studio that made the film, toga mania meant more money in the bank. Produced for a meager $2.7 million, and promoted with a $4.5 million budget, the film took in more than $50 million in its first two months. *National Lampoon* magazine's cut of the gross for that period was $3 million. Unexpected beneficiaries of toga mania were the nation's department stores, which reported sheet sales at an all-time high. Indeed, in cities like New York and Los Angeles, it was vogue for young adults to attend the movie clad in togas. Whereas the movie's popularity continued to grow, catapulting it to a cult classic, toga mania did not survive the academic year.

Mood Rings

In the Me Decade, the mood ring was the quintessential amulet to sum up the era's quest for instant self-knowledge and self-mastery. The ring's stone consisted of a heat-sensitive liquid crystal that changed colors to reflect the wearer's shifting moods: purple, bliss; blue, tranquillity; yellow-green, stability, if not dullness; reddish-brown, irritability; black, gloom, depression, despair, if not worse. During a few months in 1975, more than 20 million mood rings were sold, cheap rip-offs costing as little as $2, with the "real things" (designed by creator Joshua Reynolds) selling at Bonwit Teller and Neiman-Marcus for up to $250. Celebrities like Barbara Streisand, Ali MacGraw, and Muhammad Ali spoke glowingly of their chameleonlike rings' faithful reflection of their moods, and syndicated columnist Eugenia Sheppard gushed approvingly over the invention as a much-needed "thermometer of the mind."

To fully grasp mood ring mania, it is necessary to realize that the trinket appeared at the height of another craze.

Biofeedback is the science of monitoring hidden body rhythms and feeding back that information to more favorably alter those rhythms. Newspapers and magazines ran articles on employing biofeedback sensors to achieve creative alpha-brainwave states and deeply meditative theta-brainwave states. Attempting to capitalize on that trend was thirty-three-year-old Joshua Reynolds, alleged to be the descendent of the eighteenth-century British portrait painter Reynolds, and heir to the R. J. Reynolds tobacco fortune. After having little success establishing biofeedback seminars, which used cumbersome EEG machinery, Reynolds conceived the idea of a "portable biofeedback aid." With the help of a New York press agent, and with financial backing from an actress turned perfume executive, Polly Bergen, Reynolds kicked off one of the two biggest fads of 1975 (the other being the pet rock; see below).

The ring, an instant hit, was not without its flaws. First, it responded crudely to temperature, a variable haphazardly correlated with specific emotional states. A desired color could be easily achieved with minimal cheating; merely holding a ring tightly could turn it a tranquil blue. Over time, the liquid crystals wore out, the ring growing progressively blacker and blacker. Many companies offered lifetime guarantees, convinced that the fad would fade before the ring blackened and needed to be replaced.

And they were right. By 1976 the market for mood rings was flooded with cheap plastic imitations—as well as spin-off items like color-changing mood shoes, belts, watches, and panties. The bauble was tucked into the back of a jewelry box and forgotten. Unfortunately, Joshua Reynolds did not move fast enough in securing a patent and profited little from his invention. His meditation center in New York, Q-Tran (Tran for tranquillity), plunged into the chaotic state of bankruptcy. Had he been wearing one of his rings, its color would have been predictable.

Pet Rocks

It was the quintessential fad: an item that is needless, pointless, and profitable; one that leaves an indelible memory trace and whose popularity is short-lived and inexplicable.

One can only imagine that in 1975 more than a million Americans, fed up with feeding cats and walking dogs, opted for a pet that cost $5, required no maintenance, did absolutely nothing, and bore an uncanny resemblance to rocks in any garden, along any country road. An unemployed, thirty-eight-year-old California advertising man, Gary Dahl, dreamed up his million-dollar scheme after an evening in a bar with friends, hearing them lament the costs and inconveniences of pet ownership.

It began as a joke. Dahl announced he had the perfect maintenance-free pet. He presented several of his friends with smooth beach rocks. Their reception of the gag inspired him to order nearly three tons of rocks from a Mexican beach, and to write a clever owner's manual for the "care and training of your Pet Rock." With a bit of nudging a pet rock could "learn to roll over," and with nearly no training it would "play dead." Instinctively it knew how to roll down a hill. One instruction advised: "Place it on some old newspapers. The rock will never know what the paper is for and will require no further instruction." Like a guard dog, the rock also could protect its owner if assaulted: "Reach into your pocket and purse as though you were going to comply with the mugger's demands. Extract your pet rock. Shout the command: 'Attack!' and bash the mugger's head in." And a pet rock came in a specially designed box with air holes.

For every pet rock sold, Gary Dahl pocketed 95 cents. Following their introduction a month before Christmas of 1975, pet rocks were selling out at Hallmark card stores, Bloomingdale's and Macy's in New York, Filene's in Boston, and in fine department stores around the country. Whereas the original pet rock was merely a plain stone, later variations came with brightly painted-on sly smiles, knowing grins, and devilish grimaces—as if to say, Yes, we all know I'm a joke. The pet rock was one of the most sought-after Christmas gifts of the season, and its popularity faded only after about 5 million rocks had been sold. By that time Dahl had been featured in *Newsweek* and *Time,* and he'd introduced companion products like Pet Rock Food—a chunk of rock salt.

Happy Face Buttons and Have a Nice Day

Two black eye dots and an upcurved smile line against a solid background became the most familiar symbol for peace, love, and sentimentality for the Seventies generation. Smile buttons, as the happy faces were also called, encouraged (and perhaps originated) one of the decade's most mindlessly insincere farewells, "Have a nice day," a signoff that even Ma Bell operators adopted as a token of politeness and feigned concern. As for happy face, not since the impish Kilroy (see page 208) had a grinning insignia so thoroughly swept the country. But unlike Kilroy, the origin of happy face is, more or less, well known.

The facial expression began to appear during the button craze of the Sixties, though who first drew the irrepressibly upbeat smile is uncertain. It's known that a 1971 San Francisco publication, *Mr. Natural #2,* an underground comic strip by the pseudonymous R. Crumb, featured a character, recently released from prison, who is irritated by the ubiquitous presence of happy face expressions in store windows, on T-shirts, and on lapel buttons. He curses, "that dum' face!" laments how maudlin the world has become since his incarceration, and asks a girl sporting the smiling grin on her shirt and jeans its significance. "You don't know?" she cheerfully exclaims. "It's happy face. It means have a nice day." Thus the face and the phrase were associated in print.

I'm O.K. You're O.K.   R. Crumb's inspiration probably came from a Manhattan button manufacturer, N. G. Slater, who in 1969 began to produce happy face buttons, appliqués, and novelties that were named smilies. Two years later the items suddenly became faddish, and sales ripped through the proverbial roof. Woolworth ordered a half million buttons from Slater, and Cartier in New York offered 18-karat gold smilies, made to order. The face appeared on coffee mugs, bumper stickers, writing pads, jewelry, dolls' heads, and even trash cans, a nod in absentia to the garbage collector to "Have a nice day." Students and letter writers dotted their *i*'s with a tiny happy face, and grade school teachers abandoned the gold star of approval on a well-done assignment in favor of a smilie.

Sales figures show that the smile button was the most popular craze since the hula hoop, selling more than 20 million grinning discs in a six-month period of 1971. The *New Yorker* observed, "America is waking up once again to the importance of plain old smiling," and both *Newsweek* and *Time* ran a cartoon of President Nixon wearing a smile button. Presidential candidate George McGovern adopted the happy face as his campaign logo.

Indefatigable cheer prompts ridicule, and, not surprisingly, the spread of such a sugary symbol encouraged numerous sour-faced spin-offs: buttons showing faces in scowls, snarling toothy grins, and with tongues stuck out in a sigh of exhaustion. At the same time, "Have a nice day" became the acerbic brunt of many comedic monologues, passing from a salubrious salutation to a snide putdown. Whereas the smile button eventually slipped into obscurity (to return with less ardor in the Eighties, associated with Bobby McFerrin's song, "Don't Worry, Be Happy"), its associated phrase lingered on, supporting the decade's other upbeat exhortation, "I'm O.K. you're O.K.," from the title of a bestseller.

CB Radio

What began in 1958 as the opening to the public of a narrow 10-megahertz airwave band (460–470 MHz), for businesses and emergencies, became a countrywide obsession in the mid-Seventies, when millions of Americans, following the lead of the nation's truckdrivers, emerged as citizens band, or CB, enthusiasts. What is perhaps forgotten about this craze is that it was kicked off by the 1974 Arab oil embargo. After having languished for sixteen years, CB radio suddenly was the best means one big-rig trucker had to alert his brotherhood to gas stations that were open and selling petrol.

For reasons practical and faddish, the allure of CB radio spread. Eight months after the oil embargo began, more than a million gas-hungry truckers and hobby-hungry automobile drivers were CB-ers. In the next three months, another million drivers spent between $4 and $20 for a license and anywhere from $50 to $380 for a twenty-three-channel CB dashboard radio. And the FCC was flooded with requests for additional licenses.

A saucy, colorful lingo emerged among truckers, was picked up by car CB-ers, and was played up by the media. One CB-er might broadcast the alert that there were **smokies** (police) ahead, avoid going over **double nickel** (55 miles per hour), and receive a **10–4** (affirmative acknowledgment). CB monthlies emerged, as well as bestselling books on the in jargon, which required a dictionary: **Pick'em up truck, you git an eyeball on that Kojak with the Kodak up at the one-seven, ten what?** (Calling the pickup truck. Did you see that radar patrolman at the 17-mile marker? Do you understand?)

By the time the gas shortage was over, a segment of the country was bilingual with CB-ese. A fad was entrenched.

There were numerous spin-offs: CB bumper stickers, hit songs ("Convoy," by country singer C. W. McCall), coffee mugs, jacket patches, hats, jewelry, several grade-B films, a TV series ("Movin' On"), and more dictionaries, for

CB-ese mushroomed as Joe and Joan Public realized they could travel the nation's roads agab with one another, as well as with their big-wheeler folk heroes—for that is what many sociologists dubbed the fad-setting truckers. In an essay, "CB Radio as Icon," James Pollman pictures CB truckers as the "Last American Cowboys," who packed not the old Colt .44 but the "electronic magnum Cobra CB," and who through media coverage achieved "cult status." In devoted imitation, says Pollman, "Americans began buying CBs, listening in to these 'ghosts of the rolling nights,' investigating their mystique, learning that a diverse populace can, with a communications tool, create a community."

First Lady as First Mama.   More than a radio frequency, CB became the country's newest car culture. By 1976 electronics companies had manufactured an estimated 25 million CB radios for cars, boats, and homes, and the FCC was deluged with 656,000 license applications a month, eventually forcing the organization to broaden the range from twenty-three channels to forty. At the peak of the fad, First Lady Betty Ford admitted to being a CB-er, and to broadcasting **breakers** from the White House under her personal **handle** of First Mama. The CB craze, writes Pollman, "took in all stratums of society, from the elite in expensive cars to the rather marginal in clunkers."

Why such broad appeal?

Columbia University sociologist Amitai Etzioni suggested: "A CB allows you to present a false self. Like the traveling salesman who drops into a singles bar and says he's the president of his company, a person can project on the airwaves anything he wants to be." Indeed, it was the facelessness of the fad that allowed a milquetoast kind of Walter Mitty guy to announce himself as Big Al, or better yet, Magnum Force, and enabled a lonely woman to come off as One Hot Mama. Most sociologists who have written about the CB mania claim that the fad was driven largely by a human urge to act out one's fantasies. CB radio lost its faddish appeal when cheap, "leaky" radios began to flood the market, when the crowded airwaves became a cacophony of unintelligible babble, and when, simply, the quantity of CB-ers rendered their hobby commonplace and their in language everyone's cliché. Tens of thousands of radios gathered dust on store shelves, and the radio frequency was returned to truckers.

Minibikes and Mopeds

Beginning in the Seventies, two fast-growing fads-on-wheels involved small motorized bicycles and vehicles that are half bike, half motorcycle. It was a manifestation of the car culture specialized to accommodate kiddies.

Kids gifted in the art of mechanics had always tinkered in their family garages, fastening old lawnmower and washing machine engines to wheels to produce motorized go-carts. But in the late Sixties and early Seventies even the nonmechanically inclined could get around on pint-sized, store-bought scooters. Intended for off-road travel, they were dubbed minibikes. As an alternative to an older sibling's motorcycle, the slight (about 65 pounds), sturdily built, safely sluggish mini—4 feet tall and with wheels about 10 inches in diameter—offered the pre–driving age teen a chance to skirt along dirt trails in wooded suburban areas for as little as $130 for a cheap model or $300 for a top-of-the-line bike. With top speeds of less than 40 miles per hour, minis were disparaged as "hardly Davidsons."

The bikes had few design restrictions, until, that is, reports of accidents and fatalities began trickling in. When an eleven-year-old California boy was killed in the early Seventies, concerned parents launched a national crusade, first against the selling of minibikes, then in favor of enforcing safety features like helmets and protective clothing. Preteens were also told to turn off engines and walk their bikes across a highway or street. Though consumer magazines cautioned that the bikes were unsafe at any speed for children, the fad mushroomed as more and more suburban communities across the county constructed neighborhood dirt trails.

The marketing genius of a thirty-year-old French expatriate, Serge Seguin, was responsible for launching the fad for the hybrid half bicycle, half motorcycle moped—which was a $50 million-a-year industry mid-decade. Arriving in America in 1972 to get a graduate degree in business administration at the University of Florida, Seguin chose the then little appreciated moped as the novel subject for his master's thesis. "I knew," he told *People* magazine in 1977, "that there were a number of good European products that were unavailable in the U.S. I wanted to find out why."

For his field work, Seguin persuaded Motobecane in France to stake him to two sample mopeds and $1,000 in expenses. During the winter of 1972 he traveled nearly 24,000 miles cross-country, interviewing people about their interest in the light-framed, 150-miles-to-the-gallon bikes that had been popular in Europe since 1946. For one thing, U.S. safety regulations were keeping European mopeds out of the American market. Moving to Washington, D.C., Seguin lobbied Congress to change the law, and in 1974, amid the Arab oil embargo, the Department of Transportation agreed to grant mopeds a separate vehicle classification. Soon thirty-one states amended their laws to welcome energy-saving mopeds onto their roadways. With the market open, the rest is merchandising history. By 1977, more than a quarter million Americans were economically scooting along on their minimotorcycles.

The next motoring fad was decidedly uneconomical.

Monster Trucks

The monster truck—that is, a normal-sized cabin atop gargantuan 6-foot-tall tires with Siberian tundra treads—grew out of the practical desire for a powerful country vehicle to navigate treacherously muddy roads, ferrying sportsmen from fishing hole to campsite or weekend cabin. Bigfoot, the 1974 brainchild of Missourian Robert Chandler, is taken to be the proto-monster truck. Chandler's powerfully souped-up Ford, with modestly-sized 4-foot-high tires, caught the attention of auto buffs. And when Chandler began to demonstrate at country fairs that his monster could literally roll over lesser vehicles in its path (side-by-side junked cars) a fad was hatched.

Fan clubs, Saturday TV specials, and a slew of magazines were devoted to the monsters, which mushroomed in size, power, and eye-catching ferocity. By the mid-Eighties the fad had hundreds of thousands of fans and was under the aegis of the Monster Truck Racing Association, and the "macho" vehicles were outrageously large and lavishly expensive, often costing over $170,000. Psychologists, who had from the dawning of the love affair between the American male and his power-packed auto, equated machismo and machine (see page 62), found in the monster truck a phallic substitute to impress many a female and intimidate all rival males. Others said the fad, as engaged in by teenagers and young male adults, was merely another Eighties manifestation of shameless consumer consumption and sinful fuel excess.

Indoor Plants in Hanging Baskets

As had happened during the fern in a terrarium craze of the Gay Nineties (see page 18), in the early Seventies suburban home-owners and city apartment dwellers welcomed indoors the verdant beauty of nature. House plants were chic, plant shops trendy to browse through, and names like *coleus, dracaena marginata,* and *ficus* were dropped by middle-class collectors. Those willing to spend on exotica mentioned with pride *clivia, genista,* and *cyperus papyrus.*

The boom in plant sales created a hearty market for bestselling books, from such essential how-tos as *The New York Times Book of Houseplants* and *The Complete Indoor Gardener* to such tantalizing tomes as *The Secret Life of Plants.* The last assured readers that plants had feelings and responded favorably to gentle persuasion and kind compliments. Many parapsychologists wired the leaves of plants to polygraph recorders and claimed to detect "signs of intelligence." In one much-publicized experiment a dracaena that had "witnessed" a companion plant brutally defoliated by a "murderer" (one of the researchers) responded with frenzied electrical output when the assailant reentered the room and approached the leafy witness.

Popular too were miniature plant care kits, sporting tiny shovels and picks, as well as decorative spray bottles to mist one's verdant menagerie—indeed, misting was as much a fashionable word as a painstaking pastime. Treasured plants were periodically carried to the bathroom shower for a thorough soaking, and plant owners going on vacation hired plant sitters to care for their greenery.

Macramé.   A plant could be hung in a no more fitting basket than one of clove-hitched and square-knotted macramé—(from the Turkish *makrama,* "napkin"; or Arabic *migramah,* "veil"), a medieval embroidery art. It employed hemp, jute, and sisal cord for making church vestments and decorative castle wall-hangings. The art surfaced in America in the Sixties hippie culture as the back-to-nature craft to aspire to. A favorite plant was suspended in a macramé "cradle," around the home, and in restaurants whose motif was half plant, half knotted hemp.

As caring for plants generated bestselling books, doing macramé resulted in such how-tos as the straightforwardly titled *Macramé Hangers for Small Spaces* and the unfortunately titled *Macramé Hang-Ups,* suggesting weavers of hemp had special phobias. Before the end of the decade, true to the nature of fads, indoor plants were considered gauche and macramé too embarrassing to leave hanging around. The decorative style by then, for apartments and restaurants, was for **industrial carpeting** and **hi-tech** architecture and accessories; a man-made, technological look, the antithesis of designs from nature.

Streaking

A nude young man jumps from behind a bush, races across the campus mooning onlookers, then ducks into a getaway car. He has streaked, and, importantly, gotten away with naughtiness—which was the crux of the faddish behavior.

The affront of streaking, a short-lived undergraduate fad in 1974, began on campuses in the warmer climates of Southern California and Florida during a period when the nation was mired in a recession and suffering under the shame of Watergate. Perhaps more relevant, though, was the peaking of the sexual revolution, which made public nudity, long a taboo, an annoyance for some and an amusement for others.

For a time streakers were everywhere. On campuses the behavior was a daily occurrence. At televised NBC sporting events it was a highlight to be hoped for. On the "Johnny Carson Show" it was probably staged (a blank screen was shown when a streaker flashed). At cultural events—as when streakers disrupted a Van Cliburn keyboard performance and a Rudolf Nureyev ballet solo (the dancer observed that the streaker had a "beautiful body")—it was tolerated as the passing fad it was perceived to be. For critics of the fad, the juvenile streaker was baring all he could be. But by shedding clothes a streaker symbolically demonstrated a shedding of inhibitions, which during the sexual revolution and the human potential movement was as noble a desideratum as any. By graduation time 1974, it was expected that at most commencements some young man would discard cap and gown for a flash of flesh. And so many did.

By then the fad had infected the general male population—and been tried by a few women; the first being eighteen-year-old student Laura Barton of Carleton College, Minnesota. In Hawaii, a streaker raced through the state legislature chamber, declaring himself "Streaker of the House." Producers of live TV broadcasts, an exhibitionist's wet dream, feared a streaker would violate the ban on frontal nudity and cautioned directors to be on alert. Sure enough, one Robert Opel, au naturel, streaked the Academy Awards telecast, prompting on-camera presenter David Niven to quip stingingly about the man's all-too-apparent "shortcomings."

Exhibitionism Abroad.   Streaking was a pandemic fad, erupting throughout most of the civilized world. Yet it remained largely American: Three streakers who dashed through Rome's St. Peter's Square were visiting Americans; two men who scurried their way up the Eiffel Tower were sightseeing Americans, themselves becoming the sight; the streaker at an elegant sit-down embassy dinner in Peking was a Western junior diplomat.

Before the fad died down there were several streaking casualties. Heady in their streaking achievement, two naked young men collided on exiting a Detroit restaurant, one knocked senseless, the other coming to his senses and carrying his companion off. One man died after his burst of a streak across the deck of the *Queen Mary* ended in a getaway plunge into eighty feet of water. Another streaker was killed crossing the Dallas–Fort Worth Turnpike, victim of a motorist he had mesmerizingly distracted.

The demise of streaking itself came, not surprisingly, with the close of the academic year. Oh, there was an occasional public display of a passing derriere, but it occasioned no media coverage, nor scarcely a raised eyebrow. The latest in a long line of campus rites of spring had run its course.

Wall Climbing

As metaphor, "climbing the walls" has long been a student exam-time phrase as an expression of pent-up energy and percolating anxiety. Frustrating urges have long driven sane people "up the wall." But mid-decade the phrase, of uncertain origin, passed to literal expression as scores of college men scaled campus buildings like human flies in a craze called buildering, performed by builderers. The faddish behavior was triggered by the avalanche of media attention afforded the dizzying ascent of "professional" builderer George Willig up New York's World Trade Center in the summer of 1976.

Until Willig's public feat, most builderers were expert mountain climbers. To stay in shape or to rehearse for a climb, they'd scale any vertical wall with sufficient brick edges and finger-gripping crevices. The true-grit feat was less risky than climbing a real mountain, since avalanches and extreme weather changes were not a concern. Willig turned a little-publicized sport into a craze that swept campuses in the academic year of 1977.

For safety reasons, most colleges banned buildering. And they posted security guards in front of the most "challenging" buildings. Thus, at the University of California at Berkeley, a group of determined students, clutching with toes and fingertips, brachiated their way beneath the stadium overhang to win media attention and administration surprise. Students at Stanford University published a climbing guide to campus buildings, outlining the best routes up the math building. Female students at the University of Colorado in Boulder shinnied up a ventilation shaft.

As fads go, climbing walls took an unexpected twist. The University of Washington, hoping to wean kids off buildings, spent $45,000 in 1977 to construct a "climbing structure," filled with tempting cracks and overhangs—it began attracting about twelve hundred students a month. The school's recreational-sports director dubbed the adult play-gym "the anthill." More planned anthills surfaced, and grew into more challenging vertical structures, and by the Eighties the latest indoor-sport craze was climbing wall structures of concrete and stone that replicate sheer mountain faces. The nation's largest designed wall to date opened in April 1990, at Cornell University. Measuring 30 feet high by 160 feet wide, the $160,000 surface incorporated concrete blocks and specially constructed chunks of real rock as finger- and toe-holds. Bigger walls are already planned. The one-time campus fad and mountain climbers' exercise may turn out to be the hottest indoor sport of the Nineties.

Hacky Sack

In the mid-Seventies, fad forecasters predicted that a ball which resembled a leather beanbag, was kicked around soccer style, and bore a name like a city in New Jersey (Hackensack) would outrival Frisbee and the hula hoop in promoters' hype and buyers' sales. They were nearly right. For a time Hacky Sacks, selling for $5 each and usually stuffed with small plastic pellets, seemed to be everywhere. They were particularly popular on college campuses, where student players were hackers and the activity was hacking—words that in the next decade would apply to more intellectually oriented computer buffs.

The object of the game of Hacky Sack was to keep the soft, golfball-sized bag airborne, using knees and feet, without letting the bag touch the ground or a player's upper body. A kick counted as one point. The game was invented in 1972 by an injured football player turned entrepreneur, R. John Stalberger, age twenty-seven, of Oregon City, Oregon. For Stalberger, the Hacky Sack footbag was a means of exercising and strengthening his tendon-torn knee. Motivated by his own fun at hacking, he began manufacturing the sacks, selling them to sporting goods stores, and giving demonstrations along the West Coast. By spring of 1978 he'd sold some seventy-seven thousand beanbags and established the National Hacky Sack Association to govern the growth of the game and referee rules disputes. Several colleges started Hacky Sack teams.

Unlike most fads that quickly crest, then crash, Hacky Sack grew in popularity. Stalberger's luck peaked in the early Eighties when he discovered that thirty-five-year-old Dan Roddick, a past world champion Frisbee player and then director of sports promotion at Wham-O Company (creators of Frisbee and hula hoop), was an avid hacker. In 1983 Wham-O acquired the U.S. and Canadian marketing rights from Stalberger for $1.5 million, leaving the inventor's company, Kenncorp, the rest of the world. By then Hacky Sack had fad followings in England, France, Germany, and Denmark.

As it did with Frisbee, Wham-O legitimized Hacky Sack by elevating it from a casual pastime to a competitive sport. The company gave support to the development of a World Footbag Association, which sanctioned tournaments and championship events, standardized rules of play, and decided such arcane points as the names of particular kicks and moves players devised. By the mid-Eighties the former fad was a national sport with TV promotion, and Wham-O had sold more than 1.2 million beanbags at $6 apiece. As the Eighties drew to a close, the world record for consecutive kicks by a hacker was 32,598, completed in five hours, twenty-nine minutes, and ten seconds. For a hackerette: 12,838 kicks in two hours, ten minutes, and forty seconds. Who is to say where such devotion will lead?

Star Wars Toys

George Lucas's 1977 high-tech space fantasy *Star Wars* spawned a cottage industry of fad spin-offs. The movie, earning a quarter of a billion dollars, produced a frenzy of merchandising tie-ins; especially popular were a line of 3¼-inch-high action figures by Kenner of the film's characters: the plucky Luke Skywalker, the robot team of R2D2 and C3PO, noble Obi-Wan Kenobi, in-distress Princess Leia, evil Darth Vader, Han Solo, Chewbacca, and the imaginative rest.

When Kenner could not keep up with the Christmas season demand, risking the loss of millions of dollars in profits, the company devised a brilliant ruse: issuing IOUs that could be redeemed as soon as the toys were available. Millions of parents bent on pleasing their kids laid out cash for nonexistent toys, while Kenner merrily counted money for toys on spec. In February 1978, two months after Christmas, Kenner began to make good on the IOUs. As Richard O'Brien points out in *The Story of American Toys,* between 1977 and 1984 Kenner and another licensed company sold 300 million *Star Wars* toys, and by 1987 merchandising from the movie accounted for sales of $2.6 billion. By that time the film characters were icons, Darth Vader, R2D2, and C3PO having put their footprints in cement at Mann's Chinese Theater.

As toy fads go, *Star Wars* figures were something of a turning point. Throughout history, children had played with horses, soldiers, carriages, cars, and trains—toys that reflected their times. "After *Star Wars,*" writes O'Brien, "more and more toys emerged that had nothing to do with the past, nothing to do with the present, and very little to do with the foreseeable future." Fantasy toys were hot. "Children no longer copied their parents, other adults, or anyone else on earth," says O'Brien. "A basic tenet of playthings had been violated"—and a lucrative new market had opened up. A line of Super Heroes Action Figures—featuring **Batman, Superman, Spiderman,** and **Wonder Woman**—was for a time among the nation's ten bestselling toys. And later in the decade there was the **Incredible Hulk.** All taken from the pages of comic books.

DANCE CRAZES

Disco

For many young people in the Seventies, the style of dance became confusingly inseparable from the beat of the popular music as dance and music became one, known simply as disco. Disco was a dance style, a pulsating musical rhythm, and the name of a nightspot for dancing. The word was as much a verb as a noun: You discoed at a disco to disco. Never before had a club, a discotheque, given its name to a style of song and dance. And more: For many people disco came to mean a mode of dress, a style of life.

Discotheques existed some three decades before the birth of disco music (which is discussed in the next part of this book). The clubs, where dancers did the swing and jitterbug to music recorded on discs, originated in Paris after World War II. Because a popular club had a rich library of musical discs, it was named after a book library, a *bibliotheque,* the coined neologism combining the French *disque* (Latin *discus,* "disc") and *theque* (Greek *theke,* "library"). Disc libraries for dancing, on the order of Paris's popular Whisky A Gogo, spread from France to England to America, where chic Manhattan clubs like the Peppermint Lounge, Arthur's, and Sybil's (owned by Richard Burton's ex-wife Sybil) were discos—though the music they played did not yet bear the name disco. Most observers of popular culture agree that it was a mid-Seventies dance, the hustle, that unleashed discomania on the nation.

Hustle

Purely an American invention, the hustle was created in the early Seventies in East Harlem by black youths who could not afford to attend rock concerts or get into fashionable discotheques. Isolated, energetic, they began dancing to a Latin beat called **salsa,** inventing their own footsteps and bodyshakes. The hustle (in its Latin and New York versions) brought back touch-dancing and vigorously athletic movements in which the male would spin his partner and acrobatically toss her into the air. In addition to its strenuous style, the hustle also had set foot patterns like the fox trot; many said it was a Latinized hybrid of the jitterbug crossed with the fox trot.

"The hustle gained popularity," writes Roberta Morgan in *Disco,* "in small private social clubs in Harlem's El Barrio. Then it moved downtown, all around town, and discos started opening *en masse.*" From blacks, gay men picked up the disco beat, and many of Manhattan's trendiest discos catered to a bisexual crowd. Then in 1975 came a hit instrumental song that kicked off the disco revolution nationwide: "The Hustle," by Van McCoy and the Soul City Symphony.

McCoy had already written a string of hits for Aretha Franklin and Gladys Knight and the Pips when he created the catchy tune "The Hustle." An instant hit, from his album "Disco Baby," the song shot to number one in July 1975. The *New York Times* called it the biggest dance recording of the decade. It became an international bestseller and won a Grammy award for best pop instrumental of the year. Ironically, "The Hustle" was the last cut on the album, and McCoy almost didn't record it. "My partner kept bugging me about doing something with the hustle," he said. "We had just one hour of studio time left, so I sat down and wrote whatever came into my head."

In essence, he transformed a dance he'd only recently seen into an irresistible musical beat. Expressed another way: He took a trend in dance and music wildly popular among blacks and gays and made it mainstream. Though it is always risky to try to pinpoint when a trend began, Van McCoy's recording seems the most reasonable starting point for viewing disco as all we remember it to be (for more, see page 000). For McCoy, who tragically died of a heart attack at age thirty-five, "The Hustle" was his only single to make the top forty.

Roberta Morgan pinpoints another trend starting from McCoy's "The Hustle" and its effect on the proliferation of disco clubs and disco music. Disc jockeys and the airtime they granted a record had long determined a song's popularity. "With the discos," she argues, "dancers decided what would be popular, and the music they wanted to hear was the music they wanted to dance to." By 1978 America had over twenty-five hundred discos, and "three out of every five records cut in the country" were disco. And, too, there were disco movies like . . .

Saturday Night Fever

In 1977 TV star John Travolta, adored for his role of the sexy and lovable hood Vinnie Barbarino in "Welcome Back, Kotter," donned a three-piece white suit, shiny black shirt (open down the chest), flamenco-wedge shoes, and gold chain, and defined disco for millions of moviegoers through the hit film *Saturday Night Fever*. His characterization of Tony Manero, for which he received an Academy Award nomination, at once made disco a cliché and a commercial bonanza. The movie, about a working-class boy from the Bay Ridge section of Brooklyn whose world comes alive on Saturday night through dance, was a disco how-to: how to dance, dress, and score big with disco babies.

The story was based on an article in *New York* magazine (June 7, 1976) by Nik Cohn: "Tribal Rites of the New Saturday Night." The movie made Travolta

John Travolta in Saturday Night Fever.

a superstar and Tony an icon, and prompted hotels and airports to set up disco lounges so travelers would not be caught without a place to disco. As disco fever raged, elegant dance establishments like the Persian Room at New York's Plaza Hotel and the Empire Room at the Waldorf-Astoria reported empty floors, and old dance halls like Roseland, where folk earlier had danced the Lindy, became discos to survive. Preeminent among discos was . . .

Studio 54

Not since the Peppermint Lounge had there been a nightspot so notorious and so hard to get into. At the height of discomania, the Manhattan dance club on West 54th Street—opened on April 26, 1977, by Steve Rubell and Ian Schrager (who'd later go to jail for income tax evasion)—was the place where *Liza, Liz* and *Jackie-O* hosted private disco parties, where *Bianca* discoed atop a white horse, where the dressed-all-in-black *Halston* watched bare-chested young men boogie, where *Roy Cohn* dabbed a runny nose, where *Brooke* wore her Calvins, and where *Calvin Klein* remarked "Steve changed forever what people think of as nightlife in New York." After a visit to the club, *Andy Warhol* jotted in his diary: "Went over to Studio 54. The band struck up 'New York, New York' and they carried Liza in. Halston did photos with her."

According to *Vanity Fair* editor Tina Brown, Rubell was "a genius at social life, the greatest showman of after-eight existence." And Studio 54 was his showcase. *Newsday* summed up Rubell's formula for success: He had a knack for "creating a sense of mystique, courting the press, and hiring good-looking waiters and abusive doormen." Bob Colacello, then editor of *Interview Magazine,* claimed that no matter where in the world he traveled—"Chicago, or Milan, or Düsseldorf or Dallas"—he was barraged with the same question: "You're from New York? Can you get me into Studio 54?"

As much a tourist attraction as the Statue of Liberty or Radio City Music Hall, Studio 54 drew people to New York in the slim hope of discoing with the stars. A beefy doorman who did not recognize Warren Beatty once turned away the star; another doorman rejected Michael Douglas. To minimize embarrassment, celebrities either phoned ahead that they were coming or arrived with high-profile regulars or exotica like Divine.

Major, Major Stars.   Studio 54 defined disco life in the Seventies. "It was the most exciting period for New York nightlife in the last fifty years," Halston reminisced in *Newsday* in the Eighties. "Every corner you'd see somebody you'd read about in the paper . . . Beautiful people. Major, major stars." And, too, those lucky ordinary folk who were shuffled through the door because of their trendy attire or knockout looks. "Diana Ross would be sitting in the DJ booth," recalled Halston, "and all of a sudden take the microphone and sing. It was like a movie." The unapologetically bisexual atmosphere of Studio 54 made it a place unique to the decade, when for a time it was fashionable to know gays, dance with gays, or at the very least watch gays dance.

Studio 54 came to an end some twenty months after it opened—when the IRS charged Rubell and his partner Schrager with evading nearly a million dollars in taxes. The disco's celebrity regulars were shocked, not only because their favorite nightspot was shut, but because IRS agents, searching the premises, had come up with a list of expenses for poppers, Quaaludes, cash, and cocaine, prompting speculation that owners Rubell and Schrager were not above luring in the Beautiful People with gifts.

Roller Disco

The faddish marriage between disco dancing and roller skating, the latter a popular Seventies pastime in its own right, took place in rinks in Brooklyn and the Bronx late in the decade. By 1979 the Roller Skating Rink Operators Association of America reported that at least 70 percent of its member rinks were equipped for roller disco—an expensive conversion in terms of lights and loudspeakers, but one essential to survival.

It's believed that roller disco began among younger people, between the ages of thirteen and twenty, who, unable to get into disco clubs that served liquor, strapped on wheels and began to skate in a disco-dancing style. The fad caught on when Olivia Newton-John, Robin Williams, and Linda Ronstadt appeared in national magazines as roller disco aficionados, and when Cher and Ringo Starr threw private parties at Los Angeles's Sherman Square Rink.

What few people realized during the height of roller discomania was that the fad had a nineteenth-century precedent. Roller skates were invented by Belgian musical instrument maker Joseph Merlin in the 1700s; and by the mid-1800s people were wild about "gliding on wheels," a form of roller dancing. Many of the early pioneering roller rinks, in England and America, added music for skaters' pleasure. The more accomplished skaters, eager to display their skills, began to roller dance. Most popular were the **roller two-step** and the **roller waltz**—both markedly genteel considering the bulk and burden of Victorian clothes. During the Gay Nineties the **roller march** was popular, a ten-step dance routine created by Franz Scholler and first performed at a Vienna rink in 1889. It was also used by ice skaters.

In New York, in the Seventies, what Studio 54 was to disco, the Roxy was to roller disco. In 1979 the first roller disco magazine was published, and Pocket Books released *Jammin'*, a guide to dancing safely on wheels. Early in the next decade the fad had lost momentum, with the activity done more on streets and in parks than in rinks and converted discos.

POPULAR SONGS

In the Seventies the term rock 'n' roll was shorn to simply "rock." Though there was nothing simple about rock's multitude of sounds: **folk rock and soul rock, hard rock and soft rock, acid rock and shock rock, gospel rock and bubble-gum rock.** It got to be that any contemporary sound enjoyed by young people, or those young at heart, was, by default, rock. All that was "other" was listened to by "adults." Rock even got its own magazine, *Rolling Stone.*

There was, too, a new record-selling trend apparent in the Seventies. Prior to the late Sixties, most young people bought *singles.* Starting, arguably with the music of the Beatles (others say with that of Elvis Presley), rock fans moved away from singles and toward buying albums. The shift greatly influenced the way music was recorded and promoted throughout the decade. Mid-decade, *Billboard* paused to count up album sales from the period 1956 to 1975. Though rock music and its young audience was a commercial force to be lovingly courted, its influence had yet to dominate the purchase of albums. The top ten sellers were:

1. **My Fair Lady**—original cast
2. **South Pacific**—movie soundtrack
3. **The Sound of Music**—movie soundtrack
4. **The Sound of Music**—original cast
5. **West Side Story**—movie soundtrack
6. **Oklahoma**—movie soundtrack
7. **Johnny's Greatest Hits**—Johnny Mathis
8. **Sing Along With Mitch**—Mitch Miller
9. **Camelot**—original cast
10. **The King and I**—movie soundtrack.

It was obvious who then had the money to afford albums—though things were already changing. Number twelve was **Led Zeppelin,** followed by Carole King's **Tapestry;** climbing the list was the Beatles' **Sgt. Pepper's Lonely Hearts Club Band** (number twenty-six), **Hair** (number twenty-nine), **Blood, Sweat & Tears** (number thirty), plus albums by Simon and Garfunkel **(Parsley, Sage, Rosemary & Thyme),** Elton John, Jim Croce; and Earth, Wind & Fire.

Here, by year, are the hits, singles and albums.

Raindrops Keep Fallin' on My Head: 1970

"Raindrops," sung by B. J. Thomas, was the first big hit of the new decade (number one the week of January 3), written by Burt Bacharach and Hal David for the soundtrack of the Paul Newman/Robert Redford film *Butch Cassidy and the Sundance Kid* (which itself would launch a trend for male buddy movies). For Bacharach and David, it was their second number one single, following their 1968 smash with Herb Alpert, "This Guy's in Love With You," and the song took the Academy Award in its category.

Led Zeppelin, which would become one of the most influential rock bands of the Seventies—and, surprisingly for many, one of President Jimmy Carter's favorite groups—began the year with **Whole Lotta Love,** number four at the end of January. The band, whose first two choices for a name were Whoopie Cushion and Mad Dog, and which derived its name from the cliché "going down like a lead zeppelin," was, as the authors of *The Seventies* write, "the harbinger of the first serious split in the rock audience between those who came of age with the Beatles and their younger siblings."

In the year when Led Zeppelin gained commercial clout (voted England's most popular group by one rock publication), the Beatles broke up. Their last records together were **Let It Be** (number one in April) and **The Long and Winding Road** (number one in June), the second being the group's twentieth and final chart topper. Their final LP, also released in 1970, was **Abbey Road.** "Only two other chart acts in the entire rock era have come close to the Beatles' total of 20 number ones," writes pop chronicler Fred Bronson. "Elvis Presley had 17 and Diana Ross and the Supremes had 12." By coincidence, notes Bronson, the Beatles, Elvis, and the Supremes "all had their final number one singles in an eight-month period between November, 1969, and June, 1970."

In the first six months of 1970, Peter, Paul, and Mary scored a hit with **Leaving on a Jet Plane;** Diana Ross and the Supremes sang **Someday We'll Be Together;** heartthrob Tom Jones crooned **Without Love There Is Nothing;** Eddie Holman sang **Hey There Lonely Girl;** and Simon and Garfunkel, one of the most successful duos since the Everly Brothers, began the painful process of splitting up during the recording of their ironically titled album (and one of the bestselling of the rock era) **Bridge Over Troubled Water.** In fact, many of the album's songs feature only Paul Simon; Art Garfunkel was busy filming Mike Nichols's *Catch-22* and contemplating a new career in movies.

I Want You Back: 1970

It's ironic that a month after Diana Ross and the Supremes had their final number one single, Motown was able to "replace" them with the Jackson Five. "I Want You Back," the only single released from their first album, topped the charts in the first month of the new year and set a pattern for the immensely talented group and family (sisters Janet and LaToya would later make their marks on pop music history). In April the group was again number one on the charts with **ABC,** then in June with **The Love You Save,** and again in October with **I'll Be There.** And the pattern would be similar the following year, beginning with **Never Can Say Goodbye.**

In the summer of 1970 another family group—a brother, Richard, and sister, Karen—the Carpenters, outsold the Jackson Five with their number one hit **(They Long to Be) Close to You.** The Burt Bacharach/Hal David song had been turned down by Herb Alpert, who could not bring himself to sing such sugary lyrics as "So they sprinkled moon dust in your hair . . ." The Carpenters' hit was soon eclipsed by Diana Ross's first smash single as a solo artist, **Ain't No Mountain High Enough,** three weeks the nation's top tune. In the closely watched competition between the new Supremes and the solo Diana, Ross aggressively took the lead—and kept it.

The Carpenters were tops again in the fall with **We've Only Just Begun,** which competed closely in sales with **I Think I Love You** by the Partridge Family, members of ABC's hit sitcom of the same name (only two cast members, Shirley Jones and David Cassidy, actually recorded the song). The year ended with the Fifth Dimension scoring a hit with **One Less Bell to Answer,** Dawn with **Knock Three Times,** and solo Beatle George Harrison holding the number one single in the last week of December, **My Sweet Lord/Isn't It a Pity,** a double-sided success.

On the downside, drugs claimed the lives of two pop stars in 1970. Jimi Hendrix, age twenty-eight, died from a combination of drugs and choking on his own vomit on September 18. Hard-living Janis Joplin, age twenty-seven, was found dead in a hotel room on October 3, victim of a combination of heroin, tequila and Valium. She had a posthumous Number One hit in March 1971: **Me and Bobby McGee.**

I Feel the Earth Move; It's Too Late; You've Got a Friend: 1971

A major songwriter in the Sixties ("Up on the Roof," "He's a Rebel," "Go Away, Little Girl"), Carole King (born Carol Klein on February 9, 1942) was reincarnated in the Seventies as a combination singer/songwriter. Her solo album *Tapestry* sold over 14 million copies, ranking it then as the bestselling LP in history. In 1971 she was honored with four Grammy awards. "It's Too Late"/"I Feel the Earth," a double-sided hit, was number one in June (just ahead of the Carpenters' **Rainy Days and Mondays**). In July her close friend James Taylor was at the top of the charts with a single from her *Tapestry* album, "You've Got a Friend." In a March cover story, *Time* hailed Taylor, son of a medical school dean, as "the first superstar of the 1970s." In a decade that could be summed up in est and the human potential movement, King's "You've Got a Friend" and Taylor's song message as he told *Newsweek*—"to look deeply into your own self for answers"—were perfectly suited for the group therapy era.

In March, Tom Jones had a hit with his sexy **She's a Lady.** The Carpenters were back on the charts with **For All We Know.** Lone Beatle Paul McCartney had a double hit in April with **Another Day/Oh Woman Oh Why,** while the next month Ringo Starr scored with **It Don't Come Easy.** In the summer of 1971, the Bee Gees, the brothers Gibb (Barry, Maurice, and Robin), shot to the top of the charts with **How Can You Mend a Broken Heart?** The successful British-born group had split up in 1969, then at their father's pleading reconciled. "Broken Heart" was written by Barry and Robin for Andy Williams, but when he rejected it the brothers made their own recording. "It became," says Fred Bronson, "the first of nine number one singles for the Bee Gees."

Go Away Little Girl: 1971

Brother Donny (born Donald Clark on December 9, 1957) had been a member of the Osmonds (Wayne, Merrill, Jay, and Alan), five siblings who appeared regularly on "The Andy Williams Show." The brothers had a long list of hits, including **One Bad Apple,** number one in February 1971. Though Donny would occasionally record singles, the group remained together and highly successful, scoring ten top-selling records between 1971 and 1974. But what really unleashed the Seventies Osmondmania was the attention that teen magazines gave young Donny. First he, then his sister Marie, became teen idols; they recorded duets and in 1976 landed their own popular TV show. Their perky, pristine soda-pop image would be hard for them to shake off, but Donny, after a long absence from recording, would be reincarnated with a harder edge in the Nineties.

Donny's "Go Away" was displaced from number one by Rod Stewart's **Maggie May/Reason to Believe;** and that same week in October, Sixties phenomenon Joan Baez was back, in the number three spot, with **The Night They Drove Old Dixie Down.** And again a solo Beatle surfaced: John Lennon (Plastic Ono Band) with **Imagine,** a song that would take on new meaning following his violent death.

Theme From Shaft: 1971

If the image of blacks in movies had long been that of a Stepin' Fetchit, the stereotype changed, for better or worse, in the Seventies. *Superfly* (1972), the most controversial of the new genre, glorified a black cocaine dealer, and *Shaft* (1971) dished up a black, militant James Bond type (played by Richard Roundtree), who prompted the song lyric: "Who's the black private dick / Who's a sex machine to all the chicks?" The movie's menacing theme song won an Academy Award for writer/producer Isaac Hayes, and topped the charts in the final weeks of 1971.

Hayes, who thought he was going to actually play the movie's hero (before MGM came up with Roundtree), consoled himself by having a blockbuster single. The success of the film and its theme song produced a trend for what was called "blaxploitation" in the early Seventies. Hayes was asked to score other blaxploitation films like *Tough Guys.* Mean black "dudes" and "studs" turned up in *Black Caesar* (1973, something of a black *Godfather*), *Abby* (1974, a black *Exorcist*); and black monsters took center stage in *Blacula* (1972) and *Blackenstein* (1974). Blacks needed heroes, the NAACP conceded, but was this the answer?

Gospel rock was well represented in theater in 1971: *Godspell* opened on Broadway on May 17, and on October 12 Tim Rice and Andrew Lloyd Webber (the latter soon to be a musical theater phenomenon) debuted their *Jesus Christ Superstar* at the off-Broadway Cherry Lane Theater.

American Pie: 1972

Singer/songwriter Don McLean composed "(Bye Bye) American Pie" with his hero Buddy Holly in mind (as he only later admitted). The song's line "the day the music died" referred to February 3, 1959, when Holly and friends were killed in a plane crash. For many, the end of the Fifties was the day the music died (see page 292). But the song, coming during the homefront anguish over the Vietnam War and during the year that five Watergate burglars would be arrested and in turn bring down an American president, seemed to sum up for many a general disillusionment with American Pie and all it contained. The song was number one at the start of the year, ahead of **Family Affair** by Sly and the Family Stone.

The Carpenters returned to the charts in February with **Hurting Each Other** (number three), just ahead of Climax's **Precious and Few.** That week the top tune was **Without You,** by Nilsson (born Harry Edward Nelson), an earlier song he'd come upon while gathering research for his album *Nilsson Schmilsson.* Paul Simon, now a solo act, scored in March with **Mother and Child Reunion.**

For spring, the romantic favorite across the country was Roberta Flack's hauntingly beautiful **The First Time Ever I Saw Your Face.** She'd recorded the song, co-written by the sister of Pete Seeger, in 1969 for her album "First Take." But only after Clint Eastwood, searching for a mood-creating number for a love scene with Donna Mills in *Play Misty for Me,* included the tune in his movie did it become a smash. Number one for six weeks, "it became," says Bronson, "the longest-running chart-topper by a solo female artist since 'The Wayward Wind' by Gogi Grant in 1956."

Sammy Davis, Jr., took over the top slot in June with another tune from a movie: **Candy Man,** from the 1971 children's musical *Willie Wonka and the Chocolate Factory.* The song was written by Anthony Newley and Leslie Bricusse, who gave Davis another hit from their Broadway show *Stop the World—I Want to Get Off:* **What Kind of Fool Am I?** Both numbers became Davis trademarks.

As summer turned to fall, Mac Davis had a number one single in **Baby Don't Get Hooked on Me.** Three weeks later Michael Jackson, in his first solo effort, had the nation's top seller, **Ben,** a song from the 1972 animal movie of that title. The film, a sequel to the 1971 rodent hit *Willard,* tells of an ailing boy who befriends the leader of a pack of rats. The young Jackson, even then a passionate animal lover, was attracted immediately to the song. That same month the Moody Blues scored with a more adult song, **Nights in White Satin,** and Johnny Cash was number one with **I Can See Clearly Now.**

I Am Woman; You're So Vain: 1972

The decade would be remembered for the publication of *Ms.* magazine, promotion of the equal rights amendment, and the Supreme Court's *Roe v. Wade* decision that moved abortions out of back alleys and into clinics. The women's movement was in full swing, and Helen Reddy's hit, "I Am Woman," number one in December, quickly became an anthem for many in the ranks of the liberated. Reddy wrote the song with Ray Burton and performed it while she was pregnant. Her Grammy award acceptance speech after winning best vocal performance/female amused thousands of fans: "I want to thank everyone concerned . . . my husband and manager, Jeff Wald, because he makes my success possible, and God because She makes everything possible." To celebrate the United Nations International Women's Year, Reddy donated use of the song, and she told *Newsweek,* "I've had the chance to raise the consciousness among American women . . . I get a special feeling when I sing it. It's a chest-beating song of pride."

The year 1972 ended with the release of Carly Simon's "You're So Vain," which would be number one in the first week of the new year. An heiress to the publishing house of Simon & Schuster, wife of singer James Taylor, Simon had everyone guessing who the song was about. Was the vain cad rumored lover Warren Beatty, or Mick Jagger (who provided a backup vocal), or Kris Kristofferson? Or Taylor, whom she had married a month earlier? Simon later admitted in *Carly Simon Complete* that "I had about three or four different men in mind when I wrote that song."

The year was also notable for the February 14 debut off-Broadway of *Grease,* which kicked off a nostalgic, decade-long pining for the Fifties. The show had moved to Broadway by June, and by 1978 had grossed $40 million, and became a hit film starring John Travolta and Olivia Newton-John.

Tie a Yellow Ribbon Round the Ole Oak Tree: 1973

During the Persian Gulf conflict of 1991 thousands of American families tied yellow ribbons and bows around front yard trees. Some authorities believe the custom originated in the 1949 John Wayne cavalry saga *She Wore a Yellow Ribbon,* in which the band of fabric symbolized a woman's devotion to her fighting soldier. Others point to an old folk song, first published in 1917, "Round Her Neck She Wears a Yellow Ribbon," in which an anxious woman awaits the return of her lover. It's known that during the Civil War the custom was not uncommon.

"Tie a Yellow Ribbon Round the Ole Oak Tree," the 1973 song by Tony Orlando and Dawn, was number one in April. It celebrated the return not of a soldier but of a prisoner (and the practice was seen in 1981 for the U.S. hostages in Iran). Many authorities say the megahit, based on a true story, marked the beginning of the modern-day custom. The story told of a man returning home by bus after serving three years in jail for passing bad checks; his wife, if she wishes to take him back, is to signal her intentions by placing a yellow ribbon on a tree in a public square. Everyone aboard the bus awaits the sign, which materializes. Writer Irwin Levine cast the tear-jerker into a song that revitalized Tony Orlando's career and won the group its own TV series.

Crocodile Rock; Daniel; Goodbye Yellow Brick Road: 1973

It was a splendid year for emerging superstar Reginald Kenneth Dwight (Elton John), born on March 25, 1947, in Middlesex, England. Pained son of a despotic military father, who by his own admission endured a restrictive and humiliating childhood, Reg displayed early musical genius. He derived his stage name by combining the Christian names of two members of his first band (Elton Dean and John Baldry). "Crocodile Rock," a pastiche of the Beach Boys' sound and several of John's favorite pop songs, hit number one in February 1973, and hailed the arrival of the decade's glitz showman par excellence—a tour de force metamorphosis for a pudgy, balding, bespectacled, unhappy young man.

"Daniel" was number two in May, and "Goodbye Yellow Brick Road" was number two in December. By 1976 John, who later hurt his career by admitting his bisexuality, had sold 42 million albums and 18 million singles, with royalties exceeding $8 million. *Billboard* eventually ranked him as "one of the wealthiest rock stars of all time." By then ten of his albums had gone platinum. More than a singing sensation, John, through his outrageous platform shoes, bizarre attire, fetching wigs and hats, and bejeweled eyeglasses, launched a host of the decade's funkier copycat fashions.

The Night the Lights Went Out in Georgia: 1973

Born in 1949 in Inglewood, California, Vicki Lawrence longed for a career in show business. In college she performed with a folk group and later sang with the Young Americans. When a journalist mentioned her resemblance to comedienne Carol Burnett, Vicki Lawrence moved quickly. She wrote to Burnett as a fan, won an introduction, and soon was a regular cast member of "The Carol Burnett Show," later winning her own series, "Mama's Family." Along the way she married songwriter Bobby Russell, who composed a fact-based song for Cher about a man who murders out of passion. Cher turned down "The Night the Lights Went Out in Georgia," and wife Vicki Lawrence had the nation's number one single in the spring of 1973, two weeks at the top of the charts. When she failed to duplicate the feat (with "He Did It With Me," number seventy-five in 1973; and "The Other Woman," number eighty-one in 1975), Vicki abandoned singing for TV sitcom.

Other hits in the first quarter of 1973 were Roberta Flack's **Killing Me Softly With His Song,** Stevie Wonder's **Superstition,** the Carpenters' **Sing,** and the Four Tops' **Ain't No Woman.** And in May, Stevie Wonder was back with the country's number one romantic single . . .

You Are the Sunshine of My Life: 1973

This anthem to love featured the multitalented performer playing most of the instruments. It won Wonder a Grammy for best pop vocal performance and became a money-maker for such artists as Johnny Mathis, Andy Williams, and Frank Sinatra—to name a few who recorded it. It was "Little" Stevie Wonder's third number one single, and it marked the point in his career when fans began to drop the reference to his childhood genius; Stevie had married his secretary, Syreeta, and was no longer "Little."

His hit was soon displaced by Paul McCartney and Wings' **My Love,** top of the charts in June. By the end of the month another ex-Beatle, George Harrison, would have a chart-topper with **Give Me Love.** Climbing fast was the sexy **Pillow Talk** by Sylvia (Robinson), who as part of the duet Mickey and Sylvia enjoyed a Fifties smash single, "Love Is Strange" (see page 286). She wrote the "Pillow" song herself, hoping another artist (Al Green) might make it a hit, and recorded it herself only as a demo for Green's producer. When it was rejected, she released her own version.

During the summer Jim Croce scored with **Bad, Bad Leroy Brown;** Maureen McGovern with **The Morning After;** and Diana Ross with **Touch Me in the Morning,** a song conceived as "insurance" to give Ross a hit should she bomb in her acting debut as Billie Holiday in *Lady Sings the Blues.* "Morning" was topped in September by Helen Reddy's **Delta Dawn,** which in turn succumbed to Paul Simon's **Love Me Like a Rock.** *Billboard*'s number one hit in late September was . . .

We're an American Band: 1973

Grand Funk Railroad (named after Michigan's Grand Trunk Railroad) was a hard-rock trio who introduced many Americans to an early form of "heavy metal" music, like "We're an American Band." The group was panned by critics but worshipped by a new breed of rock followers. Many writers point to the trio's ascendancy as the benchmark for the split between rock reviewers and rock fans. Through hype, the group overcame the reluctance of radio DJs to play their music, going straight to long-haired teen audiences through continual touring. "Grand Funk ARE an experience meant to be lived, in which to participate," wrote rock critic Dave Marsh. "For they are in touch with what no one else is—the spirit of American youth, the children of the '70s."

As the year wound down, Gladys Knight and the Pips were back on the charts with **Midnight Train to Georgia,** Cher with **Half-Breed,** Marie Osmond with **Paper Roses,** the Carpenters with **Top of the World,** and Charlie Rich with the romantic **(If You Happen to See) The Most Beautiful Girl (in the World).**

Pop music hits from Broadway came from Stephen Sondheim's *A Little Night Music*—particularly **Send in the Clowns,** recorded by many artists. The Academy Award–winning film *The Sting,* with a score assembled from Scott Joplin tunes, launched a craze for ragtime. And George Lucas's nostalgic look at the Fifties in *American Graffiti* boosted the sales of oldies.

The Way We Were: 1974

It was the year Richard Nixon resigned the presidency to avoid impeachment proceedings. In the world of music, the year opened with Brooklyn-born Barbra Joan Streisand—no stranger to hits: she'd already scored with **People, Second-Hand Rose,** and **Stoney End**—in first place with the title song from her film (with Robert Redford) *The Way We Were.* The Marvin Hamlisch tune won a Grammy and an Oscar, and remained number one for three weeks. The song and the film reinforced her image as a superstar of the Seventies, though critics were already complaining that as an actress Streisand could only play Barbra—precisely what her fans wanted her to be. Composer Hamlisch enjoyed his own piano single, **The Entertainer,** written in 1902 by Scott Joplin.

In March the pop chart slots were occupied by John Denver's **Sunshine on My Shoulders,** Elton John's **Bennie and the Jets,** and Cher's **Dark Lady.** The following month Blue Swede scored a Number One single with **Hooked on a Feeling,** and a most unexpected bestseller was . . .

The Lord's Prayer: 1974

Born in Adelaide, Australia, in 1938, Janet Mead had become a member of the Sisters of Mercy at age seventeen, and began her own rock band, providing Sunday church music for the Christian Mass, which was growing decidedly communal and folksy in the Seventies. A local radio station started to play her songs, but when she put to music a millennia-old prayer that Christ had taught his disciples, Sister Mead had a million-seller; in fact, a 2-million-seller. The song "featured an earthy bass line, ominous fuzz-tone, plushly uplifting strings, and an ethereal lead vocal," reviews Wayne Jancik in *One-Hit Wonders*—and Sister Mead was a one-hit phenomenon.

It was a season for surprises: In spring, the heavy metal group Grand Funk returned to the top of the charts with a warmly nostalgic 1962 Little Eva dance hit, **The Loco-Motion,** number one for two weeks. The Jackson Five were not far behind with **Dancing Machine,** nor was Gordon Lightfoot with **Sundown.** The Stylistics scored with **You Make Me Feel Brand New,** William DeVaughn with **Be Thankful for What You Got,** and the Hues Corporation with **Rock the Boat** (from their 1973 album "Freedom for the Stallion"), a song in which the group had such little faith, they almost didn't release it as a single. "Rock the Boat" was a summer dance favorite.

Midsummer, progressive rockers Donald Fagen and Walter Becker, as the duo Steely Dan, scored with **Rikki Don't Lose That Number,** what Seventies observers Edelstein and McDonough called "an ecstatic boogie bolero that doubled as a prayer to a Buddhist Bodhisattva." High on the charts at the same time were John Denver's **Annie's Song,** and the Righteous Brothers' **Rock and Roll Heaven.**

As the summer drew to a close, prolific songwriter Paul Anka had a number one hit with . . .

(You're) Having My Baby: 1974

Fans loved this schmaltzy Paul Anka tune, but feminists complained that it cast women "in a subservient position." The National Organization for Women awarded Anka their annual Keep Her in Her Place award. Lambasted NOW's founder, Ellen Peck, "Were I 16 and pregnant, that song could keep me pregnant." Anka himself viewed the song as a joyous celebration of motherhood.

Around the same time, Elton John returned to the charts with **The Bitch Is Back.** Dionne Warwick and the Spinners were riding high with **Then Came You.** Bobby Vinton emerged from semi-obscurity with **My Melody of Love.** And John Lennon had a success with **Whatever Gets You Through the Night.** A craze for Kung Fu movies produced an unexpected hit at the end of the year.

Kung Fu Fighting: 1974

"Fu flicks," as they were called in the industry, were big box-office business, with David Carradine and Bruce Lee becoming cult heroes. As the story goes: Jamaican-born Carl Douglas had recorded "I Want to Give You My Everything," hoping it would become his breakthrough hit. Needing a flip-side filler, he suggested to his producer one of his own compositions, "Kung Fu Fighting." Quickly knocked off in ten minutes of studio time, with improvised karate-chop sound effects, the song aroused no expectations on the part of anyone involved with the record. However, it appealed to savvy Pye Record executives, who thought it could be tied in with the kung fu fad. Nine million copies were sold, the single held on to the number one spot for two weeks, and it kicked off a "fu" dance step—which in turn gave Douglas his next single, **Dance the Kung Fu.**

"Fu" was displaced from the top spot by Harry Chapin's **Cat's in the Cradle,** which in turn was topped by Helen Reddy's **Angie Baby.** Glitzmeister Elton John ended the year with his phenomenally popular **Lucy in the Sky with Diamonds,** written earlier by John Lennon and Paul McCartney. The song was inspired by Lennon's young son, as Lennon explained in a *Playboy* interview: "My son Julian came in one day with a picture he painted about a school friend of his named Lucy. He had sketched in some stars in the sky and called it 'Lucy in the Sky With Diamonds.' " Lennon denied rumors that the song's initials, LSD, were a subtle reference to the then-popular hallucinogen.

Mandy: 1975; I Write the Songs: 1976; Looks Like We Made It: 1977

The year 1975 opened with the arrival of a new pop music phenomenon, Brooklyn-born wonderboy Barry Manilow. Former arranger and pianist for Bette "The Divine Miss M" Midler, the twenty-eight-year-old Manilow—artist of advertising jingles: State Farm's "And Like a Good Neighbor"; McDonald's "You Deserve a Break Today," which he sang—launched his own career with

"Mandy," number one in January. The song, under its original title, "Brandy," and with a more upbeat tempo, had made the Hot 100 in 1972. Three years later, when Manilow was cutting his second album, he reluctantly included it as a "throwaway" cut. As the pop balladeer later said, "Who would know that this little album cut would turn out to be the beginning of my career?"

Almost exactly a year later, Manilow was at the top of the charts with his second hit single, "I Write the Songs"—a tune, which, despite popular misconception, he did not write (actually he did not write any one of his first three successes). Written by Bruce Johnston, one of the Beach Boys, and a modest hit for David Cassidy in 1975 (number eleven), the song *became* Manilow's since he did indeed write songs that, as the lyrics go, make the whole world sing.

Already famous for lushly orchestrated, escalating instrumental schmaltz, Manilow scored again in July 1977 with "Looks Like We Made It," a phrase that at that point succinctly summed up his career. From a musical standpoint, his songs were as slickly packaged as any of the many product commercials he'd worked on, and his fans loved them, one and all. From backing Bette Midler at the Continental Baths to headlining at the Copacabana, he would, by 1981, have amassed a string of eighteen consecutive top forty hits, surpassing Elvis Presley's record.

Feelings: 1975

The song, written and sung by Morris Albert, had millions of Americans intoning "whoa, whoa, whoa, feelings." "For nearly eight months," writes the author of *One-Hit Wonders,* "this lounge-lizard classic remained on the Hot 100 . . . Albert became a pop sensation—until, thanks to airplay ad nauseam, radio listeners grew weary of his sentiments." As it turned out, more than 80 percent of Albert's song had been plagiarized from a 1956 French song, "Pour Toi," by composer Louis Gaste, who expressed his own feelings in a lawsuit. In 1985 a Manhattan Federal District Court awarded Gaste a half-million dollar settlement.

In July 1975 came what many observers of pop music and dance say was a seminal single, the disco smash . . .

The Hustle: 1975

Disco—that potpourri of rock, rhythm and blues, and Latin dance fever—had been around, in song and dance, when songwriter Van McCoy's "The Hustle" hit number one in July 1975. Music writers proffer three other songs, all hits in 1974, as the first disco singles: Barry White's "Love's Theme" (number one in early February), the Hues Corporation's "Rock the Boat" (number one in early July), and George McCrae's "Rock Your Baby" (number one in mid-July)—all great to dance to. Indeed, that was an essential element in disco music.

"The Hustle," though, selling more than 10 million records and spawning a dance fever not seen since the mid-Sixties, became disco's anthem, a dance-floor sensation not only in New York clubs like the Sanctuary, the Loft, and the Flamingo, where disco was a passion, but in nightspots across the country.

"The Hustle" was a cut on Van McCoy's LP "Disco Baby," an album "specifically geared toward the discotheques," McCoy told *Essence* magazine, "because of the major role they play in getting a lot of new products started." And as a new product, disco was off on a frenzied climb: Soon there were novelty songs like Rick Dees's **Disco Duck**; the theme from "I Love Lucy" was revved up to **Disco Lucy**; Mussorgsky's 1887 "Night on Bald Mountain" came out as **Night on Disco Mountain**; Johnny Taylor hit it big with **Disco Lady.** There was a disco version of "The Star Wars Theme" and a celebrity disco club, Studio 54 (see page 387); a trendsetting disco movie, *Saturday Night Fever* (see page 386); and a kinky diva of disco, Grace Jones, who appeared on "The Merv Griffin Show" in a wedding dress and exposed black garter belt, carrying a leather whip. And Barbra Streisand teamed up with Donna Summer in the summer of 1979 to produce a disco dance-floor frenzy with **Enough Is Enough.**

Disco was proof that the Sixties were over.

As the Fifties became the doo-wop era, the Seventies would be remembered as the disco decade. DISCO TAKES OVER! announced a *Newsweek* cover story in the spring of 1979; leading off the article was a sentence that was more an expression of a trend than a fact: "Roll over rock . . . disco is here to stay." For rock and disco, as we'll later see, were about to become inextricably melded.

In addition to the arrival in 1975 of Barry Manilow and disco (and the mysteriously simultaneous appearance of newcomer Bruce Springsteen on the covers of *Newsweek* and *Time,* celebrating his "Born to Run" album), another musical phenomenon debuted that year.

A Chorus Line: 1975

Few of the privileged theatergoers who saw the May 21 opening of *A Chorus Line* downtown at Joseph Papp's Public Theater on Lafayette Street in Manhattan were ready for the visceral, moving, soul-searching experience that the musical was. On July 25 it moved uptown to Broadway's Shubert Theater and was pronounced by critics, one and all, a landmark in musical theater history. The show, conceived and directed by former "gypsy" Michael Bennett, with music and lyrics by Marvin Hamlisch and Edward Kleban, won nine Tonys and a Pulitzer, and produced a hit album and a run of smash singles, such as the much-recorded **What I Did for Love.** The longest-running show in the history of Broadway gave its final performance, number 6,137 (beating second-place *Oh, Calcutta!*'s 5,959) in 1990, having earned for Papp's Shakespeare Festival more than $38 million over the years. Bennett, the show's creator, died of AIDS in 1987.

Love Hangover: 1976

On July 4, 1976, America celebrated its bicentennial. Under Operation Sail, an armada of tall ships from around the globe sailed into New York harbor, welcomed by uncountable millions of cheering spectators. The nation's number one song that week was Diana Ross's **Love Hangover** (having displaced Wings' **Silly Love Songs,** written by Paul McCartney). Ross had begun the bicentennial year with another smash, **Theme from Mahogany (Do You Know Where You're Going To).**

Perhaps in unprecedented number, love was the subject of many of the country's top 1976 hits: **Love Rollercoaster** (Ohio Players), **Love to Love You Baby** (Donna Summer), **I Love Music (Part I)** (O'Jays), **Love Machine (Part I)** (Miracles); **Let Your Love Flow** (Bellamy Brothers); **Sweet Love** (Commodores); **Fooled Around and Fell in Love** (Elvin Bishop); **Love Is Alive** (Gary Wright); **You'll Never Find Another Love Like Mine** (Lou Rawls); **I'd Really Love to See You Tonight** (England Dan and John Coley); **Love So Right** (Bee Gees); **Muskrat Love** (Captain and Tennille)—all in a period of twelve months. On the emotional flip side was Paul Simon's **50 Ways to Leave Your Lover.**

The nation's number one tune in October was by a prolific writer of a past century, though given a disco beat.

A Fifth of Beethoven: 1976

As jingle-writer and pianist Walter Murphy revealed in *The Top Ten,* he had a "crazy idea to take symphonic music and combine it with contemporary rhythm." Not that the notion was original. In 1972 Bach's "Jesu, Joy of Man's Desiring" was a hit as "Joy." Murphy, who had composed catchy jingles for Korvette's, Revlon, Lady Arrow, and Woolworth's and arranged the music for "The Tonight Show," selected several of classical music's greatest themes, and gave each a disco punch. Then he sent the demo to industry executives. The disco version of Beethoven's *Symphony No. 5 in C Minor* appealed to one company, and in October the talented Murphy, who played most of the instruments on the single (the name Big Apple Band appearing on the label was a PR fiction), had the country's number one disco dance tune. Music stores reported that the song boosted sales of all Beethoven's music, especially *Symphony No. 5.*

Walter Murphy was, however, a one-hit wonder. Though he "discofied" other classics—Rimsky-Korsakov's "Flight of the Bumble Bee" and George Gershwin's "Rhapsody in Blue"—the record-buying public bought the gimmick in quantity only once.

As the year closed, Rod Stewart, considered by many critics the best male singer in rock, had the top single: **Tonight's the Night (Gonna Be Alright).** The unmarried, ladies-man Londoner ended the decade with the tease **Do Ya Think I'm Sexy?,** but almost before his legions of female admirers could shout "Yes!" he married George Hamilton's former wife, Alana.

You Make Me Feel Like Dancing; When I Need You: 1977

In this era of discomania, Gerard Hugh "Leo" Sayer's number one single (in January), "You Make Me Feel Like Dancing," expressed for many their Saturday night passion for kicking up their heels. The British-born singer-songwriter told *Newsweek* that the inspiration for many of his songs sprang from the emotional frenzy of a nervous breakdown, which he'd carefully chronicled in a diary. (Though his next smash, "When I Need You," number one in May and his biggest hit ever, was written by the sane and savvy Carole Bayer Sager.) His highly danceable tune was soon overtaken in sales by Stevie Wonder's **I Wish** and Rose Royce's **Car Wash.**

As the year progressed, high on the charts were Mary MacGregor with **Torn Between Two Lovers,** Manfred Mann's Earth Band with **Blinded by the Light,** and the Eagles with **New Kid in Town.** By March veteran top-seller Barbra Streisand had a megahit (as singer and composer) in **Evergreen,** the theme from her film remake, *A Star Is Born.* Though the critics panned the movie, the theme tune (co-written with Paul Williams) won an Academy Award, as well as a Grammy for Streisand as best pop female vocalist.

Gonna Fly Now (Theme From *Rocky*): 1977

The rags-to-riches *Rocky* film and its musical theme, a paean to underdogs, were more than a movie and a hit song. The film about Rocky "Against-All-Odds" Balboa, a South Philly boxer who wins fame, fortune and the rights to all sequels, launched the career of writer-actor Sylvester Stallone, whereas the Bill Conti theme song, "Gonna Fly Now," became a much-heard, if not too much heard, anthem at countless sporting events. Across the nation, high schools, little league baseball teams, even the Special Olympics used the rousing instrumental to spur athletes on to glory.

Number one in July, "Gonna Fly Now," with sparse lyrics by Carol Connors and Ayn Robbins, was a hit even before it was released. At test screenings of the movie, grown men stood on their seats and cheered, and women screamed for Rocky's victory over the Ali-like heavyweight champ Apollo Creed. Interviewed viewers agreed that the driving beat of the music roused them as much as the story (try watching Rocky's early-morning run through Philly with the sound off). A post-Watergate America was desperate for heroes and adopted boxer Balboa. The film, the sleeper of the decade (which Hollywood producers had envisioned as a vehicle for Burt Reynolds or Robert Redford; over Stallone's dead body), won three Academy Awards (best picture, best director, best film editing). The stand-up-and-cheer song, though not taking an Oscar, became the anthem of athletes. Stallone maintained that the film was not about boxing but "about a man simply fighting for his dignity. People require symbols of humanity and heroism." Rocky Balboa became an American icon.

Other summer of 1977 hits: Andy Gibb's **I Just Want to Be Your Everything,** the Emotions' **Best of My Love,** Shaun Cassidy's **Da Doo Ron Ron,**

Alan O'Day's **Undercover Angel,** Peter Frampton's **I'm in You,** and another smash from a movie soundtrack: John William's instrumental **Star Wars Theme,** which climbed to number one as the new school year got under way. Two pop musical "events" remained in the year 1977.

You Light Up My Life: 1977

What can you say about a girl who owned the nation's number one single for a Seventies record-breaking ten consecutive weeks? That she was the daughter of Fifties sensation Pat Boone; that she was twenty, remarkably wholesome-looking, and admittedly no disco baby. The single, by former advertising man Joe Brooks, garnered a Grammy for song of the year, won one for Debby Boone as best new artist, and took home an Oscar—for it was from the movie *You Light Up My Life,* about a young singer (Didi Conn) who seeks fame and fortune as a song stylist. In the movie Conn lip-synched to the voice of another vocalist; Debby Boone's voice was later laid in over the movie's instrumental soundtrack.

Though the lyrics—about lighting up a life, giving it hope and the strength to carry on—had nothing to do with the Lord, Debby Boone's singing suggested to millions of fans that the song was a Christian anthem. For her it was a religious song, as she explained in *Billboard:* "The lyrics really lent themselves to how I felt about my relationship with the Lord, that's the way I chose to sing it. I never really thought anyone would know." Of the song's record-breaking accomplishment Fred Bronson writes, "To find a single by a solo female artist that equalled Debby's achievement, one would have to return to the pre-rock era days of October, 1948, when Dinah Shore's 'Buttons and Bows' began a 10-week stay at number one."

As the year 1977 drew to a close, "You Light Up My Life" was challenged in sales by a run of songs from *Saturday Night Fever:* **How Deep Is Your Love, Stayin' Alive, Night Fever,** and **More Than a Woman.** The movie's score, by the Bee Gees (for "Brothers Gibb"), sold more than 35 million records worldwide, and "How Deep Is Your Love," which the brothers wrote (for a female vocalist) before beginning work on the score, was the country's number one single at Christmastime. As brother Maurice Gibb later explained the group's thinking when asked to score the movie: " 'Wow! A disco film. Let's get into some good disco songs.' It took about two-and-a-half weeks to write them and put them down as demos." The rest, as one must say, is disco history.

King Tut; Boogie Oogie Oogie: 1978

In this year Broadway got another dance musical (after *A Chorus Line*): Bob Fosse's *Dancin',* which opened at the Broadhurst Theater. "Wild and crazy guy" Steve Martin parlayed a new wave of Tutmania (see page 126) into a hit record, "King Tut" (in the top twenty), and through a zany production number on TV's "Saturday Night Live," unleashed a funky, short-lived Tut dance craze.

"Dance" was in the title of songs like Andy Gibb's **Shadow Dancing** (number one in June), and Donna Summer's throbbing disco hit **Last Dance** (number three in August). The film *Thank God It's Friday* exploited the nationwide fever for boogieing, being a plotless rip-off of *Saturday Night Fever,* riding to its popularity on a disco score. Closing out the summer, the disco group A Taste of Honey owned the country's number one single, the platinum-selling "Boogie Oogie Oogie."

Other 1978 hits: Dolly Parton's **Here You Come Again,** Randy Newman's **Short People,** Queen's **We Are the Champions,** the Commodores' **Three Times a Lady,** Olivia Newton-John's **Hopelessly Devoted to You,** Donna Summer's **MacArthur Park,** and an end-of-year surprise . . .

You Don't Bring Me Flowers: 1978

This last smash (number one in December), with its unexpected pairing of superstars Barbra Streisand and Neil Diamond, came about by happenstance. The song was written by Diamond, and included on his latest album. When radio disc jockey Gary Guthrie realized that Streisand also performed the song on her newest album, and in the same key as Diamond, he inventively spliced the two singles into one duet and played it on the air. The favorable call-in response was overwhelming, and fans of the two stars begged record stores for the still nonexistent disc. Sensing a blockbuster gimmick poised to take flight, Diamond's producer rounded up the two singers in one studio and quickly released the single; it won a Grammy for record of the year, and Streisand and Diamond were nominated as best pop vocal duo.

Another 1978 duo, **You're the One That I Want,** number one in June, was written for the film version of *Grease* and sung by John Travolta and Olivia Newton-John. By coincidence, it displaced from the top spot another duet: **Too Much, Too Little, Too Late,** by Johnny Mathis and Deniece Williams.

My Life: 1979

Perhaps unprecedented, in the final year of the decade a Roman Catholic pope, John Paul II, recorded an album of folk songs and joined the music union ASCAP. Equally out of the ordinary, the same year disgraced former President Richard Nixon earned a Grammy nomination for the LP of his less than completely candid TV interviews with David Frost. More predictably, the year began with Long Island songwriter Billy Joel scoring a major hit with "My Life," number three in January. Not yet the superstar he'd become in the next decade, Joel was still no novice in the realm of recording successes. His 1973 album "Piano Man" was praised by critics, and his 1977 album "The Stranger" included "She's Only a Woman to Me" and "Only the Good Die Young."

In this year that produced records by a pope and a former president, an unlikely group called the Village People, costumed as four gay stereotypes and lip-synching to prerecorded music, scored a hit with **Y.M.C.A,** number two in February. They became a nationwide sensation, performing **Macho Man** and

In the Navy in concert and on TV. In the atmosphere of the decade's sexual revolution, no one seemed to mind that their songs were unapologetic paeans to the gay lifestyle.

Other hits of early 1979: Gloria Gaynor's **I Will Survive,** the Doobie Brothers' **What a Fool Believes,** Peaches and Herb's **Reunited,** and a driving disco version of the Sixties single **Knock on Wood,** number one in April, by former cast member of *Bubbling Brown Sugar* Amii Stewart. Not a fan of disco, she later admitted in *Record Mirror,* "I've never bought a disco record in my life. And I don't want to buy one." Yet her only top-seller was a disco number. Another singer was catapulted to celebrityship by a disco hit . . .

Heart of Glass: 1979

The group Blondie, led by sexy, platinum-haired Deborah Harry, had been around in the Seventies, always on the musical fringe. The talented Harry wrote "Heart of Glass" and had performed it in several "new wave," or "punk," clubs, never imagining it would become a smash single. The highly danceable song, number one in late April, awakened many adults to the burgeoning phenomenon of **punk;** though Harry, through teasing sex appeal and knowing put-on, made new wave more palatable to middle America than groups such as Britain's chicly bored and calculatedly nasty Sex Pistols.

So nonthreatening was Harry's cheesecake and camp that in the same year she went from headlining at the trendy club CBGB to horsing around on "The Muppet Show." Nonetheless, several radio stations refused to play "Heart of Glass" because of a line that could be read innocently or otherwise: "Once I had a love and it was a gas / Soon turned out to be a pain in the ass."

Hot Stuff; Bad Girls; Dim All the Lights: 1979

In record sales, the last half of 1979 belonged to disco queen Donna Summer (born LaDonna Andrea Gaines). In June the singer, who had replaced Melba Moore in Broadway's *Hair,* held the country's number one single, "Hot Stuff." Topped briefly by Anita Ward and her **Ring My Bell,** Summer was back in first place in July with "Bad Girls," a stick of disco dynamite composed by the singer and her husband-to-be Bruce Sudano. Reviewed *Rolling Stone,* the song "cheerfully evokes the trash-flash vitality of tawdry disco dolls cruising down the main drag on a Saturday night."

Competition came from Kenny Rogers with **She Believes in Me,** Chic with **Good Times,** The Knack with **My Sharona,** Sister Sledge with **We Are Family,** and **Main Event/Fight,** by Barbra Streisand. Two unexpected hits were Randy Vanwarmer's **Just When I Needed You Most,** and **You Take My Breath Away,** by singer/actor Rex Smith, who starred in the made-for-TV movie *Sooner or Later,* about a rock star obsessed with one of his preteen fans; the song was from the soundtrack.

The disco diva was back on the charts in November with the number two single, "Dim All the Lights," and again in December, teaming up with Barbra Streisand for **Enough Is Enough (No More Tears),** by songwriter Paul Jabara, who had already given Summer the Oscar-winning "Last Dance" from the disco film *Thank God It's Friday.* By all accounts the two songstresses attempted to vocally outdo each other, Summer even holding her breath so long on one note to outlast Streisand that she fell off her recording stool. Jabara told *US* magazine: "There was Streisand, hands flaring, and Donna, throwing her head back—and they're both belting, sparking each other. It was a songwriter's dream." Streisand proved she could handle pop rock music. Summer, who graced the April 2, 1979, cover of *Newsweek* for its disco feature, and was called "Disco's Aphrodite," summed up her Seventies popularity saying, "God had to create disco music so that I could be born and be successful. I was blessed."

BESTSELLING BOOKS

From Bestseller to Superseller

"The Seventies was a decade in which the quest for the superseller came to dominate the lives of publishers," writes John Sutherland in *Bestsellers,* itself a weak-seller in which the author presents "the lurid incidents" that made so many books blockbusters. Indeed, the blockbuster was the breed of book, fiction and nonfiction, publishers were after—with unprecedented advances, staggering first printings, and nearly shameless hype. Often the sum spent by a paperback house to court an author who'd reveled in a hardcover success could never be recouped in sales; prestige came merely from having the stellar author on one's roster. A superselling book bred a sequel, which in turn got its own sequel whether the storyline merited one or not. In this section we'll look at as many "lurid incidents" as possible that, through hype and media tie-ins, made horror stories, disaster novels, and "bodice rippers" super-dooper-sellers. And we'll look at several good books, too. To begin with an overview, here are the decade's top ten fictions (with dates published, hardcovers sold, and paperbacks in print), as The *New York Times Books Review* announced on December 30, 1979:

1. **The Godfather,** Mario Puzo (1969)—hardcover, 292,765; paperback, 13,225,000
2. **The Exorcist,** William Peter Blatty (1979)—Hardcover, 205,265; paperback, 11,948,000
3. **Jonathan Livingston Seagull,** Richard Bach (1970)—Hardcover, 3,192,000; paperback, 7,250,000
4. **Love Story,** Erich Segal (1970)—Hardcover, 431,976; paperback 9,778,000
5. **Jaws,** Peter Benchley (1974)—Hardcover, 204,281; paperback, 9,210,000

6. **The Thorn Birds,** Colleen McCullough (1977)—Hardcover, 646,503; paperback, 7,450,000
7. **Rich Man, Poor Man,** Irwin Shaw (1970)—Hardcover, 99,610; paperback, 6,550,000
8. **The Other Side of Midnight,** Sidney Sheldon (1973)—Hardcover, 85,000; paperback, 6,500,000
9. **Centennial,** James Michener (1974)—Hardcover, 458,788; paperback, 5,715,000
10. **Fear of Flying,** Erica Jong (1973)—Hardcover, 100,000; paperback, 5,700,000

Everything You Always Wanted to Know About Sex but Were Afraid to Ask: Number One Nonfiction, 1970

If there was a trend in nonfiction in the Seventies it was toward sex, more sex, and the joy of sex. As the decade opened, Dr. David Reuben's *Everything You Always Wanted* swamped all other titles, with hardcover sales passing the million mark. There had been sexual how-tos in earlier decades, but in the Seventies sexual manuals were displayed on coffee tables, carried on subways and buses, frankly discussed, and, in the case of Reuben's superseller (number one for 1970), made into a Woody Allen movie.

Number three for the year was **The Sensuous Woman** by "J"; number eight was **Body Language** by Julius Fast. It is interesting to note that sandwiched between *Everything You Always Wanted* and *The Sensuous Woman* was the year's second-bestselling book, **The New English Bible,** strongly holding its own. The next year, 1971, *The Sensuous Man* by "M" was the leading nonfiction book in the country. And Dr. Reuben was back with the boldly titled **Any Woman Can!;** not many people had to ask "Can what?" Number four for the year was Thomas Harris's reassuring **I'm O.K., You're O.K.** In this swinging singles' decade, the self-explanatory **Open Marriage** was a 1972 bestseller, and the following year the decade's bible of sex arrived . . .

The Joy of Sex: Number Four Nonfiction, 1973

"The safest of all human activities" is how author Alex Comfort celebrated sex in the pre-AIDS decade. Whereas past sexual manuals had been clunky and clinical, no better than medical school texts, *Joy,* tantalizingly subtitled *A Gourmet Guide to Love Making,* was a spicy cookbook that instructed the reader that "good hand and mouth work practically guarantee you a good partner." It rated lovemaking techniques as "top grade," "cordon bleu," and "high quality."

Geared to the era of sexual liberation, the guilt-free guide to grade-A sex asserted, "All people are bisexual," assured timid readers that "Lovers will play rape games without end," and said of the taboo of bondage: "Chains create a tied up and tinkling look—fashionable now and they look good on naked skin." The tone of the superselling book was nonjudgmental: "We've deliberately not gone into the ethics of lifestyles," wrote Comfort. He said of pain as an aphrodisiac: "The idea of being beaten unquestionably turns some people on, and if it does, you should try it."

The next year, 1974, Comfort was back on the bestseller lists as editor of **More Joy: A Lovemaking Companion to the Joy of Sex**—though the book was topped in sales by Marabel Morgan's **The Total Woman.** By this time, David Reuben had turned from sex to the decade's second big nonfiction theme: dieting, his **The Save-Your-Life Diet** being a top-seller in 1975. But what Reuben was to sex in the Seventies, Robert Atkins was to the diet craze, launched in large part by his 1972 **Dr. Atkins' Diet Revolution.** The book, two years a bestseller, started a nationwide dieting mania, such that any trendy place name—like Beverly Hills or Scarsdale—suggested to one doctor or another a diet plan and a book title. Weight Watchers weighed in with **Weight Watchers Program Cookbook,** number five for 1973.

Other nonfictions that addressed trends:

Tales of Power by Carlos Castaneda (the get in touch with your inner self through drugs trend); **Winning Through Intimidation** by Robert Ringer (the aggressiveness in business trend); **The Bermuda Triangle** by Charles Berlitz (the occult craze); **Total Fitness in 30 Minutes a Week** by Laurence Morehouse and Leonard Gross (the fitness without effort belief); and **TM: Discovering Energy and Overcoming Stress** by Harold Bloomfield (the attempt to cope with all the decade's other trends). Not to be forgotten: **All the President's Men** by *Washington Post* sleuths Carl Bernstein and Bob Woodward.

Love Story: Number One Fiction, 1970

What can you say about a twenty-five-year-old girl who died?

That she was beautiful. And brilliant. That she loved Mozart and Bach. And the Beatles. And me.

So opened the novelization of the original screenplay by Erich Segal, professor of classics at Yale University. Conceived as a Paramount tearjerker, *Love Story,* a modern-day *Romeo and Juliet* about two lovers from opposite sides of the tracks, became a book largely by Segal adding an occasional "he said" and "she said" to the movie's dialogue. The tale of self-sacrificing love involved spiffy millionaire preppie Oliver Barrett IV (Ryan O'Neal) and a musically talented, tart-mouthed Italian-American, Jennifer Cavilleri, whose surname, deriving from the Latin verb *cavilor,* "to scoff," summed up Oliver's mother's feelings toward her son's "rustic" girlfriend. Indeed, the wealthy Mrs. Barrett dubbed her daughter-in-law "Cavilleri Rustica," at once playing on Jenny's love of music and her earthy manner—as authentically conveyed by dead-pan actress Ali MacGraw. The bestselling book primed fans for the film, and O'Neal and MacGraw became stars. As did Erich Segal. The story had much of America mouthing Oliver's hard-learned lesson: "Love means not ever having to say you're sorry."

"The banality of *Love Story* makes *Peyton Place* look like *Swann's Way* as it skips from cliché to cliché with an abandon that would chill the blood of a *True Romance* editor," reviewed *Newsweek*. Nonetheless, the book was a publishing phenomenon, and it launched a new trend: previously, movies had been made from bestselling books; Segal's Kleenex-special ushered in the genre of fiction as film novelization. The movie earned $50 million, was nominated for seven Academy Awards, and won one for best original score.

There are two versions of how Segal came to write the story. In one, he overheard two Yale students discussing a real-life Romeo and Juliet affair, and he dramatically affixed the girl's untimely death and the contemporary nicety that she worked to put him through law school. In the other version, Segal, while attempting to write his first novel, discovered that a friend's young wife had died and composed the fiction in her memory. Segal claims there's truth in both.

For the year 1970, the number two fiction was John Fowles's **The French Lieutenant's Woman;** number three, Ernest Hemingway's **Islands in the Stream;** number ten, Irwin Shaw's **Rich Man, Poor Man,** which would become a TV miniseries.

That year, one of America's most highly respected contemporary poets, James Dickey, published a much-acclaimed, visceral novel, **Deliverance,** several weeks a bestseller. "I wrote the right book at the right time," Dickey said, in reference to a growing environmentalism across the country. In the survivalist-type story, four urban men go canoeing for a weekend in remote Georgia wilderness and encounter hardships even their wildest nightmares could not have prepared them for. Hollywood, violating one of its own laws, allowed poet Dickey to write the screenplay for the 1972 film. The riveting drama of man against nature and man against his fellow man starred Burt Reynolds, who only three months before the film's release appeared as the nude centerfold in *Cosmopolitan* magazine—kicking off another kind of trend in the Seventies: the male-in-the-buff pin-up.

Airport: Number One Fiction, 1968; Wheels: Number One Fiction, 1971; The Moneychangers: Number Two Fiction, 1975; Overload: Number Three Fiction, 1979

Arthur Hailey, once a writer of television dramas, enjoyed bestsellerdom in 1968 with *Airport,* a novel most significant in that it launched a flight of "Airport" movies *(Airport, Airport 1975, Airport '77, Airport '79—The Concorde,* and such spoofs as *Airplane!* and *Airplane II),* as well as the genre of disaster films in which an all-star cast faces almost certain death unless it is rescued last minute by another star. Hollywood clamored for disaster novels and found two that became films: *The Poseidon Adventure* (1972; disaster via a mammoth tidal wave) and *The Towering Inferno* (1974; disaster in a burning skyscraper).

Hailey had honed his own formula for a blockbuster, beginning in 1965 with **Hotel.** What that "insider's look" novel did for hotel management, *Airport* did for airport security, *Wheels* did for the automobile industry, *The Moneychangers* did for banking, and *Overload* did for electric utilities and mass blackouts. Whereas his fans loved the melodramatic disaster aspects of his books, Hailey's publishers often highlighted the muckraking aspect of his fiction, aligning him in the fearless tradition of American journalism. "He contrasts Detroit's slums with the auto industry's tremendous wealth," read a book-jacket blurb for *Wheels,* "and covers problems experienced in hiring the hard-core unemployed."

Maybe so, but more memorable are say, the male prison gang rape scene in *The Moneychangers,* or the athletic copulation in *Overload* between a ravishing quadriplegic and a senior executive of an electric utility, whose company's failure to produce current kills the girl; or the unfortunate character who has his penis charred off by a surge of electric current and the "insider's look" at how it's replaced by sophisticated cosmetic surgery. Hailey was writing for his times.

The year *Wheels* was the country's number one fiction, John Updike published **Rabbit Redux** (number ten); Herman Wouk, **The Winds of War** (number seven), Frederick Forsyth, **The Day of the Jackal** (number four), and number two for the year was . . .

The Exorcist: Number Two Fiction, 1971

Basing his novel on a true story of the exorcism of a possessed child in 1949, William Peter Blatty produced one of the most sensational books of the decade, which, in turn, yielded one of the decade's most frightening films. A bestseller in more than a dozen countries, the book told of twelve-year-old Regan, possessed by the devil, who vomits forcefully, rotates her head dislocatingly, screams obscenities at her exorcising priests, and commits perverted acts with a crucifix. By the end of the book/movie, she, deeply exorcised, remembers none of it—though the same could not be said for readers/moviegoers. So frightening was the story that reviewer Pauline Kael called the film "a recruiting poster for Catholicism."

Lapsed Christians of all sects were said to return in flocks to the fold. The Catholic Church reported an unprecedented number of requests for exorcisms by people merely quaking with paranoia. In line with the decade's trend for sequels, Blatty's book spawned **The Legion** (1983), and the William Friedkin film prompted *Exorcist II* (1977)—Roman Numerals II and III were big business in the Seventies. (In the next decade, *Rocky* would take the count to IV, then V.)

Though the demonic possession of children had been a staple of horror fiction since *The Turn of the Screw,* the wave of religious cults and the rise of Jesus freaks paved the way for the theme to leap from the genre circuit to mass-market appeal. The success of *The Exorcist*—following on the heels of Ira Levin's *Rosemary's Baby*—encouraged a wave of occult-horror books and novelizations, like *Audrey Rose, The Omen, The Fury, Suffer the Children, The Soul of Anna Klane, Harvest Home, The Reincarnation of Peter Proud,* and *Carrie.* Indeed, it paved the way for the publishing phenomenon of Stephen King.

The film made a star of the movie's Regan, young Linda Blair (the devil's baritone voice was dubbed by breathy actress Mercedes McCambridge). Across the country fans related how Warner Brothers' special-effects department imaginatively combined oatmeal and pea soup and pumped it through a tube hidden in Blair's lower lip. Sales of pea soup plummeted.

Jonathan Livingston Seagull: Number One Fiction, 1972

Some critics claimed that Richard Bach, an aviation writer, repackaged Norman Vincent Peale's *The Power of Positive Thinking* in feathers, casting Peale's uplifting advice in the metaphor of soaring flight. Littered with clichés and truisms, the inspirational tale of a seagull preciously named Jonathan Livingston certainly soared up the bestselling lists, breaking the hardcover record set by *Gone With the Wind.*

Bach claimed that the story of a seagull (a nonconformist) ostracized by his flock (society at large), came to him in a mysterious voice, which he heard "behind and to the right." The voice suggested the title of the book, but not the ending, which would take Bach eight years to figure out. Jonathan (a human spirit piloting a gull's body) becomes a hermit, meets an elite of feathered friends (perfectionists) who teach him the secrets of perfect flight (supreme personal achievement), which he in turn teaches to the flock. "Find what you love to do, and do your darndest to make it happen," was how Bach described the book's message—which was vague enough to be many things to many people.

For a drug culture and a self-knowledge-seeking me generation, the book became something of a bible. In fact, *Publishers Weekly* called 1972 "the year of the bird and the Bible"; for whereas *Jonathan* was the year's number one fiction, the top-rated nonfiction was **The Living Bible.** That you could take your inspiration from Christ or a seagull offended many people. The *Christian Science Monitor* refused to run ads for Bach's book on the grounds that it just might be heretical. The editors pointed to lines like "Each of us is in truth an idea of the Great Gull," and the fact that Jonathan enters "heaven" (achieves perfection) without suffering and death. The volume was slight, fewer than ten thousand words, but sales were hefty.

Watership Down: Number Two Fiction, 1974

Richard Adams's bestseller told the story of a determined band of rabbits who set out to find a new home in the English countryside. It became that oxymoron of the publishing industry, an instant classic. Adams, a British civil servant turned novelist, put on paper the rabbit tales his daughters loved. In England, his manuscript was rejected by several publishers, then finally printed as a novel for children, selling over a million copies. In America, in the favorable atmosphere created by the allegorical *Jonathan Livingston Seagull,* the adventurous animal fantasy for children appeared as an adult novel.

But Adams's tale was no simple, clear-cut allegory. He imaginatively and complexly created a complete rabbit world, rich in mythology, history, and law, and embodying a profound respect for nature. Fans of Richard Bach were profoundly confused. Some critics thought rabbits were just the next pop literary fad; others labeled *Watership Down* "a serious literary work." As if to prove them right, Richard Adams never produced the much-anticipated sequel, believing that much of the charm of his story of lovable lagomorphs was in its uniqueness.

James Herriot.   Animal stories were something of a rage in the early Seventies. The books of James Herriot, a Scottish veterinarian in Yorkshire, were extraordinarily popular. From a diary he'd kept since 1937, he wrote of his own experiences and recounted anecdotes about his veterinary friends, brothers Siegfried and Tristan, weaving fact with fiction. **All Creatures Great and Small** was a hit in 1972, followed two years later by **All Things Bright and Beautiful,** then, playing on the similar titling, **All Things Wise and Wonderful** in 1977—by which time critics were complaining that the farm-animal formula, while still effective, was wearing thin. Meantime, readers were engrossed with an animal of a far more ferocious sort.

Jaws: Number Three Fiction, 1974

What Herman Melville did for the great albino whale in *Moby Dick, Newsweek* writer Peter Benchley did by way of parody for the great white shark in *Jaws.* Both the whale and the shark are portrayed as more than dangerous forces of nature; they're monsters with a malignant will and an "I'll get you yet" agenda. The novel was Benchley's first, and the movie version was the first smash hit for young director Steven Spielberg. Millions of fans recall the summer of 1975, when the film was released, as the time they abandoned ocean swimming for ankle-deep wading.

As a boy Benchley had spent his summers on Nantucket, fascinated by the surf, skin-diving, and sharks. Once a speechwriter for President Lyndon Johnson, he began writing about sharks in the late Sixties. The genesis of *Jaws* was a lunch on June 14, 1971, when Benchley pitched several book ideas to Doubleday editor Tom Congdon. Congdon liked none of them, and, to make conversation, asked if Benchley had ever considered writing a novel. Benchley mentioned an idea of "a great white shark that appears off Long Island" and terrorizes bathers. On the basis of a brief outline, Benchley got an advance, and two years later, after much in-house editing, the novel with the shark on the

Jaws.

cover appeared and began to climb the bestseller lists, earning the distinction of being "the most profitable first novel in bestseller history."

Jaws—The Movie.   Most people, though, remember Spielberg's film more than the book—and a pivotal picture it was for Hollywood, ushering in the era of huge-grossing escapist blockbusters that would dominate the box office for years to come. Benchley's novel was already a million-seller when Richard Zanuck purchased screen rights for a paltry $175,000, with Benchley getting $25,000 to write the script. The movie would eventually become the first to break the $100 million mark in theater rentals, making it the highest grossing film to that date. Though Zanuck wanted the shark sequences shot in a tank, director Spielberg, insisting on authenticity, chose Martha's Vineyard as the fictional village of Amity. Three hydraulically-operated plastic sharks were constructed, each weighing a ton and a half and costing $150,000, and affectionately named Bruce.

The huge success of the movie, though, sprang from Spielberg's masterful technique of escalating suspense. In large part this was done by letting the droning *dunn, dunn, dunn, dunn, DUNN, DUNN, DUNN, DUNN* of John Williams's score stand-in for the creature, which is not glimpsed until the film is well under way. In essence, the audience *become* the helpless swimmers who cannot see what is beneath them. Whereas the story made the careers of Benchley and Spielberg, it boded poorly for nature's real great whites, which beginning in the summer of 1975 were hunted down and strung up as if *they* had stalked their captors.

Fear of Flying: 1973

Erica Jong did the previously unthinkable: expressed female sexual horniness and orgasmic fulfillment with the kind of bald honesty and bawdy abandon of male writers like Norman Mailer and Henry Miller. Indeed, Miller called *Fear of Flying* "the feminine counterpart of *Tropic of Cancer,*" his own groundbreaking book. In her quasi-autobiographical first novel, Jong appears as Isadora Wing, who in a quest for self-discovery gives voice to feelings and attitudes women didn't dare to discuss even with other women: masturbation, erotic fantasies, playful rape, pleasure through pain, and the cultural demands a male-run society imposes on a woman's shape and overall appearance.

Many male readers saw *Fear* as a "man-hating" novel, which it wasn't. It was, as one essayist wrote, "the high point of the modern feminist movement's first phase—a phase marked by consciousness raising, rebellion, and anger." Isadora doesn't hate men, quite the contrary: "The big problem," she admits, "was how to make your feminism jibe with your unappeasable hunger for male bodies"—the book's theme and Isadora's unresolvable dilemma. The novel, born into the "your place or mine?" generation, became a classic and made cocktail chatter of Isadora's quest for the "zipless fuck."

Looking for Mr. Goodbar: Number Four Fiction, 1975

The number one fiction for 1975 was E. L. Doctorow's **Ragtime,** an inventive and complex novel that seamlessly mixed fictitious characters with realistic figures like Sigmund Freud and Booker T. Washington. It captured a theme of the Me Decade in that its cast of characters relentlessly satisfy their own egos no matter what the cost to those around them.

Equally thematic of the times was the number four fiction, Judith Rossner's *Looking for Mr. Goodbar,* a tale in which the main character, Theresa, because of low self-esteem, cannot find love or male companionship, or commit to a relationship. After a string of rejections and failures, she opts for the bar scene and one-night stands with an assortment of men, epitomizing the swinging singles' philosophy: instant pleasure without the pain of commitment.

Of all her casual lovers, the most gratifying is Tony Lopanto, whom she regards as a "delightful, tender, and energetic lover." He's ideal because he never talks, never goes out, only takes off his clothes and provides her with pure sexual pleasure. Ultimately alone, she returns to the local Mr. Goodbar in search of sex and meets the one-night man who will be her murderer. In the last moments of her life, she glimpses the futility of the existence she was living and her problems of commitment. The novel, and then the 1977 movie starring Diane Keaton and Richard Gere, cast brief encounters of the sexual kind in a horrifying light and changed the dating habits of thousands of young liberated women. Rossner based her book on the 1973 murder of schoolteacher Roseann Quinn by a man she picked up in a Manhattan singles bar and took back to her apartment. *Ms.* magazine reviewed the book as "a haunting, compelling thriller, guaranteed to make any woman terrified of the next strange man she meets."

Other bestsellers mid-decade that had film or TV spin-offs: Judith Guest's **Ordinary People** (1976), a first novel optioned for the movies by Robert Redford, and a black American family saga that launched a nationwide genealogy craze:

Roots: Number Five Nonfiction, 1976

Alex Haley (author of *The Autobiography of Malcolm X;* 1965), at lunch one day in the Sixties, mentioned to his Doubleday editor that he needed financial help to trace his family roots. He knew their probable location was the village of Juffure on the banks of the Gambia River in West Africa, and with an advance of $5,000 he began a quest that would take twelve years and eventually cost $100,000 in travel and research fees.

It turned out that Haley's forebears were the Kinte clan. Many had been kidnapped by slave traders and shipped to America. Coincidentally, *Roots* was published during America's bicentennial fervor and its theme assured it wide publicity; it remained on the bestseller list for nine months and won accolades from reviewers across the country. Its translation into a twelve-hour, eight-segment TV miniseries in 1977 became a media event of extraordinary proportions. It made an overnight star of nineteen-year-old unknown actor LeVar Burton, who starred as the young Kunta Kinte, and was nominated for an unprecedented thirty-seven Emmys.

The book and the miniseries launched a genealogy craze, as millions of Americans began searching for information about their own ancestry. Furthermore, ABC's daring decision to run the series on consecutive nights—rather than on one night a week for several consecutive weeks—made television history by abandoning decades of rigid program-scheduling philosophy. Consecutive-night airings allowed television to achieve the kind of thematic power and narrative sweep previously found only in feature films. TV was never the same.

The Search for Roots. With *Roots* a blockbuster, Haley expanded his twelve years of research into the bestselling *The Search for Roots*. On TV, two years after the first miniseries, the Kunta Kinte saga was updated in a fourteen-hour program, "Roots, the Next Generations"—which brought the story through World War II and the civil rights struggles of the Fifties and Sixties. Many point to these events as the beginning of a new trend: if "The Work" is a success, then "The Making of the Work" as a sequel has a ready-made audience. TV in the Eighties would become the home for specials titled "The Making of . . ." (fill in the original hit of your choice).

Other bestsellers that enjoyed film or TV reincarnations: John Irving's **The World According to Garp** (1978), reworked as a 1982 movie starring Robin Williams as male feminist T. S. Garp; Judith Krantz's sensational **Scruples** (1978; thirty-six weeks on the bestseller lists) and **Princess Daisy** (1979; also thirty-six weeks on the lists), which wove together trendy fashions, exotic locales, and beautiful people into page-turning fictional froth. Scott Spencer's

Endless Love, a novel of the destructiveness of unbridled passion, was nominated for an American Book Award, and as a Franco Zeffirelli movie gave the young Brooke Shields a thoroughly adolescent role. The decade drew to a close with the emergence of Robin Cook, an eye doctor turned suspense writer, scoring a chilling bestseller with **Coma,** the first in a series of medical fictions that would give anyone entering a hospital for elective surgery pause to run.

TELEVISION HITS

Prime Time, Our Time

This section opens with the title of Donna McCrohan's excellent book, as well as with a paraphrase of her premise: that popular television writes a history of our time, in many ways a more accurate history than one chronicled in newspapers by journalists. Just as historians read the story of our ancestors first from cave paintings, then from portraiture and postcards, future historians will one day screen shows such as "M*A*S*H," or "60 Minutes" or "Saturday Night Live"—even "Dynasty" and "Dallas"—to glimpse issues, lifestyles, liberties, and excesses from a particular decade. They might be wise to begin with a groundbreaking sitcom, the decade's first smash hit.

All in the Family: CBS Premiere, January 12, 1971

Featuring Archie ("Aw, chee whiz") bunker and his dingbat wife Edith, the show—based on the Britcom (British sitcom) "Till Death Do Us Part"—brought to television "real" people. And it gave television a public forum for venting tensions that had been building over the past decade between parents and children, between the sexes, and between races. Bigoted blue-collar Archie (Carroll O'Connor) and his bighearted lamebrained wife Edith (Jean Stapleton) resided in Queens, New York, with their modern-minded daughter Gloria (Sally Struthers) and her liberal Polish "Meathead" husband Mike (Rob Reiner). Every slur and sling relevant to the times got ample air play. Bunkerisms like "You're taking it out of contest," "It's just a pigment of your imagination," and "Smells like a house of ill refute to me" added to the show's humor and mitigated Archie's vitriol by playing up his ignorance.

The show, dubbed TV's first "relevant" sitcom, took a long time reaching the airwaves—and almost didn't last, due in part to dismal reviews: "A flop," deemed the *New York Post.* In fact, the Bunker clan didn't catch on until the reruns of the show in the summer of 1971. Then it set a record as the only program in TV history to be number one for the year five times. As an escape valve America needed, it was arguably the most revolutionary and influential sitcom ever on television.

The acerbic Archie character was the brainchild of producer Norman Lear, who admitted his father was the model. A CBS vice president, Fred Silverman,

"All in the Family."

believed in Lear's reworking of the Britcom and slipped it into the schedule as a mid-season replacement. Once viewers started watching, they couldn't get enough of the generational and political differences between the show's four main characters. The series brought to television issues never before hinted at. Toilets flushed. Mike got a vasectomy. Gloria had a miscarriage and befriended a transvestite ("She was a nice fella," said Archie). Edith experienced a difficult menopause, which an impatient Archie refused to comprehend: "If you're gonna have your change of life, have it right now! You got exactly thirty seconds . . . Change!"

Spin-offs Galore. The show had its critics. They argued that Archie's black and Polish jokes, and his steady stream of ethnic slurs—Hebes, Japs, fags, coons, polacks, chinks, micks, and spicks—fostered bigotry. Yet even the critics agreed the show was uproariously funny, and that Archie's shortcomings and personal flaws were always revealed.

No subject was taboo. Even the horror of rape was presented, and with a modicum of humor: In a special hour-long episode, Edith is attacked by a would-be rapist in the family living room. As the rapist tugs to open her zipper, Edith nervously whines, "Would you like some coffee?" RAPIST: I don't drink coffee. EDITH (anxious): I've got Sanka.

The show spawned spin-offs in America: "Maude" and "The Jeffersons."

And it was copied in other countries: in Germany as "One Heart and One Soul," starring a Hitler-like bigot, and in South Africa as "People Like Us," featuring a racist who must learn to live with black neighbors. Atlantic Records released two albums of the program's soundtrack, and Popular Library published *The Wit and Wisdom of Archie Bunker.* Five episodes of the series were published as plays. And when Gloria and Mike had a baby around Christmas 1975, little Joey Stivic spawned a toy advertised as "the first physically correct male doll." By the time Rob Reiner, Sally Struthers, and Jean Stapleton left the show to pursue other projects, and Carroll O'Connor remained in the retitled "Archie Bunker's Place," it had made television history and captured on film a history of the times. The Smithsonian Institution put Archie's and Edith's armchairs in its archives of national treasures. After "All in the Family," which last aired in September 1983, television would never again be the same.

The Mary Tyler Moore Show: CBS Premiere, September 19, 1970

The television production company co-founded by Mary Tyler Moore in 1970, MTM, launched a new trend in TV shows, beginning with her own "The Mary Tyler Moore Show." In less than a dozen years, MTM created such other hit sitcoms as "The Bob Newhart Show," "Rhonda," and "WKRP in Cincinnati," and such hour-long dramas as "Lou Grant," "The White Shadow," "Hill Street Blues," and "St. Elsewhere"—a track record unmatched by any other Hollywood studio.

It all began in Minneapolis with the "family" of modern-minded Mary Richards (Mary Tyler Moore), television's first single career woman, struggling to make it as an equal in a "man's" world and a "man's" profession: the TV newsroom. Her workplace family included her tough-guy/soft-guy boss Lou Grant (Edward Asner; LOU: Call me Lou. MARY: Okay, Mr. . . . Lou); her loud-mouth best friend Rhoda Morgenstern (Valerie Harper), a transplanted New Yorker; TV's most uninformed anchor, pompous, self-centered Ted "Hi, guys" Baxter (Ted Knight); Mary's bitchy, insincere landlady Phyllis Lindstrom (Cloris Leachman); sarcastic newswriter and mother hen to Mary, Murray Slaughter (Gavin MacLeod); and man-hungry homewrecker Sue Ann Nivens (Betty White), hostess of the fictional "Happy Homemaker Show." Sue Ann raised sexual innuendo on TV to a new high: "I was lying in bed last night and all of a sudden I had a great idea for the show. So I went right home and wrote it down." With action centered around the WJM-TV newsroom, the series started a trend toward job-oriented sitcoms. By the time it went off the air in 1977, it had won more Emmys than any sitcom in television history.

By moving the sitcom out of the living room and into the workplace, and centering it around a working woman, the show's producers created a revolution. In the era of women's lib, Mary Richards was single and liked it. She didn't need a man, and rather than go out on a boring date she'd stay home, and not feel stigmatized. The show's theme song, "You're Going to Make It After All," implied that Mary Richards was going to survive, and perhaps thrive, in a man's world.

Creating a Yuppie.   Mary Richards, as originally scripted, was a divorcee. But network executives, feeling that the American public wasn't ready for a divorced sitcom heroine, argued to make her a widow. But that entailed the messy task of killing off a husband. They feared that making her single—as well as determined and career-oriented—might suggest she was a lesbian; such was the sad state of stereotypes at the time the show was conceived. First given a boyfriend to underscore her sexual preference, she was soon allowed to drop him, be single (with an occasional date) and unapologetically thirtyish, and exhibit considerable spunk. As her boss-to-be Lou Grant observes, "You have spunk . . . I hate spunk!"

For millions of fans in the pre-VCR days, the Saturday night show made staying home on the "loneliest night of the week" acceptable and not that lonely. Reported a 1971 article in *The New York Times Magazine:* "Mary is so In that it's become fashionable to drift into the den at a party or even to go home at 9 on Saturday because you simply must not miss this program."

Much-loved was anchorman Ted. As real-life TV anchors were becoming celebrities in their own right, humorless, bumbling Ted provided a comic counterpoint. Around his dressing room hung photos of himself, and on hand to boost his ego at a moment's need were videotapes of his newscasts. In one episode he testifies before a grand jury:

TED: I told them I was the best newsman in the country.
MURRAY: You didn't!
TED: I had to. I was under oath.

After seven successful seasons and 168 episodes, Mary Tyler Moore decided to fold up the enterprise while it was still on top. Mary Richards's final words define the sitcom's newest kind of family. The TV station is sold and all are fired except, of course, the most incompetent, Ted Baxter. Mary says goodbye to everyone with: "I thought about something last night: What is a family. And I think I know. A family is people who make you feel less alone and really loved. Thank you for being my family." Mary's family split up to create "Rhoda," "Phyllis," "The Betty White Show," and "Lou Grant." Murray went aboard "The Love Boat." The last "MTM" episode was on September 3, 1977.

The Odd Couple: ABC Premiere, September 24, 1970

It featured two improbably mismatched roommates: neat-to-a-fault photographer Felix Unger (Tony Randall) and slob-by-any-standards sportswriter Oscar Madison (Jack Klugman). Called an adult sitcom, the show that weekly asked the question "Can two divorced men share an apartment without driving each other crazy?"—and answered with a no—was the brainchild of playwright Neil Simon.

Already a Broadway success, Simon was asked by Paramount in 1963 to develop a comedy for TV. Based on a forty-word synopsis, he received over a half-million dollars and the rights to produce an *Odd Couple* play (1965; starring Art Carney and Walter Matthau), while the studio retained the rights for a TV series and a feature film (1968; starring Jack Lemmon and Walter Matthau). Much mileage was derived from Simon's kernel of an idea, based on a real-life situation involving his divorced brother and a roommate.

And more mileage was sought. In 1975 Paramount created a female odd couple in "Laverne and Shirley" (a spin-off from "Happy Days"), then in 1982 it opted for a black version with "The New Odd Couple," starring Ron Glass and Desmond Wilson. It was not over yet. ABC developed an ethnic odd couple in "Perfect Strangers," and Simon himself wrote a female odd couple play, *Olive and Florence,* starring Rita Moreno and Sally Struthers. There was even a cartoon spin-off called "The Oddball Couple," featuring a slovenly canine and a prissy feline. The original TV show lasted five years, until July 1975.

The Partridge Family: ABC Premiere, September 25, 1970

Oscar-winner Shirley Jones, playing a widowed suburban housewife, and her sixteen-year-old stepson David Cassidy starred in this comedy about a musical family, based in part on the adventures of a real-life recording family, the Cowsills. Two months after the show debuted, the Partridge Family, as a singing group, had the country's number one single, "I Think I Love You." The series ran four years and made David a teen idol of the early Seventies; in the late Seventies his half-brother Shaun Cassidy would be a teen sensation. A month after it went off the air, ABC introduced an animated Saturday morning sequel, "The Partridge Family, 2200 A.D.," which was short-lived.

Sanford and Son: NBC Premiere, January 14, 1972

Producer Norman Lear followed his "All in the Family" success with a sitcom about a cantankerous but lovable Los Angeles junk dealer, Fred Sanford (Redd Foxx), and his picked-on partner and son, Lamont (Desmond Wilson). As "All in the Family" originated with a Britcom, "Sanford" derived from the British series "Steptoe and Son," and Lear's pilot, featuring two white actors (Paul Sorvino and Barnard Hughes), failed. The concept worked splendidly with black actors, though, and Lear, adopting Redd Foxx's real surname, changed Steptoe to Sanford and had an overnight hit. The show remained in the top ten throughout its five-year run.

Lamont was discontent with the junk business and continually threatened to set off on a more lucrative venture. Fred, to ground him, would feign a heart attack and moan to his deceased wife, "I'm coming, Elizabeth, I'm coming."

Fred Sanford was not that dissimilar in his prejudices from Lear's Archie Bunker, frequently belittling minorities: "I can't eat chink food," he said of Oriental cuisine. "Those people do their laundry and cooking in the same pot." The last telecast was in September 1977.

M*A*S*H: CBS Premiere, September 17, 1972

When television's first black-humor sitcom debuted, the country was bogged down, its citizens split apart over the seemingly endless war in Vietnam. "M*A*S*H," skirting between the brutality of battle and the mindlessness of war, was a nationwide smash. Created by Larry Gelbart from a hit Robert Altman movie (starring Elliott Gould and Donald Sutherland, from a novel by Korean War veteran Dr. J. Richard Hornberger), the series played more like a minimovie than a standard sitcom.

The action took place during the Korean War, and among medics. Its theme song, "Suicide Is Painless," struck the desired note of black humor. The loneliness, fear, and bloodshed of conflict were shown to be bearable only through humor, often of the daringly darkest sort; humor as a survival kit:

*"M*A*S*H."*

"Hey, nurse, you wanna play doctor when we're finished with this operation?"

The men and women of the 4077th Mobile Army Surgical Hospital were an unforgettable bunch of cut-ups: wisecracking-but-caring surgeon Captain Hawkeye Pierce (Alan Alda); shy and bumbling Corporal Radar O'Reilly (Gary Burghoff), nicknamed for a sixth sense that let him hear choppers before anyone else; regulation-breaking Captain Trapper John McIntyre (Wayne Rogers); sexy head nurse Major Hot Lips Houlihan (Loretta Swit), who, despite her admonitions to underlings about fooling around, was having an affair—details of which were broadcast to the base from a speaker hidden under her bed. Most unusual of all was high-heeled Corporal Maxwell Klinger, an operating room aide of Lebanese descent who paraded in women's clothes as a ruse to escape service, regularly beseeching, "If two doctors will sign a form, I'll be able to go home."

Viewers never knew quite what to expect. One week the show might be scripted strictly for laughs; the next week it was heart-wrenchingly serious or a mixture of both. Equally unusual for a sitcom (which Alda denied the show was), episodes often did not have neat resolutions. As the series progressed, Alda became the centerpiece. His humor could be poignant as when Hawkeye discussed the enemy: "I just don't know why they're shooting at us. All we want to bring them is democracy and white bread, to transplant the American Dream: freedom, achievement, hyperacidity, affluence, flatulence, technology, tension, the inalienable right to an early coronary sitting at your desk while plotting to stab your boss in the back."

Rick Mitz aptly sums up the show in *The Great TV Sitcom Book:* "Sergeant Bilko" told us "War is Fun," says Mitz. "Hogan's Heroes" told us "War is Heck." "M*A*S*H," though, "just came out and said it: War Is Hell." The final show—after eleven years, 250 episodes, and fourteen Emmys—was aired on September 19, 1983, drawing one of the largest audiences in sitcom history.

Maude: CBS Premiere, September 12, 1972

On Norman Lear's "All in the Family," Maude was Edith Bunker's cousin, an upper-middle-class, arch-liberal woman who would take on bigoted Archie Bunker. The feisty character became so popular that she was spun off in a 1972 series. Nothing sums up Maude Findlay (Beatrice Arthur) better than the show's theme song: "Enterprising, socializing, everything but compromising—right on, Maude!" Whenever she was angry with Walter (Bill Macy), her fourth husband, she'd threaten, "God'll get you for that." The series broke taboo ground by candidly discussing birth control, unwanted pregnancies, and abortions—all with irreverent humor.

After the Supreme Court legalized abortions, Maude learned she was pregnant and—in one of the most daring episodes in sitcom history—she had an abortion. Many affiliate stations aborted that show. Letters of protest poured into network headquarters. TV had come a long way; Lucy Ricardo hadn't even been allowed to mention the word pregnant. When articles on manic depression began to appear in the popular press, Maude discovered she had the ailment and started on Lithium. Almost as unusual, Maude was, unlike most perpetually youthful sitcom females, frankly fortyish and advancing—a grandmother with deepening wrinkles (she gets a facelift in one episode) and a depressing menopause. "I'm fifty and nobody loves me," she cried on her transitional birthday, on which she visits a psychiatrist. Then glimpsing herself in a mirror she adds, "Oh, God, if I could only repeal the law of gravity."

Good Times.   In typical sitcom fashion, the Findlays had neighbors: Walter's best friend, Arthur Harmon (Conrad Bain), a doctor of questionable competence (and thus the focus of many jokes), and in time his wife Vivian (Rue McClanahan), counterpoint to Maude in that her concerns were with her hair, her clothes, and what to serve for dinner. A witty black maid, Florida, (Ester Rolle), soon left the show for her own sitcom, *Good Times* (1974; with comic Jimmie Walker and his signature line, "Dy-no-mite!"), replaced by the hard-drinking Mrs. Naugatuck (British actress Hermione Baddeley)—who was herself replaced. Maude went through maids as she did husbands.

Florida was the viewers' favorite (precisely why she got her own show). To express her liberalism, Maude insists Florida enter the house through the front door, dine with the family, and schmooze with them over cocktails. Florida firmly declines.

FLORIDA: Now, the first week'll be on a trial basis.
MAUDE: Oh, Florida, don't be ridiculous—you're not on trial.
FLORIDA: I know—you are.

True to Lear's concept, when Florida leaves to return to Harlem (because her husband doesn't want her to work) her parting is poignantly realistic. "Oh, we'll visit," says Maude reassuringly. Florida responds: "Mrs. Findlay, you know we'll never visit each other." Maude says quietly: "I know." After six years and 142 episodes *Maude* was last telecast on April 29, 1978.

The Bob Newhart Show: CBS Premiere, September 16, 1972

Today it is almost expected that a talented stand-up comic will land a sitcom. But bringing the subtle humor of Bob Newhart to TV in 1972 as Chicago psychologist Dr. Bob Hartley seemed a gamble. The show, though, ended up creating "real" characters, particularly the members of Hartley's group therapy sessions. Its premise was that Bob was an expert at solving patients' problems, but a bumbling fool at handling his own. While fans enjoyed the home scenes with wife Emily (Suzanne Pleshette), they adored the wacky goings-on in Hartley's office. It was a sitcom peopled by neurotics, and often it was hard to tell Hartley's patients from his friends and co-workers. Group therapy, est, TM, and other routes to self-knowledge were then trendy, and the shrink sitcom arrived at a time in the decade when it was fashionable to have one's own Dr. Hartley—if a more competent one. The show lasted until 1978.

Happy Days: ABC Premiere, January 15, 1974

Because of the sitcom's unrealistic innocence, purity, and familial harmony, many reviewers called "Happy Days" an animated cartoon strip. "Sundays, Mondays, happy days" ran the theme song that introduced viewers to Richie Cunningham (Ron Howard), Potsie (Anson Williams), Chachi (Scott Baio), and Fonzie "Ayyyyy!" Fonzarelli (Henry Winkler), also known as "the Fonz"—whose leather jacket is now enshrined in the Smithsonian Institution.

Contrary to popular opinion, the series was not a spin-off of *American Graffiti*, which came a year later. The show originated as a skit, "Love and the Happy Day," featuring Howard and Anson Williams, in 1972 on "Love, American Style." The series could not have been more different from CBS's "Maude" or "MTM," or NBC's "Sanford and Son," and for its juvenile effort ABC was dubbed the Acne Broadcasting Company—for the show was about all you ever wanted to know of puberty. Necking was as far as the sitcom, set in the Fifties, would go. Richie's father Howard (Tom Bosley) owned a Milwaukee hardware store, and his mother Marion (Marion Ross) did what June Cleaver and Margaret Anderson had done—housework—and worried about Richie and his pals. Whereas early episodes revolved around straitlaced Richie and Potsie and their boring friends at Jefferson High, it became apparent from the low ratings that spice had to be added to the formula and fast. Enter . . .

The Fonz. He was the coolest dude in Milwaukee, a hip, kindhearted "thumbs-up" greaser. He saved the series, kicked off a cottage industry cult and a motorcycle craze, and his Fonzisms were mimicked by kids across the country. As his popularity soared (due in large part to Winkler's skillful performance), his billing in the credits climbed from fifth to second, behind Ron Howard (and first after Howard left the show). With viewers demanding more of the character, the producers conceived the gimmick of having him rent an apartment above the Cunningham's garage. Thus, at the scriptwriters' whim, he could drop in on the family to inject three-dimensional reality to their one-dimensional existence. And he became omnipresent.

The inevitable talk of giving him his own spin-off series was eventually canned. The producers realized that the "Happy Days" magic lay in the striking contrast between the smug Fonz and the sincere Richie, whom the tough guy protected: "Let him go," the Fonz would threaten bullies, "unless you want to make medical history." At its peak popularity, the show was watched by 50 million fans a week. Amazingly, Ron Howard, whose lines got fewer as the Fonz took center stage (as Winkler's salary went from $750 an episode to $80,000), got along well with Henry Winkler—which in TV land says a lot about the unselfish Howard, a screen veteran since his days as the tyke Opie in "The Andy Griffith Show" (see page 351). Howard later admitted that he was a lot like Richie Cunningham.

The show made a star of Winkler and gave Howard a chance to direct, setting him up for his later movie successes. And when actresses Penny

Marshall and Cindy Williams appeared on "Happy Days" in 1975, as dates for Richie and Fonzie, they were a season away from their own hit series: **Laverne and Shirley** (ABC premiere, January 27, 1976). And Mork (Robin Williams), who debuted on "Happy Days" in 1977, returned to TV with Mindy (Pam Dawber) in **Mork and Mindy** (ABC Premiere, September 14, 1978).

The *New York Times* faulted "Happy Days" for presenting a distorted view of the Fifties, all happiness and harmony. The show's producers realized this. At the end of the series they had Mork return and conjure up his Orson voice for a valedictory:

VOICE OF ORSON: Mork, you seem to like the fifties.

MORK: Yes, sir. It's a wonderful, naive, and romantic time. I went back to visit the Cunninghams and their friends. They're really nice people, but a little mondo-mundane . . . I'm talking white bread and mayonnaise . . . But, you know, they all seem to block out one thing, Senator McCarthy.

VOICE OF ORSON: Ah, yes—those were sad days.

MORK: I guess that's why it's so romantic—they never remember the sad things.

Barney Miller: ABC Premiere, January 23, 1975

Police departments around the country voted "Barney Miller" the cop show most accurate in the depiction of their jobs. The series originated by combining two sitcom ideas into one. Producer Danny Arnold wanted to do a show starring a Jewish New York foot cop; his partner wanted to feature a Los Angeles desk-bound detective. The combined concept set the series in New York's Greenwich Village and starred Hal Linden as levelheaded Captain Barney Miller; Maxwell Gail as discombobulated Detective Stanley "Wojo" Wojohowicz; Abe Vigoda as down-and-out Detective Phil Fish; Ron Glass as Ron Harris, a black detective hoping to be a novelist, at work on a lurid police thriller, *Blood on the Badge;* and Steve Landesberg as sarcastic know-it-all Detective Arthur Dietrich. To a station house visitor who mentions, "You guys must have a lot of fun around here," Dietrich deadpans, "We manage to have a laugh or two at humanity's expense"—which summed up the show's comic tenor.

The office-bound crew were plainclothes cops, whose lives were enlightened and disrupted by a stream of Village freaks, geeks, meeks, wackos, and petty criminals. The show's true genius was that the criminals were not all that different from the station house staff. At times a street loony came off as saner than the bickering cops. Fish whined insufferably, Dietrich was a confirmed cynic, Wojo continually fell in love with girls picked up for soliciting, and Harris was sharp-tongued and pretentious: When a woman reported her shoes were stolen and she felt violated, Harris snapped, "Well, metaphorically, yes." A visitor to Manhattan is robbed at knifepoint and complains, "I watched all those

'I Love New York' commercials . . . with Broadway actors singing and danc
ing . . . they never mentioned people with knives." Harris answers, "Well, they
only have a minute."

Overseeing the precinct was humane and even-tempered Barney. He held
the crew together, and when tempers flared he kept the cops apart. Scripts
were literate, the comedy was high-caliber, and the show won many awards.
Police, in particular, loved it. The New York City Police Department granted
the series an honorary membership award, and the Los Angeles Police Department held a Barney Miller Week. The final telecast was on September 9, 1982.

The Jeffersons: CBS Premiere, January 18, 1975

In the Seventies there was a fad for shamelessly spinning off new shows from
existing hits. To recap: As we've seen (or will), "Mary Tyler Moore" gave birth
to "Rhoda," "Phyllis," "Betty White," and "Lou Grant." "Happy Days" gave
life to "Laverne and Shirley and "Mork and Mindy." "Barney Miller" gave
Detective Fish "Fish," and "Three's Company" gave its downstairs neighbors
"The Ropers." "All in the Family" gave Edith Bunker's cousin "Maude," which
in turn gave the Findlays' maid Florida "Good Times." And the gingerly racist
show gave to Archie Bunker's black neighbors George and Louise Jefferson,
source of many of Archie's headaches and the show's humor, their own prime-
time slot in January 1975.

George was like Archie in that both characters were snobs and bigots. But
whereas Archie was financially strapped, George was newly rich. Vain and
scheming, George (Sherman Hemsley) scored a success in the dry cleaning
business and was able to escape from Queens and move his family to a "deluxe
apartment in the sky" on Manhattan's Upper East Side—though by the end of
each episode he always got his comeuppance from either his patient, long-
suffering wife Louise (Isabel Sanford), or their acerbic black maid Florence
(Marla Gibbs). To show the family had "overcome" (as in "We shall"), their
son Lionel (Mike Evans; later Damon Evans) was a college student. In fact,
"overcome" was the theme of the black sitcom, and the barb of maid Florence's
banter: Surveying the luxury flat, she shakes her head in disbelief, saying, "How
come we overcame and nobody told me anything about it?"

George's pomposity was endearing because it was always turned back on
him in a putdown, voiced or implied. As a boasting sophisticate he applies for
a loan.

BANKER: Before I give you the money, Mr. Jefferson, I'll need your John
    Hancock.
GEORGE: hat do you want with my life insurance?

Or when George is bragging about his possessions to a guest:

GUEST: Those are beautiful occasional tables.
GEORGE: Yeah, but we're gonna use them all the time.

As the Norman Lear spinoff factory made George a wealthy Archie, it created warm-hearted, level-headed Louise as an Edith Bunker with brains. When George, a racist, refuses to meet neighbors who are an interracial couple, Louise persuades him to invite them over. Black sitcoms, through "Sanford and Son" and especially "The Jeffersons" with its affluent family and interracial couple, had come a long way since the days of "Amos 'n' Andy."

Chico and the Man: NBC Premiere, September 13, 1974

As fast-talking, ambitious Chico Rodriguez, Freddie "Lookin' go-o-o-d" Prinze went overnight from an unknown comic to a TV superstar. And it would create insurmountable problems for him.

The sitcom itself was little more than an ethnic variation on "Sanford and Son," where the feisty, cynical Man, Ed Brown, played by Jack Albertson, owned a dilapidated garage in the barrio section of East Los Angeles, which Chico argued could be spruced up and made profitable. The chemistry between the two men, and moreover, the force of Prinze's screen personality, made the show a hit and its Puerto Rican lead the centerpiece. For the young comic, born in the ghetto of New York's Hell's Kitchen and once a knife-carrying member of the Royal Lords, the rapid rise from anonymity to big-bucks stardom took its toll on his private life. After his wife of fifteen months filed for divorce and his former manager initiated a business lawsuit against him, Prinze took to drugs and alcohol.

On January 28, 1977, midway through the show's third season, the twenty-two-year-old star popped a handful of Quaaludes and shot himself in the head. Four episodes with Prinze had already been filmed and were aired (even the one in which he talked about death), then the format of show was altered—though without Freddie Prinze's charisma the effort was doomed to fail. *Variety* referred to the sitcom without Prinze as "the sound of one hand clapping."

Alice: CBS Premiere, August 31, 1976

Alice Hyatt (Linda Lavin) was a widowed aspiring singer with a precocious twelve-year-old son (Philip McKeon), who worked as a waitress at Mel's Diner while waiting for her big break. Her dramatically different co-workers, fun-loving, outspoken Flo (Polly Holliday), and shy, scatterbrained Vera (Beth Howland), soon became viewer favorites, commanding larger and larger scripts. Tender, malcontent Mel (Vic Tayback), renowned for Mel's famous chili, tried to keep the women in line, shouting, "Stow it" when angry.

Flo, though, had the series' most quoted line (usually delivered to Mel): "Kiss mah grits." She also delivered the show's countless sexual double entendres, as when Mel asks her to lift a sack of sugar. "Mel, if I'm gonna get a bad back, it's not gonna be from lifting sugar." Her many boyfriends dropped into the diner for food and sassy talk. "Earl, honey," asks Flo, "what would you like this morning?" He winks: "Same thing I had last night."

Though the show broke no new ground, and though episodes could be banal or fatuous, it contained, says Rick Mitz, "the subliminal message that Sisterhood is Powerful." For the waitresses, as a unit, were a force Mel couldn't overpower. Out of true love and affection, Alice, Flo, and Vera supported each other through the myriad sitcom crises that crop up over a long run.

The humorous sitcom derived from a noncomedic film, *Alice Doesn't Live Here Anymore,* for which Ellen Burstyn won an Academy Award as the waitress who wishes for a singing career. To bring the film to the tube, Alice's love interest (Kris Kristofferson) was dropped, opening up possibilities for mismatched dates and serious relationships for Linda Lavin. If "Alice" displayed the power of sisterhood, it also showed, in a decade when the divorce rate soared, leaving many mothers single parents, that one working woman, Alice Hyatt, could raise a child, make ends meet, and strive for a dream and a better life. The show was last telecast in 1984. Flo, the most popular character, got her own spin-off sitcom, "Flo."

Taxi: ABC Premiere, September 12, 1978

The cabbies of New York's drably dark Sunshine Cab Company displayed ensemble comedic acting at its best. The idea for the show came from an article in *New York* magazine about the nighttime exploits of real-life cabbies cruising around the city. In additional to its superb scripts, the show was a smash because of its skilled cast—in fact, the entire cast was nominated for a Golden Globe award in the series' second season.

The show made stars of just about everyone on it. Judd Hirsch played Alex Rieger, a normal, level-headed character. Unknown Tony Danza, fresh from the boxing ring where he was discovered, was the resident sex symbol, and a boxer with few wins. Andy Kaufman, as the wide-eyed babbling mechanic Latka Gravas, hailed from an unspecified country and had an accent to match. Chortling, pint-sized Danny DeVito, as demented dervish Louie De Palma, Sunshine's lurid dispatcher, was the embodiment of evil and loved it. Jeff Conaway, as Bobby Wheeler, was a pretty-boy actor/model waiting for his break. The only female cabbie was art gallery receptionist Elaine Nardo, played by Marilu Henner, a single mother who drove a cab for pocket cash while her children slept. Craziest of all was Christopher Lloyd's "Reverend" Jim Ignatowski, a Sixties drug burnout who could have benefited from the latter-day commercial of the egg in the frying pan: "This is your brain. This is your brain on drugs." Lloyd took a small role and parlayed it into a *Back to the Future* career. In a sitcom sense the group was a family, with Rieger as father.

It was an immediate hit with viewers and critics alike. TV writers flatteringly referred to the cast as a repertory company, and the show won many awards for its scripts and actors. With competition like "Laverne and Shirley" and "Happy Days," "Taxi" was recognized for the quality program it was. After five successful years, the show signed off on July 27, 1983.

CHAPTER 10

━━━━━━━━ ❑ ━━━━━━━━

The Spendthrift Eighties into the Payback Nineties

1980 to the Present

The Greed Decade

The Me Decade of the Seventies passed, perhaps not surprisingly, to the Me! Me! Me! Decade of the Eighties. The keynote was greed; the underlying philosophy was image over reality. Some say the temper was struck early in the decade—on February 23, 1980, when in the New Hampshire presidential primary, Ronald Reagan, preeminent image, barked, "I paid for this microphone," giving voice to the era's credo: "I paid for it. It's mine."

Others say the notion of greed as a cardinal virtue began on Wall Street amid the push for high-risk short-term yields over simple long-term common sense. The notion was frighteningly summed up in the movie *Wall Street* when heartless corporate raider Gordon Gekko shouts, "Greed is good," embracing the belief that the relentless pursuit of self-interest "at the top" trickles down, in due time, to benefit all humankind. Hostile takeovers, leveraged buyouts, and mega-mergers spawned a new breed of billionaire: a money-man who produced no consumable product. Ivan "Insider Trader" Boesky. Michael "Junk Bonds" Milken. Donald "The Deal" Trump. Leona "Rhymes with Rich" Helmsley. All would become Eighties symbols of the meteoric rise and, in due time, the humbling fall. Trump, we'd later learn, had built his empire by using image as collateral.

An insatiable desire for wealth, status, and good time was evident everywhere: In the Michelob motto, "You can have it all." In the much-heard maxim, "If you've got it, flaunt it." In the image of the sneaker-clad, briefcase-carrying Superwoman who balanced (she wished) a career, kids, husband, housework, and happiness. In the *Forbes* tally of America's four hundred richest people, which overshadowed its rundown of the country's five hundred largest companies. And in Robin Williams's insightful quip, "Cocaine is God's way of telling you that you have too much money." Nor was religion immune from greed: The sins of Jim and Tammy Faye Bakker made it clear that in the Eighties the biblical manna was money.

Gotta Shop

Not surprisingly, Americans went on a spending spree unlike anything seen since the postwar Forties. We binged on buying—some 62 million microwave ovens, 57 million washers and dryers, 88 million cars and light trucks, 105 million color television sets, 63 million VCRs, 31 million cordless phones, and 30 million telephone answering machines. All of this conspicuous consumption in a five-year period mid-decade; and all of these products bought at a time when America had only 91 million households. In the era when "Shop till you drop" was the motto of millions, one company came out with shoes designed especially for shopping, with supports that allowed you to hurry from mall to mall to maximize your purchases with minimal foot discomfort.

Our consumption rose faster than our incomes. People saved less and borrowed more. They mortgaged their homes and mortgaged the future; as a bumper sticker read: "We Are Spending Our Children's Inheritance." From this book's standpoint of fads and trends, the "splurge generation" (as Tom Wolfe dubbed the buying baby boomers) provides an unequaled richness of material.

We begin with a look at language, always a revealing barometer of an age.

Buzzwords and Best Quotes

Language, argued Walt Whitman, never one to pass up a **photo opportunity,** is not the province of lexicographers, but arises "out of the work, needs, ties, joys, affections, tastes" of a culture. Out of its excesses too. The wordy Whitman might have had trouble fashioning a succinct **sound bite,** that ideally compact and colorful quip favored by Eighties television news shows, which tried to keep the tedium of **talking heads** to a minimum. Brevity is the soul of the sound bite.

"That was a great bite," compliments the journalist, praising short form over substance. A Harvard researcher, Kiku Adatto, analyzed network newscasts from the Sixties and the Eighties and determined that the average sound bite shortened from 42.3 seconds to 9.8 seconds—indicative perhaps of a general shortening of viewers' attention spans. Arguably the decade's most famous sound bite was George Bush's **Read my lips.**

Bites were not new, of course; *Reader's Digest* and *Bartlett's Familiar Quotations* made a business of colorful condensation. But in the Eighties, "biteability," warned the *New York Times,* "threatens to reduce culture to a mere index of what's in it."

All of us strive, wittingly or not, to sum up a sentiment or event in a smart phrase. A single word can have potent impact—and later convey an explosion of nostalgia. Can you describe the decade's trends embodied in the following catchphrases: **networking, interface, safe sex, just say no, thirtysome-**

thing, cellulite, camcorder, wannabe, in the loop, cutting edge, pet rock potential, Elvis sightings, lite, let's do lunch, call my people, oat bran, tabloid TV, Reaganomics, Black Monday, boom box, junk bonds, house music, fax, user friendly, spin control, quality time.

Collegians have always had their own in language (see page 115). In the Eighties it went something like this: **Praying to the porcelain god** meant clutching a toilet bowl while on one's knees expelling an excess of alcohol. A **hamster** was an opened beer leftover from the night before. Others as compiled by UCLA students in *UCLA Slang:*

McPaper—a term paper written quickly and without much research.
She's been fake-baking—She's been going to a tanning salon.
A party hat—a condom; also known as a **lifejacket.**
Beer goggles—blurry vision resulting from too many drinks, which makes everyone of the opposite sex look appealing.
To go ballistic—to go crazy.
Multiple sadness—when two or more things go wrong.
Are you dealing with him?—Are you involved with him?
Boinking—having sex.
Let's rage—Let's party.
Did you overserve?—Did you drink too much?
A pirate's dream—a flat-chested woman (with a sunken chest).
Hemorrhoid—a person who is painful to be with.
Fossil—a person who has been a college student for over four years.
That dude is clueless—That guy has no idea of what's going on.

From the movie *When Harry Met Sally* comes **a Sally**—a meticulous person; from the cult film *Heathers* comes **a Heather**—a superficial girl.

As for memorable quotes: Susan Sontag summed up the decade by saying, "I think there's been a decline in the capacity for seriousness—that society is dominated by entertainment values." For many Americans, Vice President Dan Quayle summed himself up when, addressing the United Negro College Fund, he said, "What a waste it is to lose one's mind, or not to have a mind . . . How true it is." Gary Hart summed up his career when he dared reporters—on the same day he'd be caught with Donna Rice—"If anybody wants to put a tail on me, go ahead. They'd be very bored." Secretary of State Al Haig summed up his ambition when, on the day Ronald Reagan was shot, he mounted the podium and presumed, "I am in control here." Dealmaker Donald Trump summed up existence itself when he said, "The ultimate deal is life." Hotel queen Leona Helmsley summed up the decade's opportunism when she said (according to testimony at her trial on tax-evasion charges), "Only little people pay taxes."

FADS, FOLLIES, AND TRENDS

Flash Fashions

We saw, in the Seventies, how the films *Annie Hall, Saturday Night Fever,* and *Urban Cowboy* inspired fashion statements: kookie conservative, lounge lizard in white, and Western chic. The first Eighties film to influence attire was the 1983 slick and sexy *Flashdance*—about a Pittsburgh charmer (Jennifer Beals) who's a welder by day, a go-go dancer by night, and a ballet hopeful round the clock. Within a few weeks of its release, the film grossed $50 million, and its bouncy title song, "Flashdance—What a Feeling," shot to the top of the charts.

The **Flashdance look** that heroine Beals inspired consisted mainly of an artfully torn, off-the-shoulder, shortsleeve sweatshirt, worn over a tank top, with tight-fitting pants and a dancer's leg-warmers bunched at the ankles (or three pairs of socks worn at different lengths). Not since Jane Russell's heyday did women get so much mileage out of peekaboo shoulders. Fashion observers commented that the *Flashdance* look caught on overnight primarily because sweat gear, already popular as jogging attire, was owned by millions of young women—they merely had to scoop out the neckline and slice off the sleeves. Young men also sported the ragamuffin shirt style, which let them showcase their progress at the gym. Among young teens, *Flashdance* fashions crimped their earlier **Valley Girl look.**

Michael Jackson Glove.   Pop singer Michael Jackson launched a fashion affectation in 1984, after dominating the Grammy awards ceremony that year. His trademark—a single, sequined white glove, worn on the right hand—had teenagers across the country decorating their mothers' old white gloves in gaudy imitation. The glove became a hotbed of controversy at many high schools. At Bound Brook High in Somerset County, New Jersey, male and female students were banned from wearing gloves because they violated the school dress code, but also because a gloved hand interfered with students' typing, climbing ropes, and shooting hoops in gym class, and operating heavy machinery in shop.

Madonna Mimics.   Pop star Madonna inspired imitation with her sexy lace and fishnet ensemble, highlighted on an MTV video and in her hit film *Desperately Seeking Susan.* The mandatory Madonna raiment consisted of bared off-the-shoulder bra straps, artfully torn fishnet stockings, sundry leather and chains, and a handcuff as bracelet, all punctuated by an exposed belly button. Tousled hair and heavy red lipstick added authenticity. The look made lace underwear a fashionable outer garment and inspired Madonna lookalike contests in schools and clubs around the country. Contestants often paraded while lip-synching to Madonna's hit "Like a Virgin."

Out of Africa Safari Style.   Women too mature to copy Madonna could in 1986 dress in the khaki chic popularized by Meryl Streep in the movie *Out* *of Africa,* in which she portrayed the legendary Baroness Karen Blixen, who recorded her experiences in the book *Letters From Africa* under the name Isak Dinesen. The costumes, designed by Italian-born Milena Canonero, in color and style combined Dinesen's mannish flair with a rugged Ralph Lauren romanticism to kick off a safari-wear craze. Army and Navy stores were ransacked for authentic gear (like pith helmets), and boutiques like Banana Republic found themselves in step with the vogue. Saks Fifth Avenue ran a "floral and khaki" line, while Macy's opted for a more direct tie-in: an *Out of Africa* boutique. Fringed shawls, khaki duster coats, riding breeches, and four-pocket safari jackets were seminal to the style, as were primitive prints in earth reds, oranges, and greens.

One humble item of attire in the Eighties became unexpectedly trendy and pricey . . .

Sneaker Mania

Long a utilitarian gym shoe to be shoved into the corner of a musty locker or under an unmade bed, the sneaker emerged as the decade's most fashionable footwear, especially among youths. Gone were the days of the simple black canvas high-top with a rubber sole. In was high-tech footgear, engineered to give an athlete a competitive edge in running and jumping.

Made variously of leather, suede, and nylon, the shoes might have shock-protective heels, or heels of molded thermal plastic, air-cushioned soles, and inflatable air-bladder collars. Designer sneakers—like Nike's $110 Air Jordan and Reebok's $170 Pump—were pitched to kids, who literally begged, borrowed, or stole to get the money for the status footwear. As the decade ended, the entire sneaker industry reported sales in excess of 400 million shoes, up from 347 million the previous year. Converse claimed that 58 percent of their revenues came from children eighteen and under.

The upscaling of sneakers began in the Sixties with companies like Adidas and Puma, and was carried to new heights in the next decade by Nike. The working Superwoman of the Seventies made sneakers a high-heels alternative for walking to the office. Furthermore, an emphasis on fitness and jogging, and the popularity of Jane Fonda–like workout videos, helped promote specially designed shoes.

But the real mania came in the Eighties when kids, particular inner-city kids, adopted footwear as a personal statement. A poll of sporting goods stores revealed that many inner-city youths bought pricey new sneakers at least once a month. Marketing experts claimed that it was these kids, often using drug-earned dollars, who set the trends for sneaker gimmickry design and shoe distribution around the country. Many parents and sportswear store owners charged that some brands of shoes were even targeted at the drug-dealing crowd. The Los Angeles Police Department accused shoe companies of cashing in on the easy drug money picked up by inner-city kids.

The shoe companies denied the charges. They said that the high price of sneakers was due to high-tech innovations. UCLA professor of social psychology Harold Kassarjian summed up the incestuous supply-and-demand cycle when he told *Newsweek* in 1989, "The world doesn't need $200 sneakers. But it doesn't need Hostess Twinkies either." By that time several shoe manufacturers, to display their social responsibility (and quell negative publicity), had begun to pump some of their profits back into the nation's inner cities by refurbishing school gyms and outdoor basketball courts.

Rubik's Cube

In 1974, Hungarian architectural professor Erno Rubik designed a challenging puzzle—a cube that was a cluster of cubelets—for his students. It was meant to be a mental exercise, if not a frustrating experience. The six-sided plastic cube had nine colored squares set in rows of three, and the rows could be rotated to achieve different color configurations. The object of the puzzle was to align the cubelets until each side of the cube displayed a single solid hue. The harrow of the challenge lay in the fact that the cube could be aligned in 43,252,003,274,489,856,000 different patterns.

Rubik's Cube—retailing for about $6 to $10—was first marketed in America in 1980, and for the next year and a half much of the country became obsessed with solving the puzzle. Worldwide sales topped 100 million, bringing lasting fortune (and fleeting fame) to Erno Rubik. Millions of people never did solve the puzzle. Others aligned the colors in under a minute; for a while, a sixteen-year-old boy held the record of twenty-eight seconds. A British mathematician solved the cube in fifty calculated moves. The media, punning with a "cult of cubists," reported that a compulsive woman developed wrist tendinitis from rotating the cube's rows, while another woman filed for divorce, citing as grounds her husband's single-minded infatuation with the cube. At the fad's height, more than fifty quickie books were published offering step-wise solutions.

Erno Rubik attempted to duplicate his runaway success with spin-off puzzles like **Rubik's Magic Snake** and **Rubik's Revenge,** but, true to a fad's one-time windfall, they never ignited a mania.

Wacky WallWalker

Harvard MBA Ken Hakuta was operating a small import-export business in Washington, D.C., when, in 1982, relatives in Tokyo sent him a box of *takos*—a Japanese term for "octopus" that described a gummy, spiderlike toy that when hurled against a wall slowly descends, limb over limb, under the grip of gravity. In takos, rechristened Wacky WallWalkers for the American market, Hakuta glimpsed his future. He dropped his import lines of ironing board covers and karate uniforms and secured U.S. rights to distribute the toys, which in Japan were popular among small children. Within five years he had sold 220 million WallWalkers—in colors of red, green, blue, yellow, and black—and rechristened himself Dr. Fad.

Mr. Millionaire could also have described him. The toy, manufactured in Japan, cost about 20 cents to make, and Hakuta sold them for about $1.90. By his own accounting he earned a profit of $20 million on a fad item that in terms of longevity outlived Rubik's Cube and the pet rock.

Not that it happened overnight, or without great effort. Lacking money for advertising, Hakuta initially made the rounds of a city's toy stores, hurling WallWalkers at the nearest wall, hoping the gadget in motion would sell itself. When the toy caught on, Dr. Fad promoted it aggressively around the country. And when peak interest began to wane, he cleverly pulled WallWalkers from toystore shelves and turned down licensing requests to use the wacky image on T-shirts—gambling that if he made the product scarce he could imbue it with a second life. As he did, by contacting food companies like Kellogg's and Wendy's, persuading them to offer the toys as premiums. Kellogg's alone stuffed 75 million WallWalkers into its cereal boxes mid-decade. Wendy's not only offered the WallWalker as a premium with the purchase of a hamburger, but also launched a national advertising campaign, saving Dr. Fad the expense of promoting his own product.

In the meantime, Dr. Fad was busy promoting himself. The savvy Hakuta published a book, *How to Create a Fad and Make a Million Dollars,* hosted a syndicated TV show for children, and was awarded the inventor of the year award from the Franklin Institute in Philadelphia. By this time the indefatigable fadmeister had followed his Wacky WallWalkers with three related spin-offs: **Sticky Hands, Space Darts,** and **Rocking Rollers**—the last also a Kellogg's cereal box premium. Dr. Fad and his Wacky WallWalkers became one of the decade's great widget success stories.

Slap Wrap Bracelets

It resembled a thin 9-inch ruler, but with a downward flick against the wrist it curled around the arm to become a bracelet. Popular among the schoolyard set, Slap Wraps sold for about $2.25 in 1990 and were dubbed by one fad observer as "a Venetian blind with attitude." Produced by Main Street Toy Company of Connecticut, Slap Wraps were initially turned down by several major toy companies that did not believe the invention of Stuart Anders, a high school shop teacher from Sun Prairie, Wisconsin, had fad potential.

Anders, in 1983, was experimenting with thin steel ribbon (0.006-inch gauge) when he observed that a strip, upon impact with a wrist, curled into a circle. He demonstrated the ribbon to a friend who represented toy inventors, and in 1989 Slap Wraps, in polka-dot and solid-colored sheaths, were ready to debut at the annual New York Toy Fair.

Unfortunately, the snappy product was easy to rip off. Soon the market was flooded with imitations—not all as safe as the originals. Slapping a strip of paper-thin metal against bare flesh lacerated many a youth's arm. As the fad was peaking, Anders said, "I'd like to think Slap Wraps will last thirty years." Then he modified that slap-happy forecast: "But I know it won't. I hope it falls somewhere between Pet Rocks and the Hula Hoop."

Nerd Pride

It was the most ironic form of popularity to be seen in the Eighties—pride in being a nerd. "I'm a Nerd, and I'm Proud" read a fast-selling T-shirt. Nerds even developed their own in language, geekspeak.

Modern popular culture has long featured with derision "brains" and "egg-heads," high IQ folk interested more in books than dates and booze. Of more recent origin is the term nerd, a milquetoast in white shirt, baggy pants, black-rimmed glasses, who carries pens in a plastic nerd-pack in a shirt pocket. The term is thought to derive from California surfer jargon of the Sixties, referring to an inept, ineffectual person. A **geek,** according to a contemporary dictionary, is a "street performer who shocks the public by biting off heads of live chickens." Thus, neither a geek nor a nerd was necessarily a brain.

The association of the slurs with high intelligence arose in popular culture at a time when Woody Allen, the nerds' national hero, began to gain popularity. The same period witnessed the rise of the computer genius, or "hacker." Whereas in movies the scrawny, neurotic Allen always got the beautiful woman, in real life the hacker wiz manifested "cool" by such acts as breaking into Pentagon computers. Or, as was the case with Apple Computers founder Stephen Wozniak, by becoming a millionaire before the age of thirty. "Nerd" took on a different light.

A seminal transformation of the nerd to hero occurred on the movie screen in 1984 with Jeff Kanew's *Revenge of the Nerds,* which depicted how a geek fraternity masterfully took over a college campus and won the respect of the shapeliest female students. Two years later came *Lucas,* featuring a gangly geek who not only is interested in girls but tries out for the football team.

Nerd Pride.

Hollywood was mining the social misfit. *Stand by Me* was the story of a skinny nerd who blossomed into a successful writer, and *Peggy Sue Got Married* showed the triumphant return of the abused nerd of the physics lab to his twenty-fifth high school reunion; he had become a famous scientist, admired by his former tormentors.

Television, too, cast nerds as heroes. ABC's hit series "Head of the Class" was the antithesis of the previous decade's "Welcome Back, Kotter," featuring a classroom not of dumb greasers but of geeky geniuses. The kids, all social misfits, wallflowers, and loners, had that prized information age commodity: brainpower. The rise of the nerd brought with it a trend for dressing like a nerd, plus nerd cereals and candies, geek greeting cards, and even a mechanical wind-up geek doll. The shouted torment "Nerd!" passed from insult to endearment—of sorts.

As members of Harvard University's Society of Nerds and Geeks point out, "There are few countries in the world where anti-intellectualism runs as high in popular culture as it does in the U.S." The group cautions that if America does not learn to laud its brains and eggheads as do our economic rivals in eastern Asia, the twenty-first century may witness a monetary battle in which Asian nerds and geeks are pitted against such American heroes as overpaid jocks, pop rockers, and sitcom heartthrobs.

Tanning Salons

For a decade that prized image over reality, what could be a more appropriate symbol than the tanning salon—after one visit you boast the rosy glow of health atop the possible seeds of malignant melanoma. But you looked *maaar-ve-lous*. Short-term. Very short-term, since your skin soon needed a further assault of ultraviolet irradiation.

This may be an exaggeration, but only slightly. For—as with other "rosy" images of the early and mid-Eighties—by decade's end reality reared its inevitable head. Tanning salons were not as safe as we'd been told; their lamps' "safe" ultraviolet A rays were not all that different from the sun's "burning" ultraviolet B rays. In fact, as the FDA reported in 1989: "As for long-term damage, the effects of UVA and UVB radiation are essentially the same."

Tanning salons were so in during the fitness mania of the Eighties that their clients and operators developed the language of salonese: Pale-skinned customers were **Caspers** (as in Casper the Friendly Ghost), while those excessively tanned, with leathery hides, were *iguanas*. To get an even **fake bake,** a Casper lay in a **clamshell** (tanning bed), called out, **Turn me on** (switch on the lamps), and later requested, **Flip me** (turn me over). It was cheaper than a winter vacation to the Caribbean, and sessions could be crammed into one's lunch hour. Customers were lulled into a false security with claims that the specially designed lamps were significantly safer than the sun. The actual difference was dangerously marginal: Sunlight contains from 1 percent to 3 percent of UVB rays; a properly functioning tanning bulb emits about 1 percent.

Unfortunately, tanning beds and their accompanying timers were not always well maintained. In addition, FDA field inspectors found that many owners removed warning labels from tanning beds, did not offer protective eyewear, ignored timers, and never gave clients a rundown of the safety measures needed for tanning under lamps. By the start of the Nineties, the salons, which once were commonplace in malls and fitness centers, were an endangered species. It remains to be seen if the healthful look of the Nineties will be one of a natural, untanned complexion.

Lottos and Legal Gambling

"Gambling," as reported in *Business Week* in the last months of the Eighties, "is part of the daily routines of tens of millions of Americans." Reported *Newsweek* during the same period: "This year Americans will spend an estimated $278 billion on everything from state-run lotteries to church-run bingo." While the practice of betting is ancient, the proliferation of lotteries, off-track betting (OTB), TV game shows, and Atlantic City's casinos—coupled with a newfound attitude that gambling was a socially acceptable way to acquire instant wealth in the greed decade—created a betting mania in the Eighties unlike anything the country had previously experienced.

Consider some numbers: In 1964, only the state of New Hampshire had a lottery. In 1990, thirty-two states and the District of Columbia had games—which took in nearly $20 billion. Or: In December 1988, when the New York State Lottery jackpot shot to $45 million, vendors were selling an average of twenty-eight thousand tickets a minute. Or (as *Time* reported in 1989): A minimum of 15 million men and women routinely bet beyond their means, making them gambling addicts.

Many factors created the mania. In addition to the legalization and socialization of gambling, modern technology helped fan the fad. Computers coughed out instantaneous odds on any kind of race, ballgame, and lottery, and the machines even simplified gambling by picking random odds for bettors. In many games all you had to do was turn over your money. A new TV technology allowed couch potatoes to gamble from the comfort of their living room sofas. Further, we were told that gambled monies went for such respectable things as improving the educational system and offsetting local taxes. Sociologists pointed out that that argument alone gave millions of timid bettors a rationale to be bold gamblers. The aggressive marketing of gambling in the decade, by government and the private sector, conveyed the message that you could have wealth without work—precisely what the average person thought the country's Michael Milkens and Ivan Boeskys were doing.

Many sociologists argue that mass gambling fever is pernicious. The more people believe in the attainment of happiness through luck and chance, the less they believe in the importance of virtues such as industriousness and thrift, and the deferral of gratification. In a 1989 essay, George Will summed up the decade's mania: "Once upon a time, mass irrationality was considered a menace to democratic government," he wrote. "In this age of lotteries manufacturing mobs is a government goal and mass hysteria is an important ingredient of public finance." As of this writing the gambling fad is still hot; it remains to be seen if the "pursuit of wealth without work" will continue as America's favorite pastime in the decade of the Nineties.

Couch Potato and Cocooning

Definition: n. (1) Male homebody who whiles away the day slouching on the couch with impunity; Motto: "Say it loud: I'm a spud and I'm proud." (2) Limbless, soft, do-nothing doll popular in 1987.

The couch potato husband or bachelor has always existed as a guilt-ridden man who'd rather forgo dancing, partying, barhopping, even sex, for another uninterrupted, uneventful, perfect night at home in his favorite chair. He'd gladly trade machismo for "spudismo." The lowly tuber, in the age of television, became the boobtuber. In 1987 Madison Avenue transformed his guilt into pride, his image into a marketing bonanza, and his do-nothingness into the trendy couples' pastime of cocooning. No longer did those who stayed at home have to feel inferior about their social life (or lack thereof). Couch potatoes captured the cover of *New York* magazine, and Coleco introduced a $35 couch potato doll, a brisk seller at Christmastime. The Company Store, an upscale mail-order house, offered the Couch Potato Down Bed Comforter, ideal for cocooning.

Much of the couch potato merriment in 1987 centered on punning. Underground cartoonist Bob Armstrong founded a group whose motto was "Couchland, couchland tuber alles." He encouraged video addicts to shed their guilt and accept the fact that "the indigenous form of American meditation is Transcendental Vegetation." He also held the federal trademark on the term couch potato, licensing the phrase to be used on T-shirts, mugs, couch pillows, blankets, and dolls. A couch potato convention was planned in January 1988, to be followed by a banquet featuring TV dinners, but the idea languished from its own inherent inertia: How do you get a couch potato off the sofa and to Chicago's Hyatt Hotel? The dilemma was never resolved. Though human couch potatoes still exist, and always will, by mid-1988 they were no longer the center of media attention. And probably thankful for it.

Deely Bobbers

They were bobbing, glitter-coated headsets that resembled insect antennas and were all the rage in 1982; a set may now be in a carton in your basement.

A quintessential silliness, Deely Bobbers were the brainchild of thirty-eight-year-old novelty manufacturer John Mincove of Bellevue, Washington. A set sold for about $2, and wearers looked as if they belonged on "Saturday Night Live" in one of John Belushi's killer bee skits. The novelty item was easy to rip off, and, indeed, one Stephen Askin of Marina Del Rey, California, claimed that he and his wife concocted the first bobbing antennas in 1981, but failed to move fast enough to gain a patent and make a killing. Askin said he commissioned a manufacturer to produce 2 million bobbers, at a cost of 11 cents each, but the fad had crashed by the time he had the product ready for stores. Deely Bobbers (the origin of their name remains a mystery) were a hot item during the Christmas season of 1982, but the headgear, once expected to outsell the pet rock and Rubik's Cube, proliferated in so many cut-price imitations that the fad survived only a few months. Due to cutthroat price competition, no one manufacturer walked away a millionaire.

Smurfs

Smurfs—small, plucky, blue gnomes with white stocking caps, who generated some $600 million in retail sales at the peak of their popularity in 1982—were created twenty-five years earlier by Belgian illustrator Pierre "Peyo" Culliford. The grotesquely adorable creatures, through book illustrations, attracted the attention of European toy manufacturers in the Sixties, creating fads in Germany, Italy, Spain, and Scandinavia, where the cuddly pint-sized pixie was known respectively as Schlumpfe, Puffo, Pitufo, and Smolf.

The Belgian-born elves' break into big-time faddom began in 1978 when, christening them Smurfs, British Petroleum launched a promotional campaign based on Culliford's creatures. In England, they spawned such Smurfanalia as T-shirts, posters, and even a record, "The Smurf Song," that ascended the British charts. In America, the 2-inch-high figurines, imported by a Los Angeles–based novelty distributor, Wallace Berrie and Company, sold for $1.50 in 1981. The craze mushroomed when NBC president Fred Silverman, impressed by his daughter Melissa's attraction to the troll-like dolls (which she thought resembled her father), commissioned Hanna-Barbera, creators of "The Flintstones," to devise a Saturday morning cartoon series. "The Smurfs" became the showcase for the images, which soon appeared on clocks, children's vanity sets, pedal cars (Smurfmobiles), lunchboxes and transistor radios.

Smurfs were *the* major toy fad of 1982. Through imaginative licensing of the image, Smurfs outsold Steven Spielberg's 1982 creation E.T., as well as George Lucas's *Star Wars* characters, such then-trendy dolls as Strawberry Shortcake, and cartoon favorites like Snoopy and Garfield the cat. So popular was the TV show that it drew NBC from last place to first in the Saturday morning ratings, was lengthened from a half hour to ninety minutes, and caused the network to shelve its plans to expand the "Today" show to weekends.

As people began collecting Smurfs, their population grew to include ninety-eight male elves with Disney-like monikers of Brainy, Greedy, and Jokey, plus a wise old Papa Smurf, and a single blonde female Smurfette. The media punned shamefully, saying a new craze was "Smurfin' USA" and that the White House's annual Easter egg roll was "besmurfed" by the gnomes, and inverting Murphy's Law to Smurfee's Law, in which "everything that can go right, does go right"—a phrase that reflected the dolls' extraordinary merchandising profits. Though overmarketed, Smurfs did not fade away, as do most fads. Instead, by 1984 the cloyingly cute elves had moved into that classification—fairy tale icon—that includes the enduring Disney characters and ageless comic book heroes. Future generations of preschoolers will never know Smurfs as fad toys but as staples of folklore fantasy.

WrestleMania and Hulk Hogan

The decade witnessed the transformation of an ancient sport of strength and agility into a show business arena, some say center-ring circus, featuring 300-pound-plus, muscle-bound behemoths as the unlikely stars and profitable pop culture icons. Pro wrestling became one of the country's most popular sports. Its practitioners, once unable to earn a living from the game, suddenly were commanding six-figure incomes. Andre the Giant, Rowdy Roddy Piper, Ravishing Rick Rude, and Sergeant Slaughter became heroes to millions of kids, though the limelight in the Eighties was stolen by Hulk Hogan, aka "the Hulkster"—born Terry Gene Bollea. The 6-foot-8-inch, 300-pound Hogan, with flowing blond locks and 24-inch biceps, set the standard for the decade's super-star wrestler.

No one expected Hogan to engage his opponents in legitimate Greco-Roman-style grappling of the sort seen in the Olympics. Rather, what was presented in Vince McMahon's World Wrestling Federation extravaganzas was choreographed roughhousing, staged for drama as much as for laughs, for athleticism as much as for stuntman special effects. As if to prove pro wrestling was really entertainment, in 1984 pop star Cyndi Lauper entered the sport as the "manager" of Captain Lou Albano, while Albano made reciprocal appearances in Lauper's MTV videos.

Celebrities from diverse occupations soon entered the ring in one guise or another. Boxer Muhammad Ali debuted as a guest referee; baseball manager Billy Martin as a guest timekeeper. Feminist Gloria Steinem and politician Geraldine Ferraro attended matches, and Andy Warhol visited Madison Square Garden and pronounced the sport "hip, exciting. It's America." Sometimes the wrestlers got caught up in the image they promoted. Hulk Hogan, as a guest on comedian Richard Belzer's cable TV show "Hot Properties," demonstrated a front-chin lock on Belzer, rendering him limp, unconscious, and bloody; the comedian's head required eight stitches. John Stossel, reporter for ABC's "20/20," was similarly roughed up when he egged the sport's colossal Dr. D. (David Schultz) with the taunt that pro wrestling's moves were faked.

In 1985 four wrestling programs, all produced by the World Wrestling Federation, were among the top ten shows on cable TV. Among the major networks, NBC joined the fray with its "Saturday Night's Main Event." Merchandisers rushed out Hulk Hogan video cassettes, action dolls, T-shirts, and sweatbands. And at Madison Square Garden a ringside seat for a bout of behemoths sold for as much as $200.

While WrestleMania started in America, by late in the decade its staged spectacles were being enjoyed via satellite in twenty-six foreign countries. Whereas promoters of the sport viewed it as harmless exportation of home-grown entertainment, many social commentators argued that it contributed to the image abroad of America as the most violent country on the planet, an image backed up late in the decade by statistics on the high rate of domestic violence and street bloodshed.

Channeling, Harmonic Convergence, and Crystal Power

Whereas the decade of the Seventies had est and the human potential movement, the Eighties turned to the occult for its own form of spiritual awakening. Channeling, as practiced by West Coast psychic J. Z. Knight—a woman who claimed to be the reincarnation of "Ramtha," a thirty-five-thousand-year-old male sage—was a form of nineteenth-century mediumship given modern-day media exposure. Knight garnered a large following, including actress Shirley MacLaine, who in turn became a channeler in her own mind, writing several bestselling books on her mediumship and "past lives."

Harmonic convergence was a repackaging of the century-old notion of a collective conscious. Specifically: If a critical mass of humanity held hands at a prearranged time, their "positive energy" would converge, setting up harmonic vibrations that would have humane reverberations into the future.

The belief that crystals possessed special healing powers was nothing more than a repackaging of the Seventies decade's fascination with "pyramid power"—the notion that the geometric center of a pyramid radiated an energy that could preserve perishable fruit, prolong human life (presuming one slept in the pyramid), and sharpen razor blades.

The umbrella rubric for all of these ideas was the **new age movement.** Many experts viewed new age as a "maturing" of the Sixties hippie movement and a marketing of that decade's flower power to Eighties yuppies. The counterculture had grown up and joined the work force. Others claimed it was a faddish extension of consciousness-raising programs such as est, Forum, Silva Mind Control, LifeSpring, and Actualization. The ancient Ramtha, channeled through the well-dressed J. Z. Knight, offered his own surmise for the New Age craze: "People realize their religions don't work anymore. They are pulling away from fear-oriented religions and beginning to discover their own divine self."

Origin.   New agers listened to "new age music" and read "new age books." But in truth there was nothing really new about new age. "The only things really distinguishing modern channeling from this earlier form of trance mediumship," writes new age chronicler Jay Kinney in an essay "Deja Vu: The Hidden History of the New Age," "are the sophistication in marketing techniques that mediums such as J. Z. Knight have brought to the field, and the ability of all the '80s spirit guides to speak the lingo of the moment."

Even the phrase new age predates its usage by Eighties practitioners, first appearing in 1914 as the title of a monthly journal, *The New Age Magazine.* A popular metaphysical quarterly in the 1940s was the *New Age Interpreter.*

If there has been a single new age belief throughout the movement it is that humankind is poised on the verge of a breakthrough in understanding, a "leap of consciousness" that will expose the "force" in the universe that leads to personal happiness and worldwide peace and unity—not unlike the "force" in George Lucas's *Star Wars* films. Those who study the latest manifestation of the new age awareness claim that the Eighties version influenced Madison Avenue advertising: from MasterCard's slogan, "Master the possibilities," to the army's recruiting come-on, "Be all that you can be." As the end of the second millenium A.D. draws closer, with the year 2000 packed with numerical portent, it is thought that the new age movement will return in yet another incarnation, spawning a fresh round of books, music, seminars and promises that the "force" will be with us sooner than ever.

Top Toy Fads

At the close of the decade, *Toy & Hobby World* published a list of the twenty top-selling toys in a year when the retail sales of toys in the United States reached a staggering $13.4 billion. A glance at the ratings reveals that one video game manufacturer, **Nintendo**—played in 20 percent of American homes— dominated all other toy fads: **Nintendo Entertainment System** (number one), followed by the company's game **Super Mario Brothers 3** (number two), its **Game Boy** hand-held system, (number four), its **Tetris** game (number six), its **Super Mario Brothers 2** game (number nine), and its **Final Fantasy** game (number twelve). A business publication reported that for the latter part of the decade Nintendo "stymied the growth of the traditional toy industry."

Nintendo videos entered the market in 1985. They offered superior graphics in a highly sophisticated computer about the size of the family Bible that rested next to the television set. The games of fantasy, sports, and combat were intricately designed by the Japanese computer company, and kids found them addictive. So, too, did many adults, especially men. The unassuming mustachioed Mario was the star character, followed by his brother Luigi— creations of Japanese software engineer Shigeru Miyamoto. Legend has it that Mario received his name from the landlord of the building that housed Nintendo's American staff. By 1989, Super Brothers Mario and Luigi were so popular they had their own Saturday morning cartoon. A cereal was named after them, and their images were emblazoned on lunchboxes, underwear, bed linens, and the licensing like. Nintendo had singlehandedly revived the home video game market—which began in 1981 with the munching menace known as **Pac-Man,** itself based on a Japanese folk hero known for his voracious appetite. Just when Nintendo madness seemed to have peaked, poised for the inevitable sales dive, the company introduced a new action-packed product: Game Boy, a hand-held version of the home video.

The mania for video games in general, and Nintendo games in particular, prompted voluminous criticism. In an article titled "Pathological Preoccupation With Video Games," appearing in a 1990 issue of the *Journal of the American Academy of Child and Adolescent Psychiatry,* the author claims that many games "deliberately promote habituation," and induce in children an altered state of consciousness akin to a hypnotic trance. Other critics argue that that is precisely the state many busy parents want their children in—mesmerized, inactive, and out of mischief for hours at a time. Is it good for kids? We will have to wait for the answer until the Nintendo generation enters adulthood.

Here's how other hit toys rated in nationwide sales:

Barbie, by Mattel, number three. First introduced at the New York Toy Fair in 1959 (see page 263), the shapely fashion model was still selling briskly at the toy age of thirty. At the close of the Eighties, Barbie accounted for more than half of the company's growth in sales. Reflecting the ethnic mix of the American population, there were **Hispanic Barbies, black Barbies,** and **Asian Barbies**—though, it's worth noting, the only doll featured in print and TV advertisements was the fair-skinned, blue-eyed original. In the Nineties, however, Barbie ads will go ethnic as Mattel attempts to capitalize on the country's ethnic spending power.

WrestleMania, which we examined earlier, influenced toy sales in the decade, with Hasbro's **World Wrestling Federation figures** ranking as the sixteenth top toy of the decade. The company's **New Kids on the Block,** based on the pop singing group, was number eighteen. Though the decade witnessed manias over **Strawberry Shortcake** in 1980, **Trivial Pursuit** in 1984, and **Teddy Ruxpin** in 1985, it was a top-seller of 1983 that caused riots in department stores and merited a Christmas season cover of *Newsweek:*

Cabbage Patch Kids

The dough-faced, chinless dolls—in high demand and short supply—were termed the "Holy Grail" of the 1983 Christmas shopping season. At a store in Wilkes-Barre, Pennsylvania, one shopper suffered a broken leg when she was caught in the hysteria of a thousand charging parents who'd waited eight hours to get at grab at the homely dolls. At another store an advancing mob of buyers was held at bay by a baseball bat–wielding department manager. A shipload of Cabbage Patch Kids was delivered to a toy store in Middletown, Connecticut, in an armored car. Fearing a riot, the manager of a Woolworth store in Lawrence, Kansas, placed his last seven dolls in a bank vault and held a lottery for the privilege of buying them.

The press was filled with reports of parents caught up in Cabbage Patch madness. A Kansas City postman, despairing of finding a doll in the Western Hemisphere, flew to London to get one for his five-year-old daughter. But the most illustrative incident of the magnitude of the mania involved a Milwaukee radio station that facetiously broadcast that two thousand dolls would be tossed out of a B-29 circling over County Stadium. The announcer said, as part of the lark, that it would be an airborne delivery and that customers should bring catcher's mitts and credit cards to be photographed from the air. Astonishingly, more than two dozen gullible adults showed up in frigid December weather, gazing skyward, searching for the great Cabbage Patch drop.

Birth and Adoption.   The soft dolls with pudgy cheeks, close-set eyes, and short, stunted arms and legs—which were not purchased but "adopted"—were based on the 1977 designs of Georgia sculptor Xavier Roberts, who took his inspiration from the work of Appalachian folk artists. Though the dolls were adorable in a facially unfinished way, their primary appeal rested on Roberts's marketing gimmicks.

As a child he'd been told that babies are found in cabbage patches, a variation on the stork fairy tale. Roberts dubbed his Georgia art gallery Baby-land General Hospital, dressed his sales clerks as doctors and nurses, placed his dolls in incubators and bassinets, and sold each doll by putting it "up for adoption," and making the transaction official with a birth certificate and adoption papers. A child had to swear to an "oath of adoption" for the doll, as well as to a list of promises to take care of the infant. The brilliant ploy, in the mass-marketing hands of Coleco Industries, brought in more than $60 million in sales in the year the dolls debuted. Each "one-of-a-kind" doll was actually manufactured in Hong Kong, with a minutely differentiated feature determined by a computer program.

The buying blitz was fanned by several celebrities. Dr. Joyce Brothers endorsed the dolls as "healthy playthings" for children, and then-pregnant host of the "Today" show Jane Pauley played with the dolls, giving them five minutes of precious airtime and priceless publicity. In addition, several real hospitals set aside days on which children could bring in their dolls for "vaccinations."

Though Cabbage Patch Kids did not achieve the classic status and accompanying sales longevity of Barbie, teddy bears, or Raggedy Ann, the dumpy, dimpled dolls were a fad of major proportions. Sales peaked in 1985 at $600 million, after which the dolls were eclipsed by other hot toys. They also generated a host of imitations: **Pumpkin Kids, Blossom Babies, Cauliflower Babies,** and **Garbage Pail Kids.**

Teenage Mutant Ninja Turtles

For a generation of children, Michelangelo, Raphael, Leonardo, and Donatello are not the names of Renaissance greats but of wisecracking, pizza-throwing, sewer-surfing superhero reptiles, masters of the martial arts. "Let's haul shell out of here," they bellow.

In an animated cartoon series, the heroes in a half shell conquered Saturday morning prime-time kiddie TV audiences. They were also responsible for one of the top-grossing movies of 1990 and generated hundreds of millions of dollars in toy merchandising. The hip, rap-music-singing dudes, originally created for comic books by Kevin Eastman and Peter Laird, became the licensing success story of 1989. The revered phrase heard throughout the toy industry was "Turtle power." In 1990, the tough-shelled quartet held three of the top ten videos for children and appeared in some three hundred Turtle merchandising spin-offs, ranging from breakfast cereals to skateboards.

The unlikely heroes debuted as static, black and white comic book figures

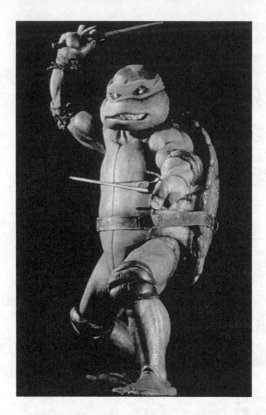

Teenage Mutant Ninja Turtles.

in 1983. At the time, twenty-nine-year-old Laird was barely earning enough money to pay his rent by illustrating vegetables for the garden section of an East Coast newspaper; twenty-year-old Eastman was a cartoonist working as a short-order cook. During a brainstorming session one night in 1983 the two friends, desperately seeking commercial success, dreamed up the idea of a slowpoke turtle transformed by a ninja mask into a swift martial arts "dude" wielding a katana blade. The incongruity amused Laird and Eastman, and by evening's end they had sketched four creatures and, borrowing from two hot trends in comic books—ninjas and mutants—christened their creations Teenage Mutant Ninja Turtles.

Cowabunga!   Gradually, Laird and Eastman developed their storyline. As any ten-year-old can explain: the four "ordinary" turtles were accidentally dropped down a sewer manhole, falling into a radioactive goo, which caused them to grow to human size and acquire the power to speak, and hiply so. The mutations, adopted by a mutant sewer rat, Splinter, master of ninja-fighting techniques, are named by Splinter after his favorite Renaissance artists: Leonardo is the group's leader, Raphael the rebel, Michelangelo the jokester, and Donatello the technical whiz.

Turtlemania struck the nation only after a New York licensing agent, Mark

Freedman, realized the creatures would make great toys and an even better TV cartoon series. Suddenly Laird and Eastman found themselves multimillionaires. By the close of the decade Teenage Mutant Ninja Turtles by Playmate was the country's number five top-selling toy, topped only by Barbie and three Nintendo products. Only time will tell if the fad wanes into nostalgic memory, or if the wacky "bodacious" dudes—whose violence was uniformly criticized throughout the media—enter the licensing hall of fame in the company of Mickey Mouse, Woody Woodpecker, and the Pink Panther. Is Turtle Power here to stay, or merely the power of the hour?

DANCE CRAZES

Smurf and Bird

Early in the decade two new dances appeared on "American Bandstand," styles that did not exactly sweep the nation. The Smurf, not surprisingly, appeared at the height of the Smurf figurine craze. It was a sidestepping dance, in which you tilted your head toward one shoulder, then, swinging your arms up and down, you sidestepped with your heels together—the way Dorothy clicked her heels in *The Wizard of Oz.* Your head then tilted toward the other shoulder and you repeated the movements in the opposite direction.

The other dance, the Bird, originated with the movie *Purple Rain.* It, too, was a sidestepping dance, though one of more exaggerated movements, involving the hips, with the arms flapping like a bird's wings. "It's a really fun dance to do," says Dick Clark in *Rock, Roll, and Remember,* "especially to the song 'The Bird.' " Viewing dance in the first few years of the Eighties, Clark argued then, "The dances we can say, with reasonable accuracy, that have been created this decade, include the Smurf and the Bird."

Rap and Slam Dancing

The Smurf and the Bird were dances quite distinct and tepid from those enjoyed at the end of the decade—like vogueing (see p. 450), and rap singer M. C. Hammer's fluid, rapid-fire rap dancing. In the latter, a seemingly boneless body in diaphanous pants, employing a feint of footwork, glides, spins, and undulates across the dance floor. It is a style of movement as punctuated and poetic as the rapper's flow of lyrics. A violent style of dance appeared earlier in the decade: slam dancing, in which young men (usually only men did the dance) slammed their bodies into each other to the further assault of loud music. Slam dancers were on the punk fringe, and usually bumped and bruised each other while wearing combat boots, T-shirt, and fatigue pants. The phenomenon was mercifully short-lived and confined to larger metropolitan cities like New York and Los Angeles.

But the first really hot dance craze of the Eighties was the exuberantly athletic and acrobatic style known as . . .

Break Dancing

"Breaking" was a grass-roots style of dance that originated in the Bronx and Brooklyn among black males. It served as a means of expressing their individuality and fearlessness through ingenious daredevil routines that few "outsiders" could copy without incurring serious injury. Spinning on one's back while lying on the ground, then spinning up onto the shoulders and perhaps up again onto the top of the head was a favorite "break"—and "breaks" originally were done during instrumental passages in a song when the beat is stripped to its barest and most driving essence. A 1983 issue of *In Performance,* a monthly guide to the Brooklyn Academy of Music, described break dancers as "twirling around the axes of their upper bodies like human coffee-grinders, using fast pedaling footwork, twisting belly-up, belly-down, finishing with elaborate leg pretzels."

Though American breaking originated with so-called B-Boys in the South Bronx, its roots, writes Curtis Marlow in *Break Dancing,* go back to "three neighboring countries in West Africa: Mali, Gambia and Senegal." The African cultures practiced a highly vigorous form of acrobatic social dancing—right down to the concluding stance in a break dance: the nonchalant "freeze"; that is, an abrupt stop as if the dancer were trapped in a film's freeze-frame.

How did this form of African social dancing find its way to New York's South Bronx?

The transformation took about sixteen years. Starting in the late 1960s, Marlow argues, many professional West African dancers—members of such companies as the Senegalese Ballet—came to America and settled in the Bronx, offering master dance classes to professional American dancers. In a reciprocal program, many black American dance companies then visited West Africa, offering their own master classes, and incorporating local dance styles into their own repertory. Upon returning home, "The knowledge that these dance companies gained," says Marlow, "was used in performances at public schools and community centers . . . these groups saturated the South Bronx with African dance, and sitting in the audience were the breakers of today, soaking it all up."

Once out on the streets, the B-Boys did their own improvisation, mixing African dance and rap rhythms with the elements of competition and one-upmanship from their own everyday experiences.

The word break was also used by inner-city kids to mean an outburst of anger. An example Marlow gives: "The bank would not cash her check, so she just started breaking on them"—translation: "She got loud and caused a scene."

Electric Boogie

Though often confused with break dancing, the electric boogie was a distinctly different style that emerged in the late Seventies. It consisted of mimelike movements such as hand waves, robotlike "popping" (stiff start-and-stop jerks), and gravity-defying "moonwalks," this last popularized by Michael Jackson. The roots of the electric boogie, claims Curtis Marlow, are to be found in the comic mime routines of Shields and Yarnell.

In the late Seventies, Robert Shields, who had studied with Marcel Marceau, and Lorene Yarnell were featured on a six-week summer replacement program on CBS TV. They introduced audiences to a robotic couple named the Clinkers, who moved by "popping." "Young black kids were all talking about the robot characters," says Marlow. "They started to imitate . . . in a matter of weeks becoming proficient in an area [mime] that professionals study for years." As the team of Shields and Yarnell used mime to tell stories, urban black youngsters began to tell their own stories on the streets of the Bronx and Brooklyn in a miming dance that evolved into the electric boogie. It was, as is all dance, a means of communication.

Lambada

Borrowing from the tango and merengue, the lambada was a Brazilian bump-and-grind that dates back to the Twenties. The word lambada is from the Portuguese verb "to whip." The dance became a brief nationwide craze after two French record producers, Jean Karakos and Oliver Lorsac, saw it performed in Brazil in 1988 and decided the steps were sufficiently passionate and sensual to market as "an alternative to sex in the age of AIDS." The savvy producers assembled a group, Kaoma, and flooded the country with the pulsing single "Lambada" and abundant lambada videos. Meanwhile, two Bolivian brothers, who claimed to have written the song's melody, sued the French producers.

Not for the bashful, the hip-grinding, pelvic-touching "dirty" dance was featured on the "Arsenio Hall Show," touted as the latest trend on "Hard Copy," and given an elaborate presentation at New York's Palladium disco. On tour, the Kaoma band played to packed houses from Miami to San Francisco. From the waist up, two lambada dancers resemble a couple doing the tango or fox trot—the man with his right arm around the woman's waist, her right hand in his left, held out to the side. The woman rests her left hand on his shoulder. The intimate aspect of the dance comes from the infamous "thigh straddle," in which the man's crotch tightly grips the woman's thigh, assuring that the partners remain locked together at the groin while they gyrate. The basic movement is up and down with the hips. "It's a bit embarrassing to do with someone you don't know," said one dance instructor at the craze's peak popularity. "You have to be open-minded." It's known that the dance was once banned in Brazil, and it's thought that the label lambada (from "to whip") referred to the fact that dancers were punished for their lascivious behavior. The craze inspired two forgettable films of 1990, *Lambada* and *The Forbidden Dance*.

Vogueing

Vogueing—an attitude as much as a dance, all about striking a pose—was popularized by Madonna and her "vogue" video. It is a lithe, languid style of dance, incorporating the struts and stances of high-fashion models of the haughtiest sort. Contrary to popular opinion, it did not originate with Madonna. Nor, as is sometimes stated, was it the concoction of promoter Malcolm McLaren, who featured the trend on his 1989 LP, "Waltz Darling."

Vogueing began underground, among flamboyant gay black and Latino men at urban dance clubs, particularly ones in Harlem. As director Jennie Livingston makes clear in her 1991 film about vogueing, *Paris Is Burning,* the dance of "Saks Fifth Avenue mannequins" moved from Harlem downtown to New York's Washington Square Park, where it was publicly performed al fresco and copied. Though not by everyone.

The original voguers, the grandest of drag queens in elaborately sequined gowns, belonged to cliques called "houses," named after couture houses like Dior and St. Laurent. Whereas the heterosexual ghetto male had his rough-house gang, at society's other extreme, the fey homosexual counterpart had "her house."

The black and Latino males imitated, in life and dance, the jet set's beautiful crowd and stylish magazine models. "These were people excluded from the mainstream in every way," Livingston says. "Yet their whole subculture was based on imitating the very people who were excluding them." For her chronicling of that particular gay subculture, with its grand balls, gaudy gowns, and couture houses, *Us* magazine christened Livingston "the voguer's Margaret Mead."

POPULAR SONGS

Music Video Madness

The popular music scene, traditionally an aural arena, underwent a profound change in the early Eighties with the arrival of the music video—debuting as a television staple in August 1981 on cable's MTV. The four-minute, audio-visual format—a marriage of pop music and quick-edit film techniques targeted at the teenaged market—was variously heralded and lambasted as (1) nothing more than a commercial advertisement for a new record, (2) nothing less than a vanguard form of video art, and (3) a new genre of TV cartoon for teens.

It turned out to be all three—and more. Music videos boosted the sales of records, mesmerized teens around the clock the way Saturday morning loony tunes transfixed tots, and attracted serious artists like John Mayberry, whose simplicity of style in Sinead O'Connor's clip "Nothing compares 2 U" (in which the Irish singer appeared as a close-cropped talking head) earned the video three MTV awards in 1990.

The way feature films created movie stars, music videos produced a new breed of pop personality, whose "look" was as important, if not more so, as voice. "Not until the creation of MTV did a Hollywood sensibility enter the world of music," observed one music writer. "Glamour and beefcake—male and female—began to shape the music industry the way they had traditionally influenced movies." Whether it's Jon Bon Jovi, M. C. Hammer, Vanilla Ice, or Michael Jackson, "men in pop get the same treatment that used to be reserved for women—tight clothes, obsessional camera angles, fetishization."

In this section, as we progress chronologically through the hits of the Eighties, we'll see the increasingly powerful role moving images played on popular music. It's been said that not since the invention of the record has music undergone a more profound change than with the birth of rock video and round-the-clock MTV.

Please Don't Go: 1980

The decade's first number one single (the week of January 5, 1980) was "Please Don't Go," a departure for K.C. & the Sunshine Band, which had been known in the late Seventies for their disco music. The group was quickly displaced from the top slot by Michael Jackson's **Rock With You,** which in turn succumbed to the Captain and Tennille's **Do That to Me One More Time,** written by Toni Tennille, who would soon be repackaged by TV executives as a "new Dinah Shore" and given her own talk show.

Come spring, Blondie topped the charts with **Call Me,** the title song for the film *American Gigolo,* written by Deborah Harry herself. The Paul Schrader movie was about a lady and a stud, and Harry's co-writer, Giorgio Moroder, originally wanted the song's title to reflect the "mechanical" aspect of a gigolo's lovemaking, suggesting it be called "Machine Man." While "Call Me" was still selling briskly, Kenny Rogers (with Kim Carnes) had a hit with **Don't Fall in Love With a Dreamer,** Paul McCartney with **Coming Up,** and Billy Joel with **It's Still Rock and Roll to Me.**

During the summer of 1980, movies provided some of the biggest hit songs. There was Bette Midler's single, **The Rose,** and Olivia Newton-John's **Magic**—this last from the critically panned film *Xanadu.* Though the movie was a complete box-office failure, its soundtrack went platinum and produced five top twenty singles: in addition to "Magic," the title song, **Xanadu;** the romantic duet **Suddenly** (with Newton-John and Cliff Richard); **I'm Alive** by the Electric Light Orchestra; and **All Over the World,** by the same group. On average, the *Xanadu* experience proved positive for Olivia Newton-John: though embarrassed by the film, Olivia scored two music successes and found a husband in actor Matt Lattanzi.

Teenagers returned to school in September dancing to Irene Cara's hit **Fame,** as well as to Diana Ross's biggest single of her solo career, **Upside Down,** four weeks at number one.

A form of emotionless singing was popularized briefly by Devo, a bizarre robotic quintet from Akron, Ohio, who had a hit with **Whip It.** The spastic-shuffling performers derived their name from the word de-evolution—which they believed was the downslide direction humankind was headed in. They, however, quickly de-evolved right off the pop music scene.

Among familiar names to top the charts in the last quarter of the year: Barbra Streisand with **Women in Love,** Kenny Rogers with **Lady,** and Neil Diamond with **Love on the Rocks.**

(Just Like) Starting Over: 1980

The year 1980 ended tragically with the murder of John Lennon. After a long hiatus from recording, Lennon, with wife Yoko Ono, released the LP **Double Fantasy** on November 17. One prophetically titled single, "(Just Like) Starting Over," slowly climbed the charts, reaching number six in the first week of December. On the evening of December 8, Lennon and Ono worked late in a Manhattan sound studio, putting finishing touches on a song, "Walking on Thin Ice," for their next album, tentatively titled "Milk and Honey." Around ten-fifty P.M. they were returning home to their Upper West Side apartment in the Dakota when a voice called out, "Mr. Lennon!" John Lennon turned around and was shot five times; he was rushed to Roosevelt Hospital where he died from internal injuries. With grim irony, "(Just Like) Starting Over" climbed the charts to number one at Christmastime, a posthumous success for one of rock music's greats.

Nine to Five: 1981

The new year opened with Blondie holding the number one song, **The Tide Is High;** the first single to displace John Lennon's "Starting Over," five weeks at the top of the charts. Climbing fast was Rod Stewart's **Passion** and Dolly Parton's "Nine to Five," which reached the top in late February. This last was a breakthrough for Dolly Parton; she wrote the song and sang it, and it was the title number for her first venture into film acting. As the dipsy Doralee, secretary to a male chauvinist boss (Dabney Coleman), Parton demonstrated she could compete with her co-stars Jane Fonda and Lily Tomlin; if anything, she was the most realistic of the three office workers in the women's lib comedy. *Newsweek* called the singer "a sweet and easy comic presence, a natural actress." The country and western singer had "crossed over," and she picked up an Oscar nomination for best song. A year later *Nine to Five* debuted as an ABC sitcom, with Dolly Parton's sister, Rachel Dennison, playing one of the leads.

John Lennon had a second posthumous hit with **Woman,** number two in late March, just behind Blondie's **Rapture,** which pop music chronicler Fred Bronson calls "the first rap song many Americans had ever heard." For live performances of the hit, Blondie admitted that she ad-libbed lyrics during the single's rap segment. Though rap was already a sensation on the streets of the South Bronx, years would pass before it exploded into a mainstream phenomenon.

As summer approached, the top songs were **Kiss on My List** by Hall and Oates, **Morning Train** by Scottish-born Sheena Easton, and **Bette Davis**

Eyes by Kim Carnes. Songwriter Donna Weiss said that Davis's film *Jezebel* was perhaps the immediate inspiration for the offbeat single, but she felt that all of the actress's riveting glances onscreen contributed to her penning of the lyrics. The song was a hit in twenty-one countries, won two Grammys, and prompted the real Bette Davis to send a letter to Kim Carnes, thanking her for making her name known to a whole generation of young people.

Endless Love: 1981

Director Franco Zeffirelli was about to bring the bestselling novel *Endless Love* to the screen, starring Brooke Shields. He wanted a lush, romantic theme song, reminiscent of the title number from *Love Story,* but he also wanted the song to capture the story's obsessive love affair between two teenagers. Lionel Richie played an instrumental he'd previously written (but not recorded) for Zeffirelli, but the director felt that lyrics were essential to sum up the film's theme. Richie composed words, and persuaded Diana Ross to spare two hours from her busy schedule to record the song with him. When she arrived in the studio, Ross had not yet seen the lyrics; within two hours the singers had a "take." "Endless Love" became the most successful Motown single of all time, holding the number one spot for nine consecutive weeks in the summer of 1981.

That year ended with Olivia Newton-John back at the top of the charts with a song that would quickly become an anthem for ladies who worked out. **Physical** displayed a sexy, athletic side of the singer, and the single became the springboard for her TV special "Let's Get Physical." It remained the country's number one song for ten straight weeks (tying Debby Boone's "You Light Up My Life"). Many who listened to the song took the word physical to connote aerobics; for others it meant activities of a more sexual nature.

Chariots of Fire: 1982

As 1982 opened, cable's MTV was four months old, and Hall and Oates had the country's number one single, **I Can't Go for That (No Can Do).** In March Stevie Wonder scored a hit with **That Girl,** and in May he teamed up with Paul McCartney for **Ebony and Ivory**—which topped Rick Springfield's **Don't Talk to Strangers.**

But the unexpected hit of the season was an instrumental movie theme by Greek keyboard artist Evangelos Papathanassiou, who shortened his first name, which means "angel of good tidings," to Vangelis. Based in London, Vangelis had already acquired a respectable reputation for his electrically synthesized music when he was approached by British film maker David Puttnam to score *Chariots of Fire,* the emotional tale of two runners preparing for the 1924 Paris Olympics. Though the tune took a torturously long twenty-one weeks to climb to number one, once there it became a theme for myriad athletic events, much as had the title song from *Rocky* in the previous decade. *Chariots* won an Oscar for best picture, and Vangelis won one for best original score.

At year's end, several familiar names topped the charts; Lionel Richie with

Truly, Olivia Newton-John with **Heart Attack,** Hall and Oates with **Man-eater,** and Paul McCartney and Michael Jackson with **The Girl Is Mine.** As 1982 ended Jackson was at the top, and about to soar into a stratum of super-stardom all his own with . . .

Billie Jean; Beat It; Thriller Album: 1983

There were, of course, other superlative hits in 1983: Irene Cara's **Flash-dance . . . What a Feeling,** the Police's **Every Breath You Take,** the Eurythmics' **Sweet Dreams (Are Made of This),** Billy Joel's **Tell Her About It,** Bonnie Tyler's **Total Eclipse of the Heart,** Lionel Richie's **All Night Long,** Donna Summer's **She Works Hard for the Money,** and the Paul McCartney/Michael Jackson duet **Say, Say, Say.** But no matter how you look at it the year belonged to no singer more than it did to Michael Jackson—featured on the cover of *Time* as pop music's event of the decade. "He's taken us right up there where we belong," producer Quincy Jones told the magazine. "Black music had to play second fiddle for a long time . . . Michael has connected with every soul in the world."

For a time it seemed that every soul in the world was buying Jackson's "Thriller" album—the bestselling LP of all time, spending a record thirty-seven weeks as number one on *Billboard*'s album chart. The young entertainer, born into a singing family, had arrived. His hits would dominate the middle years of the decade. And he would begin the next decade by signing a billion-dollar recording deal with Sony, the largest contract ever for a singer.

The duet "The Girl Is Mine" with Paul McCartney was from "Thriller." But the album began to skyrocket in sales after another single, "Billie Jean"—which the singer recorded in one take—reached the top of the charts in early March—a spot it would hold for seven weeks. No sooner had "Billie Jean" begun to slip when Jackson was back on top with "Beat It"—a feat few other artists have matched. The pulsing song, with a searing guitar solo by Eddie Van Halen, was boosted in sales by a dynamic music video, costing $160,000.

Jackson's "Thriller" album sold more than 40 million copies worldwide; his 1987 follow-up LP, **Bad,** would sell some 25 million copies. Moreover, Michael Jackson, who had his first hit at age five, set high standards for dance and movement on music videos, having mastered the visual medium better than any artist before him. Before the pop icon's lucrative 1991 deal with Sony corporation, his worth was estimated at more that $100 million, including substantial real estate holdings and ownership of the John Lennon–Paul McCartney music publishing catalogue. (Ironically, Jackson's Sony deal was concluded one week after his twenty-four-year-old sister Janet signed a $40 million contract with Virgin Records.)

As mentioned, Jackson was again number one with "Say, Say, Say" as 1983 ended. The singer, known for his passionate love of animals, closed the year with a tally of seven top ten singles—an accomplishment second only to the

Beatles' eleven hits in 1964. It seemed fitting that Michael Jackson should celebrate his final hit of the year with ex-Beatle Paul McCartney.

Hanging on firmly behind "Say, Say, Say" was Billy Joel's **Uptown Girl,** an ode to his shapely, top-model wife, Christie Brinkley.

The novelty hit of 1983, **Puttin' on the Ritz** (number four in September), belonged to Taco Ockerser, born in Indonesia to Dutch parents.

Karma Chameleon: 1984

The four singers who made up Culture Club came from different "cultures," hence their name: Jon Moss was Jewish; Mikey Craig, Jamaican; Roy Hay, British; and George O'Dowd—lead singer, and better known as Boy George— was Irish. It was Boy George, with his plucked eyebrows, facial makeup, and fey sway who garnered all the media attention. So much so that it seemed as if George Alan O'Dowd, born in London in 1961, *was* Culture Club.

The group had enjoyed two hits in 1983: **Do You Really Want to Hurt Me** (number four in March) and **Time** (number four in May). "Karma Chameleon," a song whose title and lyrics mystified many a fan, was the group's first number one single in America, three weeks at the top of the charts in February 1984. It topped Yes's **Owner of a Lonely Heart,** then succumbed to Van Halen's **Jump.**

Boy George.

In the spring, Cyndi Lauper, a funky new wave singer who became part of WrestleMania by managing one of its superstars, Captain Lou Albano (see page 441), enjoyed a hit with **Girls Just Want to Have Fun.** As if to counterbalance that feminist song title, Deniece Williams sang her way to success with **Let's Hear It for the Boys.** She was soon displaced from number one by Cyndi Lauper's **Time After Time**—this last dispelling the industry gossip that Lauper, termed by *Newsweek* as a "new-wave Gracie Allen," was destined to be nothing more than a one-hit wonder. "Time After" was soon topped by Duran Duran's **The Reflex,** which in turn gave up the number one slot to Prince's **When Doves Cry,** a single from his smash album "Purple Rain"— also the title of Prince Rogers Nelson's semi-autobiographical 1984 film. "Doves" yielded up its first place to Ray Parker's **Ghostbusters,** from the Bill Murray/Dan Aykroyd film of that title.

In the last quarter of 1984, Prince (and the Revolution) was back on top with **Let's Go Crazy,** and Cyndi Lauper had her third hit with **She Bop.** Also, two veteran singers appeared on the charts: the ever-youthful Tina Turner with **What's Love Got to Do With It,** and Stevie Wonder with **I Just Called to Say I Love You.** Bruce Springsteen, following his **Hungry Heart** hit (climbing to number five for a time in 1980), enjoyed a smash album success with **Born in the U.S.A.**

But the singing and video sensation who held the country's top song in the final week of 1984 was the decade's female counterpart to Michael Jackson, Madonna, with her hit . . .

Like a Virgin: 1984

Born Madonna Louise Veronica Ciccone on August 16, 1959, the singer had had a hit in 1983: **Lucky Star.** But her breakthrough to big time stardom was "Like a Virgin," number one for six straight weeks. And shortly after it started to slide, her **Material Girl** ascended the charts. Garnering rave reviews for her role in the film *Desperately Seeking Susan,* she established herself as a multimedia phenomenon.

As the decade progressed, Madonna's star shone brighter and brighter, flashing supernova with her worldwide Blonde Ambition tour. The week that the two-and-a-half-hour elaborately choreographed extravaganza—a trademark blend of sassy simulated sex and spiritual symbolism—hit New York, the star appeared as Breathless Mahoney in the blockbuster film *Dick Tracy.* And when in 1990 MTV banned her video for **Justify My Love,** the Material Girl—she brought back conical bustiers and championed self-crotch grabbing for females—made headlines throughout the civilized world. The video—which featured a steamy, fun-loving orgy in a Paris hotel room, highlighting simulated sex, voyeurism, and self-fondling—merited exposure on ABC's "Nightline," in which the star seemed to define a First Amendment right to free expression of sexual fantasies. Record stores could not amply stock the video for the Christmas season.

The platinum-haired chanteuse turned dominatrix, whose personal motto was perhaps best summed up in the title of her video **Express Yourself,** underscored the importance of the music video better than anyone. Can one think of a Madonna song and not be flooded with its corresponding visual imagery? The aural is inseparable from the visual. Indeed, for Madonna it can be argued that much of her success derives not from discs, cassettes, or CDs, but from music videos.

The novelty hit of 1984, **Eat It,** belonged to Weird Al Yankovic (with Michael Jackson), who in his demented style parodied Jackson's "Beat It." The next year he spoofed Madonna's "Like a Virgin" with **Like a Surgeon.**

We Are the World: 1985

It was the year that teen idol George Michael appeared on the American music scene with his phenomenally successful first effort, **Careless Whisper,** number one for three weeks in February.

That same year music impresario Maurice Starr was rounding up from the streets of Boston five wholesome would-be singers to groom and package as the **New Kids on the Block,** a fad as much as a rock group. The subteen heartthrobs would soon be a pop music cottage industry, the focus of an "official" autobiography *(Our Story),* scrapbooks, comic books, coloring books, and fan clubs. By the end of the decade the New Kids had sold 17 million albums in the United States alone and had had five smash singles, of which three made it to number one. Two unofficial paperback biographies were simultaneously on the bestseller lists at positions number two and number three, and their 1988 album **Hangin' Tough** sold 11 million copies worldwide. The group was one of pop music's marketing miracles of the late Eighties; in just the final year of the decade New Kids merchandise pulled in an estimated $400 million.

While impresario Starr was slickly packaging the New Kids, the largest gathering of American singers ever was uniting, under the rubric U.S.A. for Africa, to fight hunger in Africa with a consciousness-raising and money-raising song. Earlier a union of British artists calling themselves Band Aid had raised money with their hit **Do They Know It's Christmas?** Using Band Aid as his model, Harry Belafonte contacted Lionel Richie and Michael Jackson, who then wrote "We Are the World"—virtually effortlessly as the two performers later acknowledged. Producer Quincy Jones decided that the best way to engage as many big-name singers as possible was to hold the recording session on the night of the American Music Awards, January 28, 1985. Some of the forty-five artists who took part: Ray Charles, Bob Dylan, Hall and Oates, Billy Joel, Cyndi Lauper, Huey Lewis, Bette Midler, Diana Ross, Paul Simon, Bruce Springsteen, Tina Turner, Dionne Warwick, and Stevie Wonder. "We Are the World" was number one for four weeks, raising millions of dollars for the starving populations of Africa.

For a period that spring it topped Phil Collins's **One More Night,** and two of Madonna's songs, **Crazy for You** and **Material Girl.** In late spring, George Michael (with Wham!) was back in first place with **Everything She Wants.** In a few months Michael would split with his Wham! partner, Andrew Ridgeley, to go solo, growing a voguish patina of facial stubble and repackaging himself to his adoring subteen admirers.

Other hits of 1985: Tears for Fears' **Everybody Wants to Rule the World,** Duran Duran's **A View to a Kill,** Whitney Houston's **You Give Good Love** and **Saving All My Love for You,** and Stevie Wonder's **Part-Time Lover.** As the year drew to a close, Starship had a number one single in **We Built This City,** and the popular year-old NBC-TV crime show "Miami Vice" provided a chart topper for keyboard artist Jan Hammer with original music he'd composed for the program: **Miami Vice Theme.** The album "Miami Vice" also produced the hit single **You Belong to the City.**

That's What Friends Are For: 1985

Whereas "We Are the World" was a joint effort to help the hungry of Africa, "That's What Friends Are For," by Dionne Warwick and Friends, was a number one hit with profits going to the American Foundation for AIDS Research. The song was actually written earlier in the decade by Burt Bacharach and Carole Bayer Sager for the 1982 film *Night Shift.* Later, when Bacharach played it for his long-time friend Dionne Warwick, she felt that as a duet it could take her to the top of the charts, and she suggested Stevie Wonder as her partner.

By coincidence, actress and AIDS-fundraiser Elizabeth Taylor was in the recording studio and heard the duet. It was a stroke of genius on the part of Carole Bayer Sager to suggest that the song be used to raise funds for AIDS research. Taylor loved the idea, and Warwick felt that the plural "friends" in the song's title required additional voices be included in the recording—thus, real-life friends Gladys Knight and Elton John became part of the ensemble. The single, four weeks at number one (topping Eddie Murphy's **Party All the Time**), came about by much happenstance and, as Warwick later said, probably by the emotion in the Bacharach/Sager song that seemed to suggest it should be more than a solo, more than a duet, and more than just another chart topper.

The single was displaced by Whitney Houston's **How Will I Know.** The singer soon had another hit with **Greatest Love of All,** number one in May 1985. Houston in turn vacated the top of the chart of Madonna's **Live to Tell;** then Madonna returned to the number one spot with her highly controversial **Papa Don't Preach.** Many people felt the song encouraged teen pregnancy; others believed it encouraged fruitful discussions between pregnant teens and their parents. The Pro-Life League adopted "Papa Don't Preach" as an anthem, whereas other groups argued that Madonna should make a public statement that unwed pregnant teens have the option of abortion.

Graceland: 1986

This was the year that Paul Simon began to revitalize his career by "going Zulu," as it's been said. In the process he would discover the appeal of the big band, but not that of an Ellingtonian orchestra of saxophones and brass, but of an African-style ensemble of percussions, guitars, keyboards, horns, and a chorus of Zulu singers.

It began with his "Graceland" album, which familiarized millions of Americans with the music of Mahlathini and the Mahotella Queens. The group—consisting of one man and three women (the Queens)—had been around since the late Sixties, their unique music combining traditional South African rhythms with American-style blues. They named their hybrid sound *mbaganga* (um-ba-KON-ga), supposedly after a tasty South African vegetable stew made from sundry ingredients, as was their music. Simon's "Graceland" LP brought international attention to mbaganga, and paved the way for Mahlathini and the Mahotella Queens to score with their own top-selling records later in the decade. Employing intricate Brazilian rhythms and complex, inward-looking lyrics, Simon would score a smash success in 1990 with **The Rhythm of the Saints.**

I Wanna Dance With Somebody (Who Loves Me): 1987

The year 1987 began with Madonna and Cyndi Lauper having chart toppers with "heart" songs: **Open Your Heart** and **Change of Heart,** respectively. The titles of Samantha Fox's and Georgia Satellites' smash hits couldn't have sent more opposite signals: **Touch Me (I Want Your Body)** and **Keep Your Hands to Yourself,** respectively. Bon Jovi had a number one single in **Livin' on a Prayer,** and it was a great year for the group U2 (named after the kind of spy plane in which Francis Gary Powers was shot down over the Soviet Union, causing an international incident). U2 had two number one hits: **With or Without You** (in May) and **I Still Haven't Found What I'm Looking For** (in August).

One of the hottest dance songs for the summer of 1987 was Whitney Houston's "I Wanna Dance With Somebody." Written by the team of George Merill and Shannon Rubicam, who had already given the singer three number one hits (including "How Will I Know"), the lyrics were not about wanting to dance at a disco, but wishing to "dance through life" with a special lover. Weeks later the singer had her album "Whitney" enter the charts at number one, making her the first female artist ever to appear at the top of the album charts without having to make a climb. And weeks later still, Houston again had the country's top single, **Didn't We Almost Have It All.**

The very week that Houston's "Didn't We" was number one, Michael Jackson saw his **Bad** album enter the *Billboard* LP chart at first place, duplicating that rare feat which Houston had recently achieved. In fact, according to Fred Bronson in *The Billboard Book of Number One Hits,* only six albums in history began at the top: two by Elton John: **Captain Fantastic and the Brown Dirt Cowboy** (June 7, 1975) and **Rock of the Westies** (November 8, 1975); Stevie Wonder's **Songs in the Key of Life** (October 16, 1976); **Bruce Springsteen and the E Street Band Live/1975–1985** (November 29, 1986); plus **Whitney** and **Bad.**

As 1987 drew to a close, Belinda Carlisle had a hit with **Heaven Is a Place on Earth;** and a new sensation on the teen music scene was sixteen-year-old Debbie Gibson of Merrick, Long Island. Her **Out of the Blue** album sold 3 million copies, and two years later her **Electric Youth** would sell 2 million. The multitalented teen took to songwriting, producing, and arranging, becoming the youngest person ever to have written, produced and performed a number one single: **Foolish Beat** (number three in the summer of 1988). As she became a pop phenomenon, advertisers swarmed around her; she endorsed a line of teen cosmetics, Natural Wonder, for Revlon; a perfume was named Electric Youth after her album; and Columbia Pictures signed her to a film deal in which she was to star in a *West Side Story*–like musical (which has yet to be made). Like the New Kids on the Block, Debbie Gibson was, for a time, a merchandiser's dream.

So Emotional; Got My Mind Set on You; The Way You Make Me Feel: 1988

As 1988 opened, Whitney Houston with "So Emotional," George Harrison with "Got My Mind Set on You," and Michael Jackson with "The Way You Make Me Feel" held the nation's top songs. And for Michael Jackson, "The Way" was the third consecutive number one single from his "Bad" album. The song, says Fred Bronson, "was Michael's seventh number one single of the 1980s, giving him the most number ones of the decade to this date." Directly behind him were Madonna and Whitney Houston, tying with six each. Two months after "The Way" topped the charts, Jackson was again on top with **Man in the Mirror,** becoming, as the record-keeping Bronson tallies, "the first solo artist in chart history to pull four number one singles off one album." By this time Jackson was a worldwide solo phenomenon virtually unmatched in pop music history.

The year 1988 was also good to George Michael, who scored number one hits with **Father Figure** in February and **One More Try** in May. Michael's **Faith** won single of the year and album of the year, and he was voted male artist of the year. Debbie Gibson won female artist of the year.

Anything for You: 1988

In 1988 Gloria Estefan and the Miami Sound Machine enjoyed their first number one smash, "Anything for You," from the album "Let It Loose." Cuban-born Estefan, who suffered a nearly paralyzing back injury in 1990 when her tour bus crashed in the Poconos (her spine is now held together by two 8-inch-long stainless-steel rods), was the first Hispanic pop singer to command broad popularity in North America.

Fresh out of the University of Miami in 1978, Gloria joined the Miami Sound Machine, founded by Emilio Estefan, who soon became her husband. The group, blending pop and Latin rhythms, was known throughout the Spanish-speaking world before their hit **Conga** made the American top ten in 1985.

After nine top ten singles and three consecutive bestselling albums ("Primitive Love," "Let It Loose," and "Cuts Both Ways"), *Newsday* rated Gloria Estefan "the biggest Cuban-born pop star in the United States since Desi Arnaz." In Miami, with its nearly 60 percent Latin population, radio stations "react to a new Estefan record as if it were the Beatles," said the editor of the trade magazine *HITS.* "No other act generates as much competition among stations to get a new single on the air first."

Estefan was the daughter of Jose Fajardo, a Miami-based Cuban exile who joined in the 1961 Bay of Pigs invasion, the abortive attempt by fellow exiles to recapture their homeland from Fidel Castro. (Captured, imprisoned, then later released, Fajardo volunteered for service in the Vietnam War and died in 1980 from a degenerative neurological disease believed to have been caused by exposure to Agent Orange during the war.)

As her popularity increased, Estefan began to deal explicitly with her Cuban heritage in her music, as in her early nineties hit **Mama Yo Can't Go**—the title itself captures the mixed vernacular often heard by second-generation Latinos. A cross-over success, Estefan has recorded in all-English, all-Spanish, and in a hybrid of the two, "Spanglish," and industry insiders predict she will be a megastar of the Nineties—an event reflecting not only her talent, but a trend in the country's demographics, in which Hispanics will continue to be the fast-growing minority.

Girl You Know It's True: 1989

As the Eighties turned into the Nineties, the pop music scene experienced several controversies. The rap group 2 Live Crew was taken to court on obscenity charges, for lyrics in their album "As Nasty As They Wanna Be" that were deemed violent, lewd, and degrading to women.

Would-be singers Rob Pilatus and Fab Morvan of Milli Vanilli were revealed to be lip-synching puppets on their smash album "Girl You Know It's True" (number ten for 1989), which sold 10 million copies. Their German record producer, Frank Farian, had used studio singers and was planning the same ruse for the group's next album. It turned out that nearly penniless Pilatus and Morvan had been living in a Munich housing project when, in 1988, Farian offered each of them $4,000 plus royalties to be the visually striking, vocally silent Milli Vanilli. The boys accepted, and they later claimed that their record company, Arista, knew all along about the scam—which left millions of record-buying fans feeling sympathetic and at the same time duped. In 1990 a repentant Rob and Fab—arguing that in the age of vigorous rock videos many performers resort to lip-synching—were nonetheless forced to forfeit their 1989 Grammy for best new artist of the year.

Milli Vanilli.

Yo, Rap!

Perhaps no phenomenon so uniquely altered the pop music scene in the late Eighties and early Nineties as hip-hop, better known as rap. Rapping began more than two decades earlier as a form of expression among jailed black inmates who, in the absence of instruments, turned poetic meter into pulsating musical rhythm. The early rap heard on ghetto streets was abrasive and laced with hostility toward society in general and white culture in particular.

Music and rap poetry had merged by the Seventies. In New York basement clubs disc jockeys kept dance rhythms uninterrupted by cutting back and forth between two records on two separate turntables. As they meshed sounds during instrumental stretches, they filled in the vocal silences with their own rhymed chanting, or rapping. Depending on the DJ and the club, this filler could be incendiary or relatively benign. Rapping was a DJ's way of making himself a master of ceremonies (or M.C.; hence the initials used by many rap groups) for the evening, expanding his rap for his own self-promotion, and also to egg dancers on. The term hip-hop is thought to derive from the expression "hippity hip hop / don't stop."

The rap group Public Enemy, formed by friends who met at the radio station at Long Island's Adelphi University, was the first act to publicly incorporate ghetto expressions of hostility into their own identity. They argued that every black youth was to society "a public enemy," and their logo showed a young black man in a rifle sight. Their music spoke to a largely alienated sector of society who felt hated and despised. Bill Stepheny, who produced Public Enemy's first album, observed that in the early days, "You were considered a criminal if you just listened to rap records." Other groups selected names calculated to tease and at the same time to caricature ghetto misbehavior; the initials of the platinum-record–winning group N.W.A. stand for "Niggas with Attitude."

In time, rap's infectious sound caught the ears of larger and larger audiences. With commercialism as the carrot, more and more rappers jettisoned hostile lyrics (and off-putting names) for mass-appeal rhymes—still bawdy and harsh, but at least not so intimidating as to be unmarketable to a wide audience. Others came to view rap as a way to be "Afro-positive," itself an Afrocentric in expression.

According to *Billboard,* about a half dozen groups helped to put rap on music's mainstream map. The highest-rated albums through the end of the Eighties were: Run-D.M.C.'s **Raising Hell** (1986), L. L. Cool J.'s **Bigger and Deffer** (1987), the Beastie Boys' **Licensed to Ill** (1987), and Tone-Loc's **Loc-ed After Dark** (1989). The two fast-selling rappers of the Nineties to date are Vanilla Ice and his album **To the Extreme,** and the phenomenally successful M. C. Hammer with **Please Hammer Don't Hurt 'Em,** number one for twenty-one weeks in 1990.

Whereas Public Enemy once rapped "There's a need to get alarmed / Again I said I was a timebomb," by 1991 there was "soft rap," and "lite rap," and Bart Simpson and the Teenage Mutant Ninja Turtles created the phenomenon of "tot rap"—proving that in America anything is marketable given the right spin.

The history of trends has repeatedly demonstrated that once an in-group phenomenon is watered down and spread out across many levels of society, its originators look for a new way to define themselves. Rap music began as a child of the inner city, but when Bart Simpson and the Ninja Turtles are rapping for crass profit and tot appeal, inner-city youths must turn inward for alternate ways to express their hopes or hopelessness. What mode of release they come up with may well be the next major phenomenon on the pop music scene.

BESTSELLING BOOKS

The Official Preppy Handbook: Number Five Nonfiction, 1980

Fad-wise, the decade opened with a veritable "prep-edemic" as millions of wannabe preppies scrambled to outfit themselves in conservative L. L. Bean chic. The fashion craze gave middle-class youths the idea that by adopting Shetland sweaters, Lacoste shirts, and teak-brown Top-Sider moccasins (sans socks) they could, through costume, enter the court of WASP aristocracy. How trendy to pass by Bloomingdale's and head straight for Brooks Brothers; better yet to order your cable knits and corduroys from Talbot's in Hingham, Massachusetts.

But clothing alone does not a preppy make. What does the breed eat? Where does it water? The publication of a 224-page tongue-in-cheek how-to, *The Official Preppy Handbook,* edited by twenty-four-year-old Lisa Birnbach, a former writer for the *Village Voice,* escalated the preppy fad to a merchandising blitz. Three weeks after hitting the stores, the trade paperback was entrenched high on the bestseller list, and it inspired parodies such as *The Joy of Stuffed Preppies* and *101 Uses for a Dead Preppy,* and such spin-offs as *The Official Preppy Desk Diary* and *The Original Preppy Jokebook.*

No one was more surprised than Lisa Birnbach, whose prep credentials included graduation from the Riverdale Country School and Brown University. The book was the brainchild of an editor at Workman Publishing, who felt that Birnbach, then at the *Voice,* had the requisite sense of humor to pull off a spoof of the current preppy dressing fad. She quit the newspaper and in ten weeks, with the assistance of three other writers, produced a crash course in prepdom that mixed admiration for WASP tradition with mockery of its upper-crust do's and don't's. For instance: Pampers were out, cloth diapers in; suitable nicknames for boys were Chip or Trip, for girls Muffy or Buffy; the chapter on preppy sex was subtitled "A Contradiction in Terms"; clothes were ordered from Land's End and G. H. Bass Co.; of model prep Caroline Kennedy it was pointed out that "An un-natural fiber never went near her body."

After eighteen reprintings, the handbook achieved sales of over a million copies and made its author a sought-after speaker at colleges across the country and on TV talk shows. A planned three-week publicity tour turned into an exhausting seven-month media hustle. A year later, when the blueblood Baedeker was still selling and spawning successful spin-offs—like *The Official I Hate Preppies Handbook,* a satirical paean for the four major nonprep groups: greasers, nerds, jocks, and freaks—Birnbach admitted, "I had no idea this was going to capture people and become part of their vocabulary the way it did. It's scary."

A look at trends in nonfiction bestsellers:

Pop Icons: Real Men and Yumpies

Lisa Birnbach had launched a trend for books on "correct" personal appearance and conduct. On the more serious side of the craze was Charles Hix's bestselling **How to Dress Your Man;** on the humorous side was **Real Men Don't Eat Quiche,** a guide on how to be a male chauvinist pig. In essence, anything a sensitive Seventies man did, an Eighties real man eschewed.

C. E. Crimmins's **The Official Young Aspiring Professional's Fast-Track Handbook** dispensed advice on how to be a yuppy (young urban professional)—or as columnist George Will dubbed the breed, yumpy (young upwardly mobile professional). Yumpies were hardworking Americans between the ages of twenty-five and forty who were consumed by "extraordinary ambition and extraordinary insecurity," wrote Will. "One ambition is to assuage their insecurity by means of an elaborate, all-absorbing strategy of socially correct consumption."

How-to handbooks like Crimmins's raised snobbery to a science and conferred on certain pricey products must-have cachet. Readers learned how to network and touch base with colleagues; that they should live in a gentrified neighborhood; that the career stress disease to boast of was TMJ (Temporo-Mandibular Joint Syndrome); that children should be given quality time; that when it came to food preparation you should own a Cuisinart, an asparagus steamer, a pasta maker, and an espresso machine; and you should eat out only at restaurants where the menu was written on a blackboard and each table sported a single flower in a Perrier bottle. An ideal yumpy's meal laid out by Will: grilled tuna with sun-dried tomatoes, an arugula and radicchio salad, an insouciant Chardonnay, and cappuccino. "Yumpies buy," said Will, "to advertise their sensibilities."

Iron John. If real men and yumpies were icons of the Eighties, Iron John, a mythic figure embodying male boldness and spontaneity, would be a model for the early Nineties. Countless real men who never tasted quiche would, surprisingly, find themselves crying in the arms of other real men as they attempted to regain their "deep masculine" side under the guidance of pop guru and poet Robert Bly.

Bly's premise, put forth in his bestseller *Iron John,* was that modern society has estranged men from their fathers, given them no male mentors in his stead, and dispensed with vital initiation rites into manhood. Evolving on their own, men have become either wimps or brutes. From the phenomenal sales of Bly's book and the success of his workshops and support groups, millions of American males apparently sought in the story of Iron John—an ancient fairy tale first written down by the Grimm brothers in 1820—a "map to find their way through the mountains," as Bly wrote, to a new and balanced manhood. The book, assisted by a Bill Moyers's TV series on Bly, became a number one bestseller in the early Nineties. But for now we're still looking at the greedy Eighties and books like . . .

Trump: The Art of the Deal: Number Four Nonfiction, 1988

"The Donald," in his 1987 less-than-humble autobiography, offered a series of principles on the business deal that he called "Trump Cards," and which he'd later have to eat as crow. "The worst thing you can possibly do in a deal is seem desperate to make it," he advised. "That makes the other guy smell blood, and then you're dead."

Less than four years after the book rode high on the bestseller list, Donald Trump found himself cutting desperate eleventh-hour deals to avoid personal bankruptcy. And whereas he wrote in 1987 that he fought hard against "people—I categorize them as life's losers—who get their sense of accomplishment and achievement from trying to stop others," he later thanked such "losers" for helping him curb his profligate spending and forestalling the total collapse of his empire. His second book, **Trump: Surviving at the Top,** published in 1990, was anticlimactic in terms of sales, but also credulity.

Three similar kinds of late Eighties bestsellers were Lee Iacocca's **Iacocca: An Autobiography** (the number one nonfiction for the decade, with 2,572,000 hardcover copies sold), and the same author's **Talking Straight** (number two for 1988), and Harvey MacKay's **Swim With the Sharks Without Being Eaten Alive** (number six for 1988). First-person accounts on how to achieve success and negotiate "the mother of all deals" were a staple of the Greed Decade, selling millions of copies and making their authors icons of the moment.

Then came the crushing comeuppance: a dive in the stock market, followed by junk bond scandals and S&L closings. The aggressive CEO, and certainly the hostile corporate raider, were no longer viewed as role models but piranhas. Publishers, perceiving the mood shift in the post-Reagan era, brought out books that criticized the frenzied dealmaking once the adrenaline of Wall Street: **Barbarians at the Gate,** by Bryan Burrough and John Helyar, and **Liar's Poker,** by Michael Lewis, were two particularly successful books to ascribe straight-talking pejoratives like "barbarian" and "liar" to former denizens of the deal.

On the fiction front was Tom Wolfe's bestselling **Bonfire of the Vanities,** a novel future sociologists might turn to for a glimpse of the Eighties in a light not found in conventional journalistic accounts of the decade. Donald Trump attributed the high sales of such supersellers as *Bonfire, Barbarians,* and *Liar's Poker,* to simple psychology: "People love reading negative things about successful people." He might have added, especially successful people on the way down.

With greed out and concern in, books on the environment began appearing on the bestseller lists; notably **50 Simple Things You Can Do to Save the Earth,** self-published by the San Francisco-based Earthworks Press. Twelve weeks a *New York Times* bestseller, the book was followed by **50 Simple Things Kids Can Do to Save the Earth,** from a different press, whose vice president, Donna Martin, observed at the start of the Nineties, "People want to get involved. There's been a turn from the 'me' to the 'we' decade." We'll see.

Celebrity Confessions

While businessmen were boasting of their deals, celebrities from Hollywood, TV, and the world of politics were baring their most embarrassing shortcomings in bestselling books. Though the genre of the literary confession dates back to St. Augustine's straightforwardly titled *Confessions*—which chronicled a spell of dissolute pagan living, summed up in his plea, "Lord, give me chastity and continency, but do not give them yet"—tell-all books in the Eighties were not so much inspirational as mortifyingly personal. Did readers really need to know, from Kitty Dukakis's **Now You Know,** that the woman who was almost the country's First Lady was once so desperate for an alcoholic buzz that she downed nailpolish remover and hair spray? Did actress Mariette Hartley really need to break her silence in **Breaking the Silence** to tell readers that her booze binges left her squatting on the kitchen floor eating cat food from a can? Is this what St. Augustine had in mind when he kicked off the genre?

In **Dancing on My Grave,** ballerina Gelsey Kirkland chronicled her addiction to cocaine. "The list goes on and on," wrote *Newsday*'s David Friedman in "The Urge to Purge." In the Eighties, in print, Tina Turner confessed to suffering at the hands of an abusive husband; young actress Drew Barrymore revealed an addiction to booze; Sid Caesar to booze and drugs, Judy Carne to booze, drugs, and men. Liz Taylor, in **Elizabeth Takes Off,** confessed to the cardinal sin of gluttony, though at least this admission had long been suspected. "American culture has redefined its sense of shame," says Friedman. "Once there were vices too humiliating to reveal. Now you're only as sick as your secrets. Somewhere along the line the Me Decade gave way to the Me, Too! Decade."

Did those who confessed in the Eighties do it purely for profit?

"A tell-all autobiography by a celebrity is the easiest sale in the world," says Marty Posner, an agent at William Morris. "It's the great American way of turning misfortunes into fortunes." All of the confessionals sold strongly. Carol Burnett had a bestseller with **One More Time;** football's bad boy Jim McMahon said the darnedest things in **McMahon: The Bare Truth** about Chicago's Brashest Bear. *Elizabeth Takes Off* was the sixth bestselling book of 1988. Roseanne Barr's let-it-all-hang-out **Roseanne: My Life as a Woman** was the number eight nonfiction the following year, appearing just beneath Gilda Radner's posthumously published memoir of her courageous battle with cancer, **It's Always Something,** certainly more inspirational than the rest. Number ten for that year was former First Lady Nancy Reagan's get-even autobiography, rather willfully titled **My Turn.**

Celebrities told all not just for the money, though, but for many of the same human urges that motivated St. Augustine: for sympathy, for attention, to set an example, to purge themselves psychically. Had the former bishop of Hippo been around today he'd most certainly go on Oprah and Phil and Sally and Geraldo.

Fatherhood: Number One Nonfiction, 1986

In a different vein from the confessional autobiography was actor Bill Cosby's bestseller *Fatherhood,* which, according to *Publishers Weekly,* was then "the fastest-selling hardcover book in U.S. publishing history." Star of the country's then number one television sitcom, Cosby wrote a book about fathering that was published shortly before Father's Day 1986, and that sold nearly 2.4 million hardcover copies before the year's end—breaking the selling record (of 1,815,000 copies during 1972) held by Richard Bach's *Jonathan Livingston Seagull* (see page 411). As Cosby's editor, Paul Bresnick, who conceived the concept, said, "It was the right idea at the right time with the right author." *Fatherhood* came in as the number two nonfiction of the decade. Cosby's follow-up was **Time Flies,** published in 1987.

Competing for slots on the bestseller list in that year of 1986 were Jeff Smith's **The Frugal Gourmet Cooks With Wine** (number seven), a follow-up to his successful 1985 book, **The Frugal Gourmet** (number eight); psychologist Dr. Susan Forward's self-help guide "for men and women caught up in misogynistic relationships, **Men Who Hate Women and the Women Who Love Them** (number thirteen); the million-seller **Fit for Life** by Harvey and Marilyn Diamond (number two), a book touted by Merv Griffin, who'd lost weight on the diet regimen; Leo Buscaglia's **Bus 9 to Paradise** (number fifteen), another of his "caring and sharing" books; and *60 Minutes'* Andrew Rooney with **Word for Word** (number nine), the fourth in his collection of humorous essays that began to appear early in the decade with **A Few Minutes with Andy Rooney.**

All I Really Needed to Know I Learned in Kindergarten: Number One Nonfiction, 1989

Unitarian minister Reverend Robert Fulghum did not set out to write a best-seller called *All I Really Needed to Know I Learned in Kindergarten: Uncommon Thoughts on Common Things.* Though within less than two years the book sold 902,000 copies in hardcover, went through seventeen printings, thirteen foreign-language editions, garnered a record-breaking $2.1 million in nonfiction paperback advance, and helped him earn a seven-figure advance for his more autobiographical follow-up, **It Was on Fire When I Lay Down on It,** which went on to sell more than a half million copies between its publication in the fall of 1989 and the end of that year—ranking as number four for that year. All of this hoopla and profit over a premise that couldn't be simpler—and more appealing: that all we really need to learn in life—the sum of its major truisms—is acquired not in college but in the sandbox.

Fulghum's homespun homilies include: Share everything, play fair, don't hit others, clean up your own mess, flowers die and so do we. The simple messages, which contain more than a kernel of truth, began to appear as the themes of essays in a biweekly newsletter the author wrote between 1960 and 1984. The Seattle minister mimeographed his musings and passed them out to parishioners, and his expanding collection gradually caught the attention of variously important and high-placed individuals. As *New York Times* reporter Patricia Leigh Brown detailed the snowballing of events that led to publication (she dubbed Fulghum "a sort of Norman Vincent Bombeck"), *"Kindergarten* was picked up by the radio commentator Paul Harvey, the Rev. Robert Schuller, former Representative Barbara Jordan and the singer-activist Pete Seeger. Dear Abby and *Reader's Digest* published abridged versions."

Then one day in 1987 a real-life kindergarten student showed the essays he'd picked up in school to his mother, who happened to be a New York literary agent. The rest is Eighties' publishing history. "Fulghum's essays," said Brown, "reaffirm the sanctity of the ordinary." And arriving amidst nationwide disillusionment as the Greed Decade passed to the Payback Decade, the book, with its emphasis on honesty, innocence, and old-fashioned common sense, found an eager market.

A Brief History of Time: From the Big Bang to Black Holes: Number Three Nonfiction, 1988

British physicist Stephen Hawking's book was one of the decade's most unexpected success stories. The Cambridge author, severely afflicted with Lou Gehrig's disease and confined to a wheelchair (able to communicate only with the assistance of a computerized voice synthesizer), saw his none-too-simple treatment of modern physics go from its April 1988 publication to a year-end bestseller with 729,000 hardcover copies sold. The 1988 sleeper continued to rack up impressive sales the following year (eventually ranking as the number nine nonfiction of the decade). However, many industry insiders believed that *A Brief History,* like Salman Rushdie's superselling fiction of that period, **The Satanic Verses,** attracted countless readers dazzled more by the media spotlight shone on both authors and their particular hardships, rather than interest in their texts. The infirm Hawking and the threatened Rushdie were more than authors; they were multimedia events, and one had only to buy their books, not read them, to partake of the phenomena.

As of this writing, *The Satanic Verses*—after the author was forced into hiding by death threats from the Ayatollah Rudhollah Khomeini of Iran—scored the "highest rate of sales in a single week" of any nonfiction or fiction in publishing history; the closest book approaching that weekly sweep, according to *New York Times* figures, was Kitty Kelley's controversial 1991 megaseller, **Nancy Reagan: The Unauthorized Biography.**

A subsequent event, which merited months of worldwide attention, brought back to publishing (unofficially) a category of books not seen since the Forties.

War Books

The week the war in the Persian Gulf ended, mid-March of 1991, seven of the ten paperback bestsellers on the *New York Times* list were related to the conflict, one way or another. You could survey the Arab-Israeli conflict over the past decade with **From Beirut to Jerusalem** (number one); read of the Iraqi president and his invasion of Kuwait in **Saddam Hussein and the Crisis in the Gulf** (number two); and follow the invasion in detail, through observations of people who witnessed it firsthand and escaped to tell about it, in **The Rape of Kuwait** (number three).

The public, bombarded for months with television, newspaper, and radio reports, still wanted more information. Often from a unique angle, as found in **Not Without My Daughter** (number four), by Betty Mahmoody, an American woman held captive in Iran, whose dramatic tale became a movie starring Sally Field. For those who wanted to get to the heart of the Persian Gulf conflict, **A Peace to End All Peace** (number five) detailed how the Middle East was redrawn by the Allies in the years following World War I, and how the partitioning laid the groundwork for an inevitable latter-day imbroglio. Samir al-Khalil, an expatriate Iraqi scholar, gave an account of life under Saddam Hussein in **Republic of Fear** (number seven). Those who wanted to familiarize themselves with the geographic region at war could turn to the **Desert Shield Fact Book,** a compendium of maps and facts which was number two on the special "advice and how-to" bestseller list.

"Instant" war books were also in the making. Workman Publishing rushed out ninety thousand copies of *My Desert Storm Workbook: First Aid for Feelings,* which included a series of drawings and exercises meant to help young children overcome their fears of war. Even novels of war—any war—enjoyed sales through association with the Desert Storm assault.

But this particular war, occurring in the Middle East—and near the end of a millennium, always a time of great portent and dire augury—produced a kind of book unseen on the war books lists of the Forties.

Armageddon Books

In **Armageddon, Oil and the Middle East Crisis,** number six the week the war ended, theologian John Walvoord argued that events in the Gulf were fulfilling the Bible's promise of the second coming of Christ. The paperback sold over 2 million copies in two months, including three hundred thousand that were given away as premiums by evangelist Billy Graham. Authors like Walvoord—and televangelists like Jack Van Impe, who cautioned his viewers that "We're on the march to Armageddon"—viewed the Persian Gulf crisis as the predicted conflict between Babylon (Iraq) and Rome and Greece (represented by the modern Western world). The war supposedly fulfilled a forecast in which a worldwide coalition would force a peace settlement on the state of Israel, thus setting the stage for the rise of the murderous anti-Christ as a global dictator. The biblical battle of Armageddon follows, then comes the "rapture," a time in which all true believers are lifted up into heaven, leaving unbelievers and apostate Christians to perish at the hands of an avenging Jesus. Even singer Johnny Cash cashed in on the war mania with "Goin' by the Book," a ballad linking the Gulf crisis to Armageddon.

From the invasion of Kuwait in August to the end of the conflict the following March, Christian publishers rushed out more than a dozen books of dire prophecy, which place the rapture and the end of the world squarely in the decade of the Nineties. It seems that no more accurate pinpointing is possible since, as the Bible cautions, "you know not the day or the hour."

Megaseller Fiction

"The term 'megaseller' is an '80s word coined specifically to describe the new breed of hardcover bestseller," wrote Daisy Maryles in *Publishers Weekly.* She was speaking of seven-figure sales, the kind once expected of mass-market paperbacks but rare for hardcover books. We saw in earlier chapters that certain books sold over the million mark, but in the Eighties thirteen novels (and twelve nonfiction books) achieved that heady megamark. More remarkable still, "Ten of the 13 million-copy novels," wrote Maryles, "were by three writers—Stephen King, Danielle Steel and Tom Clancy." Here, then, is *PW*'s list of Eighties novels (with hardback figures) that we readers pushed over the million mark:

1. **Clear and Present Danger,** Tom Clancy—1,607,715
2. **The Dark Half,** Stephen King—1,550,000
3. **The Tommyknockers,** Stephen King—1,423,923
4. **The Mammoth Hunters,** Jean M. Auel—1,350,000
5. **Daddy,** Danielle Steel—1,321,235
6. **Lake Wobegon Days,** Garrison Keillor—1,300,000
7. **The Cardinal of the Kremlin,** Tom Clancy—1,287,067
8. **Texas,** James A. Michener—1,176,758
9. **Red Storm Rising,** Tom Clancy—1,126,782
10. **It,** Stephen King—1,115,000
11. **Kaleidoscope,** Danielle Steel—1,065,355
12. **Zoya,** Danielle Steel—1,000,319
13. **Star,** Danielle Steel—1,000,119

TELEVISION HITS

Trends: Nightline to Entertainment Tonight

In the decade of the Eighties, the three major networks lost their dominance, and a good deal of their luster, to cable TV—which by 1989 was in more than 60 percent of homes with television sets. The acronym VCR became commonplace as sales of the recorders soared from 475,000 at the opening of the decade to 11 million at its close. No longer did you have to stay at home to watch your favorite program; you taped it to view at leisure, and fast-forwarded past those pesty commercials.

It was the decade in which we became familiar with the bark of that nasal-toned ace of Fleet Street journalism, Robin Leach, with his tacky tag of "champagne wishes and caviar dreams"; with the crisply proficient letter-turning of the svelte and silent Vanna White. And stand-up comics came to TV in unprecedented numbers: Garry Shandling, Roseanne Barr, Jane Curtin, Robert Klein, George Carlin, Bill Cosby, Richard Lewis, Jerry Seinfeld, Tracey Ullman, and Jackie Mason—the last in the short-lived *Chicken Soup*.

The decade will also be remembered as the era in which news and entertainment became strange bedfellows, the line between the two often calculatedly blurred. On the one hand, there was the "infotainment" show, typified by "Entertainment Tonight," which offered the aura of a newscast in sets and anchors, but which delivered celebrity gossip and covered star-studded opening night parties as if each one were the Malta summit.

On the other hand, there was CBS's **60 Minutes.** It first aired on September 24, 1968, and by the Eighties (and throughout the decade) was one of the most consistently top-rated shows on television. The format was copied throughout the decade, and no more successfully than by ABC with its newsmagazine **20/20,** hosted by Hugh Downs and Barbara Walters. By the early Nineties, "20/20" was the network's most watched hour-long program.

ABC's "Nightline" became network television's first regularly scheduled late-night news broadcast. It began in November 1979 in response to the hostage crisis in Iran (the holding of fifty-two Americans for 444 days), and went on to subject all the decade's major stories and many of their stars—like the teary Tammy Bakker, and the even more teary Reverend Jimmy Swaggart—to the probing mind of Ted Koppel. The decade would be sandwiched at both ends with news shows of importance, for 1991 began the virtual round-the-clock TV coverage of the Persian Gulf conflict, which, as an historical first, gave viewers an armchair view of a war in the works. It is interesting to note that the decade in which the force of news wed the froth of entertainment to sire infotainment—the very same decade in which image took prominence over reality—America had as its President and First Lady a former actor and actress.

If the so-called media decade had one unexpected superstar, it was . . .

CNN

Ted Turner's Cable News Network was perhaps the most significant new media creation of the Eighties. The audacious Turner, cast as the biblical David, single-handedly took on the three network Goliaths and wounded them mightily with his creation of a revolutionary new force in television news. It has been credibly argued that CNN usurped the CIA in terms of providing crucial information to the highest levels of government. The global broadcasts were watched by Margaret Thatcher, Saddam Hussein, Manuel Noriega, George Bush, and even the CIA in order to learn what was going on in the world's hot spots. The Soviet news agency **Tass** admitted to monitoring the network, as did U.S. generals in the Pentagon war room.

"When Mr. Bush wanted to encourage Panama's military forces and populace to overthrow General Manuel Noriega," wrote a political correspondent in the *New York Times,* "he did it by having his press aides offer an exclusive interview to CNN, knowing that the General and the Panamanians watch it." That's power. "CNN has opened up a whole new communications system between governments in terms of immediacy and directness," admitted Marlin Fitzwater, President Bush's press secretary. "In many cases, it's the first communication we have."

Tabloid TV

Geraldo, Phil, Oprah, and Sally. Maury Povich and Morton Downey, Jr. They brought you headlines unimaginable a decade earlier, "Men Married to Practicing Prostitutes." "Nurses Who Kill Their Patients." "Gay Fathers." "Priests

Oprah Winfrey.

Phil Donahue.

Who Pimp." The talk show had originated as a comfy way for film and TV stars to shill their latest project to an adoring, noncombative host, one who allowed stars to hype themselves and promote their products. In the Eighties, the format changed radically. Talk shows dealt in trash and their guests were weirdos, wackos, and wannabe celebrities; hookers, addicts, the abused and the abusive—all willing to brazenly bare matters so private that they were once confided, and with great reluctance, to one's analyst.

In the previous section we looked at the bestselling book phenomenon of

Geraldo Rivera.

the confessional autobiography; well, Phil Donahue, Geraldo Rivera, Oprah Winfrey, and Sally Jessy Raphael brought the equivalent, known as tabloid TV, to the home screen. Wherever did they get their guests? How do you find, for show after show, a population of people with utterly no shame?

In defense of such titillations, the networks argued that the programs provided information on socially taboo subjects, helpful hints for viewers struggling with their own dark secrets. In truth, most viewers were not men married to practicing prostitutes, or nurses who killed their patients—both themes of "Geraldo" shows. In fact, during a single month, "Geraldo" alone covered such topics as a topless coffee shop frequented by truckers ("Debby Does Donuts," as the show became notoriously known), serial rapists, pregnant prison inmates, teenage prostitution, dating married men, nymphomaniacs, rape on college campuses, sex rings, lady drug dealers, transsexuals, autistic savants, Chippendale's men, and domestic violence among lesbians. Tabloid TV indulged largely in titillation and provocation; what it rarely did was present issues in context and with a sense of proportion, if not decency. It was the decade in which everyone with a secret screamed his or her way out of the closet.

Dynasty: ABC Premiere, January 12, 1981

In many ways the extravagances of the cult and camp hit "Dynasty" mirrored the times, sinfully. The hour-long soap opera was equal parts ruthless money-making, egregious ambition, dirty deals for oil, and an obsession with glamorous clothes and glitzy parties. "Dynasty" (originally titled "Oil") peaked along with

"Dynasty."

the popularity of Reagonomics, with revelations of the First Lady's lust for designer clothes, with the rise of the Trump deal, the Milken junk bond, hostile corporate takeovers, and a willful blindness to the risk of excessive debt. Most of the characters on the show would do (and did do) just about anything to "have it all"—three little words that embodied the hungry hopes of the era.

Denver's Blake and Krystle Carrington (John Forsythe and Linda Evans) lived in a forty-eight-room mansion (actually the Filoli estate in Northern California), and did continual battle with Blake's former wife, the despicably villainous, ever-glamorous, successful Alexis Carrington Colby (Joan Collins). Before Blake married his secretary, Krystle, he and Alexis sired two problem children, a sexually liberated daughter, Fallon, and a homogenized homosexual son, Steven, who, as the plot and ratings dictated, changed his sexual preference almost as frequently as his mother changed millinery. The couple's adopted son, Adam, was a lethal blend of his father's gentle demeanor and his mother's killer instincts; he continually sold out one parent for favors from the other.

The show made superstars of Forsythe, Evans, and Collins and generated "Dynasty" lines of clothing, luggage, and women's fragrances like Krystle and Scoundrel (named for Alexis), and a man's smell of success, Carrington. In a decade that revered wealth and power, "Dynasty" was something of an amoral, behind-the-scenes fictionalization of that peek-at-the-privileged show, "Lifestyles of the Rich and Famous." In its fourth year on the air, Rock Hudson, the all-American sex symbol of the Fifties, became a love interest of Krystle, the two actors exchanging a kiss that would soon be heard around the world. In real life Hudson fell gravely ill, journeyed to France for secret treatments, then, near the end of his life, publicly admitted he had AIDS. The admission heightened public awareness of the disease, caused President Reagan to belatedly voice the word in public, and made everyone in the acting profession horrified of kissing scenes. The Screen Actors' Guild dispatched seven thousand letters to producers and agents informing them that actors must henceforth be notified in advance of scenes involving "opened-mouthed kissing."

"Dynasty's" message of "you can have it all" fell on hard times in the late Eighties. The stock market had crashed, ethics as a concern in business and politics was at least being discussed if not yet practiced, AIDS had introduced the concept of safe sex, and it was apparent to all that amorality and greed carried a hefty price. Villainy was out; virtue was in. At the close of the show's 1988–89 season, Blake was shot, Alexis fell from a balcony, and horrible fates awaited other cast regulars in the cliffhanger episode—which turned out to the soap's swan song.

Dallas: CBS Premiere, April 2, 1978

The first of the soap opera oil giants, "Dallas"—a camp cartoon of evil—was set in its namesake town and was similar to the Denver-based "Dynasty" in its emphasis on unimaginable wealth and treacherous power. The villain of "Dallas," though, was a man in a cowboy hat, the much-hated and envied J. R. Ewing (Larry Hagman). He was a modern version, in businessman attire, of the

"Dallas."

old-time villain who tied virgins to railroad tacks and snickered as the train steamrolled in. One TV critic called him the "Swine of the Decade." Hagman labeled his character "a WASH—a White Anglo-Saxon hedonist" who "sleeps well at night."

The audience for the much-awaited "Who Shot J.R.?" episode of November 21, 1980, was, at the time, the largest in TV history; nearly 76 percent of Americans with their TV sets on sat poised for the revelation. Worldwide, 300 million viewers in 57 countries waited breathlessly for the most successful cliffhanger in entertainment history. (The character Kristin, played by Bing Crosby's daughter, Mary, had shot J.R. for getting her pregnant.)

Whereas in "Dynasty" the wicked occasionally felt guilt, in "Dallas" characters were of an evil unencumbered with conscience or apology. "The most glamorously back-stabbing clan since the house of Atreus," said *Time* of the show often called Lifestyles of the Rich and Pretty, which, as the magazine punned, "elevated conspicuous consumption to a secular religion: gaud almighty." The story of the Ewings, a Texas oil family headed by the unscrupulous J.R., blended avarice with hate and sex and power to paint a picture of the wealthy victimized by the wealthy, a theme nonwealthy viewers hoped mirrored reality. The show was wicked and adored for its wickedness throughout the world; *"Dallas* is to TV fiction what Gustave Flaubert's *Madame Bovary* is to the novel," assessed Donna McCrohan: "absorbing realism approaching shocking naturalism; sexual trauma; transgressions; rampant emotion."

The two oil soaps emphasized the Eighties reality that more Americans than ever before were millionaires, and billionaires. In "Dallas's" fourth season, the *Wall Street Journal* reported that on prime-time TV, "Millionaires are as common as policemen and far more common than any other strata of society. Night-time fare on the three major networks has become the electronic equivalent of an old fashioned society page." The show, whose philosophical premise was "greed works," made superstars of Hagman, Linda Gray (J.R.'s wife, Sue Ellen), Victoria Principal (Pamela Barnes Ewing), Patrick Duffy (Bobby Ewing), Charlene Tilton (Lucy), and veteran actress Barbara Bel Geddes (Miss Ellie); two characters were spun off to form the popular and long-lived "Knots Landing."

Like "Dynasty," "Dallas" remained popular throughout much of the Eighties. J. R. Ewing was a "hero" for millions because, as anthropologist Ashley Montagu argued, "we admire rugged individuals like Mr. Hagman's character precisely because they can get away with it"—it being the greedy behavior that real-life businessmen and bankers were then getting away with with impunity. It is no coincidence that during the years when shows like "Dynasty" and "Dallas" were tops in the ratings the incidence of white-collar crime scored its own ratings high. However, in real life, once people who had gotten away with it began to get caught, go to trial, and serve jail terms, greed was out and "Dallas" began to slip in the ratings. It was canceled on May 3, 1991.

If future sociologists screen TV shows to glimpse the shadier themes of the Eighties, "Dallas" and "Dynasty" should be high on their list.

Cheers: NBC Premiere, September 30, 1982

On the Boston common is a bar named the Bull and Finch, the location for the popular "Cheers," an exceptionally well-written sitcom from the producers/writers of "Taxi." Though the series about ex-Boston Red Sox baseball pitcher Sam Malone (Ted Danson) and his cast of cronies debuted in 1982, at the close of the decade it was still one of the top-rated shows on the air—despite major cast changes. Sassy, hard-edged waitress Carla Tortelli (Rhea Perlman), lethargic, beer-guzzling Norm Peterson (George Wendt), know-it-all mailman Cliff Clavin (John Ratzenberger), dense and adorable Coach Ernie Pantusso (Nicholas Colasanto), and the pretentious would-be intellectual reduced to waitress Diane Chambers (Shelley Long)—these made up the original crew who, through literate scripts, tackled issues of concern for single men and women in the Eighties. So loved was the show by its legions of fans that it survived the nearly always fatal departure of a main character, in this case Diane Chambers. In 1990 "Cheers," then eight years old—and "60 Minutes," then fourteen years old—scored number one ratings, the only shows up to that date to command such large audiences for their on-air ages.

"Cheers" began breaking television records from the start; in its first dismal season the sitcom came in dead last one week, earning it the distinction over its lifetime of being the only show (other than "Lou Grant") to have finished both last and first in weekly numbers. And the show ended the decade scoring

"Cheers."

another "bookend" TV first: winning an Emmy award for best comedy series in 1989 as well as one the year it debuted.

"How does a TV show remain so highly regarded and even become *more* popular after so many years on the air?" asked *New York Times* critic Bill Carter. After considering many possibilities, Carter concluded that "the explanations always come back to writing." Indeed, within the TV industry, "Cheers" has consistently been considered the best-written comedy on television. "We give our audience more credit than most shows," said executive producer James Burrows, who directed all but a few of the show's more than two hundred episodes. "We would always allow Diane to say *pomme de terre,* and never made her say potato. If the audience gets it, O.K." And the series is among the most literate on the air in that its humor, analyzed Carter, "is almost exclusively verbal; the episodes depend on dialogue, not slapstick action."

Instead of the show dying when Shelley Long departed to do feature films, her absence—and her replacement by the wonderfully vulnerable character of Rebecca as played by Kirstie Alley—forced the rest of the cast to expand their roles, which actually "re-energized the bar," said Burrows. As of this writing, the sitcom was still garnering new fans, still high in the weekly ratings. At the moment, "Cheers" is one of the longest-running sitcoms in TV history, with 194 half-hour episodes in syndication, each selling for $1.3 million.

Family Ties: NBC Premiere, September 22, 1982

Hard as it is to believe, when the sitcom family of Steve and Elyse Keaton (Michael Gross and Meredith Baxter-Birney) and their children, Alex (Michael J. Fox), Mallory (Justine Bateman), and Jennifer (Tina Yothers) arrived on the small screen in the fall of 1982, the show was, as *TV Guide* was quick to point out, "the only sitcom to feature an intact nuclear family"—a measure of how much the genre had changed since its early days when families like the Cleavers, the Andersons, and the Nelsons were the sitcom standard. It was the show's producer, Gary David Goldberg, who, writes Donna McCrohan, "restored dignity to a genre that had been written off as nearly extinct."

The nuclear family had withered on TV in the Seventies. In part, this was because socially hot issues involved sex, singles, abortions, homosexuality, infidelity, working women and emasculated men—elements not easily explored in the context of a conscientious mother and a concerned father with decent kids—what the Keatons were. Goldberg, a flower child of the Sixties, was by the Eighties a husband and a father, and he wanted to create a sitcom to reflect his own new family concerns. Indeed, Steven and Elyse Keaton are former flower children themselves, political activists of the Sixties; their son Alex was born in Africa when the couple was in the Peace Corps; daughter Mallory, in the counterculture capital of Berkeley; daughter Jennifer, when the Keatons were involved with the George McGovern campaign.

Much of the comedy in the series came from the fact that their firstborn,

Alex, turned out to be everything his parents weren't: staunchly conservative, ambitious, not above scheming if necessary, infatuated with money, determined to succeed whatever the cost, basically not a nice person—though not an evil one either, for when push came to punch, Alex discovered he had scruples. Whereas the series had originally focused on the parents, the conceited character of Alex ("I hate to toot my own horn, but beep, beep!") quickly stole the show—catapulting Michael J. Fox to superstar status.

"It is no coincidence that [Alex Keaton] arrived in our nation's homes at the same time that Reagan moved in," wrote Kevin Sessums in *Interview* magazine. "For Alex is the embodiment of the Reagan era, a no-deposit, no-return, nonbiodegradable product of the '80s, a pendulum reaction to an earlier generation's generosity." Interestingly, according to the White House press secretary, President Reagan's favorite TV show was "Family Ties," his favorite character Alex Keaton. This was so well known that producer Goldberg made several attempts to get the president to make a guest appearance on the show—in which he'd encourage the hard-working, determined Alex to shoot for nothing less than the presidency itself.

Whereas Alex's selfish behavior shocked his socially conscious parents, they were equally disappointed that their daughter Mallory turned out to be an Eighties airhead, obsessed with clothes, shopping, and appearance. She was a material girl, convinced that if the world were more color coordinated there'd be more harmony and no more wars. As the children aged (as did the sitcom, leaving the air by the end of the decade) they began to reflect more of their parents' concerns. By that time, the sitcom nuclear family was back in vogue, and with no family scoring higher Nielsen ratings than the thoroughly respectable black clan on . . .

The Cosby Show: NBC Premiere, September 20, 1984

It has been argued that the Huxtables, headed by successful obstetrician Dr. Cliff Huxtable (Bill Cosby) and his lawyer wife Clair (Phylicia Rashad), were an Eighties reincarnation of the Andersons of "Father Knows Best," given the Afrocentric twist that the close-knit, loving family was black and their concerns were not so much contemporary as universal.

"The Huxtables became America's favorite prime-time TV family," writes Donna McCrohan, "because they succeeded in portraying the generic family." Their appeal crossed all ethnic and racial lines because the family was neither black nor white but simply representative of humankind, and a kinder, gentler humankind at that. Family values were back in vogue, and no family embodied them better, and with more good-spirited, sugary humor, than the Huxtables. Coretta Scott King called the show "the most positive portrayal of black family life that has ever been broadcast." No actual black family duplicated the Huxtables, but then no white family in the Fifties was the Andersons.

The show's success sprang from and mirrored Bill Cosby's own. After a stint as a stand-up comic, he broke into prime time TV as a co-star (with Robert

"The Cosby Show."

Culp) on "I Spy," becoming the first black actor to head a major network drama series. After several failed shows of his own, and appearances on "Sesame Street" and in kiddie Jell-O commercials, the star returned to school under the "life experience program," earning a doctorate in education from the University of Massachusetts in 1977. After NBC's Brandon Tartikoff caught Cosby on the "Tonight" show doing one of his family-oriented comedy routines, he approached him about developing a sitcom "that people could feel good about." Cosby, as had such earlier stars as Milton Berle, Jackie Gleason, and Lucille Ball, devoted himself to every aspect of the series, from scripts to music, from casting to directing.

As with Cosby's own family, the Huxtables have five kids, and Clair's maiden name, Hanks, is that of his real-life wife, Camille. "The show became one of the most successful sitcom series in TV history," observed *Forbes* magazine in a business profile, "helping lift NBC to the number-one slot among networks in both ratings and profits." Comedian Cosby created more than a TV sitcom, though. He set himself up to be a bestselling author of record-breaking proportions (see page 432), a film star, and a one-man cottage industry. *Forbes* estimated Cosby's earnings for one year at $92 million, making him the world's second highest paid entertainer, second only to Michael Jackson at $97 million.

In typical sitcom fashion, the show had a successful spin-off when Denise

Huxtable (Lisa Bonet) left home to attend college: "A Different World," premiering in 1987, offered a positive view of college life and stressed the importance of education.

As of this writing, "Cosby" is the most lucrative, and most popular, of all reruns; it has 150 half-hour episodes in syndication, each selling for $4.4 million. For the record, number two is Tony Danza's **Who's the Boss?** with 147 rerun episodes at $2.5 million each; number three is Tom Selleck's **Magnum, P.I.** with 162 episodes at $1.6 million each; and number five is **Golden Girls** with each syndicated rerun selling for $1.4 million.

When we looked at the birth of the TV sitcom in the Forties and Fifties, we observed that the element fundamental to the genre and its mass appeal was family—not merely a collection of biologically related individuals; an array of people interacting in a workplace could constitute a sitcom family in all its dynamics and with all its potential for drama and humor. If, as mentioned, "Family Ties" marked the return of the nuclear family, "The Cosby Show" the reemergence of the generic family, television in the decade of the Eighties also witnessed the emergence of a new type of family:

Anti-Family Sitcoms: Roseanne and Married . . . With Children

The premise underlying the success (and controversy) of the anti-family show is simply this: whereas a series like "Father Knows Best" could make all viewers who did not measure up to the Andersons feel guilty, virtually every viewer could feel he or she was better off than, say, Al and Peg Bundy of "Married . . . With Children," or the blue-collar Conner clan of "Roseanne." Peg Bundy and Roseanne Conner typify what's been called the "mom no longer interested in being a human sacrifice on the altar of pro-family values." Critics of the genre claim that if there is a message in the anti-family sitcom it's the one Al Bundy continually utters to single people: "Don't marry." That is, don't have a family. To quote Al again, "Ah, home sweet hell."

Whereas Peg Bundy is anti-housework, Roseanne Conner does housework but with a continual whine and a constant chip on her shoulder. Of her kids she says in typical anti-family humor, "They're all mine. Of course, I'd trade any one of them for a dishwasher." In "Roseanne," which quickly became the country's number one sitcom, the mother (Roseanne Barr), despite her acerbic one-liner barbs, does display, if often grudgingly, a deep love for her brood. The same cannot be said of Peg Bundy.

Bickering Bundys. Husband Al Bundy, who by day sells ladies' shoes and by night suffers slurs from his sex-starved wife and perpetually hungry kids—whom he calls "the leeches"—likes nothing better than an evening at home picking his toes and sniffing his fingers. His happiest hours are spent on the toilet seat. His wife, Peg, a slothful shrew, abhors cooking, and when she's not shopping, she's seated on the living room sofa in a skin-tight outfit downing bon-bons. In brief moments that both Peg and Al find too repugnant to recall in depth, they conceived two anti-family children: their older daughter Kelly, a floozy with the morals of an alleycat, who can barely count to ten; and a son Bud, horny and forever trying to score with "the chicks," or, if not succeeding there, with, as his sister accuses, the family's long-suffering dog.

Bundy repartee is always gross, often drenched with venom. Yet the sit-com, called a "vicious cartoon," became an undeniable hit and acquired a devoted cult following. It also created a nationwide controversy when one offended viewer, Terry Rakolta, a wealthy housewife and mother from Bloom-field Hills, Michigan, sent letters to advertisers asking them to discontinue sponsorship of the show. When Coca-Cola, fearing a grass-roots boycott, backed out, the show softened its emphasis on sex and anti-family values. Irate fans protested. The subsequent media hoopla only made the show a bigger hit the next season; viewership soared by over 38 percent. The campaign to stamp out the Bundys seemed to make them bawdier and raunchier than before.

It's been said that anti-family sitcoms are not so much against family as scornful of a romanticized image of it. Yet many critics find that the shows project the subliminal message, "If I had it to do over again, I'd never marry. And I'd certainly never have kids." When Jim Anderson, in "Father Knows Best," announced "Honey, I'm home!" his wife came running and greeted him with a smile. The same announcement in an anti-family sitcom generates a cringe on the part of the wife, while the children scurry to their rooms to hide. Viewers may like the abrasive humor because it serves as a vent for their own family frustrations (and private anti-family thoughts), or because most families can feel superior to the bickering Bundys; whatever the reasons, the tremen-dous popularity of the anti-family sitcom demonstrated that the late Eighties genre filled a need—or mirrored a reality.

One wildly popular anti-family sitcom arrived in the form of an animated, prime-time adult cartoon.

The Simpsons: Fox Network Premiere, January 14, 1990

"If you buy the argument that television mirrors us more than it molds us," wrote *Newsweek*'s TV critic Harry Waters in April 1990, then "we're beginning to revolt against the tube's idealized images of domestic life—and, at the same time, lovingly embracing messed-up families." The messed-up family Waters had in mind was from the pen of cartoonist Matt Groening, who in "The Simpsons" gave the fledgling Fox network one of it biggest successes.

Homer, the father, known as Bonehead, is a reckless safety operator at a leaky nuclear power plant, who bickers with his wife, Marge, and threatens his son Bart with the expression "Why you little . . ." Mrs. Simpson sports a towering blue beehive hairdo, wears size 13AA shoes, get her homilies crossed with her clichés, and advocates smiling to get through life: "Just smile. Then you'll fit in and you'll be invited to parties . . . and happiness will follow." The Simpson's infant, Maggie, is speechless; the only sound from her mouth comes from her sucking on a pacifier. Daughter Lisa is a precocious second grader, a classic brown-noser with teachers and adults (her brother calls her a "butt-kisser"), and plays saxophone like a professional. "Like an animated *Honeymooners,*" wrote one reviewer, *"The Simpsons* is about people on whom fortune never smiles, whose ship is never coming in."

Fortune did smile on creator Matt Groening. Previously known for a cult comic strip, "Life in Hell," the idiosyncratic cartoonist created the sad-sack Simpson family ("mutant Ozzie and Harriet" by his own description) in 1987 to star in brief segments separating skits on Fox's "The Tracey Ullman Show." The network then commissioned thirteen episodes of a full-fledged half-hour series of "The Simpsons" which debuted in January 1990 to mixed reviews. The public, though, loved the hard-luck clan, and kids in particular loved the obnoxious, irreverent son Bart—who quickly became one of the hottest licensing properties of the times.

Bart Fad Blitz. Bart (an anagram for Brat) emerged as the star of the show. The brash, snotty ten-year-old, who's proud he's an underachiever, wisecracked his way onto T-shirts, lunchboxes, bedsheets—in fact, the character and his family had turned up on seventy spin-off products by April 1990, and Bart got himself a bestselling music video. Whereas the show's humor and irony is geared toward adults, Bart's expressions—like "Don't have a cow, man," "Eat my shorts," and "Aye, caramba, dude"—endeared him to viewers his own age. Pull the string on a $19.95 Bart Simpson doll and you hear his most popular put-downs and snide bon mots. Perhaps no spin-off toy is more typical of the cartoon's anti-family humor than the Simpson's pop gun, which comes with two harmless hollow ball projectiles and two Homer Simpson targets. Wally Cleaver would never have shot at his father, Ward.

That Bart is bad is depicted in the show's opening credits; typically he's at a school blackboard writing as punishment such promises as "I will not draw naked ladies in class," "I did not see Elvis," "I will not call my teacher 'hot cakes.' " While kids copied Bart's spiked crewcut, TV critics pondered the significance of the show's mass appeal. "The Simpsons," says one professor of popular culture, "are actually closer to the norm for a modern-day family than anything we've ever seen on television." Certainly the Simpsons fall somewhere between the hyper-crude Bundys and the hyperglycemic Huxtables. The most daring piece of TV programming of 1990—billed the "TV Battle of the Year"—was Fox's decision to run "The Simpsons" opposite "The Cosby Show," a match-off between family and anti-family. The Huxtables won, but the Simpsons, in their new prime-time slot, picked up thousands of new fans.

Fad forecasters predict that in the long run, it will be the Simpsons who endure in one spin-off form or another. TV and comic strip characters can exhibit great vitality. Betty Boop is still around at age sixty. Bugs Bunny has passed fifty. Only ten years younger are Snoopy and his "Peanuts" pals. The bet in fadland is that Bart and Homer and Marge and Lisa will be a commercial part of the popular culture scene well past the appeal of such cult shows as "Twin Peaks," and well into the next century. On the other hand, the Huxtables, the Bundys, the Keatons, and the Conners will exist only as a nostalgic memory trace.

For the record: The top ten TV shows for the last year of the Eighties:

1. "The Cosby Show"
2. "Cheers"
3. "Roseanne"
4. "A Different World"
5. "America's Funniest Home Videos"
6. "Golden Girls"
7. "The Wonder Years"
8. "Empty Nest"
9. "60 Minutes"
10. "Unsolved Mysteries"

Selected Reading List

IT IS NOT POSSIBLE to list all the sources and references I used to write this book. Many sources are given within the text; others are not. Below are publications I found particularly useful, and ones I believe might be of interest to readers wishing further information on themes I've covered.

Atwan, Robert, et al. *Edsels, Luckies, and Frigidaires.* Dell, 1979.

Barber, Lynn. *The Heyday of Natural History.* Doubleday, 1980. An excellent source on Victorian hobbies and pastimes.

Bennett, James. *Much Loved Books: 60 Best Sellers of the Ages.* Liveright, 1927.

Berger, Melvin. *The World of Dance.* Phillips, 1978.

Bettmann, Otto. *The Good Old Days—They Were Terrible.* Random House, 1974. Victorian times overview, humorously handled.

Bocca, Geoffrey. *Bestseller.* Wyndham Books, 1981.

Brantlinger, Patrick. *Bread and Circuses: Theories of Mass Culture as Social Decay.* University Press, 1983. Distinctions between highbrow and lowbrow culture.

Bronson, Fred. *The Billboard Book of Number One Hits.* Billboard, 1988. A superb single source for the backgrounds of popular songs and their chart ratings. Highly recommended. I found it of great value.

Brooks, Tim, and Earle Marsh. *The Complete Directory to Prime Time Network TV Shows, 1946–Present.* Ballantine, 1988.

———. *TV in the '60s.* Ballantine, 1985.

Browne, Ray. *Objects of Special Devotion.* Bowling Green University Press, Ohio, n.d.

Browne, R. B., and Marshall Fishwick, eds. *Icons of America.* Popular Press, 1978. See essay by Phyllis Boring.

Buckman, Peter. *Let's Dance.* Paddington Press, 1978. Highly recommended, comprehensive.

Cairis, Nicholas. *Passenger Liners of the World Since 1893.* Bonanza, 1979.

Canton, Norman. *The History of Popular Culture.* Macmillan, 1968.

Carner, Mosco. *The Waltz,* Parrish. London, 1948.

Chipman, John. *Index to Top-Hit Tunes, 1900–1950.* Humphries, 1962.

Clark, Dick, and Richard Robinson. *Rock, Roll and Remember.* Crowell, 1976.

Davis, Fred. *Yearning for Yesterday: A Sociology of Nostalgia.* Macmillan, 1967. Scholarly and highly informative.

Dearling, Robert. *The Guiness Book of Music.* 3rd Ed. Guinness, 1986.

Dick, H., and D. Robinson. *The Golden Age of the Great Passenger Airships.* Smithsonian Institution Press, 1985. Filled with fascinating facts.

Downs, Robert. *Books That Changed America.* Macmillan, 1970. Superb overview, highly recommended.

Dumazedier, Joffre. *Toward A Society of Leisure.* Macmillan, 1967.

Dunning, John. *Tune In Yesterday, The Ultimate Encyclopedia of Old-Time Radio, 1925–1976.* Prentice-Hall, 1976. Fascinating browsing and highly readable.

Edelstein, Andrew J., and Kevin McDonough. *The Seventies.* Dutton, 1990. A great book for browsing, amazingly comprehensive for its size.

Ewen, David. *The Life and Death of Tin Pan Alley: The Golden Age of American Popular Music.* Funk and Wagnalls, 1964.

Fischer, Stuart. *Kids' TV.* Facts on File, 1983. A delightful read; laid out show by show.

Flexner, Stuart Berg. *I Hear America Talking.* Simon & Schuster, 1976. One of the best popular sources on modern American language, word origins and regional variations in meanings.

———. *Listening To America.* Simon & Schuster, 1982. Every bit as good as his earlier book.

Flink, James. *America Adopts the Auto, 1895–1910.* MIT Press, 1970. Excellent overview.

———. *The Car Culture.* MIT Press, 1975. Highly recommended.

Frank, A, ed. *A Pictorial Manual of Ballroom Dancing.* Museum Press, London, 1959.

Fraser, Antonia. *A History of Toys.* Delacorte, 1966. Good overview.

Gans, Herbert. *Popular Culture and High Culture.* Basic Books, 1974.

Gardner, Martin. *Science: Good, Bad, and Bogus.* Prometheus, 1981. Entertaining reading; see his account of the Bridey Murphy hoax.

Gerani, Gary, and Paul Schulman. *Fantastic Television.* Harmony Books, 1977. Superb overview of TV science fiction shows.

Gitlin, Todd. *The Sixties.* Bantam, 1987.

Gutman, R., and E. Kaufman. *American Diner.* Harper and Row, 1979.

Hager, Steve. *Hip Hop: The Illustrated History of Break Dancing, Rap Music, and Graffiti.* St. Martin's, 1984.

Hackett, Alice P. *80 Years of Best Sellers, 1895–1975.* Bowker, 1977.

Hanson, Kitty. *Disco Fever.* New American Library, 1978.

Harmon, Jim. *The Great Radio Comedians.* Doubleday, 1970.
———. *The Great Radio Heroes.* Doubleday, 1967.
Hart, James, *The Popular Book: A History of American's Literary Taste.* Oxford University Press, 1950.
Hine, Thomas. *Populuxe.* Knopf, 1986. Excellent overview for styles from the late Forties through the Fifties.
Howe, Daniel Walker, ed. *Victorian America.* University of Pennsylvania Press, 1976.
Hughes, Stephen. *Popular Culture Mania.* McGraw Hill, 1984. About collectibles.
Huizinga, J. *Homo Ludens: A Study of the Play-Element in Culture.* Beacon, 1955.
Inge, M. Thomas. *Handbook of American Popular Culture.* Greenwood, 1978.
Inge, M. Thomas, ed. *Concise Histories of American Popular Culture.* Greenwood, 1982. See essay by Michael Bell.
Jancik, Wayne. *One-Hit Wonders.* Billboard, 1990. Excellent stories on pop singers who hit it big just one time.
Javna, John. *Cult TV.* St. Martin's, 1985. Highly recommended for hours of delightful browsing.
Jenkins, Alan. *The Thirties,* Stein and Day, 1976.
Jesen, Oliver, ed. *The Nineties.* American Heritage, 1967. The 1890s, of course.
Johnson, Richard. *American Fads.* Beech Tree, 1985. Highly recommended.
Kaye, Marvin. *A Toy is Born.* Stein and Day, 1973.
Lackmann, Ron. *Remember Radio.* Putnam, 1970. Excellent overview.
Landrum, Larry. *American Popular Culture.* Gale, 1982.
Lawrance, W. L. *Highbrow/Lowbrow: The Emergence of Cultural Hierarchy in America.* Harvard University Press, 1988.
Lax, Roger, and Fred Smith. *The Great Song Thesaurus.* 2nd Ed. Oxford University Press, 1989. Comprehensive and highly recommended.
Levy, Lester. *Give Me Yesterday, American History in Song, 1890–1970.* University of Oklahoma Press, 1975.
Lynch, Vincent, and Bill Henkin. *Jukebox, The Golden Age, 1937 through 1948.* Lancaster-Miller, 1981. Fascinating; all you ever wanted to know about the musical wonders.
MacDonald, J. *Don't Touch That Dial: Radio Programming in American Life.* Nelson Hall, 1978. Superb single source of sweeping scope.
MacKay, Charles. *Extraordinary Popular Delusions and the Madness of Crowds.* 1890; Harmony, 1980.
Marlow, Curtis. *Breakdancing.* Sharon Publications, 1984.
Marsh, Dave. *The Heart of Rock and Soul.* New American Library, 1989. Highly recommended.
Marum, Andrew, and Frank Parise. *Follies and Foibles.* Facts on File, 1984. A superb overview of decades of fads, presented chronologically and concisely.
McClintock, Inez. *Toys In America.* Public Affairs, 1961. Comprehensive.

McCrohan, Donna. *Prime Time, Our Time.* Prima, 1990. Highly recommended for backgrounds on the most popular TV shows

McCullock, Lou. *Photographs: A Guide to Their History and Value.* Schiffer Publications, 1981.

McCullough, E. *World's Fair Midways.* Arno, 1966. Thorough and a delight to read.

McDonagh, Don. *Dance Fever.* Random House, 1979. A wonderful source for an overview of popular dance. Highly recommended.

Milberg, Alan. *Street Games.* McGraw-Hill, 1976.

Mitz, Rick. *The Great TV Sitcom Book.* Marek, 1980. The word great in the title is well deserved; highly recommended for the stories behind your favorite sitcoms; rich in dialogue from scores of shows. The best single source I found on the subject.

Monaco, James. *Media Culture: Television, Radio, Records, Books, Magazines, Newspapers, Movies.* Dell, 1978.

Morgan, Roberta. *Disco.* Bell, 1978.

Mott, Frank. *Golden Multitudes.* Bowker, 1947. On bestselling books.

Nelson, Walter. *Small World: The Amazing Story of the Volkswagen.* Little, Brown, 1967.

O'Brien, Richard. *The Story of American Toys.* Abbeville, 1990.

Orleans, Susan. *Saturday Night.* Knopf, 1990.

Parsons, Nicholas. *The Book of Literary Lists.* Facts on File, 1986. Great to browse.

Reader's Digest editors. *Reader's Digest; Great Events of the 20th Century.* Reader's Digest, 1977.

Rearick, Charles. *Pleasure of the Belle Epoque.* Yale University Press, 1985.

Reaser, Eduard. *The History of the Waltz.* Continental Books, 1947.

Rose, Brian. *TV Genres.* Greenwood, 1985.

Rydell, Robert. *All the World's a Fair, Visions of Empire at American International Expositions, 1876–1916.* University of Chicago Press, 1984. Fascinating reading.

Sann, Paul. *Fads, Follies and Delusions of the American People.* Bonanza, 1967. Highly recommended; the best single source I discovered for extensive treatments of fads and follies. (Note: As for the similarity in titles between my book and Sann's; I discovered the latter after mine had been named.)

Schick, Frank. *The Paperback Book in America.* Bowker, 1958. Excellent overview.

Schrank, Jeffrey. *Snap, Crackle and Popular Taste.* Delacorte, 1977.

Shore, Michael, and Dick Clark. *The History of American Bandstand.* Ballantine, 1985.

Skolnik, Peter. *Fads: America's Crazes, Fevers and Fancies.* Crowell, 1972. Recommended for its overview of the subject.

Slocum, Frank. *Baseball Cards: The Golden Years, 1886–1956.* Warner, 1987.

Spaeth, Sigmund. *A History of Popular Music In America.* Random House, 1948. Excellent source on the first half of the century.

Stambler, Constance. *Encyclopedia of Popular Music.* St. Martin's 1965. Recommended for an overview.

Stern, S. L., and T. Schoenhaus. *Toyland.* Contemporary, 1990. Excellent for an overview of toy fads from an industry standpoint.

Stevenson, Elizabeth. *Babbitts and Bohemians: The American 1920s.* Macmillan, 1967.

Sudjic, Deyan. *Cult Objects.* Paladin Granada, 1985. The products consumers have elevated to American icons.

Sutherland, John. *Bestsellers: Popular Fiction of the 1970s.* Routledge, 1981.

Time-Life editors. *This Fabulous Century.* Time-Life, 1969. A volume devoted to each decade.

Ward, Edward, et al. *Rock of Ages: The Rolling Stone History of Rock and Roll.* Rolling Stone, 1986. Comprehensive.

Wertheim, Arthur. *Radio Comedy.* Oxford University Press, 1979.

Whitburn, Joel. *Joel Whitburn's Pop Memories, 1890–1954: The History of American Popular Music.* Record Research, 1986.

———. *Joel Whitburn's Top Pop Singles, 1955–1986.* Record Research, 1987.

Wilk, Max. *The Golden Age of TV.* Delacorte, 1976.

Williamson, Judith. *Consuming Passions: The Dynamics of Popular Culture.* Boyars, 1980.

Youmans, John. *Social Dance.* Goodyear, 1969.